Major Problems in American Women's History *(editor with Ruth Alexander)*

To Toil the Livelong Day: America's Women at Work, 1790–1980
(editor with Carol Groneman)

A People and a Nation *(with five co-authors)*

Liberty's Daughters: The Revolutionary Experience of American Women,
1750–1800

Women of America: A History *(editor with Carol Berkin)*

The British-Americans: The Loyalist Exiles in England, 1774–1789

FOUNDING
MOTHERS & FATHERS

FOUNDING
MOTHERS & FATHERS
Gendered Power and the Forming of
American Society

MARY BETH NORTON

Alfred A. Knopf   New York

1996

THIS IS A BORZOI BOOK
PUBLISHED BY ALFRED A. KNOPF, INC.

A portion of chapter five was originally published as
"Gender and Defamation in Seventeenth-Century Maryland"
in *William & Mary Quarterly*, January 1987.

Library of Congress Cataloging-in-Publication Data
Norton, Mary Beth.
Founding mothers & fathers :
gendered power and the forming of American society /
Mary Beth Norton.
p.   cm.
Includes bibliographical references and index.
ISBN 0-679-42965-4
1. Sex role—United States—History—17th century.
2. Family—United States—History—17th century.
3. United States—Social conditions—To 1865.
4. United States—Politics and government—To 1775.
I. Title.
HQ1075.5.U6N67   1996
306'.0973—dc20   95-43791
CIP

Manufactured in the United States of America

First Edition

for
Bernard Bailyn

Contents

Acknowledgments

As an undergraduate at the University of Michigan, I studied political theory and intellectual history, and I enrolled in graduate school at Harvard University intending to become an intellectual historian. While at Harvard, though, like many other scholars of my generation, I became enthralled by social history and—in particular—the excitement of studying the lives of ordinary Americans in the colonial period. Subsequently, I was drawn to the newer field of women's history and even more recently to its broader incarnation, the study of gender in its many and varied manifestations. Thus the research reported in this book, which has occupied me for more than a decade, combines an earlier interest in political theory and intellectual history with my more recent fascination with social history and especially women and gender.

The first stages of the intellectual odyssey just described owe much to the influence of three men: Frank Grace, who taught me political theory at the University of Michigan; John Higham, who introduced me to intellectual history and directed my undergraduate honors thesis; and Bernard Bailyn, who became my graduate mentor. That I have chosen to dedicate this book solely to the last is not to slight the influence of the other two but rather to highlight the great debt I owe to Bud Bailyn, who over the years has become friend as well as teacher. I only wish that Frank Grace were still alive to see that I have not forgotten those intriguing gentlemen to whom he first systematically introduced me—Sir Robert Filmer, Thomas Hobbes, and John Locke.

This book could never have been written without the assistance of many former Cornell graduate and undergraduate students, who spent innumerable hours immersed in the court records of seventeenth-century America, translating the details of civil and criminal cases into numerical values that could be analyzed by computer. My thanks go to Ruth M. Alexander, Daniel Alonso, Gavin Campbell, Yong Chen, Julia Chu, Joanne Gernstein, Alan Ginet, Eric Mitnick, Celia Naylor, Susan Steigerwald, and especially to Vivian Bruce Conger and Julie Curry, the two who devoted more years to this project than they probably care to recall. As I was in the final stages of preparing the book manuscript, A. Paige Shipman served as my general aide and research assistant, cheerfully tackling every assignment I gave her with good humor and assiduity.

Although this book has taken considerably longer to research and write than I anticipated when I began to work on it in 1982, it would have taken far longer had it not been for the generosity of several funding agencies. I gratefully acknowledge the financial assistance of the American Antiquarian Society's Peterson Fellowship, which supported a month of research in the society's collections in 1984; the Rockefeller Foundation, which awarded me a Gender Roles Fellowship in 1986–87 and served as my host for a productive month at the Villa Serbelloni International Center for Scholars in April 1992; the Society for the Humanities at Cornell University, which designated me a resident fellow in 1988–89; and the John Simon Guggenheim Memorial Foundation, for a fellowship that supported the writing of this book's first draft during the 1993–94 academic year. In addition, I received ongoing assistance from the Humanities Research Fund, the Return Jonathan Meigs III Fund, and the Mary Donlon Alger endowment at Cornell University.

Although much of this work is based on published materials, archivists at the American Antiquarian Society, the Connecticut State Library, the Massachusetts State Archives, the Phillips Library of the Peabody Essex Museum, the Massachusetts Historical Society, and the Maryland Hall of Records helped in essential ways. I am grateful to them all, and to the county clerk of Dukes County, Massachusetts, for dealing with a variety of inquiries.

I have learned much from the comments offered by many audiences and individual historians who have listened to or read pieces of this project over the years. In particular, I express my thanks for useful and often spirited criticisms to those who attended my Commonwealth Fund lecture at University College London in February 1987 (especially the commentators, Roger Thompson and Gwenda Morgan); to the other participants in the Harvard conference in honor of Bernard Bailyn in October 1987, especially the ever-generous Lois Green Carr; to Laurel Thatcher Ulrich and John M. Murrin, the commentators on my paper at the 1990 Berkshire Conference on Women's History; to Cynthia Herrup, who read some early article-length drafts; and to my colleagues in the Cornell Women's Studies program, who have discussed several parts of this project at different times. Drafts of the book manuscript have been read and commented upon by my graduate students Jackie Hatton and Leslie Horowitz, my former colleague Clive Holmes, and my current colleagues I. V. Hull and Rachel Weil. My editor, Jane N. Garrett, has offered sage advice. The book is definitely the better for all their contributions. Any errors of judgment that remain are mine alone.

Finally, I thank my friends on Martha's Vineyard and in Ithaca (especially the other members of the SPCC) for many years of listening to me recount at too-great length the "latest" seventeenth-century scandal. They have put up with my eccentric obsession with a world three centuries gone for far too long. I appreciate their forbearance and their support.

FOUNDING
MOTHERS & FATHERS

Introduction

THE SIGNING of the Mayflower Compact in November 1620, on
shipboard off Cape Cod, provides one of the most enduring images
of early American history. "It was thought good there should be an
association and agreement," recalled one participant, "that we should
combine together in one body, and to submit to such government and
governours, as we should by common consent agree to make and
choose." Therefore, the male passengers on the *Mayflower* created "a
civil body politick, for our better ordering and preservation," authorizing
the framing of "such just and equal laws . . . as shall be thought most
meet and convenient for the general good of the colony." The signers
promised "all due submission and obedience" to the government they
had thus established.[1]

Superficially, it seems but a simple step from the decks of the *Mayflower* in 1620 to the Constitutional Convention in Philadelphia in 1787.
The men in both contexts appear to have been engaged in the same
enterprise—mutual consent to the creation of elected governments. Yet
there was an important difference between the two documents. That
drafted in 1620, explained the Reverend William Hubbard, an early
chronicler of New England, was intended as a temporary measure, designed to last only until the signers could obtain a royal charter. The
migrants had accidentally landed outside the jurisdiction of the Virginia
Company, in whose territories they had received permission to settle,
and accordingly they "could not fall into any order of government, but
by way of combination."[2] The Constitution, by contrast, was intended
to serve as a long-term blueprint for the government of an independent
United States. Whereas the Mayflower Compact constituted a temporary
substitute for a grant of authority from a higher power, the Constitution
established a government based permanently on the consent of the
populace.

The events that occurred 167 years apart superficially resembled each
other in another way: neither had any female participants. All those who

signed both documents were white male heads of households, men of substance and standing in their respective communities. In both 1620 and 1787, women rarely played the role of independent actors in the political arena. Instead, society conceptualized them as dependents whose menfolk would speak and act for them in economic, political, and legal affairs. English men too could be the dependents of others, but most of them in reality (and all of them in theory) experienced dependency merely as one stage in their lives, during their youth. For women in both eras, on the other hand, dependency was thought to be natural and perpetual.

Yet in regard to the status of women as well the signers of the Mayflower Compact and those of the Constitution lived in very different worlds. The Founding Fathers of the 1780s were children of the Enlightenment, the political and intellectual movement that swept Europe and America after the late seventeenth century. Their ideology celebrated men's equality, rationality, and individuality. The English migrants of 1620, by contrast, still followed traditional notions of social and political organization rooted in the European past, ideas stressing inequality, collectivity, and what later ages would dub "superstition," such as beliefs in witchcraft and in God's "remarkable providences."[3] Such contrasting belief systems placed women in very different relationships to the state, in ways that historians have hitherto failed to recognize.

This book focuses on the first half-century of English colonization in North America, when—during the years between approximately 1620 and 1670—colonial society took shape within the context of a system of conceptualizing politics, society, the family, and relationships among them that differed significantly from later Enlightenment formulations. The worldview that is my principal subject is most often termed herein "Filmerian," after the great English theorist of paternal power, Sir Robert Filmer.[4] That outlook saw family and state as analogous institutions, linked symbiotically through their similar historical origins, aims, and functions. This book examines the Filmerian system by deploying a gendered analysis of power relationships in society, religion, and politics to offer insight into the initial development and operation of colonial governments, the maintenance of social order, and the experiences of individual men and women. The prevailing Filmerian worldview assumed the necessity of hierarchy in family, polity, and society at large. Authority in all aspects of life theoretically emanated from the top, not the bottom, of those essential hierarchical structures.[5]

This volume describes as well the inchoate beginnings in America, by chance rather than by design, of the very different way of thinking eventually adopted by Enlightenment theorists. Even though John Locke's great work, *Two Treatises of Government*, did not appear until after the end of the period that is of primary concern here, elements of the sociopolitical system he explicated will play a major role in the book and will usually be called (albeit anachronistically) "Lockean." The English philosopher, in company with other Enlightenment thinkers, severed the connection between family and state; he in particular contended forcefully that the state originated not in the family but in a contractual agreement among men, and that the aims and functions of the resulting polity were very different from those of the family. Not all contractual thinkers agreed with Locke in every detail, just as not all paternalistic thinkers aligned themselves with Filmer. Nevertheless, for their age and ours the writings of the two men have come to symbolize the conflict in which both participated. Accordingly, it seems appropriate not only to use their names to identify the respective positions with which they have been associated, but also to focus specifically on their own writings as epitomes of the general debate over the nature of government and society that dominated seventeenth-century political thought.[6]

Founding Mothers & Fathers links such theoretical concerns with the realities of daily life in the colonies, particularly with the contours of gender relationships in the Filmerian and Lockean systems. The term *gender* describes the cultural construction of sex; that is, the definition of masculinity and femininity. Although every society believes that its gender definitions stem "naturally" from biological sexual identity, in practice different cultures define the sexes' modes of behavior and appropriate roles in widely varying ways.[7]

For example, European colonists soon discovered that theirs was not the only method of designating work roles by sex. In the Algonkian cultures of eastern North America, women performed agricultural duties, which were masculine tasks in English eyes. Algonkian men, one colonial observer remarked, engaged in "no kind of labour but hunting, fishing and fowling." Such activities supplied protein crucial to the villagers' diet, but English people saw them solely as elite leisure-time diversions. Thus colonists uniformly and inaccurately interpreted the Algonkian gender system as one in which women were "in great slavery" and men "extraordinary idle." The Algonkians in return appear to have been just as startled by the gender system of the interlopers. Thomas Lechford, an early New Englander, reported that Algonkian men called English women "Lazie *squaes*," accusing male colonists of "spoiling good working creatures."[8]

But gender systems do more than simply assign work roles to men

and women and designate their allied behavioral traits. Gender terminology describes not only the supposedly separate characteristics of the
sexes but also the social relationships between them. In that context,
gender supplies "a primary way of signifying relationships of power," to
quote the historian Joan W. Scott.[9] Nowhere was that more true than
in seventeenth-century English America, where the inherited language
of power was infused with gendered images drawn from the familial
analogies of the Filmerian worldview. These images and their implications will be examined at length in the pages that follow.

The subtitle of this book, *Gendered Power*, refers simultaneously to
two different aspects of the relationship of the sexes in seventeenth-
century Anglo-America. First, power both inside and outside the household (in family, society, state, and even church) was conceived in
gendered ways and expressed in gendered terminology. Filmerian modes
of thought encouraged the application of common familial locutions
(husband/wife, father/child) to a variety of hierarchical relationships, and
because of their origins in the family those designations were inevitably
gendered. Second, power in colonial America lay in the hands of men,
who expected to govern women. These two aspects of gendered power
seemingly reinforced each other, yet, as shall become evident in subsequent chapters, they also clashed in significant ways. Paradoxically, the
expression and conceptualization of power as a gendered phenomenon
could create exceptions to men's hold on the reins of social, political,
economic, and religious power in the colonies.

The intimate link between gender and power in the minds of early
Anglo-Americans is revealed in a variety of ways. Take, for example, an
observation made in 1666 by a one-time resident of Maryland. George
Alsop, describing the Algonkian gender system for an English audience,
noted as had many others that women were "Butchers, Cooks, and
Tillers of the ground" and that men thought it "below the honour of a
Masculine" to do anything but hunt. Alsop then exposed his own implicit assumption about the gendered nature of power by commenting,
"I never observed . . . that ever the Women wore the Breeches, or
dared either to look or action predominate over the Men." To Alsop's
European mind, those who tilled the soil normally "wore the Breeches"
and "predominated over" the other sex. Therefore, he had to assure
both himself and his English readers that despite their work roles Algonkian women were simply—in his words—"ingenious and laborious
Housewives," rather than competitors for the power that properly resided in male hands. By asserting that an English system of gendered
power prevailed in Algonkian as well as settler families, Alsop rendered

an alien form of social organization both more familiar and less threatening.[10]

That the signers of the Mayflower Compact and their womenfolk lived in the same Filmerian world as did Alsop was revealed by one of their number, William Bradford. In the late 1640s, in his history *Of Plymouth Plantation*, Governor Bradford reflected on the reasons why the Pilgrims had abandoned their original economic system, in which property was held in common and all persons worked for the community. He explained that by spring 1623, less than three years after the colony's founding, communal labor and property holding had been found to "breed much confusion and discontent and retard much employment that would have been to [the colonists'] benefit and comfort."[11]

Bradford detailed four reasons for the failure of the communal enterprise. First, young men did not want to "spend their time and strength to work for other men's wives and children without any recompense." Second, the "strong" men thought it "injustice" to receive the same share of food and clothing as "he that was weak and not able to do a quarter the other could." Third, those Bradford termed the "aged and graver" men regarded it as "some indignity and disrespect" to be ranked and treated equally with "the meaner and younger sort." Fourth and finally, "men's wives . . . deemed it a kind of slavery" to be forced "to do service for other men, as dressing their meat, washing their clothes, etc. . . . neither could many husbands well brook it." By contrast, Bradford observed, when individual plots of land were laid out, "all hands [became] very industrious." In particular, "the women now went willingly into the field, and took their little ones with them to set corn; which before would allege weakness and inability; whom to have compelled would have been thought great tyranny and oppression."

Although several historians have analyzed Bradford's discussion of the collapse of Pilgrim communalism, no one has recognized that all four explanations he offered for the failure of the experiment were gender-related.[12] Bradford's comments demonstrate the salience of traditional English gender definitions for the early migrants to North America. In essence, Bradford explained that older men did not want to surrender the hard-won benefits of their senior status; that healthier men expected to reap advantages from their strength; that bachelors disliked working to support other men's families; and that married men believed a wife's labors should be devoted to her husband and children alone. In short, older men wanted to retain the prerogatives of status, private property, and family domination that accrued to them as English heads of

households, while younger, single men aspired to attain the same rank
through control of the profits derived from their labor.

The women in Bradford's story apparently did not anticipate achieving the same sort of autonomous status in the new land. According to
him, they recognized that their role was to serve men, but not *all* the
men of the colony. The wives of Plymouth regarded cooking and doing
laundry for the community as "a kind of slavery," even though those
were tasks customarily performed by females in English society. They
seem to have complained not about the nature or the amount of their
work—though it is possible that communal labor was more arduous—
but instead about its organization. If Bradford portrayed their attitudes
accurately (and there is no evidence to suggest otherwise), the colony's
women saw themselves as properly subordinate to a particular man and
their work as properly confined to the context of a specific household.
That the shift to private property created in women a new willingness
to do agricultural labor implies both that regular work in the fields had
not been among these women's normal tasks in England and that they
were more likely to take on unfamiliar roles when their own households
and families would benefit directly from their labors.[13]

Bradford's account does more than simply describe the gender-role
expectations held by the first English migrants to New England. It also
points up the symbiotic relationship between family and state that characterized early seventeenth-century Anglo-American thought and practice. Even if few theorists adopted the extreme position expounded by
Sir Robert Filmer—that the sources of authority in the family and the
state were identical—most English people of the day drew an analogy
between family and state, believing that the historical and theoretical
origins of the state lay in the husband and father's power over his wife,
children, and other dependents. They held, in other words, a *unified
theory of power*: all secular authority systems were said to rest on the same
fundamental base, the father's governance of his subordinates. Since that
rule was ordained by God, such systems were inextricably linked to
religious belief as well.[14]

Because state and family were so closely aligned in theory, they could
also have an intimate practical relationship. Although twentieth-century
Americans tend to conceive of that relationship as a one-way street,
emphasizing exclusively the impact of government policy on families, in
early Plymouth the street clearly ran in both directions. The government
could, and did, regulate families in a variety of ways; but family life also
affected political and economic organization. Bradford's story in essence
explained that the colony had to adapt to the family strategies preferred

by individual settlers. An economic system that ran counter to familial expectations could not survive, and the result was a lasting change in the colony.

Bradford concluded his discussion of that lasting change with a general observation:

> Upon the point all being to have alike, and all to do alike, they thought themselves in the like condition, and one as good as another; and so, if it did not cut off those relations that God hath set amongst men, yet it did at least much diminish and take off the mutual respects that should be preserved amongst them.

To the Plymouth settlers, then, God had ordained inequality. An egalitarian, communal economic system removed "the mutual respects" necessary for viable social organization. John Winthrop, the governor of the Massachusetts Bay colony, conveyed the same message in his famous lay sermon "A Modell of Christian Charity," delivered on board the *Arbella* en route to New England in 1630. "In all times," Winthrop declared, "some must be rich some poore, some highe and eminent in power and dignitie, others meane and in subjeccion." Such distinctions of rank did not, however, imply that people were of greater or lesser worth. Instead, God intended that each person "might have need of other," so "they might be all knitt more nearly together in the bond of brotherly affeccion."[15]

Bradford and Winthrop thus explicated what the historian Keith Wrightson has termed "the most fundamental characteristic" of seventeenth-century English society: "its high degree of stratification, its distinctive and all-pervasive system of social inequality." English society was composed of a series of interlocking hierarchies, in which each person occupying a superior position was responsible for directing the activities of inferiors. Within the family, parents ruled children and servants; in the wider society, people of high rank commanded deference from lower-status persons; in the polity, male officials rightly wielded authority over other men of various ranks. But outside the household the nominally all-encompassing system was conceptualized solely with respect to the status of adult men. Women and children, it was assumed, took the rank of their husbands and fathers.[16]

Bradford certainly implied as much by the way he framed his account. The governor's use of masculine terminology ("those relations that God hath set amongst *men*") more accurately described the social hierarchy when read restrictively than generically. Bradford divided men into three categories—bachelors, husbands in their prime, and older men—while the only women he mentioned were wives, the counterparts of just one of the male groups. The single women and widows of Plymouth (the analogues of his first and third sets of men) had no place in his story. Teenage daughters were lumped into the genderless category "children" and linked with their mothers; widows were simply invisible.[17]

Like other Englishmen of his day, William Bradford therefore too readily assumed that all women were always wives or daughters subject to, and controlled by, male family members. In accordance with that same assumption, the institutional structures of the seventeenth-century state were designed to control the behavior of male heads of households. They, in turn, were expected to govern the women (and the male dependents) in their families. If men failed to fulfill that fundamental duty, everyone understood that social disorder would result.

But even if men successfully ruled their female dependents, the application of Filmerian precepts to the position of individual women contained three problematic elements. First, as mothers women legitimately wielded some authority within the family; because of the intimate link between family and state, they consequently could not be wholly excluded from the category of those who wielded power in the society at large. Second, women could be widowed, thus being deprived of their male governors. And third, high-status women took precedence over low-status men, since their fathers' or husbands' rank was more important in determining their social standing than was their gender. When the three elements were united—that is, in the persons of high-status widowed mothers—the combination posed particularly knotty problems for state and society. Such women properly deserved the deference of low-ranking men yet at the same time were subject to no men themselves. High-status mothers, and especially widows, accordingly could become flashpoints for conflict in a society organized on the basis of Filmerian theory.[18]

But some seventeenth-century English people were familiar with another way of conceptualizing the nature of polity and society, one that resolved the ambiguities in women's status by rendering females irrelevant outside the household. That theory, which had originally been formulated in ancient Greece and achieved its fullest early expression in the works of Aristotle, saw the family and the state not as analogous but as different, diametrically opposed institutions. The *polis*, composed only of men, was based on equality, while the family, composed of men and women, incorporated hierarchies of age, wealth, and gender. Greek and (to a certain extent) Roman political theory drew a sharp line between the family and the state. Thus the place of women within the family could be conceptually separated from the position of women in the polity and the wider society. In a Filmerian system, rank depended on a combination of age, gender, and status, and women with high standing by those criteria could claim some types of power inside and outside the household. In the formulation developed in the ancient world, women's rank was determined entirely by gender, all females being excluded from active participation in political and social decision-making. This was, in short, a *dichotomous theory of power,* in which the sources of authority in the family differed from those in society and the polity.[19]

In the sixteenth and seventeenth centuries, this older approach, which had been abandoned because Christianity encouraged the development of a unified worldview based on the familial model, once again attracted adherents. English men perhaps found it congenial because it expressed in theoretical terms the reality of certain aspects of their political lives. In counties and villages throughout the nation, the era witnessed the development of strong local institutions based on widespread male participation and government by a consensus of at least some property-owning male inhabitants.[20] John Locke's contribution was to combine ancient political concepts with customary English practices to construct a comprehensive explanation for the origins of society that was to challenge successfully the then-dominant familial formula. The two political theories—one Filmerian and unified, the other Lockean and dichotomous—can also be characterized as systems relying for legitimacy on either authority (that is, a higher power) or consent (that is, a consensus of male household heads).

The distinction between the two approaches to conceptualizing society and government can be analyzed in anthropological terms as well. Although some cultures categorize men and women similarly (as was done, however inadequately, in the Filmerian model), others have defined men and women separately, judging women in terms of their relationships with men but seeing men in ways that have little to do with women. In John Locke's schema, men's most important interactions occurred outside the household and with other men, whereas women's took place in the context of the family, which included both men and women. Locke, in other words, divided the world conceptually into an all-male realm (politics and society) and a realm of heterosexual relationships (family), thereby breaking down the unified worldview that characterized familial theory.[21]

Prior to the publication of Locke's *Two Treatises,* the ideas he systematized comprised a series of diverse theories revolving around the belief that men should somehow consent to government. Few philosophers or rulers were as authoritarian in their outlook as Sir Robert Filmer, who denied all voice to the governed. Yet consent was conceptualized in a variety of ways and with varying degrees of precision. Debates over the nature of consent and the structure of government abounded in seventeenth-century England and America alike. The issue was further complicated by the fact that versions of consent were often incorporated into familial theory. Colonists everywhere, not just on board the *Mayflower*, recognized that men's consent could create a temporary government until a proper grant of authority could be obtained. And, as shall be seen, leading New Englanders came to liken government to a marriage, in which a wife's consent at her wedding legitimized her husband's later authority over her. Indeed, as Elizabeth Janeway has perceptively observed, legitimacy in any power relationship can be created "only *by the governed*. . . . Force of arms and physical might cannot exact this grant. Though they can compel obedience, it is not willing, committed obedience." But even when early Anglo-Americans seemingly acknowledged the need for consent, they did so within an essentially authoritarian framework.[22]

In the middle years of the seventeenth century, the subject of much of this book, the ascent of Lockean thinking lay far in the future, and only very limited notions of consent held sway among the Anglo-American populace. As shall be seen in chapter six, colonial men argued about politics and government in authoritarian rather than consensual terms. They believed that claims to wield power rightfully rested above all on grants from appropriate higher authorities. Accordingly, debates over the legitimacy of particular governments focused primarily not on whether men had consented to them but instead on whether those governments had received legal sanction from the proper English "father." Furthermore, clashes between governments based on consent and those resting on more appropriate Filmerian foundations inevitably ended with the victory of the latter.

Although all the English migrants carried with them to North America a Filmerian theory of unified authority and attempted to implement that ideology in their new settlements, certain characteristics of the early Chesapeake colonies had unanticipated consequences. This book will contend that New England and the Chesapeake developed diverse modes of political and judicial behavior as a result of demographic and religious differences between those two initial sites of English settlement.[23]

New England's Puritans stressed the importance of the family and employed family analogies to explain political, social, and religious structures. Since the Puritans emigrated in kinship groups to a healthy environment, they quickly established strong, paternally governed families—perhaps even stronger than those in England. Throughout the seventeenth century New Englanders remained committed to the hierarchical, familial model of state and society. To keep order in the early settlements, they frequently used the mechanism of the covenant—like the Mayflower Compact, an agreement through which men (and in some churches, women as well) voluntarily submitted to the governance of others. Yet the ubiquitous New England covenants were less Lockean social contracts than they were the means through which legitimacy and claims to obedience were established within a fundamentally Filmerian system, in which initial consent preceded an ongoing, obligatory acquiescence to a traditional hierarchy. The Reverend John Cotton of Massachusetts Bay suggested as much when he declared in 1645 that a "mutual Covenant" between "husband and wife in the family, Magistrates and subjects in the Commonwealth, fellow Citizens in the same citie" was the only way in which people "free from naturall and compulsory engagements, can be united or combined together into one visible body." His equating of familial and political covenants demonstrated that he viewed them and the obligations they established as comparable. If the political bond resembled the marital one, then the subject's obedience was likewise perpetual and absolute, involving no voluntary element once initial consent had been granted.[24]

In contrast to New England, where the migrant population contained only a relatively small majority of men, Virginia and Maryland attracted large numbers of men but few women. Moreover, most of the migrants of both sexes moved to the region as isolated individuals rather than in family groups. The skewed sex ratio, which was especially imbalanced in the early years of each colony, meant that it was difficult to establish the marital households English people regarded as normal. Since the vast majority of settlers were servants whose indentures prevented them from marrying for a period of several years, family formation was significantly delayed even when potential marriage partners were available. In addition, the environment was extremely unhealthy, causing high mortality rates and bringing immense instability to family life. The result was a society in which the overwhelmingly numerically dominant men quickly became culturally dominant, and in which the ideal of consensual male political interaction assumed a prominence hitherto unknown. In the Chesapeake, the family could not serve as a model for the state—or vice versa—because families were too truncated, anomalous, and unstable by English standards. The peculiar nature of family life in the Chesapeake, coupled with the absence of strong church structures in either colony, turned the region into a practical laboratory for the dichotomous theory of authority years before Locke systematically formulated his ideas.[25]

The principal sources for this study of the Filmerian system of gendered power are the court records of the Anglo-American colonies, which are particularly rich for the period before approximately 1670. Judicial systems in the first decades of English settlement were dominated by lay judges and clerks who lacked formal legal training and who accordingly paid little attention to technicalities that in England would have prevented cases from being heard. Legal codes (as shall be seen in subsequent chapters) were fragmentary and incomplete, and delinquents were often charged with "crimes" that were nowhere specifically defined. The earliest court records therefore supply a treasure trove of information about the colonists' assumptions, attitudes, and behavior. Indeed, the records incorporate materials that have little or nothing to do with litigation or prosecutions as such, but which were produced by court clerks in response to requests from illiterate colonists.

Court records furthermore are the major type of surviving documentation from an era without newspapers, magazines, or many locally printed materials of any sort, and in which only a very few people—chiefly elite men—kept diaries or wrote letters. Trial records in particular provide invaluable insight into a context in which the state and the family intersected with each other and with a third key element—the peer groups of individuals who appeared as witnesses and in the process mediated between and remarked upon the functioning of both families and the state. In civil suits and criminal prosecutions, ordinary settlers and the leaders of their colonies interacted regularly as civil litigants, criminal defendants, witnesses, judges, and jurymen, thereby bringing to light many aspects of their lives and thought that would otherwise have remained hidden from a historian's view.

In spite of the many advantages of basing this work largely on court records, it is important to acknowledge the disadvantages as well. One result of the de facto adoption of a Lockean system in the Chesapeake is that in the first section, which focuses on gendered power in the family, the documentation is more sparse for the southern colonies than for New England. The absence of abundant evidence stems from the Chesapeake governments' lack of interest in the daily functioning of households. Whereas northern governments regularly intervened in households they regarded as disorderly, Chesapeake governments assumed a more laissez-faire stance and stepped into household governance only on rare occasions. Accordingly, Chesapeake court records are far less revealing of family dynamics than are those in New England. On the other hand, because of the importance of peer-group interactions in the Chesapeake, court records in Virginia and Maryland are particularly useful for examining community relations, the subject of the second section of *Founding Mothers & Fathers*.

Moreover, few Africans, Indians, or other unquestionably non-English people appeared in Anglo-American courts as litigants, witnesses, or criminal defendants before the 1680s, and therefore this study can say less than I would have preferred about issues of race and ethnicity during the early years of colonization. In part, the omission is deliberate, for the book concentrates on the first half-century of English settlement and on a specifically English conceptual scheme that linked family, state, and community into a unified whole that diverged significantly from the concomitant structure of Indian societies. It would have been inappropriate to apply an analysis focused on English definitions of family and state to Native Americans during an era when they continued to live largely independently of Europeans.[26]

Further, the primary goal of this book is to delineate the social and political patterns that preceded the dramatic changes beginning in the mid-1670s, the most significant of which were the rapid expansion of slavery and major alterations in the colonies' relationships with nearby Indians, as reflected in Bacon's Rebellion in Virginia and King Philip's War in New England. The growing commercialization of New England, especially in the years following the Glorious Revolution of 1688–89, also contributed to the reshaping of colonial society and politics.[27] As a result of such changes in the later years of the seventeenth century, the Filmerian system of thought declined significantly in importance. By the time of the American Revolution, it survived primarily as a metaphorical language strategically employed by patriot leaders to explain their quest for independence in easily understood familial terms.[28] In the future, I plan to explore the decline of Filmerian thinking in the years surrounding 1700, and to link that decline—and the rise of Lockean ideas—to the development of an entrenched slave system and to the colonists' changing relationships with their Native American neighbors, but such a task proved impossible to undertake in the context of this volume.

If the limitation of *Founding Mothers & Fathers* to the era before the mid-1670s was intentional, certain consequences of the reliance on court records were not. Only in retrospect did I come to understand why there was so little information about Indians and Africans in the documents I was reading. During the first half-century of colonization, Indians rarely came into contact with the English court system. The earliest colonists often commented on the Algonkian societies they encountered, and those initial accounts have been used in this book. But as the decades passed and English settlement expanded, fewer English people wrote about America's native inhabitants except in the context of diplomatic contacts and sporadic warfare, which had little relevance to the explication of Filmerian thought that primarily interested me. The few Indians incorporated into English society, primarily as captured or hired servants, did make occasional appearances in the courts; their origins often proved to be relevant to the ways they were treated, as shall be pointed out in the chapters that follow.

Africans resident in mainland North America prior to the mid-1670s (there were fewer than four thousand in the Chesapeake and fewer than five hundred in New England) rarely appeared in English courts for any reason. Africans lived primarily as servants and slaves within the households of English settlers, with the exception of a few free black families on Virginia's eastern shore.[29] For reasons discussed in detail in the prologue to the first section of this volume and in chapter two, cases involving household subordinates of all descriptions (children and English servants in addition to Africans and Indians) seldom came before colonial courts. And in the absence of the sorts of plantation records and letterbooks used by scholars of the eighteenth century (including myself), it was impossible to reach many firm conclusions about the experiences of the first African residents of the colonies.[30]

Much of the time, this book will contrast "New England" and "the Chesapeake," but it is important to observe at the outset that there were significant differences *within* as well as *between* the two regions, differences that will occasionally be remarked upon. In the Chesapeake, Virginia (with an established church and political stability by the early 1630s) resembled the New England pattern more than did politically chaotic Maryland, which could not enforce religious orthodoxy because its residents were divided between largely Catholic leaders and mostly Protestant settlers. In New England, the most Filmerian government was that of New Haven; the least, Maine prior to its incorporation into Massachusetts Bay. Indeed, Maine in general resembled the Chesapeake rather than its New England neighbors: with a similarly imbalanced sex ratio—the excess men were fishermen working for wages rather than indentured servants laboring in the tobacco fields—and without an established church for a good part of its existence, Maine, like Maryland, was at least potentially a Lockean society. But the Bay Colony eventually took over the fishing communities (in a process examined in chapter six), and so in the long run Maine did not develop into the Chesapeake's northern counterpart.[31]

One of this book's major contentions is that—everywhere in theory, and in much of New England in reality—the seventeenth-century state and family were conceptually and practically related to each other. Yet for analytical purposes it is necessary to separate them and, indeed, to include another component in the discussion: the community of individuals and other families that comprised the environment within which specific families and the state functioned on a daily basis. Thus this book is divided into three sections: the first focuses on gendered power as it operated in families, the second on gendered power within communities, and the third on the gendered power wielded by political authority. Despite the primary focus of the individual sections, however, the other two elements will enter into each analysis, for the three are so entwined they cannot be fully extricated from one another, nor should they be. The central arguments of *Founding Mothers & Fathers* are designed, after all, to explicate the nature of those very connections.

SOME WORDS ABOUT WORDS

This book employs certain key concepts as they were understood in the seventeenth century, not as they are used in modern English. The most important of these are *family, public,* and *private.* To aid in analysis, it also adopts some terms not commonly utilized in the period under study; these include *status, community, formal public,* and *informal public.* It is therefore essential to define the meanings I attach to such words.

Family. In seventeenth-century English America, the word *family* applied to all persons subject to the same household head.[32] Usually, but not always, that head was a man; it could also be his widow, for whatever period transpired before her remarriage. At that point her new husband would assume the role of head of her household, merging it with any household he had previously governed. Thus the term *family* as commonly defined consisted of a man, his wife, and their children; the resident children of either by earlier marriages; resident servants; and any other co-resident dependent relatives or nonrelatives. Two major connections linked members of a family to one another: co-residence and subjection to the same person. Kinship ties were not essential to the definition of *family.*[33]

Therefore, even though households in early Maryland and Virginia looked very strange indeed by English standards, contemporaries had no difficulty applying the word *family* to them. Because of the imbalanced sex ratio, many Chesapeake men spent years as single adults; even though such men might be property-owning planters, they could not meet the usual English criterion for initiating a family—that is, forming a marital union. Chesapeake families consequently often consisted largely of male servants. Moreover, such households could be headed jointly by two male partners, known in the region as "mates." The partners might both be single, or one could be married, but in no case were both married.

Rank or *Status.*   The only contemporary term used to describe the elements of England's all-encompassing social and political hierarchy was *rank*, employed in English as early as the late sixteenth century to mean "one's social position or standing." Other roughly comparable words, like *status* or *class*, came into use later, primarily in the eighteenth and nineteenth centuries.[34] Since in twentieth-century usage *class* has taken on Marxist connotations that can be misleading in a seventeenth-century context, that term will be avoided, but I will employ *status*, which does not carry the same ideological baggage, in addition to *rank*.

Most migrants to the early colonies were drawn from the broad middle ranges of society, so the elaborate English hierarchical system was not fully reproduced in America. The few representatives of the nobility or gentry who made their way across the Atlantic were carefully designated in colonial records as "Sir," "Lord," "Lady," or "Gent.," but for the most part the top of the colonial pyramid was occupied by those persons termed "Master," "Mister," or "Mistress." Below them came the familiar "Goodmen" and "Goodwives," along with the people undesignated by title, and finally those at the bottom—the indentured servants and slaves, temporarily or permanently bound to service.[35]

The words *Master* or *Mister* and *Mistress* have often confused editors and scholars, but it is important that they be understood in a seventeenth-century context. Abbreviated in the court records as "Mr." and "Mrs.," they have been misread as the simple, uninflected designators familiar to twentieth-century readers.[36] The confusion has been particularly notable in the case of "Mrs.," which historians have tended to interpret as an indicator of marital rather than social status. Yet in early modern Anglo-America, "Mrs." exclusively designated a high-status woman, regardless of whether she was single, widowed, or married. In fact, the term's role as a sign of rank was so important that where the word *mistress* might commonly have been employed in a somewhat different context—a servant's referring to his "master and mistress"—it was often replaced by another term, *dame,* when the woman in question was of ordinary rather than high rank. Thus, for example, a servant was told by the New Haven court in 1661 that he was "a stubborne & rebellious youth, neither feareing God nor his Mr nor dame," and when a Virginia maidservant fell ill in 1629 she said to her master that she "wished that her dame were with her for her dame could give her ease."[37]

Community. Colonial historians have employed the word *community* in a variety of different ways. For some, it has meant shared value systems as expressed in such collective activities as attending the same church or signing the same town covenants. Other historians, especially those studying the Chesapeake, have applied it more broadly to groups of people who interacted regularly over an extended period of time. Some have used the word without defining it, as though its meaning was self-evident; others have developed their own definitions or relied on those drawn up by social theorists.[38]

In this book I employ the words *community* and *informal public* (of which more will be said shortly) as synonyms for the social collectivity within which individuals and families lived their daily existence, and which affected nearly every aspect of their lives. These were people who, as David Sabean has stressed, shared arguments as well as values.[39] The word used by the early colonists closest in meaning to my definition of *community* is *neighborhood.* But *neighborhood* then and now implies physical proximity, and although many participants in what I call *community* were indeed "neighbors," others were not. It accordingly seemed crucial not to define the concept spacially, and thus I have chosen not to use *neighborhood* except when referring to people who lived close to one another.[40]

It is important to distinguish between *community* and what will be called in this book *state, church, authority,* or *formal public.*[41] Such words will be applied to officially sanctioned rules and rulers, to persons elected or appointed to govern or regulate the actions of other colonists. The *community* or *informal public,* by contrast, had no such formalized regulatory role to perform, but it contributed to the formation and perpetuation of social order nonetheless. Roughly, it consisted of peers: of heads of households and their dependents who saw one another frequently and commented on one anothers' doings. Sometimes those comments were positive and approving, other times they were negative and harshly critical. A seventeenth-century colonist ignored the judgment of the community at his or her peril. If a person came into conflict with the *formal public* (the disciplinary apparatus of state or church), the opinions of the *informal public* could determine his or her fate.

Public. The word *public* (and variants) had two primary meanings in the early colonies. Both were relatively straightforward and uncontested. The first, which the *Oxford English Dictionary* dates to 1548, was "open to general observation, sight, or cognizance . . . manifest, not concealed." Thus, the Virginia General Court in 1625 decided that although a planter had acted in an "irreguler" manner by killing and eating hogs that damaged his corn crop, his offense was mitigated since it was done "Publiqly." In the same vein, the author of a 1652 pamphlet criticizing Massachusetts Bay's policy toward Baptists told his targets, "I hope you will not be offended to see this Narrative brought forth into the publick view." Often *public* and *private* appeared together as contrasting terms in both this and other senses of the two words. So a Maryland governor's proclamation about a rebel in early 1661 read: "Wm ffuller doth privatly lurke and Obscure himselfe in unknowne places [so] I have thought fitt to make the same publickly knowne to all persons."[42]

The second definition, "of or pertaining to the people as a whole," originated in the mid-fifteenth century and was employed by the colonists along with similar, earlier words like *commonweal* (for which the earliest usage found by the *OED* is 1330). In this sense it was often joined with other words, as people spoke of "those which are in publique trust," of "publick spirit" or "publick good," of a gift for "publick ends & purposes." Again, *public* and *private* commonly contrasted with each other, as in Winthrop's lay sermon, "A Modell of Christian Charity": "the care of the publique must oversway all private respects . . . perticuler estates cannot subsist in the ruine of the publique."[43]

As has already been indicated, for analytical purposes I have found it useful to divide the second meaning of *public* into two subsets, termed *formal public* and *informal public,* or, alternatively, *state/church/authority* and *community.* Such a distinction seemed essential for two reasons. First, I wanted to make it clear that peer groups of colonists (the informal public) did not always concur with the judgments or decisions of the officially recognized authorities (the formal public). Without the qualifying adjectives, the word *public* could be read ambiguously in a way that would unnecessarily obscure my meaning.

Second, and more important, is the distinction between the two subsets of *public* in terms of gender. The *Oxford English Dictionary* points out that the origins of *public* lie in a Latin word meaning "adult men" or "male population." In the seventeenth-century English colonies, the formal public—with one notable exception who will be considered at length later in this book—was indeed composed exclusively of adult men, the vast majority of whom also headed households.[44] But the informal public or community was much more inclusive: it encompassed women of all ages, younger men, and even indentured servants or slaves. Certainly within the informal public some voices, for example those of older, more experienced, or higher status colonists, carried more weight than others, but few voices could be wholly ignored, especially if they were expressing a community consensus. Moreover, on some issues, in particular female sexuality, it is clear that women's voices dominated the discussions in the informal public and that women's opinions accordingly affected the decisions of the formal public as well.[45]

Private. If the meanings of *public* in the colonies were relatively uncontested, the definitions of *private* present a very different picture. The *OED* remarks that *private* means "in general, the opposite of public." That the two terms are intricately linked is suggested by their frequent appearance together in colonial documents. Even so, *private* appears in many more guises than *public.*

Private in the sense of "concealed, secret" originally appeared in English in 1472. This definition of the word was employed repeatedly in the colonies. Thus court sessions on sensitive matters were declared "private" (and one Maine man was punished for "harkening under the window, when the Court was private"); Massachusetts law penalized people who "privately" received goods stolen from them without "legally prosecut[ing] the offender"; and the Reverend Thomas Shepard, recalling his months as a fugitive from the authorities in England, spoke of living for a time in "a very private place" in London.[46]

Yet *private* also had a myriad of other meanings for the colonists, all of which are noted in *OED* definitions. It could refer to something personal, as in "private Hours," "particular & private" spiritual concerns, or the "private comfort" of seeing one's children do well.[47] That meaning of *private* extended to economics: a Virginia law of 1631/2 referred to planters' "private labours" that could not be interrupted by the governor alone "uppon any coullor whatsoever"; if "the publique service require imployments of many hands," the House of Burgesses declared, the council's concurrence was necessary.[48] The word could also characterize a gathering that was not open to people generally or which had no official function, like the "Private Meeting" of Baptists in Lynn held "in the time of Publick exercise of the Worship of God" or the "private Fast" observed in 1688 by fifty members of the Plymouth church.[49]

More often, used in contradistinction to the second meaning of *public*, it identified a man who did not hold a public office or responsibility, such as the Marylander who came to the Upper House of Assembly in March 1659/60 to express an opinion "as a privat man . . . not one of his lordships councell," the "private men" who in the opinion of the Massachusetts General Court in 1650 had asked the court to convene too often "uppon slender grounds," or the "private brethren" who spoke regularly in the Plymouth church, to the dismay of pastors of other congregations.[50] In the same vein, *private* distinguished the personal interests of a man who held an official position from his broader responsibilities. For example, Thomas Gorges's letters from Maine in the early 1640s to his uncle Sir Ferdinando Gorges, the colony's proprietor, described both "publique" affairs and "your privat" business; similarly, one of Lord Baltimore's agents in Maryland reported in 1638 that "I have not yet had Leysure toe Attend my pryvate Conveniensy nor Proffitt, . . . haveing run myself and fortune allmost out of breathe in Pursute of the Publick good." And the phrase "private occasions" was commonly used to refer to what today would be termed the "personal business" of officeholders.[51]

Two important observations need to be made about the varying uses of *private*. First, note the common denominator: *private* meant, in essence, "not public," instead of having its own intrinsic definition. As a result, the colonists sometimes had difficulty determining what was, or should be, private, even on occasions when they had little difficulty determining what was, or should be, public.

The problem arose with all the different uses of the word *private*. Contested meanings are evident in colonists' attempts to determine what subjects should be "concealed, secret," as well as in their disputes over a man's appropriate public and private roles or what events should occur in public as opposed to private settings. Such arguments will be discussed throughout this book; the most notable examples occurred during the trials of Anne Hutchinson, which will be analyzed at length in chapter eight. There the matter of what constituted a private conversation led to considerable controversy, as did the issue of how to define a public gathering. Many such contentious discussions occurred in various contexts during the seventeenth century, indicating that the meaning of *private* was by no means fixed, and that the colonists, while acknowledging the theoretical opposition *public/private*, found it extremely difficult to draw a clear line between the two.

For instance, two different public/private disputes arose in the context of New England church governance. One involved charges against a misbehaving church member: should such accusations be considered "in public"—that is, before the entire congregation, which might include "strangers" (nonmembers)—or "in private," in front of the membership alone or perhaps even only the elders? It is hardly surprising that, in the absence of consensus about the definition of *private*, congregations engaged in lengthy deliberations and then adopted differing procedures. In the mid-1640s, for example, the newly organized church at Wenham debated the question for five months before concluding that all offenses among church members, even those "public[ly] known," should be heard in private. The Boston church, by contrast (and much to one colonist's dismay) insisted that "all matters of publique offence" be handled publicly.[52]

The second common dispute raised a gendered question: should women as well as men seeking membership be required to face "publick" examination in front of their peers, or could they be examined in private, by the elders and perhaps a few selected members? Most churches eventually opted for the latter solution, not only because some women (like those in Hampton, New Hampshire, in 1661) "professe[d] theyre inability to speake in publique" but also because some ministers, like the Reverend John Cotton, contended that women's making an "open confession . . . was against the apostle's [Paul's] rule, and not fit for women's modesty."[53]

On this question, too, though, the answer was far from universally self-evident: in Salem, one man noted, "women speake themselves, for the most part, in the Church." And the Wenham church as well insisted that prospective female members be examined in public, on the grounds that "the whole church is to judge of their meetness which cannot so well be if she speak not herself." The congregation concluded that Paul's injunction against women speaking in church referred only to "teaching a prophecy" and that "this kind of speaking is by submission where others are to judge &c."[54]

The other general observation pertains to a meaning of *private* not evident in seventeenth-century usage. None of the contemporary definitions of *private* carried undisputed gendered connotations, with the exception of those that distinguished between the familial and official roles of men who held elected or appointed positions. In other words, the English colonists did not equate *private* and *female* or *private* and *family*, even though they did largely (though not exclusively) equate *public*— that is, *formal public*—and *male*.[55] The public/private dichotomy so frequently discussed by historians of women, in other words, did not exist in the Filmerian world, with its unified rather than dichotomous conceptualization of power.[56]

True, the formal public was run by men—though exceptions were possible—but parts of the informal public were subject to women, both collectively and individually. Women, in other words, had recognized and recognizably public (in both senses: widely known, and relevant to the people as a whole) roles in colonial society. Thus in 1648, when a Massachusetts law provided that ferries should carry passengers only on a first-come, first-served basis, the sole exception was for "all Publick persons or such as goe upon publick or urgent occasions," including "Midwives and such other as are called to woemens labours."[57]

Conversely, the only time when colonial usage unambiguously termed a household *private* to distinguish it from *public* was when the household in question was headed by a man who also held an official position. That led to the possibility, though not to the necessity, that his actions in those two capacities might need to be conceptually separated. The applicability of the term *private* to a household, in short, had nothing to do with women, but rather depended on its male head's political position.[58]

Thus, in considering the meanings of *public* and *private* in seventeenth-century Anglo-America, the historian is confronted with an asymmetrial formulation. The meanings *public* ("widely known") and *[formal] public* (religious or secular authority) were clearly understood. *[Informal] public* (most often in the context of "neighbors") was less clearcut but nevertheless recognized in practice if not in theory. The meanings of *private*, by contrast, were ambiguous and obscure, open to many possible interpretations. Not one of those interpretations, however, privileged women over men with respect to the word's application.

This book will use the words *public, private,* and their variants as precisely as possible and will explore contests over their meanings, because it is impossible to comprehend the full significance of the Filmerian theory of unified power and its impact on women and men in the seventeenth-century colonies without understanding the contemporary meanings of such words and attempting to re-create fully the context within which they were applied.

GENDERED POWER
IN THE FAMILY

❧

The Government of Familyes

> The prosperity and well being of Comon weles doth
> much depend uppon the well goverment and ordering of
> particuler Familyes.
> —*Connecticut General Court, July 5, 1643*[1]

I F ANYONE HAD HELD a "most dysfunctional family" contest in
seventeenth-century New England, the clan headed by Nicholas Pinion, an iron worker, would have won easily. Other families rivaled the
Pinions for spectacular one-time misdeeds and individual long-term miscreants, but none could match the Pinions' two-generation record of
twenty-six prosecutions over two decades in four colonies, along with
other accusations that did not result in formal charges. Nicholas and
Elizabeth Pinion and their four children faced the New England courts
for offenses ranging from profanity and absence from sabbath services to
theft, adultery, and infanticide. In addition, family members were sued
for defamation and assaulted by other colonists; one was the victim of
an attempted rape reputedly instigated by her husband; and three others
repeatedly engaged in lascivious conduct. Over the years, various Pinions
were admonished, fined, whipped, and banished from two different
colonies; eventually, one was executed. Nothing ever seemed to make
them behave properly. What was the problem with the Pinions? Recounting their story as it appears in the court records suggests the answer
seventeenth-century analysts would have supplied.

The elder Pinions, who then lived at the Lynn, Massachusetts, ironworks, announced their presence in New England in notable fashion by
being charged with a total of seven offenses during three days of a Salem
court session late in the winter of 1647/8. Among them were minor
violations like swearing, drunkenness, and absence from Sunday meetings, but much more serious problems were implied in the fragmentary
record of the proceedings. Nicholas Pinion had warned one Nicholas

Russell, who had previously boarded with the family, to stay away from the house, Pinion suspecting his wife, Elizabeth, of an adulterous relationship with Russell. Two witnesses corroborated his suspicions by attesting that Elizabeth had said that if Russell left the house, she would leave too. A local justice intervened, binding her to good behavior, but she paid little attention to the admonition. She physically attacked her husband several times on different nights; he in turn beat her severely, causing her to miscarry a pregnancy and eliciting "screeching and Crying out" that disturbed the neighbors. She then charged him with the "killing off ffyve Children . . . one of them was a yeare old." Nicholas Pinion and Nicholas Russell were both fined, and Elizabeth was ordered to pay a fine or be whipped. Two months later, she was tried by the Massachusetts Bay General Court on two counts of adultery—a capital crime. Acquitted of that serious offense, she was nevertheless ordered "severely whiped for her evill & adulterous behavior & swearing," the lashing first to be performed at Boston, then again a month later at Lynn.[2]

Perhaps the penalties had a quieting effect on the Pinions, for during the rest of their stay in Lynn, which lasted for at least another fourteen years, the couple was in court only sporadically, charged with a variety of offenses, some of them minor: swearing and assault (Nicholas, 1649); involvement in sexual horseplay with three men and another woman (Elizabeth, 1650); sumptuary violations ("wearing silver lace": both, 1652); assault (Elizabeth, 1663). Each was also assaulted at least once by other colonists. By the time the family left Lynn, the younger generation had appeared in the court records for the first time: in 1660 Robert Pinion, Nicholas's and Elizabeth's son, was ordered fined and whipped for criminal defamation, although the whipping was later remitted.[3]

Assessing this sorry record at the time the Pinions left Lynn, a contemporary observer would have quickly diagnosed the problem. Elizabeth was not a proper wife, and Nicholas was not a proper husband. The brawling, profane couple sought to live above their rank by wearing silver lace. A suspected adulterer who had been publicly shamed by whipping in two separate locations, Elizabeth failed to respect her obligation to confine her sexual activity to the marriage bed. Her subsequent involvement in a lascivious episode indicated that severe punishment had not had the desired effect. But the fault was not hers alone. Nicholas was hardly a model of husbandly rectitude: in fact, he faced prosecution as often as she did, though never for a capital offense. He drank to excess, spoke profanely, and fought with other men.

Most important in this context, he could not control his wife. That was shown not only by her openly expressed interest in their boarder, but also by her physical and verbal attacks on Nicholas—actions indicating the absence of appropriate wifely deference. The most telling evidence of his failure as a husband was his having beaten her so severely that she miscarried. And had he perhaps battered her previously in similar circumstances? Her charge that he had killed "ffyve children," one of them a year old, while surely exaggerated, certainly hinted as much. In a well-run household, moderate physical correction was all that should have been required to ensure the good behavior of subordinates. That Nicholas had resorted to such violence would have implied to his contemporaries that he had no other means of winning his dependents' respect.

Thus a seventeenth-century commentator would have predicted disaster for the Pinions' children. Married couples modeled proper social relationships, so if a husband and wife behaved badly, their children would not learn suitable modes of conduct. After the family had relocated to the ironworks near New Haven, the full extent of the Pinions' failings as parents did indeed become evident. The second generation surpassed their elders, and the case records revealed what any seventeenth-century New Englander would have seen as the root cause of the difficulty: Nicholas Pinion's failings as a paterfamilias.

The Pinions first appeared in court in New Haven as complainants, not offenders. Elizabeth Pinion, her younger daughter Hannah (then about fifteen), and her older daughter, the widow Ruth Pinion Moore, reported to the magistrates in mid-December 1664 that Patrick Morran, the clerk of the ironworks where Nicholas was employed, had made sexual advances to both Hannah and Ruth. Ruth was already of "ill report" in the town; a year later, she would be convicted of having "ensnared & deluded sundry young men upon pretence & promise of marriage to countenance & cover unlawfull familiarity with them," a case about which more will be said shortly.[4] Undoubtedly Ruth's poor reputation led Morran to conclude that not just she but her younger sister as well would be receptive to his invitations for sexual encounters.

The evidence later presented against Ruth Moore showed that she enjoyed flirtatious exchanges with bachelors, but the fifteen-year-old Hannah, not yet sexually experienced, was taken aback when Morran, over a period of three weeks starting in late November 1664, began to offer her increasingly tempting bribes to "let him ly with her." First, he proffered a pair of gloves, then stockings *and* gloves, and finally gloves and a silver shilling. Hannah reported to the court that, certain the last offer would clinch the deal, "he pulled out the shilling & he went to take her up in his armes & fling her on the bed." To stop him, she threatened to call out to two other people who were then in the house where he boarded.[5]

Hannah soon told her mother and sister—but not, significantly, her father—about the troubling incidents. Goody Pinion directly confronted Morran; he in turn approached Nicholas, seeking to persuade the family not to file charges against him. Nicholas, who thereby first learned about the sexual encounters between his supervisor and his younger daughter, quickly decided not to pursue the matter. Backed by Goody Mary Russell (the wife of Morran's landlord, Ralph Russell), Nicholas even convinced the reluctant Elizabeth to "pass it over." But then Patrick made a mistake. He called at the Pinions' house one night and quietly asked Ruth Moore to meet him at the ironworks. She agreed, yet her intentions were unclear: was she seeking to warn him to leave her younger sister alone (as her testimony implied) or was she trying to add Patrick to her list of conquests (as his version suggested)? Ruth attested that while they were at the ironworks Patrick Morran told her that "he must or would have the use of her body," using such "immodest & shamefull expressions" that "shee was ashamed to speake it." John and Thomas Luddington, two brothers who lodged with the Pinions, witnessed the end of the ironworks encounter but could not testify about what Ruth and Patrick had said. Any attempt to discern the contents of the conversation is complicated by the fact that Ruth and Patrick did become sexually involved with each other at some time within the next eighteen months, a fact that emerged in a later case.

Despite the ambiguity surrounding Ruth Moore's motives that night in the late autumn of 1664, it seems to have been her meeting with Patrick that led the female Pinions to bring formal charges against the ironworks clerk. Questioned by the magistrates at his trial, Morran admitted that after Ruth had gone home that evening he told the Luddington brothers that he was ashamed to be seen under such circumstances with a woman of dubious reputation, "for it would be a scandall to the gospell & a Blemish to his name" if the tale became known. He insisted, to the brothers and later to the court, that the subject of his conversation with Ruth was the "wrong" she had done to Benjamin Graves, one of her many suitors. He "absolutely denied" having propositioned her, also denying Hannah's original charge.

After considering Ruth's and Hannah's statements and Morran's unconditional denials, the New Haven judges decided that "they find not Patricke Morran such a person as they accuse him to bee," yet at the same time that "he hath imprudently carried it, soe as renders him suspitious of something of the like nature." On the whole, Ruth Moore's poor reputation seems to have influenced the court's opinion of her and her sister's charges, just as it had undoubtedly influenced Morran's assessment of whether Hannah would be open to a proposition in the first place. New Haven's judges were unwilling to convict a man on the testimony of a woman of "ill report" and her young sister, no matter how logical or consistent their stories. The Pinions were thus caught in a melancholy circularity: Ruth's bad reputation both created the situation in which Hannah found herself and prevented an adequate resolution of it. The unsuccessful prosecution of Patrick Morran for propositioning the two young women thus provides an excellent example of the interplay of family, community, and state. The community's negative judgment of Ruth Moore thwarted her sister Hannah's attempt to win any redress from the judicial system.

Perhaps emboldened by his success in escaping punishment, Patrick Morran then sued Elizabeth, Hannah, and Ruth for defamation, asking £200 in damages. He presented three witnesses to the slander, which basically consisted of the three women's telling others about their accusations after they had complained to the authorities but before Patrick's trial. "Old goody Pinion," one man reported, had called Morran a "base rogue & Rascall" who "sought the ruine of her & her Children." One new element entered the defamation: Ruth Moore claimed that Morran had lost a previous job for the same reason—that is, lascivious conduct. Asked why he requested such excessive damages, Morran told the court that "he esteemed his name above this money." The judges, who certainly had not cleared him despite their earlier verdict, responded drily that "he might over Esteeme his name," awarding him just £5 in damages and court charges. They also gave him a "serious admonition, That he carry it more prudently for the future." The warning did not do much good: twenty-eight months later Morran was back in court, charged with "unsutable & unseasonable familiarity" with Hannah Pinion and Goody Mary Russell. Again, however, his "perumptory" denial saved him from more than another "serious admonition and Caution."[6]

One of the most remarkable aspects of the two original cases—first the prosecution of Morran, then his countersuit against Goody Pinion and her two daughters—was the role played in them (or, more precisely, the role not played in them) by Nicholas Pinion. Elizabeth, Hannah, and Ruth made the initial accusation against Patrick. When Nicholas testified at Patrick's trial, he explained that he appeared "as a witnes . . . & not as a complayner," then by his testimony revealed that he had little direct knowledge of what had happened. Indeed, he heard about

Hannah and Patrick only after his wife had already angrily confronted Morran, and his first reaction to the incidents was to persuade his wife to overlook them. Nicholas did tell the justices that he watched Patrick carefully the night he visited their house, "as he thought it behooved him to doe." But he failed to take note of the conversation in which Ruth and Patrick agreed to meet at the ironworks, and, although he noticed that Patrick "jogd [Hannah] with his foote" whenever she walked by him, Nicholas still "said nothing to him of the busines."[7]

Nicholas Pinion then compounded his inaction in the defamation suit. Named by the court as attorney for his wife and daughters and asked to respond to Morran's charges, Nicholas told the judges that "he had nothing to say for he had heard nothing of it. Therefore he should Leave it to the Court for he had nothing to object in behalf of his Clyent."[8] Such a total abdication of responsibility on the part of a household head was unprecedented in New England. Men occasionally asked the courts for assistance in controlling unruly wives, children, and servants, thereby in effect admitting their own inadequacy as family governors. In these two cases Nicholas Pinion did more—or, rather, less— than that: he abandoned any claim to authority in his household, allowing his wife and daughters to act on their own, without his guidance or even assistance. He professed ignorance of the recent events, revealing that the womenfolk in his family had successfully kept secrets from him. Nicholas refused to align himself with the complaints against Morran, and he refused to defend his wife and daughters in the slander suit, even though he would have to pay their fines. Because Morran was his supervisor, Nicholas might understandably have hesitated before taking decisive action, but contemporaries would have judged his inertia harshly. No wonder the family was in disarray, they would have remarked. It had no leader, no proper guide, protector, and counselor at its head.

The prosecutions of all four of Nicholas's and Elizabeth's children over the next three years, two of them at courts convened especially for the purpose, fully revealed the disorder in the Pinion household. The first to face the judgment of his peers was Robert, the son who had been in trouble even before the family left Lynn. Unlike his father, he was unwilling to remain silent at what he regarded as the New Haven authorities' improper treatment of his mother and sisters in the Morran cases. He uttered "some contemptuous speeches in reference to the Authority" at the January 1664/5 court session. Then he compounded his offense by telling a woman "that he had as good be bitt with a mad dog as snapt at by a company of fooles" when she asked him about his examination by the magistrates. The following month the judges decided that although they thought "his evill deserved sharpe Corporall punishment," they would be lenient. They fined him twenty shillings, directing that he also sit in the stocks on two different days.[9]

The next time he did not get off so easily. The following August, at a "Speciall Particular Court," Robert was accused of conspiring with Patrick Morran's servant, Giles Blach, to steal various items from Morran's chests and cellar.[10] On a sabbath, Robert broke into Morran's cellar to steal rum and sugar. Giles and Robert took their booty to the house of Robert's brother, Thomas; the three "burnt" the rum and sugar and drank the resulting toddy. In the afternoon, with Morran still away at church, the thieves returned for more. In addition, the Pinion brothers took stockings, gunpowder, ribbon, and linen from Morran's chest. Robert, who had previously threatened to burn Morran's account book, went through it, tearing out "sundry Leaves of the accounts of the Pinions & none else"—so when Morran produced the mutilated book at the trial, it served as crucial evidence of Robert's involvement in the theft. Giles, described by the court as "a very wicked Boy," was fined and ordered "severely whipt."

A special prosecutor then charged Robert not only with theft but also with sabbath violations, "lieing & slaundering the Authority & people here," "Lascivious & Corrupt speeches & Carriages," and "Threatening the lives" of the judges. The prosecutor accused Robert of being so frequently absent from church and so given to "mischeife" on the sabbath that "the neighbors were afrayd to leave their houses without some [people] at home, as was said by some of them." Several witnesses described Robert's speeches against the New Haven authorities and his boasts that he had persuaded young women to kiss him while he was sitting in the stocks. Others reported that "he vowed to be the death of them that punished him though it was seven yeares hence." Confronted with such overwhelming evidence, Robert admitted that "he had been apt to speake very vilely in those things" and that he had threatened people "in his wrath." He was ordered "severely whipt, for a future warneing & terror to himselfe & others against such miscarriages." He was also fined, ordered to post a good-behavior bond, and sent to prison until the sentence had been fully carried out. (Some time later, Robert left New Haven for Plymouth. In June 1667, "taken up as a vagrant" there, he was "publickly whipt" and ordered to leave the colony immediately.)[11]

The second Pinion child to be hauled into court was, not surprisingly, Ruth. In December 1665 she too was charged before a "special

court" with "sundry Crimes." By the time of the trial, she had married
one of her many suitors, Peter Briggs, but the marriage had already
proved a failure. The accusations against her involved conduct both before and after her wedding.[12]

Before she came to New Haven, the court indicated, she had promised to marry two Massachusetts men, one of them Benjamin Graves,
the man on whose behalf Patrick Morran had claimed to be speaking
with her the previous year. Graves testified that his and Ruth's intention
to wed had been announced in Boston, and that he had come to New
Haven to marry her. Asked by the judges if she had said she would
marry Graves, she replied airily, "there might be such a thing at Boston,
but shee was not to answer for that here." Although she had jilted
Graves, they were accused of lascivious conduct both before and after
her marriage to Briggs. Witnesses had seen them "kissing & embrace-
ing," and they were known to have spent time together in a "suspicious"
manner. Graves also told two other men that she was a "whore." One
of those men was John Luddington, whom Ruth had met in New Haven and whom she had also promised to marry. Luddington told the
court that Graves had asked him "if he never lay with her? to which he
answered, That he scorned to doe that before marriage: But the said
Benjamin Replied that he had, more then once or twice."

Benjamin denied having made the last statement, though he admitted he had called Ruth a whore. Ruth claimed that Benjamin had kissed
and hugged her only when he "wisht her Joy after her marriage." The
judges believed neither of them. Graves was convicted of lascivious conduct and lying, fined, told to acknowledge his guilt formally in the court
or to be "severely whipt," and ordered to leave New Haven.

Ruth Briggs faced additional charges with respect to her marriage.
She was accused of "wilfully departing" from her husband against his
wishes, then—when questioned about her action by a magistrate—of
having "pretended she had liberty from her husband to come away,
which appeared otherwise when enquired into." When Peter came after
her and ordered her to return home with him, she "in a rage" and
"contrary to the duty of a wife" refused to do so, thus "casting contempt upon Authority whoe had enjoined her returne to him." All this
Ruth admitted, including being "very abusive" to Peter and "offering
violence to him." The judges, considering such behavior on her part to
be "gross miscarriages," ordered her to pay court costs and a hefty fine
or to undergo a lashing. They also ordered that she "speedily depart"
from New Haven. She said she would pay the fine to avoid corporal
punishment.

Nicholas and Elizabeth were summoned to appear at Ruth's trial, but failed to come. Later, the court clerk noted, they satisfied the court about the reason for their absence; no details about why they were wanted or what they were doing are given in the record, but Nicholas's absence would have surprised no one familiar with his lack of action in the previous cases involving his wife and daughters.

Nine months after Ruth's trial and a year after Robert's it was Thomas's turn. In August 1666 he, Ralph Russell, and two other men were charged with drunkenness, in itself a minor offense.[13] But Thomas's wife, Mary, reported to a neighbor that William Collins, one of Thomas's drinking companions, "had been hunting her about, & . . . shee could not be quiet for him." In the Pinion clan unusual results were perhaps to be expected. After the four men had been drinking heavily one morning at Russell's house, Thomas evidently told Collins that, if Mary agreed, he could have sex with her. Mary's testimony revealed what happened next, as Collins came directly to the Pinion house and found her working outside.

> Then he strove with her & tooke her up in his armes & Carried her in a doores, but she got out from him twice, but after he threw her upon the bed & said he would ly with her, but she said he should not. He said he had a Commission from her husband, if she would give her Consent, But she answered that her husband had noe such power over her as to make her sin. He not forbeareing she Cried out & then he went away.

The cries brought Nicholas to his daughter-in-law's aid; he confirmed her description of the incident, as did two other men, both of whom had seen Collins pick Mary Pinion up and carry her inside the house. Intriguingly, neither sought to intervene in what was clearly a sexual assault. Did they fail to act because of the Pinions' reputation? It is possible to speculate that such was the case; witnesses to similar incidents usually did not let them pass without taking some sort of action.[14] But on this occasion, at least, Nicholas Pinion had acted like a proper paterfamilias by helping his daughter-in-law to fend off her attacker.

If the witnesses were not inclined to involve themselves in the attempted rape of Mary Pinion, the New Haven justices were. In this case the reputation of the family was irrelevant. They told Collins—who claimed that he had been so drunk he did not remember his actions—that "he was not fitt to live among a people," directed that he be "severely Whipt, for a warneing to himselfe & others," and ordered him to post bond for his future good behavior. The court ignored Thomas Pinion's denial that he had given Collins "a Commission to abuse his wife," instructing him on "the greatnes of his sin." It then fined him twenty shillings. Ralph Russell and the other participant in the drinking bout were fined lesser sums.

In early March 1667/8, two more prosecutions and an investigation both renewed and concluded the New Haven magistrates' involvement with the Pinions. Hannah, now about eighteen, was ordered whipped "at her fathers house," for "wicked carriage" at the ironworks and for "her bad Language as Cursing & other Corrupt base speeches." Another crime showed that the torch of misbehavior had not been passed entirely to the younger generation and that the family dynamic remained the same. Giles Blach, accused of stealing a blanket, proclaimed his innocence. He pointed a finger instead at the Pinion household, where a constable's search turned up the purloined object. Called to account for its presence in his dwelling, Nicholas, true to type, told the magistrates "he knew not of it." Ruth Briggs, however, was aware of the provenance of the blanket: she confessed that it "was stollen by her mother, wife of the said Nicholas pinion, whoe was now dead." The court told Nicholas that "he must be responsible for it, being found with him," ordering him to pay triple damages (the standard penalty for theft) to the blanket's owner. Fittingly, Elizabeth Pinion had reached out from the grave to bedevil her husband once again.[15]

But both Hannah's and Elizabeth's misbehavior paled beside that of Ruth Briggs. Her testimony about the blanket and in another concurrent investigation revealed that she had not left New Haven permanently when ordered to do so in December 1665, but had instead returned to town periodically for prolonged intervals, if indeed she had ever left at all. In February and March 1667/8, Ruth Briggs was investigated by the magistrates upon "some suspicion" that she "had been Lately with Child but now was delivered of it & made it away."[16]

Testimony by Mary Pinion and Mary Russell, along with opinions offered by midwives and other women, strongly suggested that Ruth had given birth on February 15, 1667/8. Although Ruth at first denied the charge, the magistrates continued to press her until she confessed. Ruth finally admitted that she had been pregnant, had taken savin (an abortifacient) prepared by her sister, Hannah, and had given birth in secret. Claiming that the child had been born dead "thro her neglect for want of helpe," she revealed that she had subsequently buried it "below her sisters [Mary Pinion's] garden by the swampe." She thereupon led the investigators to the body.

Questioned first as to the paternity of the child and then about her sexual conduct in general, Ruth, facing the death penalty for infanticide, declared "that she could not have peace untill she had made some further discovery of her wickednes." She accordingly confessed to a series of sexual offenses committed in New Haven over the previous three years. Her partners included Patrick Morran, with whom she said she had had sexual intercourse both before her marriage to Peter Briggs and in the months since her mother's death; Francis Tyler, "whom she said had committed wickednes with her 6 times"; and Richard Nicolls, who she claimed was the baby's father. With the last, who had insisted that she take the savin, she said she had had sex "soe often as she could not tell she thought more then she had fingers & toes." Such confessions may have—as the New Haven magistrates told Ruth—"improve[d] her little time for her soules advantage in makeing her peace with god," but they could not save her life. Tried and convicted of infanticide and adultery by the Court of Assistants in Hartford (by 1668 New Haven had been incorporated into Connecticut), she was hanged there later that year.[17]

Nicolls, an ironworker, had apparently left New Haven, for there is no record of his being questioned in the case. But Francis Tyler asserted that "he never committed any such fact with her in his life," and Patrick Morran adopted a similarly defiant stance. When Ruth reported that in the spring of 1666 he had also propositioned her sister-in-law, Morran admitted to having kissed Mary and to having been at the time tempted by "lust in his heart." Still, he denied Mary Pinion's testimony that he had offered her £10 "to let him lye with her." She and her husband had never gone to the authorities, Mary explained, because Morran "threaten[ed] them to bring them into trouble as he had some others . . . & proofe she had none & they lived in feare of him." Morran was ordered to post bond to appear for trial in Hartford. The outcome of that prosecution is unknown, but four years later, while employed at the Lynn ironworks, he was convicted and fined for making violent sexual advances to a reputable married woman whose story the local court saw no reason to doubt.[18]

The Pinion children had thus more than fulfilled whatever dire predictions contemporary observers might have made about their fate. Hannah was whipped, and on other occasions both she and her brother Thomas were formally admonished by the judges for their misbehavior. Robert, who was whipped in two colonies, escaped a similar punishment in a third and was eventually banished from Plymouth. Ruth only barely avoided whipping in New Haven in 1665, and she was eventually executed for infanticide and adultery after years of admitted sexual pro-

miscuity. In spite of repeated efforts by several courts and many magistrates over two decades, Elizabeth and Nicholas never reformed: one
of her last earthly acts was stealing a blanket, and he remained to the
end an inadequate paterfamilias. No other seventeenth-century Anglo-
American family even came close to such a disastrous record of failure.[19]

WHAT MADE HOUSEHOLDS like that of the Pinions so dangerous in
the eyes of the authorities was the crucial role families played in the
maintenance of the Filmerian social order. The family was the real—
not just metaphorical—foundation of the state. The household constituted the lowest rung on the ladder of secular and religious authority
alike; its head was the first line of defense against disorderly subordinates
for both state and church. Thus, when five Indian leaders agreed to have
their people ruled by Massachusetts Bay in early 1644, the nine propo-
sitions to which they were asked to submit included not only injunctions
against such crimes as theft and murder and demands that they convert
to Christianity, but also two that related directly to the establishment of
what the English migrants would consider to be orderly households.
First, the Indians were warned "to honor their parents & all their superiors," as the Fifth Commandment ("Honor thy Father and Mother")
required; and second, they were enjoined "to comit no unclean lust, as
fornication, adultery, incest, rape, sodomy, buggery, or beastiality." Following both rules was essential to the formation of proper families, English people believed: if men and women engaged in sexual activity only
within marriage, and if dependents showed appropriate deference to
their real and their metaphorical parents, the cornerstones of civilized
society would successfully be laid.[20]

The person primarily responsible for maintaining order in the family
was its head, usually the husband and father. Seventeenth-century English people, whether Puritans, Catholics, or orthodox members of the
Church of England, believed it essential for fathers to supervise all aspects
of their dependents' secular and spiritual lives. The father's continuous
presence in the household was regarded as so important a part of the
requisite supervision that colonists expressed hesitation about laying out
farms too distant from villagers' dwellings. A group of Plymouth men
in 1639 thus complained that "by meanes of such farmes a mans famylie
is Divided so that in busie tymes they cannot (except upon the Lords
day) all of them joyne with him in famylie duties [daily prayer]." Likewise, the migrants who settled at New Haven in 1638 did so in part
because remaining in Massachusetts would have required them to live

too far from the land they were expected to cultivate. Some, according to their leaders, Theophilus Eaton and the Reverend John Davenport, were indeed "not . . . persuaded that it is lawfull for them to live continually from the greatest part of theyre familyes."[21]

The English immigrants, then, believed that heads of households were crucial links in the chain of hierarchical authority that governed their society. Because of the absence of other well-established, accepted hierarchical relationships in the early colonies, those links became even more important in North America than they had been in the mother country. The rulers of the new settlements faced repeated challenges to their understanding of orderly political and economic relationships. To meet such challenges, they adopted legislation designed to bring sky-rocketing wages and prices under control; they also commanded that proper deference be paid to officeholders who in England had been of relatively low rank. Even more significantly, they attempted to fill the social void that confronted them by delegating a variety of responsibilities to heads of households and by assessing penalties if those duties were not carefully performed. Heads of families were therefore asked to compensate for the lack of the elaborate administrative superstructure that had surrounded households in England.[22]

The impulse was the same in each of the colonies, but the outcome varied by region, for only in New England were enforcement efforts even sporadically pursued. During the early years of all the colonies but two, assemblies drafted sets of laws specifying that household heads take on obligations novel to the American context, along with duties that in England would have been performed by local government officials or members of parish vestries. The sole exceptions were Maryland and New Haven, which adopted only a very few pieces of such legislation during their first three decades of existence. Since New Haven's magistrates (as shall be seen in the pages that follow) had an expansive view of their own authority, they closely supervised household heads even in the absence of specific statutes. Thus for the most part such laws must have seemed superfluous there. As for Maryland, its hesitancy in this regard probably stemmed from the fact that it was the only Anglo-American jurisdiction to attempt to establish a manorial system and thus to try to sustain manorial courts, English institutions that oversaw families and would have rendered unnecessary special laws placing new responsibilities on household heads. By the time the manorial system was known to have failed, the anomalous Chesapeake regional demographic pattern had made it obvious that any attempt to base a stable social order on heads of households there was doomed to defeat.[23]

In all the other English colonies founded before the 1660s, masters of families were subjected to rules and regulations that applied to no other members of society. Plymouth regarded the character of such household heads as so important to the colony's success and stability that it provided as early as 1636 that only men approved by the proper authorities would be allowed "to be housekeepers or build any cottages." The nature of the legal obligations ranged widely, from the mundane (registering births, deaths, and marriages in one's family) to the serious (assisting in the capture of runaway servants). Heads of households were directed to plant two acres of corn for each working member of the family (Maryland, 1639); to supply themselves with adequate amounts of arms and ammunition (Maryland, 1649; Maine, 1665); and to grow or process hemp and flax (Plymouth, 1639, 1640; Connecticut, 1640, 1641; Massachusetts, 1641).[24] They were also ordered *not* to do other things: not to permit the congregating of idle young people under their roofs (Massachusetts, 1651); not to allow gambling in their households (Connecticut, 1657); and not to make more than sixteen barrels of tar in one year (Plymouth, 1665).[25]

Perhaps responding to the ever-present threat of social chaos that beset Virginia from its earliest years, the House of Burgesses adopted an especially long and detailed series of such laws. In order to ensure that the responsibility was placed on the right person if a household was headed by male partners, it in 1644 specified a procedure for identifying "the master of the family" when mates grew "a joynt cropp." The requirements that family governors plant sufficient corn to feed their families (1624), supply themselves with adequate arms and ammunition (1659), register all births, deaths and marriages (1660), and grow hemp and flax (1673) only marked the beginning of their responsibilities to the province. They were also directed lead their families in prayer at least once a day (1626); to save and store for public use the ashes from trees burned while clearing their lands (1630); to plant no more than 2,000 tobacco seedlings per household resident (1630); to carry guns to church on Sundays (1643); to report accurately once a year the number of taxable persons in their families (1649); to publicize "huies and cries" for runaway servants (1658); to convey "publique" letters "imediately" from plantation to plantation until the missives reached their intended destination (1662); and to prevent their servants from holding "unlawfull meetings" (1663). Noncompliance with such directives could bring substantial fines; for example, Virginians who concealed tithables were to be assessed treble taxes, and those who neglected to carry public letters could be fined up to 350 pounds of tobacco for each offense. But there is little indication in the colony's surviving court records that any of these laws was systematically enforced.[26]

The master's role in preserving social order was seen as so crucial that the Plymouth, Massachusetts Bay, Connecticut, and New Haven colonies directed single persons to live in "well governed families." In 1656 New Haven explained that persons "who live not in service, nor in any Family Relation, answering the mind of God in the fift Commandement" were a potential source of "inconvenience, and disorder." Accordingly, the colony provided that such individuals should live only in approved households, and that

> the Governor of which Family, so licensed, shal as he may conveniently, duly observe the course, carriage, and behaviour, of every such single person, whether he, or she walk diligently in a constant lawful imployment, attending both Family duties, and the publick worship of God, and keeping good order day and night, or otherwise.

The master was directed to inform the authorities if he noticed "disorder," so that his tenant could be "questioned, and punished, if the case require it."[27]

New England courts enforced these statutes from the 1630s through the 1670s. In the early 1640s, even before the passage of the law quoted above, New Haven twice directed that "all single persons are to betake themselves forthwith to some famylyes." Local courts occasionally prosecuted persistent offenders. For example, Plymouth in 1639 charged two men with "liveing alone disorderly," and the York, Maine, county court in 1674 ordered a magistrate to ensure that a man "liveing an Idle Lasy life" was placed "under family Government."[28] The court in Hampton, New Hampshire, learning in 1672 that a man "lay in a house by himself contrary to the law of the country," gave him six weeks to "remove and settle himself in some orderly family in the town, and be subject to the orderly rules of family government." The judges justified their decision by explaining that "the companions and consequences of a solitary life" were "much sin and iniquity." The nature of the family in which such single people were to live was accordingly important. Thus when a New Haven man in December 1658 asked that two shoemakers and a saddler be allowed to live in his house until the spring, "some of the Towne" expressed concern that there would be too many "younge persons" in the family. Before reluctantly agreeing to the arrangement, the justices inquired of another boarder about the truth of reports that "their hath beene a custom of shovell board [shuffleboard] in that house of late, and that mens servants do stay there at unseasonable houres."[29]

The phrase "family government," used repeatedly in such cases, reveals the key task assigned to the head of a household in the Filmerian system: he essentially acted as a justice of the peace with respect to his dependents. The state expected him to maintain order in his family and supported his right to correct his subordinates, just as (as shall be seen in chapter six) it supported its lowest-level officeholders, the grand jury men and constables, in their efforts to carry out their regulatory duties. Dependents faced formal prosecution primarily if they had misbehaved outside the household or if the master of their family could not control them. Even then, judges in New England (in a tactic rarely employed in the Chesapeake) often ordered offenders punished not by constables but by their family governors. Penalties inflicted inside and outside the household were thus closely interrelated. Frequently, indeed, they were viewed as substitutes for one another.

When the Filmerian system worked properly at the familial level, courts did not intervene in the process through which masters punished unruly dependents for what were termed "private" offenses—that is, minor misdeeds taking place entirely within the context of the household. (Such misbehavior might include, for example, intrafamilial theft, laziness, quarreling, or irresponsibility.) Thus the few intrafamilial cases brought to the attention of the authorities—thereby being recorded in court documents available to historians—raised pressing questions the judges needed to address. The cases that involved charges of excessive use of force by household heads will be considered in subsequent chapters. Here, the discussion will focus on general issues raised by the operations of the Filmerian system at its fundamental level, that of the family.

The question of how to define a "private" offense, one not subject to public scrutiny, posed the most nagging problem. As was already indicated in the introduction to this volume, seventeenth-century English people had an expansive conception of *public* and an inchoate, contested notion of what might be described as *private*. Yet they recognized that the word had some meaning when applied to intrafamilial behavior, especially to the acts of the household head. Even when they did not specifically employ the term *private*, they disclosed their belief that some, though certainly not all, information about the events and conversations in the household should be held in confidence by its members. The problem was determining the precise scope of that confidential information.[30]

The evidence on this point is scattered and fragmentary, as might be expected in light of the unformed nature of the concept. One of the few explicit definitions of *private* in a household context was elicited when parliamentary commissioners took over the governments of Virginia and Maryland in the early 1650s. The commissioners reported to their English superiors that they had agreed with the governor of Maryland that he was "not to be questioned for praying for, or speaking well of Charles Stuart in his Family or private discourse" during the year he was given to leave the colony. They included similar language in their formal agreement with Virginia officials, noting that the governor and council were not to be "censured" for "speaking well of the King for one whole yeare in their private houses or neighbouring conference."[31]

The provisions therefore had two restrictions: one chronological (the grace period of a year) and the other spacial (any conversation shielded from the threat of prosecution had to take place in the officials' own houses or, at most, in "neighbouring conference"). Further, only one specific political comment was protected under this limited application of *private*. Presumably, had any of the men involved chosen to speak critically of Parliament, rather than positively of the King, they could have opened themselves to prosecution for sedition even if the conversations had occurred in their "private houses." Furthermore, other members of their households received no exemption from punishment for their own seditious political statements.

A May 1634 incident described by John Winthrop in his journal similarly involved some protection for political speech within a family. Winthrop wrote that "a godly minister" had, "upon conscience of his oath and care of the commonwealth," revealed to the magistrates "some seditious speeches of his own son, delivered in private to himself." But the General Court, Winthrop stated, was "loath to have the father come in as a public accuser of his own son." It therefore sought other evidence against the young man before calling him formally to account for his statements.[32] The leaders of Massachusetts, while criminalizing the conduct in question, thereby attested to their disquiet at asking a father to testify against a son for a conversation occurring within a household, even though the father had voluntarily come forward with the information. Like the parliamentary commissioners, then, they recognized that comments made within a family unit were not necessarily subject to the same rules as remarks offered outside of it.

Perhaps the incident involving the minister and his son prompted the Massachusetts Bay General Court seven years later to approve the clearest and least restricted statement about family privacy drafted in the early years of the Anglo-American colonies. In the province's first comprehensive legal code, the Body of Liberties (1641), using language that was also later incorporated into the Laws and Liberties (1648), the General Court provided that

> No Magestrate, Juror, Officer, or other man shall be bound to informe present or reveale any private crim[e] or offence, wherein there is no perill or danger to this plantation or any member thereof, when any necessarie tye of conscience binds him to secresie grounded upon the word of god, unless it be in case of testimony lawfully required.[33]

The circuitous prose alluding to "necessarie tyes of conscience" that bound men to "secresie grounded upon the word of god" clearly referred to intrafamily matters, especially those involving relationships of husbands and wives or parents and children. By providing that men, particularly those who held public office, were not required to reveal "private crimes or offences" that posed no danger to the province or to any individual settler, the General Court created a limited statutory exception to the expectation that residents of the colony would report whatever misbehavior they witnessed to the proper authorities. It also thereby created what the twentieth century would term a small "zone of privacy" within the households of Massachusetts Bay.

Significantly, however, although the other New England colonies later used the Laws and Liberties as the model for their own legal codes, none copied this provision, which was entitled "Secresie" in its 1648 incarnation. The failure of the other governments to extend such protection to family members in their jurisdictions suggests just how fragile and disputed was the seventeenth-century notion of family privacy, especially as it applied to household dependents. In New Haven in 1646, for example, the authorities did not hesitate to prosecute a group of three women—the mistress of the household, her mother, and a friend—for speaking contemptuously of the colony's political and religious leaders. The male servant who revealed to an inquiring neighbor the contents of the conversation later admitted to having qualms about what he had done, telling a magistrate that "he had sinned in reporting things out of the famyly." New Haven's judges, though, had no such misgivings, and they vigorously pursued the case against the women. New Haven also, it will be recalled, specifically ordered heads of households to report any misbehavior by their single boarders.[34]

Records from New Haven and Massachusetts disclose the nature of the disputes that could arise when the colonists attempted to draw a line between private offenses that should be handled wholly within the family and cases with public implications. In 1644, the Reverend James Parker of New Hampshire was summoned to Boston to testify as to what a former maidservant had told him two years previously about sexual advances made to her by a male acquaintance. Parker wrote to John Winthrop to describe the actions he had taken at the time and to outline the reasoning that lay behind them. His letter revealed what must have been a rationale common to many other family governors dealing with problematic circumstances they defined as private.

The ex-servant was now dead, Parker informed Winthrop; he had learned of her complaint only "accidentally," after she already had spoken to his wife about the purported incident. He had then taken appropriate measures, first by interrogating the man in question and then by forbidding him to come to the house except on business, even though the accused man had denied the charge "strongly." That had resolved the problem, Parker reported, expressing bewilderment that he had been ordered to come to court. He certainly had not intended to "countenance sin by concealing this person." Rather, Parker explained, "I love not to trouble Courte and Country . . . unless it be in case off Bloud or some notorious crime." He did not want to speak publicly about misbehavior without "cleare" evidence and believed that he had done all that was required of him. Parker, in short, had to his own mind acted precisely as he should have: confronted with potential disorder in his household, he had successfully dealt with the situation, and intervention by higher authorities was unnecessary.[35]

A year earlier, Richard Crabb, a resident of Stamford in the New Haven colony, offered a less adequate justification for his assertion that misbehavior by one of his servants should be considered private.[36] Crabb's Indian servant boy (whose name does not appear in the records) had stolen a gun, and Crabb reported to the local justice of the peace that he had punished the boy by beating him. When the judge decreed that the boy should in addition be "publiquely whipped for publique misdemeanours," Crabb objected, declaring that "itt was neither honesty nor justice so to proceed, he haveing corrected the boy att home." Even when brought before the New Haven provincial court for "affronts to magistracie," Crabb continued to insist that it was not "just to punish the boy twice for one fact." He thus contended that a penalty inflicted in his household was interchangeable with one ordered by the court, asserting in true Filmerian fashion the full integration of family and state.

Under pressure from the justices, though, Crabb eventually admitted to another motive for his adamant stance: he had feared that "if his boy were publiquely whipped, it would cause him to run away, which would be a great losse to him and a greefe to his wife." He was fined and ordered to acknowledge that he had erred in attempting to prevent the public punishment of his servant. The New Haven authorities in this instance, as they later did in the 1646 prosecution of the gossiping women and the 1656 statute about single persons, therefore advanced an expansive definition of what should be seen as public and a concomitantly restricted view of what actions might be interpreted as private.

A New Haven case that nevertheless hinted at the existence of a household realm beyond the usual reach of secular power came to court in December 1647. Theophilus Eaton, the colony's governor, told the court that he had learned from others that his slave Anthony had been drunk. He explained that "because it was openly knowne, he thought it necessarie the matter should bee heard in the courte, whereas, had it bine keept within the compase of his owne family, he might have given him family correction for it." Mr. Eaton's fellow judges heard testimony about the incident, decided that there were mitigating circumstances, and agreed to forgo "any publique corporall punishment." In light of the "governers zeale and faithfullnes . . . (not conniving at sinn in his owne family,)" they left it up to him to give Anthony "that correction which hee in his wisdome shall judge meete," thereby acknowledging that in at least this one case the court did not need to oversee the specific details of household governance.[37]

Taken together, the three incidents reveal some of the dimensions of the definitional dilemma confronting both heads of households and colonial officials when they tried to decide jurisdictional disputes between family and state within the Filmerian system. That worldview offered no unambiguous guidelines for separating *public* and *private* and little consistency in the application of the only existing standard, the ill-formed notion that some speech and perhaps some behavior within the household did not have public implications and thus should not necessarily come into public cognizance. It is not surprising that New Haven, the small colony with the broadest definition of what constituted the *public*, should have generated two of the three contentious cases, for authorities there gave family governors less autonomy in handling matters within their own households than did any other New England jurisdiction.

Yet the three 1640s cases all had elements that made them less than fully private under contemporary definitions. Anthony's offense was potentially public because it had become known outside the Eaton household. The other two were potentially public because one of the participants—in one case, the victim of the crime; in the other, its perpetrator—was not a household member. Undoubtedly, the fact that Crabb's servant was a captive Indian (perhaps a survivor of the Pequot War) also influenced the judge to order public punishment for him. In two of the three instances, the household head interpreted the incidents as private, whereas the authorities thought them public; in the third, the reverse occurred, with the family governor regarding the misbehavior as public but the court, after a hearing, determining that it should be treated as private. In the unified conception of power that characterized the Filmerian worldview, such lack of precision and ambiguity was to be anticipated. Courts and heads of households could not definitively separate the conceptually inseparable.

Nor, for that matter, did they usually seek to do so. As would be expected in a Filmerian system of goverance, most cases involving the interplay of authority in family and state in New England involved cooperation and connection between masters of families and civil officials rather than the opposite. Formal prosecutions of dependents for misbehavior inside or outside the household most commonly occurred under three circumstances, none of them involving the disagreements between family governors and local authorities that characterized the cases just discussed. These three categories were: first, instances when heads of households deliberately sought the assistance of the authorities in controlling unruly subordinates; second, occasions when the courts accepted penalties inflicted within the family as adequate punishment for disorderly conduct, wherever it had been committed; and third, prosecutions in which judges specifically ordered parents or masters to penalize their children or servants within the household as a substitute for public punishment. Other such cases will be described in subsequent chapters; a few examples here will introduce the usual patterns.

One of the cases of the first type arose in 1653, when a New Haven man complained to the town court that his servant boy, Edmund, had run away repeatedly and had stolen from another servant. He explained that "he hath given him private correction in the family for it but hee hath not bine reclaimed." The magistrates accordingly commanded that Edmund "be publiquly corrected with a rod on the backe, to try if God may give a blessing to this meanes for his recoverey out of these courses." An example of the second occurred in Suffolk County, Massachusetts, in April 1673: after a man assured the court that his daughter had been "corrected privately" for "pernicious lying & making disturbance among the Neighbours," the judges merely "admonished her & soe dismissed her."[38]

Cases in the third group are particularly significant because they illustrate with special clarity the integration of punishment systems in family and state under the Filmerian system. When judges ordered parents to whip their children or servants (as they ordered Nicholas Pinion to whip his daughter Hannah in March 1667/8), they treated the household power structure as an arm of the state and masters of families as semi-official constables. Accordingly, in Ipswich, Massachusetts, in 1674 the Essex County court declared that since two girls accused of "disturbance and disorder" in the meeting house were "under family government," their parents should "correct them for offences past and to keep them in better order for the time to come." That same year, when the son and daughter of John Chandler of Roxbury were charged in Suffolk County with "wanton uncivill & unseemely carriages," the justices ordered each "severely whip't" by the parent of the same sex "in theire own house in pursence of the constable." The court may have suspected incestuous activity, for it also directed that "the said Children bee put asunder & not suffered to dwell together."[39]

As was observed earlier, the Chesapeake governments, especially Maryland's, did not supervise their resident families with the same vigilance used in New England. Instead of involving themselves in the day-to-day governance of families, as did New Haven authorities in particular, Virginia and Maryland judges for the most part contented themselves with overseeing two crucial turning points, the formation of families in marriage and their cessation through death or divorce. The Chesapeake governments intervened in disorderly households only when asked to to come to the aid of beleaguered masters or when excessive abuse of subordinates was alleged. Virginia and Maryland courts normally did not order children or servants whipped by their household superiors, nor did they frequently substitute penalties inflicted in a family context for the public punishment of miscreant dependents.[40]

All this indicates, as was observed in the introduction to this volume, that the Chesapeake colonies became a proto-Lockean society long before Locke developed his ideas about the separation of family and state. The disrupted conditions of family life in the Chesapeake made it impossible for "normal" households to be established there and rendered irrelevant many of the settlers' Filmerian concepts of social order that remained salient in New England. Although Virginia initially attempted to prosecute a wider range of household-related offenses than did

Maryland, the authorities there largely abandoned the effort by the early 1660s, much sooner than did the New England colonies.[41]

In the Chesapeake, no cases raised the question of public/private distinctions in the same way as those involving the Parker, Crabb, and Eaton households in New England. Similar controversies never arose in the southern colonies, for heads of households there had greater leeway to rule their families as they chose, without constant supervision by the state. The Chesapeake governments created a de facto private realm of family life immune from regular oversight by civil officials. The Chesapeake intrafamily cases that will be examined in the chapters that follow therefore have a different configuration from those that appeared in the New England courts. Significantly, although household issues were occasionally involved in criminal prosecutions, accused persons were usually tried not for that misbehavior but for other related offenses.

A prime example is provided by Virginia's prosecution of Lieutenant Thomas Flint for contempt of authority in November 1628.[42] Flint's wife, Mary, the widow of Robert Beheathland, had complained to Governor Francis West about her husband's treatment of Dorothy, her daughter by her first marriage. The problem was not physical abuse but rather his "being soe familiar with the wench further then was fitting," as Governor West put it when he described the incident to the General Court. In a New England colony, such an accusation would have resulted in the investigation of Flint for incest, since the contemporary definition of that crime did not distinguish between affinal and blood relationships. In Virginia, by contrast, Governor West and his wife, Temperance, merely sought out Flint to speak with him informally about the report of his "ill Carriadge" toward his stepdaughter. After Flint denied his wife's charge, West reminded him that the previous governor, Sir George Yeardley, also "did not thinke it fitt that the maid should live with him." (The information about Yeardley's opinion had undoubtedly come from Temperance West, who was Yeardley's widow.) West further pointed out to Flint that his wife, Mary, had asked that Dorothy Beheathland "might bee drawen from" Flint's house.

Flint responded angrily to that statement, telling West "that noebody should Comaund her from him, and often repeating these words." West replied that if he so chose, he could separate them; Flint then exploded, swearing "many oathes" and raging, "you may Comaund mee and anything that I have but her you shall not." West directed that Flint be arrested and held temporarily, presumably until he cooled down. While under detention, Flint compounded his problems by attempting to stab one of the men guarding him and by repeatedly advocating the governor's removal from office. According to one witness, Flint said punningly of West, "the Dyvell confound him body and soule I hope an Easterly wind will bring in a new governor and then I shall have true Justice." In addition, when West sought to question Dorothy Beheathland, Flint evidently "sent a Count[er order] that shee should not come." For his "misdemeanour and Contempt," the Virginia General Court directed that Flint should be fined and deprived of his military commission, telling him to post bond for his future good behavior. It said nothing about whether Dorothy Beheathland would be removed from the home against her stepfather's wishes.

Flint's case is revealing for three reasons. First, as already noted, it illustrates the standard Chesapeake pattern in which the courts did not formally charge delinquents with family-related offenses, even when criminal trials raised such issues. Lieutenant Flint was tried and convicted for his contempt of West during their conversation about Dorothy Beheathland and for his behavior while he was being detained, not for his reportedly incestuous conduct toward his stepdaughter. The only element of the court's decision that offered Dorothy any protection was the requirement that Flint post a good-behavior bond, but that was presumably aimed primarily at preventing new outbursts against the governor rather than at satisfactorily resolving the situation in the household.

Second, it introduces what will prove to be a recurrent theme in this book: women's informal, often ineffective efforts to win a redress of grievances from a male-dominated judicial and legal system. Mary Beheathland Flint asked Governor West for his assistance when she feared that her husband would molest her daughter, turning to the state to counterbalance her husband's power in their household. Breaking ranks with Thomas, she actively sought intervention in their family. Probably urged on by his wife, who knew of her previous husband's anxiety about the Flint household, Governor West responded by initiating an informal conversation with Flint rather than by bringing formal charges against him. The upshot, of course, was that Lieutenant Flint was punished for contempt of the governor rather than for the original offense that caused his wife's complaint. When men's concerns about the maintenance of civil order came to the fore—as they always did when other men engaged in conduct contemptuous of the government—women's affairs were pushed aside.

Third, Lieutenant Flint, as a family governor, openly challenged

Governor West's power to direct him to live separately from Dorothy Beheathland. "You shall not" order her to leave, he told Francis West, speaking to the governor in what Mr. West later described as a "most peremptory manner." Why could Governor West "Comaund" Lieutenant Flint and whatever he owned, but not his stepdaughter? Clearly, Thomas Flint believed that in his role of head of the household he alone could oversee his dependents' activities, and that the state had no authority to tell him how to behave with respect to the young woman. Even Stamford's Richard Crabb had not gone so far in asserting the autonomy of his family: he had firmly disputed the magistrates' interpretation of how to characterize his servant's offense, but he had not questioned the New Haven authorities' ultimate power to supervise the affairs of his household.

It is not that northern family governors never challenged the court system's authority to scrutinize their dealings with their subordinates. Some did; those cases will be discussed in following chapters. Rather, the point is that Chesapeake governments rarely sought to exercise any authority over the internal operations of a household, whereas in the New England provinces such supervision was the rule rather than the exception. In the Chesapeake, men like Thomas Flint valued their freedom from control and resisted attempts by the courts to impose behavioral standards on them; in New England, men like Richard Crabb, James Parker, and Theophilus Eaton—while raising some questions about details—accepted such oversight as part of the normal course of affairs.

Examples of the sort of scrutiny vigorously rejected by Thomas Flint abound in the New England court records. Men were accused of "not provideing for" or "neglecting" their families, of permitting "disorderly carriages" in their households, and of "not ordering & disposeing of [their] Children as may bee for theire good education."[43] In 1656, for example, the town of New Haven charged a couple with allowing their children to engage in "disorderly walking" on the sabbath, stealing apples and eggs from neighbors instead of going to services at the meetinghouse. "The said chilldren are not nurtured and brought up as chilldren ought to be," the magistrates declared, ordering the children whipped by the marshal if their parents had neglected that duty. Their father was also directed to post bond that his children would behave "well and righteously amonge their neighbours," that they would begin to attend church regularly, and that they would be "nurtured as is fitt." If the family did not reform its ways, the authorities warned, it would have to leave town.[44]

In the last case, neighbors had obviously brought the complaint against the marauding children and their parents. Neighbors also went to the authorities in other instances as well, hoping to quiet disturbances that affected them in addition to the households in question. In 1677, four men informed the Bay Colony's authorities that Thomas Smith, Sr., was "continually drunk & mad," abusing "all his neighbours in very scurlious Language & actions." His chief targets, though, were "his pore wife & family," whom he failed to maintain properly. He had also thrown his wife out of the house in a drunken rage, "forceing hir to ly by the neighbours fire all night." If such behavior was allowed to continue, the men warned, "his neighbours must still be abused his family suffer & in a short time com to the town for maint[en]ance." Likewise, when an Ipswich man in 1670 charged his young servant with a variety of offenses, an observer of the household defended the boy, not by proclaiming his innocence but instead by attacking the inadequacies of his family governor:

> whear a servant is in any houes wher no Cristian duty is performed nor Regard [paid] to Instruckt[ion,] such young on[e]s wil be bad enouf and for a servant to be Cept almost nakd lick a hethen and left alone in his work and none to luck after him weeck after weeck a[n]d so [for] munths a man Cannot xspeckt much servis unles Concienc binds.[45]

On both of these occasions, then—though for quite different reasons—neighbors called the failings of the head of the household to the attention of appropriate authorities, thereby indicating that the community as well as the state recognized the importance of maintaining orderly households. Even so, the primary responsibility for the close supervision of household heads lay with the formal public; and, among New England's leaders, the New Haven magistrates were especially likely to pursue prosecutions of men found delinquent in their duties to their underlings. Two cases deserve detailed analysis because they reveal the legally enforceable obligations of heads of households to their subordinates.

The first case was heard in spring 1646, after the magistrates learned of "severall leawd passadges" involving the wife of William Fancy.[46] In a detailed statement to the court, Goody Fancy revealed that over a period of two years Thomas Robinson had repeatedly attempted to rape her, primarily on occasions when she was working for his wife. He had attacked her in his own cellar, in corn and pumpkin fields, in the "cow howse," and once while she was gathering firewood. Her account described six incidents that varied little in specifics. On the first occasion, as on the last (no more than two months prior to the trial), Robinson "tooke hold of her, put downe his owne breeches, put his hand under her coates [clothes], & with strength & force labored to satisfie his lust, & to defile her." Each time, she declared, she had successfully resisted him by one means or another, sometimes by threatening to inform his wife or the authorities, other times because his attacks were interrupted by potential witnesses.

Goody Fancy told the court that she "from time to time acquainted her husband with Robinsons leawd lustfull attempts uppon her . . . & prest him to complayne to the governor." Her husband, though, refused to take action on her behalf, claiming that her story would not be believed because she had been "publicquely punished for theevery." (Goody Fancy was convicted of theft in New Haven in July 1643 and ordered "severely whipped"; she had previously been whipped twice for similar crimes in Connecticut.)[47] William Fancy also declared that "being ignorant of the mynd of God in the Scriptures, he knew not but that it might be concealed," presumably because no rape had actually occurred. Thus the story emerged into public view only by chance, because Goody Fancy angrily exploded when Goodwife Thomas, another woman who employed her, informed her that Goodman Robinson had accused her of theft. At that Goodwife Fancy burst out "passionatly . . . , save one from the gallowes & he will hang you or cutt your throate if he can." Goody Thomas asked her to explain the heated allegation, and Goody Fancy then disclosed "Robinsons filthynesse & villeny" to her.

But no one immediately approached the authorities, for William Fancy was not the only New Haven resident who thought that Robinson's attempted sexual assaults should be kept secret. Goodman and Goodwife Robinson, Goody Thomas, and Robert Usher (to whom Goody Thomas told the story) all declared that they hoped to prevent the information from coming to the attention of the judges. Robinson, however, "provoaked" Usher by telling him that he had spoken to Goody Fancy only "in jest, & that Fancy his wife wronged him." Usher, angered by the obvious lie, then finally revealed the sordid tale to the magistrates.

By the time the case came to trial, Goodman Robinson had left town "in a sadd discontented frame," fleeing to avoid prosecution. But witnesses (including his own wife) testified that he had admitted the truth of the charges against him. And Goody Fancy, in a further revelation that shocked the town, disclosed that two other New Haven men, Mark Meggs and Stephen Medcalfe, had recently made sexual advances toward her. Meggs, she declared, "strove with her, put his hands under her coats," and offered her money to have sex with him; and Medcalfe, whom she was nursing after he had lost an eye in an accident, tried "in an basse lustfull way to kisse her by force." She disclosed that she had told her husband about both incidents, again announcing to him that "she would complayne to the magistrate." Although William this time chided both men about their behavior, he nevertheless "diswaded" his wife from filing criminal charges against them.

New Haven's magistrates were less willing than William Fancy and the other participants to let such offenses pass unpunished. They first ordered Meggs whipped for his "sinful & lustful attempt." Then they directed that Goody Fancy also be whipped for her "concealment of the forementioned vylenous & lustfull attempts by severall." But they saved their harshest words for William Fancy, who had acted, they declared, "as a pander to his wife," and who had neglected to report the attacks on her in a "timely" fashion. He "should have bin her protector, & although he was told of them, neither did discover [disclose] them him-selfe, nor would he suffer his wife to doe it." So he was ordered "se-vearly" whipped. William Fancy's failure adequately to fulfill his responsibilities to his wife thus resulted in his having to endure public humiliation and corporal punishment.[48]

The second New Haven prosecution was especially complex, in-volving not one but two heads of families charged with neglecting their duty to dependents. John Knight, a servant of William Judson and a known sexual offender, was convicted in 1655 of committing sodomy with Peter Vincon, a fourteen-year-old servant of the Judsons. Mary Clarke, a maidservant in the household, further accused Knight of having "abused her in a filthy way, discovering her nakedness" at least three or four times. The issue here is not the sexual incidents but rather the way the New Haven magistrates dealt with the Judsons and Mary Clarke's parents.[49]

Testimony in the case disclosed that Mary had immediately informed her mother about Knight's assaults on her. Goodwife Clarke then "told Goodman [Judson] and his wife of it, and prayed them to put John Knight away else, she would take away her daughter." The Judsons promised Mary's mother that "they should not be together alone, and they would be carefull of her." But, Goody Clarke told the court, the Judsons failed to carry out their pledge. Not only had they let Mary and John be "in the feild together," where he attacked her again, but also

Peter Vincon testified that on a number of occasions he saw Knight engaging in sexual horseplay with Mary Clarke, "tumbl[ing] her aboute, and put[ting] his hands under her coates." Mary informed Goody Judson about some of these incidents, but her dame "bid her she should say nothing of John Knight." Asked why she sought to conceal the information about Knight's misbehavior, Goodwife Judson replied that "she thought he had inough upon him all ready," referring to his previous punishment for similar crimes in another household. The judges declared themselves "much unsatisfyed" with that answer, accusing her of protecting John "in a sinnfull way for ends of her owne."

The New Haven magistrates found everyone culpable in this case, not only Knight and his two sexual partners, but also the Judsons and the Clarkes. The justices told James Clarke and his wife that they were "exceedingly to blame," because they knew of Knight's past offenses, were informed by their daughter of his sexual attacks on her, and still "let her stay there and [did] not complaine of him to publique authority." The Clarkes defended themselves by criticizing the Judsons, who had said they would send John away and had assured them that the two servants would be kept apart. And the judges agreed that although both couples had erred, the Judsons had committed the more significant offense. They reproached William Judson and his wife for having "neglected their trust and duty towards Mary Clarke and her parrents." Knowing Knight's history and having promised to keep him away from their maidservant, they had not only violated their word but had also concealed his criminal behavior and "counsell[ed] Mary Clarke to conceale it also," which made them "very guilty." "Much of this mischeife," the court concluded, "is come by their neglect." It ordered William Judson to pay a heavy fine of £10, expressing the hope that "it may be a warning to governors of families to be more carefull and watchfull over the charge and trust they take upon them."

In New England, therefore, male heads of households were closely supervised by colonial authorities, and even in the Chesapeake they were not free to act entirely as they pleased with respect to their subordinates. Family governors played too important a role in the maintenance of social and political authority to allow them to resist official oversight of their activities. Although men sporadically challenged such supervision, few assertions of that sort received official sanction, and those that did were of limited scope and duration.

The informal public too had its say in the functioning of families, for neighbors complained to local justices of the peace about disruptive children and abusive husbands or masters, thereby invoking the power of the state in an attempt to restore order. Even dependents within families, like Mary Beheathland Flint, could turn to the formal or informal public to combat their superiors and have some expectation that their complaints might have a beneficial effect, again because in a Filmerian system misbehavior by male household heads was too significant for the authorities to ignore. Government intervention in families was, to be sure, far less common in the Chesapeake than it was in New England, but it was not wholly absent, as shall be seen in the following chapters. In this early period, during which Lockean notions of the separation of family and state had not yet been fully formulated, expansive definitions of what constituted matters of public concern were commonplace.

THE FIRST CHAPTER ANALYZES MARRIAGE, the proper foundation of all households in the Anglo-American world. Chapter two focuses on the roles of men as family governors and on the children and servants who attempted to resist them. Chapter three then examines the unique problems confronted by widows who found themselves required to assume the mantle of family leadership. All three chapters in this first section necessarily emphasize the constant interplay of community, state, and family.

CHAPTER 1

❦

The First Society

The *first Society* was between Man and Wife, which gave
beginning to that between Parents and Children.
—*John Locke, 1692*[1]

O F THE MANY HIERARCHIES that governed seventeenth-century
English society, the most fundamental of all involved husband and
wife. Married couples established the households that were the basis of
English society, the locus of production and reproduction. Every English
person lived—or, more accurately, was expected to live—in such a
household. Since a well-ordered society was believed to rest firmly on
the family, proper ranking in the household was thought essential to the
functioning of the commonwealth. Accordingly, the wife's obedience to
her husband demonstrated the need for submission to superiors outside
as well as inside the household, and the relationship of the marital pair
that jointly governed the family served as a model for both society and
polity. Moreover, because an unmarried man could not have legitimate
children, marriage necessarily preceded the relationship between a father
and his sons, which many theorists interpreted as the foundation of all
political authority.[2]

Thus the persistent emphasis in seventeenth-century English legal
and prescriptive writings on the importance of men's dominance and
women's submission in marriage is understandable. "All of them
[women] are understood either married or to bee married and their
desires ar[e] subject to their husband," wrote an anonymous lawyer in
1632, in the first treatise in English on the legal status of women. His
last phrase alluded to Genesis 3:16, a Biblical passage that would have
been familiar to any literate English person of his day. There, God had
told Eve that "thy desire shal be subject to thine housband, and he shal
rule over thee." So, the lawyer concluded, "The common Law here
shaketh hand with Divinitie."[3]

Not everyone concurred with him that "Divinitie" was the origin of men's superiority and women's subjection, but few contemporaries would have disagreed with the lawyer's two basic premises: that women should be considered primarily as wives or potential wives; and that as wives they were properly subordinate to their husbands. Taken together, the premises implied that women could rarely, if ever, be considered as independent beings in law or in society at large. If all women were "either married or to bee married," and all wives were necessarily subject to their husbands, then a woman's fundamental calling, in the words of the English Puritan cleric William Perkins, was located "in her subjection and obedience to her owne husband."[4]

That subjection provided universally understood descriptive metaphors that clarified complicated concepts of dominance and submission. When the Reverend John Cotton wanted to defend the exclusion of nonmembers of the church from a colony's voting population and when John Winthrop defined civil liberty for the freemen of Massachusetts Bay, both grounded their theories on marital analogies. Similarly, Puritan ministers frequently found it useful to describe the church as "the bride of Christ" and to express religious dependency by employing feminine imagery.[5]

But the husband-wife relationship, though definitively outlined in theory, was filled with potential pitfalls in reality, for the universal subordination of wives to husbands was much more easily described than achieved. As the English colonists in America attempted to implement the ideal of marital subjection in their families, their laws, their communities, and their courtrooms, they encountered a wide range of practical difficulties with the concept. In a multitude of ways the unequal status of husbands and wives manifested itself in the daily life of the colonies, thus allowing a sustained analysis of the concrete results for women and men of the subordinate relationship enshrined in the marital ideal.

THE POLITICAL THEORY OF MARRIAGE

Because of the symbiotic relationship between family and state in seventeenth-century Anglo-America, political as well as domestic theorists discussed the proper configuration of the family. And since this book concentrates on that same symbiotic relationship, the theoretical discussions herein will draw on political rather than familial authors. Whether they focused primarily on politics or chiefly on the family, early modern

Anglo-American theorists concurred on three key points: hierarchy was necessary to the operations of the household; the proper director of the family's activities was its husband/father/master; and the subordination of wife to husband was the foundation of the family unit and thus of society itself.[6]

These elements were so tightly connected that it is difficult to disentangle them. Most authors simply assumed both the need for hierarchy and the presence of the husband at the top of the familial pyramid of power.[7] Of those who did speculate on the reasons for wives' subjection, the least specific explanation was produced by Mary Astell, the late seventeenth-century Tory writer best known for advocating improvements in women's education. In 1700, Astell observed that God had "allotted the Man to Govern" his family because he was "best Qualify'd" for that task. Like others in authority, "from the Throne to every Private Family," husbands were "the Representatives of God whom they ought to imitate in the Justice and Equity of their Laws." Wives, like other inferiors, "shou'd respect their Governours as plac'd in God's stead and contribute what they can to ease them of their real Cares." Although Astell sharply criticized the ways in which men actually wielded power over their wives, she did not question the hierarchical theory that lay behind the harsh reality she deplored.[8]

Sir Robert Filmer, the apologist for Stuart claims to absolutism, fully agreed with Astell that God had ordained wives' subjection to their husbands, but he was more precise in explaining how that subordination had initially been established. In tracts published in 1648 and 1652, Filmer argued that "God at the creation gave the sovereignty to the man over the woman, as being the nobler and principal agent in generation." Like the anonymous lawyer writing fifteen years earlier, he relied on Genesis 3:16, in which, he declared, "God ordained Adam to rule over his wife, and her desires were to be subject to his; and as hers, so all theirs that should come of her. . . . Neither Eve nor her children could either limit Adam's power, or join others with him in the government." In making such assertions, Filmer's major aim was to support his contention that monarchs—as the figurative, if not literal, heirs of Adam—had a right to wield absolute power over their subjects. Since establishing a father's dominion over his children was critical to Filmer's argument, it is notable that in this passage (the only occasion on which he discussed the specific reason why Adam was the "lord of his children") he chose to base that dominion on Adam's sovereignty over Eve. Only indirectly did Adam acquire sovereignty over Eve's children and subsequent generations. Thus for Filmer, as for others of his contemporaries, the subordination of wife to husband was the foundation of political as well as familial power.[9]

Of all the seventeenth-century English political theorists, Thomas Hobbes was the most willing to allow for the possibility that wives might be superior to their husbands. In *Leviathan* (1651), he remarked that "whereas some have attributed the dominion to the man only as being of the more excellent sex, they misreckon in it. For there is not always that difference of strength or prudence between the man and the woman as that the right can be determined without war." Even so, Hobbes thought that instances in which the wife was dominant would be extremely rare, explaining that in most commonwealths the law provided for a husband's superiority. The only contrary example he offered was unusual indeed—a "sovereign queen" married to one of her own subjects. Moreover, when he commented in passing that "God has ordained to man a helper," he indicated his concurrence with the traditional view of a wife's subordination to her husband, regardless of his conjecture about the possibility of an alternative marital arrangement.[10]

John Locke, the Whig opponent of Stuart power, rejected both Filmer's analogy between polity and family and Hobbes's willingness to admit that husbands might be subject to their wives in some circumstances. In his *Two Treatises of Government,* Locke joined Filmer and Astell in asserting a husband's dominance in the family.[11] Yet, because the first and second treatises had different purposes, he adopted divergent approaches in the two parts of his great work, while ultimately arriving at the same point in both: a wife's "natural" subordination to her husband.

The *First Treatise* was designed specifically as a response to Sir Robert Filmer. In it Locke confronted directly Filmer's interpretation of the relationship of Adam and Eve as described in Genesis 3:16. Pointing out that the verse in question was "the Curse of God upon the Woman, for having been the first and forwardest in the Disobedience," he contended that God was unlikely to have given Adam "Prerogatives and Priviledges" at a time when he was "declaring his Wrath against them both." Eve was only "accidentally" placed below Adam; "he too had his share in the fall, as well as the sin." Moreover, Locke noted, God in this passage did not speak directly to Adam, nor did he grant Adam anything. Rather, God's words should be read as directed specifically to Eve, or "in her, as their representative to all other Women." As such, "they will at most concern the Female Sex only."[12]

Locke then addressed the issue of how the verse should be interpreted with respect to women. The statement "thy desire shal be subject to thine housband, and he shal rule over thee" did not mean that an English queen married to an inferior would be in "Political Subjection" to him. God's words were not a "Law" laid down for a woman to obey, "if the Circumstances either of her Condition or Contract with her Husband should exempt her from it." Arguing in a Hobbesian mode, therefore, Locke allowed two exceptions to the general rule of wifely subordination: a woman's "Condition" (presumably, her status as sovereign), or a prior contract with her husband (that is, a marriage settlement). Still, he did not go as far as Hobbes and never implied that a woman could be superior to her spouse, only that she might be exempt from certain types of subjection to him.[13]

Indeed, Locke made it clear that he believed there to be "a Foundation in Nature" for wives' subordination to their husbands. He referred to "that Subjection they should ordinarily be in to their Husbands," to "the Laws of Mankind and customs of Nations" that ordained a male-dominated family order, and to "the Power that every Husband hath to order the things of private Concernment in his Family, as Proprietor of the Goods and Land there, and to have his Will take place before that of his wife in all things of their common Concernment." Such authority did not come from the words of Genesis 3:16, and it represented only "Conjugal," not political, power. God nevertheless by his words to Eve "fortels what should be the Womans Lot, how by his Providence he would order it so, that she should be subject to her husband." Whereas Filmer derived husbandly authority directly from the words of Genesis, Locke derived it from "Nature" and God's "Providence." The reasoning varied, but the result was the same.[14]

In the *Second Treatise*, where Locke was explicating his own ideas rather than responding to Filmer's, he presented the husband-wife relationship somewhat differently, but to the identical end. "The *first Society* was between Man and Wife," Locke explained, formed by a "voluntary Compact" between them. The aim of that compact was "Procreation," but it also involved "mutual Support, and Assistance, and a Communion of Interest too." Again Locke referred to the wife's ability to reach a contract with her husband either "in the state of Nature, or by the Customs or Laws of the Countrey they live in"—a contract that could, he declared, protect a wife's own property or give her custody of the children in the event of divorce. Locke's seeming emphasis here on mutuality in marriage, however, must be read within the context of his continuing insistence on the "natural" primacy of the husband, even in that "voluntary Compact":

But the Husband and Wife, though they have but one common Concern, yet having different understandings, will unavoidably sometimes have different wills too; it therefore being necessary, that the last Determination, *i.e.* the Rule, should be placed somewhere, it naturally falls to the Man's share, as the abler and the stronger.[15]

Thus authors who discussed politics with great originality and analytical power had little new to say about marriage. Given the fundamental role that hierarchical marriages played in contemporary conceptions of English society, the lack of innovation was predictable. John Locke, writing at the end of the seventeenth century, agreed on essentials with the anonymous legal treatise of 1632. Although Locke and Hobbes were willing to allow limited exceptions to the norm of women's subjection, both insisted that such exceptions would be rare indeed. The husband was—by natural law (Locke), civil law (Hobbes), or God's will (Filmer and Astell)—the proper head of the household, and his wife's duty was to submit to him in all things. He was the governor, she the subject. In theory, the lines of authority were unobjectionable; and they were widely accepted in both England and the American colonies. That was precisely why marriage could be seen as the bedrock of society and polity.

MARRIAGE FORMATION

The most basic quandary the colonists confronted was how to define a valid marriage. Before the principles of marital subjection could be applied and proper marital unions created, husbands and wives had to be unequivocally identified as such. Questions about marriage developed in the colonies because English law was complex, allowing a variety of interpretations. As the author of *The Lawes Resolutions of Womens Rights* observed in 1632, even though matrimony was "a Conjunction of Man and Woman, containing an inseparable connexion, and union of life," it was not "begotten and finished at once." Indeed, there were three distinct stages to seventeenth-century English marriage: first, a promise to marry "in words in the future tence"; second, a lawful contract in the present tense; and third, physical consummation.[16]

Although English marriage practices were therefore remarkably precise, they were simultaneously remarkably flexible, for they required no specific form. To contract a valid marriage, a man and a woman merely had to consent mutually to matrimony, preferably but not necessarily before witnesses. No person in authority (a cleric or a magistrate) had to "marry" them. Moreover, although the consent of parents was desirable "in regard of honestie," a young couple needed no one's formal permission to reach agreement with each other, as long as they had "come to such state, habit and disposition of body that they may be deemed able to procreate."[17]

Even in England these rules provided inadequate and ambiguous guidelines for establishing marital unions, and after the late sixteenth century the Church of England campaigned to regularize procedures by requiring clergymen to solemnize valid marriages.[18] Predictably, therefore, a number of complex questions involving marriage soon emerged from the disrupted demographic and political conditions in the colonies. Should colonial authorities simply accept men's and women's declarations that they were married to each other? What if a couple appeared wedded by one criterion, but not by another? Could indentured servants or slaves marry as easily as free people? Should parents or masters be required to approve the marriages of their dependents?

Lawmakers in America therefore found English practices alone insufficient to define marriage adequately in the novel colonial context, and so they began to draft specific statutes of their own. Within two decades of settlement, or about the time it took the first American-born generation to arrive at marriageable age, most colonies adopted their first laws regulating matrimony, which they then repeatedly revised and elaborated upon during the rest of the century. Such statutes commonly authorized certain persons to perform marriages (clergymen in Virginia, clergymen or magistrates in Maryland, magistrates alone in New England), provided that all valid marriages had to be announced publicly several weeks before a formal ceremony, and insisted that under most circumstances dependent children and servants could not marry without the permission of their parents, guardians, or masters and mistresses.[19]

The provisions of these first marriage laws in the Anglo-American colonies omitted any mention of race or ethnicity. No statute thus prevented the colonists' earliest Indian or African servants or slaves from entering into legal marriages with each other or with Europeans, as long as the parties concerned received permission from their masters or parents. (Free blacks were able to marry legally without such preliminaries.) Scattered references to African-American "husbands" and "wives" in the court records of New England and the Chesapeake suggest that blacks, even those held in servitude or slavery, established marriages their masters were required by law to recognize. Not until after the middle of the century were some of the marriage statutes amended to make racial distinctions.[20]

A constant theme in the marriage laws was the requirement that family governors consent to the marriages of children and servants, a provision that broke sharply with the English custom of giving priority to the young couple. Legislators in New England and the Chesapeake agreed on the basic principle: "God hath committed the care and power into the hands of Parents for the disposing their Children in marriage," declared Massachusetts Bay lawmakers in 1648; twenty-two years later, Virginians echoed that sentiment, referring to "that naturall right and just privilege" of "parents and guardians . . . of disposing of their children or orphants in marriage." Although both laws employed the plural *parents*, the assumption of wifely submission in marriage embedded in that wording effectively gave fathers in particular a legally enforceable veto over the marriages of their children and perhaps other dependents as well.[21]

Plymouth in 1645 thus defined a "lawfull" marriage contract as one that involved "the mutuall consent of two parties with the consent of parents or gaurdians if there be any to be had and a solemne promise of marriage in due tyme to eich other before two competent witnesses," a definition it maintained through several revisions of its legal code. In 1671 that colony specifically provided that "none shall be allowed to Marry that are under the Covert of Parents, Guardians, Masters, or Overseers, without their consent and approbation." Yet Plymouth, Massachusetts Bay, and Rhode Island permitted children to appeal to the magistrates if their parents or masters "unreasonably" denied them permission to make a "timely or convenient" marriage, especially, declared the Plymouth statute, if the refusal stemmed from "any sinister end or covetous desire."[22]

New England lawmakers primarily concerned themselves with children's marriages, Chesapeake legislators with those involving servants. Demography explains the difference: in the north, most nubile young people were the offspring of the settlers; in the south, the marriageable population was composed chiefly of youthful indentured servants. In both places, but especially the Chesapeake, the potential loss of valuable workers played a key role in generating the statutes. Pregnancy, the lawmakers assumed, would quickly result from any marriage—and so a master would lose the services of a maidservant for an extended period. Thus bastardy laws in Maryland and clandestine marriage acts in Virginia sought ways to compensate a master for a maidservant's inability to perform her usual tasks while she was pregnant or nursing. The New England statutes, by contrast, conjoined daughters and maidservants and usually did not require financial recompense to fathers or masters.[23]

Many of the laws, like Plymouth's statute of 1638, assumed that the major barrier to contracting valid marriages was young men's "practise-ing the enveagleing of mens daughters & maids under gardians contrary to their parents & gardians likeing and of mayde servants without leave and likeing of their masters." So Rhode Island's "Touching Menstealers" in 1647 declared that "the taking away, deflouring or contracting in marriage a maid under sixteen yeares of age, against the will of, or unknown to the Father or Mother of the Maid, is a kind of stealing of her." The Bay Colony the following year prescribed penalties of increasingly heavy fines for anyone who tried "to draw away the affections of any maid in this Jurisdiction under pretence of marriage, before he hath obtained libertie and allowance from her Parents or Governours." And New Haven in 1656 forbade similar attempts to woo "any Maide, or Maideservant," without prior permission of her "Father, Master, Guardian, Governor," regardless of "whether it be by speech, writing, message, company-keeping, unnecessary familiarity, disorderly night meetings, sinful dalliance, gifts, or any other way, directly, or indirectly."[24]

Two gendered assumptions lay behind the wording of these laws. First, by referring to "Father, Master" or to "mens daughters," the 1656 New Haven and 1638 Plymouth statutes made clear what other colonial legislation left implicit: fathers were the primary parents when it came to making decisions about their children's marital futures. Men's off-spring might not be possessions in quite the same way as indentured servants or slaves, but nevertheless children's matrimonial plans were legally subject to paternal approval. That colonists in both New England and the Chesapeake thereby altered English customs suggests the stress they placed on enforcing children's obedience to their fathers' wishes, particularly in one of the most important decisions children were likely to make. Marriage laws thus reinforced the authority of fathers over their young-adult children. The statutes confirmed fathers' ability to control their offspring's lives at a life-cycle stage when, had the family remained in England, young people would have been experiencing greater personal independence. Colonial marriage legislation therefore underscored the significance to colonial society of orderly households dominated by male family governors, households from which dependents could depart only with the approval of their superiors.[25]

Second, the laws also confronted the admittedly knotty problem of preventing clandestine marriages in an overtly gendered way. The legislation assumed that men were the active parties in courtship and that passive, naive young women could be enticed away from their families by stealth and deception. No law prescribed penalties for young women involved in secret courtships, and far fewer women than men were prosecuted for violations of the statutes.[26] Men did outnumber women in the population of all the colonies during the first years of English settlement; the imbalanced sex ratio led everywhere to a decline in the average age at first marriage for free women. Accordingly, the vision enshrined in law of men seeking wives by fair means or foul may not have been completely off the mark, especially in the Chesapeake, where there were at least four times as many men as women. Yet even so very few young men were ever prosecuted for "inveigling" daughters or maidservants.[27]

Evidence from the court records therefore suggests that colonial legislators failed to perceive accurately the most difficult challenge they faced with respect to marriage formation. Instead of violating rules regarding parental approval, posting banns, or the like, most colonists prosecuted for crimes connected to the formation of marriage committed another sort of transgression altogether—premarital fornication. That most such offenses appear to have been fully consensual both belies the statutes' focus on predatory men and passive women, and indicates that the civil officials' hardest task was persuading many ordinary colonists, male and female alike, to accede to the official definitions of matrimony contained in provincial laws.

Fornication, defined by colonial law as sexual intercourse by any man with a single woman (sex with a married woman constituted adultery, a much more serious offense), was a crime in all the colonies but was more frequently prosecuted in New England than in the Chesapeake. Northern jurisdictions also systematically pursued premarital fornicators by retroactively applying the law to couples who had full-term babies less than nine months after their formal wedding ceremony. (In England, such delinquencies had been handled by church courts, institutions that did not exist in North America.) For reasons that will be discussed later in this section, just a handful of Chesapeake residents were tried for premarital sexual offenses, though many more probably committed them. By contrast, hundreds of men and women faced such indictments in New England, where civil magistrates regularly penalized premarital fornication.[28]

That large numbers of colonists violated the laws defining marriage reveals a disagreement between lawmakers and ordinary English settlers over what constituted a valid marriage. A substantial body of evidence indicates that, in the minds of many settlers, two elements (together or separately) constituted a valid marriage: mutual consent, frequently in the guise of a formal contract, and sexual intercourse. They thus continued to follow traditional English practice, which required no intervention by civil or religious authorities to initiate lawful marital relationships. And they thereby transgressed the colonial statutes that criminalized marriages begun without official sanction.

In only eighteen prosecutions did court clerks record both birth and marriage dates for offending couples. But in two thirds of those cases (twelve), the premarital conceptions preceded the official marriage dates by three months or less. Such figures, fragmentary though they are, imply that young people began to engage in sexual intercourse after they had contracted to marry each other but perhaps prior to the formal posting of banns and certainly before the ceremony dictated by law. Thus incidents defined by New England courts as prosecutable premarital fornication might not have appeared to be serious misbehavior to the couples involved. One province's legislators recognized the key distinction: after 1645, Plymouth penalized fornication "after contract and before marriage" less harshly than the same offense "before or without lawfull contract."[29]

Some young couples clearly concluded that sexual intercourse could appropriately begin once a contract had been made, even though no formal ceremony had taken place. So in 1642 a young New Haven couple, "haveing entred into contract," embarked upon a sexual relationship. In the opinion of the colony's judges, who ordered them "severely whipped," they had "sinfully and wickedly defiled each other," making themselves "unfitt for any other." It is unlikely the young people interpreted their behavior in the same negative fashion, however, for they won the right to marry formally, despite not being able to prove that they had their parents' consent. The previous year in Virginia, Edy Hanking's wedding ceremony was unexpectedly delayed by a man who falsely claimed that her husband-to-be, Thomas Tucker, was still a servant. When the Lower Norfolk County court later ordered the Tuckers to do penance for premarital fornication, Edy responded angrily to what she regarded as an obvious injustice. The judges had directed her and her husband to stand on stools in church during sabbath services wearing "a white sheet" and to repeat "after the minister such words as he shall deliver unto them." The clerk recorded that, rather than doing as she was told, Edy "did, like a most obstinate and graceless person, cut and mangle the sheet wherein she did penance." That outburst earned her a lashing and an order to repeat the penance properly. It nevertheless accurately expressed her anger at a legal system that had denied her a timely marriage ceremony and then penalized her for engaging in premature sexual intercourse with her husband.[30]

Local officials could sometimes sympathize with couples who found themselves in the Tuckers' position. In 1664, for example, two Newbury selectmen wrote to the Essex County court, pleading for mercy for a couple who had had a baby less than six months after their wedding. Hannah and Peter Cheny, the townsmen explained, "have ever bin of unblameable conversation [behavior]"; they were "published according to law, and the time of marriage appointed, but unexpectedly delaied by their parents by reason of extraordinary accidents." Had the marriage taken place on schedule, the townsmen implied, no violation of the law would have been apparent, since the initiation of sexual intercourse and the wedding ceremony would have occurred in closer conjunction. The county judges were less understanding, levying an unusually heavy fine on the Chenys because Hannah failed to appear in court to express her repentance in person.[31]

Considerable evidence of other sorts also attests to the importance the colonists attached to marriage contracts. Contracted but unconsummated marriages led to lawsuits, and one young wife denied her new husband "conjugal respects" because she had previously been pledged to another. She was "troubled in her conscience about it," she explained to the Essex court in 1640, while her husband confessed to "deal[ing] rashly in matters of such weight," admitting that he had known of her promise to marry another when he pressed his suit. Likewise, in 1641 John Winthrop thought the marriage of then–Governor Richard Bellingham and Mistress Penelope Pelham sufficiently irregular that he discussed it at length in his journal. The "young gentlewoman," he wrote, was contracted to a friend of Bellingham's, but "on the sudden the governor treated with her, and obtained her for himself." The governor then compounded his error by not properly publishing the banns and by resisting his fellow magistrates' efforts to call him to task for his neglect.[32]

Sexual intercourse too was critical to the initiation and perpetuation of a valid marriage. The primary evidence on this point comes not from premarital fornication prosecutions but rather from other sorts of civil and criminal actions. Just as the New Haven judges thought that fornication made the sexual partners "unfitt for any other," so too a Maryland man who raped the woman he hoped to marry told her, she reported, that "now I Should nor Could not have any other Man but

him." Similarly, women whose husbands were impotent insisted to colonial courts that their marriages were consequently a sham, referring in
their divorce petitions to "him that pretends him sellfe hir husband" or
to a "pretended Contract of marriage" with a man "altogether deficient"
in the "performance of an husband." Marriages not physically consummated were only "pretended," women believed, whatever the law or
the courts might say. Conversely, for at least some colonists (male and
female), sexual intercourse by mutual consent established the presumption of matrimony.[33]

As a result, the many premarital fornication prosecutions that flooded
the Bay Colony's courts in particular appear less as evidence of immo-
rality and sexual experimentation by young couples than as signs of a
dialogue between the formal and informal publics about the characteristics of valid marriages. To legislators and magistrates throughout the
colonies, marriage primarily required parental consent and a formal wedding ceremony, whether performed by a clergyman or a magistrate. To
ordinary colonists, marriage instead consisted of a mutual contract by
the parties and the act of sexual intercourse.

In most of New England, the magistrates' definition prevailed; few
of the couples tried for premarital fornication there avoided fines or a
whipping, and prosecutions for the offense were so vigorously pursued
that in the northern colonies they constituted nearly half of all criminal
charges filed against married couples and approximately one fifth of all
prosecutions of married women.[34] Premarital fornication made up a less
significant proportion of accusations against northern men: just 5 percent
of all male criminals faced such allegations, but the comparable figure
for married men tried alone or with their wives was 47 percent.[35]

In the Chesapeake, especially Maryland, ordinary colonists were
more successful in convincing the civil courts to accept *their* definitions
of what constituted a valid marriage. They were aided in this endeavor
both by demography and by Maryland's unique religious configuration.
Since Virginia and Maryland contained large numbers of servants who
were forbidden to marry without a master's permission until their terms
of indenture had been completed, sexual activity among servants commonly resulted in prosecutions for bastardy. The determination of when
a recently married couple had initiated sexual intercourse—of great importance in Puritan New England—faded into insignificance in the
Chesapeake when contrasted to the financial problems posed for masters
and the state by unmarried servant women who gave birth to bastards.
Accordingly, the Chesapeake colonies evinced little interest in prosecuting couples for premarital fornication.[36]

Furthermore, lacking the religious unity that characterized Virginia and much of New England, Maryland became a de facto secular state even before the adoption of its famous Act for Religious Toleration in 1649. That secularization was yet another element contributing to the Lockean characteristics of its society. With the notable exceptions of bastardy and sexual slander, offenses that in England would have been heard in ecclesiastical courts—and which in New England were tried in civil courts—rarely found their way into Maryland's judicial system. Because Catholics dominated Maryland's government, whereas a majority of the colony's residents were Protestants, and because Catholics, Puritans, and orthodox English Protestants defined marriages (and who could perform them) differently, judges and ordinary settlers more than once disagreed about what constituted marriage.

In 1665, for example, a Charles County constable accused a woman "living at Gil[e]s Tomkinsons" of being "illegitimately got with Child." Tomkinson, though, assured the judges that the woman was "his lawfull wiffe" and that the child she was carrying was his. Giles declared that

> his marriage was as good as possibly it Coold bee maed by the Protestants hee beeing one becaus that befor that time and ever since thear hath not bin a protestant Minister in the Province and that to Matrimony is only nesessary the parties Consent and Publication thearof befor a Lawfull Churchman and for their Consents it is Apparent and for the worlds Satisfaction thay hear publish them selves Man and wife till death them doe part.

A similar case in 1658 involved a Protestant man who considered himself divorced "by reason of mutuall discharges from the Bond of Matrimony" witnessed by a clergyman and signed by himself and his first wife. He remarried, and was subsequently charged by Catholic judges and a grand jury with bigamy, a capital offense in the colony. Although the Maryland authorities were none too pleased with his behavior, they failed to try or convict him and allowed his second marriage to stand, just as they admitted the validity of Giles Tomkinson's irregular union.[37]

Even in New England a determined couple could occasionally resist the courts. George Garland of Black Point, Maine, was thought to have a wife in England, but nevertheless lived with Sarah Mills, a widow with grown children, for at least six years in the 1660s. The couple ignored repeated court orders either to separate or to marry properly. After years of frustrating encounters with Mills and Garland, the York County grand jury admitted in 1668 "not knowing whether they weare maryed togeather." But although the Maine courts eventually tolerated the Garland-Mills relationship, they were not willing to allow Garland to take another wife during Mills's lifetime. Thus when in 1672 George announced his intention to marry a second widow, Lucretia Hitchcock, the judges threw the book at him. In July 1673 they ordered him whipped with thirty-nine lashes, the maximum number allowable. Yet the punishment for "Incoradgeableness" did not deter Garland; he continued to resist the courts, just as he had while living with Mills, and he and Lucretia eventually had several children.[38]

But if courts, especially in Maryland and Maine, were occasionally willing to accept the colonists' self-defined marriages, some colonists conversely adopted the judges' attitudes toward premarital fornication. One young husband told the New Haven court about how he and his wife had tried "to avoyde the shame" of a birth six months after their wedding by traveling to Massachusetts Bay for the birth of their child. Other men attempted to falsify marriage records for the same reason, and in 1677 a father was not only fined by the Essex County court but also admonished by his church for testifying that his daughter had been married "about six or seaven months" before she gave birth to a premature infant. In reality, her wedding—which took place in Boston in hopes of confusing matters—had predated the birth by less than three months.[39]

Such actions reveal the shame that could be felt by young couples and their families when an overly advanced pregnancy disclosed premarital sexual relations. Another Essex County prosecution showed that misbehavior of this sort could poison family relationships for a substantial period of time and that at least one mother shared colonial lawmakers' opinions about who bore responsibility for initiating premarital sexual relations. In December 1661 judges in Salem fined Beatrice Cantlebury for uttering "many revilinge speeches" against her son-in-law, Thomas Woodrow, who eighteen months earlier had been convicted of premarital fornication with her daughter Rebecca. Neighbors reported that Beatrice ignored their advice to "doe him the best good you can & give him good counsel for now he is your son," instead insisting that the "divel should picke his bones before she would owne him to be her son." She termed Thomas "theife" and "rogue"—"a theife for that he had stolne the best flower in her garden, & a rogue because he had brought her body to shame." Even though Rebecca told her mother that "she had him that God had appoynted for her" and that she was happier with Thomas than she would have been with any other husband, Beatrice repeatedly called her son-in-law "a wretch" who "deserved to be hanged." No amount of cajoling by neighbors or "weeping" assurances from her daughter had persuaded her to change her mind, and so the court intervened to try to restore harmony to the family.[40]

Thus the colonial conversation on the subject of marriage formation was not unambiguously dichotomous: ordinary colonists and officials were each found on both sides of the argument. Beatrice Cantlebury concurred with the analysis her colony's leaders had enshrined in their laws regulating courtship, whereas Maryland's magistrates acknowledged the validity of Giles Tomkinson's marriage. Nevertheless, more magistrates tended to support formal ceremonies and more settlers adhered to English tradition. And by their actions, particularly by their active engagement in consensual premarital sexual relations, Anglo-American women like Rebecca Cantlebury Woodrow demonstrated that they were not the passive, easily deceived daughters described by the laws but rather the active shapers of their own lives. They resisted officials' attempts to define marriage as a formal ceremony performed by a man in authority, instead collaborating with their husbands-to-be in emphasizing the importance of sexual intercourse preceded by mutual consent as the appropriate initiator of matrimony.

Whether marriages began regularly or irregularly in official eyes, those beginnings did not end colonial authorities' interest in wedded couples. Because of the significant role properly functioning marriages played in the maintenance of social order, in New England in particular courts intervened in marriages when judges or community members believed that married couples were not behaving properly. In the Chesapeake, where society was not so firmly grounded on households headed by married couples, such intervention was less common but not entirely absent. In both regions, women who had participated equally in the formation of their marital unions found that after marriage that equality did not persist.

MARITAL SUBORDINATION IN PRACTICE

American legislators and judges, like their English counterparts, assumed an "identitie of person" between spouses after marriage. As the anonymous lawyer explained in 1632, "the prerogative of the Husband is best discerned in his dominion over all externe things in which the wife by combination [matrimony] devesteth her selfe of proprietie in some sort, and casteth it upon her governour." Any moveable property a woman owned before marriage "is presently by conjunction the husbands, to sell, keepe or bequeath if he die." (Thus a man might specify in his will that his widow would inherit "all her wearing cloathes her bed & furniture" or "her own Jewels and other peculiar things fitt for her owne use.") A wife's real estate became her husband's to manage; they could no longer contract with each other; she could not make a will; and "it is seldom, almost never that a married woman can have any action to use her writt onely in her owne name: her husband is her sterne, her *primus motor*, without whom she cannot doe much at home, and lesse abroad."[41]

A dramatic example of the application of the doctrine of "identitie of person" in the colonial context came when Maryland adopted its first slave code in 1664, providing for lifetime service for "all Negroes or other slaves." When the upper house considered the draft legislation, it raised the question, what "shall become of such weomen of the English or other Christian nacons being free that are now allready married to negros or other Slaves?" The assembly answered the inquiry in the wording that was ultimately adopted: "whatsoever free borne woman shall inter marry with any slave from and after the Last day of this present Assembly shall Serve the master of such slave dureing the life of her husband And that all the Issue of such freeborne woemen soe married shall be Slaves as their fathers were." Children already born from such unions were ordered to serve their father's master until they reached the age of thirty. The assembly specifically noted that it intended to deter "such freeborne weomen from such shamefull Matches," but the method it selected accorded with English thinking about the legal unity of husband and wife.[42]

A woman's subjection to her husband could be enforced by physical coercion. The author of the *Lawes Resolutions of Womens Rights* put it this way: "there is some kind of castigation which Law permits a Husband to use," as long as he avoids "any bodily damage, otherwise then appertaines to the office of a Husband for lawfull and reasonable correction." One positive result for women, he noted, was that a wife could not be convicted of felony for a crime committed with her spouse, because she was assumed to be acting at her husband's instigation, nor could she ever be tried as his accessory, "inasmuch as shee is forbidden by the Law of God to betray him."[43]

Massachusetts Bay's first comprehensive legal code, the Body of Liberties of 1641, modified English practice by providing that "everie marryed woeman shall be free from bodilie correction or stripes by her husband, unlesse it be in his owne defence upon her assalt." Yet the provision did not free wives from all physical punishment. It went on to state that "if there be any just cause of correction complaint shall be made to Authoritie assembled in some Court, from which onely she shall receive it." Thus the marriage law reformers of the Bay Colony at first merely shifted to the courts the responsibility for "correcting" an unruly or disobedient wife. Nine years later, though, Massachusetts lawmakers repealed that language, declaring instead that "no man shall strike his wife, nor any woman her husband," on penalty of either a fine or corporal punishment. Like the Bay Colony law on household privacy, this prohibition of spouse abuse was unusual in that it was not widely copied in the region. Only Plymouth eventually followed the Bay Colony's lead, and then not until 1671. Legislators in all the other colonies ignored the subject altogether, thereby allowing English custom permitting "lawfull and reasonable correction" of a wife to prevail in their jurisdictions.[44]

In two other areas of the criminal law a wife's subordinate status affected statutory provisions. Rhode Island's first legal code in 1647 was unique in the colonies in applying the gruesome penalties for treason—hanging and drawing and quartering for men, burning at the stake for women—to wives convicted of killing their husbands, or to children or servants who murdered parents or masters and mistresses. The statute explicitly linked all three groups of inferiors, defining petty treason as "when willful murder is committed (in the estate Economicall or household order of government), upon any subject by any one that is in subjection and oweth faith, dutie, and private obedience to the partie murdered." Significantly, the law placed wives in the same category as persons who, in a household context, were inferior to them. It also explicitly linked family and state: the killing of a domestic governor was the equivalent of killing a political ruler, and the demands of "private obedience" to "household government" were the same as those of "public" obedience to the state.[45]

The other criminal offense in which wives' position played a key role was adultery. Four New England colonies—Massachusetts Bay, New Haven, Plymouth, and Connecticut—officially prescribed the death penalty for persons convicted of adultery, a crime that by definition involved "a married or espoused wife" as one of the parties. The marital status of the woman's partner was irrelevant; she was as liable to hang for having sex with a single man as with a married one. By contrast, as was noted in the last section, a married man who had illicit sexual intercourse with an unmarried woman was guilty only of fornication, which was usually punished by fine or whipping. Adultery was considered a more serious crime than fornication because it violated a husband's exclusive sexual access to his wife and directly challenged his supremacy in the household. That juries and judges alike proved reluctant to impose capital punishment in adultery prosecutions is less important than the fact that the statutes remained on the books for years, symbolically if in no other way reinforcing a wife's subjection to her husband and writing a sexual double standard into the law.[46]

Although colonial civil and criminal legislation emphasized women's subordination in marriage, wives did have some rights, most of them implicitly and incompletely described. Perhaps the most important was the right to a husband's physical presence and financial support. The Bay Colony required husbands and wives to live together and prosecuted spouses of either sex who disobeyed that order. Testation acts (analyzed in chapter three) forbade dying men from disinheriting their wives under most circumstances, and, as was already observed in the prologue to this section, New England men were sometimes prosecuted for neglecting their families.[47]

Yet colonial statutes in essence codified the ideals of marital subordination that suffused Anglo-American society. Adult women were rendered incompetent by what the anonymous English lawyer termed "wise fiction of Law." He told his female readers that a wife might wonder "whether shee bee either none or no more then halfe a person." That was not true, he assured them: "bee of good cheare," for "in nature & in some other cases by the Law of God and man, they remain divers." Even so, from the assumption that a female criminal was acting at her accomplice husband's direction to a wife's loss of the ability to act independently in civil cases, the law merely detailed the consequences of the widely held belief that, as Mary Astell put it in 1706, there could be no "Society, great or little, from Empires down to private Families, without a last Resort, to determine the Affairs of that Society by an irresistible Sentence," and that, in marriages as in the state, the reins of government were best held by a man.[48]

In 1665, the Massachusetts General Court neatly summed up the universal message to colonial husbands and wives when it tried to reconcile an estranged couple: he should "provide for hir as his wife" and she should "submitt hirselfe to him as she ought." In other words, the man's primary obligation to his spouse was financial, whereas she had an equally compelling responsibility to submit to him. A Puritan minister put it this way in a letter to his soon-to-be-wed offspring: "the husband should love, provide for and be tender-hearted to the wife; . . . the wife should reverence the husband, and obey him, and endeavor to be an helpmeet for him."[49]

Undoubtedly many seventeenth-century husbands and wives fulfilled, or came close to fulfilling, such a loving if asymmetrical ideal. The
well-known poetry of Mistress Anne Dudley Bradstreet, who told her
husband, "If ever two were one, then surely we. / If ever man were
loved by wife, then thee," expressed the same sentiments as less familiar
verse by other authors.[50] Similarly, in his autobiography, the Reverend
Thomas Shepard described his first wife as "most incomparably loving
to me & every way amiable & holy," and his second wife as "a woman
of incomparable meeknes of spirit, toward my selfe especially & very
loving." Nor were tender observations offered only in verse or after a
spouse's death. The decade-long correspondence of John Winthrop and
his third wife, Margaret Tyndal, surely ranks as one of the greatest collections of love letters ever published.[51]

In the eyes of contemporaries, the best evidence of a loving marriage
was the offspring produced by it. As was already indicated, a properly
consummated sexual relationship was deemed crucial to successful matrimony, and the birth of children confirmed the existence of such a
relationship. That was all the more true because of the contemporary
belief that women could not conceive without having reached orgasm.
(So the New Haven justices informed a young woman who claimed to
have been impregnated while in "a fitt of swooning" that "no woman
can be gotten with child without some knowledg, consent & delight in
the acting thereof.")[52] Accordingly, the absence of children called into
question the character of a marriage and, in particular, the husband's
ability to satisfy his wife sexually. On several occasions childless colonial
wives reported facing insults directed more at their husbands than themselves. In 1639 in the Bay Colony, for example, a man approached a
woman "& offered to put his hands under her coats & sayd he came of
a woman & knew what belonged to a woman & because her husband
was not able to give her a great belly he would help him." Two years
earlier, at a cowpen in Virginia, two women "in a jeering manner" told
Grace Waltham that her husband "hade his Mounthly Courses as
Women have, and that . . . John Waltham was not able to gett a child."
In the mind of the community, in short, childlessness indicated a husband's failings as a man and the unsatisfactory nature of a marriage.[53]

Good marriages were characterized not only by the presence of children but also by husbands and wives who behaved in ways appropriate
to their respective stations. For a husband, that meant caring for his wife
and (as a group of men remarked) "putting honour upon her as the
weaker vessell" while nevertheless firmly asserting his authority over her.
Men who were "unkinde" to their wives and those who allowed their

spouses to dominate them were both at fault. So husbands were equally likely to sue defamers who accused them of neglecting their spouses' welfare and those who charged that they were ruled by their womenfolk. New Haven's judges, indeed, formally admonished three men who had acceded to their wives' demands that they resist court decisions. The magistrates successfully convinced one of these miscreants that he had been guilty of "a breach of the 5th commandment" both for his failure to submit to the state and for his willingness to let his wife direct his actions, which indicated his inability to govern her properly.[54]

For a wife, submission to her husband's will was essential. Such deference did not imply that she could not have opinions of her own, but rather that if she and her spouse disagreed, he had to prevail in the end. Strong-minded women accordingly had to walk a tightrope between expressing dissenting views and openly challenging their husbands' decisions. Lucy Winthrop Downing, for example, was well aware of the perilous path she was taking when she opposed her husband's plans to move the family to Massachusetts Bay in the mid-1630s. "Now you may saye I take to much apon me, I am but a wife, and therfore it is sufficient for me to follow my husban," she told her brother, John Winthrop, but went on to assure him that though she thought it her "duty" to raise practical objections to the idea, she had never been "peremptory against his goeing." Although she "utterly den[ied]" having prevented the family from emigrating, Lucy filled her letters with reasons why such a move would be inappropriate. In 1637, after several years of effort, Emmanuel Downing finally prevailed and moved his family to the Bay Colony.[55]

Wifely subjection was so fundamental to Anglo-American belief structures that it could override other ideals. In Rhode Island, founded in 1636 by Roger Williams and a group of religious dissenters from Massachusetts Bay, the settlers directed that "no man should be molested for his conscience." As a result, John Winthrop noted in his journal, "men's wives, and children, and servants, claimed liberty hereby to go to all religious meetings, though never so often, or though private, upon the week days." But Joshua Verin, a young man notable for his "ungodlines," refused to let his wife, Jane, attend such gatherings as often as she wished. In the opinion of Roger Williams, Joshua treated his spouse "tyrannically and brutishly," regularly beating her so severely that he endangered her life. The colony's leaders proposed that Verin be "censured," thereby instigating a debate in which one man insisted that liberty of conscience should not "extend to the breach of any ordinance of God, such as the subjection of wives to their husbands." John Winthrop applauded his "good solid reasons," concurring that only a misguided policy would give official approval to wives' disobeying their husbands for any reason. Although the Rhode Islanders considered the possibility of divorce as a means of settling the dispute, in the end they decided merely to disfranchise Verin. Williams remained critical of Joshua's "fowle and slanderous and brutish Cariage," but took no further steps to protect Jane Verin from her spouse's violent behavior. The couple later returned together to Salem, whence they had come.[56]

Thus even free-thinking Rhode Island reaffirmed the authority of a brutal, ungodly husband over a pious wife because to do otherwise would have violated God's law requiring wives' subordination to their spouses. And like Joshua Verin, men of both ordinary and high status, confronted with similarly undeferential spouses, thought it their right to use force to ensure their wives' obedience. All the colonies occasionally prosecuted both men and women for mistreating their spouses, and incidents of verbal and physical abuse are also mentioned in other contexts. Yet most of the prosecutions occurred in Massachusetts jurisdictions, undoubtedly because of that colony's 1650 statute prohibiting either spouse from striking the other.[57]

Cases that resulted in prosecution probably represent only the small tip of a very large iceberg of behavior, given men's expectations of dominating their spouses. Moreover, as was already observed in the discussion of the Pinion family, when a husband administered a brutal beating (the very sort that would draw the attention of neighbors and magistrates) the act revealed a man's failure to fulfill his proper role as family governor. If a man could not control his wife through moderate physical correction, it reflected negatively on him and raised the possibility that others might intervene, not only to protect his wife from harm but also to instruct him in the responsibilities of household leadership. Thus prosecutions and expressions of community concern did not necessarily stem from the belief that a husband was wrong to use force against his wife, although that was what the Massachusetts statute stated. Rather, the state and the community stepped in to mediate marital disputes when one or both parties seemed to have lost sight of their appropriate roles—when wives failed to submit to their husbands' rule, when husbands ceased to govern wisely.

One third of the colonists accused of spouse abuse were women, a proportion that at first glance might appear high. That percentage, however, probably resulted from neighbors and judges paying closer attention to disruptions of the household hierarchy than to actions that nominally accorded with proper power relationships. Even so, that men found themselves haled into court for mistreating their wives indicates that battered women could find some allies outside the family, in the realms of the formal or informal publics, and that on occasion neighbors or local officials would intervene to prevent egregious abuses of husbandly authority.

Men repeatedly signaled their assumption of marital superiority and their unwillingness to submit to supervision of their conduct. A Virginian in 1625 pointed a gun at a group of neighbors who were attempting to interrupt his wife battering, shouting at them, "what have you to do heere, you were best kepe back or I will make ye stande back." Four decades later, a man from York, Maine, confronted a local magistrate who had chided him for "sleighting & abuseing of his wife," asking, "What hath any man to do with it, have I not power to Correct my owne wife?" The following year in the same jurisdiction Mr. Francis Morgan, accused by his wife, Mistress Sarah, of "abusive speeches & Actions" that endangered her life, told the court "obstinatly" that "hee had strucke his wife & would doe it [again], for it was below him to Complayn to Authority aganst his wife." And a man brought before the Dukes County, Massachusetts, court in 1679 on similar charges exclaimed "in a scornfull way" to the justices, "you have nothing to do to Examine things as you doe."[58]

The March 1647/8 prosecution of Richard Pray of Ipswich is especially revealing because it, like a number of other incidents, shows that husbands did not bother to conceal their mistreatment of wives from observers, thereby graphically illustrating their belief that such behavior on their part was acceptable. In front of a boarder in their house, Richard spoke of having beaten his wife, Mary, declaring he would do so again "20 times a day beefore she Should bee his master." Later, accusing her of telling some high-status neighbors about the abuse, he attempted to strike her with a large stick. Thwarted by the boarder, who intervened to ward off that blow, Richard instead kicked her so hard she fell against the wall. On another occasion he threw a heavy dish at her in the presence of several people, hitting her hand and wrist and making her fear that her arm was broken. Warned by the boarder that "the court would not allow him to abuse his wife," Richard responded that he cared little for the court's opinion. When the boarder persisted, remarking that the judges "have tamed as stout hearts as hee," Pray retorted, "if ever hee came in trouble for abusinge his wife he would cripple her & make her sitt on a Stoole, and there hee would keep her."[59]

Mary Pray enlisted the boarder's sympathy for her plight by showing him the black and blue marks on her body incurred during the first beating. Like her, other battered wives sought assistance from neighbors, bystanders, or civil or religious officials; of the twenty-three incidents in which information about the origins of the prosecution is available, more than half (thirteen) involved wives who complained of mistreatment to church elders, grand jury men, or neighbors. Thus in 1660 a wife from Dover, New Hampshire, went to an elder of her church, asking "to be secured from the feare & danger she stood in of her husband"; an Essex County woman in 1675 came "weeping" to a member of the grand jury to say "she was afraid of her life"; and four years later another woman from the same county showed several male and female neighbors "the marks of her husband beating her" and told them he had nearly killed her.[60]

Witnesses to such abuse did not always intervene, or at least failed to do so immediately. This was especially true in the Chesapeake colonies, where the courts took less interest in the daily functioning of marriages than did those in New England. That only a minuscule number of Chesapeake men were prosecuted for beating their wives indicates not that they behaved better than their northern counterparts but rather that the courts there—and perhaps even neighbors—largely eschewed the task of trying to counterbalance a husband's authority in his household. In that nascent Lockean society with a dispersed pattern of settlement, there was little judicial or neighborhood supervision of a man's behavior in his family, and the dependents of brutal men suffered the consequences. Further, in a pattern remarked upon previously, incidents of spouse abuse in the Chesapeake tended to be revealed during prosecutions for other offenses, so the small number of known cases in fact overrepresents the tally of men called to account for mistreating their wives.

Thus, for example, even though many witnesses heard Anne Moye complain in 1639 that her husband, Roger, had threatened to kill her and that she was terrified of him, they did not report the alleged abuse for three years. At that time, a man Roger had accused of attacking her used the retrospective testimony to suggest that whatever injuries she had suffered had probably come at her husband's hands rather than his. Roger Moye was never charged with spouse abuse, and the attacker's defense failed because there was considerable evidence that he was indeed guilty as charged. But even when witnesses did come forward, Chesapeake authorities did not pursue the complaints. In September 1656, two women informed the Maryland Provincial Court about a man who had brutally battered his pregnant wife, causing her to miscarry. The court required the husband in question to post a bond, but remitted it six months later and declined to prosecute him.[61]

In both regions, wives who were dissatisfied with their husbands' treatment of them wisely did not always wait for hesitant neighbors or civil and religious officials to come to their aid. As Mary Astell pointed out late in the seventeenth century, the constant submission required of wives was "not over easie" to achieve, and some women resisted marital subjection vigorously. Some fought back, returning blow for blow and insult for insult; others tried to kill their spouses, one evidently succeeding. Even such a paragon as John Winthrop's second wife reluctantly admitted on her deathbed that "the devill went about to persuade hir to cast of[f] hir subjection to hir husbande."[62]

Yet only one colonial wife advanced a positive rationale for challenging her spouse's authority. Unruly and undeferential wives abounded in Anglo-America,[63] but the vast majority of such women did not develop reasoned defenses of their actions. The sole prominent Bay Colony woman who did present just such a formal justification for her behavior revealed both the possibilities and the limits of contemporary thinking about the appropriate relationship of husbands and wives. That only a high-ranking woman produced such a rationale confirms the earlier observation that high-status females could potentially pose serious challenges to male dominance within the Filmerian conceptual system.

Mistress Ann Hibbens was the wife of Mr. William Hibbens, a wealthy merchant, civil officeholder, and pillar of the Boston church.[64] In September 1640, she was excommunicated, in part because she had failed to submit herself to her husband, whom the church described as "so wise [and] discreet a head . . . unto whom you ought to have been obedient in the Lord." She served as an "evil example" to "diverse other wives," the church charged, for she had "against nature usurped authority over him, grieved his spirit, and carried yourself as if he was a nobody, as if his wisdom were not to be compared to yours." Despite the church's heated accusations, Mistress Hibbens nowhere frontally challenged the traditional position on wifely subjection, readily admitting to the Reverend John Cotton that "I am bound to obey my husband in all lawful things, and that it is a sin to do the contrary." Instead, she presented a twofold defense to the charge of disobedience: first, she insisted that she had done no more in a business matter than her husband had authorized; and second, she argued that God had advised husbands to listen to their wives, citing as her source a passage from the Old Testament.

The text Mistress Hibbens had in mind was Genesis 21:12, in which God instructed Abraham to "hearken unto" his wife, Sarah. During her trial, several men reported that she had quoted it to them when they accused her of lacking "wifelike subjection." Proper interpretation of the verse was obviously of great significance to Mr. Cotton and the lay members of the church, for they spent a considerable amount of time discussing the passage, her usage of it, and its subversive implications. The Reverend Cotton was particularly disturbed by Mistress Hibbens's statement that in one of his sermons he had described the statement that "a man should hearken to the counsel of his wife" as "an ordinance of God." Did you hear me say that? he asked her; no, she replied, a friend informed her that he had said it. Who? inquired her interrogator. "It was my Sister Bellingham, that told me so, that you delivered such a thing at our Elder Leveret's daughter's marriage," Mistress Hibbens responded.[65]

Mr. Richard Bellingham, then deputy governor of the colony, immediately jumped to his deceased wife's defense. "This I can testify, that it was neither the opinion nor practice of my wife—but if she had at any time given offense in any such way, she would speedily come in with submission and much melting of spirit." In so attesting, Mr. Bellingham was defending himself as well as his wife; to admit that she agreed with Mistress Hibbens was to admit to a disordered hierarchy in his own household. His wife could never have said such a thing, he proclaimed, because most of the time she did not behave as though she believed it—and when she did, she quickly apologized for her fault. The Reverend Cotton too declared that the pious Mistress Bellingham could not have believed the statement Mistress Hibbens attributed to her, and therefore that Mistress Hibbens must have misinterpreted her meaning, "for I dare confidently assert that I never delivered any such thing." He insisted that the Biblical text in question referred only to those rare occasions "when a wife speaks as the oracles of God. . . . But that wives *now* should be always God's oracles to their husband, that is a false principle." Unless husbands ordered their spouses to commit "a plain sin," wives "ought to obey them and be subject to them in all things."

Far more likely than Bellingham's and Cotton's hastily concocted retrospective version of events, though, was that one high-ranking woman had shared with another (a distant relative by marriage) their pastor's positive and perhaps somewhat unguarded reading of wives' marital standing, delivered on the occasion of the wedding of a third high-status woman. Mistress Hibbens, the recipient of the information, then made enthusiastic use of that interpretation as one of the few available justifications for her position. For example, she asked one male critic "whether it is better to obey God or man," thus implying, he told the congregation, "that disobedience to the counsel of her godly husband was her obedience to God, and that God would have her to do what she did." By "tak[ing] it for a principle that the husband must hearken to his wife in the counsel she shall give," she had made "a cipher of her husband and his authority," the church member maintained.

Mistress Ann Hibbens's bold assertions clearly struck a negative chord among the men of the Boston church. John Cotton told her that "the brethren" were deeply troubled by "the frame of your spirit and carriage toward your husband," an observation fully borne out by the record of the proceedings. In addition to Cotton and Bellingham, four different men publicly reproached her for her behavior and statements, terming her guilty of "a plain breach of the rule of Christ" and of acting "to the great dishonor of God and of [her husband]." Mistress Ann Hibbens's resistance to her spouse's authority united the men of the Boston church against her, and the interpretation of a single biblical text, transmitted through a network of high-status women, was insufficient to protect her from their anger. No one objected to her excommunication.[66]

Mistress Hibbens was unique in her attempt to develop a rationale for arguing that husbands should pay attention to their wives' opinions. Like her, other women resisted their spouses' supervision, but no other woman so consistently advanced a position contrary to the traditional belief that husbands should always dominate their wives. Even Ann Hibbens did not dispute the overriding principle of wifely subordination, but she nevertheless unhesitatingly contended that, if women had a duty to submit, men had a concomitant obligation to "hearken unto" their wives' advice. She shocked the men of Boston by claiming orthodox backing for her position: the Reverend John Cotton's explication of a verse from the Old Testament. For refusing to surrender her insistence that husbands should respect their wives, she paid the ultimate price extracted from a church member: excommunication.

THE LAW OF MARITAL SUBORDINATION

Anglo-American law stated that married women, known legally as femes covert, could come into court as plaintiffs or defendants only in conjunction with their husbands. That conjunction could take different forms, for husbands and wives sometimes filed or responded to lawsuits jointly, while at other times husbands alone sued (or were sued) on their wives' behalf.[67] Although legal procedures in seventeenth-century English America diverged in many ways from standard practice in the migrants' homeland—both because the early settlements contained few lawyers and because the migrants deliberately modified some provisions of English law—all the colonies enforced these rules of marital unity. That meant that anyone who wanted to sue a wife (for example, for debts she incurred prior to her marriage or property she detained illegally) had to sue her husband. Conversely, a wife could not pursue her own interests in court but instead needed her spouse's cooperation. The only legal procedure requiring a wife to act independently of her husband was the obligation that she consent formally and separately to any sales of family-owned real estate.[68]

Over the course of the century, four fifths of the married women who appeared in court did so accompanied or represented by their husbands. Of the one fifth who did not, nearly half were participating in just two anomalous categories of civil suits: divorces (in which a wife by definition could not sue in conjunction with her husband) and defamation cases, which in England had been handled primarily by ecclesiastical courts. Since church courts did not apply the common-law rules of marital union, when colonial judges allowed married women to file or respond to slander suits on their own they merely continued standard English practice in such cases, even though they were doing so in a secular context. It is also likely that some of the remaining wives who came to court independently had husbands' authorizations that went unnoted in the record. Therefore, the colonies violated common-law procedures in fewer than one tenth of the standard civil suits involving married women.[69]

The restrictive common-law rules allowed little flexibility to married couples or to people who wanted to do business with them. Thus on many occasions the colonists chose to circumvent those rules, acting in ways that were technically illegal but which accomplished desirable goals. So couples drafted postnuptial agreements, husbands deeded property to their wives or permitted them to write wills disposing of "their" property, and friends and relatives made gifts to married women to the explicit exclusion of their spouses.[70] Wives also negotiated bargains independently of their husbands. When a thirteen-year-old maidservant came to live in a Massachusetts household, for example, its master recorded in his diary the details of the "verbal Covenant" his wife and the girl's mother had reached regarding her service. Virginia wives sold or exchanged servants; another Virginian hired a married washerwoman; and a mother-to-be promised to pay a midwife "12 hens" for taking care of her in childbed. All such actions were prohibited under the common law, but could nevertheless be upheld in colonial courts if no one objected to their enforcement.[71]

In addition to acting for themselves, wives served as agents for their husbands even without formal powers of attorney. Court records are replete with narratives of wives' selling or purchasing items, receiving or making payment of debts, and bargaining for services.[72] Some of these arrangements were later formally confirmed by their husbands, others were understood to be valid unless husbands repudiated them. So, for example, a Stratford, Connecticut, man argued in 1654 that his purchase of a boat from a married Long Island woman should stand (though her husband was now trying to renege on the deal) because she "had formerly told her husband that she would sell the boate and he contradicted it not." He also presented evidence that the woman had frequently sold items "in her husbands absence, which her husband hath alowed of." Similarly, in 1637 a Virginia wife agreed to sell a hogshead of tobacco, assuring the buyer "that she wold acquaint her husband with it, and if he heard not from her, he might make use of it."[73]

Yet men and women who made such bargains with wives did so at their peril. If the women or their husbands later decided to back out of the arrangements, the law would protect them, since wives could not make valid contracts without formal powers of attorney. Thus in 1668 four suits were filed in York, Maine, against "Joan or John Andrews" by two men to whom Joan owed money. The confusion about the name of the defendant reflected the plaintiffs' problem: Joan was indebted to them, but she could not be sued directly for debts she had incurred during her marriage. Joan Andrews, like other women in similar situations, hid behind her status as feme covert, and though the suits were refiled regularly as late as 1674 (by then being directed at her second husband, Philip Atwell), they were just as regularly thrown out of court. One of the two plaintiffs was so frustrated by his inability to collect the sums he was owed that he ended up being ordered to post a substantial good-behavior bond "for his Contemptuus speches & carages towards this Court."[74]

Even if wives had powers of attorney, husbands could subsequently repudiate their actions. The guiding principle was that the husband's will should prevail if at all possible. Take, for example, the case of Mr. John Hammond of Maryland, who during a six-year absence from the colony in the late 1650s empowered his wife, Ann, to act on his behalf. While her husband was in England, Mistress Hammond represented him on fourteen occasions, mainly in suits for debt, most of which she won. But twice she made major mistakes, and when her husband returned in 1661 he petitioned the Provincial Court, citing her "want [lack] of experience" and asking for "Reheareings" of the suits she had lost. He had reason to be upset: the evidence demonstrated that in one case she had been a "foole" (as a witness called her at the time), selling a plantation without retaining proper documentation; and in the other that she had acknowledged the validity of a falsely backdated claim on part of the estate. The Provincial Court agreed to reconsider these two cases, but in the first the lack of documentation prevented Mr. Hammond from winning (as it had previously kept his wife from prevailing), and no decision is recorded in the second.[75]

Perhaps fears that their wives might likewise (as Mr. Hammond put it in his petition to the court) subject their estates to "strange and unjust Engagements" led other husbands to designate male friends and relatives, rather than spouses, as their attorneys. Whatever the reason, wives formally served as their husbands' attorneys in only a small number of civil cases.[76] That fact, coupled with the enforcement of marital-union rules in all but a tiny proportion of lawsuits, meant that, as the law intended, wives for the most part lacked the ability to act independently within the legal system.

The common-law procedures could subject men to unanticipated liabilities. Husbands were responsible for any debts their wives had contracted prior to marriage, and many men faced suits asking them to repay such preexisting obligations. Husbands often tried to contest the claims, but to little avail.[77] Also damaging to husbands was the legal responsibility to pay any fines assessed on their wives for criminal misbehavior. Financial penalties were the most common punishments inflicted on both male and female offenders in colonial English America. But when the guilty party was a married woman, a fine penalized her husband rather than herself, since she possessed no property of her own. Sometimes judges formally imposed the fine on the woman, sometimes on her husband, but he always had the obligation to pay, even when he had nothing to do with his wife's offense. So a Virginian was penalized because his wife had killed another man's hog, although a witness reported that he had been "angry" at his wife's act; and Mr. Francis Morgan of Maine was fined because his wife, Mistress Sarah, kept "a disorderly house in her husbands absence."[78]

The height of irony was achieved when wives were convicted of lascivious conduct with other men, but husbands nevertheless had to pay costs or post bond for their spouses' future good behavior. One can only sympathize with such men as John Pearce, whose wife, Ellen, was found guilty of "light behavior" in 1639 and who was directed to supply a £10 bond for her; Charles Glover, who had to pay court costs when his wife was presented for adultery in early 1649; or Thomas Scelling, whose wife was accused of "many suspicious carriages with Thomas Patten" and who was "bound for his wife's good behavior in rejecting the company of said Patten." In most such cases the courts also inflicted penalties on the women themselves—Ellen Pearce had to "stand in the market place the next market day with a paper" detailing her offense and Goody Glover had to sit in the stocks—but even so, a majority of married women charged with committing crimes in which their husbands did not participate were given some sort of financial penalty, for which their spouses then became liable.[79]

Conversely, though, men could also benefit greatly from their wives' dependent legal status. In addition to controlling or at least having the ability to manage any property their spouses brought to the marriage, husbands gained immeasurably from their wives' labor. Because of the gendered division of household work roles, women were a valuable economic asset. Skilled at such tasks as cooking, baking, laundering, sewing, making butter and cheese, and supervising household servants, wives not only improved the quality of their husbands' lives but also augmented the family's income.[80]

Accordingly, when in 1666 the married Alexander Davis broke a contract to work for Daniel Glover, an unmarried planter in Talbot County, Maryland, the disgruntled Glover filed suit as much for the loss of Davis's wife's labor as for Alexander's failure to complete the planting and fencing he had promised to accomplish. "The said Davis wife was to doe all theire houshould imployment, and to make and mend, theire Lining [linen]," Glover complained. A sympathetic jury awarded Glover damages if the Davises failed to fulfill the contract. Bay Colony arbitrators in 1640 similarly recognized the value of a wife's work: although an employer declared that his servant's wife had been "a charge and no benefit" to the household, when the servant pointed out that his wife "provided diet for 5, 6, 7, 8 workmen in hay tyme," managed the dairy, and occasionally helped to "tend the cattle," he won his claim for higher wages. In such a context, husbands unsurprisingly regarded the value of their wives' labor as wholly at their disposal. One demonstration of that came in 1659, when a Maryland planter responded to a suit by claiming that a debt he owed had been partially repaid "by his wife for helping the sayd Plantives wife to wash and milke."[81]

Wives, indeed, were so submerged in their husbands' legal and economic identities that in court records they are often called "[John Doe] his wife," with their own first names never appearing anywhere. Al-though prenuptial agreements could circumvent the common law and permit wives to retain control of any property they might have owned before their marriages, only a handful of women other than widows—and just a few of those—took advantage of that opportunity. It is no more than suggestive, but still revealing, that a tally of livestock earmarks registered in Maryland after 1648 lists as the owners thereof 428 men and just 44 women, only 7 of whom were specifically identified as wives (28 were "daughters" and 6 were "mistresses" of unknown marital status). Such figures imply that only a tiny proportion of married women in seventeenth-century English America possessed property in their own right.[82]

The assumptions of marital union and of husbands' primacy per-meated colonial society, extending far beyond the courts. Institutions in which legal technicalities should have mattered little were affected by common-law procedural rules and the concepts they incorporated. Consider, for example, the tangle that enveloped the new church at Wenham, Massachusetts, in late 1644 and early 1645. Previously, most of those joining the congregation had worshiped at Salem, where the church had formally dismissed only the male members, wives being "conceived to be dismissed with their husbands . . . because women are supposed to go with their husbands." But in Wenham "some agitation" arose about the status of the wives, because "these sisters did not join in that request [for dismissal]" at the time or subsequently. Not all the founders of the church agreed that the women had been "orderly dis-missed," and therefore questions arose about their ability to join the Wenham congregation. In addition, someone realized that the married women had never even been asked whether they wanted to participate in the new church; when questioned, three women indicated that they had serious doubts about the proceedings. A particular problem was posed by a married "sister" whose husband had not been a member of the Salem church: people challenged her status, since she could not have been included in the dismissal document even by implication. In the end, it took months of exchanges with the Salem church and lengthy consultations in Wenham before all the issues were clarified and some of the women formally admitted to the congregation.[83]

Although the New England and Chesapeake colonies differed in many other respects, therefore, courts in both regions rigorously en-forced the principles of marital unity. By mutual consent, husbands and wives or parties to business transactions could ignore legal technicalities and proceed as though wives had the ability to make contracts or to own property. But if disputes later arose, the courts in all the English colonies uniformly decided that wives could not act independently of their husbands, with the sole exceptions of seeking divorces, filing or responding to slander suits before the mid-1660s, or consenting to the sale of land. In law as in practice, the key to marital unity—and thus to social stability—was wives' subordination to their husbands. In marriage, the fundamental social hierarchy, there could be but one dominant force, and that was the husband. When wives acted alone, they did so only at the sufferance of their spouses, the courts, and the people with whom they did business. In short, wives' legal subjection to their husbands restricted their capacity for autonomous participation in the colonial economy.

DIVORCE

Marital unity based on wifely subordination was thus both ideal and reality in seventeenth-century Anglo-America. Still, all the colonies except Virginia reluctantly acknowledged that perpetuating every marriage, however desirable in theory, was impossible to accomplish in fact. Maryland had no divorce law, but in practice its courts endorsed separations when marriages seemed to have broken down irretrievably. New England Puritans regarded marriage as a civil contract rather than as an irreversible sacrament; such a contract could legally be voided, especially when desertion, bigamy, or adultery was involved. Further, the New Haven colony formally recognized the importance of sexual intercourse to the constitution of a valid marriage by explicitly permitting a wife to divorce her husband for impotence. As the statute delicately put it, if a woman "needing and requiring conjugall duty, and due benevolence from her husband," found "after convenient forbearance and due tryall" that he "neither at the time of marriage, nor since, hath been, is, nor by the use of any lawfull means, is like to be able to perform or afford the same," she could sue for divorce and permission to remarry. The law also provided that if the man had known of his incapacity before marriage and had deceived her, she could be awarded monetary damages.[84]

Divorce in the colonies was rare but not entirely unknown. Most "divorces" were, in effect, separation agreements, allowing husbands and wives to live apart and providing for a distribution of the property or the continuing maintenance of the wife, but not permitting remarriage for either partner. On occasion, it is difficult to distinguish such divorces from a court's declaration that a deserted wife should regain feme sole status so that she could support herself and her children. For instance, in July 1667 the court in Casco, Maine, announced with respect to an innkeeper whose husband had absconded that

> what estate shee hath hitherto procured by her owne Industrey or shall obtayne for the future without her husbands assistance shall be & remaine to bee her owne reall & proper estate, & shall not bee lyable upon any reason or pretended cause whatsoever to bee at the disposing of . . . her husband, nor In any Course of Law to answere or respond his debts.

Although the Casco justices did not explicitly grant the woman a divorce, their order had the same effect as a separation decree.[85]

Just as colonial courts proved willing to endorse settlers' self-defined marriages, so too they occasionally acceded to self-defined separations. Maryland judges, for example, ratified agreements drafted by divorcing couples when all attempts at reconciliation had failed. Thus in October 1656 the Provincial Court confirmed a division of assets worked out by a husband and wife who "were minded to live a sunder," and a decade later it decreed that the profits from a plantation Hannah Price had acquired during a previous widowhood should be used for her separate maintenance "and that William Price her husband be for ever debarr'd from any Claime thereto." Likewise, even though in June 1658 the court ordered an estranged couple to live together, a year later its officials recorded without comment the couple's declaration that they mutually "disclayme[d]" each other as marital partners and would not "molest or trouble" each other further.[86] Such actions resembled the de facto separations acknowledged by Bay Colony judges when they failed to order the reunification of couples who seemed determined to live apart.[87]

A second form of divorce, considerably less common, allowed an innocent party to remarry. In Connecticut, a spouse's desertion alone provided adequate grounds for such a divorce, but elsewhere in New England judges required additional evidence of misconduct, usually adultery or bigamy committed by the absent spouse, before permitting the other party to enter matrimony anew. In such cases, the evidence had to be conclusive. Given the perceived significance of inviolable marital unity, mere suspicions of adultery or bigamy, even when coupled with desertion, were inadequate to win divorces.[88]

Definitive proof was also required when a wife sought to end a marriage by alleging that her husband was impotent. Even without New

Haven's statutory language allowing such a result, the other Puritan colonies acknowledged the key role of physical consummation in matrimony by voiding unions in which sexual intercourse had never occurred. Only impotence predating a wedding could serve as grounds for divorce; a husband's becoming impotent during a marriage was interpreted as an act of God, a trial a woman would have to bear patiently. So when Mary Drury refused to live with her husband, Hugh, claiming that "he never had a fellow ship with me, nor was abull" and that he had been at the time of their wedding "incapasitated for a mariage Estate," the Suffolk County court took testimony from a series of witnesses who had spoken with Hugh's first wife, Lydia, about *their* marriage, during which she had had a son. Although some of the testimony suggested that an accident during his marriage to Lydia had rendered Hugh impotent, the Court of Assistants refused to nullify Mary's marital bonds, regarding the evidence as inconclusive.[89]

Wives not facing Mary Drury's problem—proving that a husband who had fathered a child during a previous marriage had never been capable of sexual intercourse in a second union—had a somewhat easier time winning divorces on grounds of impotence, as long as they were patient. In March 1662/3 a Marblehead man admitted, as his wife had charged, that he was "Infirmous not able to performe that office of marriage." Still, the Court of Assistants initially denied her request for a divorce, advising them instead "to a more loving & suitable Cohabitation one with the other" and suggesting they use "all due phisicall meanes." Seven months later, the Essex County court granted what the higher court had withheld: a divorce, with permission for her to remarry. Likewise, a Salem woman requesting a divorce from her husband for "insufficiency" had to wait more than a year before her request was fulfilled.[90]

Such wives successfully pleaded their cases in court, but couples and those who formally judged them were not the only people with opinions relevant to the conduct and perpetuation of individual marriages. That community members joined the courts in emphasizing the inviolability of matrimony and the importance of its preservation is illustrated with remarkable clarity by the experiences of a divorced woman and her second husband in the Bay Colony during the late 1660s and early 1670s.

In 1651, the Essex court divorced Martha Bradstreet Rowlandson of Ipswich from her husband, Thomas, whom she had "proven impotent." Within a year or two, Martha married William Beale. The couple settled in Marblehead, and they eventually had several children. Then, during the winter of 1666, Martha Beale became embroiled in an

unusually bitter and violent altercation with three of her neighbors—
Richard Downing, his wife, Mary, and Mary's mother, Margaret Bennett. The confrontation nominally occurred because the Downings had
purloined four cartloads of dung promised to the Beales by another
neighbor, Alexander Gilligan, but the court record makes it clear that
much more was involved.[91]

Martha Beale accompanied Mary Stacy, a young woman, and
Frances Gilligan, Alexander's wife, when they went to the Downing
household to investigate the theft of the dung. Mary's mother, though,
warned Martha not to go. Jane Stacy later testified that she "haveing
Herd of some passages Before by my Husband . . . told her severall
Times that They Would Beate her." Martha replied that "shee Would
doe Them noe Hurt" but instead would "give Them good Words &
noe Cause to beate Her." According to Mary Stacy and Frances Gilligan,
that is exactly what Martha did. She "did not any way molest them then
by any kind of affront," the two recalled. Even so, Jane Stacy's wariness
proved to be completely justified.

When the three women arrived at their destination, Martha Beale
was greeted with anger by the Downings and Bennett, the two women
armed with "scragged clubbs." They repeatedly threw her down on the
"Hassoky frozen ground," not allowing her to get up; Richard "with
his cluch fist smote her in the ey"; and all the while the three called her
such names as "whore," "Base whore," and "whor and drabb." With
Mary Stacy standing to one side "Crying out with teares in her eyes . . .
doe not kill the woaman," Frances Gilligan intervened, rescuing Martha Beale but in the process receiving a severe beating herself. Indeed,
witnesses eventually suggested—though the Downings and Bennett
were never formally accused of such a crime—that lingering effects of
the beating caused Frances's death less than a year later.

As shall become evident in chapter four, "whore" and its many
variants were the slanderous terms most commonly directed at women.
Yet the vicious nature of this confrontation, and the repeated use of the
word in it, implies that the epithet had unusual resonance for the participants. "You whore get you of[f] my ground or els ile slatt out your
braines," shouted Richard Downing; "Margaret Bennit & Mary downing cald good[y] Beale whore whor & drabb searvall times," attested
Mary Stacy and Frances Gilligan. That the brawl was in fact directly
related to Martha Beale's marital history became clear several years later.

In June 1669, the Beales formally complained to the county court
about a long and violent campaign of harassment. Adding to the preexisting tensions evident in the 1666 confrontation at the Downing

houselot was Martha's admission to church membership. That sign of favor infuriated the Beales' neighbors, who thereafter hurled insults at family members at different times and in a variety of locales: William was an "adulterouse Roge" and "Cuckolly Curr," Martha a "base Jade," their son Samuel "a bastard." A manservant from the nearby Gachell household struck Samuel and threw rocks at his parents while they were milking their cows, one of the family's lambs was deliberately crippled, and two young men from the Gachell family attacked the Beale house with clubs, yelling, "we are come to beatt thee: thou Livest in adultery."[92]

Neighbors did more than wield clubs and shout epithets. Thomas Gachell, for one, lectured the Beales on "the scripture": "No Man shall put away his Wife exept it bee for adulterie & he that Marrieth her Comits adulterie." The comments, including that of a woman who told Martha that "you are another mans wife you were married to another man you were divorced from an honest man," indicate that the neighbors believed that the Rowlandsons' 1651 divorce had been improperly granted. Martha might have successfully convinced the court that her first husband was impotent, but the neighbors did not concur with that judgment, for they deemed Thomas "an honest man." Perhaps they suspected Martha Rowlandson of manipulating a weak husband who had experienced some sexual problems early in their marriage, a circumstance not without precedent in New England.[93]

Furthermore, an old story about the Beales was dredged up and retold to their disadvantage. In the early 1660s the couple had had some marital difficulties, instigated by William's jealousy about Martha's possibly too-friendly relationship with a former lodger. Before they were reconciled through the intervention of a high-status neighbor, William spent several nights at others' homes, the constable was called to their house one evening, and Martha complained to acquaintances of physical abuse, telling them in addition that William had once charged that "all her children wer bastards save one." William filed a successful slander suit against Mr. William Hollingworth in an attempt to stop the circulation of this story, which lent credence to the community's negative judgment of their morals. Most damningly, it even suggested that William himself agreed that his wife was guilty of adultery.[94]

One of the most trying confrontations elicited an emotional plea from the Beales to the Essex County court. A year after they filed their initial complaint, they informed the judges that because of the "anullitie" of Martha's marriage to Thomas Rowlandson and despite her being "innocent" of any wrongdoing therein, "Som persons Take ockacion

To abuse us in most revileing speches." In particular, they pointed to
the actions of Mistress Elinor Hollingworth, wife of Mr. William, "Who
Came to our dore the Last fall & charged us with Liveing in Adullterry
a Capitall Crime worthy of death & [said] that the church was a Cover
for her Rogery." Mistress Hollingworth's accusations were important
not only for their own sake but also because they were responsible for
"setting on edg [the] younger & ruggeder sort," such as the men who
had previously attacked them, for youths "thinke the thinge is truth."
Cleverly, the Beales reminded the judges that the slander injured the
church by claiming that one of its members "hath twoo husbands alive,"
in addition to "dishonor[ing]" the secular authority that had decreed the
Rowlandsons' divorce, namely the Essex court itself. The magistrates
fully agreed with the Beales that Mistress Hollingworth had not only
defamed Goody Beale but "reflected also upon civil justice and the
church." They ordered Elinor Hollingworth to pay a fine and directed
that part of it be remitted if she made an abject apology in the Marblehead church within ten days, admitting that she had spoken "to the
dishonor of God, the church & court & to the great reproach to the
partys & evill example of others." It is unknown whether she so acknowledged her error.[95]

THE INCIDENTS involving William and Martha Beale and their angry
neighbors provide a vivid reminder that seventeenth-century marriages
did not exist in isolation. When young people married, their entire families, especially their fathers, actively participated in the decision-making
and in the consequences, positive or negative, of those decisions. If
husbands and wives could not live peaceably with each other, neighbors
might intervene, offering advice, criticism, or sympathy. Everywhere in
the colonies the judicial system oversaw the process of marriage formation and dissolution; in New England, judges did far more than that,
supervising the day-to-day functioning of marriages and trying to ensure
the maintenance of proper familial hierarchies. The only colonists who
attempted to argue that such collective involvement in marital affairs was
inappropriate were men accused of excessive brutality to their wives.
And even they never claimed a right to "privacy" by using that word,
which at the time had no meaning applicable to the circumstances in
which they found themselves. Instead, men insisted that they were
merely exercising a proper husbandly prerogative.

Although both state and and community intervened in marriages,
the judgments of the formal public, as embodied in statutes or court

decisions, did not necessarily accord with those of the informal public. The Essex County court had decreed that the union of Martha Bradstreet and Thomas Rowlandson could be annulled because it had never been consummated. To Martha Bradstreet Beale's later neighbors, however, Thomas Rowlandson was "an honest man," she a woman with two living husbands and therefore an adulteress, and William was the man who had cuckolded Rowlandson. The neighbors accordingly called her children by Beale "bastards." Yet until Martha was admitted to the church only the brawl over the dung revealed any unusual antagonism between her and the neighbors. The indication that she was believed to be among the saved was more than the community (particularly the Hollingworths, for Mr. William had not yet been allowed to join the church) could stand. The Hollingworths and others erupted in a rage that did not subside until the Beales convinced the justices of the county court to weigh in on their side of the dispute and to quash the disturbances by making an example of Mistress Hollingworth and the other attackers.

Marriages drew such concentrated attention because of their crucial importance to the maintenance of social order. Peacefully dominant husbands, quietly submissive wives, marriages for life, and a conjunction of interests symbolized by common-law rules of marital unity: these were the fundamental bases of the colonial hierarchical social structure. Few colonists, no matter how disruptive their individual actions might have been, ever formally challenged the assumptions that lay behind traditional notions of social stability. Even Mistress Ann Hibbens accepted the basic premise of wifely subordination while nonetheless insisting that husbands show respect for their wives' judgment—and citing scripture to support her position. That her confrontation with orthodoxy, limited though it was, elicited such an uncompromising response reveals the tenacity with which men held onto the reins of gendered power in the context of matrimony.

CHAPTER 2

❧

A Little Monarchy

It appears that a great family, if it be not part of some commonwealth, is of itself, as to the rights of sovereignty, a little monarchy—whether that family consist of a man and his children, or of a man and his servants, or of a man and his children and servants together—wherein the father or master is the sovereign.

—*Thomas Hobbes, 1651*[1]

WHEN THOMAS HOBBES described the "little monarchy" that was the family, women became invisible. Although wives and mothers were essential to the functioning of households—indeed to their very creation—Hobbes left adult women out of his description. For him, households consisted only of men, their children, and their servants. The omission was significant, representing more than a blind spot in Hobbes's vision. He excluded women because, from the vantage point of the head of the household, a wife and mother was peripheral to the main lines of authority in the familial power structure. As a subordinate legally subsumed into her husband's identity, she worked under his direction even as she oversaw the household's daily affairs.[2]

For Hobbes and other seventeenth-century philosophers, the key questions about power in the family context revolved around fathers' control of their children; the theorists uniformly ignored or glossed over the possibility that women might wield independent authority in the household. As shall be seen in chapter three, that gendered view of familial power was inaccurate in many respects, but practical experience did not alter the common understanding of desirable family dynamics. Thomas Hobbes, Sir Robert Filmer, and John Locke concentrated their attention exclusively on exploring the bases of paternal power and outlining its potential uses.

Hobbes acknowledged that families existed within commonwealths, but failed to recognize that they were also embedded within communities of peers. Neither the colonial husbands who occasionally had to answer to the formal and informal publics for the treatment of their wives nor the "sovereigns" of Hobbes's "little monarchies" existed in isolation. Formally supervised by the courts and informally overseen by the community, male heads of households in the Anglo-American colonies wielded authority with considerable support from others. Yet if they overstepped the boundaries of the proper exercise of paternal power, that support could become condemnation.

THE THEORY OF PATERNAL POWER

Just as seventeenth-century English people universally believed that wives should be subjected to their husbands, so too they held that children should be subordinated to their parents. And by *children* they meant not just blood descendants but also servants and any other household dependents, the fictive sons and daughters who participated in most families. The Fifth Commandment, "Honor thy Father and Mother," was interpreted broadly, enjoining obedience to all superiors, religious or secular.[3] But the commandment's primary import, like its words, was familial.

Its meaning derived precisely from the words of the commandment. Children, asserted John Locke, had a "perpetual Obligation" to honor their parents, "by the Law of God and Nature." This was an "indispensible Duty of the Child, and the proper Priviledge of the Parents." Locke insisted that mothers and fathers were owed equal respect; neither parent (nor anyone else, for that matter) could free a child from obligation to either. Although Sir Robert Filmer consistently referred only to fathers, he too wrote once of the "obedience to parents . . . immediately due by a natural law."[4] When the relationship of parent and child was described from the child's perspective, in other words, seventeenth-century authors observed that the child, real or fictive, had an equal duty to both mother and father.

Yet that observation came in the context of the husband's firmly established marital primacy. From a parental perspective, the person who wielded power was the father. Filmer even went so far as to recast the Fifth Commandment, usually rendering it as "Honour thy Father." Hobbes adopted the same practice, declaring that "the right of dominion by generation is that which the parent has over his children, and is called PATERNAL." Locke, by contrast, contended that the commonly employed phrase "paternal power" was erroneous and should more accurately be termed "Parental Power." Nevertheless, even he repeatedly employed such phrases as "the *Father's Power* of commanding" or "the *Power of the Father*" while developing his argument.[5]

Just as the theoreticians thus equated the words "parent" and "father," so too they employed "children" to mean "sons." Filmer and Locke (though not Hobbes) extensively discussed the relationship of fathers and sons in the context of the family. Their observations centered generally on the origins, extent, and uses of fathers' power over sons, and the ensuing debate between the two over the nature of paternal authority masked a far deeper consensus.

Sir Robert Filmer's message in *Patriarcha* and his other writings was that fathers had absolute, uncontrollable authority over their sons. "Every man," he asserted, "is born subject to the power of a Father," who "governs by no other law than by his own will." The process, according to Filmer, started with Adam, by natural right "the Father, King and Lord over his family." Adam, and hence subsequent fathers, even had the "power to dispose [of], or sell his children or servants." To Filmer's mind, such paternal power was unrestrained unless the father himself remitted some or all of it.[6]

John Locke initially questioned Filmer's account of father-son relationships, insisting that fathers' power was subject to two limitations. First, it did not (or at the very least should not) include the "most shameful" and "unnatural" practices of exposing or selling children, as Filmer had claimed. Second, paternal power was not perpetual. Employing gender-neutral terminology at the outset of his discussion, Locke declared that so-called parental authority was in reality the "Duty" of parents "to take care of their Off-spring, during the imperfect state of Childhood." Derived solely from a child's need for care in infancy, such power was a temporary obligation that ceased when the child matured. As Locke examined that process, his language changed: "parents" became "fathers," and "children" became "sons." Thus he presented the growing independence of the child wholly in masculine terms: once a son reached the age of discretion, he and his father were "equally *free* . . . equally Subjects of the same Law together, without any Dominion left in the Father over the Life, Liberty, or Estate of his Son" in either civil society or the state of nature.[7]

Locke allowed fathers one effective means of wielding authority over adult sons: the ability "to *bestow their Estates* on those, who please them best." Although he asserted in the *First Treatise* that inheritance rights accrued equally to all children rather than simply to first-born sons, in the *Second Treatise* Locke admitted that fathers could favor one child over another. Thus his position on paternal power was not as different from Filmer's as it might appear at first glance. He argued with Filmer only about the source of dominion over sons "past Minority," not about its existence or its legitimate exercise. Fathers' authority came not, he declared, from "any peculiar right of *Fatherhood*," but rather "by the Reward they have in their hands." Locke's was a distinction without a difference, for the result was the same: both he and Filmer stressed that through control over the distribution of his property a father could ensure the continuing obedience of his adult sons. Neither he nor Filmer ever dealt explicitly with the potential inheritance rights of daughters.[8]

Indeed, the two men mentioned daughters only briefly, while citing specific examples to score debating points on opponents. Thus Filmer used Judah's declaration that his widowed daughter-in-law, Thamar, should die for conceiving a child out of wedlock (Genesis 38:24) as evidence of a father's power of life or death over his children. Likewise, Locke introduced daughters into his narrative only to show how problematic was Filmer's insistence on the inheritance of political power by the eldest son of the eldest son, in perpetuity. In the event of the failure of a direct male line, he asked, is "the Grand-Son by a Daughter" to be preferred to "a Nephew by a Brother?" Or "a Grand-Son by a Younger Daughter, before a Grand-Daughter by an Elder Daughter?" Or even "a Sister by the half Blood, before a Brothers Daughter by the whole Blood?"[9]

Daughters thus appeared in Locke's and Filmer's political writings solely as disruptive influences. They wrecked a male line of descent or a logical argument, and they misbehaved, thereby shaming their fathers. The impression one receives is that headstrong daughters, largely ignored by theory though they were, could do their families great harm. Yet Locke and Filmer proposed no mechanism to control them comparable to that which could be wielded with respect to sons (landed inheritance); the death sentence pronounced by Judah could hardly suffice as a normal remedy for daughterly misbehavior—indeed, even he did not implement it. In an unpublished essay, "In Praise of the Vertuous Wife," Filmer stated that daughters had to be "broke of the[ir] will when they are younge" if they were to grow up properly, but he offered no ideas about how to achieve that goal.[10]

The theorists' writings, then, pointed to two possible areas of conflict between fathers and their children. The first, involving sons, they confronted directly. As a child, a son was clearly subject to his father and even his mother. As he grew older, the potential for conflict with his parents, especially his father, increased considerably. Sir Robert Filmer and John Locke discussed both the desire of fathers to control their adult sons and the means that could be adopted to achieve that end. In spite of Locke's reassuring comments about the need for sons to become more independent as they grew older, his emphasis on the use of inheritance as a weapon suggests that he shared Filmer's more overt interest in the potential problems posed to fathers by disobedient male offspring.

The two men clearly were speaking to a major concern current in their society. Yet disputes between fathers and sons rarely turned up in colonial courts; few sons dared to risk their claim on a share of the family's real estate by publicly challenging their fathers. Such quarrels tended to be resolved within the family in favor of the father. In short, inheritance proved to be an exceptionally powerful weapon in the struggle for paternal control of male children, just as Filmer and Locke recognized. Evidence of father-son conflicts comes from sources other than lawsuits; most intrafamilial suits involved siblings or in-laws rather than fathers and sons.[11]

The other possibly contentious parent/child relationship received little attention from either the seventeenth-century authors or subsequent historians. Daughters have been the forgotten children, especially when considered relative to their fathers or to their families as a whole, rather than in conjunction with their mothers.[12] The theoretical neglect of daughters paradoxically implies that a father's relationship to a daughter was even more problematic than his relationship to a son. Since no one seems to have thought systematically about daughters, they had the potential to be enormously disruptive of family life—just as they were in Locke's and Filmer's narratives.

A third area of conflict involved households' fictive children, the servants. Not considered by political theorists and seldom treated at any length by the writers of prescriptive familial tracts, servants—other people's children—were potentially the most troublesome participants in colonial families. Although they were expected to behave like the children born into the household, they often failed to do so, for a variety of reasons ranging from discontent with their lot to social backgrounds that differed significantly from that of their employers. Their status was further complicated by the fact that, in New England though not in the Chesapeake, their own birth families frequently lived nearby, thus providing them, in effect, with two sets of parents. The presence of their mothers and fathers offered some young servants a means to challenge the authority of the fictive parents with whom they lived, an opportunity denied to children who remained in their families of birth.

Like the theory of husbandly power, then, the theory of paternal authority, though superficially complete, offered colonists few specific solutions to the sorts of everyday challenges that confronted their families in New England and the Chesapeake. Inheritance could perhaps control sons, but it was not immediately clear what would serve the same purpose for daughters and servants. Through statutes adopted by their legislatures and enforced in their courts, men tried to ensure the paternal dominance in the family that theorists regarded as appropriate. But theory and reality did not always coincide.

PATERNAL AUTHORITY AND THE LAW

Colonial law required heads of households to fulfill certain duties to their dependents. In early 1632, for example, the Virginia House of Burgesses ordered all masters either to teach their children and servants the catechism or to send them to church on Sundays to be instructed by a clergyman. Massachusetts Bay, in a 1648 statute subsequently imitated by New Haven (1656) and Plymouth (1671), went further, requiring "masters of families" not only to catechize their offspring and apprentices but also to ensure that they gained "so much learning as may inable them perfectly to read the english tongue, & knowledge of the Capital Lawes." The act further warned "parents and masters" to "bring up their children & apprentices in some honest lawfull calling, labour or employment." In all three colonies' versions of the statute, masters who persisted in their dereliction—thus producing children who were "rude, stubborn, & unruly"—could lose custody to another man who would "force them to submit unto government." In 1660, New Haven added a proviso that, subject to the same penalty, "the sonnes of all the inhabitants . . . [shall] be learned to write a ledgible hand, so soone as they are capable of it."[13]

A key component of a household head's responsibility to his subordinates (and to the community at large) was making certain that they learned to behave properly, both inside and outside the familial context. In Rhode Island, a master who permitted his "sonnes or servants" to engage in "licentious courses at unseasonable times or places" was to be fined £5; in New Haven, "family governors" who did not "observe & give information" to the authorities about disorderly servants or children in their households were "to be accounted accessary to the offences of such as are under their power, & to be dealt withall accordingly." And the Massachusetts Bay General Court ordered in 1653 that all "parents and governors" of children between the ages of seven and fourteen were to be liable for admonitions and fines if the youngsters misbehaved on the sabbath.[14]

Colonial legal codes were largely silent on the question of just how the paterfamilias was to keep his subordinates in line. Rhode Island's definition of "Batteries, Assaults, and Threats" in 1647 was one of the few laws that made even a passing reference to the assumption that lay behind the statutory emphasis on the importance of family governance as the colonies' first line of defense against social chaos. After describing the offenses to be punished under the rubric of assault and battery, the assembly added that "this is intended in respect of such to whom there is not allowed a naturall or civill powre over others; for a Father, Master, Schoolmaster, Keeper, may, with moderation correct those that are under them." Likewise, a Virginia act of 1668 specifically noted that "moderate corporall punishment inflicted by master or magistrate" on a runaway servant did not free the servant from the additional term of service imposed on such miscreants, thereby acknowledging masters' right to coerce their subordinates physically.[15]

In addition, laws alluding to excessive abuse of children or servants by a superior implied that "moderate correction" should be anticipated by anyone in subjection. New Haven ordered that a master maintain or compensate a servant injured through his "cruelty, or miscarriage," and Massachusetts Bay freed any servant who had been "mayme[d] or much disfigure[d]" by a master, "unlesse it be by meere casualtie [accident]." In its statute applying the death penalty to a son or daughter over sixteen who cursed or hit a parent, the Bay Colony permitted as a defense the claim of provocation "by extream, and cruel correction; that they have been forced therunto to preserve themselves from death or maiming." Virginia made the assumption explicit in 1662. The burgesses ordered masters to provide servants with "competent dyett, clothing and lodging," declaring that a master "shall not exceed the bounds of moderation in correcting them beyond the meritt of their offences."[16] Yet the laws offered no guidelines for determining what was the appropriate amount of correction for a master to give a servant or child, and the state and community alike had considerable difficulty distinguishing acceptable from unacceptable force.

The questions were even more complicated when the treatment of enslaved people was at issue. Although slaves too were subordinates seen as part of the household, in the 1640s and 1650s (prior to the adoption of formal slave codes) Virginia and Maryland first passed laws distinguishing among indentured English servants and enslaved Africans and

Indians.[17] Eventually, a wide range of statutes made such distinctions, culminating in a series of Virginia laws that subjected slaves to a variety of regulations not imposed on servants, authorized the killing of runaway slaves, and, strikingly, declared that "if any slave resist his master . . . and by the extremity of the correction should chance to die, . . . his death shall not be accompted ffelony." The legislators explained their reasoning thus: "it cannot be presumed that prepensed malice (which alone makes murther ffelony) should induce any man to destroy his owne estate." No comparable statement was ever made about English servants.[18]

Slaves had little protection, then, from a master's excessive cruelty. By contrast, along with attempting to limit the coercion of free children and indentured servants to "moderate correction," colonial legislators adopted policies designed to prevent heads of households from defrauding or cheating them. The Chesapeake colonies, afflicted with high mortality rates and thus with large numbers of wholly or partially orphaned children, enacted elaborate rules intended to forestall the embezzlement of orphans' estates by their guardians, who were often their stepfathers.[19] Colonies required that all contracts with servants be properly recorded; developed rules setting forth appropriate terms of service for those who arrived without indentures; and forbade the apprenticing of orphans without court approval. New Haven proscribed the sale of servants outside the New England region, and Virginia in 1662 provided that masters who impregnated their maidservants could not gain the benefit of an earlier law requiring a woman who bore a bastard to serve her master for two additional years.[20]

In spite of such statutes, which offered some protection to household subordinates, most legislation was aimed at enforcing inferiors' subjection to family governors. Virginia lawmakers declared that servants who resisted their masters with "audacious unruliness" would have a year added to their terms; Massachusetts Bay, that "unfaithfull, negligent, or unprofitable" servants would not be freed until they had "made satisfaction according to the Judgement of Authoritie." Maryland and Virginia both mandated harsh penalties for runaway servants and those who harbored them. Although in its 1647 code Rhode Island set out mutual obligations for masters and servants, the colony also insisted that "no inferiour shall rise up or rebell against his superiour, especially such to whom he more directlie owes faith, dutie, and ready obedience; it being altogether unsuitable to civill order." Accordingly, the law prescribed severe penalties for servants or children who threatened or assaulted their masters or parents, since, its preamble noted, crimes against "Fathers and

Mothers"—fictive as well as real—were "the highest and most unnatural" of all.[21]

The most important such statutes were the provisions in the Bay
Colony's Laws and Liberties of 1648 (later copied by New Haven in
1656 and Plymouth in 1671) inflicting the death penalty on rebellious
children—sons and daughters over sixteen who cursed or struck either
of their parents, or a son of the same age who would not "obey the
voice of his Father, or the voice of his Mother," who was "stubborn &
rebellious" and "live[d] in sundry notorious crimes." Both laws provided
that the parents in question had to be "natural" (that is, not stepparents),
a distinction rarely made in the seventeenth century and one implying
that legislators and courts would be more tolerant of a child's misbehavior if it were directed at an affinal parent. Besides the possible defense
of parental cruelty already noted, the first law also exempted from its
coverage parents who had been "very unchristianly negligent in the
education of such children," and the second explicitly required that the
mother and father themselves bring the rebellious son to court.[22]

Few northern sons and daughters were ever prosecuted under these
laws, but in conjunction with the statutes requiring parental consent to
marriages they underscore the significance for New England's legislators
of children's subjection to parents in general and fathers in particular. In
Of Plymouth Plantation, William Bradford explained that one of the primary reasons why the Pilgrims decided to leave Leiden to migrate to
North America was the fear that "many of their children . . . were
[being] drawn away by evil examples into extravagant courses, getting
the reins off their necks and departing from their parents."[23] Once settled
in the colonies, the Pilgrims and their fellow New Englanders were no
less determined to avoid that fate than they had been before emigrating.
Like the subordination of wife to husband, the dependence of children
on their parents was emblematic of a harmonious society, one in which
proper order was being maintained.

The statutes outlining the powers of the paterfamilias, along with his
obligations to the community and to his subordinates, represented the
colonial ideal rather than the reality. Not every child in Massachusetts
Bay and New Haven was taught a useful trade and how to read, nor
was each child or indentured servant in Virginia properly catechized
every week, whether by parent, master, or cleric. Indeed, the Massachusetts General Court complained in 1668 that town selectmen were
not enforcing the law as they should, which had proved "a great dis-
couragement to those family governors who conscientiously endeavour
to bring up their youth in all Christian nurture."[24] Certainly in many

households the master did not easily enforce his authority, through whatever means he selected. And New Haven, which sought most insistently to maintain proper family governance, had as much trouble with disorderly young people as did the other colonies.

Even so, colonial legal codes, like theoretical works on the family, do more than simply expose an unattainable ideal. They reveal the mechanisms through with the colonists hoped to turn their ideas into practice, thus highlighting their most basic beliefs about the operations of the household and the actions (both proper and improper) of its head. The property of orphans should be preserved, rather than purloined by guardians; "moderate correction" of inferiors was acceptable, but fathers and masters could not go too far in trying to subdue their subordinates, with the exception of slaves; children and servants should be properly educated; parents and masters were to be held legally responsible for many of the actions of their subordinates. Most important of all, heads of households were the key members of the community—the persons upon whom all else depended. The laws were thus designed to bolster their authority and to ensure their primacy in the family. The details of the laws varied (southerners were more concerned about unruly servants and slaves, northerners about disobedient children) but the vision of household order embodied in the two regions' statutes was more similar than not. Where New England and the Chesapeake differed was not in the content of their laws but rather in the enforcement of them.

PATERNAL POWER IN THE HOUSEHOLD

Viewed from the perspective of the diary kept for six decades by its head, the family of the Reverend Increase Mather mirrored both Thomas Hobbes's "little monarchy" and John Locke's male-dominated household. In a Hobbesian mode, Mather largely omitted his wife (the mother of all his children) from his diary's description of the daily life of the household, and in true Lockean style he ignored his six daughters except when they disrupted his life. Increase's diary entries mentioned his wife and daughters when they fell ill (thereby interrupting his sleep or his daily routine), but the only family members he referred to regularly were his sons, Cotton and Samuel. At intervals throughout the year, Mather observed private days of thanksgiving or humiliation, times at which he listed the blessings or current trials of his life. Those entries commonly thanked God profusely for his "dearest" children, Cotton and Samuel, both of whom followed him into the ministry. His daughters, by contrast, more often appeared among the listed "grounds for humiliation," especially when he began to worry obsessively about "disposing of" them properly in marriage. Of all his children, the most troublesome was Hannah, who resisted conversion, "occasioned a Scandalous Name to her selfe" by "being in vain Company," and married a man of whom Increase did not wholly approve. With the exception of Hannah, though, Increase Mather was the family governor of what, from his standpoint at least, appears to have been a model, male-dominated seventeenth-century household.[25]

The Reverend Mather was not the only successful domestic governor in early New England. The correspondence of John and Margaret Winthrop with their adult children shows a family in which parental (and especially paternal) superiority was for the most part unquestioned. John Jr., as his father repeatedly stated, was the quintessential "dutyfull well deservinge childe," who treated his father with a "Filial Respect" that—John Sr. proudly remarked in 1643—"was not forced from you by a Father's Power, but freely resigned by your self." The Winthrop daughters too learned their lessons well; for example, in June 1636 Mary Winthrop Dudley closed a letter to her stepmother, Margaret, by pledging "that duty and respect I owe you whenever occasion shall be offered," signing herself, "Your dutyfull daughter till death." The only one of John Winthrop's many children who showed any signs of rebellion was his second son, Henry, who married without his parents' consent, lost his inheritance in the West Indies, and died shortly after arriving in New England in 1630.[26]

Fathers like John Winthrop believed, as he once wrote, that "he is worse then an Infidell whoe throughe his own Sloathe and voluptuousnes shall neglect to provide for his family." Concomitantly, though, Winthrop would also have agreed with (and perhaps even applied to his son Henry) an aphorism a Bay Colony resident copied into his notebook: "Disobedience to Parents is against the Lawes of Nature and Nations . . . And the Vengeance of Heaven sooner or later followes it." The obligation, as Winthrop and others throughout the northern and southern colonies understood it, was mutual: fathers protected and cared for their children and servants; in return, such subordinates owed their fathers respect and obedience. Because of the widespread insistence on the need for filial acquiescence in elders' desires, Winthrop was probably not surprised by a letter he received in 1640, asking him to "admonish . . . unto submision" a recent migrant. The young man was violating his English father's wishes by moving to a different settlement from the one in which his distant parent wanted him to live and by planning to marry "a stranger," when "his father alreddy hath made a worthy choyse for him heare in Ingland." The expectation that the "obeadience unto his father which God commandeth" could be enforced even from across the Atlantic Ocean speaks volumes about fathers' perspectives on their offspring's proper behavior.[27]

As has been pointed out, colonial law held household heads responsible for misbehavior not only by their wives but also by other dependents. Husbands always had to pay any fines levied on their spouses; sometimes they were assessed financial penalties for crimes committed by their children or servants as well. Parents had to post bond for children's court appearances, which they forfeited if the children failed to show up for trial. Like one Maine man, the parents of delinquents also risked being admonished for "overmuch Indulgence & unfatherly neglect" of a daughter or, like a New Haven resident, being told "that he had not furthered his sonnes conviction [for drunkenness] as he should."[28]

Yet such assignments of penalties to family governors were not as uncontroversial as the insistence on husbands' liability for wives. For example, after the Essex County court in 1667 convicted five young men for vandalism, ordering them fined and sent to jail, a bystander named Thomas Bishop contested the choice of penalties. "To punish with fineing & prisoning was to punish there parents & not them," he asserted to his seat mates in church one Sunday, observing that the young men's fines and detention both imposed a financial burden on their parents and deprived them of essential labor. Instead, Bishop declared, the court "were better to have given them a like [lick] of the whipp." The judges did not appreciate the criticism: at the next session they fined Bishop for "speaking reproachfully and defaming the court."[29]

Still, a father's obligation to protect his offspring was so compelling that when one prominent Bay Colony settler failed to fulfill that responsibility, he was widely criticized, both at the time and subsequently.[30] In John Winthrop's opinion, Mr. John Humfrey, a magistrate who was among the founders of Massachusetts, "much neglected his children, leaving them among a company of rude servants." Lacking adequate supervision, two of his young daughters, Dorcas and Sarah, frequented the home of a married neighbor, Daniel Fairfield, who sexually abused them. When Mr. Humfrey, dissatisfied with life in the Bay Colony, returned to England with his wife, he left Dorcas and Sarah, both of whom were still under ten, in the care of a former servant, who also sexually abused Dorcas, as did yet another servant. The story eventually came out after Dorcas told an older female relative about the repeated incidents of abuse.

In June 1642, when the three men were tried by the General Court, they—in John Winthrop's words—"confessed all but entrance of her [Dorcas's] body." Although at the time the colony had no statute governing the sexual abuse of children (the law was immediately rewritten), Fairfield's penalty was severe: a combination of whipping, facial mutilation (both his nostrils were slit open), and symbolic hanging—he was ordered to wear a noose around his neck in perpetuity. He was also confined to the Boston town limits. The other two men received lesser penalties, and Dorcas, whose complicity was suspected (as was frequently the case when abuse went unreported for lengthy periods and who, Winthrop noted, admitted that she "took pleasure" in the sexual activity), was ordered "privately severely corrected by this Cort." Yet contemporaries reserved their greatest opprobrium for Mr. Humfrey, who had left "without taking due care for [his daughters'] governing and education." The Reverend William Hubbard, one of New England's first historians, regarded the abuse of Dorcas and Sarah as God's judgment on their father, who had mistakenly abandoned the colony "against the advice of his best friends."[31]

Beyond protecting their young dependents' well-being, parents were expected to prepare them for life as adults. That responsibility had several facets: seeing they learned necessary skills of farming, artisanry, or housewifery; teaching them to read and perhaps to write and do basic arithmetic; overseeing their choice of spouses, as the law required; and supplying them with an appropriate share of the family resources, especially through gifts at the time of their marriages or through inheritance. Fathers attempted to fulfill such obligations in a variety of ways. Some hired tutors or sent their offspring to a nearby school, while others chose instead to apprentice them to acquaintances who had desirable skills.[32] In addition, fathers, particularly those in the Chesapeake, gave even very young children livestock and their increase, thus supplying sons and daughters (if all went well) with substantial herds of cattle by the time they married. As John Winthrop wrote in 1629 before emigrating to New England, the colonists believed that a proper "father of a family will not send forth a Childe without a blessing and portion."[33]

The duty to oversee a child's choice of a spouse was among the most important of a father's responsibilities. Accounts of marriage negotiations reveal that the father of the young man would take the first step in a proper courtship, approaching the father of the young woman "to make a motion of marriage." Older men or orphans might act for themselves, but also first spoke to the woman's father (or mother if he was absent). Thus when the orphaned Mr. John Cogswell of Salem wanted to court Mistress Margaret Gifford in early 1673, the young woman told him politely that "she could not [receive him] except it was her mother's mind or will," her father being in England. Margaret's mother agreed that John could court her daughter; some months later, the two became engaged, but delayed the wedding until after her father's return from England to ensure his concurrence in the match.[34]

Letters written by Lucy and Emmanuel Downing about marriages proposed for their children illustrate the variety of concerns that fathers had to consider when negotiating matches.[35] In August 1639, Mr. William Pester's courtship of one of Emmanuel's daughters from his first marriage aroused criticism from church elders, who informed Emmanuel that "yt wilbe a scandall to marry my daughter to such a man that hath noe religion." Although Emmanuel was warned that a marriage to a wealthy but impious man would confirm people's opinions that he "preferr[ed] the world above all," he worried about the fact that his daughter had already "lost fayre opportunityes" and noted that she "feares that if shee should refuse mr. Pester, shee may stay long ere shee meet with a better, unles I had more monie for hir then now I can spare." The match, however, did not take place, and Emmanuel's daughter married another man several years later, after her father had been "blame[d]" by others for the delay.

When Emmanuel's son James decided he wanted to wed Rebecca Cooper, a ward of Mr. John Endicott, in early 1641, still other questions arose. "The dispotition of the mayde and her education with Mrs. Endicot are hopefull, her person tollerable, and the estate very convenient," reported Lucy to her brother John Winthrop. But there were questions about who had the "disposing of" Rebecca. The trustees of her father's estate favored James's suit and said she was old enough at seventeen to decide for herself, but Mr. Endicott declared that "he had the wholl dispose of the maid and would provide a better match for hir." Emmanuel asked John Winthrop to intercede on James's behalf; after first resisting Winthrop's intervention, Endicott acquiesced in the match, declaring, "the Lord knowes I have alwaies resolved (and so hath my wiefe ever since the girle came to us) to yelde her up to be disposed by yourselfe to any of yours."

Seven years later the Downings' daughter Lucy was the central figure, and for the first time in the correspondence the young person's desires played a major role in the discussions. Her first suitor, Thomas

Eyers, "had not yet art enoughe to carye his ship," in the opinion of the elder Lucy. Next on the scene was Mr. William Norton, to whom Lucy junior had "some objections," but Emmanuel proceeded to negotiate with William's brother John nonetheless. They reached agreement on an acceptable dowry, Emmanuel being assured that the young man had "great expectation from help of freinds having 3 unkles in London Childles." William then won Lucy's "free and cheerfull" agreement to the match. Yet the matter was not settled, for another suitor entered the picture—John Harwood, who "unseasonably" and "sinfully" began to woo Lucy. Lucy further complicated the situation by speaking "unwisely," declared her mother:

> her indiscreet words both hear and theer, havinge bin spoken to people noe wiser then her selfe have given much ocasion of offence, and unjust suspisions of our inforcement of her to mr. norton, and her seemeinge love to mr. eyers and yet as they nowe suspect, by her owne late words, her affections to be most inclininge at least to Jhon harwood.

Lucy senior's opinion of her daughter's waffling was characteristically blunt: "I wishe luce maye rather looke into her selfe, then over curiouslye apon others, and then it maye be more for her good." What led to Lucy's decision is unknown, but she did marry William Norton, the man her parents favored.

The courtships of the Downing children thus involved—in unequal mixes and to varying degrees—financial considerations, religious concerns, personal preferences, issues of timing (was Rebecca Cooper old enough to pick her own spouse? was a Downing daughter so old that a marriage to a less than ideal husband might be her last chance for a good match?), and interventions by a wide variety of individuals in addition to parents—uncles, brothers, guardians, trustees, church elders all had their say. The wishes of the courting couples appeared insignificant by comparison. In particular, John Endicott's statements about Rebecca Cooper implied that children were parental property to be "disposed of" wholly as their elders pleased. No wonder, then, that throughout the process the community held the senior Downings, especially Emmanuel, responsible for what happened to the children. If Emmanuel's daughter married a well-off but irreligious man, the "scandall" would reflect on him; if his children had not married by the times the community thought appropriate, it was his fault; if he and his wife forced his daughter into marriage with one man when she favored another, that too was unacceptable. Many fathers similarly arranging their offspring's marital unions must have felt themselves trapped in a situation from which it was impossible to emerge with their reputations intact. Still, they could not escape the responsibility, for marriages without paternal consent led to family ruin and legal chaos.[36]

Fathers not only had to find suitable partners for their children, they also had to give the young couples a proper start in married life. Two conversations about wedding gifts, one in the Chesapeake and one in New England, reveal the community's expectations about such presents. In 1657, neighbors in Kent County, Maryland, gathered to celebrate the marriage of Thomas Hill, Jr. Mr. Joseph Wickes, an attendee, "perswaded The said Mr Hill to give his sunn som Thing being now new begeners." Wickes first suggested a plantation, an idea Mr. Hill rejected. Then Wickes proposed a heifer. After Mr. Hill responded that he had none, Mr. Wickes reminded him that he himself owed Hill a heifer. "Give him That," Joseph urged, and Thomas Sr. "amediatly" acquiesced, writing out a deed of gift for the animal, which was still in Mr. Wickes's hands. The other celebrants then gave the newlyweds "several somes of Tobacco as every one was willing under There hands in A paper." Thus neighbors not only convinced a father to make an unanticipated wedding gift, they also augmented that present with offerings of their own.[37]

The other conversation demonstrated that, in addition to aiding "new begeners," the community thought that parents should provide adequately for all their children. That was what Thomas Spencer of Maine learned when he told a couple that he had given as a dowry "the on[e] half of his half part of the mill & Timber thereunto belonging" to his daughter's new husband. The couple responded, as they later deposed when a question arose about the gift: "neyhbouer Spenser I wish you well to Consedar what you doe for you had many Children & every on[e] would have a lettell & you cannot give every one such A Portion & he answered & said that shee wase the Eldest dafter & hee had don yt."[38] Thus the size (as well as the fact) of a wedding gift was seen as the proper subject of community comment.

A father's final duty to his children and his widow was the drafting of a will that would distribute his property appropriately among his heirs. Even this last act of a man's legal existence did not take place in isolation; it too was subject to supervision by statutes, the courts, and his peers. If a man wrote a will, he could disinherit his children but not his wife, to whom he was legally required to leave approximately one third of his real and personal estate. Intestacy law, on the other hand, protected both widows and children, particularly eldest sons. If a man died intestate, New England statutes gave his eldest son a double share of the paternal estate, and Maryland provided that all the father's real property would descend intact to the eldest son, with the rest of his property being divided among his widow and children. The intestacy laws favoring the oldest son conformed to a Filmerian emphasis on maintaining male prerogatives and an orderly familial hierarchy.[39]

Some men wrote detailed wills that attempted to account for all possible contingencies. The best known and most elaborate such testament was the one drafted by the Boston merchant Robert Keayne in 1653, but other men also tried to govern their families long after their own deaths, by specifying legacies to possible posthumous offspring or by directing that daughters would receive their inheritance only if they married men approved by their mothers or by overseers of the estate.[40] In the Chesapeake, where high mortality rates and the shortage of women made it likely that widows would remarry within a year (or even a few months) of a husband's death, dying men tried to make certain that their children's inheritance would not be lost to a greedy stepfather. One asked that "the said Man" post bond to manage the children's property, providing that his plantation should be leased for the children's benefit if "my wife doth leave the plantation before the Chilldren be of age." Another directed that if "the head whom [my wife] shall marry doth not doe the parte of an honnest man, and loving father in lawe towarde my deare Children," then his overseers could remove his children from the home and place them elsewhere.[41]

But even carefully drafted wills could not prevent all arguments among heirs. Such disputes often involved the competing claims of different generations, especially when remarriages had complicated the picture, but they could also arise among siblings.[42] Most lawsuits in which widows participated in some capacity will be considered in detail in the next chapter. Here the focus is on a prolonged inheritance dispute that developed primarily because a prominent man failed to favor his eldest surviving son in his will.

The December 1672 death of Massachusetts Bay's Governor Richard Bellingham sparked a complex series of lawsuits.[43] Mr. Bellingham's will had two shortcomings: first, the legacies to his widow, Penelope (the woman whose marriage to Bellingham had troubled John Winthrop in 1641), did not comprise one third of the estate; and second, the former governor left his only surviving son, Samuel, and Samuel's daughter, both of whom lived in England, nothing but a life interest in his real property. After their deaths, control of his substantial real estate holdings (essentially, the entire modern city of Chelsea) was to revert to "som godly ministers and preachers," who were to use the proceeds for religious purposes. The trustees named in the will quickly negotiated a settlement with one of Penelope's male relatives, redefining her thirds in a satisfactory manner, but the provisions that in the long run disinherited Samuel's descendants aroused great controversy.

One trustee deposed that a key factor in Mr. Richard Bellingham's thinking had been the death of his and Penelope's son, John, whom he had intended to make his primary heir. The elder Bellingham had explained to the trustee that Samuel was well provided for financially by inheritance from the family of his mother, Bellingham's first wife, Elizabeth. Moreover, Richard Bellingham believed that Samuel would probably not come to New England to take over the estate and would instead "give it away for a Song." He predicted that Samuel's daughter would never marry and thus that she would have no children to inherit the property. Accordingly, Bellingham declared, "I will dedicate it to God; and benefitt of this Contry."

In spite of the evident logic supporting such statements, rumors soon spread that the testament had been surreptitiously altered by the trustees, that the trustees had cheated the widow, that Bellingham was "Discomposed in his mind" when he wrote his will, and that the governor had "manifested an affectionate & fatherly Kindness" to Samuel while on his deathbed. That these contentions contradicted each other, overdetermining the results, did not matter to Samuel's American attorney, who advanced all of them simultaneously. After four years of legal maneuvering, which eventually included intervention on Samuel Bellingham's behalf by King Charles II himself, the General Court in 1676 nullified the will, thereafter handling the property as though Mr. Richard Bellingham had died intestate.

That did not stop the litigation, which persisted, astonishingly, until 1787. After Mistress Penelope Bellingham died in 1702 and her one-third life interest reverted to the estate, the trustees tried to win reinstatement of the will. In 1709, a group of ministers petitioned the General Court to that end, observing accurately that "the principal Reason, which sway'd those who did so far disannul the Will . . . was their Doubt, that He had not done well in leaving so little of his Estate unto his onely Son." Mr. Richard Bellingham's decision to allot nothing more than a life interest in his real estate to his sole surviving son and his heirs in fact led many contemporaries to conclude that he was "not Compos Mentis when the will was made." Sons (and everyone else) expected sons to inherit land outright from their fathers; a life interest in real property was the prerogative of widows, not of sons or even of daughters. Samuel Bellingham's attorney won his case because Englishmen, Bay Colony judges, and ordinary folk alike believed that only a man "Discomposed in his mind" would decide not to pass his real estate on to a son's heirs.

As scholars have recently pointed out, daughters as well as sons inherited land from their fathers, both through wills and by intestacy distributions.[44] But sons, especially only surviving sons, were not thereby to be disinherited. In the absence of or in addition to sons, land could pass to daughters. Land could also go to collateral heirs of both sexes if the deceased had no direct descendants. But real estate, in the minds of the formal and informal publics alike, was expected to pass first to sons, then to daughters, or in the absence of both, to blood relatives of some description. It was not to go entirely out of the hands of the family, even for pious purposes. By violating those rules, Governor Bellingham unwittingly set into motion well over a century of litigation.

So the governor's last act created chaos in what had probably been a well-ordered family life, despite Elizabeth Bellingham's suspicious association with Mistress Ann Hibbens and his hasty second marriage to a woman already promised to another. Other heads of households experienced disorder much earlier in their lives, as they proved incapable of ruling their families without resorting to the use of excessive force. Not every father benignly supervised his children and servants; not every father actively looked out for his subordinates' well-being. Many family governors exercised their authority with brutality or, at the very least, with a lack of regard for the welfare of their dependents. Such an approach to the maintenance of orderly households was the ultimate expression of gendered power in the family.

PATERNAL POWER IN A PUBLIC CONTEXT

Whereas the community and the state had clear expectations concerning the wielding of paternal power in households under normal circumstances, colonists were much less certain about the proper boundaries to impose on paternal authority when something went wrong. The formal and informal publics found it easy to intervene when fathers committed sins of omission—by not arranging appropriate marriages for their children or by not leaving them sufficient legacies, for example—but they were much more hesitant to intercede when sins of commission were at issue. A number of civil and criminal court cases thus revolved around one central question: what restrictions should be placed on family governors' ability to punish their subordinates? Since a father's role in the Filmerian system was crucial to the maintenance of social order in general, and since fathers served as putative justices of the peace for their households, were there any limits to their authority? When, if ever, should neighbors or judges step in to protect a man's dependents from punishment? At what point did legitimate correction become mistreatment? In the seventeenth-century colonies, no consistent answers to such inquiries emerged. Moreover, as might be anticipated in light of their other differences, New Englanders and Chesapeake residents responded to the questions in divergent ways, leading to contrasting patterns of litigation and prosecution.

Prosecutions for servant or child abuse were rare in all the colonies, representing less than 1 percent of the charges brought against either sex in the north, and about 5 percent of charges against either in the south. A large majority of the defendants were men, and, with the exception of one widow, the accused women were all married at the time of the incidents. As a result, the female offenders' husbands were legally responsible for their conduct, and, indeed, half the accused women were formally charged in conjunction with their spouses. In other words, in both New England and the Chesapeake such prosecutions explicitly posed questions about the extent of a man's power over his children and fictive children, even when the nominal defendant was the man's wife rather than himself.[45]

Yet behind this broadly comparable picture lay three striking variations that reflected the differences between the two regions. First, although in both regions the most commonly prosecuted crime of this sort was mistreating servants, in the Chesapeake two thirds of those cases began as complaints filed by the servants themselves. In New England, by contrast, only a handful of servant-abuse accusations were brought by the victims. The others resulted from interventions by neighbors, the authorities, or the servant's own family. Second, accusations of servant murder made up a significantly higher proportion of abuse cases in the Chesapeake than in New England. Third, northern defendants were more likely to be convicted than were southerners. More than four fifths of the New Englanders accused of these offenses were found guilty, whereas fewer than three fifths of Marylanders and Virginians met a comparable fate.[46]

Taken together, the figures confirm that the formal and informal publics in the north supervised the internal dynamics of family life more closely than did their counterparts in the south. One major consequence of intercessions by people from outside the household was fewer murders of servants, because abuse was thereby halted before it reached that final extreme. Accordingly, it is particularly telling that although fully 40 percent of those prosecuted for servant abuse in the Chesapeake were charged with murder, only 10 percent of New England servant-abuse cases fell into that category. New Englanders were probably not, as a group, kinder to their servants than were Chesapeake masters and mistresses; but neighbors, constables, and others in the north were more willing to step in to prevent the worst excesses. When offenders were brought to court, northern courts then proved more likely to convict abusers than were judges and juries in the Chesapeake. As in cases of spouse abuse, which were much more likely to be prosecuted in New England than in the Chesapeake, a Filmerian emphasis on the maintenance of orderly households therefore afforded some measure of protection to dependents. Because a family governor's restraint in exercising his authority was a crucial indicator of a properly functioning domestic unit, the lack of such restraint was concomitantly seen as a fault that should be corrected by civil authorities.

It is nevertheless essential to emphasize that the right to strike subordinates defined the position of family governor. The 1647 Rhode Island law that exempted fathers and masters from prosecution for assault and battery on their dependents codified a widely held assumption. Fathers, mothers, masters, and mistresses could legitimately correct their children and servants; other persons could not. Thus, in effect, one's ability to strike a person determined one's standing as that individual's proper superior. So, when Samuel Marsh of New Haven hit a boy with whom he had argued at a mill, he admitted—when sued by the boy's father—that "he did not well to strike the boy (though he deserved it,) which belonged to his parents or Governors to doe, when they doe that which is evill." So, too, when neighbors complained that Elizabeth Woodbury of Salem had wrongly struck a maidservant of Mr. Jeremiah Hubbard's, the Hubbards wrote a letter to the Essex County justices explaining that they had left their cousin Elizabeth in charge of their household while they were absent. "If we had power to discipline such an unruly servant, so had shee from us," they told the court. The maidservant was notoriously "unfaithfull"; Elizabeth Woodbury "did noe more then she had o[u]r authority for, & . . . [Mistress Hubbard] if present would have done the same."[47]

Given the legitimacy of wielding paternal power, whether directly or as a designated proxy, it was often difficult for outside observers to identify the line between acceptable and unacceptable coercion of subordinates. That was true even in New England, where outside intervention in the family was more common than in the Chesapeake. A dramatic incident in the Bay Colony in the late summer of 1639 provides an excellent illustration of the colonists' reactions when they witnessed an altercation between a superior and someone rightfully subject to him.

After a minor disagreement one evening, Mr. Nathaniel Eaton, the head of the new college in Cambridge, ordered his live-in assistant Nathaniel Briscoe to leave the house immediately.[48] Briscoe replied that he would depart in the morning, but that was not soon enough for Mr. Eaton. He took what John Winthrop later described as a "cudgel . . . big enough to have killed a horse," told two of his servants to hold Briscoe, and then hit him approximately two hundred times, a task which occupied nearly two hours. At one point Briscoe drew a knife, at another he began to pray, which, according to Winthrop, only caused Eaton to beat him harder "for taking the name of God in vain." Briscoe's cries of pain eventually attracted attention from passersby, including the Reverend Thomas Shepard, pastor of the Cambridge church. Mr. Shepard and the other witnesses did not come to the young man's aid, though the arrival of outsiders did cause Eaton to stop the beating. Instead, Shepard accompanied Mr. Eaton as he went to see Governor Winthrop, "complaining of Briscoe for his insolent speeches, and for crying out murder and drawing his knife." The two men asked that Briscoe be brought before the Court of Assistants to acknowledge his fault publicly.

When the magistrates inquired into the circumstances that had led to the beating, they discovered not only that Nathaniel Eaton had overreacted on this occasion but also that he had mistreated his pupils. The students boarding in the house testified that they had been fed an "ill and scant diet" consisting primarily of "porridge and pudding" and that they had been beaten repeatedly for minor failings. Mr. Eaton, they declared, would not stop striking them "till they had confessed what he required." Asked for his response to these charges, Eaton blamed his wife for any problems with the students' food and said that "he had this rule, that he would not give over correcting till he had subdued the party to his will." A group of church elders spent hours trying to convince Mr. Eaton that his brutality was inappropriate; finally, they thought they had succeeded, and Eaton made what Winthrop termed "a very solid, wise, eloquent, and serious (seeming) confession" of error during a public court session. But when the Assistants nevertheless fined him and barred him from teaching in Massachusetts Bay, Winthrop recorded,

Eaton "turned away with a discontented look." He soon fled the colony for Virginia, leaving behind his wife and family and a large number of disgruntled creditors.

The significance of this story lies not in Mr. Nathaniel Eaton's severity as the head of an expanded household composed of teachers and students as well as his own wife and children. Rather, it lies in the fact that the Reverend Thomas Shepard, a key witness to the beating of Nathaniel Briscoe, initially allied himself with Eaton rather than with the victim. In retrospect, Mr. Shepard blamed himself for his "want of wisdom & watchfulnes over" Eaton, admitting that "the sin of mr Eaton was at first not so clearly discerned by me."[49] But Shepard was not the only man who made the same choice. Winthrop noted in his journal that after Eaton was called into court, but before the full story became widely known, a church elder came to him in private "and showed himself much grieved, that he [Eaton] should be publicly produced, alleging, that it would derogate from his authority and reverence among his scholars."

At least two prominent men, therefore, instinctively sided at first with another prominent man whom they knew had cruelly beaten a subordinate. Only when Shepard learned that Eaton's justification for his action was inadequate did he "discern" Eaton's sin. The vicious assault by itself did not prove Eaton to be an improper family governor. What instead caused Mr. Nathaniel Eaton's disgrace was that the state and the community both judged his treatment of Nathaniel Briscoe to be an excessive response to a minor slight. Had Briscoe's offense been more serious, or had Eaton not exhibited similarly cruel tendencies in his treatment of his students—at least one of whom was the son of a magistrate—Eaton's authority over Briscoe would undoubtedly have been upheld.

Although the prosecution of Nathaniel Eaton differed from the trials of other household heads in that the dependents he had mistreated were students and an assistant, in another respect it was typical. The Eaton case, like a majority of such incidents that reached the courts, involved a superior's power over other people's children residing in his household rather than his authority over his own biological descendants. Only in Massachusetts Bay is there much evidence of fathers or mothers being charged with mistreating their own children.[50] The silence of the records on this point raises a difficult question: did parents treat their own children better than they treated other dependents in their households, or was the mistreatment of other children simply more likely to come before the judicial system, because such dependents (servants, orphans, or stepchildren) had more allies outside the confines of the immediate family?

It is impossible to answer that question definitively, yet the latter response appears more likely. In the seventeenth-century colonies beating one's children seems to have been taken for granted. The records of the few prosecutions of parents use such words as "immoderate and cruel" or "crewell, unnaturall, and extreame" to describe their conduct, thus implying that more "natural" or "moderate" correction would not have been censurable. Two spouse-abuse incidents began when mothers attempted to protect children from beatings by their fathers; courts in Salem and New Haven assessed penalties for striking the spouses but not for beating the children. And in 1662 a New Amsterdam woman, questioned about a loud noise in her house one night, matter-of-factly explained that "she beat her children for coming so late home." Although no similar statements survive in the records of the English colonies, an intriguing case in Maryland pitted two children against their own mother, who was said to have beaten a maidservant excessively. The two teenaged boys joined other witnesses in describing their mother's repeated whippings of the maid. Since children rarely appeared in court and even more rarely testified against a parent, it is possible to speculate that the sons were retaliating against a mother who had severely abused them as well.[51]

Unquestionably, having kin or trustees outside one's family of residence helped to protect a child from harm. In both New England and the Chesapeake, trustees appointed in wills occasionally sued a widow's new husband for mistreating children of the earlier marriage, and relatives of young servants, especially parents, tried to rescue them from abusive households. In Plymouth in 1655, for example, a father regained custody of his son after arguing that the boy's master had "unreasonably" hit and kicked him, and a Salem father some years later successfully sued his son's master for not taking proper care of him while he was ill. When Henry and Jane Stacy of Marblehead learned from friends in 1680 that their younger daughter was being mistreated by her master and dame in Newbury, they visited her, learned that the story was true, and asked the Essex County court to intervene. Their neighbor, William Beale, returned to Newbury to gather evidence on their behalf, for they were too poor to take such a step themselves. (Beale thereby repaid the Stacys for the support Jane and her older daughter had given his wife fourteen years earlier in her physical confrontation with three other neighbors.)[52]

Because of the important role relatives could play in protecting subordinates from brutal superiors, children and servants in the Chesapeake were at a distinct disadvantage. The migrant generation, especially the servants, traveled to the region as individuals without their families, and high mortality rates sundered marriages, thus depriving even native-born children of helpful kin. It is therefore understandable that most accusations of mistreatment in the south came from the victims themselves. Unusual indeed were incidents such as that in Virginia in 1632, when a couple "togeather with many other men & women of the neighbours" reported that an orphan had run away from the house in which he was living because he had been "starved and misused" or that in Maryland in 1673, when "some of the Neighbourhood" brought a young girl to court, complaining that her stepfather had "inhumanely beaten and abused" her.[53]

Far more common in the Chesapeake were cases that began when a maidservant described "diverse unjust and rigorous abuses" or a manservant spoke "most Lamentably" of "his hard and Cruell usage from his Master." The complaints, which usually though not always received sympathetic hearings in the courts, included charges of overwork and lack of adequate food and clothing along with "beating and abuseing." Sometimes servants deliberately sought out officials to file charges against their masters. On other occasions they offered the accounts of abuse to judges as their justifications for running away. For example, a man who had taken refuge with the Indians asserted that he and a companion "had rather live with the Pagans than Come home to be Starved for want of food, Cloathing and have their Brains beaten out."[54]

Because of the nature of the offense, one form of mistreatment—the sexual abuse of maidservants by masters and their sons—seems to have been underreported in both regions. Sexual molestation was less often prosecuted than were other sorts of assaults or deprivation of food or clothing, but it is unlikely that the offense was as infrequent as the few criminal cases in this category would suggest. The power imbalance between male superiors and their female subordinates in families was substantial, leading to the inference that many such incidents must never have been reported. Furthermore, two characteristics common to publicized descriptions of sexual misconduct within households imply that such behavior was often kept secret.

First, the records of the criminal cases including such allegations—all of them heard in New England—usually disclose not one but repeated offenses by the men, involving the same or different women. For example, in Essex County, John Jackson's maid Mary Somes attested that Jackson had made sexual advances to her three times before she reported the fourth incident, and Hannah Downing, a servant of the

Leonard family, in 1674 described a long series of sexual and physical abuses by the three Leonard sons. Likewise, Elizabeth Dew, a maidservant of Mr. John Endicott's in Salem who complained to another maid in the house about the "unseemly words and actions" of her master's son Zerobabell, was assured, "I know thy condition, alas, pore wench": the same thing had happened to her confidante previously.[55]

The incidents divulged in court documents, in other words, represented not one but long chains of events, involving both the narrator and other women. Most of those encounters had gone unreported for months, even years, before they finally came to public attention. Such circumstances strongly suggest that many maidservants simply never revealed acts of sexual misconduct by masters or masters' sons. That maids had good reason to fear retaliation or to suspect that their stories would not be believed is demonstrated by what happened to the women in the examples just cited. The Essex justices decided that Elizabeth Dew had lied when she accused the younger Endicott of fathering the child with which she was pregnant; they ordered that she be whipped twenty lashes, directing further that she stand in public wearing a sign that read, "A SLANDERER OF MR. ZEROBABELL ENDICOTT." For her part, Hannah Downing revealed that she was afraid the Leonard boys "would kille mee if the athoriaty dos not take some corse with them." Finally, several of John Jackson's Gloucester neighbors worried about his wife's reactions to Mary Somes's accusation, warning the townsmen that Goody Jackson might kill Somes or injure her seriously. The townsmen thereupon alerted the local constable in hopes of forestalling such violence.[56]

Second, the fortuitous ways in which these descriptions of sexual misconduct came to the attention of the judicial system imply that many other similar incidents probably escaped official notice. Only Hannah Downing submitted a formal complaint to the authorities; Mary Somes does not appear to have approached officials directly. Although the records do not make fully clear the mechanism through which her accusation came to be heard by the court, it appears that Mary's informing her master's daughters and then the neighbors started the rumor that attracted officials' attention. Elizabeth Dew told her story publicly only when asked to identify the man who had impregnated her; neither she, the other maid, nor the neighbors to whom she had previously complained about Zerobabell Endicott had said anything to the authorities before that time. Had she not become pregnant, her tale would never have been revealed.

A like inference may be drawn from a tale disclosed in a Maryland civil suit. In April 1659, Mr. Joseph Wickes successfully sued Richard

Owens for the cost of the servant Anne Gould, whom he had purchased from Owens in February 1655/6. Gould, Wickes declared, was "very much diseased with the Pox, commonly called the ffrench Pox," and lived only about six months after he bought her, even though Owens had promised that she was "sownd and in perfect health" at the time of the sale. Gould fell seriously ill shortly after arriving at Wickes's house, and when questioned about the origins of her illness "allwayes" said that "That Rogue Owens had undone her. And that hee had gyven that disease unto her, after the said wicks had bought her." Gould told at least two women and three men that Owens had raped and infected her. One of the women revealed the maid's story to a magistrate, but he replied dismissively that Owens "did not looke by his Countenance to bee such a man" and failed to take any action on the complaint. Anne Gould's tale of sexual abuse thus became publicly known only because Joseph Wickes decided to seek compensation for her loss nearly three years after her death. Richard Owens was never charged with any crime.[57]

An unnamed female slave's story, told to an English traveler in New England in October 1639, reveals that enslaved African women might have been even more likely to be subjected to sexual abuse than were indentured English women. The woman, who had been "a Queen in her own Countrey" and who sought out the traveler to express her despair, had been raped by a male slave at her master's orders. Her owner, the traveler reported, "was desirous to have a breed of Negroes." Since she would not voluntarily have sex with the man in question, the master ordered him "will'd she nill'd she to go to bed to her." Once the rape was completed, she "kickt him out" of her bed immediately. "This," the traveler recounted, "she took in high disdain beyond her slavery, and this was the cause of her grief." How many other enslaved women endured the same sort of sexual abuse is not known, but the number must have been substantial, given the economic rewards offered to a master by the prospect of "a breed of Negroes."[58]

The community's handling of the incident of sexual abuse involving Anne Gould suggests that in the Chesapeake peers outside the household rarely took steps to end sexual misconduct within it. One of the women who heard Anne Gould's story did try to help, though ineffectually; the other witnesses evidently made no effort to see the rapist punished. The formal public concurred in such inaction: the incident came up in a civil suit, not a criminal prosecution, and a magistrate refused to take any action against the accused man. Thus sexually abused southern maidservants probably had little hope of obtaining any redress for injuries. Anne

Gould did not report that she had been raped until her new owner questioned her about the origins of her venereal disease. Her silence undoubtedly resulted from an accurate assessment of the relative costs and benefits of telling her story publicly.

In New England, maidservants troubled by sexual abuse found themselves in only marginally better circumstances, and the one slave whose narrative has survived located a sympathetic listener who recorded her story in his journal but evidently did nothing to help her. Mary Somes, whose neighbors had sufficient concern for her well-being to seek assistance from local officials, was the sole complainant to receive some aid from the ordinary folk to whom she spoke. New Englanders whose tales more directly reached the ears of the authorities fared somewhat better, for the men they accused of abuse were usually tried for that crime, though they were not always convicted.

In many of the reported instances of mistreatment of all sorts, the victim's action or inaction had a major impact on the result. Servants and children who described what had happened to them—whether they spoke to fellow servants, neighbors, relatives, or court officials—could thereby acquire allies who might assist them in various ways. But such strategies did not always work. Sometimes victims' appeals for help were ignored or not taken seriously until it was too late. Prosecutions of masters and mistresses for killing their servants, particularly in the Chesapeake, demonstrate that even in extreme cases witnesses, juries, and judges were reluctant to blame superiors for the deaths of their subordinates, and that they found it difficult to identify what constituted excessive use of force in a household context. So, even though Virginia and Maryland authorities systematically investigated servants' deaths, in the absence of eyewitness testimony coroner's and grand juries inevitably returned verdicts blaming the servants for their own deaths.[59]

Moreover, witnesses to the fatal abuse of Chesapeake servants, while showing compassion for the sufferings of the victims, rarely intervened to halt the violence. So, for example, when John Bessick saw Pope Alvey viciously beating his servant Alice Sandford in the Maryland woods in February 1663/4, Bessick offered her water and helped to carry her when she could no longer walk, but by his own account did nothing to stop Alvey from mistreating her. (Alvey, Bessick reported, broke three sticks by striking Sandford on her bare back, and when she "to save the blowes of[f] put up her hand," Alvey "sett her hand under his foote & beat her againe.") Likewise, when Edward Fuller of Talbot County twice in the space of three weeks found that Francis Carpenter's servant Samuel Youngman had serious head wounds caused by blows from his master, he cleaned and dressed the injuries but did not tell local authorities about them until after Youngman had died.[60]

One of the most tragic cases involved Elizabeth Abbott, a Virginia maidservant who in 1624 repeatedly but futilely sought help from neighboring planters as she tried to escape a series of beatings with "smale lyne or whip corde," sometimes with fishhooks attached.[61] The beatings were administered by her master and mistress, Mr. John and Mistress Alice Proctor, and by other servants acting at their direction. For example, a sixteen-year-old boy attested that he had whipped her "some six tymes" on his master's orders, "and once he thinketh he gave her about 200 stripes and some tymes less"; on one occasion, Mr. Proctor told him to "fleay her or ells his Mr wold flay him."

One day Abbott sought out Mr. John Burrows, a "gentleman" superior in rank to her own high-status master and potentially a valuable ally. She informed him that "she was so beaten that she could not tell what to doe." Abbott showed Burrows her wounds, which he said were "grevous to behold," but all he did was to inform her fellow servants that her master "were best send for A Surgeon to looke to her otherwyse she must needs perishe." Another day at a well Elizabeth went up to a neighbor, Alice Bennett, telling her "shee was so beaten that she durst not tarry at home." Bennett examined her body and discovered that Abbott was covered with sores "dangerously raunckled and putrified," which Elizabeth said had come from a beating by her mistress. On another occasion Bennett found Abbott hiding near Burrows's plantation, "her body raw and Runinge with sores from her wast upwards." But instead of caring for Abbott or reporting the abuse to local authorities, Alice Bennett and her husband took Elizabeth Abbott home. They "delivered her to her Mr entreatinge him to pardon her for that fault and not to Corect her but he said he would nott pardon her." Testimony from another witness indicated that that was one of the times Proctor ordered Abbott to be whipped.

To modern sensibilities, Abbott appears to have been badly mistreated, but contemporary witnesses did not necessarily concur in that assessment. One man testified that she "hath divers tyme[s] been Corected, but never ymmoderately to his knowlege," and another insisted that "shee was a very lewd wench & such a one as noe good perswations nor moderate corection could reclame her." He and another witness attributed Elizabeth's eventual death not to the beatings she had endured but rather to "her lyinge in the woods some tymes 8 or 10 days together." The authorities seem to have agreed with that conclusion: although fourteen depositions were collected and recorded, there is no evidence that the Proctors were ever formally charged with killing Elizabeth Abbott.

Even in the cases that were brought to trial the testimony is depressingly similar to that describing the maltreatment of Elizabeth Abbott: vicious beatings, often inflicted in front of witnesses who did little or nothing to intercede for the victim; angry superiors who, accusing servants of laziness or malingering, increased the frequency or the brutality of the punishment; confusion about the cause of death, with considerable speculation that it was attributable to disease or some action of the servant's; and, finally, verdicts from grand or petty juries that usually either cleared the accused masters and mistresses or let them escape with fines or other minimal penalties.[62] Only three of the men convicted of killing their servants were hanged—two in Maryland and one in Massachusetts Bay.[63]

Most of the narratives of the deaths of English indentured servants offer little evidence that the doomed servants behaved much differently from other subordinates who were not killed by their superiors. Masters and mistresses often complained that servants in general did not do enough work, worked too slowly, made too many errors, or were generally untrustworthy. Those were precisely the same complaints offered about the vast majority of the subordinates who were fatally beaten or otherwise mistreated by their family governors. But one case stands out from the others for two reasons: first, it involved not a white indentured servant but an African slave; and second, the mistreatment began specifically because of the slave's uncompromising resistance to his master.

In the Maryland Provincial Court in late November 1658, Hannah Littleworth, a former maidservant of Mr. Simon Oversee, swore that twenty-six months earlier she had witnessed the death of Antonio (or Tony), a slave. She accused both Mr. Oversee, an English-born merchant of Dutch descent who had settled in Maryland, and his recently deceased wife, Elizabeth, the daughter of a wealthy, well-connected Virginia family, of complicity in Antonio's death. Probably fearing retaliation from her master, Littleworth had waited until she had completed her term of service before coming forward. Also surely relevant to the timing of her accusation was the fact that the Calvert family had recently regained control of Maryland's government, which had for several years been in the hands of a group of Oversee's friends and relatives.[64]

Littleworth's narrative constitutes one of the earliest depictions of a slave's resistance and death in the mainland Anglo-American colonies. Antonio must have been a recently imported African, because Oversee's brother-in-law Job Chandler described the slave as a "Brute" without "any speech or language" and revealed that they could communicate solely through the use of signs. Antonio, whom Oversee purchased about March 1656, was killed because he refused to work, first at Chandler's plantation and then later at Oversee's house at St. Mary's City. An overseer reported that "hee could not make him doe any thing, noe not soe much as beate his owne Victualls [grind his own corn]." Antonio also ran away frequently, "lurking about the Plantation" and stealing food, then evading capture for weeks.

One day in September 1656, Mistress Oversee ordered him "chayned up for some misdeamenors." After he was freed, Littleworth recounted, Antonio "layd himselfe downe & would not stirre." The African remained prone while his master beat him with "Peare Tree wands." Oversee then ordered Littleworth to melt some lard, which he poured on Antonio's wounds. When William Hewes, a manservant in the house, tried to help Antonio, Oversee "threatned him to runne his knife in him." Oversee next had an Indian slave tie Antonio to a ladder that was leaning against the side of the house. "Still the negro remayned mute or stubborne," Littleworth testified, "& made noe signs of conforming himselfe to his Masters will or command." The Oversees left, and the servants watched Antonio die. Hewes and Littleworth pleaded with the overseer to cut him down and save his life, but the overseer refused, probably fearing the wrath of his master and mistress.

To the Marylanders who considered the witnesses' testimony, the most important question (judges and jury asked it of both Littleworth and Hewes) was whether Antonio had "stood uppon the grownd." The former servants said that he had, and the grand jury that met in early 1659 refused to indict Simon Oversee for causing the death of Antonio. Presumably, the fact that Antonio was not suspended in the air was decisive; it could be seen as demonstrating the absence of malicious intent.

The resoluteness of the enslaved Antonio, who died in agony far from his African homeland, directs attention away from the public context of the household and instead suggests a renewed focus on its inner dynamics. As has been seen in this section, representatives of state and community alike commonly offered support to fathers in their exercise of paternal power over their children and fictive children. Only in the most extreme cases of abuse or when subordinates or their families of origin were especially aggressive in seeking outside assistance—and sometimes not even then—would eyewitnesses, judges, or juries step in to halt the excessive use of force within the household, even in New England. That rendered all contests within the household between superiors and inferiors truly unequal. But contests they were nevertheless, for household subordinates were not without weapons to wield in the struggle with their governors.

RESISTING PATERNAL POWER

In 1666, the former Maryland servant George Alsop painted a benign verbal portrait of the system in which he had been indentured for four years. His pamphlet, *A Character of the Province of Mary-land*, not only described the colony to prospective settlers but also offered a justification for the province's social structure. He explained that subordination was necessary to society, for just as there could be "no King without subjects, nor any Parents without . . . Children," so too "neither can there be any Masters, unless it be by the inferior Servitude of those that dwell under them, by a commanding enjoynment." Indeed, he asserted, "good Servitudes are . . . so requisite, that the best of Kingdoms would be unhing'd from their quiet and well setled Government without it." Accordingly, Alsop declared, "there is no truer Emblem of Confusion either in Monarchy or Domestick Governments, then when either the Subject, or the Servant, strives for the upper hand of his Prince, or Master, and to be equal with him, from whom he receives his present subsistance."[65]

Alsop's account constituted an extended paean to the virtues of temporary dependency in youth as a necessary preparation for adult life. It also unwittingly identified the reason why resistance by a household subordinate could be viewed as (to use the words of a decision rendered by the Massachusetts Bay Court of Assistants) a challenge not merely to a master but also to "the peace, & welfare of this whole Comon welth."[66] Since "good Servitudes" and obedient children were as essential to the maintenance of public order as were hierarchical marriages, in a Filmerian system unruly dependents represented "Emblems of Confusion" with implications far beyond the families in which they resided. Uncontrollable children and servants raised serious questions not only about the functioning of their own families and the authority of their parents and masters but also about the social structure as a whole. Alsop, one of the few Marylanders who wrote in a Filmerian mode, had identified a potent weapon potentially wielded by servants or children. By refusing to acquiesce in the system based on their subordination, they could call into question the legitimacy of authority generally as well as the power of their own immediate superiors.

New Englanders understood the dire implications of children's resistance to parents and stepparents. On the basis of statutes defining such
behavior as a potentially capital crime, the northern colonies punished
both sons and daughters for resisting their elders, though no child was
ever executed for that offense.[67] Most such insubordination was verbal
rather than physical, involving at most the threat of violence. Thus a
young Bostonian was convicted of reviling his "naturall father by Calling
him Liar & Drunckard & holding up your fist against him," a New
Haven girl was found guilty of profanity and "rebellion to her Mother"
for swearing and saying "a pockes of the devill what ayles this madd
woman," and Samuel Ford of the same colony was ordered publicly
whipped for—among other offenses—saying to his mother, "you [and
your friends] get a gossiping together, and when my father and I come
to dinner wee cannot have it." The two New Haven cases involved
insolence and disrespect rather than outright opposition to parental authority, but that mattered little to the province's judges, who saw in
Ford's conduct "a high breach of the 5th Commandement." Even the
most important such prosecution, caused by the "Dolefull falling out"
over inheritance between John Porter, Jr., and his father, John Sr., primarily involved a son's impassioned oral outbursts against his parents
instead of physical confrontations. Significantly, John Jr. avoided execution under the rebellious-child laws only because—in the words of
Bay Colony authorities—his mother, "overmooved by hir tender &
motherly affections," failed to join his father "in complaining & craving
justice," as was required by the statute before the death penalty could
be imposed.[68]

Since mere lawsuits filed by sons against their fathers were viewed
as "scandalous," John Porter, Jr.'s open and militant resistance to his
father's authority, which lasted for nearly two decades, must have been
truly shocking to contemporaries. Indeed, indications of intergenerational conflict among the men of the same family are exceedingly rare,
and the small number of arguments that did find their way into the
public record focused chiefly on inheritance. Sir Robert Filmer and John
Locke were clearly correct in their belief that a father's control of the
family property provided him with a nearly unassailable weapon in any
contest with a son. Few members of the younger generation dared to
oppose their fathers directly; most men who did so, like Samuel Bellingham, acted only after a father's death, filing suit against his estate
rather than against him.[69]

But what about the problems potentially posed by misbehaving
daughters and stepdaughters? A father confronting a rebellious female

child would have found little useful advice had he consulted a contemporary work on governing the family. Daughters may have felt freer than sons to violate family norms, since although they needed a dowry to make a good match, that inheritance was less important to their futures than were the legacies of real property, tools, and livestock on which their young male contemporaries relied. In a society in which demography dictated that the vast majority of women would marry, many of them more than once, a father's command of the family property would not have carried as much weight with daughters as with sons. Even so, like sons, they rarely filed suit against their fathers or their fathers' estates—although their husbands occasionally did, especially when seeking the payment of their dowries.[70]

Nonetheless, daughters could, and did, tarnish their family's reputations through sexual misconduct, one of the few avenues of rebellion available to young women. The strategy, though, could backfire badly. A series of four New Haven cases suggests the nature and consequences of such sexual rebellions. The incidents also imply (despite the theorists' silence on the subject) that property considerations could have affected the behavior of daughters as well as sons.

The prosecutions involved four high-status families. The most scandalous (John Winthrop even noted the outcome in his journal) occurred in early 1643 in the household of Mr. Richard Malbon, one of the colony's magistrates. There Will Harding, "a lewd and disorderly person," engaged in "uncleane filthy dalliances" with three "yong girles," among them Mr. Malbon's daughter Martha and one of his maidservants. Harding was sentenced to be "seveerly" whipped; he was also directed to pay substantial fines to the father of the third woman and to Richard Malbon, "whose famylys and daughters he hath so much dishonored and wronged in attempting to defile them." But the girls had not been innocent participants: all three were also whipped, Martha Malbon for agreeing to attend a "venison feast" with Harding, "for stealing things from her parents, and yeilding to filthy dalliance." John Winthrop found the public whipping of a high-status young woman "not unworthy to be recorded," especially since "her father join[ed] in the sentence." The daughter of Richard Malbon was surely not the only family member humiliated that day.[71]

Another young woman from a high-status family punished for sexual misbehavior was Rebecca Turner, daughter of one of the colony's early leaders. The flirtatious Rebecca reportedly did not like her stepfather, Mr. Samuel Goodenhouse, a wealthy Dutch merchant who had settled in New Haven, and so she undoubtedly felt little desire to please him.

In addition, her legacy from her deceased father was secure and could not be diminished, regardless of her behavior. In mid-1649, Rebecca Turner bore a bastard child fathered by a low-status man, Thomas Meekes. Rebecca and Thomas were ordered whipped, but after her mother's plea for mercy and a physical examination by a midwife, Rebecca was merely fined. Her stepfather promised to pay, and Rebecca married Meekes. Subsequently, the couple lived a financially straitened existence (Thomas slowly sold off the property she had inherited from her father), whereas one of her better-behaved sisters married the stepson of New Haven's governor, Theophilus Eaton. Rebecca Turner Meekes's sexual rebellion certainly did not benefit her in the long run, and for the rest of her life she suffered the consequences of her youthful fling.[72]

Unlike Martha Malbon and Rebecca Turner, Mary Hitchcock was not born into a high-ranking family, but she was a servant in the household of a magistrate when she engaged in the sexual misconduct that brought her before the New Haven court in early 1662. Her father, like Rebecca's, had died, and she had already received her inheritance by the time of her trial. Although she had previously been punished for theft—by her father, acting at the court's direction—she came from a family of church members, and a judge pronounced himself "much greived" that "a child of the Church . . . should so miscarry." Her misbehavior involved her fellow servant in the magistrate's household, Richard Matticks; both admitted to a consensual sexual relationship, but each accused the other of having initiated it. Probably because Mary told the court that she thought she was pregnant, the justices, though sentencing her and Matticks to a whipping, postponed the execution of her penalty. That delay proved vital in enabling her to escape corporal punishment, for when she returned to court some months later her expressions of remorse were seconded by several church members (friends of her "godly mother"), who asked the court to show her mercy. The judges, "hoping she would become a new woman," thereupon changed Mary's sentence to a fine. Whether the court later regretted its lenity is unknown, but Mary Hitchcock married Ralph Russell and, with her husband, played important supporting roles in several phases of the Pinion family drama described at length earlier in this book.[73]

A final telling example of youthful sexual rebellion in New Haven involved another servant born into a church member's household. The court did not doubt that the young woman brought before it in late 1663, Hester Clarke, orphaned daughter of John Clarke and his wife, had been "inveigled" by a high-ranking young man, Isaac Melyen, the son of a wealthy Dutch merchant, Mr. Cornelis Melyen. What made the matter so serious was that Hester was employed in the household of Mr. John Davenport, the colony's minister. Isaac was charged with wooing her without the permission of her master or his parents; of taking her out on horseback rides after the Davenport family had gone to bed; and, most important, of going into her bedroom secretly at night. Like Mary Hitchcock and Richard Matticks, each accused the other of having initiated the intimate relationship. In court, Hester and Isaac both abjectly apologized for their behavior. Perhaps their repentance had some effect, for Isaac's family was allowed to post a substantial good-behavior bond for him, and Hester was simply fined and "seriously warned" about her behavior, even though the judges lamented her sinfulness, "considering how she hath been educated."[74]

Several common threads connect the stories of the four young women over two decades. First, all came from high-ranking or respectable families of origin; each had at least one parent who was a church member. Second, they had directly challenged the authority of their family governors by engaging in flirtations, breaking the law against secret courtships, meeting clandestinely with their lovers, and perhaps initiating sexual relationships. Third, although the natural fathers of three of the four had died, they did not lack proper family governors; indeed, all were living under the direction of a leader of the colony at the time of their offenses. That, in the eyes of the New Haven judges, was what made their behavior so inexplicable and reprehensible, yet it was precisely because they were well connected to respectable folk that three of the four were treated leniently. It is probably no accident that only the first such prosecution, that of Martha Malbon, ended with a harsh sentence: her whipping may well have elicited negative reactions that caused the New Haven justices subsequently to render more lenient decisions.

Fourth, that three of the four misbehaving young women were at least partly orphaned supplies some suggestive indirect evidence for the hypothesis that inheritance, or the threat of its loss, could influence the behavior of daughters as well as sons. Since the fathers of Rebecca Turner, Mary Hitchcock, and Hester Clarke had died, the girls' legacies were guaranteed and could not be denied them, however serious their misconduct. Unlike daughters with living fathers, who could be threatened with the loss of a dowry, they were governed only by the moral teachings of the church and their surviving parents or stepparents, combined with the oversight of the heads of the households in which they lived. Their disreputable actions called into question the effectiveness of the training of respectable children in the New Haven colony and reflected badly on the supervisory abilities of some of the best-known men of the province. That is why the judges expressed their shock and outrage at the young women's behavior, telling Mary Hitchcock that "it was an affliction to the Court that they had occasion to call her to answere for such wickednes," and reminding Hester Clarke that she had brought "griefe [to] the family where shee lived, & many others of her friends" because of her "grosse miscarriages . . . in such a family." That such events could have taken place in the household of the Reverend John Davenport, the colony's spiritual leader, even led the judges to suggest that Isaac Melyen had a "diabolicall art to draw maydes affections." A supernatural cause of the "wonderful [amazing]" phenomenon would have helped to explain the unthinkable: how a servant in one of the best-run households in the colony could have gone so far astray.[75]

Hester Clarke and Mary Hitchcock were servants, not daughters, of the households in which they resided. And servants—those fictive children imported into colonial families—were more likely to contest the authority of their superiors than were the household's own children. Most prosecutions for resistance by dependents involved servants rather than children, even in a New England that emphasized the need for obedient offspring. Furthermore, servants had many more weapons at their command than did children: lacking a financial stake in the long-term welfare of their households of residence, they could run away, steal from their masters, or misbehave in a wide variety of ways largely denied by circumstance to children. They could also file suits for their freedom or, as was seen in the previous section of this chapter, complain to the courts about mistreatment.[76]

Yet, as the four young New Haven women learned from their experiences with the court system, if not before, civil authorities generally supported family governors in their efforts to maintain order in their households. Thus the overwhelming majority of servants accused of such crimes were convicted in both New England (100 percent) and the Chesapeake (86 percent). The penalties in the two regions did, however, differ significantly. In the Chesapeake, most servants were punished by lengthening their terms of service; in New England, most were punished by whipping. The regional variation arose from the divergent priorities of the two societies. In the Lockean Chesapeake, servant resistance was primarily a concern of individual households; accordingly, over half the prosecutions originated as civil suits brought by masters against their servants, and the appropriate remedy for misbehavior was a "fine" paid to the servant's household, in the form of additional service. In Filmerian New England, by contrast, servant misconduct was seen as having broad implications for society as a whole. All the prosecutions were initiated by the state, and the most common penalty, public whipping, carried a symbolic message to those who viewed it: resistance to superiors would not be tolerated, be those superiors family governors or political officials.[77]

That their resistance had little chance of success in either region did not deter servants from disobedience. With greater frequency than sons and daughters, servants engaged in a variety of verbal offenses against masters and mistresses, confronting them with "base revileing speaches" or "filthie language." Servants lied to their masters, threatened them (one Virginian said he would give his master "a Kinge Henry knocke" on the head), falsely accused them of assorted crimes, and defamed them.[78] Unlike children, who were never charged with such offenses, servants occasionally refused to work at certain times, to do some types of labor, or even to work at all. In Maryland, for example, a hired (not indentured) servant in 1645 "refused to doe his labour on Satturdayes in the afternoone"; six indentured manservants went on strike in spring 1663, complaining that their master fed them only "Beanes & Bread," rather than the "flesh" they preferred; and in 1657 another male servant won relief from a court after he successfully accused his master of forcing him and his fellow servants to "beate their Victuals in the Night." Indeed, the "beating of victuals" (more precisely, pounding dried corn kernels into meal with a heavy mortar) was so despised an occupation that as early as the mid-1640s knowledgeable servants were drafting contracts providing that they would "doe all labours except beating bread."[79]

Indentured servants had another legal weapon to wield against their masters: the insistence that they not be held beyond a specified term. Remarkably, about three quarters of the indentured servants suing for their freedom in the Chesapeake won their cases, which implies either that the courts (and juries largely composed of former servants) were sympathetic to their plight or that masters in the region were particularly venal and given to deceit in such matters.[80] The lawsuits also demonstrate that many servants had learned about their rights under Maryland and Virginia law. Not only did they successfully challenge their masters' reckonings of the times they had to serve, they also relied on laws defining terms by "the custom of the country" for those arriving without indentures and on other statutes forbidding them from making valid contracts while still in service.[81]

Many servants chose to contest their masters' authority by other than legal means. The most common form of resistance was running away, an act that for some fictive children in New England merely meant returning to their parents' houses—or, for captive Indians, to their own people.[82] Chesapeake servants, few of whom had nearby relatives, could rarely avail themselves of a like opportunity and, when recaptured, often spoke of having hoped to gain their freedom by reaching "the Dutch plantation" or "the Sweades." In 1643, two Virginia maidservants who ran away from their master achieved such a goal by going no farther than Maryland, where men desperate for wives refused to return them to him.[83]

Despite the problems caused by runaway servants, masters appear to have been reluctant to bring them to court, preferring instead to deal with their absences by punishments inflicted within the household. A New Haven master explained in early 1663 that "it was a great afliction to him to accuse his servant, he had kept servants these twenty yeares & had never the like excersise with any but seeing this was become publicke & other private meanes not prevailing," he had decided to report a manservant who had run away three times. Other masters offered less detailed accounts, but described servants they brought to court as "often running away," "a Constant Runnaway," or declared that he "hath Absented himselfe from his sarvice at severall tymes."[84] The New Haven court, consistent with its overall approach to governance, insisted on levying public penalties on runaways, a policy the judges explicated to a servant in April 1661, giving him a seventeenth-century civics lesson. The judges insisted that they would have punished the delinquent even had his master not complained, for "he was an Apprentice & stood Bound to doe faithfull service." Responding to the servant's explanation of his behavior, the judges asserted that if he had a complaint about his master, "the Authority must decide it, & [he was] not upon every dislike to run away."[85]

In addition to running away, the other common form of resistance engaged in by servants but not a family's own children was theft.[86] In New England in particular, servants (who often came from poor families, or at least poorer households than those in which they worked) occasionally seemed overwhelmed by the cornucopia of clothing, household goods, foodstuffs, and money with which they were surrounded. Northern servants stole chickens, pigs, cheese, grains, apples, linens, coins, wine and beer, and various items of clothing such as shirts, handkerchiefs, and scarves from their masters and household visitors. In the Chesapeake, where even wealthy planters had far fewer belongings worth stealing, servants concentrated on killing their masters' hogs and pilfering liquor. Frequently in both regions successful thieves shared their bounty with other servants, feasting together on "fresh Pork rosted" or enjoying "ffellowship . . . in drinkeing &c."[87]

Sometimes the plundering was both prolonged and organized. In early 1650, New Haven authorities uncovered a ring composed of four manservants, who had at various times stolen tools, wheat, corn, a heifer, beef, gunpowder, sheets and blankets, wampum, a pistol, and candles from their own and other households. The primary recipients of this bounty were Thomas and Rebecca Meekes, who frequently entertained the servants and welcomed their gifts of foodstuffs and other supplies without questioning their provenance. The newlyweds, penalized less than a year previously for bastardy, were charged with hosting "disorderly night meetings" of servants and concealing their thefts. Both denied having known that the items were stolen, but the court found everyone guilty, sentencing the servants to whippings and heavy fines, ordering Thomas and Rebecca fined, and directing the young couple "to come to the whipping post, and stand ther" while the thieves were whipped, "that they may have part of the shame which ther sinn deserveth." Once again Rebecca's wealthy stepfather agreed to pay the fines.[88]

The New Haven judges made a point of telling Rebecca Meekes that "servants may be incouraged to steale when they have such to receive it from them," observing that the couple set a "mischeivous example" tending to "nourish unrighteousnes & disorder in a plantation: for who can be secure, of his Chilldren or servants, or goods, if this be allowed." They had put their finger on a problem also evident in the cases of other theft-prone servants: the willingness of poorer colonists to ask no questions about the origins of goods they obtained from servants in wealthy households. It was precisely to forestall such complicity that colonial legislatures passed laws forbidding trading with servants, but those laws were difficult to enforce and widely ignored.[89] The frequent involvement of complaisant neighbors in servants' thefts is yet another indication that family governors could not rule their dependents in isolation from the surrounding community, and that the actions (or inactions) of the informal public had a major impact on the functioning of individual households.

Few servants went beyond threats or slanders, running away, and theft in resisting their masters. A handful of male servants physically assaulted masters or mistresses, and an even smaller number of servants and slaves of both sexes killed family governors.[90] Arson, a somewhat more common offense, posed a particular problem in New Haven, where three servant arsonists—one described as a "litle girle," the others boys aged twelve and fourteen—set damaging blazes in 1656, 1660, and 1663. The court did not quite know what to do with the criminals, whom it thought too young to hang, even though they had committed a capital offense. It ordered all three whipped, subjected two to symbolic hangings by ordering them to wear halters around their necks, and proposed to send two out of the colony.[91]

Such violent acts thus did not necessarily achieve much more than momentary elation for their servant perpetrators, since they were more likely than not to be caught and punished severely for their misdeeds. Sometimes less dramatic methods of resistance could bring greater satisfactions. Such was undoubtedly the case in August 1663 with an "incorrigable and impudent" Virginia maidservant named Elizabeth Leverit. Having been punished for her "insolent demeanor" toward her master Robert Brace at his complaint, Elizabeth nevertheless shortly thereafter became involved in a public squabble with him and another woman, Alice Boucher. The county court ordered the two women ducked, and then declared that since "the said Brace hath degenerated so much from a man, as neither to beare Rule over his woman Servant nor govern his house, but made one in that scolding society, wherefore the said Brace is censured to be ducked with his woman servant & Alice Boucher." Elizabeth Leverit had made her master suffer the ultimate indignity: to be told he was an inadequate family governor and to be treated like a woman.[92]

ROBERT BRACE must have been thoroughly humiliated by his sentence, which denied his stature as a male household head. And that was exactly what the justices intended: a man who had so "degenerated" as not to be able to "govern his house" did not deserve the respect reserved for men who wielded paternal power forcefully and effectively. A proper paterfamilias, unlike Brace, could expect the support of the state and the community as he ruled his family, for both the formal and informal publics understood that disorderly households threatened social stability.

Consequently, even in New England fathers had a considerable amount of freedom to govern their households as they wished. Outsiders like the Reverend Thomas Shepard or the Virginia neighbors of Mr. John Proctor instinctively sided with heads of households against such subordinates as Nathaniel Briscoe or Elizabeth Abbott. They were reluctant to intervene in the relationship between a father/master and his various children and fictive children, taking such a step only under unusual circumstances. Servants and slaves, who had no long-term stake in the households in which they lived, were the most likely to oppose the authority of family governors, but sons and daughters also occasionally rebelled against paternal power. Yet the strength of the father's position in a world organized by Filmerian principles is revealed by the fact that the most common form of filial resistance was indirect: filing a lawsuit not against a father himself, but rather against either his estate or a father by marriage (an in-law).

In the Filmerian schema, then, paternal power was secure from much outside interference unless, like Robert Brace or (in a different way) Mr. Nathaniel Eaton, a man proved himself unworthy to wield it. At that point the state, the community, or both would step in to restore order and to chastise the man who had demonstrated his inability to handle the prerogatives of power. When men headed households, the process worked with clarity and vigor. But not all family governors were male. Widows too could lead households, and the handling of them within a Filmerian context discloses additional facets of the system of gendered power.

CHAPTER 3

❦

Free in Liberty

Why mourne you so, you that be widowes: Consider
how long you have beene in subjection under the pre-
dominance of parents, of your husbands, now you be free
in libertie, & free *proprii juris* at your owne Law.
                        —*English legal treatise, 1632*[1]

THE ANONYMOUS AUTHOR WHO published *The Lawes Resolutions
of Womens Rights* in 1632 described more clearly than most of his
contemporaries the freedom that women would experience if their husbands predeceased them. He even recognized what the common law (in
its linkage of all unmarried females) did not: that women, subject to
their parents before marriage and to their husbands afterwards, would be
truly free "at their own law" only in widowhood. But neither he nor
anyone else examined what such freedom might mean for seventeenth-
century women. No one asked whether a woman could unproblemat-
ically assume the role of household head, or considered whether the
gendered definition of power was so deeply embedded in her society
that she might encounter difficulties not experienced by her male
contemporaries.

It was not as though a married woman, or even a daughter under
some circumstances, was without a claim to authority in the early modern Anglo-American household. As the supervisor of the family's daily
functioning, an adult woman directed the work of her children and
servants and could act as her husband's agent in his absence. An older
daughter in the home might serve as her assistant and thereby also
acquire certain limited power. Under the injunction of the Fifth
Commandment, "Honor thy Father and Mother," children owed their
mother continuing respect throughout their lives, even long after they
had left home to establish households of their own. No one questioned
these presumptions, so the notion that women wielded some sorts of

power and deserved deference from their children was not threatening in and of itself. Yet the change of context that occurred when a woman's husband died raised questions merely hinted at in the lawyer's formal exposition of the legal status of widows.

Indeed, his own words elsewhere in his book implied an ambiguity beyond the common law's capacity to resolve. As was noted earlier, the lawyer remarked that in English law "all of them [women] are understood either married or to bee married."[2] Widows, though, *had been* married and might not choose (or have the opportunity) to marry again. They did not fit either of the two basic categories English law established for women, and their anomalous position could accordingly pose perplexing problems.

As has already been observed, in a Filmerian system the institutional structures of the state were designed to control male household heads. In turn, they were expected to rule their subordinates of both sexes. Although theoretically it might seem that the gender identity of a household head was irrelevant to the functioning of that role, in truth it was not. Pervasive Filmerian assumptions about fatherhood presupposed male rulers at the heads of both familial and political structures. Certainly, in some ways a widow was able to take her dead husband's place at the head of the family. Her position as sole household governor afforded her unquestioned primacy over her children and servants. If she took on the responsibility of administering her husband's estate, as was customary, she became liable for paying his debts. Unless she remarried, she could sue or be sued in her own name, make contracts, and draft a will.

In other important ways, though, a widow did not resemble a male household head, precisely because she was not a man. She assumed her husband's familial roles, but not most of his political responsibilities. Although she had to pay taxes, she could not vote, serve in the militia or on juries, or hold any sort of elective or appointive office. Her inability to perform those functions resulted solely from her being female, not from age, social standing, or lack of sufficient property—all of which might disqualify a male contemporary. Thus a widow's gender identity fundamentally affected her social, political, and economic roles, especially those beyond the confines of her household. She was simultaneously both female and male: female, in that like other women she was excluded from certain political and military obligations; male, in that like men she had economic responsibilities and automatic rule over her own household. The ambiguity of her status left open the issue of whether she should be treated more like other adult women (who happened to be married), or more like other property holders (who happened to be men). Colonial authorities vacillated in their dealings with widows, because in the context of Filmerian thinking a widow's proper role was by no means clear. A wholly Lockean response could have resolved the matter by stressing a widow's gender identity to the exclusion of her masculine qualities, but not even the Chesapeake region was wholly Lockean in the seventeenth century. So confusion remained endemic.

The problem of definition was especially acute if the widow in question was high-ranking, because when a high-status woman had no obvious male supervisor, her social position in the Filmerian hierarchy became deeply problematic. As a widow, such a woman had no male superior in her own family, while simultaneously her status gave her precedence over all low-ranking men. The mere presence of high-ranking widows in their communities could accordingly confront officials and other colonists with complex conceptual issues. And if high-status widows openly challenged the structure of authority, the problems became even more pressing. The ambiguity of such widows' positioning in a sociopolitical hierarchy universally analogized to the family helps to explain why a number of colonial conflicts centered on high-status women, especially widows or those who can be termed fictive widows—that is, married women whose husbands, for one reason or another, were unwilling or unable to govern them.

THE POTENTIALLY POWERFUL WOMAN IN THEORY AND LAW

The same theorists who wrote at length about the relationships of husbands and wives or fathers and sons had little to say about women in their role as mothers or widows. Although one might hypothesize that their omission of daughters was simply an oversight resulting from their much more immediate interest in the dynamic interactions of fathers and maturing sons, it is difficult to advance the same argument with respect to their neglect of mothers and widows. Rather, another factor was at work: a concerted reluctance to consider the possibility that women could be the wielders, rather than the subjects, of power.

For example, Sir Robert Filmer's reliance on the Fifth Commandment, in which God subjected children to mothers as well as fathers, would seem logically to require the presence of a powerful mother or widow in his thinking. Yet that prospect was sufficiently dangerous to his intellectual construct that he—as was pointed out in chapter two—wholly omitted mothers from consideration in *Patriarcha*, thereby opening himself to John Locke's devastating attack, which (as shall be seen shortly) in part took the form of reinserting mothers into the words of the commandment. In an unpublished essay, Filmer commented in passing that a husband could trust his wife to govern *"Daughters and maidservants"* and *"even . . . sonnes when they be younge."* Aside from a one-sentence reference to the need for children to obey their mothers, that constituted Filmer's entire discussion of motherhood anywhere in his writings.[3]

Thomas Hobbes and John Locke, therefore, were the most important political philosophers who confronted the problems posed by powerful female images. Hobbes, the theorist most interested in the exercise of absolute power, recognized that with respect to their offspring mothers could be said to wield independent authority. In *Leviathan* he observed, "in the condition of mere nature, where there are no matrimonial laws, it cannot be known who is the father unless it be declared by the mother; and therefore the right of dominion over the child depends on her will, and is consequently hers." Hobbes contended that under such conditions a child properly belonged to its mother, and "she may either nourish or expose it." Any child nourished by its mother in the state of nature "is therefore obliged to obey her rather than any other," but a child abandoned by its mother would owe obedience to whoever raised it. No other contemporary theorist took such an uncompromising position on the prospect of maternal power.[4]

But having created a vision of an omnipotent mother, holding the same power of life and death over her children that Sir Robert Filmer had attributed solely to a father, Hobbes proceeded to modify it substantially. Not only did such a possibility obtain only in the state of nature—because "for the most part" in civil societies fathers controlled the children—but also it occurred only if the mother and father had not previously "dispose[d] of the dominion over the child by contract." Just as Hobbes had offered a unique example of a powerful wife (a queen married to one of her own subjects), so too he provided a similarly rare instance of a contract giving control of (some) children to their mothers: the arrangements reached by the Amazons with the fathers of their children, in which they kept the daughters while allowing the men to have the sons. Although Thomas Hobbes was willing to allow for the theoretical possibility of maternal power, in other words, he defined it in such a way as to make its actuality unattainable under normal conditions. He then concluded his discussion by putting the argument into conventionally masculine language, referring to "paternal dominion" and declaring in Filmerian fashion, "*He* that has the dominion over the child has dominion also over the children of the child and over their children's children [my italics]."[5]

John Locke, while eagerly taking advantage of Filmer's omission of mothers to reveal the flaws in *Patriarcha* and Filmer's other essays, was less willing than Hobbes to hold out even the theoretical possibility of maternal power. Although he too described a state of nature predating the creation of what he termed "*Political Society*," even in that natural state women were not (indeed, could not be) free of men's control. Locke's assertion in the *Second Treatise* that "the *first Society* was between Man and Wife, which gave beginning to that between Parents and Children" was crucial. Locke thereby refused to admit, as had Hobbes, that a woman could be a mother (that is, a powerful figure) without first being a wife (that is, under the control of a man). For Locke, only *wives* could be *mothers*; even in a state of nature, in the absence of all civil law, the relationship of husband and wife necessarily preceded and gave rise to that of mother and child. In the *First Treatise* Locke made the same point in a different manner when he declared that "the main intention of Nature" was "the increase of Mankind, and the continuation of the Species in the highest perfection," which required "the distinction of Families, with the Security of the Marriage Bed, as necessary thereunto." In other words, a monogamous marital relationship was "natural," predating the births of children.[6]

Unlike Filmer, Locke could not ignore mothers: he needed to use them against his opponent. But he also had to find ways to circumscribe their authority. That led him to adopt some revealing strategies. Throughout the *First Treatise*, Locke asked repeatedly: what happens if mothers are added to Filmer's statements about the powers of fathers? Locke's own answers to that question fell into two categories. The first pointed to mothers' role in producing and dealing with children. "The Mother cannot be denied an equal share in begetting of the Child," he wrote, "and so the Absolute Authority of the Father will not arise from hence." In the same vein were his comments, recounted in chapter two, about mothers and fathers deserving equal respect from their offspring. Thus one of his responses to Filmer was to acknowledge formally what Filmer had not: that there were two parents in every family; that those parents had "joynt Dominion" over their children, however that authority might be defined; and that, from a child's standpoint, neither parent could command its primary loyalty.[7]

The second was necessitated by the first. Having formally designated mothers as at least potentially powerful, Locke nevertheless insisted on maintaining male primacy, both within the family and in the society at large. He accomplished that goal in part by referring chiefly to "paternal power" when he discussed the role of parents. Although occasionally employing the phrase "parental power," he could assume his readers understood it in the context of his emphasis on the "natural" dominance of husbands over wives. Thus the primary determinant of "parental" policy would always be the father. Significantly, Locke never used the terms "maternal power" or "the power of mother and father" in the *Treatises*. He gave women dominion solely as part of a pair designated "parents," a pair in which he had explicitly stated that wives were to be seen as subordinated to their husbands' authority. He listed "mothers" separately from "fathers" only when he was considering the respect children owed their parents and when he was attempting to demonstrate the absurdity of Filmer's reasoning about the extent of paternal authority.

Locke's rhetorical practice is succinctly illustrated in a remarkable paragraph in the *Second Treatise*. Summarizing his views, he wrote:

> *First*, then, *Paternal* or *Parental Power* is nothing but that, which Parents have over their Children, to govern them for the Childrens good. . . . [The child] having received Life and Education from his Parents, obliges him to respect, Honour, Gratitude, Assistance, and Support all his Life to both Father and Mother. And thus, 'tis true, the *Paternal* is a natural *Government*. . . . The *Power of the Father doth not reach* at all to the *Property* of the Child.

In this one passage, Locke moved from the power of *parents* in the context of childrearing, through the honor due to *father and mother* as a lifelong obligation of an adult, to the actual wielding of power by a *father* alone and the "natural" character of "paternal" governance. He adopted the same terminology throughout the *Treatises*.[8]

The theorists' difficulty in dealing with the issue points to the likelihood that potentially powerful female figures could become the focus of conflict in the seventeenth-century colonies. The fact that some widows and fictive widows were positioned within the ranks of those persons who deserved deference outside their own households had broad implications for politics, society, and economics, as well as for the family. And not surprisingly (since they had to deal with the day-to-day practicalities of governance), colonial legislators were more willing than political theorists to come to grips with at least some of the problems posed for them by mothers and widows.

Women in their capacity as mothers rarely appeared in American laws. Most mothers were wives, and as such they were subsumed into

their husbands' legal identity. As was noted in chapter two, a few statutes
(like Rhode Island's law of 1647 or Massachusetts Bay's of 1648) prescribed particularly harsh penalties for subordinates who killed or resisted
mothers or fathers, following the Fifth Commandment in treating the
two parents equally.[9] At all other times but one mothers were invisible
in legal codes. The sole occasion on which they attracted the attention
of lawmakers was when they bore children—or, in New England, when
they became pregnant—out of wedlock. All the American jurisdictions
penalized women who bore bastards; in New England, as was seen in
chapter one, censure extended as well to women who had babies conceived premaritally. The New England governments made more vigorous attempts than Chesapeake authorities to locate and punish the
fathers of bastards, but in both regions female offenders (perhaps because
their guilt was so visible) endured the bulk of the punishments meted
out for such crimes.[10]

In contrast to the invisibility of properly married mothers in colonial
law, widows had a major presence in American legal codes, as legislators
confronted the necessity of arranging for the maintenance of women
after their husbands' deaths. Thus the Massachusetts Bay Body of Liberties of 1641 gave a widow the right to "a competent portion" of her
husband's estate, and in 1647 Rhode Island provided that a town's leaders should "make an equal and just distribution" of any intestate's estate
"among those to whom it does belong." In 1633 Plymouth similarly
directed its officials to "allow the widow and fatherless or motherless"
what they needed "for their present comfort," even if the estates' owners
had died bankrupt.[11]

Such statutes, however well intentioned, lacked sufficient specificity,
and within a few years most of the colonies adopted more precise policies
dealing with widows. The laws attempted to resolve two distinct problems but occasionally intermingled the solutions. The simplest problem
was created by intestacy. Since as many as one third of all men may
have died without making wills, colonial lawmakers had to determine
the appropriate distribution of an intestate decedent's property. Maryland's 1642 law, for example, provided that if a man left a widow but
no children, she would inherit all his "goods & Chattells"; if a widow
and one child, they would divide the moveable property; if a widow
and more than one child, she would receive one third, with the children
inheriting equal shares of the remainder. Any land would pass directly
to "the next heire . . . by the Law of England," except that a widow
would "succeed to the cheife mansion house (to hold it during her
widdowhood) and to the thirds of all the lands whereof her husband

died seised." After her death or remarriage, the house and her thirds of the land would also go to the proper heir as defined by English law.[12]

The second problem was more complicated, caused by a husband who died testate but left a will that made inadequate provision for his wife. Virginia burgesses solved it in 1673 by drafting a statute that applied universally. In that colony, the intestacy distribution became the minimum amount a man could leave his widow; he had the option of giving her more, but could not allot her less. Plymouth legislators chose a different strategy: in 1671 they allowed their colony's courts great discretion in certain testacy cases, providing that if a man wrote "an irrational and unrighteous Will, whereby he deprives his Wife of her reasonable allowance for her subsistency," she could complain to the court, which would then "relieve her out of the estate." Such a remedy was particularly appropriate, the Plymouth assemblymen believed, when "the Wife brought with her good part of the Estate in Marriage, or hath by her diligence and industry done her part in getting the Estate."[13]

Although the Plymouth policy promised special assistance to widows who deserved it, the reasoning also worked in reverse. Provisions for widows in the Bay Colony's 1648 code (applying to both testate and intestate estates), which were copied word for word by New Haven in 1656, applied only to a woman "living with her Husband in this Jurisdiction or other where absent from him with his consent or through his meer default, or inevitable providence, or in case of divorce where she is the innocent partie." In the same vein, a detailed intestacy law adopted by Plymouth in 1685 limited its property distribution to "every married woman, who hath not demerited the contrary by her wilful Absence or Departure from her Husband or other notorious fact without reconciliation to him in his life time."[14]

Through such provisions New England lawmakers expressed their determination to decide whether widows were worthy of receiving a substantial share of their husbands' estates and furthermore gave local judges considerable authority to divide a man's property among his widow, his children, and other possible heirs, especially in the event he died intestate. Consequently, in most of New England a widow's right to a share of her husband's property was not absolute: if she had deserted him or perhaps had lived with him discordantly, he could legitimately disinherit her. If she lived in Plymouth and her husband died intestate, the court could assess her character before awarding her a portion of the family's property. Such statutes required courts to render judgment on the wife's contributions to a marriage and her treatment of her husband.

The laws of widowhood in the northern colonies thus underscored a wife's dependence on her husband during his lifetime. A woman who offended her husband could be risking her livelihood as a widow, not only because he might leave her a small proportion of his property, but also because judges could take her past behavior into account in allotting her a share of the estate. The asymmetry of Anglo-American marriage law is nowhere better illustrated than by the fact that no colony ever adopted comparable edicts basing a man's access to his wife's estate on his ability to live peacefully with her, or depriving him of legal control of her property if he abandoned her.

That the legal codes of the Chesapeake colonies did not contain similar provisions allowing for official discretion in the distribution of men's estates is not surprising. In the first place, few Chesapeake women remained widows for very long: the heavily imbalanced sex ratio ensured that most widowed women would remarry quickly, often within months and commonly within a year. Any estates they inherited would soon come under the control of another husband; thus, a judgment of their "worthiness" to manage the estate rapidly would become moot. Second, as has already been seen repeatedly in this book, Chesapeake legislators were simply not as concerned as New Englanders with the internal functioning of families within their jurisdictions. Indeed, they could not be. Those families were so peculiar by English standards that it would have been difficult for the courts to intervene to uphold behavioral norms. It was far easier for Chesapeake authorities to establish clear rules and then to apply them universally than to decide cases on an individual basis, which is what often happened in New England.

As in so many other areas of family life, therefore, colonial laws and practices governing widowhood differed by region. Just as Virginia and Maryland legislators and judges showed little regard for protecting subordinates from the excesses of their husbands, fathers, or masters, so too they evinced no interest in assessing the propriety of women's behavior in marriage before allotting to them shares of their husbands' estates. In New England, though, civil authorities not only prosecuted spouse abusers, those who mistreated their servants, and, in particular, couples who were sexually active prior to marriage, but also judged women's reputations before awarding them a portion of their husbands' estates. Such supervision of individual families had both risks and benefits for women. On the one hand, a wife who was badly treated by her husband, in life or in death, could seek (and sometimes find) redress from New England courts. On the other hand, a wife who misbehaved in the eyes of the judges could be deprived of what she probably regarded as her rightful share of her husband's estate. Chesapeake wives had neither the courts' protection nor the courts' interference to contend with. Which system a woman would have preferred undoubtedly depended on her circumstances.

WIDOWS AS FAMILY GOVERNORS

In many ways, widows' experiences resembled those of other (male) household heads. They, like their masculine counterparts, sought to protect their children from abuse by others and to give them appropriate wedding gifts; had to cope with unruly servants and faced occasional charges of mistreating their dependents; and found themselves being sued by disgruntled sons-in-law claiming that dowries or legacies had never been properly paid to daughters.[15] But such similarities were more than outweighed by significant differences, contrasts that became evident from the very beginning of a woman's widowhood.

When new widows first assumed the responsibilities of family governors, they encountered difficulties clearly distinguishable from those confronted by young, recently married men embarking on the same tasks. Although little direct evidence describes their emotional state, many (like one Bay Colony widow in 1679) must have been stricken with "griffe" and therefore liable to make decisions they subsequently regretted. Others, especially in New England in the later decades of the century, were described as "ould," and widows everywhere often complained that they were "very poore" or "Destitute."[16] Such women had to rely on judges to allow them to retain the bare necessities and on creditors to lessen or entirely relinquish claims on the estate. A Salem widow told John Winthrop in the spring of 1631 that she needed a man's help for a variety of jobs, especially fencing her property and planting corn, and asked him to find someone to assist her. None of these conditions, except possibly initial economic woes, would have affected young newlywed men.[17]

Moreover, although widows (as a Marylander put it in 1661) "[ac]cording to the usuall Custome of the Countrey" commonly administered their husbands' estates, they did not have the same degree of control over their possessions as men did. Dying husbands frequently restricted their wives' ability to manage or dispose of all or parts of the family property, both by providing that the widow would inherit her share of the estate only for life or until she remarried and by outlining in great detail the eventual division of the property among other heirs, usually their children. Men also often named male friends as overseers of their children or estates; widows were then not able to act without consulting the overseers. Few widows were as assertive as Frances Axey of Salem, who, when her husband was on his deathbed in June 1669, complained that "you will give away all" and asked him not to make a will, telling him, "Cannot you Confide in mee that I will performe what yor minde is." Men present at James Axey's bedside tried to convince him that "it was an Apoyntment of God for him to sett his house in order," but James replied that "I can dispose of none of my estat" because his wife would not permit it. When Frances Axey herself died about a year later, she left a will containing a long list of bequests of money, clothing, and livestock—property she was able to distribute because her husband had not done so.[18]

Even if a husband's will left his wife relatively unencumbered by restrictions, northern widows often had to obtain a court's permission to take certain necessary steps with respect to their husbands' estates. New Haven judges supervised widows' payments of legacies to their children, and in Massachusetts Bay widows who needed or wanted to sell their husbands' real estate had to seek permission to do so. Significantly, the General Court itself devoted a considerable amount of time to discussing widows' petitions, and approval of their requests was not automatic. That the magistrates and deputies did not simply delegate such chores to the county courts or dispense with them altogether reveals the emphasis the colony's leaders placed on retaining real estate in the hands of a man's own heirs if at all possible and on their perceived need to supervise widows' actions.[19]

Not all widows submitted to such judicial oversight without protest. For example, when the townsmen of Providence in 1657 attempted to settle the estate of Nicholas Power, who had died without leaving a will, they reported in puzzlement and frustration that his widow, Jane, "refuseth to yeald obedience to the Law of the Colony," which, as already indicated, gave local officials the right to determine the division of such estates. Successfully resisting the townsmen, Goody Power skillfully managed her husband's property for ten years, after which she asked the townsmen for a final division, because her children "grow neere the age of possessing." The Providence officials, applauding her "industrye" and the increase of the estate under her direction, seem to have accepted Jane's proposal for the disposition of the property, giving her a generous share of it and noting in passing that a mare and a foal designated for her son's inheritance "are already made knowne to him by his Mother." By the simple device of refusing to accept the town's initial decision about the disposition of her husband's property, Jane Power won herself a decade of freedom and financial responsibility, which she did not surrender until it was to her advantage to do so.[20]

As she capably managed her dead husband's estate, the widow Power evidently encountered little concerted opposition from either local officials or her husband's relatives. In that she was fortunate, for many widows had to confront challenges to their authority far more serious than those experienced by male household heads. As has been seen, fathers rarely had to deal with overt defiance from other family members, especially children or stepchildren. By contrast, significant numbers of widows, particularly those with adult stepchildren, aggressive in-laws, or male collateral relatives, became involved in extended intrafamilial disputes over the control of property.[21]

Three such conflicts, one from Maryland and two from Massachusetts, provide examples of the types of opposition that widows could face. They illustrate, first, problems arising from specific statutory provisions, most notably the preference for the inheritance of land by the eldest son; second, presumptions against a widow's unequivocally asserting her rights; and third, the vigor with which competing male heirs could advance claims to manage or inherit the property.

A complex battle of several years' duration, instigated at least in part by the contents of intestacy law, involved a shifting alliance across generations in St. Mary's County, Maryland. Pitting two widows in the same family against each other, the struggle revealed that whether a man died testate or not could have significant and long-lasting consequences for his widow. It also exposed the ways in which a colony's statutes could constrain widows, reducing their ability to manage or dispose of their husband's real estate as they thought best.

The first indication of trouble in the household headed by Elinor Martin, a widow whose husband, Francis, had died without leaving a will, came in October 1658, when Elinor complained to the Provincial Court that her son-in-law, George Wilson, was abusing her "in her own howse."[22] Three witnesses described two separate incidents, one three years earlier (probably shortly after Francis's death) in which Wilson had "knockd the Widdows head against the howse side, & made it bleed," and a recent shouting match, during which Wilson "sayd that shee cheated him of his wifes portion, & shee sayd that hee was the ruine of her husband." Neither the origins of this dispute nor the court decision that resolved it are known, but in April 1661, shortly after the death of William Martin, Elinor's and Francis's older son, the conflict escalated and the parties regrouped.

At that time, Elinor, George Wilson, and another son-in-law,

Thomas Ward, joined forces against Patience, William Martin's widow. Under the provisions of Maryland law, which adopted English practice favoring the oldest son, William had inherited all his intestate father's land, along with a share of the moveable estate. Elinor earlier clashed with William over issues of housing and fencing, leading to the drafting of a formal agreement between them in late 1660. William died shortly after that agreement was signed, leaving a will that gave his entire estate to his wife and her three daughters by a previous marriage. Elinor, George, and Thomas were outraged, and according to Patience they "barbarously . . . halled me out of my howse and shoved my Children out head long alsoe soe that wee were forced to lye out in the plantation all night, and they have nayled up the doores of my howse and the tobacco howse."

Elinor Martin complained to the Provincial Court that William's will deprived her younger son, Ludowick, "the right heire" of Francis Martin, of property that should now go to him as their only surviving male offspring. She claimed the land on Ludowick's behalf and asked that Patience Martin and her daughters be ejected from the property. But despite the usual presumption that land should descend to male heirs in a direct line, the judges ruled that William Martin's will should stand and that Elinor was entitled only to a lifetime third interest in the property that had once been Francis's. She, Ward, and Wilson were fined for their treatment of Patience Martin, and her younger son and two daughters were deprived of any claim on their father's real estate.

It is not clear whether Elinor Martin genuinely believed that her younger son was her husband's appropriate primary heir once her older son had died, whether she was using Ludowick—who was still a minor—as a mask to hide her own interest in controlling the property, whether she simply did not like her daughter-in-law (who had not been married to her son for very long), or whether she and her two sons-in-law had joined forces in an attempt to bring about a more equitable distribution of Francis's landed property than Maryland intestacy law allowed. That the last may indeed have been the motive is suggested by the fact that Ward and especially Wilson joined their mother-in-law in attacking Patience Martin and her daughters. Wilson had had his own differences with Elinor Martin over the handling of the estate; surely he would not have aided her in the contest with Patience had he not hoped to gain substantially by the alliance. In the end, though, the elder widow Martin and her sons-in-law lost the battle for control of Francis Martin's real estate to the younger widow Martin, who benefited first from the preference given to the eldest male heir in the intestacy statutes and then from the absence of that preference in her husband's will. Elinor Martin, who nominally advanced a contention favoring a male line of descent, could well have hoped that if she won the case she could not only manage the property—presumably with the assistance of her sons-in-law—until Ludowick came of age, but also perhaps ensure its division among all her surviving children rather than having it pass to the widow and stepdaughters of her dead son and eventually to their husbands. But Maryland's laws and judges together thwarted that aim.[23]

Another widow who adamantly defended her right to control land she regarded as rightly hers was Mary Smith of Ipswich.[24] Her antagonist was a son-in-law, Richard Rowland, who had a history of conflict with the Smith family. On at least one occasion Richard had physically attacked his father-in-law, James Smith, and had, in the eyes of the neighbors, "grosely abused" him for years before James's death. Rowland asked his mother-in-law to allow him to bring cartloads of hay and dung across her property, promising that he would rebuild her stone wall after he had finished his work and that he would pay her a reasonable fee in exchange. In a family in which cordial relationships prevailed, that might have come as an easily granted request, but Mary Smith vehemently refused it, warning Rowland that "he should come on his perill." After Richard took matters into his own hands and tore down the fence so his carts could pass through, they clashed violently. According to Goody Smith, Richard "tooke a sticke & strucke her upon her arme & her legg" and then "pusht her downe & Stunned her" before hitting her in the back with a fence rail.

In the immediate aftermath of the confrontation, Mary Smith told the neighbors who ran to assist her and later came to her bedside that, if she died, her son-in-law had killed her. But eventually, perhaps influenced by a female friend, who warned her that "she should be carfull what she sayd, that she should not wrong her sonn, because it would be bruted abroad to his discreditt," she belittled the importance of both her injuries and Richard Rowland's conduct. Mary Smith might also have been concerned about her future well-being if she pursued the complaint against her violent son-in-law; she told a female acquaintance that she was afraid "he would kill her, or do her Some harm." In any event, in court she accepted partial responsibility for the altercation and explained that she had made her accusations against him "out of passion—being greeved & vexed." Indeed, she declared that she did not "make anie Complaynt" against him; instead, the primary complainant in the case was a neighbor worried about Richard's "violent carriadge toward his mother." Despite the concern expressed by that neighbor and others, the Essex justices penalized Mary Smith rather than Richard Rowland for the confrontation, chiding her for her "passionate distempers" toward her son-in-law. Thus in this instance a widow who asserted herself too firmly against an abusive male relative, although gaining the sympathy of some of her neighbors, erred in the eyes of the county court and perhaps in her own estimation as well. Either fear or the persuasive argument that she should not "wrong her sonn" led her to rethink her initial position and to pull back from a defense of her property rights.

Children's spouses challenged both Mary Smith and Elinor Martin. The antagonist of Frances Swan Quilter, another widow caught up in a bitter dispute over control of her husband's property, was instead her husband's brother, Joseph Quilter.[25] Although some details of the case were contested and remain obscure in the court record, certain facts seem clear. The controversy began as Mark Quilter lay dying in the autumn of 1678. He tried to tell two men how he wanted to dispose of his property, but, one reported, he was "faint & weake" and "they could not understand one word of many he spake." A doctor called to attend Quilter concluded that "he was altogether uncapable of making a will his understanding & speech being so taken away by his distemper."

After Mark's death the two deathbed witnesses nevertheless wrote a document that they presented to the Essex court as his "will." One of the witnesses admitted to being troubled that the childless Mark "had not done enough for his wife," since (apparently concerned primarily with her maintenance) he had left Frances only a life interest in his house and land, along with all the household goods and half the livestock. After her death, the house and land were to descend to Mark's "owne relations"—that is, his brother. Because the purported will did not meet technical requirements, the justices declared that Mark had died intestate. Even so, they named Joseph Quilter, who presented the document to the court, as administrator of the estate, evidently with instructions to distribute the property as much in accordance with Mark's expressed wishes as was possible.

In court that day, Frances Quilter—who had not previously seen the "will," though she had been told of its contents in general terms—pointed out to the court an internal contradiction in the document. She subsequently came under considerable pressure from her brother-in-law, the two deathbed witnesses, and one of the judges to accept arbitration as a means of resolving the problem. She signed an agreement to that effect, but (in the opinion of a later witness) "the poor widdow is much wronged [,] they Coming so Suddenly upon hir being a poore weake woman and Joseph hasty in getting the Estate, into his hands." Frances, reported the woman who had nursed the dying Mark, was also "full of trouble . . . and nobody there Could give her good Advice," so she "set hir hand to that . . . she did not now well understand." The identity of the arbitrators (the same deathbed witnesses who had produced the "will" in the first place) certainly suggested collusion with Joseph. Not surprisingly, they rendered a decision in his favor.

Within a few weeks Frances Quilter's male relatives began seeking information about the "will" on her behalf. Her brother, Robert Swan, approached one of the deathbed witnesses to "in quier what the reson was his sister was left so poorly." The witness responded that "thay did not know that Marke had such an estat as it proofed to bee" and admitted that "wee did not well know what hee did say." When Swan specifically asked, "what was the reson that his sister had nothing to dispose of when shee died" (that is, why was Frances not given outright ownership of any part of the house or land?), the witness defensively replied that "hir husband gave hir her portion forever." Since, according to other witnesses in the case, Frances's "portion"—the amount she had brought to the marriage twenty-three years earlier—was quite small, such a legacy appeared niggardly at best to all the observers, not just to Frances's relatives.

So, in May 1679, Frances Quilter and a group of her supporters successfully convinced the General Court to declare the "pretended will" void. Frances won the right to the entire estate during her lifetime and the ability to dispose of half of it at her death. The remainder would eventually go to Mark's relatives. But Joseph did not surrender easily. In September he persuaded the Essex court that several of Frances Quilter's proponents had made false statements to the General Court. He also sued Frances for violating the arbitration agreement, a clever mechanism for winning a review of the prior decision in her favor. Joseph again won his case in the county court, but Frances appealed to the Court of Assistants. By the time the appeal was heard there, the two parties had reached a satisfactory settlement providing for the disposition of the estate, but the court did not record its specifics.

Just as the cases involving Elinor Martin and Mary Smith illustrate what could happen when widows' claims to their husbands' estates conflicted with the perceived interests of the next generation, the experience of Frances Quilter points up potential pitfalls in intragenerational relationships. The link among all three disputes is men's desire to circumscribe widows' freedom of action in a central aspect of their role as family governors, the control of real property. Elinor Martin clashed with her son, William, and her son-in-law, George Wilson, before she and George joined forces in the name of another male (her younger son, Ludowick) to try to prevent Francis Martin's plantation from falling into the hands of women who were related to him only indirectly. Richard Rowland physically assaulted his mother-in-law, Mary Smith, enraged that she could prevent him from having easy access to his land—which was undoubtedly the part of the Smith family property that had been allotted to his wife when they married. And when Mark Quilter died without a son, his brother moved quickly to cement the Quilter family's long-term claim on his real estate by every means possible, which included probably influencing the deathbed witnesses' account of the purported oral will, getting himself named as executor of the estate, pressing Frances Quilter to accede to a tainted arbitration agreement once the "will's" shortcomings had become evident, and eventually pursuing lengthy litigation.

Such bitter challenges to widows' rights to control and dispose of property did not end with their deaths but could continue into the next generation. Richard Rowland began by arguing with Mary Smith but continued to fight for years with his two brothers-in-law. The three men (and their respective wives and children) initially disagreed over the handling of a legacy the widow Smith had left to her only son and then over a number of other issues involving family lands and the normal daily interactions required among persons whose property holdings adjoined each other. Another prolonged dispute developed in a Dorchester family because a high-status widow chose to distribute her husband's estate to his four sons in a different way from that specified in his will. Long after the widow's death and two decades after her spouse's, her granddaughter's husband filed suit against the estate, claiming that his wife and her siblings had not received their fair shares of the property.[26]

Several such lawsuits arose because one heir claimed to have been given a gift by the widow, but had no formal record thereof. Rachel Haffield Clinton of Ipswich, for example, said in 1666 that the £21 she had paid to buy out the time of her indentured-servant fiancé, Lawrence Clinton, had been given to her by her mother, the widowed Martha Haffield. But Rachel's brother-in-law, guardian of the insane Martha and later the executor of her estate, contended instead that the money properly belonged to Martha and should be repaid to him by Lawrence Clinton's former master. Likewise, William Nickerson in 1661 told the Bay Colony's Court of Assistants that his widowed mother-in-law had promised Anna, her daughter and his wife, that she would forgive the debt Nickerson owed to her estate, at least in part because Anna tended her with great dedication during her final illness. But Anna's brother, who was the executor of his mother's estate, successfully sued to collect the sum in question, informing the court that "he doth not know that his mother was ever satisffied or did thinke herselffe indebted to her sonne & daughter Nickerson" for Anna's services.[27]

The continuing dispute among the Smiths and the Rowlands does not seem to have resulted from any specific act of Mary Smith's, but the other widows bore some responsibility for the later contentions that divided their descendants. If Martha Haffield genuinely gave that money to her daughter Rachel, she told no one about it while she was still mentally alert; if Anna Nickerson's mother intended to reward her daughter by forgiving the debt Anna's husband owed her, she neglected to tell her son, the designated executor of her estate. For her part, the Dorchester widow failed to obtain the explicit consent of all her sons to the alteration of her husband's legacies. Had these widows shown more foresight, subsequent litigation could well have been reduced in frequency or intensity, perhaps even avoided altogether. That they did not act to formalize their arrangements with sons and daughters indicates both a naive assumption that their wishes would be carried out and an unfamiliarity with the technical requirements of the law. Men did not make the same mistakes. Men's estates were subject to litigation, but not commonly of this type. The vast majority of men knew enough to record gifts in writing or to obtain witnesses when they wished to dispose of their property. The fact that women failed to do so opened their decisions to prolonged contestation and provided their male relatives with a mechanism to attack the widows' attempts to distribute their property as they wished—a right men both took for granted and knew how to effect.

One occasion on which widows did sometimes act to distribute their property to their heirs in accordance with legal technicalities was when they planned to remarry. Although prenuptial agreements were relatively rare in the seventeenth-century colonies, widows participated in most of those that were drafted. In such documents women not only reserved property for their own use but also divided their holdings among their children, often with the formal consent of their husbands-to-be. Both strategies—retaining control of some property for themselves and ensuring that their existing offspring were protected from possible "imbezill[ment] & wast[e]" at the hands of their new husbands—revealed that women had learned important lessons from the months or years in which they had been "free in libertie." Premarital contracts allowed widows to continue to wield some of the power they had acquired as family governors, even as they nominally surrendered their independence to new household heads.[28]

And women tenaciously held onto that power. When Beatrice Cantlebury, the woman who in 1661 vilified her son-in-law for premaritally impregnating her daughter, married for a second and then a third time, she signed prenuptial agreements with both husbands, Francis Plummer and Edmond Berry. Plummer seems to have observed the terms of the marriage settlement, but Berry balked at fulfilling the contract and refused to support Beatrice because "she would not join her estate to his." Presented in 1676 for failing to live with Edmond, Beatrice Berry explained to the county court that before they married Edmond had declared that he "desired nothing of my estate he desired nothing but my person; but alas how he carried it to me afterwards." She accused Edmond of having told a friend that "if I would not give up the writings that were made between us he would make me weary of my life"—"& so indeed I found it," she informed the justices. She complied with their order to return to her husband, but a year later, testifying when Edmond was formally charged with mistreating her, Beatrice disclosed that "I am not onely continually abused by my husband, with most vile, threatening & opprobrious speeches but also his son who lives in howse with him hath in his Father's presence threatened me to throw me downe head long down the stairs." Edmond was fined for abusing her, Beatrice remained adamant in her refusal to surrender the premarital contract, and they subsequently lived apart.[29]

The twice-widowed Beatrice Berry's insistence on maintaining her financial independence in a third marriage, even though that insistence led first to physical abuse and then to a separation, speaks volumes about the value some women learned to place on the "libertie" that came with widowhood. As female family governors, widows faced more serious intrafamilial challenges to their authority than did their menfolk, but at the same time they gained stature in their own eyes, in their households, and in the wider community. Those gains were sufficiently important that some chose to maintain them even when entering a subsequent marriage.

WIDOWS IN A PUBLIC CONTEXT

The most daunting task facing a new widow was settling her husband's estate. As was already pointed out, dying men usually named their widows as sole or joint executors, which meant that such women were required to participate actively in civil lawsuits, often for the first time in their lives. Single women rarely appeared in court as plaintiffs or defendants in civil suits, and, as was noted in chapter one, because of common-law requirements married women came to court largely in conjunction with their husbands. Widows, by contrast, most often had to act on their own. Occasionally overseers or hired attorneys assisted them, but they bore the ultimate responsibility for probating the will, producing an accurate inventory (commonly with the aid of court-appointed appraisers), paying off their husbands' debts, and collecting sums owed to the estate.[30]

As a result, among women who were named as civil plaintiffs or defendants, more than half were widows, and most of the cases involving them were suits for debt.[31] Understandably, widows inexperienced in estate administration or civil litigation complained to judges that they "knew not how to doe it" or accused opponents of taking "advantage of her widowhood and Ignorance" of the matters at issue. Some asked male acquaintances to assist them, which could work to their detriment if the men did not take their affairs seriously. Widows also made mistakes, failing to probate their husbands' wills through "ignorance of the law," bringing into court accounts "not formall and according to Method" or submitting inventories "not under oath of the appraisers according to the generall courts order."[32]

Fortunately, the courts usually made allowances for widows' lack of expertise, although sometimes they had to pay costs and refile lawsuits that had been improperly submitted. Yet most widows were surely overwhelmed when, shortly after their husbands' deaths, they were hauled into court to face perhaps as many as twelve creditors eager to register their claims on the estate.[33] Still, many widows soon learned the tactics men had long employed in such situations. One creditor complained, for example, that a widow was paying off only the debts "she is forced too by lawe." A Virginia widow "by pretence of a bond found invalid . . . deteyned the said estate from her husbands creditors," earning the condemnation of the authorities for her "illegal proceedings." A Maryland widow's male attorney acted "fraudulently" to avoid a debt judgment against her, then married her shortly thereafter; it is unlikely that she had no knowledge of what he had done. And Mistress Ann Hammond, who as her husband's attorney in the late 1650s had made serious errors while managing the estate in his absence, handled herself more confidently in court after his death in 1663.[34]

Despite their initial difficulties, widowed litigants' overall success rates matched the success rates of married couples, with one significant exception. A majority of widowed plaintiffs in both New England and the Chesapeake won their cases, as was true of married couples and, indeed, of all civil plaintiffs. Conversely, most widowed defendants lost the suits in which they were involved, just as did most civil defendants of other descriptions, male and female. Only one category of widows, those who were defendants in the Chesapeake, did considerably less well than married couples under the same circumstances. One might plausibly infer from such results that the nature of the Chesapeake economy, with its heavy dependence on debt relationships, placed widows who knew little of their husband's business affairs at a particular disadvantage when they confronted claims against the estate they were administering.[35]

In addition to taking such statistical snapshots and describing widows' experience in general terms, it is instructive to examine the litigious career of one Chesapeake woman, the thrice-widowed Mistress Jane Smith Taylor Eltonhead (1617–59). She had two daughters by her first husband, Thomas Smith, and a son and daughter by her second, Philip Taylor, but no children by her third, a fact that proved relevant to the lawsuits in which she became involved as William Eltonhead's widow.[36]

Most of the recorded litigation in which Mistress Jane engaged was as Eltonhead's widow, although there is scattered evidence of prior legal activity on her part as the widow of both Smith and Taylor. After her third husband's death she filed three lawsuits and responded to four as the administrator of his estate. Each suit required several court appearances before being resolved. In addition, she, and eventually her heirs, became enmeshed in litigation contesting the validity of her husband's testament. Just prior to his death in 1655, unable to obtain "pen, inke or paper to make a formall Will," Mr. Eltonhead told John Anderton, the husband of one of his stepdaughters, that he left "all his lands with all his other goods & Chattles" to his wife "for the good of her & her Children," while asking her to give "som part of the lands" to his nephews. Although at Jane Eltonhead's request the Maryland Provincial Court declared this oral will valid in October 1658, her son and principal heir, Thomas Taylor, later had to respond to challenges to his possession of his stepfather's property from both his step-cousins and William Eltonhead's English brother, all of whom claimed to be the proper "heirs at law" to Eltonhead's landed estate.[37]

Thus Jane Smith Taylor Eltonhead and her heirs confronted many of the problems encountered by other colonial widows and their families. In attempting to pay and collect her third husband's debts, she had to deal on the one hand with recalcitrant debtors (one claim she filed in September 1656 was still only partially paid by April 1659) and on the other with importunate creditors (she managed to postpone one judgment against her for eleven months, from April 1658 to March 1659). Her handling of the estate was further complicated because the only witness to her husband's disputed oral will was an interested party, her son-in-law, and because her status as her husband's only heir opened her to serious challenge. Her son Thomas Taylor, a male heir—but not, significantly, the son of the man whose property he inherited—had to defend his possession of the property from lawsuits instituted on both sides of the Atlantic by his stepfather's collateral male relatives. Finally, as so often happened in such cases, the heirs in the next generation also fought with each other: in 1664, Thomas filed suit against his half-brother-in-law John Anderton for possession of some of the Eltonhead property.[38]

Although Mistress Jane Eltonhead appeared in court repeatedly as a civil litigator during her years as a widow, she faced no criminal charges in that same period. Indeed, only once was she accused of a criminal offense: she and her third husband were penalized for mistreating a maidservant in 1652. In this, Jane Eltonhead was like other widows, the least likely of all women to be charged with crimes. About 5 percent of female miscreants were widowed, as opposed to the approximately one fourth who were single, and the two thirds who were married. This small number of widows was charged with a wide range of offenses, the two most common of which (unlicensed liquor sale and fornication) amounted to just one fourth of the accusations against them. All categories of women were charged with fornication, but alcohol-sale violations, largely a consequence of widows' most common occupation, innkeeping, were more characteristic of widows than of other groups of female defendants.[39]

Two Maryland criminal cases involving recently remarried widows are of particular interest for the insights they offer into the economic pressures widows must have regularly confronted. Few women chose the illegal tactics adopted by Blanch Harrison Oliver Howell or Elizabeth Potter Greene, but others must have felt similar temptations in like circumstances. Although the women's motives are nowhere specified, they can be inferred from the legal record.

A two-time widow, Blanch Harrison Oliver administered her second husband's small estate during Maryland's chaotic "plundering time" in the mid-1640s. After order was restored to the province in early 1647, she declared that she had lost several head of cattle under circumstances that appeared to entitle her to compensation from the colony. Livestock undoubtedly comprised a substantial portion of her estate, and so such a loss was by no means of negligible importance to Blanch and her two children. In October 1648, she and a man named Thomas Baker submitted mutually supportive depositions to the Provincial Court. Endorsing Blanch's claim, Thomas swore that a cow thought to be hers had been illegally killed at the house of his former master. Concomitantly, she deposed that she had seen Walter Coterill deliver a particular yearling bull to Thomas. Shortly afterwards, however, Coterill attested that, although he had indeed given a bull to Baker, Blanch Oliver had not witnessed the transfer of the animal. Moreover, Coterill declared, the bull he had turned over to Baker was not the one Baker now claimed. Other evidence then demonstrated that the bull currently in Baker's possession had probably been stolen from a third man. The judges accepted Coterill's testimony rather than Oliver's and Baker's. Accordingly, Blanch Oliver, by then married to Humphrey Howell, was tried for and convicted of perjury. The court ordered that she "stand nayled in the Pillory, & loose both her eares," and that the sentence be carried out "before any other busines in Court be proceeded uppon."[40]

Elizabeth Potter Greene met a similar fate—being "sett on the Pillory, & Loose[ing] one of her eares," in addition to being fined and imprisoned—for a comparable offense. She did not offer false testimony for someone else but instead in September 1663 persuaded her servant boy to forge a receipt purporting to show that her first husband had paid in full for a maidservant she had purchased during their marriage. Although she claimed to have "fownd this Reciept amongst her husband Potters papers," witnesses concluded that the handwriting was that of her servant. When questioned, the boy admitted "that hee writt the Receipt or discharge now produced in Court, . . . And that shee caused him to write it." The false document seems to have been a desperate attempt by Elizabeth to forestall a substantial claim against the estate of her first husband (who had died in late 1659 or early 1660), a claim that could well do significant damage to the holdings of her second husband and thus adversely affect her and her children.[41]

Few men or women were ever accused of perjury or forgery in the colonies, and fewer still were sentenced as harshly as were Blanch Oliver Howell and Elizabeth Potter Greene.[42] That the former widows tried such ultimately self-defeating and unusual tactics suggests both the depth of their desperation and, perhaps, a lack of knowledge of the possible consequences. Since the crime was so rare, and since women had so little experience with the demands of the courtroom setting and its heavy reliance on oaths, one is tempted to speculate that they did not understand fully what would happen to them if their crude dissembling were discovered. Blanch Oliver, seeking to replace precious cattle lost during a chaotic period, could easily have negotiated a reciprocal arrangement with Thomas Baker, who, after all, really had acquired a bull from Walter Coterill—just not the one he now had in his possession. Elizabeth Greene, whose second husband had already responded to several suits against her first husband's estate, could well have concluded that this particular claim might be the one that would bankrupt her family or irrevocably enrage her husband.

Whatever their motives, the two Maryland women demonstrated by their actions that they did not completely comprehend the rules by which men transacted business. Not only were they probably unaware of the brutal penalty meted out to perjurers and forgers (thereafter, the loss of ears would communicate their untrustworthy character to all who saw them, and they would no longer be allowed to take oaths of any sort) but also they probably did not realize the extent to which they had violated the standards of interaction upheld by the male informal public, standards that will be examined in detail in chapter four. As women, they had not been required to meet those standards or to operate within the judicial-economic milieu dominated by men until they were widowed. But at that time they were expected to behave with nearly instant comprehension of what had previously been an alien world.

Seventeenth-century women were not hermetically sealed off from the world of men before they experienced widowhood. Obviously, they would have heard their husbands and other men discussing business and legal affairs. Moreover, as was pointed out in chapter one, they themselves probably engaged in a variety of business activities while married. But as femes covert they had not borne final legal responsibility for their actions. Widowhood accordingly made different demands on them. Women who as widows had to undertake unfamiliar tasks not unexpectedly made mistakes, some of them more costly than others. Additional episodes similarly suggesting that women did not understand the largely unspoken communal rules that governed men's behavior will be discussed at length later in this book. Here, by way of introducing the theme, it is useful to focus on an incident already previously considered in part—the Boston church's excommunication of Mistress Ann Hibbens in 1641.

Mistress Hibbens, it will be recalled, not only resisted her husband's authority but also cited scriptures and a sermon delivered by the Reverend John Cotton to contend that husbands should listen to their wives' advice. The events that led to her excommunication developed in the context of a dispute over carpentry work done in their home under her direction.⁴³ Her husband, William, had given her permission "to order and carry on this business to her own satisfaction," thus making her a fictive widow for the purposes of the negotiations. She hired a joiner, John Crabtree, to make a bed and other items, but was dissatisfied when he charged her more than she thought appropriate. Accusing Goodman Crabtree of "deceitfulness in his work and slight doing of it, . . . and neglecting his work after he began it," she told the church that "I have but only desired to find out the truth." The search for that truth led her first to other Boston joiners who, led by John Davies, a church member, sided with Crabtree's assessment of the value of his workmanship. Mr. William Hibbens was willing to accept the Bostonians' estimate but could not persuade his wife to concur. Instead, linking her experience to the "general complaint of oppression in work and workmen"—that is, to widespread concern at the time about excessively high wages and prices—she began to search actively for men who would support her low estimation of the quality of Crabtree's work.

As was appropriate, the first person she consulted was the pastor of the Boston church, the Reverend John Wilson. After she told him "in private" that she feared "an agreement among our joiners to keep out the prices of their work," Wilson advised her (she later claimed) to seek proof of her charges. Mistress Hibbens thereupon embarked on a vigorous one-woman campaign against the carpenters, whom she accused of having "compacted together to deceive her." She recruited two Salem artisans to evaluate the workmanship (on the grounds that "the truth of it would hardly be found out by the joiners of this town"); she "in an unsatisfied way sent from workman to workman and from one to another to view the work and to appraise it"; and she used "indirect means to make men undervalue the work by stirring them up to judge it before they have well viewed it" and by "speaking disgracefully and slightly of it."

John Winthrop's account of her attempt to enlist him supplies a useful description of her methods. Mistress Hibbens employed, he said, "many hard expressions to me of their unconscionable dealing in the thing, and would never be satisfied till I had come and viewed her work, and to judge of it." Mr. Winthrop at first fell prey to her "skill and patience," admitting that he initially "did undervalue it, upon my own want of experience in such work." And when "upon better grounds I altered my judgment, she would never be satisfied, and would know my reasons. And when I did give my reasons, yet she was still unsatisfied, and came again and again to know my reasons, till at last I was fain to turn my back upon her and to say no more."

When Mistress Hibbens persisted in her belief that she had been wronged even after "twenty, or forty several meetings" with the carpenters and church elders, the ministers and the congregation lost patience with her. After a series of hearings in September 1640 and February 1640/1, the Boston church excommunicated her for nine reasons, only one of which—slandering the carpenters—related to the original dispute. Three others were lying (changing her story), selective memory, and failure to subject herself to her husband, who had indicated his willingness to accept the Boston joiners' judgment. But a majority of the enumerated offenses pertained to Ann Hibbens's refusal to pay attention to communal norms of behavior. She had not compromised, despite having been pressed to do so by the elders and "our honored magistrates and diverse other Brethren and friends." Even had she been correct in her assessment of the carpenters' actions, she did not properly "labor to bring them to repentance." She had rejected the "council and advice of diverse . . . Brethren and Sisters" who had "taken pains with [her] in private," cautioning her to pay heed to the church's admonition. Finally, she had caused "discord and jealousies" in the congregation and had maligned its actions as "unrighteous."

In the end, then, whether Mistress Hibbens was correct in her assertion that the carpenters had deliberately united to cheat her was less important than her failure to comply with the unwritten rules by which the male members of the community resolved their differences. Her excommunication stood even though in June 1641 the General Court, with members drawn in part from the Boston church, sided with her by ordering John Crabtree to repay money to Mr. William Hibbens "for so much overpaid for the worke formerly done" and "admonished" John Davies for his role in the affair.[44] Isolated, having antagonized the other members of her congregation, Mistress Hibbens was expected to yield gracefully to the communal judgment that she had erred in her unrelenting obstinance, even if not in her initial position.

She would previously have had little experience with such intense pressures to conform. As a high-status married woman, Ann Hibbens was accustomed to deference, not resistance, from those inferior to her on the social scale—as the joiners most certainly were. While taking pleasure in the fact that her husband had allowed her to negotiate with the carpenters and thus to assume a supervisory role usually reserved for male and female household heads, she did not realize that that same role would bring her into conflict with men unaccustomed to dealing with an outspoken woman who proclaimed her own authority in the face of both her husband and the church. Indeed, as a fictive rather than a true widow, she was resisting not only the informal public but also her own spouse, which compounded her error. Convinced she was right and never having been socialized into a male world that valued consensus among household heads and especially among high-status men, Mistress Hibbens ran dramatically afoul of the rules of gendered power. It is perhaps not surprising that less than two decades later she became the only high-status colonial woman ever hanged as a witch.[45]

Just as widows and fictive widows were uncertain of their proper role in a public context, so too the state and the community had difficulty in categorizing such anomalous household heads. Widows were awarded land grants when New England towns were first established; they had to pay taxes, just like other property owners; and at least once (in Plymouth Colony in 1653) they, along with men over sixty, were ordered to "beare their parte [of militia service] by finding one to watch according to theire proportions [the size of their estates]." In addition, widowed New Englanders occasionally joined men from their towns in signing petitions and other official documents. For example, in 1640 the "proposals for a form of Government" at Providence were signed by thirty-seven men and two widows; and one widow and seventeen men from Sudbury addressed a statement of thanks to the Bay Colony's authorities in 1656 for helping them to resolve a local dispute.[46]

Yet at the same time widows could not vote or hold office, and they stood in an ambiguous relationship to authority, particularly at the local level in New England. Since the early Chesapeake lacked institutions that would allow for widespread participation in local governance, widows there (like most men) had no formal voice in local political affairs; and in both regions the further up the hierarchical ladder of politics one went, the clearer was widows' exclusion from the formal public. But in New England towns there is scattered evidence that widows occasionally attended and spoke at meetings, though only on matters pertaining to their own property. And when in 1662 an issue arose concerning the commonage rights of property owners who were not present at a New Haven General Court session, the colony's leaders sent several emissaries to learn the opinions of the absentees, explicitly including "widdowes" in their directive. New Haven officials thereby revealed that they recognized widows' right to be consulted on topics relevant to their property holdings.[47]

Whatever the ambiguities of their relationship to the formal public, widows of ordinary rank were of negligible importance in the broad context of colonial politics. High-status widows and fictive widows, on the other hand, had been (or still were) married to the leading men of

English America. Their social standing gave them a right to deference from their inferiors, male and female, and, since their status was more important than their gender in determining their position in the theoretically all-encompassing Filmerian hierarchy, they were not clearly distinguishable from other potential wielders of legitimate power. As John Locke was later to observe, in a Filmerian system based on the Fifth Commandment, women with claims to being "mothers" had as much right to power as did "fathers."[48] It might therefore be anticipated that the New Haven colony, that most Filmerian of all the Anglo-American mainland settlements, would experience a remarkable and protracted series of confrontations involving high-ranking widows and fictive widows.

MISTRESS ANNE EATON AND HER FRIENDS: A CASE STUDY

Two public altercations, the first in the church in 1644–45, the second in the court in 1646, created intense disturbance in the small New Haven colony. Each generated additional religious and secular proceedings of various sorts, and the reverberations continued at least until 1649. The principal combatants were, on the one hand, the two primary leaders of the colony, Governor Theophilus Eaton and the Reverend John Davenport; and, on the other, four high-status widows or fictive widows: Mistress Lucy Brewster, Mistress Moore, Mistress Leach, and Mistress Anne Lloyd Yale Eaton—the governor's own wife.[49]

Mistress Eaton was the focal point of most of the battles. Daughter of an English Anglican bishop, she was a "prudent and pious" widow with three children when in 1627 she married Theophilus Eaton, then a widower with two children. Ten years later they emigrated from England to North America, where in 1638 her husband became the first governor of the New Haven colony. There they, her children, his children, their children, and eventually his mother all lived together, in a blended household that created not a little friction. After her husband's death in 1658, she returned to England, dying shortly thereafter.[50]

Anne Eaton's friend Mistress Lucy Brewster was the widow of Mr. Francis Brewster, a wealthy merchant who had been assessed the seventh highest tax in the colony in 1643. Mistress Brewster, a church member, had a considerable local reputation for intelligence and perspicacity; one man was quoted as having declared, "I had rather be questioned by any boddy than her, for she hath a notable patte." By early 1647 she married

Mr. Thomas Pell, a prominent physician. In 1650, they left New Haven for Fairfield, and several years later they settled in New Netherland, where he founded the town of Pelham. She died there around 1668.[51] Less is known about the other two women, who were mother and daughter. Recent arrivals (the family was not enumerated on the 1643 tax list), they were not church members. The widowed Mistress Moore evidently lived with her daughter and son-in-law, Mr. Edmund Leach. He, like Francis Brewster, was a wealthy merchant with wide-ranging business interests.[52]

The events that enmeshed the four women, the colony's leaders, and indeed many of New Haven's residents in half a decade of controversy began when Anne Eaton started to question a key Puritan doctrine, infant baptism. Seeking information about the practice, Mistress Eaton consulted another high-status Englishwoman in America, Lady Deborah Moody. Lady Moody, who had been excommunicated from the church in Lynn, Massachusetts, for being an Anabaptist, supplied her friend with a recently published book opposing infant baptism, which Mistress Eaton read "secretely." Anne Eaton then compounded her error, said the Reverend John Davenport, "for she neither asked her husband at home [for assistance] . . . nor did she seek for any light or help from her pastor . . . nor did she seek help from the body whereof she is a member, nor from any Member." Instead, "she showed her book with the charge of secrecy" only to one or two people, whom she hoped to convert to her beliefs.[53]

Not by coincidence did Mistress Eaton turn for advice to another high-ranking woman like herself. Only another gentlewoman, she implied by her actions, could offer her appropriate guidance as she rethought her religious views. Significantly, the Reverend Davenport was bothered not only by Anne Eaton's heretical ideas, but also by the method through which she arrived at them: obtaining a book from another high-status woman, reading it "secretely," and reaching her own independent conclusions. Crucially, she had failed to consult men, including her husband, at any point in the process. Davenport cited scripture to prove her error. First Corinthians 14:35, he observed, ordered wives to direct their religious questions initially to their husbands. And Theophilus Eaton would have "held forth light to her according to God," because the governor was widely known for his piety and his leadership of daily religious exercises in his own home.[54]

Since Mistress Eaton reached her decision through her own personal reflection, the first inkling John Davenport, Theophilus Eaton, or the congregation as a whole had of her change of mind was strikingly dramatic: "by her departing from the Assembly, after the morning sermon, when the Lord's Supper was administered, and the same afternoon, after sermon when baptism was administered judging herself not to be baptized, nor durst she be present at the latter, imagining that predo baptism is unlawful."

The governor's wife sat in the front row of the meetinghouse, so her abrupt departures that sabbath could not have been overlooked by anyone in the colony. Within a week the Reverend Davenport convened a meeting of the church, at which Anne Eaton for the first time explained to others her spiritual struggle and her newly acquired Anabaptist beliefs. Mr. Davenport then took it upon himself to refute the contentions in the book she had read, responding to them point by point, first in a sermon and later in writing. Her husband and two church elders went over the book and Davenport's document with her in minute detail, but she refused to change her position. During Davenport's sermon she muttered *sotto voce*, "it is not so." She was later openly "contemptuous" of the men's arguments and "neither would object nor yield" during their sessions with her. Moreover, she continued to leave the church whenever infant baptism was being administered, sometimes even "absenting herself from the sermon and from all public worship in the congregation." This, declared Mr. Davenport, was a "public offence, which she knows is grievous to us."[55]

Mistress Eaton's refusal to defer to her husband or her pastor with respect to her religious beliefs had its counterpart in what John Davenport termed "her scandalous walking in her family." While the Reverend Davenport was striving to make her abandon her Anabaptist convictions, "divers rumors" spread through the town about dissension in the Eaton household. Once these tales had become "common fame," Davenport and the elders decided that they were required by scripture to "inquire, make search and diligently ask whether it were true." Since the Reverend Davenport and Governor Eaton were longtime friends, such an investigation must have been mutually embarrassing in the extreme, and the clergyman was probably reluctant to embark upon it. Indeed, his account of the decision to undertake the inquiry suggests as much: although the two families lived next door to each other, Mr. Davenport later said that he was one of the last to hear the stories, explaining his lack of information by noting that he was "almost continually in my study and family except some public work or private duty called me forth." In all likelihood, the minister had instead turned a blind eye to the goings-on next door until the scandal could no longer be ignored.[56]

The Reverend Davenport and the elders first asked Mr. Eaton about the rumors; he referred them to his wife, who in turn referred them to "her mother and daughter and servants." From these witnesses the investigators not only learned that the tales were true but also discovered "more evils . . . than we had heard of." They concluded that "these evils would by the just judgment of God hinder [her] from receiving light"; in other words, that Mistress Eaton's conduct in her household would, unless corrected, prevent her from recognizing her theological errors. Accordingly, they decided to "deal with her in a private way" about the familial disorders prior to resuming their attempts to wean her away from Anabaptism.

In adopting that course of action, the New Haven church leaders revealed their staunch adherence to a Filmerian worldview. To their minds, religion and family, like state and family, were tightly linked: disarray in one indicated disarray in the other, and problems in one could not be resolved without a similar resolution of problems in the other. Domestic misbehavior and intellectual error were inseparable, all of one piece. If they could make Mistress Eaton see the error of her ways with respect to her household affairs, that would be the first step on the road to reforming her heretical religious opinions as well.

The Reverend John Davenport, Theophilus Eaton's old friend, undoubtedly had another motive for trying to rectify conditions in the governor's household. Davenport must have been well aware of the Puritan doctrine expounded by the Reverend William Perkins in 1603: "Such as beare publike callings, must first reforme themselves in private. . . . How shal he order publike matters for the common good, that cannot order his owne private estate?" The conflict in the Eaton household, in short, reflected on Governor Eaton as well as on his wife. If he could not control his own family, could he claim the ability to rule the colony? Certainly the implied negative response to this question (in addition to a normal interest in gossip about the powerful) caused the rapid spread of rumors about the family's disorders. So Mr. Davenport, once roused, eagerly took a hand in the matter. By convincing Mistress Eaton of her multiple offenses, he could both return a stray lamb to his fold and salvage his friend's battered reputation.[57]

He and the elders thus returned to speak with Anne Eaton, reviewing with her what she had done and the rules she had broken in so acting. They then left her alone after "exhorting her to repent." When some time had passed with no signs of repentance on her part, they informed her that because of "her hardness of heart" they were being forced to go to the church as a whole. Trying to prevent at least some of the details from becoming widely known, they urged her to agree to discuss them "in private, by holding forth her repentance privately for such particulars as were not commonly reported; for we were unwilling to bring forth such things into public." A few of her sins were minor and not generally known, they acknowleged, and they would conceal those from public view if she would admit her errors.[58]

Yet Mistress Eaton obstinately resisted the three men. Davenport reported that "she refused to give any private satisfaction for any. Told us that these [the "not commonly reported" stories] were also common talk, and that she herself had met with reports of them in other houses." Clearly seeking precisely that public confrontation the church leaders were hoping to avoid, the highest-ranking woman in the colony utterly refused to cooperate with the elders. Eventually, Mistress Eaton "told us we labored with her in vain and should have no other answer, and wondered that the Church did not proceed." Consequently, Mr. Davenport informed the congregation at the opening of Anne Eaton's first church trial in August 1644, "we are compelled to bring sundry particulars of which she was privately admonished into the public notice of the Church, because she refused to hear us in a private way, according to the rule in Matt. xviii, 17."[59]

At this point it is useful to reflect briefly on the usage of the terms *public* and *private* in the language of the combatants. Two of the oppositions identified in the introduction to this book appear in the contemporary prose elicited by this confrontation. The most prominent was the dichotomy of such overriding concern to the Reverend John Davenport and the elders: between public (widely known) and private (concealed). They conducted as many conversations with Anne Eaton "in private" as they thought possible, preferring to deal with her "in a private way." Then, once they believed they were required by scripture to make the matter "public," they sought to limit the number of incidents discussed. The governor's wife, on the other hand, refused to acquiesce in the men's stated goal of restricting general knowledge of her reputed transgressions. By rejecting their repeated pleas to keep matters "private," she insisted on a "public" airing of the charges against her.

The other meaning appears in remarks by both John Davenport ("public work"/"private duty") and William Perkins ("publike callings"/"private estate"). Although expressed in somewhat different terms, both referred to the same phenomenon: the dual roles played by men who simultaneously headed households and fulfulled responsibilities to the state or the church. As was seen previously, that distinction was commonly made and widely employed with respect to men holding some sort of official position.

The presence of this latter binary opposition in the men's language, though, directs attention to the absence of a third potential pair. Mistress Eaton's leaving the church when infant baptism was administered was, Mr. Davenport averred, a "public offence." But nowhere did he concomitantly describe her behavior in the family as "private." As was observed earlier, that particular oppositional meaning of public/private —one that could be applied to *women* in the family rather than to a few men with official positions—did not yet exist, precisely because the household and the wider community were not yet definitively separated. The absence of the third possible public/private pairing, coupled with the presence of the two others, reconfirms the prevalence of a Filmerian mode of thought in seventeenth-century New Haven. That worldview both established Anne Eaton's importance and turned her resistance to the authority of her husband and the church into a fundamental challenge to social order in general.

In the record of Mistress Eaton's 1644 trial, the discussion of infant baptism occupies three pages, less than half the space consumed by the recital of her conflicts with other members of her household. Confrontations with her servants, her stepdaughter Mary, her mother-in-law Elizabeth, and her husband—but not, significantly, her own children by either marriage—formed the core of the elders' case against her. She was accused of having slapped her mother-in-law in the face twice at the dinner table; of having falsely implied that her unmarried stepdaughter was pregnant; of twice alleging witchcraft on the part of members of the household; of having made numerous unfounded complaints against her male and female servants; and of having told her husband she would be better off if he left the house. All these offenses, the church concluded, violated one or more of the Ten Commandments (primarily the Fifth, Sixth, and Ninth).[60]

The impression received from reading the charges is of a hot-tempered woman who lacked patience with her underlings, clashed repeatedly with her elderly mother-in-law, and detested her adult stepdaughter. But some of the grievances enumerated by the servants— that she had called one maid a liar and a thief, had termed two of them "wicked wretches," and had accused the black slave, Anthony, of ruining the beer—would hardly have been unusual in other households. The maids furthermore described their mistress's "unquietness with them" and their seeming inability "to give her content." These sorts of commonplace complaints from servants were usually ignored by masters, mistresses, neighbors, and justices of the peace alike. Yet in the context of the other allegations against Mistress Eaton, they were solemnly heard without questioning their validity.

One confrontation with her husband seems particularly significant. One morning, the story went, she criticized a male servant for not bringing water into the house, and complained to Theophilus about the servant's negligence. But Mr. Eaton failed to back up his wife: "he not seeing cause for it did not reproach the man according to her mind." With "much heat of Spirit," Mistress Anne then told her husband, "you and this man may go together," and (the elders added) "that desire of getting from her husband she has prosecuted importunately," which was "against the Covenant of Marriage." Behind this homely tale, which reported the escalation of what surely must have been an ordinary disagreement between husband and wife over household governance, appears to lie Mistress Eaton's intense frustration at her husband's failure to support her management of their large household, which at times included as many as thirty people. From the prominence of her mother-in-law in many of the charges, including four of those involving the servants, one suspects that Anne Eaton felt her authority continually undermined by Elizabeth Eaton's presence in her home and that Theophilus often sided with his mother in the event of conflicts.[61]

After all the tales were told, the congregation considered whether to excommunicate Mistress Eaton or merely to give her "public admonition." Mr. Davenport argued strongly for the latter option, contending that it was not yet clear whether the charges "could be proved to proceed from a habitual frame of sinning in her, so as that she may not be counted a visible saint." He also pointed out that some of her misdeeds were minor, not perhaps requiring the ultimate church penalty. Given the deep concern he had expressed about her behavior, it is highly likely that the clergyman initially sought no more than an admonition for two reasons: first, to avoid further embarrassing his friend Theophilus; and second, to try one last time to keep Anne Eaton in the church. The congregation followed his lead, and despite Mistress Eaton's last-minute request that "there might be no censure passed upon her," she was publicly rebuked and directed "to attend unto the several rules that you have broken, and to judge yourself by them, and to hold forth your repentance according to God."[62]

The congregation then waited for signs of reformation. Mistress Eaton submitted a written statement to the elders, but they deemed it inadequate. They insisted that she had to acknowledge the truth of the charges against her, repent fully of her sins, and reform her behavior to the satisfaction of those "that ordinarily conversed with her"—presumably, her husband, stepdaughter, and mother-in-law. Although she initially indicated that she would comply with the elders' instructions, months passed without any noticeable change in her behavior. Finally, Mr. Davenport reported, other churches in Connecticut and Massachusetts began to criticize the New Haven congregation for their failure to adopt "the last remedy" available to churches in such circumstances.

So the elders once again approached Anne Eaton in private to ask why her repentance was delayed. She reluctantly admitted that "she was not convinced of the breach of the Fifth Commandment, . . . for she did not acknowledge her husband's Mother to be her Mother." Faced with such an "obstinate" response, the elders threatened her with excommunication. Attempting to avoid this fate, she sent another written document to the elders, but this they deemed even more unsatisfactory than the first. Thus in May 1645 she was again called before the church. In two separate meetings the old charges were rehashed and five new ones added, four pertaining to her family relationships and one to the limited nature of her acknowledged repentance. The most important again involved Theophilus and his mother: "She charged Mr. Eaton, her husband, with breach of promise, in bringing his Mother into the house against her will, but it was proved it was with her consent." Just how that point was "proved" the record does not make clear, but once more it highlighted the theme of intergenerational conflict among the adult women in the Eaton household. Late in the month, at the end of the second meeting, Mistress Eaton was excommunicated. Henceforth, like other New Haven excommunicates, she must have been prevented from attending church services and forced to stand outside the door if she wished to hear the sermon.[63]

The 1649 excommunication trial of Ezekiel Cheever, one of the original leaders of the New Haven church, adds some useful information to the official record of Anne Eaton's dealings with the congregation. Testimony elicited in Cheever's trial revealed that at some point, probably following her admonition but prior to her excommunication, Mistress Eaton became frustrated with her interactions with the elders and asked to defend herself before the church as a whole. Some members of the congregation, including Cheever, regarded her request as reasonable. Accordingly, the elders proposed to allow her to speak to the church, but with the proviso that only her critics could respond to her in her presence. Not until she left the meeting were her defenders, like Cheever, to be permitted to express their views. Cheever recalled that "this did not satisfy Mrs. Eaton's desire, and therefore she accepted it not." When the church members then agreed that Anne Eaton would have to satisfy the elders prior to any appearance before the congregation, Cheever made the remark that ended up as one of the charges against him five years later. He grumbled to several men, "This I apprehended, was so to subject the Church to the Elders, that they had nothing to do in this case but to consent with the Elders, or to say Amen."[64]

Theophilus Eaton endured one last public embarrassment as a consequence of his wife's activities and her confrontation with John Davenport and the elders. In September 1646 he presided over a case in which the point at issue was a deposition drawn up for an illiterate woman by Richard Perry, the colony's secretary, who was the son-in-law of Mr. Richard Malbon. The testimony intended to be included in the deposition revealed that a woman named Susan (perhaps one of the Eatons' servants) had disclosed to several people that "Mrs. Eaton would not lye with her husband since she was admonished, but caused her bedd to be removed to another roome." Even more scandalous was Susan's assertion that Anne Eaton had "denyed conjugall fellowship" to Theophilus. Mr. Perry tried to suppress the most embarrassing part of the oral statement by writing only that Susan had reported that the Eatons "lay apart," thus omitting the reference to the cause of the difficulty and ignoring the consequences for the marriage. Confronted with sworn testimony exposing Perry's falsification of the deposition, Eaton and the other magistrates were forced to render judgment for Perry's accuser.[65]

The chain of events surrounding Anne Eaton's church trial demonstrates the intimate connection between her religious beliefs and behavior and her actions in her own household. In the minds of seventeenth-century New Englanders, Anabaptist ideas threatened the stability of family, state, and society as well as that of the church, and so such opinions had to be exterminated at all costs. Reasoning thus, in November 1644 (after Mistress Eaton had been admonished but prior to her excommunication) the Bay Colony formally banished all known Anabaptists, terming them "incendiaries of comon wealths."[66]

New Haven did not follow suit, but the presence of an Anabaptist in the household of New Haven's governor was an affront to order in the most fundamental sense, because that family was the model for every other household in the colony. If Anabaptism took root in the colony, other families might well experience the same discord. What if every New Haven wife refused to take religious instruction from her husband or pastor? Fought bitterly with her mother-in-law? Could not get along with her stepchildren or servants? Refused her husband "conjugall fellowship"? The possible consequences were alarming. The implication of Mistress Eaton's heretical religious beliefs, therefore, was at one with her misbehavior within the household: both threatened political and social order at its core. Her resistance to her husband's authority (in short, her insistence on being a fictive widow), along with her violations of the Fifth Commandment in her treatment of superiors and inferiors, lay at the heart of all the charges against her. In true Filmerian fashion, her religious, domestic, and political offenses were so entangled they could not be separated.

About a year after Mistress Eaton's excommunication, some time in early May 1646, she and three friends—Lucy Brewster, Mistress Moore, and Mistress Leach—gathered at Mistress Leach's house to gossip about recent events. Evidence suggests that they must have come together frequently in the same way, four high-ranking women meeting for casual, sociable conversations that ranged widely over a number of topics and incidents. They expressed their opinions to each other freely and without reserve, knowing that they (a church member, an excommunicate, and two nonmembers) generally concurred in their criticisms of the magistrates and the church. Such gatherings of female friends were commonplace, but this one received a remarkable amount of official attention because of the prominence of the participants and the explosive implications of the ideas they expressed. On June 2, Mistress Eaton's three friends were brought to trial, charged with "severall miscarriages of a publique nature."[67]

Just as Mistress Eaton's servants had been among her primary accusers in the excommunication proceedings, so too the chief witnesses in this secular prosecution were Mistress Leach's servants, Elizabeth Smith and Job Hall. Elizabeth, who at the time of the trial was visibly pregnant by her husband-to-be, deliberately recruited the other servant, Job, to eavesdrop with her on the women's conversation. She later told the court that she thought he could "better remember the perticulers of such a conference then herselfe." Mistress Brewster repeatedly referred to Elizabeth's pregnancy in an attempt to discredit her, calling her "slutt," "whore," and "harlott," and charging—probably with considerable accuracy—that Smith hoped "to currey favor to keepe her whores back from whipping." Edmund Leach, trying to impeach Elizabeth's damaging testimony, declared that she always "was of a crooked disposition, & apt to speake untruthes," but Hall had a good reputation. One witness commented that Mr. Leach had declared himself "satisfied with [Job's] service & carryadge," a statement that was not disputed.[68]

Job Hall seems to have been the first to report the incident in detail. While he was on an errand at the house of Mr. Richard Malbon, Mistress Malbon asked him "about the meeting at Mr. Leeches howse." Job later explained that "his owne sperit being then burdened, he had accounted it a call to speake what he had heard, though some doubts after returned." Those doubts led to his eventual conclusion that he had "sinned in reporting things out of the famyly but Mrs. Malbon had sinned more in drawing them [the facts] from him." He also tried to soften some of his original testimony, informing the judges that he "was somewhat doubtfull whether he heard the words from Mrs. Brewster herselfe, or only heard Elizabeth repeate them from Mrs. Brewster."[69]

Thus the women's conversation came to the magistrates' attention when Mistress Malbon, the wife of one of them, deliberately interrogated the Leaches' servant about the gathering, which had clearly already aroused some public speculation. After Job Hall and Elizabeth Smith had formally told their stories, Lucy Brewster was summoned to appear before the magistrates for a private hearing. The examination infuriated Mistress Brewster; she evidently went immediately afterwards to the Leaches' house, where she confronted the two servants. She loudly told Job that "shee had bin where she had justified herselfe agaynst a great manny of his lyes & added, she would have him & his slutt, you & your harlott, to the whipping post." She accused Elizabeth of telling "half truthes & halfe lyes." When Elizabeth retorted that "her half truthes will prove [to be] whole truthes," Mistress Brewster shouted at her, "you brasen facd whore."[70]

The conversation that worried Job Hall, occasioned the servants' tale-telling, and elicited deep concern from New Haven's magistrates had been sharply critical of both the Reverend John Davenport and the colony's political leaders. The women discussed two recent trials that would have occasioned a great deal of talk in other New Haven households as well. One was the prosecution for sexual misconduct of William Fancy, his wife, and Mark Meggs, which had taken place in mid-April. As will be recalled from the prologue to this section, Meggs and the fugitive Thomas Robinson attempted to commit adultery with Goody Fancy; the Fancys and Meggs were then publicly whipped. The outspoken Lucy Brewster (according to Elizabeth Smith) remarked that the criminals had been "cruelly whipped & that her son said he had rather fall into the hands of Turks, & hath rather be hanged then fall into their [the New Haven magistrates'] hands." The second trial was that of Thomas Fugill, formerly the colony's secretary. In March of that year, Fugill had been deprived of his position in disgrace after an inquiry revealed that he had falsified some of the colony's records. Fugill sub-sequently came to see Mistress Brewster, who openly sympathized with his claim of partial innocence and his charge that at least one of the accusations against him was groundless. She declared of the magistrates that "they goe two and two together, & writt down what scandelous persons say & soe hurrey them & compare their writeings, & if they find any contradictions they are chardged for lyes." In words reported by Job Hall, she then added, "I pray God keep me from them [the magistrates]."[71]

In her comments on these incidents, therefore, Mistress Brewster frontally challenged the magistrates' authority. She questioned the righ-teousness of their conduct with respect to Fugill, implying that they had deliberately entrapped him, and in the case of the sexual offenders lik-ened the magistrates' cruelty to that of the hated infidel Turks. Neither remark, obviously, recommended her to her judges.

The other topics of conversation that aroused the magistrates' con-cern related to religion, but they were of three different sorts. The first subject was a series of doctrinal disputes between the women and the Reverend Davenport and the elders; the second questioned the church's collective actions with respect to excommunicates; and the third per-tained to Mistress Eaton and her troubles with the New Haven congregation.

According to the testimony of both Smith and Hall, Mistress Moore, Mistress Leach, and Mistress Brewster all denounced some of Daven-port's doctrines. Part of the servants' testimony on this point related not only to the crucial conversation in early May, but also to remarks made by Mistress Moore and Mistress Leach at other times—for example, during family prayer. Several of the women's criticisms revolved around Mr. Davenport's assertions that only members of the New Haven church would be saved, and that clergymen had a special status in God's eyes, indeed that they should properly be regarded as the heirs of the angels. Mistress Moore in particular was skeptical of the latter contention, de-claring that "pastours & teachers are but the inventions of men." She compared New Haven to "the wildernesse of Sinai" and commented that "a vayle is before the eyes of min[i]sters and people in this place, & till that be taken away, they cannot be turned to the Lord." On one occasion, she reportedly prayed that no one in her family should "have any fellowshipp with them." Mistress Brewster was accused of having said that Davenport's ideas turned her stomach, making her "sermon sicke," and Mistress Leach with having asserted that she would not try to become a church member because there were too many liars in the church.[72]

Mistress Brewster also questioned the church's policy concerning excommunication. Elizabeth Smith charged that she spoke "in a scoffing manner" about the impending excommunication of a male church member, and Job Hall revealed that she had interested herself in the affairs of Edward Parker and the widow Potter, the local midwife. The widow, an excommunicate, wanted to marry Parker, a church member, but the elders had hitherto forbidden the marriage. Further complicating the issue was the fact that Parker had angered Mr. Malbon by accusing him of neglecting his duty as a magistrate. The couple had come several times to seek her advice, Lucy Brewster told her friends, revealing that she believed the church was seeking revenge against both by preventing the marriage. She advised Potter and Parker to present the magistrates with a fait accompli by simply declaring themselves to be married in front of witnesses—that is, adopting the English folk tradition—and remarked that a couple in the Bay Colony had dealt with a similar situation in just that way. When Potter and Parker joined those testifying against her on June 2, Mistress Brewster accused them (as she had Elizabeth Smith) of trying to "currey favor" with the authorities so that the widow could rejoin the church and they be allowed to marry. Indeed, after the magistrates had tried and fined Parker for defaming Mr. Malbon, the two were permitted to wed.[73]

Governor Eaton made a special point of informing Mistress Brewster that—with respect to her repeated discussions with the widow Potter about the marriage difficulties—"for her to eate, drinke, & to shew such respect to excommunicate persons did expressly crosse the rule." With that remark the governor disclosed how fine a line he and the other magistrates were walking in this prosecution, since the fourth, and seldom mentioned, participant in the conversation was none other than his own excommunicated wife. Only two remarks of Mistress Eaton's made it into the official trial record. She defended the congregation's practice of having members come forward publicly to donate money to the church, a custom criticized by Lucy Brewster, who compared it to "going to masse." She also commented that she had confessed her faults, "but not to the churches satisfaction." At one point the friends discussed Mistress Eaton's status. Lucy Brewster told Anne Eaton that

> they could not banish her but by a Gennerall Court, & if it came
> to that shee wished Mrs. Eaton to come to her & acquaynt her

with her judgment & grownds about baptizing, & she would by them seduce some other weoman, & then she, the said Mrs. Brewster would complayne to the court of Mrs. Eaton & the other weoman should complayne of her as being thus seduced, and soe they would be banished together & she spake of going to Road Island.

Mistress Brewster, admitting that she had said this, explained that "she spake it in jest & laughing." The magistrates were not amused: "she was told, foolish & uncomely jesting are sinfull, but to harden one agaynst the truth who already lyeth under guilt, may not passe under a pretence of jesting."[74]

Lucy Brewster was the only one of the three women who consistently disputed the servants' accounts of her words or tried to persuade the judges that her statements had been taken out of context or should not be taken seriously. Even so, after the testimony against her had been concluded and she was asked if she had any response, the clerk noted that "shee was full of speech" characterized by "boldnesse," and that "she seemed to chardge the court as if she could not be heard." Mistress Moore and her daughter were still more defiant. A church member who before the trial had advised Mistress Moore that, if she was troubled about doctrine, she should listen to the clergy, reported to the court that "she answered in a great rage, she would goe to none of them all for any truth of her salvation, she was as cleare as the sunne in the firmament." When he returned to speak to her again, she "would not heare him, giveinge only this answer, if she were in an error it was to herselfe, he had noe authorye to examine her about it." In court, she cited scriptures to support her positions, arguing about biblical exegesis with the judges. As for Mistress Leach, she "spake uncomly for her sex & age," and by "her carryadge offended the whole court."[75]

In behaving with such obstinance when confronting the colony's judicial authorities, the three women adopted the same defiant stance employed earlier by their friend Mistress Eaton in her contests with the church. She had been "contemptuous" of efforts to wean her away from Anabaptism, had refused to "object" or "yield" to arguments directed at her, had rejected all attempts to keep secret some of the charges against her, had tried to force the elders to bring her before the entire congregation, and had failed to respond positively to the initial admonition. Now her friends with equal adamance refused to repent for their slanderous statements: Lucy Brewster contested the servants' testimony, and Mistress Moore persisted in her criticisms of the church. The leaders of

New Haven were not accustomed to such obstreperous opposition to their authority, especially not from women. Accordingly, they fined the miscreants heavily and thereby seem to have successfully dissuaded them from subsequent outspokenness. At any rate, none of them appeared in court again under comparable circumstances.[76]

To what cause would contemporary observers have attributed this sort of defiance on the part of women? The response would have been obvious: none of the offenders was under the effective supervision of a male church member. Mistress Moore and Mistress Brewster were widows; and Edmund Leach, who consistently sided with his wife, never seems to have thought about joining the church, unlike her—who at least considered, but rejected, that option. Theophilus Eaton was a pious gentleman, but he, like the church, had completely lost control of his excommunicated wife. Seventeenth-century New Englanders would have concluded that without pious men to give them appropriate religious guidance, these headstrong women had gone seriously astray.

But even in light of their expression of unorthodox views, what had given the women's conversation its significance and led to the prosecution of three of the four participants? How had a visit by two women to the home of a female friend and her mother been transformed into an event of "a publique nature"? The answer to that question is twofold.

First, and fundamentally, the conversation was "publique" because it did not qualify as "private" by any contemporary definition of that term. As has been seen, political conversations among male heads of households, and even perhaps the contemptuous words of their sons, could be deemed private if those conversations occurred in their own families or in the homes of associates. But such rights of privacy accrued solely to men, and primarily to those who held positions that carried with them obligations to the people as a whole—to the public. Then their public and private roles could be separated, and the latter accorded some measure of protection from official scrutiny.

Women, especially those acting outside the purview of men, had no such privilege. All their words and actions were subject to supervision —if not by their husbands (if the men were ineffectual, compliant, or, in the case of widows, nonexistent), then by neighbors, the state, or the church. *Private* was, emphatically, a word irrelevant to women: it did not apply to them in any of its many guises. Appropriately, therefore, the gossiping women's defense did not include any claim of privacy; at no time did they contest the authorities' right to try them for their conversation by rejecting the notion that their statements had "publique" implications. Rather, they either questioned the specifics of the witnesses' testimony or directly confronted the judges on doctrinal issues. Thus Mistress Eaton's insistence upon dealing with the New Haven congregation as a whole, instead of with the elders "in private," in one sense merely expressed a preference for a mode of operation fully in accordance with the principles usually applied to women.

Second, the evidence presented at the trial demonstrated that Lucy Brewster in particular, as a prominent, high-ranking female church member, had become a focal point for discontent in the small colony. Both Thomas Fugill and Edward Parker had sought her out, asking for her advice and assistance as they contested the authorities' handling of their cases. Mistress Moore too presented New Haven's leaders with a frontal challenge. By openly criticizing the doctrines propounded by the Reverend John Davenport and through her ability to match scriptural references with citations of her own, but by still operating within a Puritan framework, she offered an alternative vision of religion that differed markedly from the one offered in the colony's church. She thus had the potential to become a locus of religious dissent nearly as dangerous as the Anabaptist Mistress Eaton herself.

Both Lucy Brewster and Mistress Moore, like Anne Eaton, achieved their status as menaces to social and political order in the eyes of New Haven's officialdom not simply because of their intelligence, their forcefulness, and their willingness to criticize the authorities openly. Rather, they significantly challenged the colony's leaders precisely because as high-ranking widows they, like male officials, had a claim to wielding gendered power: in the Filmerian schema, they were symbolic mothers who deserved deference from the colony's ordinary residents even though they held no political positions. Their power flowed simultaneously from their rank in the social hierarchy and from the worldview that informed their contemporaries' conceptualization of the society in which they all lived. The four gossiping women of New Haven thus demonstrated, by their actions and by the reaction to them, the extent to which high-status widows and fictive widows could contest masculine dominance in a Filmerian world.

GENDERED POWER
IN THE COMMUNITY

Searchers Againe Assembled

Those searchers being againe assembled . . . were againe
desirous to search the said Hall, and having searched him
. . . did then likewise find him to bee a man.
                                        —*John Atkins, 1629*[1]

O N APRIL 8, 1629, a person named Hall was brought before the
General Court of the colony of Virginia. Hall was not formally
charged with a crime, although witnesses alluded to a rumor about fornication. Yet Hall's case is one of the most remarkable to be found in
the court records of any colony. If no crime was involved, why was
Hall in court?

Hall had been reported to the authorities for one simple reason:
people were confused about Hall's sexual identity. At times Hall dressed
as a man; at other times, evidently, as a woman. What sex was this
person? other colonists wanted to know. The vigor with which they
pursued their concerns dramatically underscores the significance of gender distinctions in seventeenth-century Anglo-America. The case also
provides excellent illustrations of the powerful role the community could
play in individuals' lives and of the potential influence of ordinary folk,
both men and women, on the official actions of colonial governments.

The Hall case offers compelling insights into the process of defining
gender in early American society. Hall was an anomalous individual, and
focusing on such anomalies can help to expose fundamental belief systems. Since in this case sex was difficult to determine, so too was gender
identity. Persons of indeterminate sex, such as the subject of this discussion, pose perplexing questions for any society. The process through
which the culture categorizes these people is both complex and revealing. The analysis here will examine the ways in which seventeenth-
century Virginians attempted to come to grips with the problems
presented to them by a sexually ambiguous person.[2]

After narrating the story of the person known variously as Thomas or Thomasine Hall, this account will reflect on what that tale reveals about the role of gender divisions in the structure of community life in the Anglo–American colonies and about the relationship of the formal and informal publics to each other and to those gender distinctions. The concern is not so much with Hall's personal dilemma, but rather with other Virginians' reactions to this anomaly in their midst, this person who resisted being defined irrevocably by both sex and gender.[3]

Describing my usage of personal pronouns and names is essential to the analysis that follows. The other historians who have dealt with the case have referred to Hall as "Thomas" and "he," as do the court records (with one significant exception). Yet the details of the case, including Hall's testimony, make such usage problematic. Therefore the practice here shall be the following: when Hall is acting as a female, the name "Thomasine" and the pronoun "she" will be used. Conversely, when Hall is acting as a male, "Thomas" and "he" are just as obviously called for. In moments of ambiguity or generalization (as now) "Hall," or the simple initial "T" will be employed (the latter as an ungendered pronoun).

THOMASINE HALL WAS BORN "at or neere" the northeastern English city of Newcastle upon Tyne.[4] As the name suggests, Hall was christened and raised as a girl. At the age of twelve, Thomasine went to London to stay with her aunt, and she lived there for ten years. But in 1625 her brother was pressed into the army to serve in an expedition against Cadiz. Perhaps encouraged by her brother's experience (or perhaps taking his place after his death, for that expedition incurred many casualties), Hall subsequently adopted a new gender identity. Thomas told the court that he "Cut of[f] his heire and Changed his apparell into the fashion of man and went over as a souldier in the Isle of Ree being in the habit of a man."[5] Upon returning to Plymouth from army service in France, probably in the autumn of 1627, Hall resumed a feminine identity. Thomasine donned women's clothing and supported herself briefly by making "bone lace" and doing other needlework. That she did so suggests that Thomasine had been taught these valuable female skills by her aunt during her earlier sojourn in London.

Plymouth was one of the major points of embarkation for the American colonies, and Hall recounted that "shortly after" arriving in the city Thomasine learned that a ship was being made ready for a voyage to Virginia. Once again, Hall decided to become a man, so he put on men's clothing and sailed to the fledgling colony. Thomas was then approximately twenty-five years old, comparable in age to many of the immigrants to Virginia, and like most of his fellows he seems to have gone to the Chesapeake as an indentured servant.

By December, Hall was settled in Virginia, for on January 21, 1627/8, a man named Thomas Hall, living with John and Jane Tyos (T's master and mistress), was convicted along with them for receiving stolen goods from William Mills, a servant of one of their neighbors. According to the testimony, Hall and the Tyoses had encouraged Mills in a series of thefts that began before Christmas 1627. Some of the purloined items—which included tobacco, chickens, currants, a shirt, and several pairs of shoes—were still in the possession of Hall and the Tyoses at the time their house was searched by the authorities on January 14. Although Thomas Hall is a common name (indeed, John Tyos knew another Thomas Hall, who had arrived with him on the ship *Bona Nova* in 1620), a significant piece of evidence suggests that T and the man charged with this crime were one and the same. William Mills had difficulty carrying the currants, which he piled into his cap during his initial theft. Since that was clearly an unsatisfactory conveyance, when Mills was about to make a second foray after the desirable dried fruits he asked his accomplices to supply him with a better container. Thomas Hall testified that Jane Tyos then "did bring a napkin unto him and willed him to sowe it & make a bagg of it to carry currants." It is highly unlikely that an ordinary male servant would have had better seamstressing skills than his mistress, but Thomasine was an expert at such tasks.[6]

Although thus far in Hall's tale the chronology and the sequence of gender switches have been clear—for T specifically recounted the first part of the tale to the Virginia General Court, and the timing of the thefts and their prosecution is clearly described in court testimony—the next phase of the story must be pieced together from the muddled testimony of two witnesses and some logical surmises.

A key question not definitively answered in the records is: what happened to raise questions in people's minds about Hall's sexual identity? Two possibilities suggest themselves. One is that John and Jane Tyos, who obviously recognized that Hall had "feminine" skills shortly after T came to live with them, spoke of that fact to others, or perhaps visitors to their plantation observed Hall's activities and drew their own conclusions. Another possibility is that, after traveling to Virginia as a man, Hall reverted to the female clothing and role that T appears to have found more comfortable. The court records imply that Hall did choose to dress as a woman in Virginia, for Francis England, a witness, reported overhearing a conversation in which another man asked T directly: why do you wear women's clothing? T's reply—"I goe in weomans aparell to gett a bitt for my Catt"—is difficult to interpret and will be analyzed later. In any event, a Mr. Stacy (who cannot be further identified) seems to have first raised the issue of T's anomalous sexual character by asserting to other colonists that Hall was "as hee thought a man and woeman." Just when Mr. Stacy made this statement is not clear, but he probably voiced his opinion about a year after T arrived in the colony.[7]

In the aftermath of Mr. Stacy's statement, a significant incident occurred at the home of Nicholas Eyres, perhaps a relative of Robert Eyres, who had recently become John Tyos's partner. "Uppon [Mr Stacy's] report," three women—Alice Longe, Dorothy Rodes, and Barbara Hall—scrutinized Hall's body. Their action implied that T was at the time dressed as a woman, for women regularly searched other women's bodies (often at the direction of a court) to look for signs of illicit pregnancy or perhaps witchcraft. They never, however, performed the same function with respect to men—or anyone dressed like a man. Moreover, John Tyos both then and later told Dorothy Rodes that Hall was a woman. Even so, the female searchers, having examined Hall, declared that T was a man. As a result of the disagreement between Tyos and the women about T's sex, T was brought before the commander of the region, Captain Nathaniel Basse, for further examination.[8]

Questioned by Mr. Basse, T responded with a description of a unique anatomy with ambiguous physical characteristics. (The text of the testimony is mutilated, and the remaining fragments are too incomplete to provide a clear description of T's body.) Hall then refused to choose a gender identity, instead declaring that T was "both man and woeman." Captain Basse nevertheless decided that Hall was female and ordered T "to bee putt in weomans apparell"—thus implying that T was, at that moment at least, dressed as a man. The three women who had previously searched T's body were shaken by the official ruling that contradicted their own judgment; after being informed of the commander's decision, they reportedly "stood in doubte of what they had formerly affirmed."

John Tyos then sold Hall, now legally a maidservant named Thomasine, to John Atkins, who was present when Captain Basse questioned T. Atkins must have fully concurred with Mr. Basse's decision; surely he would not have purchased a female servant about whose sex he had any doubts. Yet on February 12, 1628/9, questions were again raised about T, for Alice Longe and her two friends went to Atkins's house to scrutinize Thomasine's body for a second time. They covertly examined her while she slept and once more decided that the servant was male. But Atkins, though summoned by the searchers to look at his maid's anatomy, was unable to do so, for Hall's "seeming to starre as if shee had beene awake" caused Atkins to leave without viewing her body.

The next Sunday, the three women returned with two additional female helpers.[9] On this occasion, the searchers had the active cooperation and participation of John Atkins, who ordered Thomasine to show her body to them. For a third time the women concluded that Hall was a man. Atkins thereupon ordered his servant to don men's clothing and informed Captain Basse of his decision.

By this time not only Hall but also everyone else was undoubtedly confused. Since Hall was now deemed to be male, the next curiosity-seekers to examine T's body were also male. One of them was Roger Rodes, probably the husband of Dorothy, who had joined in all the previous searches of Hall's body. Before forcefully throwing Thomas onto his back and checking his anatomy, Roger told Hall, "thou hast beene reported to be a woman and now thou art proved to bee a man, i will see what thou carriest." Like the female searchers before them, Roger and his associate Francis England concluded that T was male.

A rumor that Hall "did ly with a maid of Mr Richard Bennetts called greate Besse" must have added considerably to the uncertainty. Hall accused Alice Longe, one of the persistent female searchers, of spreading the tale. She denied the charge, blaming the slander instead on an unnamed male servant of John Tyos's. If the story was true, what did it imply about Hall's sexual identity? Whether Hall was male or female would obviously have a bearing on the interpretation of any relationship with Bennett's maid Bess. Clearly, Virginians now had reason to seek a firm resolution of the conflict. Since Captain Basse, the local commander, had been unable to find an acceptable solution, there was just one remaining alternative—referring the dilemma to the General Court.[10]

That court, composed of the governor and council, was the highest judicial authority in the small colony. The judges heard from Hall and considered the sworn depositions of two male witnesses (Francis England and John Atkins), who described the events just outlined. Remarkably, the court accepted T's own self-definition and, although using the male personal pronoun, declared that Hall was "a man and a woeman, that all the Inhabitants there may take notice thereof and that hee shall goe Clothed in mans apparell, only his head to bee attired in a Coyfe and Crosecloth wth an Apron before him." Ordering Hall to post bond for good behavior until formally released from that obligation, the court also told Captain Basse to see that its directives were carried out. Since most court records for subsequent years have been lost (they were burned during the Civil War), it is impossible to trace Hall's story further.[11]

WHAT CAN THIS TALE REVEAL about gender definitions and the role of the community in the formative years of American society? Six different but related issues emerge from the analysis of Hall's case.

First, the relationship of sexual characteristics and gender identity. All those who examined T, be they male or female, insisted T was male. Thus T's external sex organs resembled male genitals. Roger Rodes and Francis England, for example, pronounced Thomas "a perfect man" after they had "pulled out his members." Still, T informed Captain Basse "hee had not the use of the mans parte" and told John Atkins that "I have a peece of an hole" (a vulva). Since T was identified as a girl at birth, christened Thomasine, and raised accordingly, T probably fell into that category of human beings who appear female in infancy but at puberty develop what seem to be male genitalia. Such individuals were the subjects of many stories in early modern Europe, the most famous of which involved a French peasant girl, Marie, who suddenly developed male sex organs while chasing pigs when she was fifteen, and who in adulthood became a shepherd named Germain. It is not clear whether early Virginians were aware of such tales, but if they understood contemporary explanations of sexual difference, the narrative of Marie-Germain would not have surprised them. Women were viewed as inferior types of men, and their sexual organs were regarded as internal versions of male genitalia. In the best scientific understanding of the day, there was just one sex, and under certain circumstances women could turn into men.[12]

What, then, in the eyes of Virginia's English residents, constituted sufficient evidence of sexual identity? For the male and female searchers of T's body, genitalia that appeared to be normally masculine provided the answer. But that was not the only possible contemporary response to the question. Leaving aside for the moment the persons who saw T as a combination of male and female (they will be considered later), it is useful to focus on those who at different times indicated that they thought T was female. There were three such individuals, all of them men: Captain Nathaniel Basse, who ordered T to wear women's clothing after T had appeared before him; John Atkins, T's second master, who purchased Thomasine as a maidservant and referred to T as "shee" before bowing to the contrary opinion of the female searchers and changing the pronoun to "him"; and, most important of all, T's first master, John Tyos.

It is not clear from the trial record why Captain Basse directed T to dress as a woman, for T asserted a dual sexual identity in response to questioning and never claimed to be exclusively female. Perhaps the crucial fact was T's admission that "hee had not the use of the mans parte." Another possibility was that Mr. Basse interpreted T's anatomy as insufficiently masculine. As was already indicated, the partial physical description of T included in this portion of the record survives only in fragmentary form and so is impossible to interpret, especially in light of the certainty of all the searchers.

John Atkins acquired T as a servant after Captain Basse had issued his order, and he at first accepted Thomasine as a woman, referring to how "shee" seemed to awaken from sleep. Yet Atkins changed his mind about his servant after he and the five women subjected T's body to the most thorough examination described in the case record. It involved a physical search by the women, then questioning by Atkins, followed by an order from Atkins to Hall to "lye on his backe and shew" the "peece of an hole" that T claimed to have. When the women "did againe finde him to bee a man," Atkins issued the directive that contradicted Captain Basse's, ordering T to put on men's clothes. For Atkins, Hall's anatomy (which he saw with his own eyes) and the women's testimony were together decisive in overriding his initial belief that T was female, a belief presumably based at least in part on his presence at Mr. Basse's interrogation of T.

Unlike Atkins, John Tyos had purchased T as Thomas—a man. And for him the interpretive process was reversed. After just a brief acquaintance with Thomas, John and his wife learned that he had female skills. Approximately a year later Tyos "swore" to Dorothy Rodes that Hall "was a woman," a conclusion that contradicted the opinion of the female searchers. It also seemingly flew in the face of what must have been his own intimate knowledge of Hall's physical being. The lack of space in the small houses of the seventeenth-century Chesapeake is well known to scholars.[13] It is difficult to imagine that Tyos had never seen Hall's naked body—the same body that convinced searchers of both sexes that T was male. So why would Tyos insist that T was Thomasine, even to Dorothy Rodes, who forcefully asserted the contrary? The answer must lie not in T's sexual organs but in T's gender—that is, in the feminine skills and mannerisms that would have been exhibited by a person born, raised, and living as a female until reaching the age of twenty-two, and which would have been immediately evident to anyone who, like John Tyos, lived with T for any length of time.

Thus, for these colonists, sex had two possible determinants. One was physical: the nature of one's genitalia. The other was cultural: the character of one's knowledge and one's manner of behaving. The female and male searchers used the former criterion, John Tyos, the latter. John Atkins initially adopted the second approach, but later switched to the first. Nathaniel Basse may have agreed with Tyos, or he may have refused to interpret T's anatomy as unambiguously as did the searchers: it is not clear which. But it is clear that two quite distinct tests of sexual identity existed in tandem in early Virginia. One relied on physical characteristics, the other on learned, gendered behavior. On most occasions, of course, results of the two tests would accord with each other. Persons raised as females would physically appear to be females; persons raised as males would look like other males. Hall acted like a woman and physically resembled a man. Thus in T's case the results of the two independent criteria clashed, and that was the source of the confusion.

Second, the importance of clothing. Many of the key questions about Hall were couched in terms of what clothing T should wear, men's or women's. Captain Basse and John Atkins did not say to T, "you are a man," or "you are a woman," but instead issued instructions about what sort of apparel T was to put on. Likewise, although the General Court declared explicitly that Hall was both male and female, its decision also described the clothing T was to wear in specific detail. Why was clothing so important?

The answer lies in the fact that in the seventeenth century clothing was a crucial identifier of persons. Not only did males and females wear very different garb, but persons of different ranks also were expected to reveal their social status in their dress. In short, one was supposed to display visually one's sex and rank to everyone else in the society. Thus, ideally, new acquaintances would know how to categorize each other even before exchanging a word of greeting. In a fundamental sense, seventeenth-century people's identity was expressed in their apparel. Virginia never went so far as Massachusetts, which passed laws regulating what clothing people of different ranks could wear, but the Virginia colonists were clearly determined to uphold the same sorts of rules.[14]

Clothing, which was sharply distinguished by the sex of its wearer, served as a visual trope for gender. And gender was one of the two most basic determinants of role in the early modern world (the other was rank, which was never at issue in Hall's case—T was always a servant). People who wore skirts nurtured children; people who wore pants did not. People who wore aprons could take no role in governing the colony, whereas other people could, if they were of appropriate status. People who wore headdresses performed certain sorts of jobs in the household; people who wore hats did other types of jobs in the fields. It is hardly surprising, therefore, that Virginians had difficulty dealing with a person who sometimes dressed as a man and other times as a woman—and who, on different occasions, did both at the direction of superiors. Nor, in light of this context, is it surprising that decisions about T's sexual identity were stated in terms of clothing.[15]

Third, the absence of a sense of personal privacy throughout the proceedings. To a modern sensibility, two aspects of the case stand out. First, seventeenth-century Virginians appear to have had few hesitations about their right to examine the genitalia of another colonist, with or without official authorization from a court and regardless of whether that activity occurred forcibly, clandestinely, or openly. The physical examinations were nominally by same-sex individuals (women when T was thought to be female, men when T had been declared to be male), with one key exception: John Atkins joined the women in scrutinizing the body of his maidservant. A master's authority over the household, in other words, extended to the bodies of his dependents. If a master like Atkins chose to search the body of a subordinate of either sex, no barrier would stand in his way.[16]

Second, Hall seems not to have objected to any of the intrusive searches of T's body nor to the intimate questioning to which T was subjected by Captain Basse and the General Court. Hall too appears to have assumed that T's sexual identity was a matter of concern for the community at large. Such an attitude on Hall's part was congruent with a society in which the existing minimal privacy rights were seen as accruing to households as a unit or perhaps to their heads alone. Subordinates like Hall neither expected nor received any right to privacy of any sort.

Fourth, the involvement of the community, especially women, in the process of determining sexual identity. One of the most significant aspects of Hall's story is the initiative taken throughout by Hall's fellow colonists. They not only brought their doubts about Hall's sex to the attention of the authorities, they also refused to accept Captain Basse's determination that Hall was female. Both men and women joined in the effort to convince Virginia's leaders that T was male. Nearly uniformly rejecting T's self-characterization as "both" (the only exception outside the General Court being Mr. Stacy), Virginians insisted that Hall had to be either female or male, with most favoring the latter definition. They wanted a sexual category into which to fit T, and they did not hesitate to express their opinions about which category was the more appropriate.

Women in particular were active in this regard. Three times groups of women scrutinized T's body, whereas a group of men did so only once. After each examination, women rejected T as one of their number. Because of the vigorous and persistent efforts of female Virginians, Hall was deprived of the possibility of adopting unambiguously the role with which T seemed most comfortable, that of Thomasine. Here Hall's physical characteristics determined the outcome. Accustomed to searching the bodies of other females, women thought T did not physically qualify as feminine—regardless of the gendered skills T possessed— and they repeatedly asserted that to any man who would listen. For them, T's anatomy (sex) was more important than T's feminine qualities (gender).

Male opinion, on the other hand, was divided. The three male searchers of T's body—Roger Rodes, Francis England, and John Atkins—agreed with the women's conclusion. Other men were not so sure. John Tyos and Nathaniel Basse thought T more appropriately classified as a woman, while Mr. Stacy and the members of the General Court said T displayed aspects of both sexes. It seems plausible to infer from their lack of agreement about T's sex that men as a group were not entirely certain about what criteria to apply to create the categories "male" and "female." Some relied on physical appearance, others on behavior.

Moreover, the complacency of the male searchers can be interpreted as quite remarkable. They failed to police the boundaries of their sex with the same militance as did women. That T, if a man, was a very unusual sort of man indeed did not seem to bother Rodes, Atkins, and England. For them, T's physical resemblance to other men was adequate evidence of masculinity, despite their knowledge of T's feminine skills and occasional feminine dress. That opinion was, however, in the end overridden by the doubts of higher-ranking men on the General Court, who were not so willing to overlook T's peculiarities.

Fifth, the relationship among sex, gender, and sexuality. Twice, and in quite different ways, the case record raises issues of sexuality rather than of biological sex or of gendered behavior. Both references have been alluded to briefly: the rumor of Thomas's having committed fornication with "great Besse," and T's explanation for wearing women's clothing—"to gett a bitt for my Catt."

A judgment about T's body would imply a judgment about T's sexuality as well. Yet was it possible to reach a definitive conclusion about T's sexuality? If T were Thomas, then he could potentially be guilty of fornicating with the maidservant Bess; if T were Thomasine, then being in the same bed with Bess might mean nothing—or it could imply "unnatural" acts, the sort of same-sex coupling universally condemned when it occurred between men. The rumor about Bess, which for an ordinary male servant might have led to a fistfight (with the supposed slanderer, Tyos's servant), a defamation suit, or a fornication presentment, thus raised perplexing questions because of T's ambiguous sexual identity, questions that had to be resolved in court.[17]

T's phrase "to gett a bitt for my Catt," as reported by Francis England, was even more troubling. What did it mean, and was that meaning evident to England and the members of the General Court? As an explanation for wearing female apparel, it could have been straightforward and innocent. One historian reads it literally, as indicating that Hall wore women's clothing to beg scraps for a pet cat. Hall might also have been saying that because T's skills were feminine, dressing as a woman was the best way for T to earn a living, "to get a bit (morsel) to eat." But some scholars have read erotic connotations into the statement. Could T, speaking as a man, have been saying that wearing women's clothing allowed T to get close to women, to—in modern slang—"get a piece of pussy" by masquerading as a female?[18]

There is another more likely and even more intriguing erotic possibility. Since Hall had served in the English army on an expedition to France, T could well have learned a contemporary French slang phrase —"pour avoir une bite pour mon chat"—or, crudely put in English, "to get a penis for my cunt." Translating the key words literally into English equivalents (bite=bit, chat=cat) rather than into their metaphorical meanings produced an answer that was probably as opaque and confusing to seventeenth-century Virginians as it has proved to be to subsequent historians.[19] Since much of Francis England's testimony (with the exception of his report of this statement and the account of his and Roger Rodes's examination of T's anatomy) duplicated John Atkins's deposition, England could have been called as a witness primarily to repeat such a mysterious conversation to the court.

If T was indeed employing a deliberately misleading Anglicized version of contemporary French slang, as appears probable, two conclusions are warranted. First, the response confirms T's predominantly feminine gender, for it describes sexual intercourse from a woman's perspective. In light of the shortage of women in early Virginia, it moreover would have accurately represented T's experience: donning women's garb unquestionably opened sexual possibilities to Thomasine that Thomas lacked. Second, at the same time, Hall was playing with T's listeners, answering the question about wearing women's apparel truthfully, but in such an obscure way that it was unlikely anyone would comprehend T's meaning. In other words, Hall was having a private joke at the expense of the formal and informal publics in the colony. Hall's sly reply thus discloses a mischievous aspect of T's character otherwise hidden by the flat prose of the legal record.

Sixth, the court's decision. At first glance, the most surprising aspect of the case is the General Court's acceptance of Hall's self-definition as both man and woman. By specifying that T's basic apparel should be masculine, but with feminine signs—the apron and the coif and cross-cloth, a headdress commonly worn by women at the time—Virginia officials formally recognized that Hall contained elements of both sexes. The elite men who sat as judges thereby demonstrated their ability to transcend the dichotomous sexual categories that determined the thinking of ordinary Virginians. But their superficially astonishing verdict becomes explicable when the judges' options are analyzed in terms of contemporary understandings of sex and gender.

First, consider T's sexual identity. Could the court have declared Hall to be female? That alternative was effectively foreclosed. Women had repeatedly scrutinized T's anatomy and had consistently concluded that T was male. Their initial determination that T was a man (in the wake of Mr. Stacy's comment that T was both) first brought the question before Captain Basse. Subsequently, their adamant rejection of Captain Basse's contrary opinion and their ability to convince John Atkins that they were correct, coupled with the similar assessment reached by two men, were the key elements forcing the General Court to consider the case. A small community could not tolerate a situation in which groups of men and women alternately stripped and searched the body of one of its residents, or in which the decisions of the local commander were so openly disobeyed. Declaring T to be female was impossible; ordinary Virginians of both sexes would not accept such a verdict.

Yet, at the same time, could anyone assert unconditionally that Hall was sexually a man? Francis England, Roger Rodes, John Atkins, and the five female searchers thought so, on the basis of anatomy; but John Tyos, who was probably better acquainted with T than anyone else, declared unequivocally that Hall was a woman. And T had testified about not having "the use of the mans parte." Hall, in other words, revealed that although T had what appeared to be male genitalia, T did not function sexually as a man and presumably could not have an erection. To Captain Basse and the members of the General Court, that meant that (whatever T's physical description) Hall would not be able to father children or be a proper husband to a wife.

As was observed in chapter one, the ability to impregnate a woman was a key indicator of manhood in seventeenth-century Anglo-America. Childless men were the objects of gossip, and impotence served as adequate grounds for divorce. A person who could not father a child was by that criterion alone an unsatisfactory male. T had admitted being incapable of male orgasm. Given that admitted physical incapacity and its implications, declaring Hall to be a man was as impossible as declaring T to be a woman.[20]

Second, consider T's gender identity. In seventeenth-century Anglo-America, as in all other known societies, sexual characteristics carried with them gendered consequences. In Hall's life history those consequences were especially evident, because what T did and how T did it were deeply affected by whether T chose to be Thomas or Thomasine.

Whenever Hall traveled far from home, to France in the army or to Virginia, T became Thomas. Men had much more freedom of movement than did women. Unlike other persons raised as females, Hall's unusual anatomy gave T the opportunity to live as a male when there was an advantage to doing so. Even though T seemed more comfortable being Thomasine—to judge by frequent reversions to that role—the option of becoming Thomas must have been a welcome one. It permitted Hall to escape the normal strictures that governed early modern English women's lives and allowed T to pursue a more adventurous lifestyle.[21]

Thus whether T chose to be male or female made a great difference in T's life. As Thomas, Hall joined the army and emigrated to the colonies; as Thomasine, Hall lived quietly in London with an aunt, did fancy needlework in Plymouth, and presumably performed tasks normally assigned to women in Virginia. T's most highly developed skills were feminine ones, so T was undoubtedly more expert at and familiar with "women's work" in general, not just seamstressing.

It was, indeed, Hall's feminine skills that convinced some men that T was female; and those qualities, coupled with Hall's physical appearance, must have combined to lead to the court's decision. T's gender was feminine but T's sex seemed to be masculine—with the crucial exception of sexual functioning. Given T's sexual incapacity, all indications pointed to a feminine identity—to Thomasine. But Virginia women's refusal to accept T as Thomasine precluded that verdict. On the other hand, the judges could not declare a person to be male who had admitted to Captain Basse an inability to consummate a marriage.

Ordinary men might possibly make a decision on the basis of physical appearance alone, but the members of the General Court had a responsibility to maintain the wider social order. If they said Hall was a man, then Thomas theoretically could marry and become a household head once his term of service was complete. That alternative was simply not acceptable for a person of T's description.

So, considering sex (incompletely masculine) and gender (primarily feminine), the Virginia General Court's solution to the dilemma posed by Hall was to create a unique category that combined sex and gender for T alone. Unable to fit Hall into the standard male/female dichotomy, the judges preferred to develop a singular definition that enshrined T's dual identity by prescribing clothing that simultaneously carried conflicting messages.

The court's decision to make Hall unique in terms of clothing— and thus gender identity—did not assist the community in classifying or dealing with T. After the verdict, Virginians were forced to cope with someone who by official sanction straddled the dichotomous roles of male and female. By court order, Hall was now a dual-sexed person. T's identity had no counterpart or precedent; paradoxically, a society in which gender—the outward manifestation of sex—served as a fundamental dividing line had formally designated a person as belonging to both sexes. Yet at the same time it was precisely because gender was so basic a concern to seventeenth-century society that no other solution was possible.

Hall's life after the court verdict must have been lonely. Marked as T was by unique clothing, unable to adopt the gender switches that had previously given T unparalleled flexibility in choosing a way of life, Hall must have had a very difficult time. T, like other publicly marked deviants—persons branded for theft or adultery or mutilated for perjury or forgery—was perhaps the target of insults or assaults. The verdict in T's case, in its insistence that T be constantly clothed as *both* sexes rather than alternating between them, was therefore harsh, though it nominally accorded with T's own self-definition. Hall's identity as "both" allowed movement back and forth across gender lines. The court's verdict had quite a different meaning, insisting not on the either/or sexual ambiguity T had employed to such great advantage, but rather on a definition of "both" that required duality and allowed for no flexibility.

It is essential to re-emphasize here what necessitated this unusual ending to a remarkable case: the opinions and actions of the female neighbors of John Tyos and John Atkins. Captain Nathaniel Basse, confronted with basically the same information that the General Court later considered, concluded that Hall should be dressed and treated as a woman. In a sexual belief system that hypothesized that women were inferior men, any inferior man—that is, one who could not function adequately in sexual terms—was a woman. Thus, charged the women at an Accomack cow pen in 1637, John Waltham "hade his Mounthly Courses as Women have" because his wife had not become pregnant.[22] Undoubtedly the General Court's first impulse would have been the same as Captain Basse's: to declare that T, an inferior man, was female and should wear women's clothing. But Virginia women had already demonstrated forcefully that they would not accept such a verdict. Hall's fate therefore was determined as much by a decision reached by ordinary women as it was by a verdict formally rendered by the elite men who served on the General Court.

No CONTEMPORARY THEORY could explain what happened in Virginia in the case of T Hall. Whereas people could easily explicate the dysfunctional Pinion clan by referring to the failings of its head, the way in which Virginians arrived at their solution to the dilemma posed for them by Hall would have been as unfathomable to contemporary observers as was T's phrase "to get a bitt for my Catt." As was indicated in the introduction to this volume, seventeenth-century theories of social interaction were hierarchical, excluding from their fundamental conceptualization any possibility that inferiors might influence superiors. Those theories also tended to assume the existence of a wholly male community. Such a hierarchically organized and male-dominated view of society was utterly inadequate to elucidate the process through which Virginians, justices and people alike, reached their verdict on T Hall.

The dynamics of the case thus exposed the shortcomings of the seventeenth-century theoretical understanding of interactions within the informal public. Few thinkers addressed the subject systematically, and those who did took an approach that blinded them to social realities.

At the outset, contemporary comments about the composition of the community overlooked the possibility that women might participate independently in the development of collective norms and values. Such words as "inhabitants" and "persons" and such phrases as "all residing in the collonie" were employed as the equivalents of "male inhabitants," "men," or "male residents" rather than being used in sexually inclusive ways. For example, in 1637, Governor John Winthrop asserted that "all the godly of this common-wealth" had agreed to a new law, when of course no women had done so; and both the Bay Colony legal codes adopted in the 1640s declared that "all persons" aged twenty-one and over could make wills, even though the legislators understood that under the common law married women (that is, the vast majority of females over twenty-one) were not comprised in the superficially all-inclusive language.[23]

In 1644 Winthrop defended such usage by arguing that "an universall affirmative proposition may be true, though it comprehend not every partic[ular], as when we saye All the Country was Rated to such a charge, no man will conceive that everye person and everye woman, etc, was rated." In the course of advancing his contention, Winthrop therefore not only admitted that women were not included in such phrases as "All the Country," he also revealed that they were not comprehended by the word "person" either: "everye person" and "everye woman" were two different groups of individuals. Such exclusionary ways of conceptualizing and describing the community offered women no theoretical space in which to participate in collective decision-making.[24]

The problems that began with such a limited conception of the number of social actors continued with a focus on hierarchy as the only acceptable basis for community interaction. John Winthrop's famous formulation in "A Modell of Christian Charity" that "some must be rich some poore, some highe and eminent in power and dignitie, others meane and in subjeccion" expressed the consensus. God's plan, Winthrop went on to explain, involved different roles and responsibilities for rich and poor, rulers and ruled. Leaders should show "theire love mercy, gentlenes, temperance" while inferior members of society should exhibit "faithe patience, obedience." The system was designed so that "the riche and mighty should not eate upp the poore, nor the poore, and dispised rise upp against theire superiours, and shake off theire yoake," because God wanted to ensure that his people were "all knitt more nearly together in the Bond of brotherly affeccion."[25]

One of the fullest contemporary explications of how such a social system should work was produced early in the century by the English Puritan cleric William Perkins, who utilized a common metaphor to begin his discussion. "In mans body there be sundry parts and members, and every one hath his severall use and office," Perkins declared; "the office of the eye, is to see, of the eare to heare, and the foote to goe." Since "all societies of men, are bodies," it followed that "in every society one person shall bee above or under another; not making all equall, as though the bodie should bee all head and nothing else." Those assigned a "meane place & calling" by God should not complain, Perkins observed, for "by performance of poore and base duties they serve God," and God would reward them for that service.[26]

As a result of their emphasis on the importance of social differentiation for the creation of a viable community, the colonists worried about the relative absence from their ranks of "persons of special eminency" —in other words, the sorts of men who in England would automatically have been expected to lead such enterprises. Early New Englanders corresponded with high-status acquaintances back home, trying to recruit them with a multitude of tempting arguments. By emigrating to North America, the settlers wrote, high-ranking men would simultaneously "advanc their owne estates," work "for the honor & benefit of old England," and find themselves truly appreciated by "this poor commonwealth." When the Lady Arbella Johnson, daughter of the Earl of Lincoln, and her husband died during that first difficult winter at Boston, a barely literate colonist accordingly lamented the loss of "the cheiffeste man of estate in the land and on[e] that woold a don moste good."[27]

Yet while universally stressing interaction based on status differences, the colonies' founders did understand on one level that, if the fragile settlements were to survive, English people in America would have to cooperate with each other in more egalitarian ways than the theory allowed. So the Reverend John Robinson, the spiritual leader of the Pilgrims (who did not himself emigrate), advised the Plymouth migrants, "Let every man repress in himself and the whole body in each person, as so many rebels against the common good, all private respects of men's selves, not sorting with the general conveniency." So too John Winthrop told the first Massachusetts Bay settlers, "wee must delight in eache other; make each other's Condicions our owne; rejoyce together, mourne together, labour, and suffer together, allwayes haveing before our eyes our Commission and Community in the worke, our Community as members of the same body."[28]

But how could such a laudable and essential goal be accomplished? Contemporary theory provided no guidance to men or women for egalitarian dealings with one another; it outlined duties to superiors and inferiors in great detail, but said little if anything about relationships with relative equals. Colonial laws were no help; only one early statute, a provision of the first Plymouth Colony code in 1636, formally attempted to prevent "all such misdemeanors of any person or persons as tend to the hurt & detriment of society Civility peace & neighborhood." Even in the absence of statutory authority, some of the colonies eventually prosecuted those kinds of misdemeanors, but the lack of legislation suggests that legislators did not see peer-group interaction as a pressing issue, or at least not one on a par with familial disorder or ensuring obedience to political edicts.[29]

Virginia did try to enlist neighbors in the process of enforcing laws. The same burgesses who compensated for the lack of administrative infrastructure in the colony by assigning many new duties to household heads did the same for neighbors as well. For example, the laws limiting tobacco plantings ordered men to have their fields viewed by a neighbor to attest that only the proper number of seedlings had been planted, and statutes to prevent the illegal killing of hogs required that men show the ears of dead hogs to neighbors. Neighbors were also seen as the first line of defense against fraud in the reporting of tithables and as the appropriate mediators of boundary disputes. In other colonies as well, neighbors made occasional appearances in laws and court orders; for example, in 1666 a Maine county court directed any man whose crops had been damaged by "unruly Mayres & horses" to enlist "seaven of the Neighbours" to appraise his losses, which would then be tripled and assessed as a fine on the horses' owner.[30]

Such statutes outlined but did not always distinguish two possible roles for neighbors. In one capacity, neighbors were viewed as potential spies and informers (in reporting illegal hog killing or undercounts of tithable workers); in the other, they served as expounders of a collective voice (by appraising losses or settling disputes). The latter appeared unobjectionable, but in 1664 Lord Baltimore, the proprietor of Maryland, pointed out the problems with the first. Miscreants could not be identified, he argued, "without either encouraging servants to inform against their Masters, or next Neighbours one against another, both which wilbe odious and dangerous for perjury and setting families in combustion both within themselves, and one against another." Consequently, he thought the tactic counterproductive, and perhaps for that reason Maryland never adopted it.[31]

But even if men did not cause "combustion" by informing on their neighbors for killing hogs or planting too many tobacco seedlings, the harmony termed "good neighborhood" was not always easy to produce, as shall be seen in the two chapters that follow. And the desire for consensus in the informal public went far beyond the physical boundaries of neighborhoods. Social ideals in both the Chesapeake and New England, but especially the latter, valued collectivities and scorned individual resistance to shared judgments. Consequently, dissidence that could not be readily resolved became a matter of considerable public concern.

Thus it was that the failure of communal dispute resolution processes in the cases of Mistress Anne Eaton and Mistress Ann Hibbens was particularly notable. Neither Eaton nor Hibbens was willing to bow to a collective judgment that differed from her own. The sustained independence of behavior and mind they exhibited was frowned upon; the key to reconciling differences among persons of roughly equal rank, the colonists soon learned, was the willingness of all parties to submit to a consensus defined by the community at large. If, like Hibbens and Eaton, the individuals concerned would not concur in the general will, the only remaining option was to cast them out of the community—which led, for the two women, to excommunication.

But why were Ann Hibbens and Anne Eaton unwilling to accept the judgment of other settlers that they were in the wrong? The answer to that question lies in gender difference. The community of peers, such as it was, was conceptualized as male. Men (especially high-ranking men) were carefully taught the rules of conformity and consensus. But women, who were not seen as part of the community in the same way as men —because each woman was always supposed to be subject to a man who would control her—had little exposure to the unwritten rules governing men's behavior. This was particularly true of high-status women like Mistress Hibbens and Mistress Eaton, who were accustomed to commanding others, rather than listening to them and acceding to their judgment. In contexts outside the family, in other words, and especially in circumstances in which peer rather than hierarchical interactions were at issue, women could find themselves in situations in which it was difficult to discern an appropriate course of action.

Yet at the same time it was precisely in that sort of context (within the informal public, in short) that women, as was demonstrated by the Hall case, could influence collective actions and even affect the formal decision-making process. Women acting independently in the community faced both dangers and opportunities: dangers, because more frequently than men they encountered difficulties in interacting with social peers, as opposed to superiors or inferiors; and opportunities, because in the wider community they were not constrained by their menfolk or by the law as they were within their own households. Thus women's participation in the informal public, while potentially effective, was frequently problematic, raising many questions about the wielding of gendered power.

THE TWO CHAPTERS in this section examine gendered power in two different community settings: chapter four analyzes same-sex groups, and chapter five looks at neighborhood interactions, often among persons of the opposite sex. Both chapters are concerned with exposing the behavioral norms for men and women, and with understanding the rules of nonhierarchical associations—the sorts of groupings that, under familial theories, should not have existed at all, but which nevertheless played a vital role in the colonists' daily lives.

CHAPTER 4

Communities of Men, Communities of Women

We hope it shall be found that we are not the men as we are censured to be . . . if we be true to that which is just and right or not repugnant to the lawful authority, nor injurious to our neighbors.

—*William Fuller and others, 1654/5*[1]

The honord Magistrates and many men more can speake but by hearesay; wee and many more of us can speake by experience [of the midwife Mistress Alice Tilly].

—*26 Boston women, c. 1649*[2]

CRISES IN TWO of the communities of men and women that comprised the colonial population elicited the statements quoted above. The first derived from a heated political dispute in Maryland, the second from a gendered conflict between the women of the Boston area and the Massachusetts Bay General Court. It is appropriate that the men's statement pertained to formal politics (a masculine preserve) and the women's to midwifery (a feminine prerogative), because the separate communities of men and women in the early colonies revolved around just such divisions. To men belonged the world of politics and business, for they were legally the heads of households and the components of the polity; to women belonged the world of reproduction, sexuality, and childbirth, epitomized in the person of skilled midwives like Mistress Tilly.

The Maryland crisis, which ended in a pitched battle between William Fuller and his associates, on the one hand, and William Stone and his followers, on the other, was precipitated by contention over who should properly be regarded as governor of the colony. In the mid-1650s,

William Fuller held authority from commissioners dispatched by Parliament to ensure that Maryland and Virginia were loyal to the Lord Protector of England, Oliver Cromwell, rather than to the Stuart monarchy. Stone, Lord Baltimore's governor, who had been removed from office by the commissioners, received word in January 1654/5 that Cromwell had confirmed the Lord Proprietor's title to Maryland. He accordingly set out to reclaim the leadership of the province from Fuller, a project that ended in disaster as Stone's men were defeated at the Battle of the Severn in late March 1655. Four of Stone's allies were subsequently executed, and he and five other leaders of his forces were saved from a similar fate only by the intervention of the wives of the victorious soldiers.[3]

The details of the dispute are less significant here than are the male combatants' perceptions of their proper collective role. The statement of William Fuller and his political associates reveals common patterns of men's thinking: they spoke of being "true to that which is just and right" and not "repugnant to lawful authority" or "injurious to our neighbors." That summarized neatly the goals of men's interactions with other men: ideally, men would obey the law, hurt no one, and uphold high standards of personal conduct. They would behave with integrity and honesty in their dealings with each other, and their exchanges would be marked by trustworthiness. Above all, men would judge their own actions and those of others by the extent to which they adhered to norms of justice and correct behavior.

Women's primary concerns diverged from men's. Not bearing the responsibility for political and economic affairs, they collectively focused instead on the subject of greatest personal concern to them: reproduction. Skilled midwives were essential to adult women's well-being. And in Boston in early 1649 the forty-seven-year-old Mistress Alice Tilly, whom other women regarded as "the ablest midwife that wee knowe in the land," was in prison, accused of "the miscarrying of many wimen and children under hir hand." (No detailed description of the charges against her has survived.)[4]

The women of Boston and Dorchester were certain that the authorities had listened only to "the black side of her actions," to accusers who lacked Alice Tilly's knowledge and ability and who, faced with difficult deliveries, "either sent for her or left the work undone." Accordingly, over the course of a year, both before and after Mistress Tilly's trial by the Bay Colony's Court of Assistants in the spring of 1649, five groups of women ranging in size from 21 to 130—each claiming to represent "a greate many more"—flooded the General Court with petitions attesting to Mistress Tilly's "skills, & redines, & paynfulnes, help-fulnes, & Courage." They expressed their confidence in her, writing of how they were "affrayd to putt our selves into the hands of any besides our midwife that wee have had experience of," for she had helped them "even in such tymes as in the eye of sence or reason nothinge but Death was to be expected."[5]

To the women living in and near Boston, the demands of abstract justice were secondary to their physical needs. Although they insisted that Mistress Tilly's skills were unparalleled, that "shee hath ben a woe-man of singular use," they were at first less concerned with disproving the charges against her than with ensuring that she would continue to be available to tend them in childbed. Prior to her trial, they indicated that they did not seek to halt the legal proceedings against her but rather merely asked that she be allowed to leave the Boston jail whenever her assistance was required. After Alice Tilly had been convicted, fined, and ordered imprisoned for a lengthy period, Boston women again requested the same dispensation, referring to "sad events" that had occurred since her detention. Led by Mistress Elizabeth Wilson (wife of the Reverend John Wilson), twenty-six female Bostonians begged the Court of Assis-tants to "heare the cryes of mothers, and of children yet unborn."[6]

The deputies in the Bay Colony's lower house joined the women they termed "sisters & neighbors" in requesting approval of the plan, contending in their recommendation to the Assistants that "Authority may be aswell manteyned, by Clemency in Remitting: as by Constancy in upholding, a Sentence at Court." The magistrates responded posi-tively, permitting Mistress Tilly, though officially jailed, to leave prison to attend childbirths without posting bail, a requirement at which her husband had balked. But William and Alice Tilly eventually grew dis-satisfied with an arrangement that so restricted her freedom of move-ment. Mr. William Tilly began threatening "to remove himselfe & her also . . . unless her innocencie may be cleared." Consequently, in spring 1650, evidently at Mistress Tilly's instigation, the women of Boston and Dorchester again submitted petitions on her behalf, entreating the Gen-eral Court to free her from custody absolutely.[7]

The renewed campaign angered the Assistants, who excoriated Mis-tress Tilly's "excessive pride." They accused her of seeking "nothinge but a compleat victory over magistracy" and testily asserted that there was "as much need to upphold magistracy in their authority as Mris Tilly in her midwivery." Yet the Boston women, while admitting that they regretted Alice Tilly's "over-much selfe conceitednes," pointedly reminded the General Court that they wrote not just for themselves but also on behalf of "the security of your children." That the 130 signatories to the final petition intended that phrase to be taken literally is demonstrated by the fact that included among their number were Mistress Elizabeth Winthrop (daughter-in-law of the recently deceased Governor John Winthrop) and Esther Houchin, Governor John Endicott's daughter. The female Bostonians also wrote of their desire to further "the publick good," thus linking what might have appeared to be an exclusively feminine concern to the officials' own families and to the welfare of the "churches and Comon wealth God has cast us in."[8]

The varying tones of the statements of the groups of men and women are instructive. The Maryland men led by William Fuller spoke firmly and in an egalitarian style to other men, secure in the knowledge that they and those they addressed shared the same priorities. The women, by contrast, spoke to the male leaders of their colony from the standpoint of importuning outsiders. Although one of the Boston groups expressed a willingness to "attend the Command of the Court," for the most part the women's language emphasized that they collectively occupied a position quite different from that of the men they addressed, even though some of those men, individually, were their own husbands, fathers, friends, and other relatives. They wrote "in childlike boldnes," representing "the weakest sexe," said the largest Boston group; as "poore trembling Petitioners," they admitted to harboring deep fears about their future welfare if deprived of their most trusted midwife. Thus, although women together oversaw the processes of reproduction—a task known to men only by "hearesay"—men nevertheless held the ultimate reins of power, and women in the end were subjected to male authority in this, as in other aspects of their lives.[9]

Even so, the power relationship of the communities of men and women rested to some extent on reciprocity. Like the Virginia women who collectively helped to determine the verdict in the Hall case, the female petitioners from Boston and Dorchester refused to accept the initial judgment of elite men, insisting instead on the correctness of their own independent assessments of the relevant evidence. The Virginia women proved by physical examinations that Hall was not a woman; the Bay Colony women knew from personal experience that their beloved midwife was skilled rather than incompetent. In both instances the women's judgment prevailed at least in part, as the male rulers of Virginia and Massachusetts bowed to women's special expertise in the areas of reproduction and women's bodies, issuing decisions that took that expertise into account. Such dynamics in specific cases, along with other evidence drawn from a variety of sources, disclose the values and inner workings of the separate seventeenth-century communities of men and women—communities that interlocked in complex ways, but which nevertheless existed independently of each other.

CREDIT, KNAVERY, AND THE PROCESS OF CONSENSUS-BUILDING AMONG MEN

Men of all ranks sought the qualities of openness, straightforwardness, and honesty in those with whom they did business on a daily basis. The civil litigation that filled the dockets of colonial courts for the most part represented dealings gone awry—debts not paid on schedule, contracts not carried out as promised, damages done to another's property or reputation. Yet the specifics of the seemingly ubiquitous lawsuits graphically reveal men's expectations of each other and expose the assumptions on which they based their interactions. Although male colonists of ordinary rank rarely kept diaries or wrote personal letters, the records of the suits they filed or to which they responded offer considerable insight into the values that informed their lives.[10]

Repeatedly the cases disclose agreements reached on the basis of oral assurances and men's willingness to trust one another. So a Maryland planter left his tobacco in the possession of a neighbor, "because he knew It was Sure in [his] hands." Another Marylander accepted a job offer when promised that "whatsoever worke he . . . should doe for him . . . hee would satisfy him therefore." A third planter in the colony relied on a fellow colonist who traded him two hogsheads of tobacco and told him that the cured tobacco "was as good below as at the top, which [he] saw." A fourth unhesitatingly purchased a manservant after having been assured by the seller that the servant was "able" and experienced, and a fifth paid a carpenter in advance for building him a house, "confideing in his honesty to performe [the contract]."[11]

Since the courts concurred that oral contracts were fully binding, men engaged in negotiating these agreements had to pay attention to their own words, and those of the other party to the deal, if they were to avoid committing themselves to undesirable bargains. The Maryland defendant who offered a hogshead of tobacco said to be "good and merchantable" to a plaintiff "with this caution if you like it take; if not refuse it" was later rewarded with a court decision in his favor, because the plaintiff, who complained that the tobacco was wet and of poor quality, "received it at his owne perill." Finding themselves in similar circumstances were two Virginia buyers, who asked the seller of four hogsheads "if it were good tobacco." The planter responded cautiously to one of them, "if he did like it there it was, if not he might leave it." When both men thereupon accepted the tobacco, having seen its "Imperfection," they were left without legal recourse. Similarly, a Marylander who initially agreed to buy ten head of cattle but changed his mind just one day later, saying he only wanted five of them, was held to the original oral contract (which had been negotiated in front of two witnesses) by the Charles County court.[12]

Sometimes, as in the last example, the parties summoned other men to serve as witnesses to the negotiations, as when John Salter of Kent Island asked Captain Thomas Bradnox and another man to "beare wittnes" to his purchase of a plantation from Mr. Francis Brooke, or when two Virginians were enlisted as witnesses to an oral agreement in which one man paid another's substantial "ould debt" in exchange for one year of his labor. Likewise, when two Marylanders reached an out-of-court settlement of their dispute over the sale of a plantation, they requested that the two witnesses subpoenaed to testify in the case "take notice . . . att the ending of our busines" before they informed the judges that the suit was being dropped.[13]

The parties' mutual concurrence, not the witnesses who might have been present, was the most important element of colonial contracts, oral or written. Witnesses could provide corroborating testimony if the details of the transaction were ever questioned or disputed, but the trustworthiness of the parties involved constituted the primary foundation on which contracts rested. Men of integrity were expected to fulfill their agreements, regardless of how disadvantageous those bargains later proved to be or whether they had formally been witnessed by others. That was true even if the arrangements had been made by an agent rather than by a man himself. So, when Governor John Winthrop discovered in late 1639 that his property had been badly mismanaged by an employee who had entered into a series of inopportune and costly business deals, he nevertheless thought himself obligated to carry them out. Although he drafted a letter complaining about "some of my Christian frends" who had taken advantage of "my servants unfaithfulnesse" —for he believed that anyone bargaining with his agent had to have known that the deals being offered were detrimental to the governor— Winthrop never sent it. Instead, he pronounced himself pleased that he had sufficient resources to pay his debts, even though doing so put him under considerable financial strain.[14]

If disagreements arose over the contents of contracts or the amounts of debts owed, the oath of one of the parties would decide the issue.

So important was this method of resolving disputes that a Marylander observed in 1664 that if "mens Oathes" could not be relied upon to decide a case, then "Noe man shall ever have either security for his debt or Certainty of his Cause," and "Lawes and Courts" would be "totally overthrowne." Few if any men would have disagreed with him. When all other means of finding the truth had failed to achieve the desired end, oaths could settle the matter. But only, of course, if they could be relied upon absolutely and without question. That was why perjury was such a heinous offense.[15]

In disputed Maryland cases, plaintiffs were customarily asked to swear to the truth of their demands; if they refused to do so, defendants were then offered an opportunity to deny the plaintiffs' claims under oath. The outcome of many cases accordingly hinged on the willingness of one party or the other to swear that what he stated was true. On Kent Island in early 1657, Mr. Thomas Ringgold sued Mr. Joseph Wickes for a barrel of corn, and "Referd The same to The said Mr Wickes his owen Oath." When Wickes swore that he did not owe Ringgold the corn, the court dismissed the suit. About a year later Ringgold was the defendant under similar circumstances; asked to swear whether he had repaid a debt in its entirety, he declared that he had done so and consequently was discharged from his obligation. Later in 1658 a Charles County plaintiff won his case by initiating an oath-taking duel. After Mr. Arthur Turner denied that he owed Henry Lillie 330 pounds of tobacco, Lillie

> told him in open Court that if hee woold thear Sware upon the Evangelist that hee owed him no Such Some that then the Plantive woold give the defendant a discharge in generall but the defendant denied his profer to performe whearupone this Court tendered the bible unto the Plantive to have him sware upone those sacred lines that his account was trew and just which the Sayd Plantive did.

The judges then ordered Turner to pay Lillie the amount in question, plus costs.[16]

One consequence of the heavy reliance on oaths was that men found guilty of perjury or merely of speaking less than the whole truth were thereinafter not allowed to submit sworn statements in court. That placed a man at a considerable disadvantage in civil litigation, as the Marylander Edward Commins learned in 1648. Sued twice during that year, Commins insisted both times that he did not owe the sums at issue, but he was not permitted to take oaths to that effect because the commander of Kent Island declared that Commins had "formerly taken a rash oath in the Court afore him, concerning an account." Commins counterattacked by accusing one of the plaintiffs of himself having taken "a rash oath," but his complaint seems to have had little effect.[17]

It is thus not surprising that men "adjudged un Capable of an oath" fought that designation vigorously and tenaciously. As an early Virginia governor observed, such a determination destroyed a man's "good name and reputation . . . for ever," and men were thereby (in a Marylander's words) "much disturbed boath in mind and person." And because a man's reputation played such a crucial role in shaping his interactions with other men, not only formal court decisions but also the opinions of his peers about his veracity affected his ability to function effectively within the male community.[18]

As a result, maintaining their "credit" was all-important for seventeenth-century men. By that word, they meant not the twentieth-century definition that privileges financial dealings but rather a more general sense, now obsolete, which originated in the late sixteenth century—"the reputation of being worthy of belief or trust," to quote the *Oxford English Dictionary*. Male colonists understood that "such is the Credit of the person, such wilbe the creditt of his acts"; accordingly, men asserted that "a good name" was "next to his life" or "to be desired above great riches," and they tirelessly defended their reputations from attack.[19]

Although men could use a variety of means to protect themselves when their good names were questioned, the tactic they most commonly selected was filing defamation suits or bringing criminal charges against their accusers.[20] The courtroom was an appropriate forum for repairing a damaged reputation because a target could directly confront a defamer with the slanderous statements and demand public satisfaction, often in the form of a fine, a retraction, or an apology. Since truth was not always an acceptable defense (the point at issue was often not whether the insult was true but rather merely whether the defendant had uttered it), court cases offered offended parties an excellent opportunity to win official redress of their grievances. A favorable decision, moreover, placed the community as a whole squarely on the side of the defamed man and helped to isolate and marginalize both the slanderer and the insults that person had promulgated. A defamation suit, in short, offered a collective solution to a personal problem. If successful, it would repair a man's credit and enable him to retain the good opinion of his peers.[21]

A substantial majority of men who filed suit against their slanderers used that mechanism to seek redress from men of the same rank. Although high-status men proved particularly sensitive to invectives uttered by lower-ranking men (more than two thirds of the suits they filed were aimed at such defendants), nearly 70 percent of the slander litigation with exclusively male participants pitted a man of ordinary status against one of his peers. Thus defamation suits provided men of roughly equal rank with a useful method of dispute resolution in circumstances in which hierarchical relationships were lacking.[22] Prosecutions for criminal defamation, by contrast, were more likely to involve high-ranking men and low-status defamers: well over half of the prosecutions fell into that category. Overall, about two thirds of the victims in criminal-defamation cases were officials or other high-ranking men, for the state's interest in upholding social and political order led it to intervene on behalf of defamed officials, especially when their slanderers were of ordinary rank.[23]

Although the pattern of the status relationship of defamers and targets in civil suits differed from that in criminal prosecutions, the slanders at issue in the two types of cases were the same. In light of the centrality of financial and political affairs in men's lives, it is not surprising that the insults which most concerned men—to judge by the frequency with which they led to both lawsuits and prosecutions—challenged a man's financial or political integrity.

In those cases in which generalized epithets alone were employed, nearly one half involved the use of the terms "rogue," "knave," or such equivalents as "rascal." Another one third of the insults eliciting lawsuits or prosecutions fell into a closely related triad alleging theft, lying or perjury, or cheating. All these charges were essentially the same, since, as the *Oxford English Dictionary* points out, in the seventeenth century *rogue* meant "a dishonest, unprincipled person, a rascal" and *knave* was used to refer to "an unprincipled man, given to dishonorable and deceitful practices; a base and crafty rogue."[24] Moreover, when specific accusations rather than universal terms of opprobrium were the subject of defamation suits, fully one half involved allegations of theft, lying, or dishonesty, and more than one tenth explicitly charged political malfeasance or challenged an official's authority in some way.[25]

The insults that brought targets into court to seek redress varied considerably within this limited spectrum. Male colonists sued each other over such epithets as "old cheating Rogue," "idle pratinge and lyeinge knave," "devillish Raskall & Roge," or "parjured Fellow."[26] Others sought to repair their injured reputations after being accused of such offenses as "gitt[ing] his liveing by shifting sharking And Cossoning" or being "A hogg stealing fellow from his Cradle."[27]

Most male plaintiffs filed defamation suits in response to specific charges rather than general epithets. Men sued after other men accused them of stealing "about half a lode of hay" or "a barrell of corne," forging a bill of sale for a servant, or taking "a false Oath" while testifying as a witness in a court case.[28] One recent arrival went to court after a former fellow passenger gossiped that it was "comonly reported in the shipp that they came over together in" that he "did come out of England for stealeing of a calf." Prosecutions for criminal defamation likewise responded to specific accusations of dishonesty as well as to opprobrious name-calling; thus, in 1673 Mr. Richard Wharton, Samuel Bellingham's attorney, was indicted by the Suffolk County grand jury for accusing the Reverend James Allen of Boston of altering Governor Richard Bellingham's will "after hee had Signed & Sealed it."[29]

Like Mr. Allen, high-status men had to be especially careful of their good names if they wanted to maintain their positions. So a New Haven merchant who sold goods on consignment from others insisted in 1658 that the charge that he had stolen two barrels of beef was "of a high nature, & in respect to the place wherein God had set him, it was greatly prejudiciall to him, for if he bee a theife, who will put anything into his hand." Similarly, a Maryland attorney responded by filing suit when a county court judge publicly declared that he should no longer be permitted to practice law in the colony because he "made it his businesse to make and urge men to goe to Law"—that is, that he was guilty of barratry.[30]

Government officials in particular were vulnerable to defamatory challenges to their position, but they, even low-ranking men like constables, could rely on the state to come to their aid by prosecuting vilifiers. The slanders directed at officials of all levels that subjected their authors to criminal action ranged from accusations that judges were biased to complaints that constables or magistrates neglected their duties. Defamed political and military leaders were protected by the courts, from 1634, when the Massachusetts Court of Assistants ordered the whipping of a disgruntled New Englander who had characterized Governor John Winthrop as "but a Law[y]er's clerke," to 1697, when the Prince George's County court in Maryland fined a man who declared "in the presence of and heareing of Verry many of his Majesties: good Leige Subject" that "All the beasts of the Forrest meaning the Suitors to the Said County Court are Come in to wait upon an Ass."[31]

Slanders were particularly damaging if they became widely known. Thus targets were especially likely to file suit or a criminal complaint if the defamatory remark had been uttered in front of large numbers of people or had been repeated several times. In 1677, for example, an English mariner sued a Maryland planter who "openly & publickly" at a county court session had called him "a cheating rogue & a knave." A Plymouth resident likewise sought redress from a man who had accused him of theft and lying "on a lecter day, . . . in the publicke meeting house . . . before sundry people," and another Plymouth plaintiff noted that his vilifier had "severall times" reported that he "had taken a falce oath against him in the Court att Scittuate."[32]

That judges and juries agreed that complainants' reputations were seriously harmed when other men called them "rogue" or "knave" or accused them of cheating or lying in general terms is shown by the results of lawsuits. Whereas plaintiffs won over 80 percent of the cases in which they alleged having been the targets of such epithets, they prevailed in just two thirds of other sorts of defamation suits.[33] Men charging that they had been defamed by specific charges of theft or dishonesty were no more successful in court than were men suing for other types of slanders. Perhaps individual charges did not carry the same weight as general attacks on a man's character, or (more likely) the defamers in such cases were better able to prove that their statements had been accurate and thus perhaps not defamatory. For instance, a Marylander sued for accusing another of theft convinced the court that "it was noe defame" by presenting two depositions to demonstrate that his charge was true, and a New Haven man who complained of having been falsely accused of stealing failed to win redress, for the court decided that his behavior had "some appearance of unrighteousnes." The judges even warned him, not the alleged defamer, to "take heed of these wayes."[34]

Four defamation suits, two each from New Hampshire and Maryland, reveal some of the circumstances that elicited slanders, led to legal responses by their targets, and eventually enveloped larger communities of men (and a few women) in their dynamics. Two developed out of specific incidents—one a dispute over the ownership of a heifer, the other a business deal—and two arose because of men's concerns about neighbors' trustworthiness.

In late May 1654, in Salisbury, New Hampshire, Robert Swan accused Henry Palmer and Abraham Whittaker of making defamatory statements about his conduct in a lawsuit he had won six weeks previously.[35] Palmer and Whittaker, Swan charged, had slandered him in the interim by claiming that he suborned perjury when he successfully wrested possession of a stray heifer from John Williams, Jr. Shortly after the verdict, Palmer had publicly expressed skepticism about the testimony of Robert Ames, a servant who appeared for Swan; and Whittaker, who originally supported Swan's claim to the heifer, recanted after the case was won, openly voicing suspicions about a deposition offered by Swan's sister Frances. She "seemed to be uncertayne at her first comeing yet after speech with hir brother swore positive," Whittaker informed one man. Both Palmer and Whittaker thereafter spoke "slanderous words" against Robert Swan, Palmer going so far as to accuse Swan of fraud "before neere twenty men." After more than a month during which the stories spread far and wide, Robert Swan could no longer ignore the insults and filed suit.

The court records (which intermingle depositions submitted in the initial dispute with those from the slander suits) reveal that many people talked about the charges against Robert Swan in the weeks after he gained title to the heifer, and that information about Palmer's and Whittaker's accusations spread rapidly along local gossip networks. Witnesses recounted hearing that Swan's case had been won with perjured testimony, questioning others to confirm that rumor, then spreading the scandalous tale even farther. As the story became more widely known, neighbors began urging John Williams, Jr., to ask for a rehearing of the original case. The relevant community of gossipers was almost exclusively male; just three women participated in the discussions that preoccupied about two dozen men.

The documents offer a remarkable case study of how Henry Palmer's initial skepticism quickly snowballed into a community consensus that challenged a court verdict and undoubtedly forever damned Robert Swan in the eyes of those who had to deal with him on a daily basis. Both his sister and Ames eventually admitted that they had given testimony of dubious validity—Frances because she had been "inveagled" into it by her brother, Ames because he was angry with his master and bribed by Swan's promise to help free him from his indenture. Robert Swan's slander suits were a calculated gamble undertaken to retrieve a badly battered reputation, a gamble that failed because he had wholly lost his credibility with the community even before he filed them.

Probably Philip Chesley hoped to be as successful in influencing public opinion as Henry Palmer had been.[36] That, at least, was what Mr. Samuel Hall charged when he sued Chesley for slander in Portsmouth in 1662. He accused Chesley of trying to ruin his reputation, of traveling to Boston, Newbury, Salisbury, Hampton, and elsewhere "to inquire of any persons that had difference with the plaintiff to trye if hee could gather up any matter that might reflect upon or further Defame" him. These actions, Mr. Hall contended, adequately proved Chesley's "malchous wicked purpose" and should entitle Hall to compensation of

£500. "No man will Credditt a man that is a cheating Knave & a Couzning Knave," he explained to the court, detailing the epithets Chesley had employed against him; "publique Slaunders spreads over all the Contry (as lightning from one side of the heavens to another) So that the plaintiffe to have his good Name stayned and taken away itt is irreperable." Proclaiming his "In'ocence," he insisted that "I know in my Conscience that all the men in the world can'ott prove any such fact against me in all my transaccons."

Philip Chesley had defamed Samuel Hall because of Hall's behavior in a business deal. First, Mr. Hall had failed to pay Chesley in full for some moose hides, and then—when Chesley won a court judgment—he withheld the costs Chesley had also been awarded, thereby forcing Philip to return to the authorities for assistance in obtaining payment. Chesley defended himself in the slander suit by accusing Mr. Hall of "deluding and abusinge the law to keep men frome there Just debts." "If a man brings it Justly on himselfe as the playntiff hath don the lawe will not releive him," he declared. Chesley also produced two depositions alleging that Hall had behaved unethically on other occasions, asserting darkly that Hall "hath not suffered at all in this case for that his name and practice is known and well understood."

Even though the judges undoubtedly agreed with Chesley that Samuel Hall's business practices were disreputable, the plaintiff was awarded damages of 50 shillings plus costs, probably because Chesley had spoken to at least a dozen people, using what one witness called "terms som what of the groser sort." The award was far less than the £500 Hall had claimed, but it was more than Chesley could easily pay. He petitioned the court for relief, admitting to "Some inconsiderat Speaches" while still complaining of Mr. Hall's "Evill and unjust dealling." The court's response to his plea is unknown.

If the evidence in the Swan suits reveals the elements of a successful defamation, that in the case of Hall and Chesley suggests the perils that could await a man who chose to embark on a less well-grounded slanderous campaign against another. The evidence proved that Hall had deliberately avoided paying the debt for months. Mr. Hall relied on a legal technicality (the lack of proper documentation); Chesley, on the same well-understood though unwritten rules of honest dealings that led John Winthrop to honor his agent's promises and many Maryland planters to obey oral agreements. Philip Chesley had good reason to be frustrated with Samuel Hall's behavior and equally good reason to believe that other men would also judge that behavior negatively, but after he won his initial suit against Hall he made the mistake of continuing to complain bitterly about the way the merchant had treated him. Mr. Samuel Hall's rhetoric was overblown, but it expressed a truth: if he, a merchant, became widely known as a "cheating knave," his business would be destroyed. The judges had to find in his favor, for Chesley had gone too far. In particular, he produced inadequate evidence that Hall habitually engaged in questionable financial practices.

Two Maryland defamers were more successful at such a task. Both their targets had longstanding reputations for double dealing, and the defamers (though responding to specific incidents) were expressing an already existing local consensus at the time of their slanders. In Charles County in May 1663, James Bouling told several men that Mr. Arthur Turner had killed and eaten a calf belonging to someone else, and the following February at a Calvert County store "afore a great Company of people" Thomas Paggett called Mr. Hugh Stanley "Knave Cheating Knave" and said that he would prove it.[37]

When Turner and Stanley reacted by filing defamation actions, Bouling and Paggett defended themselves by soliciting testimony from neighbors about the men's past behavior. James Bouling called seven male witnesses, four of them high-status men like Turner (one, indeed, was a county justice). All reported other occasions on which Mr. Turner's actions had aroused suspicion: three related a tale of how Turner had earmarked two piglets he did not own; two described his duplicitous handling of debt repayments; and two, remarkably, recalled separate incidents involving Turner's appropriation of others' livestock that had taken place at least a decade earlier. Turner's five male and three female witnesses focused not on his reputation but on the specifics of Bouling's slander, one man revealing that Bouling had apologized to Turner after the suit was filed. Whether for that reason or because the judges agreed that Arthur Turner's reputation was sufficiently dubious to justify Bouling's charge, the court decided that the plaintiff had "no Cause of action" and ordered him to pay all costs.

Mr. Hugh Stanley too was thought to have purloined livestock (a cow and perhaps a boar), but the primary reason Paggett accused him of behaving "Knavishly" was his administration of the estate of his wife's second husband. Dorothy Stanley had married Daniel Goulson, Giles Sadler, and Hugh Stanley in quick succession. At the time of Paggett's slander, Mr. Stanley was entangled in a series of legal battles involving both the Goulson and Sadler estates; settling the latter was an especially complex task because Sadler, the county sheriff, had been engaged in collecting both private debts and provincial fees at the time of his death.

The testimony of Paggett's seven male and two female witnesses revealed that Mr. Hugh Stanley's neighbors believed him guilty of sharp dealing, perhaps even fraud, in his handling of Giles Sadler's estate, for they told numerous stories of Stanley's having lied about Sadler's accounts. Even Mr. Stanley's eight witnesses offered him at best lukewarm support. One of the six men, while confirming Paggett's slander, remarked, for example, that "he knew Nothing of an actuall damage to Mr Stanley." Another declared, "I cannot say any thing in this Bussiness that I cann remember," and a third refused to back up Stanley's claim that a storekeeper had been unwilling to do business with him after he heard Paggett's defamatory statement.

That a man's own witnesses for the most part failed to endorse his position was remarkable, indicating that the informal public had already reached a verdict about Mr. Hugh Stanley's credit, regardless of what the Provincial Court decided. The jury wisely rendered a split decision: they found "no actuall damage Susteyned by the plaintiff" and ordered him to pay all costs, but at the same time declared that Paggett had not presented proof "soe valid as to repute him a Cheating Knave."

The four suits from Maryland and New Hampshire thus make it clear that slanders, though nominally involving only two people, did not occur in a vacuum. James Bouling and Thomas Paggett spoke not just for themselves, but for larger groups of men, when they defamed Mr. Arthur Turner and Mr. Hugh Stanley. Philip Chesley got into trouble by attempting to enlist others to support his negative assessment of Mr. Samuel Hall's business practices, and Henry Palmer and Abraham Whittaker successfully convinced the men of the community that Robert Swan had indeed suborned perjury. Except with respect to Chesley—who incurred a fine he could ill afford—the court decisions in these cases were almost beside the point. Essentially, they confirmed communal judgments arrived at independently by the men with whom the plaintiffs came into regular contact. So it was that communities of men collectively endorsed the same values that informed the interactions of individuals.

Heavy pressure was placed on dissidents of various sorts to acquiesce in such communal judgments. Collectivities of men, whether they were based on geographical proximity, shared professional identity, church membership, or political or military office, believed in the necessity of achieving consensus within their own ranks. Men who refused to join such an evolving consensus were viewed as presenting dangerous threats to social order, and they faced constant pressure until they surrendered to the general will. If they obstinately resisted calls to conform, they risked expulsion from the community in question—excommunication from the church, removal from public posts, loss of clerical authority, figurative if not literal "banishment" from the neighborhood in which they lived. Yet the wielding of collective power by groups of men of roughly equal status was problematic. In the absence of the hierarchical relationships that theoretically were to determine the outcome of contests, many men could find justifications for maintaining independent opinions. Only the most patient and careful negotiations could then persuade them to return to the communal fold.

The magistrates of Massachusetts Bay were particularly adept at averting potentially disruptive disputes among themselves. One of the best descriptions of the process they employed is contained in Governor John Winthrop's account of a prolonged confrontation between himself and the Bay Colony's deputy governor, Thomas Dudley. In the spring of 1632, after several conflicts with Winthrop, Dudley attempted to resign his post to preserve, he said, "public peace; because he must needs discharge his conscience in speaking freely; and he saw that bred disturbance." Such a solution to the problem of dissent was unacceptable to Governor Winthrop and the other magistrates. They accordingly initiated a series of dialogues with Mr. Dudley, during which he was invited to air his criticisms of Winthrop (many of which revolved around possible abuses of power), and the governor reciprocated with his own complaints about Dudley. At times the two men were "in passion" or "very hot," but, with the assistance of Massachusetts clergymen and other mediators, the two were fully reconciled by the early autumn. Although he noted some subsequent disputes, Governor Winthrop commented in his journal that they "ever after kept peace and good correspondency together, in love and friendship."[38]

Even so, a further flare-up of contention between the two men in 1636 led to the adoption of a formal policy (by concurrence among the assistants and the clergy) outlining procedures for minimizing conflict within the ranks of the colony's rulers:

> The magistrates shall be more familiar and open each to other, and more frequent in visitations, and shall, in tenderness and love, admonish one another, (without reserving any secret grudge,) and shall avoid all jealousies and suspicions, each seeking the honor of another, and all, of the court, not opening the nakedness of one another to private persons.

The goal was, then, to resolve differences among themselves by openly sharing their views and criticisms of each other "in tenderness and love" so that the magistrates could then present a united front to people without public responsibilities ("private persons"). The policy adopted by some churches of having members alone hear disputes among "brethren," rather than discussing such matters in front of the congregation as a whole, had the same aim: preserving harmony within a specific community.[39]

Mr. Dudley and Mr. Winthrop behaved appropriately during the process of reconciliation mediated by other high-ranking men in the colony. They understood the necessity of compromise to preserve the nominal unity of the magistracy; Winthrop in particular wanted to avoid irrevocable divisions in the ranks of the colony's rulers. Consequently, while always advancing his position forcefully and defending himself avidly, the governor would retreat if opinion turned against him. Each man listened to what the other had to say, and both then paid attention to the collective judgments of the magistrates and clergy on the subjects in dispute between them. Mr. Winthrop admitted to having exercised faulty judgment on several matters that had angered Dudley, and Mr. Dudley assured Winthrop that the questions he raised about the governor's having misused his power "were but for his own satisfaction, and not by way of accusation." In the end, the disagreements were satisfactorily laid to rest, and by 1638 the two men termed themselves "brothers," partly because John Winthrop's daughter had married Thomas Dudley's son but also in recognition of their permanent reconciliation.[40]

In the congregations of New England as well as in the region's governing bodies, men went to great lengths to achieve consensus. Although churches included female as well as male members, and sometimes more of the former than the latter, as institutions they were wholly male-dominated. (Little evidence, for example, suggests that women regularly took an active role in debates over church policy; Mistress Anne Hutchinson was threatening precisely because she was an exception to that rule.) So churches provided yet another locale in which men were required to interact with each other while deprived of the guidance offered by hierarchical theories. To be sure, Puritan congregations were led by pastors and elders, but such men were regarded as firsts among equals rather than definitively superior to ordinary members.[41]

Congregations were usually satisfied by outward conformity to a decision if genuine consent could not be obtained. As a clergyman who served in Plymouth for many years explained, the elders "never called for a negative or contrary vote," thus presuming the existence of a consensus unless someone actively objected. Moreover, he noted, "care was taken before the vote was called for in any case to gaine the consent of every brother, & in case any could not actually vote, yet they expressing, that they could rest in the act of the church, it was satisfying." That individual members concurred in the necessity for such procedures was indicated when a Bostonian who dissented from several decisions made in his congregation nevertheless declined to oppose them openly, informing a correspondent that "the peace of the Church ought to be prefer'd before the Opinion of any man" as long as "Fundamentall Truth" was not at issue.[42]

Yet not all attempts at enforcing communal judgments among New England's male church members were successful. For example, during his 1649 church trial, New Haven's Ezekiel Cheever refused to recant his criticisms of the congregation's elders, particularly with respect to their treatment of Mistress Anne Eaton five years earlier. Instead of joining in an opinion that cleared the elders of any wrongdoing in that and other matters, he insisted that "I know no order appointed by Christ, that the Church shall require every member to act with them in every vote." Technically, he was correct (some churches did decide some questions by majority vote rather than by unanimous consent), but the congregation's leaders disagreed, pronouncing Cheever's failure to submit to the consensus a violation of the Fifth and Ninth Commandments, and they excommunicated him.[43]

The powerful forces supporting consensus in New England churches and governmental bodies had no counterparts in Virginia and Maryland. Although, as has been seen, men in the informal public there were able to arrive at uniform assessments of the trustworthiness of neighbors, formal political and religious institutions in both colonies were filled with dissension and discord. The process that ensured Winthrop's and Dudley's acquiescence in a broader consensus developed by men of equal status was alien to the Chesapeake during the first decades of English settlement there. Even though men of ordinary rank in the region commonly deferred (of necessity) to higher-ranking men, political leaders had great difficulty resolving disputes among themselves, since no existing hierarchy gave any one of them clear preeminence over any other, and since (unlike the Bay Colony's leaders) they proved unwilling to defer to collective judgments.

Take, for example, the dispute that wracked Virginia in 1634–35. The governor, Sir John Harvey, disagreed with members of the Council about a number of issues, including the relationship of the colony to Lord Baltimore's new province. A Virginian, William Claiborne, had been running a trading post on Kent Island, which fell within Maryland's jurisdiction. He, backed by the Council, violently resisted the imposition of Maryland's authority on the island, whereas Governor Harvey sided with Lord Baltimore. Harvey pronounced his opponents "rude ignorant, and an ill conditionde people, . . . more lykelye to effect mutiny then good lawes and orders," while for their part the councilors accused Harvey of having "usurped" power and having engaged in "Tyrannical proceedings." Outnumbering and overpowering the governor, they arrested him and shipped him back to England. In short, they could resolve a heated dispute only by removing the source of the dissidence—and they showed none of the patience demonstrated by New Englanders, who adopted similar solutions only as a last resort.[44]

Maryland was even worse. There, contention among the colony's leaders led to such spectacles as the 1642 arrest and trial of Mr. Giles Brent for failures as a military commander in an expedition against the Indians and for "discontent or disaffection to the good & wellfare of the goverment"; an armed rebellion in 1645; the Battle of the Severn in 1655; and still another rebellion (led by Josias Fendall, the governor) in 1660. Since Maryland had neither a stable government nor an established church, the mechanisms that in other colonies worked to dampen dissent (or, in the extreme, to expel insistent dissenters) were utterly lacking, and the result—often for years on end—was chaos.[45]

Thus the elected and appointed leaders of the Chesapeake colonies for the most part failed at the crucial task of building a consensus among themselves. Without an authoritarian, paternal voice above them to direct their behavior, they proved incapable of resolving disputes effectively or easily. Ordinary male settlers in the region did better, for they were usually able to reach agreement on assessments of each other's trustworthiness, the subject of greatest immediate concern to them. But in the event of serious dissent they could always turn to a higher authority—the courts—to resolve their disputes. Chesapeake judges and legislators themselves had no such recourse.

New England's leaders were far more successful, but only because they made achieving harmony within their ranks one of their most important goals. They did not entirely avoid dissension, but each time contention flared they were able to control it, if not through a process of reconciliation, then ultimately by banishing the dissenter. Only in Maine, which in many ways resembled the Chesapeake rather than the other northern settlements, did political disputes repeatedly fail to be resolved peacefully.[46]

Paradoxically, then, men living in the most Filmerian region were also the most likely to succeed at mediating disputes in circumstances in which Filmerian rules did not apply; that is, in which men of roughly equal status had to agree on a solution in the absence of orders from a superior. Male New Englanders' commitment to achieving a harmonious society and an orderly government usually led them to peaceful solutions to their disagreements. Only a few dissenters, Ezekiel Cheever among them, resolutely resisted communal judgments.

MIDWIVES, GOSSIPS, AND WOMEN'S COMMUNITIES

If the quintessential forums for men's activities in the colonies were the courtroom, the church, and the legislative chamber (often the same physical space though used for different functions), the preeminent female-dominated space in seventeenth-century Anglo-America was the birthing room. Childbirth was the central experience in the lives of nearly all adult colonial women, for most married in their late teens or early twenties and remained married—though perhaps having two or more husbands in sequence—until their deaths or the end of their fertility. There is no evidence that married couples engaged in any form of contraception, and most women spent much of their lives caught up in a repetitive cycle of pregnancy, nursing, weaning, pregnancy, nursing, weaning.[47]

The timing of that cycle was as apparent to the colonists as it has been to subsequent demographic historians. Marriage was usually followed by pregnancy within a year. After a live birth, the baby would be nursed for a period of one to two years, then weaned. Once a woman's ovulatory and menstrual cycle was fully re-established, usually after her child was weaned, she would again become pregnant within a year, assuming normal fertility and a normal sexual relationship with her husband. Thus most married women became pregnant every two to three years during their fertile period, although not all of those pregnancies resulted in surviving children. As has already been seen, these norms were so well known to contemporary observers that departures from them could cause comment (in the event of childlessness) or prosecution (in the event of "early" births).[48]

Childbirth was as central an experience for the women's community at large as for its individual members. Although women often casually encountered each other during the course of their daily lives, sometimes in such largely female settings as a local cowpen (where they milked together) or a shared well, only birthing rooms provided women with environments that consistently excluded men. There midwives, their assistants, and the mother-to-be's female relatives and friends joined together, sometimes for several days at a time, to supervise a woman's labor.[49] Given the number of fertile married women in any specific geographical area, childbirths would have been a regular occurrence, creating a shifting series of all-female neighborhood communities.[50]

By the late sixteenth century, such women were known as "gossips" and their gathering as a "gossiping." The word *gossip* derived from the eleventh-century English term *godsib*, a child's sponsor at a christening (godparent). Before 1600, it had come to mean both "a woman's female friends invited to be present at a birth" and a woman "who delights in idle talk; a newsmonger, a tattler."[51]

Although the conjunction of definitions might seem curious, it was not accidental: women did talk at other women's childbeds, and that talk took place outside the presence of men—thus, to men's minds, it must have been idle or "tattling." Court records contain only scattered and fragmentary evidence of events and conversations that occurred at childbeds, precisely because the courts were male institutions and no men witnessed the discussions or actions in question. Nevertheless, even the few surviving fragments are highly suggestive, disclosing the hidden world of women that revolved around frequent gatherings at childbirths and which seems to have been at least partly predicated on the absence of men.[52]

An example from Massachusetts vividly illustrates the potential importance of events in this all-female society and demonstrates that men could be kept ignorant of occurrences within it. In October 1637, Mary Dyer, a follower of the religious dissenter Anne Hutchinson, gave birth to a deformed stillborn child described by contemporaries as a "monster." Present at the stillbirth were the midwife Jane Hawkins, Mistress Hutchinson herself, and at least one other (unnamed) woman, who was reputed to be the source of the information about the monstrous birth that, one observer later wrote, was "whispered by s[ome] women in private to some others (as many of that sex as[semble] in such a strang business)."[53]

Although a sizable group of Boston women thus evidently knew what had happened, John Winthrop and the other magistrates did not learn the story, which turned out to be of great interest to them, until more than five months had passed.[54] Winthrop remarked that "the manner of the discovery was very strange," for the tale came to light only by chance. In March 1638, when Anne Hutchinson was leaving the Boston church after having been excommunicated, Mary Dyer walked out with her in a show of support. Winthrop recounted in his journal that, seeing Dyer depart, "a stranger asked, what young woman it was. The others answered, it was the woman which had the monster; which gave the first occasion to some that heard it to speak of it."

John Winthrop should have written "speak of it to *men*" in his account, since his own narrative discloses that "rumor [about the monstrous birth] began to spread" among women months prior to the March incident in the meetinghouse. In short, like the other contemporary commentator, he recognized that *women* talked among themselves about the tale long before male officials learned of it. Even after the initial revelation, obtaining facts about the stillbirth proved difficult for Massachusetts Bay's leaders: a church member, Winthrop recalled, "enquired about it from one to another, and at length came to Mistris Hutchison, with one of the Elders of the Church, to whom she revealed the truth of the thing in generall onely." Not until then did Governor Winthrop himself hear the story. In the presence of another magistrate and the elder who had talked with Mistress Hutchinson, Winthrop closely questioned Jane Hawkins. In April, fully six months after the stillbirth had taken place, the men finally exhumed the body of Mary Dyer's dead child and examined its characteristics for themselves.

Just as in the later case of Mistress Alice Tilly, in other words, the magistrates of the Bay Colony learned of events at childbirths only by "hearesay" and perhaps even months afterwards. Women were far better informed about such matters. The sole surviving deposition presented at Mistress Tilly's trial certainly indicates as much. The midwife Liddea Williams attested that many of the practices of which Alice Tilly stood accused were commonplace rather than unusual or to a woman's benefit rather than her detriment. A child might be "putt backe" in the womb "after the midwifes hands had the knowledge of it, because shee might have the major & greater advantage to bringe it fforth." Under some circumstances, "the midwife cannott pluck out her hand out of the woamans boddy many times before the child be delivered, & this I cann speake by myne owne experience." Or again, "ffor puttinge of fingers & feathers in woamens mouthes I have known myne owne mother to desire others to putt fingers in my mouth." She also explained to the court a phenomenon that would have been no news to most women: "I myself have had a child allive just cominge at the birth, & yeat dead born, & several others hath had experience of the same."[55]

That magistrates had to be told such things speaks volumes about the extent of men's ignorance of the processes of childbirth. They then further confirmed that ignorance by convicting Mistress Tilly, in spite of Deputy Governor Thomas Dudley's admission at the trial that she was indeed "the ablest midwife in the land." In this context, the insistent petitioning of the Boston and Dorchester women becomes explicable. The General Court had trouble understanding why the female petitioners would in the end be satisfied with nothing less than Mistress Tilly's complete exoneration, whereas the women repeatedly expressed their frustration that the men would not accede to their greater expertise in these matters. They had had experience of Alice Tilly "not in ordynary wayes but in extraordynary wayes"; they were well acquainted with her "skill & ability"; they believed that she "hath through the goodnes of God bin carried through such difficulties in her calling that none of those who are her accusers could Doe." The women's words leave no doubt about what the verdict would have been had *they* comprised the Bay Colony's Court of Assistants in 1649.[56]

Such evidence establishes the crucial role played by experienced midwives within the women's community. Midwives like Mistress Tilly and Jane Hawkins were of necessity central figures in other women's lives, so central that they were selected with great care, as the petitioners suggested when they wrote of their fears that Alice Tilly would be unable to tend them or, worse yet, that she would leave Boston altogether. So a superstitious Virginia wife in 1626 rejected her husband's choice of a midwife for her, Goody Joane Wright, because Wright was left-handed. Yet women's choices were sometimes limited by geography or availability. Mary Courtney Clocker, a midwife in St. Mary's County, Maryland, could not have had a very good reputation in late 1659: she had recently barely escaped the gallows after having been convicted of stealing the belongings of Mistress Elizabeth Oversee, who had died in childbed under her care. Even so, Mary White employed Clocker to attend the birth of her baby, and then she too died in childbed, which must have raised further questions about Clocker's abilities.[57]

When groups of women were consulted by colonial courts in matters involving women's bodies and reproduction, midwives nearly always participated in the discussions. Because of their recognized expertise, judges named them as members of female juries that examined the bodies of accused witches, bastard-bearers, and suspects in infanticide cases.[58] In addition, when a midwife presided over the birth of an illegitimate child, she was expected to interrogate the mother about its paternity, since it was believed that a woman could not lie about the identity of her child's father while giving birth. Although all women might at some point be called to testify in civil suits or criminal prosecutions (to report on events they had seen or to recount conversations they had heard or participated in), only midwives repeatedly appeared in court as witnesses.[59]

Most commonly, they testified, along with the other women who had been present at the birth of a bastard, about what the mother had said "in her extremyty" or "in the time of her travail" about the father of her child. The men named were then declared financially liable for child maintenance and sometimes punished in other ways as well.[60] Because the midwife's interrogatory role in such circumstances was so well understood, women who failed to summon assistance when they went into labor were immediately suspected of trying to hide the identity of the child's father. Thus an Isles of Shoals woman was accused in 1673 of "being with child before Marriage, & neglecting to send for helpe in the time of her Travell & . . . denying she had any child to the women that came in after her delivery." She was ordered whipped on two separate occasions "with a halter about her neck," and her suspected lover was also whipped, in addition to being fined and ordered to post a substantial good-behavior bond.[61]

A Maryland prosecution illustrates the interplay of gossip and childbed questioning in cases of illegitimate birth. Three women attested to the Kent County court in April 1661 that while in labor Matthew Read's nineteen-year-old maidservant Elesabeth Lockett "Confest . . . that it wase thomas Brights Child." The women, however, were not initially convinced by her statement. Obviously relying on the neighborhood rumor mill, they asked her "what hur master Dide to hure in the husks in the tobaco house." Lockett replied that "Hur master Did butt tickell hur," adding that "she never knew any other mane in three quarters of a yeare [but Thomas Bright] and that she never knew hur Master but by his face and Hands." The examiners were not satisfied with this description of nonprocreative sexual activity, clearly swayed by a negative neighborhood assessment of Read's character. So the highest ranking woman among them took a further, unusual step: "when the Childs heed wase in the Birth [canal] Mrs Blunt tooke the booke and swore hure & all that she said it wase thomas Brights Child." With that confirmation, the women and the judges were at last convinced. Bright, not Read, was declared to be Lockett's child's father.[62]

Groups of women led by midwives were also enlisted to investigate cases of bastardy or infanticide at times other than at a woman's "travail." In addition to the women's juries occasionally convened as a part of a criminal trial, masters or local officials often asked midwives and other women to question female servants or free women they suspected of being pregnant or of having committed infanticide, or to examine the bodies of dead infants born secretly to such women for indications of how they had died.[63]

Thus midwives and a group of six "able women" played a key role in New Haven's investigation of Ruth Pinion Briggs for infanticide in early 1668: two midwives attested that she had recently given birth, then the women verified that her "petticoate must be the first receptacle of a child borne into the world very lately," and finally a coroner's jury consulted "those that had skill in physick & midwifery" while they were examining the child's body. In a similar 1664 Maryland case, that of the Calvert County maidservant Elizabeth Greene, the testimony of a mid-wife proved decisive. Greene admitted that she had been pregnant, but claimed that she had miscarried at four months and that she "did not see what she had whether it was a Childe form'd or not." Although the fetus was never found, Greene's fate was sealed after Grace Parker, the local midwife, testified that "(to the best of her knowledge) the said Elizebeth Greene had gone neer her full time and had had a Childe" and that "there was milke in her breasts And it was a goeing away being hard and Curdled." Greene was convicted and sentenced to be hanged.[64]

Women's relationships with midwives, and with other women who gathered at childbeds, were therefore complex. On the one hand, mid-wives' expertise was necessary for women's very survival. On the other hand, that same expertise could expose wrongdoing and render mothers liable to penalties for bastardy, premarital fornication, adultery, or infan-ticide. Midwives and their helpers often learned secrets that women would rather have kept hidden from public view; Mary Dyer's "mon-strous birth" was only one of many such, the most common of which involved out-of-wedlock births or premarital conceptions.

Three cases involving the Maryland midwife Mistress Ann Johnson Dorrington cast light both on midwives' interpretations of their roles and on the intricacies of their relationships with other women. Mistress Ann Johnson immigrated to Maryland in 1651 with her husband, Peter; in 1656, shortly after Peter's death, she married Mr. William Dorring-ton.[65] In 1653, 1658, and 1669 she played major roles in prosecutions for adultery, bastardy, and infanticide, respectively.

In all three instances she took the initiative without a court directive. In 1658, recognizing the signs of pregnancy in Jane Palldin, a maidservant her husband had hired out to John Norton, she and another woman questioned Palldin until the servant admitted that the married Norton had impregnated her. Eleven years later, Mistress Dorrington joined her fellow midwife Grace Parker and a large group of women in petitioning the Provincial Court for a reprieve for another maidservant, Joane Colledge, who had been sentenced to death for "concealeing the birth of her Child." Some of the female petitioners (but not the two midwives) had been witnesses in the case, and it is not clear whether the group questioned the verdict or if they instead saw injustice in the English statute declaring that single women who gave birth to dead bastards in secret were presumptively guilty of infanticide. In any event, the court acceded to their request and postponed the execution. Whether it was ever carried out is uncertain.[66]

The two cases suggest that Ann Johnson Dorrington, and perhaps by extension other midwives as well, felt herself under an obligation to intervene independently in matters lying within her area of expertise. Yet her role in the 1653 adultery case was less straightforward, and the depositions submitted therein describe a far more tangled tale.[67]

In December 1652, Mistress Johnson attended Mary Taylor when she gave birth to a son, but she waited for four months before informing the authorities that she suspected her patient of having committed adultery. Significantly, what precipitated her action was a confrontation with Goody Taylor that occurred in April 1653 at the childbed of a third woman, Ann Pope. Mistress Johnson signaled her intention to "have a bout with Mary Taylor if She were there" as she approached the Pope house. Yet her assistant Sarah Goulson persuaded Mistress Johnson that such an act "would disturb her Self and the woman that was in travail," so Ann Johnson postponed talking to Mary Taylor until the birth attendants were departing.

Then her promised "bout" took the following form. "I must have a paire of Gloves of you [if not] of mr Catchmey," Ann Johnson told Mary Taylor. "Why of mr Catchmey?" Goody Taylor asked. Because "he is the father of your Child," Mistress Johnson responded provocatively. Mary retorted, "he is noe more the father of mine then he is of yours for ought I know." That insult led Mistress Johnson to call Mary Taylor "an Impudent whore." Taylor replied spiritedly, "it hath pleas'd God to make us both alike." Goulson described what happened next: "mrs Johnson Struck Mary Taylor Soe they were busling a Little while Soe when they had done mrs Johnson Said that that Nights work Should Cost her a whipt back." Later that month, Ann Johnson carried out her threat by going to court officials to describe the scene at the Taylor household in late December.[68]

According to her deposition, several birth attendants and later callers—including Sarah Goulson, Robert Taylor's sister, and Margaret Broome, the Taylors' "cousin"—quietly voiced their suspicions to each other at Mary's childbed. What worried the women was not just previous "Scandall" that had circulated about Mary and her flirtations with two men other than her husband, not just that the "black headed boy" to whom she had given birth resembled one of those men, but that, as everyone well knew, Mary had been absent in Virginia for an extended period the preceding spring. The timing was wrong for Robert to have fathered what Johnson termed a "full time . . . lustyable Child." Johnson and Goulson "were Sory to See how it was," and Margaret Broome reluctantly admitted that "the thing proved it Self." Robert Taylor was as well aware as the women of when the baby must have been conceived. After Mary gave birth, he told Margaret Broome that "he would turne his wife and the Bastard out of doors," a threat he repeated several times, twice to Mr. Peter Johnson, to whom he also said that his wife had "disgraced her Self and me and her Children afterwards."

So the women and Robert Taylor knew that Mary's baby had been conceived in an adulterous relationship: but with whom? Sarah Goulson proposed asking Mary Taylor that question while she was in labor, but Mistress Johnson vetoed the idea, saying, "She had Sorrow Enough at that Instant." Even so, several days later, when she returned to the house to help Mary Taylor out of bed for the first time, Ann Johnson asked Margaret Broome "whether her husband nor No body Else had put the question to her." When Broome answered, "Noe," Mistress Johnson then took on the traditional midwife's responsibility of initiating a childbed interrogation.

"I wish you good Sitting up, but I doubt it will prove the worst that Ever you had in your Life," she began by informing Mary, who responded with the question, "Why?" You know the reason, Ann replied: "your husband he taks Notice of it, he Sees the Matter is badd." In partial justification, Mary explained that "he used to be Soe to her." Rejecting that argument, Mistress Johnson lectured Taylor, telling her that "She had both offended God and Defamed herself and wronged her husband and Children." Margaret Broome then entered the conversation, joining Johnson in urging Mary "to Speake the truth of the matter . . . that he might take part of the Shame as well as She." "O!" interjected Margaret, "doe not let your Husband worke to Maintaine another Man's Child." Yes, chimed in Mistress Johnson colloquially, "truely I would lay the Saddle upon the right horse."

At that point, Mary Taylor surrendered to the inevitable. As Johnson recalled it, "She burst out Crying and Said that wicked man had overcome her upon a Court day at Night being the 12th of Aprill." And she identified the father: Mr. George Catchmey, a Virginia planter, one of the two men whose names had previously been linked to hers—and the one her son resembled. Mistress Johnson and Margaret Broome then advised Mary to give the baby to Catchmey and "to Submitt her Self to her husband," so "She might in time gett the Love of her husband againe for the Love of the Children he had already by her."

This uniquely detailed account of a series of childbed conversations has five elements that underscore observations made previously. First, it reveals women's widespread familiarity with the details of pregnancy and childbirth. Although Mary Taylor adamantly proclaimed her innocence and repeatedly asserted that "if She might never come out of bed She could find no other father for it then her own husband," the women who attended her childbed declared her guilty of adultery. Even before she gave birth, Taylor's female relatives and neighbors knew that her pregnancy was too far advanced for the baby to have been conceived after she returned to Maryland. That verdict was confirmed when her son proved to be full-term rather than premature.

Second, the events reaffirm the midwife's central role in investigating illicit births. Neither her husband nor her female relatives asked Mary Taylor the crucial question; they left that task instead to Ann Johnson, who willingly fulfilled it but did show sufficient compassion to permit Mary to avoid the shame of responding while she was in labor. The account also suggests the reason why women took on the role of interrogators under such difficult circumstances: so that men "might take part of the Shame" in addition to women, who (unlike their male partners) were unable to deny their guilt. And there was an added financial motive, more direct in bastardy than in adultery cases, but nevertheless significant: here it took the form of Margaret Broome's injunction, "doe not let your Husband worke to Maintaine another Man's Child."

Third, the circumstances substantiate the importance of midwives and the women's childbirth community as the keepers of secrets. Mistress Ann Johnson questioned Mary Taylor and ascertained the identity of her child's father, but she did not immediately inform the authorities of what she had learned. Instead, she held her tongue, allowing the Taylors to try to reach a settlement with Mr. George Catchmey (an aspect of the case examined in chapter seven). Neither she nor the other women involved disclosed what they knew for several months. The midwife, the first to come forward, did so only after her attempt to elicit a bribe to ensure her continuing silence led to a physical and verbal confrontation with Mary Taylor. And that conflict itself occurred in the context of the childbed of another woman, the primary occasion when women gathered outside the presence of men.

That Mistress Johnson kept her silence in 1652 in the case of Mary Taylor when she did quite the opposite six years later while dealing with the pregnant servant Jane Palldin raises the question of her motivations. Although the record gives no indication as to why her actions differed in the two apparently similar cases, some speculations are possible. Her recognition of the potentially serious consequences of an adultery accusation for Mary Taylor, coupled with the Taylor family's decision to hush up the story, perhaps led her to keep quiet until her greed and Mary Taylor's insults combined to change her mind. In the later case, the fact that Jane Palldin was her husband's servant probably proved decisive. If the paternity of Palldin's child had not been satisfactorily established, Mr. William Dorrington would undoubtedly have incurred child-maintenance costs, and he might even have been suspected of fathering the child, just as Matthew Read was thought to have impregnated his servant Elesabeth Lockett. Under such circumstances, it was clearly in her interest to discover the truth about Palldin's sexual partner.

Fourth, the story of Mary Taylor points up once again married women's dependence on their husbands, which was explored at length in chapter one. Robert Taylor's repeated threats to throw his wife and her baby out of the house appear in the depositions as a counterpoint to the women's whispered fears and insistent questions. Although Margaret Broome protested that Taylor's plan was "too Cruell," Broome and Mistress Johnson advised Mary Taylor to turn her son over to George Catchmey. They saw no alternative for her but to submit herself wholly to her husband and to hope that he would show her mercy.

Finally, it verifies that women, like men, had to be concerned with preserving their reputations. For what brought this incident of adultery to the attention of the Maryland authorities was the exchange of insults between Ann Johnson and Mary Taylor while they were leaving the childbed of Ann Pope, undoubtedly in the company of other women and perhaps one man. As soon as Mistress Johnson indicated in the presence of someone other than Sarah Goulson (who already knew the story) that she believed that Mary Taylor had committed adultery, Mary felt forced to defend herself. But she went too far, returning the precise insult that had been aimed at her, and thereby angering Johnson, who responded—by one account—"I have kept your Councell Soe Long and would not goe to my Neighbours, and have You requited me thus, I have not Stured in it yet but now thou hast urged me to it I will . . . I will Cause thee to have a whipt back." Both women, in short, felt that their good names were at stake in their slanderous encounter, and both took what they regarded as appropriate action.[69]

For women as well as men, then, maintaining their "credit" was key. And that indeed was what Robert Taylor told his wife after she admitted her adultery to him. Declaring that he would have given ten thousand pounds of tobacco to have "Saved thy Creditt," he reminded her that "I bid thee to have a Care of thy Creditt when thou wentest away" to Virginia.[70] What should be obvious in this context is that women's "credit" arose from a very different source than men's. Whereas men were primarily concerned about their reputations for honesty, truthfulness, and fair dealing in business matters, women's good names rested almost exclusively on their sexual conduct.

Accordingly, just as the insults that led men to file defamation suits clustered around the terms "rogue" and "knave," and around accusations of theft or lying, the slanders that most bothered women alluded to sexual behavior. Since three fourths of those insults came from women of the same rank, for women, as for men, defamation suits primarily offered a weapon against a vilifier of the same status. The most common single epithet, accounting for more than half of the lawsuits brought by female targets against women who applied such terms to them, was "whore" or a synonym like "jade." In addition, allegations of sexual misconduct comprised nearly half the specific charges at issue in female-only defamation suits.[71] The only other sizable category of insults (constituting about one fourth of the whole) charged the slanderers' targets with theft—not with thefts of hay or livestock, as was characteristic of men, but with stealing linens, lace, jewelry, items of clothing, or foodstuffs.[72]

So, most frequently, women's slanders of other women that elicited defamation suits or prosecutions consisted of such epithets as "hoore, theife, and Toade," "common Carted hoare," "pissa bedd Jade," or "you slutt."[73] On other occasions the defamation was more specific, but of the same sort: one Maryland woman was said to have "lyen with an Indian for peake [wampum]"; a second was accused of fornicating with two men; and a Virginian sued a female slanderer who declared that she had been "delivered of a child and that the said child was provately [sic] made away." Sometimes husbands were enmeshed in such insults as well, as when a Suffolk County widow charged that a local woman "had severall Children by other men and that the Cuckoldley old Rogue her husband owned [acknowledged] them."[74]

A woman successfully tagged with such an epithet had to deal with the consequences for many years thereafter. Take, for example, the case of Hannah Marsh Fuller Finch, of New Haven. Over two decades and through spinsterhood and two marriages, she filed three defamation suits and was herself sued once for slander. All four incidents were related to the same scandalous story.

In December 1645, shortly after arriving in the colony as a servant, she sued Mr. Francis Brewster for having called her a "Billingsgate slutt" on board ship en route from Boston to New Haven. When the judges investigated the "ordynary acceptation" of that phrase, they discovered that "some that were soe called were convicted scolds and punished at the cuckeing stoole for it, & some of them chardged with incontinency [sexual misconduct]." Mr. Brewster contended that both implications were true of Hannah Marsh and at first refused to retract either, although he eventually admitted that he had no direct evidence of sexual misbehavior on her part. With respect to the other meaning of his words, the court agreed that Hannah had been "froward and contentious," and, while rendering a decision in her favor, reminded her that "meeknes is a choise ornament for weomen, and wished her to take it [the slander] as a rebucke from God."[75]

Four years later Mr. Brewster's charges came back to haunt Hannah, who was by then married to Lancelot Fuller. Mistress Newman, a magistrate's wife, began spreading the story that she had "interteined young men or a young man . . . in her husbands absenc."[76] When Hannah Fuller, insisting the tale was untrue, asked Mistress Newman for an apology, she elicited only a grudging personal acknowledgment—"she was sorry for it"—rather than what she wanted, which was clearing her name "where it had bine spoken and to her husband when he comes home." Mistress Newman not only refused the request, she warned Hannah of further disclosures: "she were best hold her tongue & say no more in it, for if she did not put up [with] that, it would bring out worse." Mr. Francis Newman even took a hand in the matter, telling Goody Fuller "that she was onc[e] brought to the court for her tongue, and in a thretning manner said he would tame her tongue, for he knew well what she was." Hannah then called Mistress Newman a liar, and he also, since "he and his wife were one."

The New Haven justices again rebuked Hannah Fuller for her conduct, telling her that she had overreacted from "pride & selfe confidenc[e]" in attacking Mr. Newman. Still, they agreed that she had been defamed by Mistress Newman, who had been guilty of "receiving a reproach against a neighbour," then "increased the sinn" by "spreading of it." They also chided Mr. Newman, "both in not pressing the rule upon his wife, that by due satisfaction the matter might have bine ended in private, and that himself instead of speaking healing words did unnecessaryly provoake." After rereading the 1645 case record, they declared that Mr. Newman was "out of his way in making such use of that suit in this case," ordering him to pay a substantial fine to the Fullers.

Yet that did not end the persistent rumors. In April 1652, another woman spoke "naughty, sinnfull, corrupting words" about the recently widowed Goody Fuller and, unlike Mistress Newman, publicly apologized to avoid a court judgment. Finally, nearly thirteen years later (February 1664/5), Hannah, now married to John Finch, was the defendant in a slander suit filed by Ellen Thompson. Goody Thompson, a witness when Hannah's daughter, Mary Fuller, was convicted of lewd conduct during the same court session, proved that Hannah had ranted to a local couple that "goodwife Tompson had told a great many lies of her, & . . . That if one should rake hell & skim the divell they could not find such a liar." Although the precise lie of which Hannah Finch was accusing Ellen Thompson is nowhere noted, it does not take much imagination to conclude that it was some variant of the comment "like mother, like daughter." And that would indeed have been a lie, for the court records contain no indication that Hannah was ever charged with sexual misconduct of any sort other than by Francis Brewster's 1645 insult, which the court had decided was not supported by adequate evidence.[77]

If the case of Hannah Marsh shows what could happen when a woman became the target of a female gossip network, other examples suggest the ways in which women attempted to profit from information gained from such sources. When in late 1640 Mistress Welthian Richards, of Weymouth, Massachusetts, was involved in a prolonged business dispute with her absent husband's partner, she cited five instances of his "lacivious cariage" with different women over a period of years in order to prove that he was not "fitt for honest company"—and thus, presumably, that her position should prevail. The only way she could have collected so many nasty personal stories was through talking to large numbers of women. Likewise, when Mary Drury wanted to divorce her husband for impotence in 1677, she turned for evidence to the female friends of Hugh Drury's first wife, Lydia, who reported a series of conversations with her "some years since" on the subject of her husband's virility. For example, in response to a comment that she looked pregnant, Lydia had replied that although she was not too old to have children, "she never was with child since she had her son John; & said alas my husband hath a great weaknes upon him along time." On another occasion Lydia remarked to an acquaintance (who then told another woman, who reported it to the court) "that if the Case were not with

[her] husband as it was formerly shee might have more children as we[ll as] other weomen."[78]

Information passed along gossip networks could also lead to collective actions of various sorts. In a deposition submitted to the Essex County court in 1664, two older women described their actions upon learning of a scandalous incident involving two young married couples in their Ipswich neighborhood. While John Howe was away for several days, his wife, Mary, asked her friend Faith Black to stay with her. The women were in bed together when John, who had been drinking, arrived home late one night. Faith's father, hearing of the incident from Mary Howe, remarked that "faith had dieprived hur of all hur comfort that night," but Mary demurred, revealing that while Faith was still present they "had t[w]o mery boutes." (A male witness put it differently, reporting that John "did her over twise that nite.") Faith Black's shocked father told the story to several others, and it eventually reached the ears of Elizabeth Perkins and Agnes Ewens. They enlisted a third woman, then went to see Mary Howe about "her simple & foolish Carriages & words." Subsequently, they assured the court, she had behaved "very gravely & soberly." When Goody Perkins and Goody Ewens asked the judges to excuse them from public testimony in a case involving the contentious relationship of Faith Black and her husband, they insisted that "what was their spoken to us . . . was spoken privately, in a way of Confession of a miscarriage, which wee have never to this day divulged." They thereby in effect claimed a family governor's privilege not to reveal a private household offense, defining their "household" as the community of women.[79]

Women, like men, opposed a settled consensus of opinion among their peers only at their peril. Goody Staplies, of Fairfield, Connecticut, learned that the hard way in 1654 after she watched the execution for witchcraft of Goody Knapp, one of her fellow townswomen.[80] Prior to her trial, Goody Knapp had been examined for "witch's teats," which were places (usually near the genitals) where animal familiars sent by the devil were believed to suck on a witch. A female jury led by an unnamed midwife and Mistress Lucy Brewster Pell concluded that Goody Knapp had such teats, but numerous witnesses later deposed that at Goody Knapp's grave Goody Staplies "handled her verey much, and called to goodwife Lockwood, and said, these were no witches teates, but such as she herselfe had, and other women might have the same, wringing her hands and takeing the Lords name in her mouth, and said, will you say these were witches teates, they were not."

Eventually, with "all the women rebuking her" and declaring that "they were witches teates" and that "no honest woman had such," Goody Staplies "yeilded it." Yet her conduct at Goody Knapp's grave aroused deep suspicions that she herself was a witch. Fairfield residents subsequently speculated wildly about stories that Goody Knapp had named Goody Staplies as a witch before her execution or, at the very least, that Knapp had accused Staplies of possessing effigies of Indian deities. Agreeing with Goody Staplies and her husband that she had been slandered by all the talk, the New Haven magistrates awarded Thomas Staplies a substantial sum "for reparation of his wives name."

Communities of women like those who gathered at the grave of Goody Knapp or at the childbeds of innumerable mothers-to-be lacked the permanence or formality of some of the male communities they paralleled, but that rendered them no less identifiable and concrete. Time and again, as this analysis has indicated, the women who assumed leadership roles were either midwives or the wives of high-ranking men or both. Such women were the focal points of the female communities, those who served simultaneously as opinion leaders, spokeswomen, and moral arbiters. Through their participation on women's juries or their work as semi-official investigators of sexual or witchcraft offenses, they linked the communities of men and women, conveying the consensus of women's thinking to such masculine institutions as courts or legislatures. Although on most occasions judges or other officials requested their assistance, at other times they acted on their own. In the cases involving Joan Colledge, Mistress Alice Tilly, and Mary Howe, one can discern the shadowy contours of the women's communities and can gain insight into their values and inner workings.

The leaders of such all-female societies had long memories; they were able to summon up recollections of abuse that had occurred years earlier. That was certainly implied by Mistress Welthian Richards's ability to obtain information about a series of long-past episodes of sexual misconduct when she wanted to discredit her husband's partner. An even more dramatic illustration of the same phenomenon came in Virginia in May 1625.

At the end of her testimony about contemptuous speeches against the government by Captain John Martin, Mistress Isabell Perry added what must have seemed to the members of the General Court to be an irrelevant aside. "In the time of Sir Thomas Dales Goverment," she recounted, Ann Laydon, Jane Wright, and other women were ordered to make shirts for the colony's servants. Each woman was allotted a limited amount of thread for each shirt, "which yf they did not performe, They had no allowanc[e] of Dyett." Because some of the thread was bad and Laydon and Wright had no other thread to use, "they tooke owt a ravell of the lower parte of the shirte to make an end of the worke." Their shirts were thus shorter than those made by the other seamstresses, and "the said Ann leyden and Jane Wright were whipt, And Ann leyden beinge then with childe (the same night therof miscarried)."[81]

An "Ancient Planter" who had arrived in Virginia with her first husband before 1616, Mistress Perry had undoubtedly witnessed the whippings she recalled with such distaste. Although the date cannot be ascertained exactly, the incident she described had occurred about a decade earlier (Sir Thomas Dale was the governor briefly in 1611, then again from 1614 to 1616). The clerk recorded her statement without comment, and it sits anomalously in the midst of testimony collected to prosecute a man for contempt of authority in 1625. So what was Mistress Perry's purpose in retelling the tale of injustice done to two ordinary women ten years earlier? She could only have intended to use a public forum to which she rarely had access—she had first appeared as a witness earlier that same month, which perhaps emboldened her to speak out on this occasion—to document her continuing outrage over the long-ago treatment of Laydon and Wright. Yet there is no indication that the judges reacted in any way to Mistress Perry's recollections.[82]

The same conjunction of outrage and opportunity seems to have occurred when the Maryland midwife Rose Gilbert Smith and her acquaintance Elizabeth Claxton came unbidden to the Provincial Court in September 1656. On September 22, Smith and Claxton served as members of a female jury that cleared a recently arrived maidservant of the charge that she had committed infanticide on shipboard en route to the colony. Three days later, they each offered an unsolicited deposition to the court, describing an event that had clearly enraged them as much as the whippings of Laydon and Wright had angered Perry.[83]

Elizabeth Claxton, who had never previously appeared as a witness before the court session in question, volunteered the information that while Mr. Francis Brooke and his pregnant wife were staying at her house at some unspecified time in the past, he hit his wife with "a Cane" until it shattered, broke "an oaken board . . . in two pieces on her," and also struck her repeatedly with "the great end" of a pair of tongs. Claxton reported that when she remonstrated with Mr. Brooke about his behavior, he replied that "he did not Care if She did Miscarry, if She were with Child it was none of his." Since Claxton gave no indication as to the timing of the beatings, they could have taken place

months or even years previously. So why did she tell the story at that
court session? Answering that inquiry requires both some reading between the lines and a close look at the other witness, who probably
encouraged Claxton to testify.[84]

In 1656 Rose Gilbert Smith, who was then in her late forties, was
a midwife, an experienced witness, and one of the few surviving early
migrants to Maryland. She had immigrated to the colony with her first
husband, Richard Gilbert, and two daughters in the mid-1630s; after
Richard died, she quickly remarried. Her 1651 testimony about her attempt to intervene in a troubled marriage revealed that she did not
hesitate to speak her mind. After Rose learned from the unhappy Dorothy Holt that she and her husband had separated, Rose advised Dorothy
"to return to her husband," reminding her of her unbreakable marriage
vows. Dorothy ignored Rose's suggestion and later found herself on trial
for adultery.[85]

Rose Smith was the midwife summoned to the side of Francis
Brooke's wife when she went into premature labor after the last brutal
beating by her husband. Rose delivered a dead fetus, "all bruised one
Side of it," and asked Mistress Brooke what had happened. "He did it
with a pair of Tongues," she replied, and so the midwife, having heard
that "the[y] Lived discontentedly," showed the little body to Mr.
Brooke. Goody Smith pointedly told him "that it Came Soe through
his Misusage, . . . he would dearly Answer [for] it although he [e]Scaped
in this world, yet in the world to Come he Should Answer for it before
a Judge that useth no partiality." In response, Mr. Brooke claimed that
"She fell out of the peach tree, And he asked her if She did not fall out
of the Peach Tree and She Said yes."

Rose Smith had thus been given conflicting information about the
circumstances of the miscarriage: first, Mistress Brooke declared that she
had been beaten with tongs, but then—challenged by her husband—
she withdrew that story and agreed that she had fallen from a tree.
Elizabeth Claxton assisted the midwife at the stillbirth and knew the
truth (that a vicious beating had caused the miscarriage) but perhaps did
not reveal that information to Rose Smith at the time. Regardless of
whether Claxton told Smith then or during the September 1656 court
session, it was service on the female jury that brought the two women
together, probably led them to talk further about the incidents at Claxton's house, and afforded them the opportunity to inform the judges
about Mr. Brooke's brutal treatment of his wife.

The Maryland Provincial Court formally charged Mr. Francis
Brooke with "Murther," but required him only to post a bond to return

six months later. At that time, the judges remitted the bond without comment and did not pursue the prosecution further. Rose Smith's prediction had been correct: the "partial" justice of the Maryland courts did not accord with the verdict she and Elizabeth Claxton had already rendered in the case.

Although the outcomes of the trials in question differed, therefore, Rose Smith and Elizabeth Claxton's encounter with the Maryland judges in 1656 resembled the experiences of Massachusetts Bay's female petitioners with their colony's General Court in 1649–50. In both instances, women and men collectively reached opposite conclusions about the guilt of a person charged with a crime, and on both occasions the men's opinion prevailed because their communal judgments had the official standing that women's decisions lacked. Yet, as has been seen, men did not always ignore women's opinions. Not only did the Maryland Provincial Court reprieve Joane Colledge, Bay Colony authorities also proved amenable to suggestions that the conditions of Mistress Tilly's confinement be eased. Moreover, male judges and juries relied heavily and regularly on women's testimony in prosecutions for bastardy, infanticide, and witchcraft.

Thus the men's communities, reinforced by laws that made men responsible for financial and political affairs, sought to achieve consensus among men on such matters as the need for trustworthiness and straightforwardness in their mutual dealings with each other. They were not always successful, especially in the Chesapeake, but the goals were well understood and accepted by the vast majority of male Anglo-American settlers. And so too women's communities sought consensus on the subject of sexual behavior. They cooperated with civil officials to ensure that men as well as women were penalized for such crimes, but they did not hesitate to express opinions opposed to those advanced by men, especially on childbirth and women's bodies, their particular areas of expertise. When the separate collectivities of men and women clashed, men's positions usually prevailed, but such an outcome was not foreordained. That was equally true when the interactions of individual men and women were at issue, as is evident in the neighborhood confrontations that are the subject of chapter five.

CHAPTER 5

Amongst the Neighbors

The defendant on a training day, before a great part of the traine band, did endeavoure by his words to take away his repute & esteeme amongst his neighbours, & lay him below the heathen, & to that end spake words to this effect, or the same words following, vizt., that John Concklin was a neighboure not fitt for an Indian to live by.

—*Concklin* v. *Corey, 1660*[1]

JOHN CONCKLIN'S COMPLAINT that John Corey had called him a bad neighbor was one of four cases involving the same group of men heard by the New Haven Magistrates Court in May 1660. The neighborhood in question, known as Hashamommock, was on Long Island, the eastern end of which fell under the jurisdiction of the small mainland colony. The troubles began, Concklin recalled in the other suit he filed against Corey that day, when "his now wife in her widdowhood" sustained substantial losses of wheat and peas from Corey's marauding hogs. That dispute was arbitrated on Long Island, but Corey was so dissatisfied with the outcome of the mediation that he not only refused to abide by the agreement but also vilified both Conckin and Concklin's principal witness, John Budd, Jr., whom Corey accused of having given false testimony to the arbitrators.[2]

Consequently, Concklin sued Corey for the loss of his wife's crops, and both Concklin and Budd sued Corey for defamation. Concklin easily won his two cases, as the magistrates accepted the arbitrators' ruling and, with respect to the slander, Corey admitted that "his was a guilty person & could not justify himself, he had done evill & he saw it." John Corey was ordered to pay fines for both offenses, to make good the damages, and to give Concklin a written apology. But Corey proved that he had already adequately apologized to Budd, for, although Budd rejected such a solution, he "did tender John Budd to give him such satisfaction as indifferent men (who John Budd should chuse) should judg meet." Accordingly, the court—while assessing Corey costs—did not fine him further, though still directing him to acknowledge his fault publicly.

The fourth case pitted Concklin and two other men against John Budd, Sr., whom they charged with "breach of an ancient order made for the preservation of good neighbourhood . . . at our first sitting downe." The agreement declared that "our comfort & quiet settlement would consist & stand in the enjoyment of good neighbourehood," providing that "what man soever should desire to remove, & so endeavour to make sale of his accommodations, should put in such neighbour as the other inhabitants liveing with him shall approve of." Asked by John Budd, Jr., representing his father, whether they thought this agreement was appropriate, the New Haven magistrates pronounced it "righteous in itself and bindeing to those that did first engage and to their successors." But the magistrates indicated that the case would turn on the key question of whether John Budd, Sr., had known about the agreement. Since neither of the parties was prepared to argue that point, the judges referred the issue to the local Long Island court. The outcome is unknown.

The suits involving Concklin, Corey, and the Budds disclose three important elements of neighborhood interactions in seventeenth-century Anglo-America. First, a man's credit rested in part on his being regarded as a good neighbor. To say that a man was "not fitt for an Indian to live by" was to vilify him, "to take away his repute & esteeme." Everyone familiar with the case, including the defamer, understood how serious an accusation had been leveled at John Concklin and recognized that reparation of some sort would be demanded for the damaging insult.

Second, part of being a good neighbor was bowing to the collective judgment of one's peers. The first settlers at Hashamommock had tried to formalize that understanding with respect to the composition of the neighborhood itself by declaring that none of them could sell property to anyone not previously approved by the other residents. Corey recognized his obligation to such a community consensus when he offered John Budd, Jr., whatever "satisfaction" was thought "meet" by "indifferent men" of Budd's choice. The New Haven court subsequently acknowledged the adequacy of Corey's response by declining to levy additional penalties for his offense to Budd. Yet simultaneously Corey violated the same obligation by rejecting the arbitrators' award to John Concklin, and the court ordered him to pay dearly for his failure to accede to the judgment rendered by his neighbors. Thus in three distinct ways the Long Island cases underscored not just the importance of good relationships among individuals but also the necessity for people to acknowledge the compelling nature of their duty to acquiesce in an established community consensus.

Third, that a key participant in the dispute, though a silent one, was a woman—John Concklin's "now wife in her widdowhood"—points up once again the inadequacy of a scheme that conceptualizes men as the only actors in colonial communities. The initial dispute over crop damage was between a widow and John Corey; Concklin became involved only because he married that widow and thereby acquired the legal obligation to represent her at the arbitration hearing and later in court. Corey would presumably have had no reason to vilify Concklin as a bad neighbor had not the marriage taken place. Although in this particular case Concklin's wife's legal status and the absence of female witnesses placed women in a wholly passive role, that was by no means the norm within the informal public, as shall be seen in the pages that follow.

In addition to the same-sex associations detailed in chapter four, then, the English colonists regularly interacted with neighbors of both sexes during the course of their daily lives. People struggled for position in the "small politics" of the neighborhood, in contests that depended on their personal reputations, their relationships with other individuals, and their connections to the collectivity as a whole. In such interactions, individuals' placement in the hierarchy of their own families or in the broader range of social ranks was influential but not wholly determinative. Recall from the last chapter, for instance, that the high-ranking men Mr. Arthur Turner and Mr. Hugh Stanley were so distrusted by their neighbors of ordinary rank that they were unable to win judgments from the Maryland courts after that distrust had been publicly expressed. Or, conversely, that the reputation of Hannah Marsh, the New Haven servant unjustly accused of sexual misconduct by the high-status Mr. Francis Newman, was formally vindicated by the judges' decision in her favor.[3]

Daily life in colonial neighborhoods accordingly proceeded largely without reference to the hierarchical order that, at least theoretically, characterized the separate households comprising those neighborhoods. Family governors could rule their own subordinates, but their relationships to other heads of households or to the dependents of those household heads was unclear. To be sure, higher-ranking individuals expected deference from persons of lower status, but such expectations were not always fulfilled when social rather than political obligations were at issue. And, in any event, most interactions in the neighborhoods occurred among people of similar social rank. How was a family governor to resolve his dispute with the wife of a neighbor? How did a married woman react when she had a grievance against a neighbor's son or daughter? How did a servant of one household deal with the child of another? And what if groups of people from several different households, not just individuals, were involved in altercations?

Neighborhood residents adopted a variety of tactics to advance their positions within the context of small politics. Some handled grievances orally, through face-to-face insults or perhaps through gossip and innuendo. Others reacted physically, while still others sought formal or informal intervention by outsiders. Whatever the method selected, the small politics of the neighborhood often ended up enmeshed in the larger politics of the colonial legal system, as the inability of neighbors to resolve certain arguments in the absence of clearly defined hierarchies regularly led to judicial intervention.

LIVING "AMONGST THE NEIGHBORS"

"It was very unComfortable for neighbours to live in Contention," declared a plaintiff in the New Haven town court in January 1665/6. The judges surely agreed with the sentiments, but they were not impressed with the complainant's commitment to local harmony. Thus they decided that *he* was the primary cause of the contention at issue. That same day the court also rendered judgment in a slander case involving the man's neighbors, rebuking a widow for having said that "the worke of the divell was done" at a nearby house. Taken together, the two "vexatious suits" troubled the magistrates, so they "left a serious Advice with these neighbors at farmes, that they live more quietly & peaceably for the future." But although the New Haven justices often expressed the hope that the settlers in their colony might "live in neighborly love together," those hopes were just as frequently dashed.[4]

The ideals of "good neighborhood" were more readily advocated than achieved. The early colonists were a contentious lot, quick to anger and prone to physical violence or verbal abuse of others, especially when they drank to excess—which was often, judging by the many reports of drunkenness that fill the pages of surviving court records.[5] Men and women were charged with "setting differences between Neighbours," "scoulding & abuseing of her neighbours," or setting "neighbours togather by the ears."[6] Yet neighbors also needed each other. The Plymouth Colony court recognized as much when it took up the case of Joseph Ramsden, who "lived with his family remotely in the woods from naighbours." Ramsden, the court proclaimed, lived "in an uncivell way" that caused "great inconveniencies" to his family and especially endangered his wife, who was "exposed to great hardship and perill of loosing her life," presumably because she lacked experienced female attendants when she gave birth. Twice, in 1652 and again in 1656, the authorities told Ramsden to move "to sum naighborhood," and on the second occasion they ordered his house to be "pulled downe" to ensure his compliance with that directive.[7]

The Plymouth judges therefore understood the vital role neighbors played in each others' lives, a role repeatedly confirmed in the records of civil and criminal court proceedings. For instance, when in 1656 a Marylander wanted to prove that a house and fencing he had recently purchased were in poor condition, he asked a neighbor to assess their value for him, submitting that deposition to support his claim for compensation. A decade later in the same colony, a group of neighbors rallied around Peter Elzey, who was suing the third husband of his former sister-in-law Sarah. The witnesses attested that Sarah's first husband, Peter's brother, had taken possession of five of Peter's cattle six years earlier. They recounted numerous conversations with Sarah and her second husband during the intervening years, all acknowledging that Peter owned the cattle. Convinced by the neighbors' depositions, the Somerset County court ordered Sarah's third husband to turn five cattle over to Peter Elzey.[8]

The testimony of neighbors proved especially valuable when the ownership of a specific animal was in question—as, for instance, when a stray horse or cow was claimed by two or more people. Then the accounts offered by disinterested parties with nothing to gain from the victory of either side often proved decisive. So in Maryland in early 1659 thirteen male witnesses helped a widow gain possession of a horse she said she had lost two years earlier. A Stamford, Connecticut, man's testimony in such cases was particularly compelling, for others attested that he was "well experienced in the knowledg of most mens horses aboute Stamford, and is much imployed by others to looke up horses for them, and is judged to be one of the ablest in towne for that purpose." On the other hand, if neighbors disagreed among themselves the courts found it difficult to render verdicts; the New Haven judges were confronted with two such cases, which they declared themselves reluctant to decide.[9]

One Virginian's low-key approach to advancing a claim to a hog that he said was his, though it bore a neighbor's earmark, must have pleased the Accomack County justices in 1640. Thomas Gascoyne presented strong evidence that his neighbor had disregarded even his own cowkeeper's doubts about the hog's ownership when he ordered it earmarked. Gascoyne could have accused his neighbor of deliberate theft, yet he declared that he felt no "malignancy or malevolenc" toward the man, instead desiring "the tranquillity and peace of himselfe, as alsoe of his neighbors." All he asked was to be "fullie satisfied for his damage and losse." The county court acceded to Gascoyne's description of the incident as a "mistake" and awarded him the compensation he requested.[10]

Thomas Gascoyne therefore cleverly won his case yet at the same time preserved his "tranquil" relationship with the neighbor he suspected of stealing other hogs in addition to the one he formally claimed. Unfortunately for local peace in the English settlements, not all were as willing as he to adopt such a diplomatic means of resolving their differences. One endemic source of contention was disputes over the ownership of land, and some colonists asserted their claims by deliberately destroying a rival's crops or fences. Thus Hannah Walford Jones, a New Hampshire woman, persisted for several years in the late 1650s in a challenge to George Walton's hold on a piece of marsh that she believed had been her father's wedding gift to her and her husband. Walton's witnesses attested that they had seen Hannah Jones repeatedly "pull downe the fence of George Waltons feild." Each time, Hannah would pasture her cow there, and as soon as Walton's servants drove the cow out, she would put it back again.[11]

Moreover, men and women alike came to blows when cattle, pigs, or horses ravaged fields of corn or peas. An Ipswich man, John Lee, angered his neighbors by being (to their minds) too quick to kill, injure, or impound roving livestock that invaded his property. Although he defended himself by arguing, "shud a man have other mens cattell eate up his foder and he have no way to help [himself]," his neighbors concluded that he regularly overreacted in such circumstances. When Lee was accused of wounding an ox and killing a pig in May 1660, nineteen men and a woman testified against him, recalling many incidents in which he had abused others' livestock. And they did more than appear in court: a year later his son deposed that during the intervening period Lee's cart had been overturned, his ropes cut into pieces, and "his cattel turned loose in the barne, in the night when there was corn on the floore."[12]

Sometimes more personal matters were raised in neighborhood contests, especially when the combatants were well fueled by alcohol. Take, for example, an incident at the house of Mr. Thomas Bradnox on Kent Island in the fall of 1657.[13] Mr. Joseph Wickes and another man arrived at Bradnox's plantation before dawn one October morning, bringing with them from the mainland "a rundlett of drams." Mr. Bradnox welcomed the travelers with "some Expresiones of his Joy," but it is not clear whether he was more pleased to see them or the liquor they carried. He quickly distributed the alcohol to his wife and several men—family members and neighbors—who were at the house. Soon Mr. Bradnox, Wickes reported, was "much disguised with drincke," and he fell and bloodied his nose. Mr. Wickes and Mary Bradnox then put Thomas to bed in his room.

Thomas Snockes, one of the neighbors who had been drinking with the Bradnoxes, described what happened next. Another neighbor, John Salter, "went & sate downe by Mrs Braadnox [sic] & he raised her up by the armes & tooke her in his armes & . . . laid her upon the Hall bed & he askt her to have to doe with her & she said noe, but noe resistance made that your deponent could see or hear." Snockes told the local justice of the peace that he tried "stamping & makeing a noise" to alert Salter and Mary Bradnox to his presence, but without success. So he enlisted a maidservant, Ann Stanly, "to see a sight." Stanly, however, hesitated to enter the hall until Mr. Bradnox, roused from his drunken stupor by the commotion, called to her "for witnesse." Then she saw "John Salters breches downe in his hand & my Mrs upon the bed with her coats up as high as her brest as the Said Salter came from her."

Salter left the room, and, Stanly recounted, "my Maister would have had society with his wife . . . [but] she would not yeald caleing forth for helpe." Her cries brought Salter back, and he attacked Bradnox, nearly strangling him before Snockes and three other men forcibly intervened to end the struggle. Mr. Bradnox then accused Salter of having "laine with his wife"; Salter retorted, "it is noe more than yow have don to my wife." The neighbors hustled Salter out of the hall, then out of the house.

Eventually, Salter left, Mr. Bradnox went to bed in his room, and Mistress Bradnox took refuge in another chamber with her maidservant. Ann Stanly told the justice of the peace that the next night, as they lay together in bed, "my Mrs . . . bid your deponent have a care, & said if I did sweare that I did see rime in ree [sexual intercourse] between my Mrs & Salter that shee would have me whipt." Although a total of eight depositions were collected by the Kent Island authorities from six witnesses, no prosecution or civil suit ever resulted from the incident. Mary Bradnox, her husband, and John Salter all had good reason to want to keep the affair out of the courts. Had any one of them pursued a case against any other, multiple charges of adultery would have had to be adjudicated. It was in the best interest of all three principals to let matters drop.

The drunken debauchery at the Bradnox plantation not only reveals that neighbors could be entangled in intimate ways but also reconfirms the lack of privacy in seventeenth-century houses and the omnipresence of neighbors in families' lives. When Joseph Wickes and his companion arrived without warning at the Bradnox household before sunrise that October day, those present (in addition to Thomas and Mary) were two servants, John Salter, three other male neighbors, a "negar," and a "child" (each of the latter two mentioned briefly in passing). All of them, including the two travelers, observed the subsequent events, though not all offered depositions about what they had seen. And there was nothing unusual about the number of people at the Bradnox household that night. Consequently, as male and female miscreants discovered time after time, concealing criminal conduct from their neighbors was nearly impossible. That was true even in the Chesapeake, where settlement was more dispersed than in New England.

Testimony in theft prosecutions provides an excellent example of the oversight exercised by neighbors. People knew each other's possessions, and unexplained acquisitions aroused comment. So when William Vincent of Talbot County, Maryland, called at the home of William Dell in 1666 and "found the pott boyling," he asked Dell whether he had killed a deer. Dell replied that he had not, but had instead slaughtered one of his hogs. Yet three days later, when Vincent returned, "he saw all the hoggs thatt dell had of that age, that hee said hee killed." As a result, another neighbor who had recently lost several hogs charged Dell with stealing them. Likewise, in Virginia in 1626 a witness's mysterious early-morning encounter with a man carrying a sack (the contents of which he would not reveal), coupled with the sack-carrier's reputation as a "ffelonious and pillferinge fellow," led to the filing of theft charges against him.[14]

Several incidents in Maryland reveal that lawbreakers recognized and feared the role of neighbors in such cases. One man concealing stolen goods was convinced that four female callers at his house were "spies" sent to search his place informally. Another planter, who brought home a slaughtered hog without ears, found a female neighbor visiting his spouse when he walked in the door. He then quickly attempted to cover up his malfeasance, but fooled no one. A witness reported that "(Seeing a Stranger in the house) when he Came in with the hog, [he exclaimed] O! wife I have left the hogs Eares in the Indian Cabinn, and forgott them." So when Thomas Bradnox killed a steer under suspicious circumstances in 1648, a servant testified that "it was eaten in private; & none of it brought forth, when any stranger was present." Not surprisingly, therefore, when the midwife Mary Clocker proposed stealing the belongings of her deceased patient Mistress Elizabeth Oversee, her accomplice warned her "that these things could not be used here but they would be knowne." Clocker was so intent upon theft as a means of obtaining payment for her work, however, that she told the other woman that "rather then ever hee [Simon Oversee] shall have them, I will burne them, & further sayd that shee would bury them in a Case in the Grownd."[15]

Since they had such comprehensive knowledge of one another, neighbors could play a decisive role in verdicts rendered by colonial courts. When a Suffolk County man "strongly denied" having fathered a bastard in January 1672/3, "an Attest of severall of his neighbourhood of his good conversation" prevented his conviction on criminal charges, and the fine levied on a Plymouth man who confessed to liquor-sale violations was halved after his neighbors testified that "he hath not been used to transgress in such kind." Similarly, eight "next neighbours" of a New Amsterdam suicide in 1664 convinced the city court to allow him a proper burial and to relax the stringent rules declaring his property forfeit to the government by affirming that he was "an old Burgher here, of whom no bad behaviour was ever heard." Conversely, a man whose neighbors said that he was "of very loose behavior at home, given much to lying and idleness," fared poorly in a Bay Colony courtroom in 1644.[16]

Colonists like him must have fared equally badly in their daily interactions in the community. Life could be very difficult for men or women who had poor relationships with their neighbors, just as John Lee discovered when he too readily killed or maimed the livestock that invaded his Ipswich farm. If irreconcilable contentions developed in neighborhoods, the objects of general opprobrium could suffer serious consequences. In the most acrimonious cases, dramatic evidence of the disruption of local harmony could surface as witchcraft accusations—the seventeenth-century verbal equivalents of nuclear weapons. Recall, for example, that one of the lawsuits from the strife-ridden neighborhood called the "farmes" considered by the New Haven town court in early

January 1665/6 involved the allegation that "the worke of the divell was done" at another house.[17]

That case was atypical because the person accused of doing "the devil's work" was a man. As is now well known, witchcraft charges, which brought explosive power to bear on the disputes of small politics, were more commonly employed against women than men. And the women charged with sorcery tended to be those who, for one reason or another, had especially contentious relationships with neighbors and sometimes their own relatives. These women's designation as witches came not so much from any "supernatural" act of their own as from suspicions in the minds of the men and women who dealt with them on a daily basis and who found those interactions troubling in a variety of ways. Such women, as the focal points of neighborhood conflict, differed little from men in the same position—men who, like Ipswich's John Lee or the Marylanders Mr. Arthur Turner and Mr. Hugh Stanley, were widely distrusted by their neighbors and who thereupon became the targets of physical or verbal abuse. But why, then, were such men not also charged with witchcraft?[18]

Some historians have answered that question by positing that misogyny lay at the heart of all witchcraft accusations.[19] Although there is no denying that seventeenth-century Anglo-Americans, like their European contemporaries, believed women inferior to men,[20] the specific implementation of that belief must be understood in the context of the small politics of the neighborhood and within the nexus of gendered power. Men and women—particularly men—who were angry with their male neighbors had many means of expressing that anger. A man could be hounded with nuisance lawsuits, he could be deprived of whatever offices he held, his fences and other property could be vandalized or his pigs and cows stolen or injured. The possibilities for a creative and vengeful person were literally endless.

But successfully attacking a woman was more difficult. Recent research has demonstrated that the majority of women charged with witchcraft in the colonies were married at the time of the accusation. A married woman owned no property; not she but her husband would come to court to respond to any lawsuit; she held no public offices and thus could not be humiliated by being thrust out of them. She could, it is true, be accused of a crime committed independently of her husband, but the opportunities for charges of that sort were few and far between. There was also little chance that a physical assault would accomplish much of lasting impact. Within the confines of a society organized on the basis of gendered power, in short, most adult women were shielded by their social and legal standing from the sorts of tactics that could easily be employed against men.[21]

Of necessity, then, neighbors' attacks on mature women often took verbal form. And the most damaging charges that could be leveled against women were those that accused them of capital offenses, chiefly witchcraft, infanticide, or—in New England—adultery (which was not a capital crime in the Chesapeake). A charge of infanticide was credible only when used against a young unmarried woman, and the Bay Colony's law providing for the execution of adulterers was implemented only once. That left an accusation of witchcraft as the one viable verbal bombshell that could be employed as a last resort against a married woman. So in the 1680s George Walton used that weapon against his long-time antagonist Hannah Walford Jones,[22] and so too it was utilized against Salem's Edith Crawford in 1666.

Crawford was initially charged with vengefully burning down a house from which she and her husband had recently been evicted.[23] A woman who expressed confidence in Goody Crawford's innocence learned from several men that "there was but few of my beleefe in the Towne." Yet the Court of Assistants nevertheless acquitted Crawford after witnesses deposed that she had been at her new dwelling with her husband at the time the fire broke out and, furthermore, that the fire had in all likelihood been started by careless workmen who were repairing the building. The house's owner was not satisfied, however, continuing to insist that Edith Crawford had caused the fire. It did not matter that she was nowhere near the scene, he declared, for "shee was A witch & if shee were nott A witch allreddy shee would bee won." He thus adopted the only course left open to him after Goody Crawford's acquittal on the arson charge, developing a supernatural explanation that allowed him to maintain his firm belief in her guilt and spreading a rumor that he hoped would place her under a perpetual cloud. Deprived of other weapons, verbal or physical, he advanced the witchcraft charge as a last resort.

A case allowing the exploration of these observations in greater depth is that of Mistress Elizabeth Godman, a resident of New Haven in the mid-1650s. Unlike most other women accused of witchcraft, Mistress Godman was not married. But, like wives, she was not vulnerable to direct attacks on her property, because her substantial estate was in the possession of the magistrate Mr. Stephen Goodyear. In compliance with the colony's order that all single people live in households where their behavior could be monitored, she resided with Goodyear, his wife, Margaret, and Margaret's two daughters by her first marriage. Mr. Goodyear, probably thought to be a suitable family governor for Mistress Godman because of their mutual high rank, controlled about three fourths of her assets. Perhaps as a result of her ambiguous position within the household, Elizabeth Godman's relationship with the Goodyear clan was uneasy: Margaret's daughters spied on her repeatedly; she once directed a "fierce looke" at Mr. Goodyear that caused him to fall into "a swonding fitt"; and Mistress Goodyear suspected her of sorcery.[24]

Even so, most of the encounters that led first to gossip about Mistress Godman, then to her 1653 defamation suit against nine people, and finally to a formal witchcraft accusation two years later, involved neighbors rather than members of the Goodyear household. Goody Larremore "thought of a witch" when she saw Elizabeth Godman because she exhibited the "froward discontented frame of spirit" that the Reverend John Davenport had declared "was a subject fitt for the Devill to worke upon." Mr. William Hooke, a second New Haven clergyman, believed that Mistress Godman had bewitched his son, for he found her "mallitious," and his boy was sick "in a verey strang manner." The Hookes' Indian servant woman joined others in attesting that Elizabeth Godman had unusually detailed knowledge about what happened in church meetings she had not attended, and Mistress Atwater "forwarned her of her house" for "sundrie things which render her suspitious." Goody Thorpe thought that Mistress Godman had bewitched her chickens and cows, Goodman Allen Ball that she had bewitched his calf and pigs, Mr. Hooke that she had soured several barrels of beer, Goodwife Elizabeth Hotchkiss that she had spoiled the butter in her churn. And many people believed that she envied Mistress Bishop, the wife of a man she had hoped to marry.

When Elizabeth Godman responded wrathfully to the suspicions voiced against her, her rage compounded her problems. Thus when Mistress Bishop had a "sore fitt" and Mr. Goodyear called Godman to "looke upon" the invalid, openly expressing his fears that Mistress Elizabeth was a witch, she became "exceeding angrie" and asked, "who bewitched her[self] for she was not well." At that, one of Goodyear's stepdaughters "fell into a verey sore fitt in a verey strang maner." Mistress Godman's reply to Goody Thorpe's charge of bewitching chickens also elicited results deemed "strange." About a week after Goody Thorpe had accused her, the two women met on the street. "How doth Goody Thorpe?" asked Elizabeth Godman sarcastically. "I am behoulden to Goody Thorpe above all the weomen in the Towne: she would have had me to the gallowes for a few chickens." Then, said

Thorpe, Mistress Godman "gnashed and grinned with her teeth in a strang manner."

The neighbors' repeated use of the word "strange" to describe happenings related to Mistress Elizabeth Godman suggests how anomalous she was in early New Haven. Evidently resisting the attempt to integrate her into the community, she chafed at her lot in life. Her high status could well have contributed to her discontent; like Mistress Ann Hibbens, she would not have been accustomed to deferring to others' judgments about her best interests. That for the five years between 1655 and her death in 1660 she resided without incident in the house of an ordinary settler (where presumably she received the deference she thought she deserved) supports the speculation that she did not readily yield to supervision by the Goodyears.[25]

In the tale of Elizabeth Godman's contentious relationships with her family of residence and her neighbors, stories of direct confrontations intermingle with echoes of gossip. Mistress Godman "heard" that the Hookes "had something against her aboute their soone [son]"; "some sisters . . . told her some thing" about what went on in church meetings; many people knew that Elizabeth had said that "Mris. Bishop was much given to longing and that was the reason she lost her children"; Goody Thorpe "had some speech with Mris Evance aboute this woman." Mr. Hooke "heard" that witches "would hardly be kept away from the houses where they doe mischeife," and he knew that "shee was shut out at Mr. Atwaters upon suspision."

Clearly, each meeting with Mistress Godman generated more talk, which then circulated further among all those who had regular contact with her, looping back upon itself to create even more fear. Thus a young woman, having observed Elizabeth Godman "cutt a sopp [a piece of bread] and put in pan," told Mistress Atwater's maidservant that Elizabeth "was aboute her workes of darkness." The girl put herself into "a most misserable case" that night, apparently because she feared that Mistress Godman would retaliate for the revelation of her sorcery, and "in the morning she looked as one that had bine allmost dead."

In such circumstances, gossip carried as much weight as actual encounters, and talk was as important as eyewitness judgments. It is accordingly examples like that of Elizabeth Godman which prove that gossip, which was universally disparaged by commentators and legislators alike, played a vital role as community members reached their collective assessments of fellow colonists. Not just direct experiences of each other but also knowledge of what people *said* about others contributed to the creation of a neighborhood consensus.

THE SOCIAL FUNCTIONS OF GOSSIP

Reputations were sustained and lost in the early colonies primarily through gossip. The "brabling women," "idle and busy headed people," and practitioners of "tale bearing or back biteing" targeted in Anglo-American slander statutes in fact served an important social function.[26] Their gossip identified misbehavior and singled out misbehavers for community attention. The constant talk alerted colonists to potential problems in their daily interactions with others by raising questions about trustworthiness, sexual conduct, and less-than-admirable aspects of people's lives. In other words, gossip, for all its negative connotations, was a crucial mechanism of social control—one used by ordinary people themselves, and especially by women, who lacked men's easy access to courtrooms and other forums of the formal public. Married women in particular might be prohibited from taking independent legal action to protect their interests, but no law prevented a woman, whatever her marital status, from *talking* about a fellow colonist. Gossip was thus above all a woman's weapon, although men too employed it. Women were both major wielders of gossip and its frequent targets.[27]

The never-ceasing gossip offered colonists the chance to share their views of each other with their neighbors. Gossip served as an adjunct to other tactics in the small politics of the informal public: one man might sue another over a business deal gone sour, as Philip Chesley sued Mr. Samuel Hall, and simultaneously talk in ways designed to damage his reputation; a woman might attack another both verbally and physically. Thus in Portsmouth in 1661 Goodwife Alice Cate accused Sarah Abbott, the wife of the local innkeeper, of causing her recent miscarriage. She not only assaulted Sarah, nearly biting off her thumb and bloodying her face, she also told at least three women that "Goody Abbot was the Caues of Loosing her Child." She publicly warned that she would "make her the said sarah Keep ordinary noe Longer, & bring her . . . children to the parish [that is, impoverish the family]," presumably by spreading the tale of Sarah's alleged misconduct far and wide.[28]

Colonists like Sarah Abbott confronted a perplexing dilemma: what many quite correctly regarded as their most important possessions, their good names, were largely controlled not by themselves but by their peers, individually and collectively. People were well aware of their vulnerability to nasty tales. One Maine man bedeviled by rumors that he drank to excess observed in 1638 that since he could not determine "what other men thinke or speake of mee," he would at least try to live in such an "honest" way that "no man shall speake evill of mee but by

Slanndering." Another New Englander troubled by widespread reports that his neighbors distrusted him consoled himself with the thought that "to have every man speacke well of me is unpossible: because howsoever I carry my selfe: some Cynick will barke at my course."[29]

Prudent men and women understood that permitting negative gossip to circulate unchecked could have a detrimental effect on their relationships with both the formal and informal publics. Like one Maryland planter, a man too little concerned with protecting his credit might find that an unrefuted report that his tobacco was "funkd' & rotten" meant that "noe Merchant would soe much as looke on [his] Tob[acco]." Like a New England shipper, he might discover that "severall base and scurrilous words" spoken to some sailors had "discouraged [them] from his Service," thereby "hindring him from proceeding in his buisness." Or, like a Maine widow, a woman who permitted stories of her "excessive Lascivious carriage" to spread for two years without refutation could well experience "reproach in the mouthes of many, & hinderance of her preferment in any match which might otherwise have been attayned."[30]

The most serious consequences awaited those colonists whom the gossip networks accused of criminal conduct. When such reports reached the ears of colonial magistrates, investigations, indictments, and punishments might follow. In Maine, "common fame" led to grand jury presentments for such offenses as fornication, keeping a disorderly house, bigamy, and fighting with neighbors; when one year a York grand jury "omitted" certain presentments the judges thought warranted by "some publique reports," they called in two members of the jury for questioning about possible negligence.[31] In Maryland, "common fame" caused the prosecution of a planter for killing his servant; in Massachusetts Bay, a prospective immigrant's "ill fame" led to his being barred from the colony; and in New Hampshire, "a fame of suspition of to much familiarity" between a man and a married woman caused him to be ordered "not to lye in hir house in the night time exept sum woman or girll above seven years ould be in bead with hir," on penalty of a substantial fine.[32]

Two colonies formally acknowledged the importance of gossip networks in bringing possible misbehavior to the attention of the authorities. In 1646, the Virginia assembly ordered churchwardens to report persons reputed by "evil fame" to be guilty of profanity or sabbath offenses, extending that directive sixteen years later to include such additional crimes as drunkenness and fornication. Likewise, in early 1663 the Connecticut General Court officially approved and ordered continued "what the Magestrates have done formerly, upon a fame or report of misdemeanour, in calling the persons suspected of delinquency before them, and in examining the case and testimonies." Furthermore, the New Haven judges, just as Mistress Lucy Brewster charged in June 1646, made a practice of listening to "what scandelous persons say" and acting upon the knowlege they thereby gained, even though they nowhere formally codified that practice.[33]

For example, when the New Haven magistrates called Sergeant William East of Milford before them in October 1657, they told him that "there is a sad fame spread abroad of his excessive drinking and drunkenness, so that people as they goe in the street doe say, that Serjant East was drunke yesterday before ten a clock, and now he is drunke againe to day allready." Two witnesses attested that there were "common reports of his being drunke," though one admitted encountering East so "seldome" that he could not testify "of his own knowledge." Another witness offered his observations of the sergeant's "distempered" behavior, then repeated gossip from other men who had also seen "signes of drunkenness" in East. In addition, the witness recounted a rumor he had heard from a "sufficient man" about East's conduct in New Amsterdam: "that his cariage ther was exceeding gross, that the Vergenia men and sea-men would scoff at him and reproach religion for his sake, saying, This is one of your church members." The case against East, who did not admit his guilt, thus rested almost exclusively on "common fame," but he was nevertheless convicted and fined for drunkenness.[34]

Sometimes court records reveal the origin of the "common fame," either by happenstance or because judges for one reason or another explicitly sought out the speaker from whom the damaging gossip had emanated. In Maryland in early 1661, for instance, officials questioned eight men during two successive court sessions in order to identify the source of a widely circulated rumor that thirty (or fifty: the number varied) Charles County men were to be hanged in the wake of the recent suppression of a rebellion. Similarly, in 1656 New Amsterdam authorities spent four months and thirteen court sessions tracking down the "first promulgators and calumniators" of a quickly disseminated tale that a high-ranking married woman "whom no one would suspect" had been seen "in the bush" with "a little sailor" whom she had kissed and bribed to keep silent.[35]

That same year, testimony at the trial of three suspected hog stealers in Kent County, Maryland, revealed that key evidence in the case had come via a female gossip network.[36] In the autumn of 1655, Goodwife Margaret Winchester called at the house that John and Jane Salter then shared with William Price. Jane hospitably fed her "sum singed porcke which was a good groth." Yet Goody Winchester and the neighbors were well aware, as one of them later told the county court, that Price and the Salters "had no hogs of theire owne to kill." After Winchester reported the meal to her friends, curiosity spread about the origins of the roast pork she had been served.

Accordingly, when Jane Salter soon thereafter visited Mistress Frances Morgan, the wife of one of the county's justices, Mistress Morgan assumed the role of interrogator. She asked Jane "if she had kild any hog alate," indicating dissemblingly that she wanted to "borrow sume." When Jane answered that no, they had not killed hogs recently, Mistress Morgan zeroed in on her target. "Then wheare had thu [sic] the singed porke that was eaten in your house"? she inquired. Jane replied that a local widow had given her husband some meat for helping another man slaughter and carry home two of her hogs. Were these the hogs whose "gutts [were] Cast into the Creecke"? Mistress Morgan next asked, clearly drawing on other information obtained from the local gossip network. When Jane Salter responded that they were, Morgan pointed out that such a procedure was "strange" because the slaughterers would thereby "loose the fatt." Her implication was clear: the only people who would throw away valuable hog entrails were seeking to hide the illicit slaughter of someone else's swine. Jane nevertheless stuck to her problematic story.

John Salter told an entirely different tale when he was questioned during the subsequent trial. Presumably, he had concluded that the claim that the widow gave him the meat was too easy to refute. So he insisted that the fat pork found in their house when it was searched by the constable "was part of a wild small hog that was kild," a hog whose ears his dog had (conveniently) eaten, so that his account could not be disproved by earmarks. And his partner William Price denied any role in the goings-on: "I kild none but hee kild a Couple," he asserted, failing to back up Salter's story of the meat's origins directly but rather merely repeating that "hee sayth it was a wild hogg."

The judges easily saw through the muddled, contradictory, and self-serving narratives. They ordered Salter not to kill any hogs "without sume twoe of his honest neighbores with him at the killinge of them, or beefore the[y] bee cut up," fined Jane Salter, and told William Price to move out of the house. They also sentenced him to acknowledge his fault publicly, to repair a local bridge, and to "in open Court stand with a papper upon his breast declaringe his offence," since he had no money to pay a fine.

Such a decisive and favorable outcome was possible primarily because the authorities could compare the account Jane Salter gave to Frances Morgan with the story John Salter told the magistrates, among whom was Frances's husband. Despite the fact that those living near the larcenous Salter-Price household had previously suspected theft, with "many hoges beeing lost amongst the neighbors . . . very strangly," and even though the Salters and Price had earlier offered inconsistent explanations for the "pork offten seene in theire house," the evidence from the female gossip network clinched the convictions. In the hands of the inquisitive and intelligent Mistress Morgan, Goody Winchester's account of homely hospitality proved to be the key to uncovering the source of the hog stealing that had plagued the neighborhood for some time.

John and Jane Salter and William Price do not appear to have tried to stop the circulation of the gossip that eventually helped to convict them, undoubtedly because such a course of action appeared fruitless under the circumstances. Other subjects of gossip and targets of insults were more aggressive in defending their reputations, adopting a variety of means to maintain their credit.

Some retaliated in kind by attacking the integrity of their defamers. For example, a western Massachusetts man who had been termed a thief declared that his accuser was a well-known slanderer who "made it his Trade to abuse men." A Marylander called a "whore Master" quickly retorted that "it was better be a whore Master then a Theife as he [the defamer] was." In a similar vein, a couple charged with "unsivel caridg" persuaded several people to attest that "little credit is to be given to any thing which hath noe other & better evidence then [their accuser's] testimony."[37] Others replied to insults with violence. In 1643 Rebecca Jackson, a Virginia woman who was called a "whore" by Robert Woolterton, responded by hitting her defamer in the face. She thereby started a brawl that ended with her husband's losing a tooth and Woolterton's lip "almost bitten off." Another Virginian who was defamed as a "theefe" instigated a fight that ended with his own death, and in New Hampshire a man termed a "Cheating Knave" began a scuffle that endangered his pregnant wife and included his being pulled to the ground "by the hair & the Neckcloth."[38]

Such physical reactions to slanders were particularly common among high-ranking men defamed by lower-status colonists. Three incidents in early Virginia serve to illustrate the pattern. In January 1624/5, one of the colony's leaders responded angrily when an ordinary settler questioned his integrity, telling the man he was "an idle knave" and then hitting him "over the pate with his Trunchione." Eighteen years later,

Mr. Philip Taylor, accused by an undersheriff of deliberately avoiding the service of warrants and executions against his estate, replied by beating the man "soundly," proudly declaring that he "would have beaten him moore but hee kneeled downe and asked forgivenes." And in 1644, Captain William Stone, the future governor of Maryland, insulted by a Virginian, confronted him with sword in hand. When the man thereupon hit Stone in the face, Stone responded by grabbing the man's hair. Finally, a witness reported, "the Company there present parted them."[39]

Colonists whose good names were questioned could also seek formal and more peaceful settlements of the conflicts. Frequently, slanderous statements were made in the context of other legal actions; when those criminal or civil cases were decided, insults uttered before the verdict by the losing party were implicitly included in the final determination, and separate actions for defamation were unnecessary.[40] On other occasions, offended parties convinced their defamers to offer public apologies, possibly by threatening to file suit against them. So, for example, in August 1660 a Marylander, expressing a desire "to live peacablye as naybours ought to" with John Smith, registered a statement with the Kent County clerk denying that he ever intended to implicate Smith in the death of one of his hogs and acknowledging his "Sorow for any wrong or Injury that ever I have Donne to the said Smith." Likewise, in 1679 a Boston chirurgeon admitted he was "ashamed" for having reported that an innkeeper's wife "had had the French pox."[41]

Most commonly, though, it took a lawsuit by the target and a court-ordered apology to achieve public reparation of one's credit. And those who pursued legal actions against their defamers had to meet the criteria set forth in the colonies' slander laws, criteria that became more restrictive over time.

English ecclesiastical and secular courts had traditionally discouraged slander suits. In England, the only actionable words were those that accused the target of violations which could, if true, lead to prosecution by the appropriate authorities. Common-law courts in particular applied strict rules of procedure to defamation cases, requiring most complainants to prove specific damages and insisting that the alleged insult be construed as positively as possible. (Only if no nondefamatory meaning was conceivable could a plaintiff win a case.) These rules made it difficult for plaintiffs of either sex to win redress for slanders, but worked especially to deny women a common-law remedy for sexual insults, unless they could prove that the slander had cost them a marriage.[42]

The English migrants to North America deliberately abandoned such restrictive procedures for handling defamation complaints, thereby indicating their recognition of the importance of reputations in the new settlements. In the early 1630s Virginia adopted a law providing for the punishment of all those who "shall abuse their neighbours by slanderinge, tale carrying or backbitinge." Massachusetts Bay drafted a similar broadly based criminal defamation statute in 1648, and Maryland followed the other colonies' lead by adopting its own expansively worded law in 1654, declaring that the statute should apply to anyone who "shall Scandalize the Good Name of any person or persons directly or indirectly in such words and Expressions as in the Common acceptation of the English Tongue . . . shall be counted Slander." (The law thereby explicitly broke with the English precedent of narrowly interpreting potentially slanderous phrases.) When Rhode Island identified actionable defamations in 1647, its list included statements that "another is a Traytor, a Fellon, a Thiefe, . . . a Bankrupt, a Cheater, . . . a whore [as applied to a single woman], . . . a whoremaster [a single man]," or which constituted "disparagement of a Man's goods that he putts to sale."[43]

Yet the statutes' early emphasis on allowing colonists to file defamation suits or initiate prosecutions in response to a wide variety of insults ended by the late 1660s, as provincial governments imposed new restraints on complainants. Confronted with a flood of slander suits, Maryland at the end of that decade first limited the monetary damages that plaintiffs could win and then attempted to restrict access to the courts to defamed officials only, thus depriving ordinary settlers of the ability to win redress for slanders directed at them. Virginia in 1662 explicitly adopted English practice, ordering that henceforth the only actionable words would be "such, as if true might have brought the person to suffer punishment by law; any other to be cast out of the court."[44]

Even though legal rules and judges' attitudes thus determined what suits could be filed and what criminal prosecutions would be pursued, defamation cases still provide the most systematic evidence for the study of colonial gossip. Such cases do not comprise the entire universe of relevant sources, for gossip played an important role in many other types of civil and criminal actions as well. But since nearly all slander cases involved neighborhood talk to some degree, it is worthwhile to subject them to specific quantitative analysis.

As was seen in chapter four, the civil and criminal defamation cases that involved men or women exclusively resembled each other in some respects but diverged in others. Most notably, in the vast majority of civil cases targets and their defamers were of roughly equivalent social rank, thus indicating that this particular response was employed most often where no rules of deferential behavior helped to resolve disputes. In only one category of these legal actions—criminal prosecutions with solely male participants—did the cases primarily involve people of different status (high-ranking targets and low-ranking defamers). Also, men and women were both more likely to sue if accused of specific misbehavior than if subjected to a general epithet. But if overall patterns of litigation and prosecution accordingly resembled each other, the slanders that led plaintiffs to file suit or press criminal charges did not. Men overwhelmingly found accusations of theft or dishonesty, or terms like "rogue" and "knave," most threatening, whereas women complained equally overwhelmingly of epithets like "whore" or "slut" and specific allegations of sexual misconduct.[45]

What happened to these patterns when men and women sued or prosecuted someone of the opposite sex, usually a neighbor, for slanderous statements? Defamers and targets in incidents involving both sexes were also of similar status, although cases with high-ranking plaintiffs or victims and lower-status vilifiers of the other sex constituted a significant minority of the whole.[46] In addition, women sued men for essentially the same insults for which they sued women: two thirds of the epithets at issue in such cases were "whore" and equivalents, and more than half the specific charges were sexual in nature.[47]

But when men complained of women's slanders the contents of the insults that concerned them differed significantly from the pattern in same-sex cases. To be sure, the actionable epithets were largely the same: "rogue" and its equivalents constituted well over half the general defamations for which men sued or prosecuted women. And specific charges of theft were also commonly at issue. The major difference lay in the fact that men rarely sued women for accusing them of cheating or perjury, but frequently cited sexual slanders as the cause for the suit or prosecution. Thus men and women of the neighborhoods of colonial Anglo-America concurred that sexual charges emanating from women could significantly affect their reputations, whereas (if one were male) such accusations from male defamers either carried little weight or simply were unlikely to be uttered in the first place.[48]

Therefore, just as a survey of all civil litigation and criminal prosecutions points up the importance of defamation cases in illuminating women's role as gossipers, so too a survey of defamation cases reveals the significance for women of sexual gossip in particular. Gossip was women's primary weapon against male or female adversaries, and because women were known to be especially knowledgeable about sexual matters, slanders that fell into that category were viewed as particularly damaging by their targets, men and women alike. Such insults required a response, and analysis of the resulting lawsuits and prosecutions, along with other evidence of sexual gossip, offers invaluable insights into the dynamics of colonial neighborhoods.

SEXUAL GOSSIP

Sexual talk played a major part in the small politics of the neighborhood. A gossiper, especially one who discussed sexual matters, claimed to know secrets hidden from most people. Knowledge of sexual wrongdoing could accordingly convey power—the power to talk or not to talk, the power to decide whether, when, and to whom to reveal one's knowledge. Since nearly all sexual encounters involved two or more participants and often witnesses as well, it was difficult if not impossible to · prevent such tales from circulating through the neighborhoods. Either or both parties had only to tell a friend or two, or a witness had only to report what he or she had seen or heard, and the story would thereafter spread rapidly, perhaps eventually reaching the ears of the authorities. Even if the scandal were wholly fabricated, as some slanders surely were, adding a few plausible details could help to provide necessary credibility and encourage the tale's dispersion. One such detail seems to have been attributing sexual scandals to women, even when those women denied having been the source of the gossip.[49]

Judging by the descriptions of gossip that survive in court records, everyone was interested in talking about sex. Titillating scandals found an eager audience of listeners, who then might turn into gossipers themselves as they spread the tales or insults even further. The subjects of the talk could only hope that lawsuits, prosecutions, or persuasion would stop the wagging tongues, in time either to preserve their reputations or to prevent their own prosecutions on sexual charges. Surviving court records reveal an intimate and intricate connection among the triad of neighborhood gossip, sexual offenses, and formal criminal charges, so targets were quite properly worried when such stories circulated about them. Few sexual offenders were as fortunate as Mary Taylor and George Catchmey, whose adultery was concealed from local officials by at least twelve knowledgeable witnesses (eight men, four women) before the thirteenth, Mistress Ann Johnson, revealed the truth.[50]

The types of sexual slanders spread by gossip networks ranged widely in nature. Some were blunt and straightforward: a Marylander "had got one of his Negroes with Child" and "had a black bastard in Virginia";

an Ipswich man "had three or four bastards at Road eyland"; two young Plymouth women "were withchild"; a third "is as very a strumpett as any in New England."[51] Others were indirect: a prominent Virginian's mother "was a middwife not to the honorable citizens but to bye blowes." Still others arose from innuendo-filled jokes: a New Haven resident reported to several men that he "heard Edmund Dorman at prayer in a swampe for a wife, & being asked who the person was . . . he answered that . . . it may be his mare that God would make her serviceable."[52]

Evidence occasionally reveals how gossip began: with an overheard but misunderstood remark, with a shouted jest, with returning travelers who eagerly reported stories they had heard elsewhere about their neighbors. So in late 1655 Mistress Mary Bradnox came home to Maryland from a trip into Virginia and immediately recounted an anecdote she had picked up there about another Kent Islander. Mr. Henry Carline had been traveling with a woman other than his wife, Mistress Bradnox disclosed, and had disrupted the sleeping arrangements planned by his Virginia host to share a bed with her. His host "was verie angerie & Cald to his folkes & bad turn them out at dores." The woman was whipped, and Mr. Carline "Could not have the Face to Come to kent to shoe his face." Unfortunately for Mistress Bradnox, Carline not only returned to the island but also sued her for defamation once he was informed of the tale she had told about him.[53]

Witnesses who had seen sexual horseplay also started chains of gossip. Two Plymouth women informed their friends in 1668 that they watched a man "kisse his mayde . . . in the feild upon the Lords day." When he sued for slander, the judges decided that although "there had bine some appeerances of truth in theire report," the women should be fined because "theire way of devoulging it was manifestly scandulous." Similarly, a youthful New Haven resident told several acquaintances about how, when passing a yard, he had seen Caleb Horton and two or three young women "& that he threw them downe upon heaps & sate on them, & that he called upon him to help him, for he could not serve three at once." Horton sued the gossiper, assuring the judges that the ribald story was not true, but the young women admitted that the incident had occurred largely as described. So, in typical New Haven fashion, Horton, who had filed suit to repair his credit, became the defendant in a criminal case, charged with "uncivell & corrupt carriage . . . at an unseasonable time." He was heavily fined and the two girls were firmly rebuked, warned "to fly the lusts of youth & vaine company . . . & to take heed of sinfull daliance, least they provoke God to leave them to some wick-ednesse that may bring shame & punishment upon them."[54]

Sometimes the gossip originated with boasting by a participant in a sexual escapade. A Maine resident informed others that "hee lay with a hoore"; a Virginian declared that a local goodwife was so pleased with his lovemaking that she "doth perswade me from Marrying"; and a young New Havenite told two male acquaintances that "he had bin gathering water millions with Margeret, & sitting downe he fownd her plyable, he might have done what he would." All these boasts set off chains of talk that eventually led to court dates for the men who were too proud of their sexual feats to hold their tongues about their own actions.[55]

Boasting was not the only means through which participants indis-creetly revealed what had happened, thereby initiating a damaging out-pouring of gossip. Occasionally women attempting to deal with unwanted sexual advances unwittingly set off a gossipy reaction that later returned to haunt them. Thus in the early 1640s a Bay Colony maid-servant was troubled by a married man's sexual advances and told her dame's sister about what had happened. Later, when her dame proposed sending her to the man's house to do some work for him and his wife, she refused to go. Her dame asked why, and "hir sister standing by told hir, and shee made hir husban aqunted with his Carage to me and hir husban told a neybor of it and that man told master Carter." Subse-quently, Mr. Carter spoke to the man in question; having so learned about the spread of the story, he confronted the maidservant. Three decades later, a Salem woman's repeated encounters with a sexually ag-gressive brother-in-law created gossip that led him to sue her and her husband for defamation. She had, she told the Essex court, sought "a privet healing," delaying formally reporting the series of sexual incidents (which occurred over several years) because she was "discouraged by others" from doing so. Yet she "foolishly" repeated to two "pretended friends" what she had previously told no one but her sister, and as a result the stories had "come to the mouths of such talkers as have per-verted the truth and made the matter appere far worse then ever it was." Although her brother-in-law challenged her veracity, he lost the case, for she was supported by a group of twelve "nere neighbores" who attested that she "would not wrong the truth in her speches."[56]

Occasionally, malicious gossipers drew on old calumnies to wound their targets. Like Hannah Marsh, whose experience was discussed in the last chapter, other women had to confront recurring tales about their conduct on shipboard en route to their new homes. In 1638 Mary Lewis, later Gibson, of Saco, Maine, was accused by "troublous spirits" of having misbehaved so badly on her Atlantic crossing two years earlier that "the block was reaved at the mayne yard to have duckt her." The slander persisted and became the subject of a suit filed by her and her husband in 1640: a prominent Maine man, they charged, had recently asserted that she "was already proved a whore . . . and that she the said Mary had or should have had a bastard three years since." Likewise, Hannah Baskel was reputed to have lain in the ship's cabin with Henry Phelps and to have put her head in his lap on their voyage to New England. It was further rumored that a high-status man on board the same vessel had called her "Strumpet." At least eight years later, after Hannah had married Henry's brother Nicholas, talk about the relationship continued, and Henry was ordered to post bond to appear in court to respond to questions about it.[57]

Of even longer duration was the gossip that circulated about another New England woman. In September 1639, in Plymouth Colony, Mary Mendam was convicted of "dallyance divers tymes" with an Indian named Tinsin and of "committing the act of uncleannesse with him." Moreover, the court declared, she bore the primary responsibility for the crime, which "arose through [her] allurement & inticement." She was ordered subjected to the penalty reserved for prostitutes in England: "to be whipt at a carts tayle through the townes streets." Goody Mendam was also sentenced to Plymouth's standard punishment for adultery: "to weare a badge [with the letters AD] upon her left sleeve during her aboad within this government; and if shee shalbe found without it abroad, then to be burned in the face with a hott iron." Nearly thirteen years later, in the town that was to become known as York, Maine (to which she and her husband had moved in 1645), a local woman derided Mary Mendam as "Indean Hoare"—a unique insult surely not chosen by coincidence.[58]

Goody Mendam had already been convicted of the crime her defamer charged her with, but those targets who feared prosecution for the sexual offenses of which they were accused often tried the same tactic employed by reputed witches: filing slander suits in the hope of forestalling criminal proceedings against them. In the vast majority of cases, the defendant in such a lawsuit was a woman who charged the male plaintiff either with having made improper sexual advances or with having had illicit sex with her. Much of the time the legal strategy worked. Plaintiffs usually won at least nominal compensation, and no subsequent criminal complaints were filed against them.[59] Even when the charge was manifestly true, plaintiffs could sometimes win judgments against gossipers who had "maliciously published many reproachfull words" against them outside the courtroom. So a week before he was convicted of committing adultery with two women in September 1640, the notoriously lecherous Maine cleric Mr. George Burdett won slander suits against two gossipers, one his former servant, who had widely reported his extramarital sexual activities.[60]

Yet if sexual slanders could thus sometimes be stopped, more often their dispersal led to the exposure of offenses that otherwise would probably never have come to light. Such was the case with a series of defamation suits involving the Marylander Jacob (later John) Lumbrozo, a Portuguese Jew who immigrated to the colony in 1656. Lumbrozo, a dark-skinned doctor (one woman called him "the blacke man"), had difficulty finding a sexual partner despite his education and relative wealth, presumably because he was a Jew of exotic origins. His search for a woman willing to engage in sexual intercourse with him—licitly or illicitly—can be traced largely through slander cases. As was already observed in chapter one, Maryland rarely prosecuted sexual offenses other than bastardy, and Lumbrozo did not run afoul of the province's criminal-justice system until he had lived in the colony for seven years. But his sexual activities can be followed nonetheless because they aroused considerable talk among his fellow Marylanders.[61]

The first woman with whom Lumbrozo was involved was Mistress Ann Hammond, whose husband, John, was absent in England for six years, from 1655 to 1661. Just when their sexual liaison began is not certain, but Mr. Hammond discovered its existence after his return to Maryland. He informed the St. Mary's County court in August 1662 that the preceding autumn he had purchased some goods from Dr. Lumbrozo, but that Lumbrozo had "delayed to take" payment for the items, "professing very much kindnes & severall extraordinary Curtesyes" to the Hammonds. The doctor had subsequently spent a good deal of time at the Hammond plantation, "and by some discourse dropt from his wife and the said Lumbroso," Hammond disclosed, "he found cause to forwarne him his howse."[62]

Dr. Lumbrozo then sent an emissary to demand payment for the goods he had sold Mr. Hammond, insisting on a larger sum of tobacco than the initially agreed-upon amount. Hammond refused to supply a requested promissory note and told the court that in retaliation for his refusal Lumbrozo reported that your petitioner would have had him layn with his wife for sattisfaccon and broached the same soe Confidently and frequently that itt became a General discourse and hath soe blemisht your petitioner that he is become the by word and Scoff of many and hath so irrepayrable injured him both in this Province and Virginea that itt hath woly taken away his hope of Lively hood.

One of John Hammond's witnesses attested that in the spring of 1662 he heard the rumor, attributed to Lumbrozo, at another man's house. When he next met Mr. Hammond, he accordingly "did reprove the said Hamond for proferring his wife to the said Lumbroso." At that, Mr. Hammond angrily informed the witness (while swearing "many Bloody oathes") not only that the story was false but also that Lumbrozo had concocted it to explain his liaison with Ann Hammond. In truth, John Hammond recounted, Dr. Lumbrozo had admitted giving his wife gifts "for the tymes he had layne with her." Mr. Hammond won a substantial judgment against Dr. Lumbrozo for spreading the malicious slander, and the court declined to order Hammond to give Lumbrozo the bill he wanted.

Next, John Lumbrozo sought sexual access to Margery Gould. Margery, who with her husband, John, was indentured to Lumbrozo, intended to accuse him of sexual misconduct, but in May 1663 Lumbrozo preempted her by suing both Goulds for defamation. He charged the Goulds with spreading the scandalous story that he tried to gain their acquiescence to a proposal that he share Margery's sexual favors. The Goulds did not deny Lumbrozo's accusation but instead insisted on the truth of their statement and on the sheer "audacitie" of the slander suit. They asserted that "docter Lumbrozo woold have laine with her . . . and told them that if shee woold bee willing that hee shoold ly with her hee woold give them half his Plantation and halfe his stocke of hogs." Further, they averred, he promised to put the agreement in writing and to record a deed of gift with the county clerk. The Goulds' attorney reminded the court that "publicke fame" gave Lumbrozo "no good report" and emphasized that "men upon such enterprises did not use to Call witnesses," arguing that the lack of extensive corroborating evidence should not be used to impugn the Goulds' claims. Lumbrozo's other servant, Joseph Dorrosell, offered partial confirmation of the Goulds' tale.[63]

Dr. Lumbrozo did more than attempt to bribe the Goulds: he also, according to Margery, "tooke mee in his armes and threw mee upon the bed and thear woold have the use of my bodie and I Crying out aloud and then hee let mee goe and afterwards I asked him if hee was not ashamed and hee sayd to mee that hee was not that hee woold show mee scriptur for it."[64] In response to Lumbrozo's suit, the Goulds asked the court to release them from their two-year service contract, for Margery reported that "when my housband is out of the way hee is still at mee to delued mee to fulfill his Lust." The Goulds' attorney then threatened to prosecute Lumbrozo for a criminal offense if he did not withdraw his defamation suit. Faced with such a prospect, the doctor wisely decided not to pursue the case and was assessed court costs. It is likely that he also freed the Goulds from his service.

Just a few months later, in July, Dr. John Lumbrozo's sexual activities brought him to the attention of the authorities once more.[65] Again talk played a major role in the case, even though on this occasion no defamation charges were involved. Having failed to work out an arrangement with the Goulds, Lumbrozo purchased an unmarried twenty-two-year-old maidservant, Elizabeth Wild. Wild, who thereupon found herself in a difficult situation, spoke to at least five men and four women about her plight. Those nine witnesses supplied depositions detailing what she had told them.

Wild disclosed to several people that soon after her arrival at the plantation Dr. Lumbrozo began to try to to persuade her to have sexual intercourse with him. "Hee tooke a booke in his hand and swor many bitter oaths that hee woold marry mee," she recalled, but she resisted his importunities for "a long time," and the doctor proved unwilling to wait until she consented. Elizabeth Wild thus described an experience much like Margery Gould's, though with a different outcome: "When hee did see that shee woold not yeald quiatly, hee tooke her in his armes and threw her upon the bed she went to Cry out he plucked his hankerchif of his pocket and stope her mouth and forch her whether shee will or noe." Lumbrozo, Joseph Dorrosell disclosed, thereafter lay with Wild "except if thear was any stranger in the hows."

The servant and several other male and female witnesses went on to offer graphic testimony about how, after Wild became pregnant, Dr. Lumbrozo had successfully administered an abortifacient to her. In speaking to a number of people about the abortion, Wild repeatedly asked for advice: was it "not best for her to runaway for hee woold never com after her"? she inquired of one man, who replied discouragingly that "her Case was now bad enough and her runing away woold make it wors." Was it "best for her to Cleare him or no"? Elizabeth asked a woman after Lumbrozo had been formally accused of abusing her. The woman offered little help: "god hee knows wheather you wear best or no for I doe not know what belongs unto such things."

In the end, Elizabeth Wild did decide to "Cleare" Dr. John Lumbrozo. Already married to him by the time she appeared to testify, she told the court that her previous statements to witnesses were "fals" and that "I desir hee may bee Cleare from the scandall and what was spoaken I did rays of my one head." Without her cooperation, Lumbrozo could not be convicted. When he died in early 1666 she inherited his estate, which later passed into the hands of her second and third husbands.[66]

What connected all the cases involving Dr. John Lumbrozo was gossip: gossip initiated by him about John and Ann Hammond that then backfired when Mr. Hammond revealed the truth; gossip about him spread by John and Margery Gould; gossip that resulted from his maid-servant Elizabeth Wild's attempts to solicit advice or seek help after he had raped and impregnated her, then forced her to take an abortifacient. Without all the neighborhood talk, none of these events would have become known, since (just as the Goulds' attorney observed) "men upon such enterprises did not use to Call witnesses." Unlike many of the other incidents that aroused sexual gossip, the Lumbrozo cases involved no eyewitnesses outside his own household. Those who testified against him fell into just two groups: his servants, and people who had talked to him or his servants or had heard rumors spread by him or his servants.

Moreover, talk was intimately intertwined with every aspect of the cases. "Some discourse" between Ann Hammond and John Lumbrozo had revealed his affair with her to her husband. Dr. Lumbrozo then enlisted the weapon of talk against John Hammond, spreading his scandalous tale of having been offered sexual "payment" for a debt "soe Confidently and frequently" that it destroyed Mr. Hammond's reputation. That led the frustrated Hammond to take legal action to halt the slander, even though he would be publicly branded a cuckold.[67]

Lumbrozo too sought to stop talk as well as start it: when he learned the Goulds intended to file suit against him, he attempted to preempt their attack by striking first with a defamation suit, hoping that the tactic that worked for others in sexual-abuse cases would work for him. That it did not suggests the significance of the "publicke fame" that gave him "no good report" and tended to make his servants' sordid story more believable.

Finally, talk was just as crucial a component in the incidents involving Elizabeth Wild. With the exception of Joseph Dorrosell, all the witnesses knew nothing more than what Wild or Lumbrozo had told them.

When Wild insisted that she had "rays[ed]" the whole story "of my one head" and declared that her vivid descriptions of rape and abortion had been "fals," the authorities could not proceed with their case against the doctor. What gossip could create—the possibility of a prosecution—the lack of gossip could take away. Nothing could more strikingly illustrate the vital role of neighborhood talk than such a case.

GOSSIP IN A MARYLAND NEIGHBORHOOD: A CASE STUDY

A detailed examination of a series of linked cases heard in the Charles County court during the late 1650s and early 1660s can, by providing a case study that extends over a period of years, expose more fully the social functions of gossip and its complex gender dimensions within specific neighborhoods.

The best point at which to enter the sequence of cases is April 22, 1662, on which date the Charles County justices considered two suits filed by Mr. Thomas Baker against William Robisson. Baker, who may have been an ex-servant and who apparently never married, had been appointed a county magistrate (or commissioner) in January 1660/1 by Governor Philip Calvert. His opponent, Robisson (sometimes called Robinson), was a carpenter who had lived in Maryland for at least seven years.

Mr. Baker's first suit charged Robisson with defaming him by declaring that "for all your Petitioner is a Commissioner he is boath a Roage and A Rascall." Robisson's slander had arisen from a longstanding dispute between the two men: in late 1658, Robisson believed, Baker's then partner, William Empson (who had since died), had cheated him out of two cows by giving fraudulent testimony in a lawsuit that also involved Baker. Despite some evidence that Baker and Empson had indeed defrauded Robisson, Baker won his suit for slander by presenting three witnesses who testified that they had heard Robisson call him a rogue. Robisson was then required to apologize in open court and to pay court costs. Baker next pursued his second complaint, accusing Robisson of killing his hogs and later altering the earmarks. Mr. Baker's fellow commissioners ordered Robisson to post bond "that hee shal not hunt by himself alone nor without a sufficient inhabitants Companie" until he had cleared himself of the charge and paid the costs of suit.[68]

Nothing about either suit seems very remarkable, but the response of Thomas Baker's male neighbors to his two victories over Robisson

was extraordinary. On the next court day, July 9, 1662, they joined
forces to attack him in three separate cases. The first blow was struck
by John Nevill, who sued Mr. Baker for defaming his wife, Joan, "in
so grose a manner that if trew and with a probable desir spoken shee
woold not bee a Creatur modest enough to keepe the brutalls of the
forrest Companie." He called Mr. George Thompson, the court clerk,
as his first witness; when Baker objected that Thompson "woold defame
himself by Perjurie to injure him," Mr. Thompson replied that Baker
"hath bin A Common defamor of most of all his neighbours and profers
to prove it and particularly by the neighbourhood who can testifie hee
never lived in any good fame since thay knew him." The judges allowed
Mr. Thompson to be sworn, and he then attested that Mr. Baker had
told him and two other men that Joan Nevill was scheduled to testify
for Robisson (presumably in one of the April 22 lawsuits), and that if
she did so "hee woold have put her by her oath for that she was a
Common whore."[69]

George Thompson then told the story that Thomas Baker intended
to use in court to impugn Joan Nevill's testimony against him:

> beeing newly delivered of a Girle as shee lay in bed shee invited a
> man that accidentally happened to bee thear [William Empson,
> whose wife, Mary, had assisted at the childbirth] to Come to bed
> to her and get her a boy to her Girle at which speach . . . the party
> turned himself about and Caled his doge Trogian to Performe the
> office as more fitting for a dog the[n] a man.

Mr. Baker, said Thompson, had then asked him "wheather or no I
thaught so wicked a woman was a Computent witnes against any man."
Nevill's next witness was William Robisson, who, over Baker's objections, said that Baker had told him the same tale and had also reported
of one John Blackwood that "he fukes her [Joan] oftener than John
Nevill himself." Three more witnesses (all men) then appeared to bolster
Nevill's case. Mr. Baker responded by calling three witnesses of his own,
Mary Dod and Mr. Thomas and Mistress Elizabeth Hussey. All attested
to hearing the story of Joan Nevill's childbed outburst not from Mr.
Baker but from Susan Robisson, William's wife, who had attended the
birth along with Mary Empson and two other women.

In his original petition to the court, John Nevill suggested that his
wife had "spoken through overmuch Joy of her safe delivery of a Child"
and that consequently "it is a most Malicious and injurious infamie Cast
on her and altogeather unbeseeming so modest a man as he by his place

[as county commissioner] is bound (or at least to counterfet himself) to bee." The court agreed with Nevill's argument, concluding that "it was against natur that such a thing coold bee spoken with a desier and thearfor aught not to have bin reiterated as an infamie unto her." The judges ordered Mr. Baker to apologize to the Nevills in open court "upon his bended knees" and to pay court costs, but the Nevills "desiered the sayd baker to aske god forgivenes and with the leave of the board [court] not them."

The testimony in the suit revealed an important characteristic of the gossip about what Joan Nevill had said to William Empson: it spread along two sex-differentiated lines, one emanating from Thomas Baker, the other from Susan Robisson. Mr. Baker spoke solely to men, Robisson primarily to women, thereby confirming the significance of separate male and female communities and allied gossip networks. But if Susan Robisson was also defaming Joan Nevill, why did not John sue her as well? Two reasons probably explain his inaction: first, her husband had been Mr. Baker's initial target and was the key to the neighborhood's campaign against Baker; and second, her gossip, while certainly damaging to Joan's reputation, had circulated chiefly among women and had not received official sanction. Thomas Baker, by contrast, indicated to Mr. George Thompson that he intended to accuse Joan Nevill of being a "whore" in court. Indeed, his threat may well have been the reason why Joan Nevill did not testify for William Robisson in one of the April cases.

The next case scheduled on the July 9 court docket was a defamation suit that Mr. Baker had filed against Thompson. Baker "let fall" the suit, but Mr. Thompson, in an unprecedented move, asked the court to allow him to justify his statement (as Nevill's witness) that Baker was "A Common defamor of most of all his neighbours." The judges allowed him to proceed, and a series of male witnesses, including William Robisson, then testified concerning Baker's general reputation and his specific slanders of both men and women. Edmond Lindsey, Thompson's first witness, expressed the consensus of the neighborhood men: "ever since hee lived in thees parts Mr. Baker hath bin Reputed by almost all his neighbours to bee a Common hog stealer." He and others recounted a series of incidents that had aroused their suspicions, most of which involved the mysterious appearance of large hog carcasses at the house Baker shared for a time with William and Mary Empson. Robisson told of an occasion on which Baker had showed him a pair of ears taken from a hog and had said, "looke hear wee are forced to keepe owr hogs Ears owr neighbours doe so much suspect us for hogstealing." Thus was explained the neighborhood's unified reaction to Baker's having charged Robisson with that same crime; the planters all believed that *Baker* was the hog thief and therefore found his action doubly galling.[70]

The testimony also made clear that Baker had indeed been an active scandalmonger. In 1658, he had defamed Mr. Job Chandler, then one of the leading men of the colony, by calling him "spindel shanke Doge" and had been sued and punished for that offense; Lindsey testified that Baker had insulted Chandler after Mr. Chandler accused him of hog stealing. Baker had also engaged in "Baudie talke," primarily about high-status women, but those slanders did not result in defamation suits, probably because no one at the time informed his targets of what he had said. In the mid-1650s, Robisson and Richard Roe both testified, Baker had told them that "Popes Wifes Cunt was licke a shot bagge and Mis [Alice] Hatches Cunt woold make Souse Enough for all the dogges in the Toune." He also "Jeear[ed]" Roe, then a servant of Mr. Francis Pope, "with putting his maggat in Popes Wifes flesh." Roe replied that unlike Baker and the Empsons "wee doe not lye all three togeather," to which Baker retorted, "my hows is my owne and my bed is my owne and I may lodge whome I Pleas in it." After producing this evidence of Baker's misbehavior, Mr. Thompson requested and was awarded a non-suit. Despite the fact he had earlier tried to withdraw his complaint, Mr. Baker had to pay a fine plus the costs of all the witnesses.

Finally, William Robisson returned to the court not as a witness but as a petitioner to ask that the April 22 order against him be removed, now that Thomas Baker's true character had been exposed to public view. After challenging the case Baker had presented in April and asserting that Baker's current financial situation was so shaky that he was probably planning to steal hogs once again, Robisson boldly expressed one of the chief grievances of Baker's male neighbors:

> all you Commissioners of Charles Countie doe in the minds of Men Reape sum kind of disgrace by not informing the liuetennant Generall of this Province of the disgrace that hangeth over your heads in having so ignominious a Person as Thomas Baker is and always hath bin esteemed Equalised with you and of the disgrace that hangeth over all the inhabitants of this Countie in that thear Coold not thearin bee found a man of an honester Reputation to Supply his place.[71]

Mr. Baker did not give up in the face of this frontal assault. He called three witnesses who attested to Robisson's keeping a vicious dog,

which he had been repeatedly asked to destroy because neighbors suspected it of attacking their hogs. The judges did not officially comment
on Robisson's plea that they have Thomas Baker removed from the
court, but they rescinded their order of April 22 and decided that both
men should pay their own own costs. William Robisson, they concluded, "hath partly bin the occasion of [Baker's] suit or complaint by
not killing his doge upon the Complaint of his neigbours." So Robisson,
who had presumably mobilized the neighborhood men against Thomas
Baker, also ultimately had to yield to his neighbors' collective judgment.
It is doubtful whether he minded very much, however: he had made
his point, and Thomas Baker never sat again on the Charles County
bench.

Although this set of cases, which might best be termed *neighboring
planters* v. *Baker*, is unique in the Maryland records, it reveals general
standards of neighborly interaction widely accepted among seventeenth-
century men. Nearby planters had for years suspected Thomas Baker of
hog stealing, and his foul mouth had won him few friends, except perhaps among male servants who enjoyed bawdy banter about unattainable
high-status women. Yet the planters had, on the whole, tolerated him
and his disreputable behavior, which included regularly sleeping three in
a bed with William and Mary Empson. Little in the court records before
1662 (except Job Chandler's 1658 defamation suit) suggests Baker's low
standing among his immediate neighbors. He and his partner Empson
participated in the usual lawsuits, he testified in court and witnessed
documents, and he was cleared of any wrongdoing in the death of one
of his male servants.[72]

But two events changed all that. The first was Baker's appointment
to the Charles County court early in 1661 and thereby his acquisition
of the title "Mr."; the other, Baker's obtaining the judgments against
Robisson in April 1662. The statements of both John Nevill and William
Robisson make it obvious that Baker's elevation to the court astonished
and shocked the men of the neighborhood. They all knew his reputation; how could a foul-mouthed hog stealer properly merit a place
among the county's rulers? Nevill spoke of how a commissioner should
at least "counterfet himself" to be "modest"; Robisson, of how Baker's
high position disgraced not only the other judges (because "so igno-
minious a Person . . . hath bin esteemed Equalised with you") but also
the county as a whole (because it seemed that no one "of an honester
Reputation" could be found to fill that role). Even so, they had continued to hold their tongues, as least in public—although undoubtedly
the situation aroused many expressions of consternation in small gath-

erings. Then came the last straw: Baker's suits against Robisson. Even though other planters had also complained about Robisson's dog, the sight of a man who had always been known as a "Common hog stealer" piously charging another (especially one he had assisted in defrauding four years before) with the same crime was simply too much for the neighborhood to endure.

The men's collective triumph over Baker in the courtroom represented the victory of ordinary planters' behavioral standards over those of the colony's leaders. Governor Philip Calvert, after all, had named Baker to the Charles County commission, and there is no evidence that the other commissioners had formally complained about the appointment. But Baker's male neighbors knew what qualities they respected in their peers and required of their superiors. Baker, in their opinion, exhibited neither, and they forced Maryland officials to accept their judgment, a judgment based on years of assessing his character in their gossip networks.

The saga of Thomas Baker and his neighbors has another chapter. In this episode Baker was a witness rather than a litigant, but his role was nonetheless central. If the three court cases of July 1662 revealed the ways in which male Marylanders judged the behavior of their fellow men, then the three cases heard a year later disclosed the workings of similar systems among their womenfolk.

In June 1663 John and Joan Nevill became involved in a violent altercation with several of their neighbors, which began when Joan Nevill quarrelled angrily with Mary Roe at a log house Mary and her husband, Richard, were then renting from the Nevills. The origin of the dispute is not recorded, but the two women pushed and shoved each other after Joan tried to set fire to the house. John Nevill knocked Mary Roe down with a stick; she responded to the attack by crying "murder," thereby attracting the attention of Thomas Baker, Richard and Mary Dod, and a passerby named Robert Cockerill, all of whom came running to see what was happening. The incident led to three lawsuits against the Nevills: the Roes sued both Nevills for assault and battery, and the Dods each sued Joan Nevill for defamation. The Roes' suit for assault and the suit charging Joan with calling Richard Dod "a perjured fellow" were both relatively straightforward; the case involving the slander of Mary Dod is much more revealing because it contains detailed accounts of a name-calling match between the two women.[73]

Cockerill, Baker, the Roes, and Richard Dod all testified that Joan called Mary Dod "Capt Batten whore," charged that Mary "lay with

Capt Batten at Patuxon [Patuxent] in the sight of six men with her Coats up to her mouth," and alluded to her "black eyed boy in her armes licke the Roge its father [Batten]." Thus Joan Nevill employed the standard slander of another woman and added supporting details to the epithet "whore." The witnesses' testimony makes obvious the continuing bad blood between the Nevills and Baker; when Thomas Baker arrived on the scene, Joan insultingly "asked him wheather hee was Come [down] from a Commissioner to a Constable," and during the court hearing Baker twice "submissively" asked that certain statements Joan made in court be recorded as "a hughe Confirmation of thear [the witnesses'] oaths." Not until John Nevill asked the witnesses to swear to the circumstances surrounding the slander, however, did it become clear that there was also considerable ill feeling between Mary Dod (who had testified for Baker in the 1662 Nevill suit) and Joan Nevill, and that Mary was simultaneously slinging some mud of her own.[74]

Mary Roe gave the most detailed account of the confrontation between Joan Nevill and Mary Dod. She testified that when Mary Dod came onto the property to see what was happening in the altercation between Joan and Mary Roe, Joan Nevill said to her, "thou jaed get thow out of my ground for what buisnes hast thow heare." They exchanged a few heated words over Mary Dod's right to be on the Nevills' land, and Mary Dod then struck Joan Nevill in the face. After Cockerill took Mary Dod's child from her arms, Joan Nevill "strooke her a good blow in the Chops and sayd by god you shall have one for the other and sayd thow jaed I will have my Revenge of thee yet." Mary Roe also attested that Mary Dod warned Joan Nevill not to threaten her, "for threatened foulkes live long," and Joan said:

> bauld Eagell get the[e] home and Eate sum of gammer belaines fat Porke and mary dod sayd if shee did eat fat Porke shee did not Eate Rammish boare and goodie nevill sayd who did and goodie dod sayd shee did not and with that goodie dod Cryed he[r]e Troge and goodie nevill sayd thow whore who is that thow Callest Troge and goodie dod sayd she was no Scoatchmans whore and goodie nevill sayd that nether scotch Irish or English came amis to her and with that goodie dod sayd to goodie nevill cum will you go hom and eat sum of goodie belaynes fat Porke if I have any and goodie nevill spit at her and sayd shee scorned to go with such Companie as shee was and with that mary dod went away and goodie nevill held up her hands and hollowed at her.

Richard Roe was more precise than his wife in his description of Joan Nevill's gesture: "goodie nevill held forth her fingers to wit her forfinger and her littell finger."[75]

The epithets Mary Dod threw at Joan Nevill clearly demonstrate the continuing impact of slanders even after a successful lawsuit, for they were based on what Thomas Baker and Susan Robisson had reported of Nevill years earlier. By her comment on eating "Rammish boare" Dod implied that Nevill was guilty of bestiality, a charge she buttressed with the sly aside, "here Troge," a reference to Empson's long ago retort to Nevill as she lay in childbed. She also alluded to John Blackwell (the Scotchman), whom Baker had claimed "fuke[d]" Joan more frequently than John Nevill did. Although Mary Dod, evidently regretting the name-calling, then tried to smooth things over by inviting Joan Nevill home to eat with her, Nevill refused to be mollified and made an obscene gesture to show what she thought of her antagonist.

This unusual confrontation is as revealing of women's values as the men's campaign against Thomas Baker is of masculine standards. The female gossip network had a long memory; each of the combatants drew on it to challenge her opponent. The insults were exclusively sexual and revolved primarily around whether the women had been faithful to their husbands. Joan Nevill, of course, had the additional burden of dealing with the scandal symbolized by the phrase "here Trojan," which was used so consistently in the testimony in both this and the 1662 case that one suspects it had become a kind of neighborhood shorthand and that it was frequently employed to refer to her. This is presumably why she and her husband did not countersue Mary Dod; they had, after all, already won a case based on that slander and it had done little good. Why should they revive it formally once again? Although Thomas Baker had had to apologize to Joan Nevill, he had certainly in this instance been a successful gossiper: he and Susan Robisson had tagged their target with a label from which she would never escape and which would forever after be available to those who, like Mary Dod, wanted to insult her. It was a considerable victory in the small politics of the neighborhood.

ALTHOUGH THE PLETHORA OF CASES from Charles County, Maryland, created a record of neighborhood interactions more detailed than most, the same process through which neighbors assessed the character of Joan Nevill and Thomas Baker was at work in all other regions of the colonies as well. Gossip enabled people of similar status to judge one another and to reach collective opinions on crucial questions of credit and trustworthiness. Those who obeyed the rules of community consensus won acceptance and respect; those who violated such rules—like Mr. Thomas Baker or Mistress Elizabeth Godman—ran the risk of inciting concerted action against themselves, endangering their reputations and livelihoods, even occasionally their lives.

As might be anticipated within a context of a society organized on the basis of gendered power, men and women differentially employed gossip, the chief mechanism through which community consensus was formulated. For men, gossip was one of many possible tactics that could be pursued in the battles of small politics. For women, though, gossip was their major weapon, one employed primarily by and against them. *By* them, because they had little means other than talk to attack their enemies, since they held no offices and controlled little money; *against* them, for precisely the same reasons: because little other than talk could seriously damage a woman who owned no property and had no economic interests to protect. Likewise, the most damaging gossip aimed at women was necessarily sexual in nature, for most women had complete control over few other aspects of their lives. Men, by contrast, were involved in a variety of different sorts of activities and could be attacked through reference to any one of them, including sex.

Almost by definition, community interactions such as gossip defied categorization within the Filmerian system, since they involved dynamics that the seventeenth-century conceptual world failed to recognize: household subordinates serving as shapers of community mores, wives acting independently of their husbands and young people of their parents or masters and dames, groups of women influencing the judgments reached by groups of men (otherwise known as courts or legislatures). Yet even within the relatively egalitarian context of neighborhoods, the system of gendered power held sway. In critical ways, men and women were affected by their access—or lack of access—to the instruments of political and economic authority. As has already been suggested in chapter four through the discussion of midwives, their testimony, and specifically the circumstances surrounding the conviction of Mistress Alice Tilly, men and women stood in strikingly different relationships to the seventeenth-century Filmerian state. Those relationships are the subject of the third section of this book.

SECTION III

GENDERED POWER
IN THE STATE

❧

His Lordship's Attorney

> Came Mrs Margarett Brent and requested to have vote in
> the howse for her selfe and voyce allso for that att the last
> Court 3d Jan: it was ordered that the said Mrs Brent was
> to be looked uppon and received as his Lordships
> Attorney.
>
> —*Maryland Assembly, January 21, 1647/8*[1]

MISTRESS MARGARET BRENT'S appearance before the Maryland
Assembly in January 1647/8 has been difficult for historians to
interpret. Because she requested a vote and speaking privileges in the
assembly, Mistress Brent has sometimes erroneously been termed America's first feminist. Yet Margaret Brent sought nothing for others of her
sex and consequently should not be regarded as a spokeswoman for
women in general. Moreover, she asked for the right to vote in the
assembly not because of (or in spite of) her sex, but rather as a result of
her recent appointment as the provincial representative of Lord Baltimore. In that position, the gentlewoman reasoned, she should be permitted to vote and speak in the colony's assembly. But the governor,
Mr. Thomas Greene, "denied that the said Mrs Brent should have any
vote in the howse." Margaret Brent responded to the snub with anger:
the clerk recorded that "Mrs Brent protested against all proceedings in
this present Assembly, unlesse shee may be present and have vote as
aforesaid."[2]

A focus on Mistress Brent's thwarted quest for the vote is misplaced,
though understandable in light of the unique character of this episode
in the history of the Anglo-American colonies. The intriguing question
raised by her appeal for a vote in the assembly is not, as most historians
have thought, why she made her request—for, as she indicated, the
petition rested logically enough on her new position and would surely
have been granted had she been a man not previously accorded voting

privileges in that body. Rather, the significant issue is why she had earlier been designated as the Lord Proprietor's attorney. The answer to that key inquiry lies conjointly in two topics that have already been explored at length in this volume: first, her standing as a high-status woman; and second, the Filmerian worldview. If Mistress Brent's action on January 21, 1647/8, seems nearly inexplicable by twentieth-century standards, it was wholly in accordance with the assumptions about gendered power that characterized her own day.

MISTRESS MARGARET BRENT, a Roman Catholic who was born around 1600, never married and may well have taken vows as a lay sister. Accompanied by her sister Mary and her brothers Giles and Fulke, she immigrated to Maryland in 1638. Their family had close ties to the Calverts, the founders of Maryland, who (as has been seen) initially envisioned a colony organized in Filmerian fashion, with an extensive system of manors directed by lords drawn from the English aristocracy and gentry. The Brent siblings, parties to that scheme, each took up a large land grant, and Giles became one of the colony's early political leaders. Although Fulke soon returned to England, the other three remained in America. After falling out of favor with the Lord Proprietor, they moved to Virginia around 1650 but retained ties to Maryland, including some landholdings.[3]

During her first four years in Maryland, Mistress Margaret Brent left no mark on the colony's records. But a lawsuit she filed in the spring of 1642 initiated a long chain of court appearances that eventually made her the most litigious woman in the province. Many of the suits, which she almost invariably won, sought repayment for debts owed to herself or her siblings. She must thereby have gained a good local reputation as a financial manager, for, on his deathbed in June 1647, Governor Leonard Calvert (younger brother of Lord Baltimore) named her as the sole executrix of his estate, telling her, "Take all, & pay all." At the same time, he designated Thomas Greene to succeed him as governor of the colony.[4]

Calvert's decision to make Mistress Brent his executrix, which was unusual because women were rarely named to administer the estates of men other than their husbands, was rendered even more remarkable by grave political circumstances. From early 1645 to early 1647, Maryland experienced near-total anarchy known as "the plundering time," a result of the English Civil War having reached its shores. Seeking to protect the "poore distressed Protestants" of the colony, an English ship captain and supporter of Parliament named Richard Ingle had attacked the "wicked Papists and Malignants" who dominated the province, initiating a prolonged period of chaos. Just a few months prior to his death, Leonard Calvert restored order to Maryland by leading a small invasion force from Virginia. The governor thus died at a critical juncture for the fragile colony.[5]

The Virginia soldiers, who had made possible the resumption of the proprietorship, deepened the crisis after Calvert's death. The few remaining Maryland settlers, whose plantations had been pillaged during the Ingle Rebellion, could barely afford to provide the soldiers with adequate food, much less to compensate them for their unpaid wages. In October 1647, the soldiers formally demanded that Calvert's executrix, Mistress Brent, pay their salary arrears. They enlisted witnesses who had heard the former governor promise at the time of the invasion "That his own Estate & his Brothers should pay the Soldiers." Since Calvert's personal estate had been devastated by the civil war, it was insufficient to supply the large sums needed. In the assembly's opinion, the soldiers' grievances threatened "divers disturbances" that might cause "the utter subversion & ruine" of the province.[6]

So, on January 3, 1647/8, Thomas Greene and the other members of the Provincial Court replied to the Virginians' demands by declaring that Margaret Brent "should be received as his Lordships Attorney" until Cecilius Calvert named a replacement. Like Leonard Calvert, who had also been his brother's attorney, she accordingly gained access to the proprietor's personal estates and the provincial customs revenues. That enabled her to pay the potentially rebellious soldiers and to avert a possible renewal of warfare. For the next eighteen months, she served as Lord Baltimore's attorney as well as Leonard Calvert's executrix.[7]

Clearly concerned about the possibility that Mistress Brent might overstep her bounds and lay claim to more power than it thought she should wield, the court, including her brother Giles, cautiously provided that her role as Cecilius Calvert's attorney should extend only to "recovering of rights into the estate, & paying of dew debts out of the estate, & taking care of the estates preservation: But not further." Yet that restriction had little effect. It neither stopped Margaret Brent from claiming a vote in the assembly nor prevented her from later appearing in court as Lord Baltimore's agent to prosecute several miscreants, including the perjurer Blanch Oliver Howell, the steer-killer Thomas Bradnox, and a man who had acted and spoken "in contempt of his Lordships Authority & government." Even though such actions transgressed the limits the Provincial Court had outlined, no one seems to have challenged her right to represent the Lord Proprietor as she saw fit.[8]

Why did the Maryland Provincial Court make such a dramatic and unparalleled move, formally conferring public responsibility on a woman? At no other time in the history of colonial Anglo-America did anything comparable occur. In part, the explanation lies in the perilous state of the colony and the lack of good alternatives. The Virginia soldiers, originally the saviors of the colony, now endangered its very existence; they could be compensated only by drawing on Lord Baltimore's resources. Someone had to be designated as the proprietor's attorney to accomplish that task, and the other obvious candidates (Giles Brent and Governor Thomas Greene) each had significant drawbacks. As was noted in chapter four, Giles was a controversial and divisive figure in provincial politics, a man who had once formally been charged with treason. Greene's hold on the governorship was tenuous: in the weeks after Leonard Calvert's death, he had had to fend off Captain Edward Hill, a rival claimant to the office. Moreover, judging by the number of contemptuous remarks attributed to them, Marylanders had little respect for Greene. One man, for example, punningly derided him as "The Greene Governor," while another dismissively declared that "he cared noe more for the Governoure . . . then hee did for any of the rest [the Virginians]," because "they were all Rogues." A third insisted that "there was now noe Governor in Mary-land. ffor Capt Hill was Governor & him only he acknowledgeth."[9]

That the naming of Mistress Margaret Brent as Baltimore's attorney presented a viable alternative to the appointment of either Greene or her brother rested on the fact she was a gentlewoman and on two aspects of Filmerian ideology. In practical terms, Brent's identity was a major asset in the tangled circumstances of early 1648, for because of her sex she had had no previous formal involvement in Maryland politics, yet because of her high rank she deserved deference from others. She was not identified with any faction—not even that of her brother Giles— and so she could be seen as disinterested as she attempted to save the colony from economic collapse. But more important than the fact that she was a gentlewoman were the implications of two key tenets of the Filmerian system of thought.

First, since in that schema the sources of authority in state and family were identical and the unified conception of power made it difficult to separate public from private obligations, her well-established position as the executrix of Leonard Calvert's personal estate made her the primary claimant to succeed Leonard as the caretaker of his brother's properties.

At the governor's dying request, she had already taken on responsibility for settling his affairs; it seemed appropriate to her and others that she assume the same role with respect to Lord Baltimore's personal and public finances as well. Indeed, Mistress Brent did not wait for the Provincial Court's official imprimatur to proclaim that she should properly be regarded as Cecilius Calvert's representative in the colony. On December 13, 1647—or three weeks *before* the court formally named her as such—she identified herself as "his Lordships Attorney" when she complained to the Provincial Court about a man who had exported tobacco without paying the required customs duty and requested an attachment on his property "on behalfe of the Lord Proprietor."[10]

Second, even though the assertion might appear paradoxical because of Sir Robert Filmer's well-earned reputation as a theorist of masculine power, within the context of familial thought Margaret Brent's sex did not absolutely disqualify her from assuming formal responsibilities to the public at large. Her fellow Marylanders may have prevented her from joining the all-male assembly, but a few weeks earlier they were following the logic of Filmerian thinking when they designated her as Lord Baltimore's attorney. That was not only because they thereby combined the roles of executrix and public representative in the same hands, but also because the action indicated their recognition that, as an unmarried gentlewoman owing deference to no male superior, she occupied a special status within a social system organized in accordance with the Filmerian principle that all authority flowed from the power of symbolic parents (including "mothers") via the Fifth Commandment.

Sir Robert Filmer himself made that status explicit. Since, for him, "economical [household] and political power differ no otherwise then a little commonweal differs from a great one," female heads of households—especially high-status, accomplished ones like Mistress Brent—could not categorically be denied access to authority in the polity. In his unpublished essay "In Praise of the Vertuous Wife," Filmer accordingly contemplated with equanimity the potential within his intellectual system for the existence of politically powerful women. "There is no vertue in men so differen[t] which weomen may not hope in some sort to attaine," he declared, "for e[ven] sayling and warre and goverment of kingdomes have been often times well handled by weomen." Moreover, he interpreted Proverbs 3:16 ("she handles the wheel and spindle") broadly, remarking that "by the wheele and spindle are ment all labour not onely of body but of mind." Therefore "if any woman excell in . . . *goverment* of a commonwealth she shall be no more bound to the *wheele* then a prince is to the *Plough*."[11]

That the Virginia soldiers as well as Mistress Brent and the Provincial Court accepted the social and political vision Filmer outlined was revealed in the assembly's response to Lord Baltimore's expression of displeasure at the court's action. Cecilius Calvert complained about Mistress Brent's "medling" with his property and commented that "the meanest Planter . . . would thinke it a great wrong don unto him, if an Attorney should (upon any pretence of authority whatsoever[)] be made without his Consent or Warrant to dispose of his Estate." The assembly defended the court by declaring its confidence in Mistress Brent: "we do Verily Believe and in Conscience report that it was better for the Collonys safety at that time in her hands then in any mans else in the whole Province after your Brothers death for the Soldiers would never have treated any other with that [same] Civility and respect." The Virginia soldiers, the assembly leaders declared, were ready to mutiny several times, "yet she still pacified them till at the last things were brought to that strait that she must be admitted and declared your Lordships Attorney by an order of Court . . . or else all must go to ruin Again and then the second mischief had been doubtless far greater than the former." In short, Mistress Brent "deserved favour and thanks" from Lord Baltimore for her efforts to preserve "publick safety" rather than the "bitter invectives" to which he had subjected her.[12]

Because of her status as an English gentlewoman and the respect with which she was regarded in the province, therefore, Margaret Brent commanded even greater deference from the soldiers than a man of comparable rank would have. When matters reached the point of crisis, she *had* to be named as Lord Baltimore's attorney; Maryland's male leaders simply saw no alternative. Their words confirmed the symbolic importance of unifying the familial role of executrix and the public one of attorney for the proprietor in the same hands and revealed their adherence to a Filmerian vision of society.

Cecilius Calvert's response to his assembly's exposition of a unified conception of authority was to contest it and to attempt to draw a line between the *public* and the *personal* (he did not employ the word *private* at any time). Yet although the distinction between public and personal affairs that he sought to define was already being used by others in somewhat different contexts, he proved incapable of explaining it without contradiction.[13]

In an August 1649 letter to Maryland's political leaders, Cecilius Calvert reacted angrily to the taking of his "personall Estate" for what he described as "publick charges." No "Prince" of a "Christian Countrey," Lord Baltimore asserted, should be expected to defray the expenses of a war out of his own pocket. The proprietor's argument made it appear that he was successfully distinguishing between public and private obligations, at least as they pertained to his property. Yet at the same time Cecilius admitted that, as his attorney, his brother Leonard "had had power to dispose of our personall Estate there"; that is, to promise to pay the soldiers from Cecilius's own holdings. Leonard must have done so, though, "upon confidence of making up againe out of the Customes what should be disbursed . . . for that purpose." And Lord Baltimore defined the customs as a revenue "appointed by Gennerall consent for the defraying of publick charges."[14]

Therefore, although Cecilius Calvert objected vigorously to the taking of his "personall Estate" for "publick" reasons, he thought it only fair that a fund established for "the defraying of publick charges" be used to replenish that same personal estate. The explanation for his apparently paradoxical statement is not venality and illogic of the most blatant sort, but rather the same conceptual difficulty evident in other contemporary uses of *public* and *private*. Lord Baltimore was struggling to create categories of thought that would separate his private role as the largest Maryland landowner from his public role as the ruler of the colony, likewise distinguishing between their respective revenues. Neither he nor Maryland's leaders could accomplish that feat in the 1640s, which was precisely why Mistress Margaret Brent had to play her prominent dual role in the colony's economic and political life.

Yet Margaret Brent was unique. Not only did no other woman ever again assume the same sort of role in the colony of Maryland, no man did either. In fact, the period of her prominence represented the last time at which the lingering influence of Lord Baltimore's Filmerian plans for the colony can be discerned. From 1650 until the last decades of the century, the province was dominated by small planters espousing nascent Lockean ideals of egalitarian interaction among male property holders rather than by manorial lords enforcing a family-like hierarchy. When hierarchy re-emerged in Maryland late in the seventeenth century, it had a very different cast, for it was based on the development of large-scale slaveholding.[15]

THE ROLE PLAYED by Mistress Margaret Brent in restoring order and proprietary rule in Maryland in 1647–48 introduces a key question not yet systematically explored in this volume: the relationship of women to the Filmerian state. That relationship had two aspects, both of them problematic. The first involved women as objects of the system of gendered power; the second, women as potential wielders of gendered power.

As was indicated in section I, under normal circumstances women (like all household dependents) were expected to be governed in the first instance by their husbands, fathers, or masters. Only if they proved uncontrollable by family governors were they to become the objects of state power. Thus in theoretical terms all women stood one step removed from the polity; their conceptual relationship with the Filmerian state was indirect, conducted through their family governors. Although male dependents too dealt with the Filmerian state only indirectly, because of their sex that situation was temporary. Unless the men in question were enslaved Indians or Africans, they would eventually be allowed to participate actively in whatever political activity was open to all male colonists of their social and economic rank.

Yet, as has already been seen, for two reasons the Filmerian theory describing the ways in which women were the objects of state power did not wholly encompass reality. First, women, like men, made independent contributions to the community. Not all of women's activities were confined to their own households: many of their most influential actions (for example, their participation in gossip networks) took place outside the household context. Consequently, on many more occasions than the theory would have suggested—such as when they were officially called to account for defamatory statements—women were directly rather than indirectly subjected to the power of the Filmerian state.

Second, widows and a few other women became household heads, the key figures in the Filmerian system. As such, they had responsibilities both to their subordinates and to the public at large. Since these women had no male family governors to serve as their intermediaries with the state, political authorities had to deal with them directly, listening to their requests in town meetings, assessing them for tax payments, or penalizing them for such misdemeanors as not maintaining their fences or not properly controlling their servants. Accordingly, widows and other female household heads presented colonial officials with constant definitional challenges: should they or should they not be included in the ranks of those property holders who deserved to be consulted about matters of general concern? Should they be liable for supplying manpower to the militia? Should they be included among the signers of political petitions? Should they be ordered to take oaths of allegiance to the state?[16]

Women, in other words, could not neatly be categorized as only the indirect objects of gendered political power. Some of women's actions occurred in contexts beyond the reach of their menfolk, and other women were not under men's domination at all. Thus the Filmerian system, which conceptualized women as always subject to the authority of male family governors, was incomplete in its treatment of women as the objects of power. It contained too many anomalies to be definitive.

Even more ambiguous and indeterminate was the Filmerian approach to women as the potential wielders of gendered power. The family analogy that explained the origins of the state explicitly numbered women among the powerful. When the Fifth Commandment, "Honor thy Father and Mother," was cited as the source of social and political authority, women qualified to rule by criteria other than sex were conceptually included in God's all-encompassing grant of power. True, female household heads, even those of high status, were excluded by their sex from formal participation in the collective ranks of political and judicial decision-makers. Yet if their sex prevented women from being included in the collectivities of the all-male formal public, it did not foreclose the possibility that *individual* high-ranking widows and fictive widows could see themselves, and be seen by others, as proper wielders of familial-based authority. Amid the chaos of early Maryland, that fact helped to re-establish the rule of the Lord Proprietor, for it allowed Mistress Margaret Brent to assume effective control of the colony's finances. In New Haven, by contrast, the potential power of high-status women posed a serious challenge to the maintenance of social order, because a group of prominent women—Mistress Anne Eaton and her friends Mistress Lucy Brewster and Mistress Moore—overtly expressed their dissent from the province's political and religious orthodoxy.

The implications of women's relationship to the state within the system of gendered power are best exposed not just by explicating familial ideology on its own terms, but also by examining the arguments advanced by that system's key critic, John Locke. Because Sir Robert Filmer, the most prominent proponent of the family analogy, developed his ideas systematically only in response to early expositions of contract theory, and because Locke wrote primarily to combat Filmer, the ideas the two men espoused during their wide-ranging dialogue on the origins of political power and the nature of governmental authority can be most fully understood in conjunction with each other.[17]

In his *Two Treatises of Government*, a reply to the belated publication of Filmer's *Patriarcha*, John Locke set forth a theory of women's relationship to the state that differed sharply from Filmer's. Most notably, it contained none of the anomalies so evident in the Filmerian view of gendered power. Because Locke denied that family and state were anal-

ogous (a point to be discussed at length in chapter six), he avoided
precisely those aspects of Filmerian thought that opened the door to
claims of authority by symbolic mothers and removed the presumption
that symbolic fathers of all descriptions bore responsibility for the
actions of their subordinates. For Locke, women's relationship to the
polity was defined solely by sex, and political power rested not on a
metaphorical claim derived from the authority of a single male progen-
itor but rather on the collective will of all the male household heads in
a given society.

Locke's assertion (already explored in chapter three) that monogamous marriage existed in the state of nature was the foundation of his
treatment of women's standing in the polity. Locke emphasized that in
the state of nature men had the freedom to dispose of their property as
they wished, and indeed that "the great and *chief end* . . . of Mens unit-
ing into Commonwealths" was "*the Preservation of their Property.*" Yet
Locke's insistence on wifely subordination both in the state of nature
and thereafter left little possibility that women could ever become proprietors, either before or after the constitution of civil society. Wives by
definition owned no property and therefore had no reason to form governments.[18] When Locke remarked that "I have truly no *Property* in that,
which another can by right take from me, when he pleases, against my
consent," he categorically omitted wives from his class of property holders, for throughout his narrative he gave husbands' decisions about family
property precedence over their wives' desires. If property holders by
definition could not be subject to the whims of another person, then no
wife—no woman—could be the sort of property owner who could
participate in the establishment of government.[19]

Locke's discussion of how commonwealths were perpetuated likewise excluded women. "*A Child is born a Subject of no Country or Government,*" he wrote, and only upon reaching the age of majority would
"a Free-man" decide "what Body Politick he will unite himself to." At
that time, men joined existing polities by acquiring property in them
(an act of tacit consent) and by "entering into it [the government] by
positive Engagement, and express Promise and Compact."[20] Since wives
(women) could neither acquire property nor, presumably, contract to
join a government independently of their husbands, they had to be incorporated into a state in some other way. Locke never explained how
that might be accomplished, but his narrative implied that women became subjects of a state solely as adjuncts of their husbands or fathers.
They had no direct relationship to the polity, but instead stood at its
periphery. They were members of it by proxy alone. Not they but only

their menfolk could choose a political allegiance or participate actively in government.

As has been seen, most women in a Filmerian state also had only an indirect relationship to the polity. Still, the households in which they lived and wielded power were integral components of that polity and fully integrated into its operations, even to the extent that (as was shown in the first section of this book) punishments meted out within them were seen as interchangeable with those inflicted by the courts. In a Lockean system, by contrast, the household power structure was irrelevant to the polity. The dependents found therein were the direct objects of state power instead of being subjected primarily to the authority of their family governors. In a Lockean world, male property holders alone comprised the state, from which women were wholly excluded as actors.

Neither the Lockean nor the Filmerian system allowed women a formal voice in creating or directing government. (As the author of *The Lawes Resolutions of Womens Rights* remarked in 1632, women "have nothing to do in constituting Lawes, or consenting to them, in interpreting of Lawes, or in hearing them interpreted.")[21] But in a polity organized along familial lines, *some* women—those who were high-ranking heads of households—necessarily constituted exceptions to the general rule of exclusion. As Filmer himself concluded, women could "excell in . . . *goverment* of a commonwealth." Accordingly, in their colony's direst emergency, Maryland officials could turn to a woman to save the colony from financial ruin. Such a solution was unthinkable in a state defined by Lockean principles, because all women, with no exceptions, were therein denied a political role by virtue of their sex alone.

Thus, although they were largely silent as Filmer, Locke, and other political theorists argued about the origins of the state, women had a very large stake in the outcome of the debate. In a Filmerian world guided by the family analogy, some women could become political actors; in a Lockean world, no females could—or at least they could not until, generations later, the definitions of Lockean individualism were widened to encompass both women and non-property-owning men. In the seventeenth-century Anglo-American colonies, that moment was far in the future.[22] But, as has already been noted, for demographic and other reasons the Chesapeake colonies became de facto Lockean states after mid-century, long before Locke systematized his ideas. As a result, the female residents of Maryland and Virginia experienced the consequences of a transition to a society organized along Lockean lines long before that same transition occurred in New England.

For men too, the nature of the state in which they lived made a difference in their experiences. In the Filmerian systems of New England, heads of households bore heavy responsibilities and were closely supervised by public officials. The Lockean societies of the Chesapeake placed less onerous burdens on male residents and were less inclined to intervene in disorderly households. At the same time, though, men in Virginia and especially Maryland had to cope with governments in which the lines of authority were by no means clear, and with polities in which dissent and unrest were endemic. The confusion about the organization of politics inevitably affected their lives in a myriad of ways.

THIS SECTION considers the gendered consequences of the colonists' varying political experiences in New England and the Chesapeake. Chapter six focuses on theoretical formulations and on the dialogue between the Filmerian and Lockean systems that took place sporadically throughout English America during the half-century between 1620 and 1670. Chapter seven analyzes the repercussions of the different systems for women and men accused of criminal activity, and chapter eight examines the single greatest crisis of gendered power in Filmerian America: the controversy instigated by Mistress Anne Hutchinson in Massachusetts Bay in 1636–38.

CHAPTER 6

Fathers and Magistrates, Authority and Consent

All the duties of a King are summed up in an universal
fatherly care of his people.
                              —*Sir Robert Filmer, c. 1639*

The Power of a *Magistrate* over a Subject, may be distinguished from that of a *Father* over his Children.
                                    —*John Locke, 1692*[1]

IN A SERIES OF DIALOGUES that occurred in a variety of Anglo-
American settings—from the floors of Parliament and the battlefields
of the English Civil War to the crude statehouses of the American
colonies—seventeenth-century men argued about the origins of political
power, the nature of their responsibilities to the state, the determinants
of allegiance, and the limits (if any) to governmental authority. The
questions posed during such debates elicited a diversity of responses that
ranged widely across a spectrum defined at one end by an ideology of
absolute authoritarianism and at the other by an equally uncompromising
insistence on consent as a necessary precursor to legitimate government.
Both sides incorporated elements of traditional English theory and practice into their ideas. Sir Robert Filmer turned the vague, but widely
accepted, analogy between family and state into a concrete justification
for absolute monarchy, and John Locke's men in the state of nature
resembled nothing so much as English property holders engaging in the
daily work of local government, in which long-standing custom required
attempts to reach consensus.[2]

Both Locke's and Filmer's formulations also contained novel elements, and both drew heavily on the specific concerns of seventeenth-
century Englishmen confronting a political crisis of such massive

proportions that it precipitated first a civil war and then a prolonged dispute over the nature of the constitution. The theories reflected the polarized thinking characteristic of an era that had to turn to armed conflict as a means of resolving its differences, an age in which the political process no longer achieved the desired ends.

The American colonists are not usually regarded as participants in the English political dialogue. In several obvious senses, of course, they were not: no writers who remained in America contributed pamphlets to the political publication wars that raged in England; few men who had resided in the colonies returned to take part in actual combat; and the colonies' leaders did their best to steer clear of involvement in the convulsions that were shaking their homeland. Yet the dialogue over the origins and nature of political obligation was just as intense in the colonies as it was in England. The very act of founding new governments, some of them with but tenuous claims to independent existence, raised questions that forced male settlers to confront the same kinds of issues that faced their relatives who had remained in England, albeit in different form. The Filmerian side of the debate, that which emphasized the demands of inherited allegiance to a higher secular authority ordained by God, inevitably triumphed in these years, but not before those colonists who alternatively argued for the importance of consent by the governed had had their say.[3]

FILMER, LOCKE, AND THE FAMILY ANALOGY

Sir Robert Filmer titled the first section of *Patriarcha* "The Natural Freedom of Mankind, a New, Plausible and Dangerous Opinion." The idea of natural liberty that Filmer found so abhorrent had two interrelated components: first, that all men were born free, subject to no higher earthly power; and second, that they accordingly could choose whatever form of government they wished, for rulers directed the affairs of states only with the consent of their subjects. To Filmer, such notions contradicted "the doctrine and history of the Holy Scriptures, the constant practice of all ancient monarchies, and the very principles of the law of nature." Thus in *Patriarcha* and a series of shorter tracts Filmer set out to disprove what he saw as the erroneous and misleading contentions of the early contract theorists.[4]

Filmer based his argument firmly on the identity of family and state, or what he termed "the Agreement of Paternal and Regal Power." Other seventeenth-century English writers on government and the household used such an analogy loosely; Sir Robert Filmer employed it rigorously and with considerable gusto. A comparison of the responsibilities of a father with those of a king, he declared, would find them to be exactly the same, "without any difference at all but only in the latitude or extent of them." Thus, "as the Father over one family, so the King, as Father over many families, extends his care to preserve, feed, clothe, instruct and defend the whole commonwealth."[5]

Establishing the identity of monarchical and familial authority was crucial for Filmer, because, as was pointed out in chapter one, he derived both from God's grant to Adam of sovereignty over Eve and her children. The text of Genesis 3:16 was, he declared, "the original grant of government, and the fountain of all power placed in the Father of all mankind." In Filmer's words, Adam thereby possessed "power monarchical, as he was a Father, immediately from God. For by the appointment of God, as soon as Adam was created he was monarch of the world . . . by the right of nature it was due to Adam to be governor of his posterity." As first parent, he was "lord paramount to his children's children to all generations, . . . and this subordination of children is the fountain of all regal authority, by the ordination of God himself."[6]

Having demonstrated Adam's absolute, universal authority to his own satisfaction, Filmer drew analogies between the first parent and all subsequent fathers and kings. Every child ever born, he declared, "becomes a subject to him that begets him: under which subjection he is always to live." Although monarchs were not "the natural parents of their subjects," they should be regarded as "the next heirs of those progenitors who were at first the natural parents of the whole people, and in their right succeed to the exercise of supreme jurisdiction." Such an argumentative strategy allowed Filmer to move back and forth easily between paternal and kingly power, drawing on the former to bolster his more extreme claims about the latter. Thus, to prove that a monarch could not be limited by laws adopted by his subordinates, he reminded his readers that "the Father of a family governs by no other law than by his own will, not by the laws or wills of his sons or servants." Similarly, he relied on a familial commonplace when, in advocating kingship over other forms of government, he asked, "Do we not find that in every family the government of one alone is most natural?"[7]

Filmer ridiculed the notion of universal consent to a social contract by raising the troublesome question of how women and children could be said to agree to the establishment of government. In addition to noting the impossibility of obtaining consent from an infant, he observed that women (especially the unmarried) "by birth have as much natural freedom as any other, and therefore ought not to lose their liberty without their own consent." The contention of some contract theorists that "parents" spoke for their children when the contract was constituted therefore conceded the key point: "If it be allowed, that the acts of parents bind the children, then farewell the doctrine of the natural freedom of mankind; where subjection of children to parents is natural, there can be no natural freedom." Theorists who admitted "an original subjection in children, to be governed by their parents" and simultaneously wrote of "an original freedom in mankind" contradicted themselves, he concluded triumphantly.[8]

Filmer thus took the family analogy to an extreme, structuring his argument not so much on the hackneyed metaphorical relationship of state and household as on a novel insistence on the universal application to politics of domestic aphorisms that exalted paternal powers. His equation of familial and political authority and his emphasis on the primacy of male heads of households allowed him to avoid the contract theorists' dilemma of simultaneously maintaining both that all persons were born free and that husbands and fathers represented their dependents when they entered the social contract. Just as Sir Robert Filmer recognized, any contract theorist unwilling to jettison the family analogy completely faced an insuperable problem. Only one of their number did so, and that was precisely why John Locke's writings had such an immense impact.[9]

One of the major aims of Locke's *First Treatise*, his detailed and specific response to Filmer, was to expose the logical complications caused by Filmer's equation of political and domestic government. If God's statement to Eve in Genesis 3:16 was an initial grant of governmental power, Locke asserted, then "there will be as many Monarchs as there are Husbands." Similarly, if the Fifth Commandment granted political authority, "every Father must necessarily have Political Dominion, and there will be as many Sovereigns as there are Fathers." The way to resolve this quandary, Locke insisted, was to recognize that neither Genesis 3:16 nor the Fifth Commandment had any relevance to politics. The biblical description of Eve's subjection was nothing but "what every Wife owes her Husband." Likewise, the injunction to "Honor thy Father and Mother" pertained only to "Natural Parents," not to political superiors: "it cannot concern Political Obedience, but a duty that is owing to Persons, who have no Title to Sovereignty, nor any Political Authority as Magistrates over Subjects."[10]

In the opening paragraphs of the *Second Treatise*, Locke thus stated without equivocation that "the Power of a *Magistrate* over a Subject, may be distinguished from that of a *Father* over his Children, a *Master* over his Servant, a *Husband* over his Wife, and a *Lord* over his Slave." Such a theory, Locke pointed out, explained more successfully than Filmer's how a man could be both the subject of a monarch and the governor of his wife, children, and servants. "These two *Powers, Political and Paternal, are so perfectly distinct* and separate, are built upon so different Foundations and given to so different Ends," he declared, that it was no contradiction for the ruler of a state to owe "filial Duty and Obedience" to his parents. A household did not correspond to a commonwealth in "its Constitution, Power and End," Locke maintained; its master had "a very distinct and differently limited *Power*, both as to time and extent, over those several Persons that are in it" than did a ruler over his subjects. There was "no Legislative Power of Life and Death over any of them," nor did a master wield "absolute Power over the whole *Family*" in the same way a ruler did in a state. Furthermore, the head of a household had no authority "but what a *Mistress of a Family* may have as well as he."[11]

Building on that insight, Locke, as was observed earlier, used women to score debating points on Sir Robert Filmer. To demonstrate the absurdity of Filmer's arguments, Locke frequently inserted into his polemics references to women's familial roles. Mothers effectively helped to establish his key point that family and polity were separate institutions. If a father died while his children were still young, he asked, would they not owe the same obedience to their mother that they had once owed their father? But

> will any one say, that the *Mother* hath a Legislative Power over her Children that she can make standing Rules, which shall be of perpetual Obligation . . . ? Or can she inforce the observation of them with Capital Punishments? For this is the proper *power of the Magistrate*, of which the Father hath not so much as the shadow.

By referring to a mother's power rather than a father's and drawing implicitly on his readers' assumptions about familial authority, Locke created a clear distinction between parental and political dominion.[12]

On the other hand, women (particularly unmarried daughters past childhood) also caused conceptual trouble for Locke. He had a ready response to Filmer's complaint that contract theorists could not logically claim that "*natural Freedom and Subjection to Parents* may consist together": children, he argued, were only temporarily subordinated to their parents; at maturity they would attain their natural rights. He also implied that wives were incorporated into the state via their husbands. Yet he did not even assay a solution to the problem of obtaining the consent of adult unmarried women to the social contract. As has already been seen, Locke's intellectual construct effectively required that women be married.[13]

Thus both theories in their purest form presented logical difficulties. Filmer (as Locke showed) had trouble deriving the power of monarchs from Genesis 3:16 and the Fifth Commandment; contract theorists (as Filmer showed) had trouble deriving political authority solely from the actions of adult men while simultaneously claiming that all people were naturally born free. As the American colonists set out to establish their new governments, such paternalist and contractual ideological extremes demarcated the boundaries within which the bulk of political dialogues occurred. Concepts of authority and consent intermingled in the migrants' minds; struggling with the practical problems of setting up viable polities, they did not look so much to the clearly defined ends of the spectrum as to the murky and obscure area in the middle.

In that middle ground, the notion that men should have some input into government leavened the prevailing Filmerian emphasis on the need to gain the official imprimatur of a higher authority for any legitimate political entity. As was indicated in the discussion of the Mayflower Compact that opened this book, the consent of male household heads could temporarily substitute for proper authorization from a superior power. But ultimately seventeenth-century colonial governments could justify their continued existence only through reference to grants of authority from appropriate symbolic fathers. Without those, all was lost.

FAMILY GOVERNORS AND THE
FOUNDING OF STATES

Although John Locke and Sir Robert Filmer disagreed on the theoretical origins of government, their accounts of how states must actually have been formed were remarkably similar. Indeed, Locke's reconstruction of the historical beginnings of government resembled familial theory more than his own speculative model. " 'Tis obvious to conceive," Locke wrote in the *Second Treatise*, "how easie it was in the first Ages of the World . . . for the *Father of the Family* to become the Prince of it." He had ruled his children since their infancy, and because "without some Government it would be hard for them to live together, it was likeliest it should, by the express or tacit Consent of the Children, when they were grown up, be in the Father." The head of the household did not gain his power by any "*Paternal Right*," Locke emphasized, but "only by the Consent of his Children." The father's dominance did not end when the children reached maturity, because they needed his protection and saw no reason to leave his domains. Thus, Locke concluded in words worthy of Filmer, "the natural *Fathers of Families*, by an insensible change, became the *politick Monarchs* of them too."[14]

The two men also concurred on what would happen when a father/king died without a recognizable heir, which would have been a not uncommon occurrence. Locke postulated that under such circumstances the heads of several allied families would gather to choose a successor to their ruler. Such men, according to Locke, used "their natural freedom, to set up him, whom they judged the ablest, and most likely, to Rule well over them." Remarkably, Filmer saw the process in similar terms. "The Kingly power," he declared, devolved upon "the prime and independent heads of families" when there was no obvious heir. Those masters of households, he averred, could place "their fatherly right of sovereign authority on whom they please." The man thus chosen would not, however, hold his position through election by the people; rather, "from [God] he receives his royal charter of an universal Father, though testified by the ministry of the heads of the people."[15]

Sir Robert Filmer never wholly explained the relationship between his paternalist theory and the quasi-electoral role he thus outlined for household heads, and John Locke never formally attempted to reconcile his historical and theoretical narratives, except by emphasizing sons' implicit consent to their father's sovereignty. Yet Locke's stories—one deliberately hypothetical, the other trying to represent a historical process —are not as divergent as they might appear. That Locke's men in the state of nature were already heads of households is evident from his insistence that monogamous marriage predated the formation of civil society. Before they entered the social contract, men had wives and (implicitly) children dependent on them. As a result, the fathers of families who in his historical account chose a ruler when there was no obvious heir were also the men who in theory consented to organize a government to protect their property rights. The actors were the same in both cases: property-owning men who were the heads of households created both the conjectural contract and real states.

That Locke and Filmer would view the historical process of forming polities in such similar terms suggests the extent of the agreement among seventeenth-century Anglo-Americans about the familial origins of government and the consequent political importance of family governors.

For Filmer, male householders merely designated one of their number to take on the fatherly role that descended from God through Adam; for Locke, they elected such a ruler and consented, actively or tacitly, to his authority. But both recognized that the formation of states required a consensus among the men who headed households, and with good reason. Agreement among such men was the foundation of seventeenth-century English government.

Englishmen who remained in their homeland did not have to confront the practical problems of creating governments *de novo*. But those men who immigrated to the North American colonies did have to deal with such matters. On two occasions, in Rhode Island and New Haven, they followed the theorists' model with remarkable precision. Both colonies were settled by migrants from Massachusetts Bay—Rhode Island by dissident Puritans, New Haven by a group of pious merchants.[16]

When in late 1635 Roger Williams was forced to leave the Bay Colony because of his unorthodox religious views, he and a few followers moved southward to Narragansett Bay, settling on lands that fell outside the jurisdiction of the existing English settlements. In mid-1636, he described the settlers' mode of governance to John Winthrop, then the deputy governor of Massachusetts. "The Masters of Families have ordinarily mett once a fortnight and consulted about our common peace, watch, and planting," Williams explained, "and mutuall Consent hath finished all matters with speede and peace."[17]

Such an informal system worked well for a time, but, as Williams discovered, it could not be long perpetuated. Indeed, his need for political advice had prompted the letter to his old friend and adversary. The arrival in the tiny enclave of "some young men single persons (of whome we had much neede)" had caused a serious problem. The newcomers were formally admitted as inhabitants, and they promised "to subject [themselves] to the Orders made by the Consent of the Howseholders." But they subsequently became "discontented with their estate, and seeke the Freedome of Vote allso, and æqualitie etc." As a result of the controversy, Williams was considering the drafting of a "Compact in a Civill way."

So he informed Winthrop that he wanted to propose to his fellow settlers a "double subscription." The first would be signed by masters of families, who would formally promise each other that

> for our common peace and wellfare (untill we heare further of the Kings royall pleasure concerning our selves) we will from time to time subject our selves in Active or passive Obedience to such

Orders and Agreements, as shall be made by the greater number of the present Howseholders, and such as shall be hereafter admitted by their Consent into the same Priviledge and Covenant in our ordinarie meeting.

The second was intended for the single men, who would be asked to agree in writing to obey the orders of present and future family governors. Williams did not comment on the fact that he proposed no concessions to the young men; perhaps he assumed that Winthrop would, like him, regard their claims as patently illegitimate. To him, it was obvious that only male household heads had a right to participate in governing Rhode Island. When other men complained, the proper response was to demand their formal adherence to the current system, not to modify it to conform to their wishes.

Winthrop's advice to Williams, if any, is unknown. But Williams did implement his plan, for over the next few years male Rhode Island residents in several towns signed documents forming themselves into "a Bodie Politick," agreeing to submit to the rule of masters of families, and promising "to yield all due honour unto [their elected leader] according to the lawes of God." The Rhode Island household heads renewed their covenant in 1641, proclaiming themselves "a DEMOCRACIE, or Popular Government" of "Freemen," who would "make or constitute, Just Lawes, by which they will be regulated," and who would choose governors to execute those laws "faithfully."[18]

Yet such arrangements proved inadequate to satisfy the perceived need for legitimacy, and other New Englanders began to charge that the tiny colony was "void of Goverment." Late in 1641, a group of Rhode Islanders complained that it was impossible to enforce arbitrators' rulings in civil cases (no formal courts had yet been organized). Writing to Bay Colony officials, they painted an apocalyptic picture of the probable outcome: "if men should continue to resist all manner of order and orderly answering one of another in different causes," the petitioners declared, they would "disorderly take what they can come by, first pleading necessity, or to maintain wife and family, but afterwards boldly to maintain licentious lust, like savage brute beasts, they will put no manner of difference between houses, goods, lands, wives, lives."[19]

Without a properly grounded government, in other words, all civil order would collapse, and men would fail to respect each other's property or families. Though at first only "disorderly," they would ultimately revert to "savage brute beasts," acting solely on the basis of "licentious lust." Roger Williams took the only course of action open to him.

Because of the "frequent" complaints that "we had no Authoritie for Civill Government," he later explained, he went to England in 1644 to obtain a charter from Parliament. Once that task was accomplished, the challenges to the government's legitimacy disappeared, for the proper Filmerian conditions for establishing order in Rhode Island had been fulfilled.[20]

By contrast to Rhode Island's casual and sequential development of governmental institutions, the New Haven colonists engaged in a solemn and deliberate process. Yet the idea was the same: just as Filmer and Locke hypothesized, a group of male heads of households together created a political entity and chose a ruler.[21]

On June 4, 1639, "all the free planters assembled together in a ge[neral] meeting to consult about settling civill Government according to God." The meeting began with a prayer, followed by an exhortation from their minister, the Reverend John Davenport, "nott to be rash or sleight in giveing their votes to things they understoode nott, butt to digest fully and th[o]roughly whatt should be propounded to them." All their votes, he declared, should be "in such sort as they would be willing they should stand upon recorde for posterity." A secretary was directed "to read distinctly and audibly in the hearing of all the people whatt was propounded and accorded on."

The meeting continued with remarkable unanimity for a time, as question after question was decided with "no man dissenting." The householders all concurred that scripture would provide "a perfect rule for the direction and government of all men in all duet[ies]," including those in their families, polities, and churches. They agreed to be governed by scripture in all secular and religious matters, to establish "such civill order" as would best produce the desired end, and to elect rulers who would lead them in the proper direction. Then the one issue that caused some dissension was raised: should officeholding and voting (that is, the status of freeman) be restricted to male church members? At first, all seemed to agree, but after the vote was taken a man stood up to declare that although he believed that magistrates and voters should be God-fearing, and that church membership would seem to guarantee those qualities in both groups, he nevertheless objected to the plan to restrict voting, for he thought that "free planters ought nott to give this power out of their hands." The group, however, overrode his objections, and the clause was reaffirmed.[22]

The polity thus established by the first group of family governors in New Haven endured for more than two decades. But in 1662 Connecticut obtained a charter from Charles II, confirming its independent status and giving it the sanction of the highest possible English authority. Although the charter did not explicitly empower Connecticut to take over the hitherto autonomous New Haven colony, its designated boundaries encompassed the smaller jurisdiction. So the two governments began a formal dialogue, in which New Haven tried to retain its independence and Connecticut asserted its newly acquired preeminence. In that unequal exchange, all of New Haven's arguments, which emphasized consent, cooperation, and its history of autonomy, fell victim to Connecticut's now-superior claim to Filmerian dominance.

New Haven met Connecticut's first avowal of supremacy with a statement observing accurately that the new charter said nothing specific about New Haven, and suggesting that both sides await further information about the monarch's intentions. "If it shall appeare . . . to have beene his Majesties pleasure soe to unite us as you understand the Pattent, we must submitt according to God," they admitted in appropriate Filmerian fashion, while nonetheless accusing the larger colony of failing to treat them "in a Christian, neighborly way." Matters proceeded far enough for negotiations over the conditions of union to begin in August 1663, but that effort went nowhere.[23]

In early March 1663/4, New Haven addressed a formal statement of its case to Governor John Winthrop, Jr., of Connecticut. In this document the colony pulled out all the stops, employing both authoritarian and consensual themes. It began by threatening Connecticut's leaders with the highest authority of all—"the wrath of God"—because of that province's "unrighteous dealing with us." It then accused Connecticut of violating the king's will, because in a letter written after the issuance of the Connecticut charter he had recognized New Haven as a "distinct colonie." Finally, the New Haven residents described themselves as "your neighbours, your bretheren, your confœderates," asking in good contractarian fashion that "we may for the future live in love & peace togeither as distinct neighbour colonies." Personal letters also passed between the leaders of Connecticut and New Haven, as John Davenport and others tried to convince their friend John Winthrop, Jr., that the colonies should agree on "rational & æqual termes, for the settling of neighbourly peace & brotherly amitie betweene them & us, mutually."[24]

New Haven, however, had a weak case, as Connecticut's response demonstrated. That colony employed a wide array of authoritarian arguments to attack New Haven's position. First, Connecticut claimed prior rights to New Haven's territory via an Indian land cession. Next, it declared that a search of its provincial records had turned up no evidence that it had ever formally recognized New Haven's independence.

But Connecticut's trump card was the new charter from Charles II: "You well know a king in his owne dominions is by all men tearmed pater patriae, & in scripture record he is said to be a nursing father, & then all his subjects or his children bound to obey." In short, New Haven was "withstanding your ready obedience to the order & appoyntment of your noursing father" and "disturbing of us in our just rights." New Haven could not assert its autonomy against the wishes of its father, Charles II; the smaller colony was a child, whose agreements could be "disanull[ed]" by its parent. "The dispose or gift of goverment is onely the gift of the nursing father within his owne territories & dominions," Connecticut explained, and so New Haven's union stood on an inadequate basis. That Connecticut's government too had until recently rested on exactly the same questionable foundation was conveniently overlooked.[25]

Confronted by this overwhelming display of Filmerian might, New Haven surrendered. At two meetings attended by as many freemen as possible, the residents of the colony agreed that in the new charter the king had given power over them to Connecticut and thus that "in testimony of our loyalty to the kings majesty," they would submit. Responding to the submission, Connecticut addressed them as "deare brethren," acknowledging an egalitarian, contractual relationship only after the authoritarian battle had been won.[26]

Rhode Island and New Haven were the American settlements that most closely resembled in their founding Locke's and Filmer's visions of historical processes. Thus in those colonies Englishmen could most easily apply their common understanding of how governments should be instituted in the absence of prior authorization from a ruler. Not surprisingly, in light of the key role male heads of households played in the maintenance of social order in general, they were also the crucial participants in the founding of states. A viable polity could rest on such a foundation—but only until it encountered a serious challenge. When groups of Rhode Islanders openly resisted the authority of their "Popular Government," or when Connecticut gained a better claim than New Haven to the favor of their mutual "father," there was no choice but to submit to the Filmerian imperative. Rhode Island acquired a charter, and the less-fortunate New Haven lost its battle for autonomous survival.

In the other American colonies, the issues were often far more complex than were those that arose in the small New England polities. The mix of Filmerian and Lockean approaches to government combined with tensions between colonial leaders and ordinary settlers and with conflicts between English proprietors and colonists in general to create an extraordinarily volatile political environment. Competing claims to territories (and thus to the allegiance of the people settled thereon) added to the instability. In the ensuing debates ordinary colonists, their leaders, and their English superiors all drew on their common store of political theories that stressed both consent and submission, both inherited claims to authority and artificially created states. The resulting discussions exposed the bases of Anglo-American political thought in considerable detail.

DIALOGUES OF CONSENT AND AUTHORITY

References to the need for consent and uses of the family analogy alike came easily to the minds and pens of English colonists in America. Such allusions ranged from casual to elaborate, from well-developed arguments to brief citations of accepted commonplaces. When men termed the English monarch or the leaders of their colonies "fathers," or when the Rhode Island code of 1647 listed laws against "High Treason, Pettie Treason, Rebellion, Misbehaviour, and their accessaries" under the rubric "murdering Fathers and Mothers," they were drawing on the tradition employed by Sir Robert Filmer.[27] On the other hand, when the Reverend Thomas Hooker asserted in a 1638 sermon that "the foundation of authority is laid, firstly, in the free consent of the people," or when the Virginia burgesses in 1658 disputed the governor's power to dissolve their assembly on the grounds that they were "the representatives of the people," they were applying the precepts that later informed the theories of John Locke.[28]

Yet despite the ritualistic acknowledgments of the need for consent, in seventeenth-century political contests appeals to authority inevitably prevailed. Many times in these battles the matter of consent was never even *raised*; rather, combatants often couched their contentions entirely in authoritarian terms. They commonly used three major types of argumentative strategies, singly and in tandem: preemptive strikes (proclaiming that their opponents had no legitimate basis for the position they advanced); dueling documents (insisting that their authority was superior to an authority claimed by their opponents); and prior allegiance (explaining that, whatever the merits of their opponents' case, they already owed fealty to another and could not alter their stance). All added up to an insistence that the authority on which they based their position should prevail over whatever authority was claimed by the other side.

When political dialogues were framed in such ways, consent might never enter into the discussion at all.

For example, when Captain William Claiborne came to Kent Island during the winter of 1644 to urge the residents to take arms against the Maryland government and to attack the house then inhabited by Mr. Giles Brent, the men responded not by asking him to persuade them of the benefits of pursuing the course he advocated, but rather "requyred to see the Authority by which hee was enabled to goe uppon the accon then in hand." In response, Claiborne "shewed them a peice of parchment & a Letter, which hee sayd was a Commission & a Letter from the King." But, for unknown reasons, a majority of the men, "doubting of the validity of his Authority, to justify them in the said accon there gave over the designe & left him." Neither side in this exchange mentioned the need for the men to consent to Captain Claiborne's proposal; both he and his hearers saw the key issue as whether or not he had adequate authority to order them to accompany him.[29]

William Claiborne, when his authority was questioned, adopted the strategy of referring to a document that he said supported his position. In the mid-1660s, Stephen Horsey, an illiterate Marylander resisting Colonel Edmund Scarborough's attempt to claim his eastern-shore lands on behalf of Virginia, took the same tack, producing a piece of paper (which Scarborough scoffingly described as "a [land] pattent instead of his Comission") and declaring that "their [sic] was his Authority, and that hee was put in trust by the Lord Lieutenant of Maryland and he would not be false to his trust."[30] Sometimes such tactics as this led to a prolonged duel of documents and historical citations, as the sides alternately exchanged their bona fides.

A notable instance occurred in the debate over control of the area that was to become Delaware. In autumn 1659, the Dutch sent an embassy from New Amsterdam to Maryland to discuss the two jurisdictions' respective claims to the region. When the Dutch negotiators learned that Lord Baltimore's patent had been issued in 1634, they pointed out that theirs predated it by more than a decade. Augustine Herrman, the leader of the group from New Netherland, recorded the documentary competition that followed: "They claimed to derive theirs originally from Sir Walther Ralegh since the year 1584, and we, on the other hand take our origin, as vassals and subjects from the King of Spain, then the first finder and founder of all America." The dialogue, which involved consultations of maps and a copy of Baltimore's patent, continued for several days without any resolution, since the Dutch ambassadors had not come equipped with a copy of their grant from the West India Company.

Without reference to the competing historical source, the matter could not be satisfactorily ended.[31]

The 1663 contest between Edmund Scarborough and Stephen Horsey employed the other two authoritarian arguments as well as such documentary dueling. Scarborough assayed a preemptive strike by informing Horsey that Lord Baltimore's territory did not encompass his plantation and that consequently Horsey had no alternative but to submit to Virginia's rule. "That question was determined by a power beyond private mens controverting," Scarborough explained loftily. But Horsey countered with the third tactic, a claim to prior allegiance. Since he had sworn to uphold Lord Baltimore's government, he told Scarborough, if he switched sides Maryland's governor "will Come so soone as you are gone and Hang me & them at our doores" for committing treason. When Scarborough replied that such an action would be "a tiranny not imaginable to be done," Horsey reminded him that "such things has bin done in Maryland, and therefore I dare not subscribe."[32]

Similarly, in the early months of 1655, when Marylanders were attempting to decide between the gubernatorial rivals William Fuller and William Stone, consent played little formal role in the contest. Rather, each man emphasized his superior claim to represent the proper authority—in this case, Oliver Cromwell, the Lord Protector of England. Both men could allege that their power derived from Cromwell because Fuller was named to his post by Cromwell's commissioners, who were based in Virginia; and Stone's appointment by Lord Baltimore was, Stone argued, implicitly affirmed when Cromwell accepted the validity of Baltimore's patent.

So, when Stone's forces marched on the Protestant stronghold at Anne Arundel, Fuller and his allies challenged him to prove to them "if you have any other or higher power than is here established by the Commissioners of the Commonwealth of England." One of Fuller's supporters assured Stone, "we must and will own and obey the Government of the Lord Protector of the commonwealth of England and am sure if you do but once produce that from His Highness you need not think the people will do anything else but obey you." Stone's backers responded not by exhibiting any specific document (for they had none) but instead by charging that the commissioners had acted "without Authority" when they put Fuller in office. Consequently, they asserted, "the Lord Baltemore and his Officers had just reason to rectifie the same by all lawfull means."[33]

Each side then buttressed its position by accusing the other of enforcing its will by coercion rather than through the appropriate use of authority. A Fuller supporter's narrative of events insisted that when Stone's men "were desired to shew by what power or Commission they so acted, they would in a proud bravado clap their hands on their swords, and say, Here is a Commission." The pro-Stone version, by contrast, emphasized that Fuller's men scoffed at "any pretence of Law or Justice," relying on an armed merchant ship "to awe the whole Countrey."[34]

In Maryland at that time, Oliver Cromwell was the undisputed Filmerian father, and so the combatants sought only to prove the superiority of their competing claims to his favor. Under circumstances in which the correct lines of authority were less certain, though, consent could become relevant. Just as Filmer and Locke recognized, if there was no obvious symbolic father with an axiomatic claim to the obedience of his subjects, male heads of households could create viable polities. Nowhere in Anglo-America was that option more frequently pursued than in the region that lay north and east of the Bay Colony.

In the scattered settlements of fishing and farming folk that eventually became the provinces of New Hampshire and Maine, disputes over the wielding of governmental authority were commonplace occurrences. Overlapping and conflicting grants to English proprietors and subsequent ill-defined land sales to other purchasers often made it difficult if not impossible for settlers to determine just whom they should obey. There were three major contenders for political legitimacy in the region: the proprietors John Mason and Sir Ferdinando Gorges (and their heirs), who based their claims on a 1622 grant from the Plymouth Company; the holders of a grant known as the Plough Patent, issued in 1632 by the Council for New England, successor to the Plymouth Company; and Massachusetts Bay, which contended that its 1629 royal charter encompassed not only John Mason's New Hampshire towns but also much of Gorges's Maine and the Plough Patentees' province, known as Lygonia.[35]

Matters first came to a head in the series of tiny settlements lining the Piscataqua River, an area in dispute among John Mason, the Bay Colony, and various other claimants, some of whom held title via Indian land cessions. Governor John Winthrop responded to the latter with a preemptive strike. "We deny that the Indians heere can have any title to more lands then they can improve," Winthrop declared in 1639, definitively rejecting any rights derived from tribal cessions. That left the settlers with a choice between Massachusetts and Mason. The town of Hampton acknowledged the Bay Colony's jurisdiction, but Captain John Underhill, the early leader of the town of Dover, opposed the imposition of the larger colony's authority.[36]

In a freeholders' meeting in early 1640, Underhill raised the authoritarian claim of prior allegiance. How could they submit to Massachusetts, he asked, "and not breake theier Alegence"? What if the king, as they anticipated, issued them a charter, but it arrived only after they had put themselves under the Bay Colony? The heads of households considered the problem, concluding in good authoritarian fashion that:

> if the[y] could not have leave to com of[f] from theier voluntuarey Subjecktion to the masatewsetes to live under the poure and Athoratey that his magestey shall be pleased to sett up . . . then the[y] could sell their estates and houses heare and Remoove to the masatewsetes without breach of theire Alegence.[37]

That prospect, however, was unappealing, and the possibility that they might too precipitously "tourne theier backes of [*sic*] the king and his Authoratey" was equally unsettling. Consequently, they accepted Captain Underhill's suggestion that they establish an interim government based on consent. They "voluntarily agreed to combine ourselves into a body politic" that would be governed by "all such laws as shall be concluded by a major part of the freemen of our Society" until the king "shall give other orders concerning us." They then asked Massachusetts to bear with them, "and not any way to enforce us to any act whereby wee should break promise or covevant [*sic*] with the patentees or amongst ourselves." About eighteen months later, after the patent holders surrendered to the Bay Colony their political rights in the region (thereby confirming the legitimacy of the Bay's power), all the Piscataqua towns formally submitted to Massachusetts.

The tangled situation further north was less easily resolved. In the early 1640s, Sir Ferdinando Gorges sent his nephew Thomas to govern Maine, and for a time the province had a semblance of consistent rule. But after Thomas's return to England, the proprietor's interests were represented less capably by Mr. Richard Vines and Mr. Henry Jocelyn. Meanwhile, the holder of the Plough Patent designated Mr. George Cleeve as the governor of Lygonia. Through the mid-1640s, Vines and Jocelyn (on behalf of Gorges) sparred with Cleeve (on behalf of Lygonia) over their respective claims to wielding authority in the northern coastal settlements. Both sides repeatedly but futilely appealed to Massachusetts Bay, the pre-eminent regional power, to support their positions.[38]

Several years of fruitless contention led to a classic documentary duel in Casco (later Falmouth) on March 31, 1646. Mr. George Cleeve was holding a court session under the government of Lygonia when Mr.

Henry Jocelyn and a large group of armed Gorges supporters appeared, demanding in writing "to have a sight of his originals, promising a safe returne." Mr. Cleeve hesitated, then agreed if the documents did not actually leave his possession. His papers were "publikely read and scanned," and the next day the Gorges group formally challenged Lygonia's authority. Mr. Cleeve in his turn "demanded a sight of their originals for goverment." Since Mr. Jocelyn and his allies produced no documents in response, Mr. Cleeve "disclaimed obedience, and told them ther was no equality betweene his something, and their nothing."[39]

The waters were subsequently further muddied by the death of Sir Ferdinando Gorges and by his heirs' lack of response to repeated pleas from the Maine settlers to establish their government on a firmer footing. Finally, in desperation, the residents of several towns—deprived of any direction from authority—turned to the only other mechanism open to them for the creation of government, a consensual union. "The Inhabitance are for present in sume distraction about the regulating the affayres of these partes," they explained in July 1649, and so until further orders arrived from England they "with one Free and unius animus Consent doe bynd themselves in a boddy politick" to make laws and to choose their governor and magistrates.[40]

But that weak contractarian polity could not survive the onslaught when the Bay Colony decided to lay formal claim to the region in late 1651. In its exchanges with Maine officials, Massachusetts employed two authoritarian arguments, contending first that its charter boundaries encompassed the northern settlements and then initiating a duel of documents—or, more precisely, eliciting comments on the lack thereof by both sides. The Bay Colony men disdainfully pointed out that Governor Edward Godfrey and his fellow magistrates (chosen under the 1649 agreement of the settlers) declared themselves empowered to rule Maine, "thoe the said persons produced noe Comission thereunto." For their part, Mr. Godfrey and his allies informed the Massachusetts delegates that had they "shewed us any Comnission [sic] or power, of Comand from the parlament of England, or Consell of state," they would have been obeyed. In the absence of specific orders from Parliament, Governor Godfrey insisted, Maine would remain independent. But his government could not long persist in defying its much larger neighbor. In November 1652, Kittery and York, the southernmost Maine towns, acknowledged the Bay's authority, followed several years later by more northern outposts such as Scarborough and Falmouth, which had been regarded as part of Lygonia.[41]

The Massachusetts takeover, seemingly so complete, was nonetheless called into question when the Stuart Restoration emboldened Gorges's adherents to press his heirs' case once again. In July 1663, the county courts upholding Bay Colony authority considered a flood of cases involving opposition to their rule. Mr. Henry Jocelyn, for one, was charged with "renou[nc]ing the authority of the Massatusetts, useing meanes for the subvirting thereof under pretence of a sufficient power from Esquire Gorges to take off the people." A second man offended by interrupting a clergyman who had prayed for God's guidance on a sabbath, "In respect they were under 2 Claymes of Goverment," to insist that "hee neede not make such a preamble for we were under Esquire Gorges authority." A third declared that the Massachusetts men "were none of his magestrates nor never should bee," and a fourth called the Bay Colony's governor "a Roge & [said] all the rest thereof were Trators & Rebells against the King."[42]

Some Maine residents sought to opt out of the renewed conflict. One group addressed a petition to Charles II, asking him to demonstrate a "fatherly care for us" by ruling the province directly and rejecting both the "usurpations" of Massachusetts and the "Invalidd" claims of the Gorges heirs. Another group formally stated with weary resignation that "we are not willing to contend or Determine who shall be our Governours butt in that to submitt to whom itt shall please the Lord & our Soveraing to appoint over us." Commissioners dispatched by Charles II then complicated matters further by arriving on the scene in May 1665, for they appointed magistrates (including Mr. Henry Jocelyn) to rule in the king's name, promising to protect the people "from the claimes of both the Bay & Mr Gorges."[43] Still, the issue was not finally resolved until there was yet another dramatic confrontation between the opposing sides three years later.

In York in July 1668, first Bay Colony representatives and then Maine justices led by Mr. Henry Jocelyn (and claiming authority from the king) convened successive, competing court sessions. At the meetinghouse, the Massachusetts men "read their Comission from the Generall Court" and received the submission of five towns. They conducted some business, then adjourned to eat dinner. Before they returned, the Maine justices summoned people to the same meetinghouse for *their* court session, took the seats previously occupied by the Bay Colony officials, and planned "to shew their power, and from whome, soe to see which was of most waite." But when the Bay Colony's magistrates reappeared to confront them, the two sides "withdrew in private, being loft [loath] to cause a disturbance among the people." The Maine officials decided not to press their case further at that time, perhaps because the Bay's justices were accompanied by a dozen well-armed men. When one of their number later traveled to Boston to protest the arrival of the Massachusetts magistrates, he was thrown into jail, and thereafter Massachusetts met with few challenges to its authority in the region.[44]

The incidents in Maine from the 1640s through the 1660s demonstrated that, in the context of a Filmerian worldview, claims to government by consent could not withstand the demands of adherence to authority. The combinations of property-holding men that sporadically ruled local areas in New Hampshire and Maine all collapsed when confronted by the more compelling mandate offered by the Bay Colony charter, misrepresented though it was. No matter how much the Maine settlers might have wanted to maintain their independence, that they had no appropriate authoritarian claim to autonomy ultimately sealed their fate. Just as "ther was no equality betweene [George Cleeve's] something, and [Henry Jocelyn's] nothing," so too a proper symbolic father—Charles I's 1629 grant to the Massachusetts Bay Company—consistently vanquished derivations of legitimacy from consent alone. But the Massachusetts interpretation of Filmerian thought was not as rigid as Filmer's own formulation, allowing instead for a limited form of consent. In its most mature version, as explicated by Governor John Winthrop, it rendered consent acceptable by casting it in terms that were both gendered and irrevocable.

AUTHORITY, CONSENT, AND JOHN WINTHROP

The only resident of English North America who developed an intellectual system comparable to those of Filmer and Locke was John Winthrop, the most important political leader in the early years of Massachusetts Bay. Winthrop was elected governor before the migrants left England; thereafter he served continuously in the colony's government for the nineteen years until his death in 1649, alternating as assistant (magistrate), deputy governor, and, for a total of nine years, governor. Winthrop's ideas evolved over time, in response to a series of bitter political disputes in the Bay Colony.[45]

Women were the central figures in two of the most significant conflicts—one that nearly tore the colony apart, the other with indelible political consequences. The former, the so-called Antinomian crisis of 1636–38, led Winthrop to write his first lengthy treatise on government. Mistress Anne Hutchinson, the focal point of the controversy, will be considered at length in chapter eight. The second incident, that involving the uncompromising Goodwife Elizabeth Sherman, had a decisive impact on Winthrop, initiating the most creative phase in his political thinking. Not by coincidence, then, did women play a major role in Winthrop's fullest statement of his political theory.

During the first six years of the Bay Colony, most political debates revolved around challenges to the discretionary power of the magistrates. The Massachusetts freemen, who by definition had to be both church members and the heads of households, repeatedly pressed Winthrop and the colony's other leaders for a greater voice in the government and for a codification of the laws. In 1634, the General Court was formally constituted as a unicameral assembly consisting of deputies elected in town meetings and assistants chosen annually by the deputies, along with a governor and deputy governor selected by the General Court each year from among the assistants. Two years later, it was agreed that no law could be passed without the concurrence of separate majorities of the assistants and the deputies. Under nearly constant pressure to move toward a more representative form of government—which Winthrop thought unwise and which he consequently opposed at nearly every turn—he nevertheless failed to produce a comprehensive document outlining his political views until spring 1637, when the colony was attempting to bring Mistress Hutchinson and her followers under control.[46]

The first step the Massachusetts authorities took against the Hutchinsonian group was to banish her brother-in-law, the Reverend John Wheelwright, along with some of his supporters. In the aftermath of his trial, the assistants, who believed that recent arrivals comprised a substantial proportion of the dissident party, adopted a regulation that forbade any newcomers from remaining in Massachusetts for more than three weeks without the permission of a magistrate.[47] That order ignited critical comments sufficiently heated to lead John Winthrop to compose a detailed defense of the court order in June 1637. Therein he systematically examined the origins and ends of government for the first time.

As he sought to justify the magistrates' policy, Winthrop began by defining the nature of "a common weale or body such as this is." Massachusetts Bay was based on "the consent of a certaine companie of people, to cohabite together, under one government for their mutual safety and welfare." Indeed, he wrote in a contractarian vein, "the care of safety and wellfare was the original cause or occasion of common weales and of many familyes subjecting themselves to rulers and laws." The consenting participants in a commonwealth thus acquired "a public and relative interest each in other, and in the place of their co-habitation and goods." No one else, he declared, "can claime priviledge with them but by free consent." So it logically followed that "no man hath right to come into us etc. without our consent." Churches and towns could each prevent unwanted persons from joining their ranks; "why then should the common weale be denied the like liberty"?[48]

Thus far John Winthrop sounded like nothing so much as a precursor of John Locke. But then, to drive home his point, he turned to that standard source of authority, the household analogy: "A family is a little common wealth, and a common wealth is a greate family. Now as a family is not bound to entertaine all comers, no not every good man (otherwise than by way of hospitality) no more is a common wealth." In both cases the purpose of the exclusion was "to preserve the wellfare of the body; and for this ende to have none received into any fellowship with it who are likely to disturbe the same." Two years later, in the midst of another controversy, Winthrop drew further on reliable Filmerian arguments. A small group of men should not petition the magistrates to alter established policies, he contended in 1639, for such an act "amounts to a plain reproof of those whom God hath set over them, and putting dishonor upon them, against the tenor of the fifth commandment."[49]

The same axiom also served as one of John Winthrop's key reference points (he accused his opponents of "a manifest breach of the 5th Commandment") during one of the strangest and most important episodes in the political history of the Anglo-American colonies: the affair of Goodwife Elizabeth Sherman and her missing sow.[50]

The case began in the autumn of 1637, when Goody Sherman, a poor woman whose husband Richard left for England soon after the dispute arose, accused Captain Robert Keayne, one of the wealthiest merchants in Massachusetts, of having killed her sow. The previous year, the sow had disappeared, and a stray resembling it ended up at Keayne's house. Keayne followed the standard procedure in such cases, announcing to the community that he had a stray and asking any claimants to come forward. "Many came and sawe her," John Winthrop noted in a summary of the case, but no one claimed ownership. Keayne kept the stray penned with one of his sows, and in October 1637 he slaughtered one of the two, which he unwaveringly insisted was his. Soon thereafter Goody Sherman came to view the remaining hog. Declaring that it did not belong to her, she charged Keayne with having killed the stray, which she said must have been hers.[51]

Goody Sherman and Captain Keayne were both church members, so she first complained about his behavior to the elders of the Boston congregation. After hearing both sides, they rejected her accusation, which brought the matter to a close for a time. But in November 1639, both the General Court and the church publicly reprimanded Keayne "for selling his wares at excessive Rates," an experience that wounded him deeply and called his reputation into question.[52] Still dissatisfied with the church's decision in her case more than two years earlier, and undoubtedly emboldened by universal censure of Keayne, in April 1640 Goody Sherman again raised the issue of her sow by filing suit against the captain. Keayne, however, won the case, along with £3 in damages. If the victorious defendant had been satisfied with that sum, perhaps the affair would have ended. But the thin-skinned merchant countersued for slander, winning an additional award of £20, assessed against both Elizabeth Sherman and her attorney, Mr. George Story, a merchant who lodged at her house.

Goody Sherman, aided by Story, then bypassed the Court of Assistants, appealing the original £3 judgment directly to the General Court. She collected new evidence, including a deposition from the man hired to kill the sow for Keayne. Peter Pettford swore that he thought the pig he had slaughtered was Goody Sherman's, though he had previously said the opposite because "mr kean told him that all his servants would swear against him which . . . made him afraid to stand to what he saw." And so in May 1642 the Massachusetts legislature heard nearly a week of testimony from a host of witnesses about the description and possible ownership of the sow. The result was a deadlock: a majority of the elected deputies supported Goody Sherman, while most of the assistants voted for Keayne. The overall vote total favored her, but because a majority of both houses had failed to concur in the judgment, nothing could be done. A year later Goody Sherman petitioned for a rehearing via the church elders (some of whom now supported her), but her husband, who had finally returned to the Bay Colony, instead negotiated an out-of-court settlement with Keayne, who agreed to forgo the £20 judgment and even to refund the original £3 in damages.[53]

John Winthrop found the affair intensely frustrating. To his mind, the evidence favored Robert Keayne. If the merchant's many witnesses were telling the truth, Winthrop concluded, "Itt is not possible the defendantt should be guiltye or anye of these Sowes the plaintiff['s]." Yet at the same time he understood why some people supported Goody Sherman's claims. The testimony offered in her behalf had some plausibility, and furthermore Keayne was "of ill report in the country for a hard dealer in his course of trading," being "very worthy of blame in that kind." The excessive slander judgment had increased the sympathy for the poor goodwife. Many people, Winthrop observed, "could not distinguish this from the principal cause, as if she had been adjudged to pay 20 pounds for demanding her sow." Since Keayne was wealthy and she impoverished, "this so wrought with the people, as being blinded with unreasonable compassion, they could not see, or not allow justice her reasonable course." Winthrop's assessment was accurate: the version of the story that reached a remote island in Maine was that the Massachusetts court "had doon great wrong to a pore woman about a sowe, and that none could have Justice [there] but such as were membars of the church." A sailor reported that in spite of "19 wittnesses sworne against Mr. Cane . . . he being a membar caried the mattar against the poore woman." The tale, told by men opposed to the Bay Colony's possible takeover of the region, concluded that "they weere as good live in turkie as live undar such a goverment."[54]

As was seen in chapter five, disputes over the ownership of stray livestock were commonplace. What was unusual was the length to which this case was carried. Elizabeth Sherman, a fictive widow of low rank, believed she had been wronged by one of Massachusetts Bay's elite and refused to surrender her claim to minimal damages for a lost sow. A man would have known better. Properly socialized into the communal values of the male informal public, he would have abandoned his quest for compensation once the church elders had ruled against him, or at the latest after the first loss in court. That, indeed, was precisely what Thomas Lechford, Boston's most experienced lawyer, advised Goodwife Sherman to do, recommending (after the loss in the church) an attempt "to compound it upon reasonable terms" before the 1640 trial, then after the subsequent loss in court advising Story and Goody Sherman "to beare themselves silently at least if they could not be satisfied." But Goody Sherman nevertheless spoke publicly of her anger at the verdict, thus opening herself to Keayne's defamation suit. She also later rejected Captain Keayne's offer to "remit the whole" if she would acknowledge that she had done him an injury.[55]

Instead, she pursued her case with vigor to the highest court in the colony. The resulting political impasse developed in part because of the identity of the parties: the recalcitrant woman came to symbolize an ordinary colonist's struggle against control by a profit-seeking, dominant elite of male church members. That she too belonged to the church was a fact conveniently overlooked as the story spread through New England and developed into a moral tale about the dangers of rule by Massachusetts Bay.

John Winthrop recorded that because of Keayne's poor reputation and the "clamors" against him, the General Court had been expected to rule in favor of the plaintiff. When the legislature deadlocked, he remarked, many colonists began "to speak unreverently of the court, especially of the magistrates." Some declared that the assistants' veto "hindered the course of justice" and started to argue for the separation of the legislature into two distinct bodies. Even though the idea was dropped for the time being, in the long run the pressures grew too strong to resist. In 1644, the two houses met separately for the first time. Thus bicameralism was established in the Bay Colony.[56]

In the wake of this prolonged controversy, John Winthrop composed his two most extended essays on the nature of government and political power. The first, his "Discourse on Arbitrary Government," was written during 1644 to support the magistrates' claim to discretionary judicial authority as pressure was mounting for a more detailed legal codification than the Body of Liberties supplied. He delivered the second, his famous speech "On Civil Liberty," in May 1645, after he had been acquitted by the General Court of charges that he had violated the people's freedom by his actions in a complicated altercation over the choice of a militia captain in the town of Hingham.[57]

Winthrop proposed in the former to distinguish the political system of Massachusetts, which critics had termed "arbitrary," from genuinely autocratic regimes. If "a people have men sett over them without their choyce, or allowance," a government could be deemed arbitrary, Winthrop averred. That was not, however, true of the Bay Colony, where the people "have Libertye to admitt, or reject their Governors; and to require the Rule, by which they shalbe governed and Judged." In form, the government was "a mixt Aristocratie," in which the governor and assistants together personified "Authoritye," and the freemen represented "Liberty; which . . . hath power to Acte upon the cheife meanes of its owne wellfare." Their "bodye politike" was, in its public aspect, "as one single person consistinge of severall members: and appointinge to eache, its proper place: it regulates their power and motions, as might best conduce to the preservation, and good of the wholl bodye."[58]

Perhaps Winthrop realized when composing that description that it resembled the standard portrayal of marriage. In any event, when he next ventured a theoretical statement about politics he drew on familial metaphors in a new way, one through which he for the first time successfully integrated the authoritarian and contractarian themes in his thought.

Accused of arbitrarily rejecting protests against the magistrates' handling of the disputed Hingham militia election, Winthrop, then the deputy governor, demonstrated a remarkable flair for the dramatic when he replied to the charges at a General Court session. After entering with the other magistrates, he (as he described the scene in his journal, no doubt with considerable satisfaction) "placed himself beneath within the bar, and so sate [with his head] uncovered." This humble posture, he reported, "grieved" many members of the public and the court, but he told them "that, being criminally accused, he might not sit as a judge in that cause." His brilliant theatrical sense must have brought home to everyone present the seriousness of the charges being pressed against him, and surely it contributed to his acquittal. At the close of the lengthy proceedings, after he had been cleared, Winthrop was "desired by the court to go up and take his place again upon the bench, which he did accordingly." At that richly symbolic moment he was granted permission to address the assembled crowd.[59]

He wanted to prevent future imbroglios of the sort Massachusetts Bay had just experienced, Winthrop explained, reminding the freemen that "it is yourselves who have called us to this office, and being called by you, we have our authority from God, in way of an ordinance."[60] Thus he neatly combined initial consent with a Filmerian view of the power of rulers. Winthrop conceded that magistrates were fallible, like other men, and he asked the people to be tolerant of their elected officials' errors. Then he moved to his key point: the contemporary misunderstanding of "liberty" in the Bay Colony. There were two kinds of liberty, the deputy governor declared: first, "natural" liberty, which men shared with beasts and which "cannot endure the least restraint of the most just authority," the sort of freedom that was a "great enemy of truth and peace." The second type of liberty, "civil or federal," was, by contrast, "the proper end and object of authority, and cannot subsist without it; and it is a liberty to that only which is good, just, and honest." This kind of freedom was "exercised in a way of subjection to authority"; it was, said Winthrop, that very liberty in which Christ had made men free.

To explicate his concept of civil liberty in terms that his listeners would understand, Winthrop then employed a marital analogy that made explicit the implied comparison contained in his essay on arbitrary government:

> The woman's own choice makes such a man her husband; yet being so chosen, he is her lord, and she is to be subject to him, yet in a way of liberty, not of bondage; and a true wife accounts her subjection her honor and freedom, and would not think her condition safe and free, but in her subjection to her husband's authority. Such

is the liberty of the church under the authority of Christ, her king and husband. . . . Even so, brethren, it will be between you and your magistrates.

If the freemen of Massachusetts behaved like dutiful wives, "quietly and cheerfully submit[ting] unto that authority which is set over you," their liberties would be preserved. But if they instead followed "natural corrupt liberties," they would "murmur, and oppose, and be always striving to shake off that yoke." Just as insubordination in a wife could destroy a family, such behavior in a state would lead to disaster for all concerned.

Thus Winthrop linked authority and consent by alluding to a familial relationship that involved both. Furthermore, his formulation employed a household metaphor that applied much more accurately to the colonial situation than did his earlier reliance on the Fifth Commandment. The reason the marital analogy was especially appropriate in the North American context was made clear by the Reverend John Cotton, Winthrop's friend and ally. Responding to those who had criticized Massachusetts Bay for making church membership a prerequisite for political participation, Cotton drew a distinction "between a Common-wealth already setled, and a Common-wealth yet to be setled, and wherein men are free to chuse what Form they shall judge best." Saint Paul's admonition to Christians to obey appropriate secular authorities, he contended, referred only to previously established governments. Just as Paul had advised women to choose Christian husbands if possible, so too the residents of a new state should decide to be ruled by Christians if it was in their power to do so.[61]

The key element, then, was *choice*: the Puritans had chosen to leave England to establish new governments and societies in North America. Therefore it was difficult for them to draw systematically on the Filmerian brand of paternalistic thought, which stressed a subject's *lack* of choice. A child, after all, could not decide which family he or she was to be born into; accordingly, the explicit message of the paternal version of the family analogy was people's inability to challenge the authority structure of their polity and society. New Englanders had already challenged that structure by their decision to emigrate, but at the same time their leaders did not want to abandon wholly the authoritarian model of the state. Consequently Winthrop's analogy to the wife's role in marriage—which allowed free choice prior to subjection—mirrored the colonists' circumstances more precisely than would reference to a child's role in a Filmerian household. From a theoretical perspective, the new formulation had an additional asset: a wife was subject to her husband

for the duration of the marriage, whereas children, while ideally remaining deferential to their parents, would eventually grow up and leave
the household of their birth, thereby implying a subject's inevitable pro-
gression toward greater independence for everyone except Sir Robert
Filmer.

Further, casting women metaphorically solely as wives removed the
disturbing implications of motherhood in Filmerian thought. To be logically consistent and to draw most usefully on the Fifth Commandment,
paternalist writers had to acknowledge that the power of mothers was
essentially equivalent to that of fathers. As has been seen, when societies
and governments were described in the same terms as families, women's
potential for power could not be definitively denied. John Winthrop
and John Locke both realized that viewing women primarily as wives
made it easier to maintain women's overall subordination to men. Winthrop, less innovative than Locke, did not discard the family analogy but
instead reshaped it in marital rather than parental terms. His use of the
analogy may well reveal a certain wishful thinking that developed after
his encounters with two outspoken women who were notably independent thinkers and certainly not the sort of wives his model had in
mind.[62]

John Winthrop's successful creation of a unified political theory that
coherently tied consent and authority together through a marital metaphor ensured the continuing use of the family analogy in the Bay Colony
after his death. For example, when the Massachusetts General Court
sought to defend its sanguinary anti-Quaker policies in 1659, an essay it
endorsed and distributed employed the same reasoning that Winthrop
had used in 1637 against recently arrived supporters of Anne Hutchinson.
"If private persons may . . . shed the blood of such intruders [into their
homes], may not the like be graunted to them that are the publicke
keepers and guardians of the comonwealth?" the author asked. Since
magistrates are the "nursing fathers & nursing mothers" of the society,
it was surely their responsibility to protect their metaphorical children
from "the daingerous company of persons infected with the plague of
pestilence or other contagions," including the Quakers' "corruption in
minde & judgment."[63]

Yet despite the powerful logic that lay behind the combination of
consent and authority in Winthrop's marital metaphor, when Massachusetts Bay confronted its greatest external threat prior to the formal rev-
ocation of its charter it abandoned all reference to consent and relied
wholly on authority for a defense of its position. The challenge to
the colony came from the four commissioners sent by Charles II in

1664–65 to "vissit all & every the severall colonies" in New England, "to heare, . . . & determine all complaints & appeales," and to work toward "setling the peace & security of the said country, according to their good & sound discretions." The Bay Colony's leaders resisted the commissioners' attempts to impose their authority within Massachusetts, reluctantly giving in on some points (for instance, abandoning both the prosecution of John Porter, Jr., under the rebellious-child statutes and their hitherto adamant insistence that only church members could have the right to vote for the colony's officers) while nevertheless engaging in a prolonged dialogue with the commissioners over political legitimacy. Throughout that dialogue they counterposed their 1629 charter to the commissioners' instructions, expressing the crux of their dilemma during a meeting in May 1665:

> either they must be charged with deniall of his majesties authority over them, or else must yeild to the prostrating of his majesties authority, orderly established heere according to the grant of his royall charter, under the broad seale of England, & submit them-selves, their lives, & estates, & their liberties, farr dearer then them both, to another authority, whose rule is theire oune discretion.[64]

In short, the circumstances in the Bay Colony in 1665 resembled those in Maryland ten years earlier: two different claims to wielding legitimate authority had clashed, and there seemed no way to decide between them. Whereas it might appear that the consent of the residents could have been factored into the equation, thus providing Massachusetts officials with an additional edge in the argument, they never employed such a contention, perhaps understanding that a claim based even par-tially on consent had no chance of prevailing against the far more com-pelling demands of the king's authority. Only an act of a monarch (the charter) could contest another act of a monarch (the commissioners' instructions).

In theoretical terms, then, Filmerian thought dominated the political thinking of the seventeenth-century Anglo-American colonies prior to the Indian wars of the mid-1670s and the Glorious Revolution of 1688–89—and perhaps even later, though that is beyond the scope of this book. Northerners and southerners alike conceived their govern-ments in familial and authoritarian terms, though Chesapeake residents were less likely than New Englanders to employ familial metaphors to explain the operations of politics. That was not only because they lacked a leader with the intellectual power of John Winthrop; it was also because, as was seen in the first section of this volume, such metaphors had an attenuated meaning in a region where traditional households headed by a husband and a wife comprised a relatively small proportion of all families. The consequences of the nascent Lockean society that thereby emerged in the Chesapeake were significant. They can best be identified through an analysis of criminal prosecutions in the two regions, especially those that focused on matters involving state authority and sexual offenses.

❦

CHAPTER 7

Marvelous Wickedness

> Marvelous it may be to see and consider how some kind
> of wickedness did grow and break forth here, in a land
> where the same was so much witnessed against and so
> narrowly looked unto, and severely punished when it was
> known, as in no place more, or so much, that I have
> known or heard of.
>
> —*William Bradford, 1642*[1]

GOVERNOR WILLIAM BRADFORD'S REFLECTIONS on the incidence of "wickedness" in Plymouth were elicited by a crime wave
of sorts that hit the colony in the early 1640s. In recent months, he
commented, there had been "too many" prosecutions for "drunkenness
and uncleanness," a term he and other colonists employed to refer to
sexual offenses, including fornication, adultery, and, he noted, "that
which is worse, even sodomy and buggery (things fearful to name)."
The analytical Bradford concluded that the outbreak of misbehavior had
three causes: first, the devil's attempts to discredit the holy experiment;
second, an understandable if lamentable reaction to the constraints imposed by the colony's "strict laws"; and third, the possible consequences
of law enforcement itself. Perhaps, he hypothesized, the residents of
Plymouth were no more prone to commit crimes than anyone else, "but
they are here more discovered and seen and made public by due search,
inquisition and due punishment; for the churches look narrowly to their
members, and the magistrates over all, more strictly than in other
places."[2]

To a twentieth-century historian, Bradford's first two explanations
are questionable, but his third has the ring of perceptive truth. The New
England colonies in general, not just Plymouth, prosecuted proportion-
ally more offenders than did Maryland and Virginia; criminal cases comprised a much larger share of court business in the north than in the

Chesapeake.[3] Moreover, as shall be seen in the pages that follow, the nature of those crimes and the legal disposition of them differed significantly in the two regions. So, too, did the colonies diverge in the ways offenses came to the attention of the legal system: in New England, constables, grand jury men, and other officials regularly reported criminal conduct to the proper authorities, whereas in the south victims themselves were usually responsible for registering their complaints, often by filing civil suits against the persons who had injured them or stolen their property. As a result, it is hardly surprising that certain types of misbehavior (especially minor, victimless crimes) were more frequently prosecuted in the north than in the south.[4]

The variations had several causes, demographic and religious differences prominent among them. Conduct criminalized in one region was acceptable (if not laudable) in the other; the same behavior could have considerably different consequences, depending on one's colony of residence. Yet the overarching explanation for the difference lies in the persistent Filmerian thinking of New England's Puritan leaders and in the divergent approach to governance adopted by their Chesapeake counterparts—by necessity rather than design. In the demographically disrupted Chesapeake, where families were truncated and scattered settlement patterns rendered impossible the neighborhood surveillance that characterized most parts of New England, the criminal-justice system was more passive than active. Chesapeake officials rarely searched out offenders; instead, they commonly waited for a formal complaint from a victim. Consequently, criminal laws were less systematically enforced in the south than in the north.

REGIONAL PATTERNS OF LAW ENFORCEMENT

Colonial legal codes reflected the interests of elected and appointed officials and the landholding men who voted for representatives to the provincial assemblies. Accordingly, statutes everywhere in Anglo-America initially focused primarily on political and financial affairs, the subjects of deepest concern to men. Not until several decades had passed did the legislators begin to adopt laws pertinent to women, such as those containing specific provisions for widows. At first, laws were written and approved in piecemeal fashion, but within three decades after their founding most of the colonies had formally codified their existing statutes. (Virginia, for example, comprehensively revised its laws in 1643, 1657, and 1662.)[5]

The civil codes drafted to cover such issues as inheritance and land conveyances did not differ significantly from colony to colony, but criminal laws varied considerably. Each legislature understandably focused on particular problems of local concern: the Chesapeake colonies adopted many laws governing servants and penalizing hog-stealing, while New England legislators drafted statutes pertaining to familial relations or communal obligations. Moreover, Virginia and Maryland for the most part assumed that English criminal statutes continued in force within their borders, whereas Massachusetts Bay based its criminal code partly on the Old Testament, a practice that was then copied by all its neighboring colonies except Rhode Island.[6]

Because of the significant regional impact of the Bay Colony's codification, it is important to examine its origins in detail. Pushed by the freemen, who insistently advocated the adoption of an explicit compilation of statutes, the leaders of Massachusetts as early as 1636 began to consider formulating "a draught of lawes agreeable to the word of God, which may be the ffundamentalls of this comonwealth." Still, little progress was made for several years. The Reverend John Cotton finally drew up a model code, which was published in London in 1641 as though it had been enacted. That same year, Massachusetts adopted the Body of Liberties, which seven years later served as the basis for the broader, more comprehensive Laws and Liberties. That 1648 code was then imitated by the other Puritan colonies: Connecticut in 1650, New Haven in 1656, Plymouth in 1671, and New Hampshire in 1680 all copied many aspects of the Laws and Liberties.[7]

The different law-enforcement emphases in New England and the Chesapeake are evident in their assemblies' respective definitions of capital offenses. Crimes carrying the death penalty are *ipso facto* the most abhorrent in any given society, so the designation of capital offenses can reveal the colonial leaders' scale of values. In largely replicating English legal practice, Virginia and Maryland leaders adopted their homeland's policy of primarily applying the death penalty in cases of theft and murder. The Puritan colonies, by contrast, also targeted a variety of familial and religious offenses for the ultimate penalty. In addition to rebellious children, those miscreants in danger of execution in New England included adulterers, blasphemers and idolaters, some rapists, and anyone convicted of bestiality or sodomy.[8]

Patterns of conviction and sentencing under the capital laws revealed the same emphases as the statutes themselves. Two thirds of the persons sentenced to die in Chesapeake courts had been found guilty of theft or murder, whereas over half their northern counterparts had been convicted instead of sexual or religious offenses. Southerners were more likely to escape the gallows than were New Englanders, because first offenders charged with capital crimes in Maryland and Virginia (but not in New England) were usually allowed to plead benefit of clergy, thereby enduring branding on the thumb but avoiding the death penalty. The primary exceptions were women convicted of infanticide; the privilege of pleading clergy was not available to any female, and so women found guilty of infanticide in the seventeenth century were almost invariably hanged, regardless of their place of residence.[9]

Just as the handling of the most serious crimes therefore disclosed significant regional differences in law enforcement, so too did the general distribution of prosecutions across broad categories of cases. Logically enough, in light of the statutory emphasis already discussed, male and female residents of the Chesapeake were relatively more likely to be accused of crimes against persons or property than were New Englanders.[10] Moreover, the politically chaotic Chesapeake produced a greater proportion of prosecutions for various transgressions against the authority of the state than occurred in the more stable northern governments.[11] Regional differences in the treatment of minor violations of public order—such offenses as swearing, disturbing the peace, unlicensed liquor sales, and sabbath breaking—were particularly dramatic. Whereas in the Chesapeake these sorts of infractions constituted just 5 percent of prosecutions of women and about one fifth of prosecutions of men, in New England they accounted for considerably more than one third of the charges brought against defendants of both sexes.[12]

Indeed, victimless crimes of all descriptions (not just such violations of public order) were more likely to be prosecuted in the north than in the south. Although everywhere in English America defendants were more commonly charged with victimless offenses than with crimes that had injured someone, in New England prosecutions of victimless crimes outnumbered crimes with victims by more than two and a half to one. In the Chesapeake, by contrast, the ratio of such prosecutions was approximately one and a half to one. These figures confirm once again the divergent nature of law-enforcement activity in the two regions—New England's overriding concern with the maintenance of social order, the Chesapeake's primary focus on preserving the lives and property of its residents.[13]

A particularly telling example of differential law enforcement is the two areas' treatment of the congeries of offenses revolving around the consumption of alcohol—drunkenness, unlicensed liquor sales, disorderly conduct, and hosting disorderly gatherings. All the colonies licensed taverns, prosecuted drunks, and penalized those who permitted or assisted others to drink to excess.[14] Yet criminal charges of this nature were pursued far more often in New England than in the Chesapeake, where prosecutions for such misbehavior were relatively few and far between. Since there is no reason to believe that Chesapeake residents imbibed alcohol less frequently or more moderately than New Englanders, the explanation for the divergent patterns of prosecution lies in the respective priorities of officials of the two regions. Those priorities become even clearer when specific evidence is examined.[15]

Just as incidents of family violence in the Chesapeake came to light in court cases that had little or nothing to do with the misbehavior, so excessive drinking was exposed in the same way. For example, a 1662 lawsuit against the executor of an estate disclosed that a Maryland woman's funeral had turned into a "merry meeting" because of the three barrels of beer consumed by "Carousing" mourners. Similarly, an inquest into a man's accidental drowning revealed that he had shared both "a Pint of Drams" and the "most part" of a quart of alcohol before setting out one morning in a canoe. Drunkenness likewise led to civil suits rather than prosecutions; thus in early 1653 Governor William Stone sued a man for "Entertaining his overseer to drink in his house," causing the overseer to neglect the timely planting of tobacco seedlings. The men and women tried for drunkenness in the region were the exception rather than the rule, and usually they had seriously misbehaved while drunk, for instance by appearing in court "much in Drink" or by "Committinge of a ryott."[16]

In New England, men and women were prosecuted not only for comparable offenses but also simply for being drunk. The New Haven colonial records are replete with such cases: nine men fined for "a drunken disorderly meeting at the prison on a Lords day att night" in 1644; two young men sentenced to "correction in their famylyes" (one by his master, the other by his father) because the first had been seen to "stagger & reele" in the street and the second had supplied him with liquor; an inebriated Dutch traveler fined heavily not only for being drunk but also for challenging New Haven's right to try him and insisting that "at the Mannadoes [Manhattan] they were not punisht for drunkenness."[17]

Officials in Maine perceived drunkenness (probably correctly) as a particularly intractable problem in their jurisdiction. The many unattached fishermen in the province seem to have spent a considerable proportion of their time ashore drinking heavily. Such behavior led to numerous prosecutions for unlicensed liquor sales (including some by captains who retailed alcohol from their boats and simply upped anchor when challenged), drunken brawls, and attacks on constables who tried to arrest the malefactors. Residents of the Isles of Shoals, rocky out- croppings seven miles off the coast inhabited almost entirely by fisher- men, were especially notorious for such behavior. For example, of thirteen presentments from the Shoals at one 1666 court session, all but four included a charge of drunkenness; and it does not take much in- terpolation to conclude that the November 1665 presentments of an unruly couple for abusing a constable by calling him "Roge and Rascal" and "horne headed Roge & slow headed Roge" arose from the consta- ble's concurrent attempt to arrest the husband for unlicensed dispensing of alcohol.[18]

Since Maine resembled the Chesapeake demographically—that is, both areas had a population containing a high proportion of single male laborers and relatively few women or families—it seems reasonable to hypothesize that the behavior so frequently prosecuted there prevailed in the south as well. But because drunkenness in the Chesapeake was interpreted as individual behavior with few significant consequences for society unless it led to the injury of persons or property (as did the scattered incidents described above), it was but rarely punished. Puritan New Englanders, by contrast, viewed the maintenance of proper order in general as essential to the survival of their Filmerian vision of a hi- erarchical, family-based society. So Governor Theophilus Eaton of New Haven could tell one early offender that "drunkenesse is among the fruits of the flesh, both to be witnessed against, both in the church and civill court, and its a brutish sinne," and the New Haven magistrates could convince a young man in 1662 that a refusal to admit he had been at fault for "great & grosse miscariages in this way of drunkenesse" con- stituted a "breach of the 5th commandment."[19]

New England's emphasis on systematic law enforcement is con- firmed by the conviction rates for crimes in that region. Remarkably, no category of offense had less than an 86 percent conviction rate, and in most types of prosecutions 92 percent or more of defendants were convicted.[20] In the Chesapeake, by contrast, conviction rates ranged pri- marily between 60 and 80 percent, with only one category of defendants (men and women charged together for sexual offenses) being convicted at a rate as high as was common in New England.[21]

Differences in sentencing also characterized the two regions. Al- though a majority of male and female defendants in both north and south incurred financial penalties (and most of those had no other punishments inflicted on them), New England courts were more likely to sentence those found guilty to multiple or alternate penalties than were judges in the Chesapeake.[22] Whipping was the second most common punishment in all the colonies, with shaming penalties also frequently applied, especially in the case of a crime such as defamation. Yet guilty New Englanders suffered such penalties more often than did Marylanders and Virginians.[23]

Thus misbehaving colonists were considerably more likely to be tried and convicted in New England than in the Chesapeake. Once found guilty, New Englanders were also somewhat more likely to be given harsher punishments than were Chesapeake residents. Yet within that general pattern, two categories of cases—authority crimes and sexual offenses—reveal significant variations that point up key elements of the disparate Filmerian and Lockean approaches to governance and of the regional differences that helped to produce them.

CRIMES AGAINST AUTHORITY

Two major components comprised the bulk of offenses committed against the authority of the colonial state: first, neglect of an assigned duty; and second, contempt of a government official or body, along with a more serious counterpart, treason. The incidence of these two categories of crimes diverged in the two regions. In New England, more men were charged with neglecting their obligations to the government than were accused of contempt, whereas in the Chesapeake the reverse was true.[24]

The explanation for this differential lies both in the politically unsettled situation in the Chesapeake colonies for much of the century and in the sorts of responsibilities placed by polities in the two regions on the shoulders of their male residents in general and on heads of households in particular. Although early statutes in Virginia (though not Maryland) placed heavy obligations on family governors, such laws do not appear to have been enforced vigorously there.[25] In New England, by contrast, men were frequently haled into court to face charges of failing to fulfill their communal duties. Since female colonists had many fewer obligations to the state, they were much less likely to confront such accusations, but they too occasionally had to respond to similar charges.

Men's responsibilities ranged from sporadic assignments to assist in the building or maintenance of roads or bridges to such duties as carrying arms and ammunition to church on Sundays to help protect the settlements against Indian attack. Common to both regions were obligations to serve on juries or to give testimony in civil and criminal cases if summoned as witnesses by litigants, prosecutors, or defendants (the last duty was the one civic responsibility also borne by women).[26] Military obligations of various sorts were probably the most onerous and time-consuming duties demanded of all able-bodied men between the ages of 16 and 60. Because the New Haven authorities were more meticulous than most in chronicling their attempts to enforce militia regulations, the records of that colony shed considerable light on the impact of such responsibilities on men's daily lives.

New Haven required all men to be furnished with adequate arms and ammunition, ordered militia officers to inspect such arms at least quarterly, and directed that there be six militia musters a year in each locality. Men were fined if they failed to maintain their arms or to appear at musters; officers were also subjected to fines if they neglected inspections or did not hold a sufficient number of training days. Moreover, from early March to late October, the town mounted a nightly watch (composed of at least four men each night) to guard against surprise Indian attack.[27]

New Haven's men grumbled at these burdens, expressing their resentment at the requirement to participate in the night watch by adopting either a legal tactic (hiring a substitute) or an illegal one (not showing up). When Mr. William Tuttle in 1657 hired "Isack that lives at Mr Gilberts to watch in his roome," the magistrates informed Mr. Tuttle that "he is an idle slight youth and not alowed of in such cases," reminding the high-status man that it had been "publiquly" announced on a training day that "those that hire must hire sufficient men." When William Bassett defended his failure to watch one night, he tried to pass the buck by declaring that "the master of the former watch did not warne him." That, admittedly, was true; nevertheless, the judges elicited testimony that Bassett had known it was his turn but told others that "so long as he had no warning he was well inough." As a signal to others who might try the same ploys, the magistrates fined both men double the usual amount.[28]

Even more burdensome than an occasional night as a watchman were the six militia training days each year. The excuses men offered for their absences disclose the ways in which the regular musters could disrupt their work and family lives. One man explained that "his wife being forth he stayed with the children," another that he did not come "in regarde of his mothers weaknes." Other explanations centered on farming needs: "he had that day a teame to plow for him, which he could not obtaine at another time"; "he had lost his cowes, and was that day looking [for] them"; and (the same William Bassett who failed to watch) "he had some haye . . . that if he had not fetched it that day it would have bine eaten up [by cattle] & spoyled, & he had indeavored to fetch it the weeke before, but it was so wett that he could not."[29]

Sometimes the magistrates accepted the excuses, but more often they pronounced the defenses "a common case which many men may plead" and refused to make exceptions to the rules. Yet exceptions *were* made for prominent residents of the colony, and that aroused resentment. For example, when several men were dispatched to work on the Reverend John Davenport's house on a training day in 1648, the mustered company made "much stirr" and "was offended at it, insomuch as some said if this was put up they would trayne no more." Denied the opportunity to take care of their own pressing needs on a training day, the men of New Haven were understandably angry when Mr. Davenport's schedule was not disrupted for the same reason.[30]

In addition to these obligations, which were the responsibilities of all men, family governors had the further burden of serving in public office. Such duties were so onerous that by 1647 Massachusetts Bay, which like New Haven had deliberately restricted the right to vote and hold office to male church members, found that some men who had joined churches were failing to take the freeman's oath solely "to exempt themselves from all publike service in the comon wealth." To circumvent the difficulty, the General Court ordered that all male church members were eligible for selection as "cunstables, [grand] jurers, selectmen, & surveyers of high wayes," and that they were subject to the same penalties for failure to serve as were freemen. In addition, the court opened the post of grand jury man to nonchurch members of good character, rewarding those men with the right to vote in town elections. For its part, New Haven did not allow men to refuse election, instead instructing reluctant officeholders that "what was done had not been done rashly" and that the voters were free to "chuse men whom they judged fit, for such imployment."[31]

Although men named to such minor posts as fence viewer, surveyor of highways, or "publique pounder" in New England had time-consuming tasks and occasionally encountered recalcitrant colonists as they attempted to carry out their duties, the officeholders who met with the most resistance were grand jury men and constables. In the Bay Colony and other regions under its jurisdiction grand juries were standing bodies elected annually with the responsibility "to inform the Court of any misdemeanours that they shall know or hear to be committed by any person or persons whatsoever," and members of grand juries were directed to "admonish all offenders." Not surprisingly, conscientious grand jury men could become the targets of opprobrium from those they reported or rebuked: jurors complained to judges of men for "defaymeing," "reviling and abuseing," or swearing "very desperatly severall oaths [at]" them. The sentiments of the Maine resident who exclaimed, "the divill take all the Jury men," were surely shared by many others whose misdeeds were revealed by grand jurors.[32]

Constables met with the most concerted resistance as they tried to carry out their duties, and men were accordingly especially reluctant to assume such posts. To force residents to serve in the undesirable office, Plymouth in 1660 provided that anyone declining election would have to pay a larger fine than those refusing other positions. In 1671, trying to make the job more attractive and to ensure that it was passed around, the colony exempted constables from militia duty and also excused from service anyone who had held the post during the past seven years. Since constables represented the first level of law enforcement outside the household, they had a myriad of responsibilities—ranging from arresting drunks and violators of the sabbath to serving warrants and executions, collecting taxes, pursuing runaway servants and other fugitives, announcing lost items, and informing justices of the peace about the presence of newcomers or men prone to idleness in the town. In 1658, Massachusetts Bay enumerated twenty-six such tasks and ordered them printed "so each connstable may understand his duty."[33]

New Englanders opposed the constables in a variety of ways. Some rebuffed constables' requests for assistance; others abused them verbally.[34] Still others met the beleaguered men with physical attacks. For example, when in early 1664 the constable of Portsmouth, New Hampshire, tried to collect tax levies from Walter Abbott, the innkeeper "sayd he would nocke the Constabells Brains outt if hee tocht any oxcon of his and stod with his axe Redy to stricke the sayd Constabell." Two Plymouth men hit a constable "on the head with a certaine stick or club, thereby fetching blood," and a drunken Shoals fisherman attacked the islands' constable in 1647, "calling him wich, divell, roage, and divers other opprobious [sic] speches, and assalted him with many blowdy œath violently."[35]

When the courts penalized colonists who physically attacked constables or defamed grand jury men, they were not only punishing men for assault or criminal defamation, they were also upholding the authority of the state. And that was critically important, especially in the early years of each colony or at times when strong challenges had been mounted to a government's legitimacy. Accordingly, prosecutions for contempt—as opposed to other authority crimes—clustered in those colonies (Maryland, Maine) in which control of political structures was particularly contested and during years of special turmoil, rather than being distributed more or less evenly across place and time.[36]

Contempt of authority cases fell into three categories. One group of contempt defendants brought trouble on themselves by vocally questioning a court's ruling, often while they were still in front of the judges. Men who reacted to the loss of lawsuits by "swearinge in a Contemptuous manner in the face of the Court" or by uttering "rash speches" or "abussive Words" were immediately hit with additional fines or orders to sit in the stocks.[37] The second type of contempt prosecution involved oral attacks on colonial leaders or governments that did not raise questions concerning the legitimacy of their authority. Men were fined, forced to apologize, and occasionally whipped for such offenses as calling the Maryland lower house "a Turdy shitten assembly" and "a Company of pittiful Rogues, & puppyes," accusing the Virginia House of Burgesses of adopting "unjust laws," terming the New Haven government "tyranicall," or stating dismissively, "hee cared not what the Governer sayd nor never a Governer In the Countrey."[38]

But the most important such cases involved participants in colonial political struggles. The men in command of a government at any given time regularly charged both adherents of earlier regimes and vocal proponents of other current contenders for power with contempt of authority. During the late 1640s and early 1650s, for example, Maryland officials repeatedly prosecuted men for injudicious comments on contemporary events. In January 1646/7, the restored proprietary government ordered the whipping of a man who had remarked of the recently arrived Virginia troops that "rather than he would have come up upon Such employment as they did he would have gathered Oysters for his liveing." Six years later, a Catholic-dominated court heard a report about a group of Protestants who had exclaimed, "hang them Papists Dogs they Shall have no right here," and after their own victory at the Battle of the Severn, Protestant judges considered the case of a man who had declared that "there was no law nor Government in Maryland" and that Protestants "did not grant true Justice."[39]

Men convicted of neglecting a duty to the state overwhelmingly incurred small monetary penalties, to the nearly complete exclusion of other punishments. In both New England and the Chesapeake, the vast majority of defendants were fined, with an additional handful in the north being admonished or required to post bond for future good behavior.[40] Most of the men convicted of contempt of authority were also fined, although the sums assessed tended to be larger, because the offense was more serious. Furthermore, a substantial minority in both regions had to endure more serious punishments, such as whipping and mutilation. In general, men in New England were both less likely to be fined and more likely to receive multiple penalties than were Chesapeake defendants, thus suggesting that northern authorities were particularly concerned about challenges to their position in the political hierarchy.[41]

The small number of women accused of crimes against authority (just 3 percent of all female defendants in the Chesapeake and 10 percent of those in New England) had committed offenses similar to those for which men were tried. The few women charged with neglecting a duty had usually failed to appear in court when summoned as witnesses or, widowed, had not fulfilled such community responsibilities as properly maintaining their fences.[42] Those accused of contempt had, like men, uttered "reproachfull speeches against the magestrats," termed a judge "a lying Justice," or resisted constables.[43]

Although only a few women were prosecuted for this type of crime in either north and south, the numbers in the Chesapeake were remarkably small.[44] An examination of the evidence in relevant cases indicates that even when Chesapeake women engaged in contemptuous conduct they were often not prosecuted. Thus when an Accomack County woman in 1641 called a constable a "Rouge" and started a brawl that eventually involved a third man as well as her husband, only the two male attackers were punished; and in two separate incidents involving Maryland women who joined their husbands in assaulting law-enforcement officials (in one case, the couple ingeniously cut off half their adversary's hair, "deformeing" him to his "disgrace and contempt"), again only the men were penalized.[45]

The relative paucity of prosecutions of women for authority crimes was a consequence of their indirect relationship to the state in both Filmerian and Lockean schemas. Men bore the burden of civic responsibilities, and men primarily had to pay the price when those obligations were not fulfilled or when contempt of colonial officials had been expressed. Yet, as was seen in the prologue to this section, women's place in the two systems of thought differed, and within a Filmerian worldview women were not wholly excluded from politics by virtue of their sex alone. Rather, their relationship to the polity was defined by their marital status and their rank in the wider socio-economic hierarchy. Accordingly, it should not be surprising that women seem to have been more likely to have been prosecuted for authority crimes in Filmerian New England.

The numbers and percentages are too small to allow for a definitive conclusion, but the difference is nonetheless telling. In the Chesapeake, women were seen as so far removed from the state that their statements and actions were of little or no political consequence. Surely Chesapeake women shared their menfolk's opinions and occasionally voiced contemptuous statements to skeptical audiences. But no one appears to have reported those remarks to the proper authorities or, if such opinions were reported, officials did not bother to initiate prosecutions except in unusual circumstances. Even wives who had physically attacked constables were not penalized directly—only their husbands suffered the punishments deemed appropriate for the offense.

In New England, by contrast, women *were* prosecuted, convicted, and penalized for crimes against authority, including those committed in conjunction with spouses. There, a woman's "reproachfull speeches" or loud complaints of injustice had sufficient relevance to the political stability of the state that they could not be safely ignored. Moreover, when New England women were accused of crimes against authority they were just as likely to be found guilty as their male counterparts, whether they were tried alone or as part of a couple; and the sentences they received also resembled those given their menfolk.[46]

Yet if women in general and Chesapeake women in particular were rarely prosecuted for crimes against authority, women, especially Chesapeake women, predominated within the category of sexual offenses. Just as women were the primary purveyors and subjects of sexual gossip, in short, they were also the primary objects of sexual-law enforcement. Thus an analysis of sex-crime prosecutions offers further insights into the relationship of women and the colonial state.

CONSENSUAL SEXUAL OFFENSES

The most frequently prosecuted sexual offenses in both New England and the Chesapeake involved heterosexual relationships among men and single women. Such sexual misbehavior was easily defined in law, and since these relationships could result in pregnancy, their existence was often disclosed in spite of their participants' best efforts at concealment. Clauses dealing with fornication were among the shortest and most straightforward statutes in the criminal codes; the Laws and Liberties of 1648, for example, defined the offense simply as sex with "any single woman" and prescribed as penalties for both parties any or all of the following: fine, whipping, and "enjoyning to Marriage." Disagreements over the constitution of valid marriages occasionally caused some confusion for the courts but were usually readily resolved. Consequently, it is hardly surprising that more than two thirds of the sexual offenses prosecuted in the Chesapeake and three fifths of those heard in New England fell into this category.[47]

But patterns of prosecution in the two regions nevertheless varied significantly, because two separate offenses, bastardy and fornication, combined to make up the whole. The distinct demographic, religious, and legal configurations in north and south led to dramatically different emphases in their respective court systems. In the Chesapeake, half of all sex-crime prosecutions were for bastardy and fewer than one fifth for fornication; in New England, the relationship of the two types of crimes was reversed: half of sex-crime prosecutions were for fornication, and just one tenth for bastardy. Moreover, as was already pointed out in chapter one, more than two fifths of the fornication charges pursued in the Puritan colonies were brought against couples who had married after they initiated a sexual relationship, whereas only a tiny handful of such prosecutions were recorded in Virginia or Maryland.[48]

The explanation for the differential prosecution of bastardy and fornication lies in part in the consequences of the divergent legal status of the majority of young women in the two regions. In New England, most single women were the daughters of free households; in the Chesapeake, they were indentured servants. Servants everywhere were forbidden to marry without their masters' permission, but northerners were not subject to the same long-term legal constraints as their southern counterparts, for most worked under contracts of a year or less. Thus the common behavior that in New England could well have resulted in a prosecution for premarital fornication—that is, a single woman's consensual sexual intercourse with a single male lover she planned to marry—could just as easily have led to a prosecution for bastardy in the Chesapeake, because there the couple would not have been allowed to wed.[49]

More than demography was involved as well. As has already been demonstrated in this book, authorities in the Chesapeake showed little interest in closely supervising the daily lives of ordinary colonists. As a result, only that sexual activity which caused illicit pregnancy, thereby raising the question of the financial burden of caring for a bastard child, aroused much concern in the court systems of Virginia and Maryland.[50] There, sexual misconduct without economic consequences, such as premarital fornication, was viewed without grave alarm. In Puritan New England, on the other hand, the stress on orderly families as the essential foundation of social and political stability led grand jurors, constables, and judges alike to respond to reports of sexual misdeeds with presentments and prosecutions. Any sexual activity that occurred outside the context of valid marriage was perceived as threatening the future of the Puritan commonwealths; consequently, behavior that in the Chesapeake led to gossip but few other tangible results became the basis for prosecutions in New England.

Evidence of the laxity of the Chesapeake colonies in prosecuting sexual offenses (including even some cases of bastardy) abounds in the court records of Virginia and Maryland. One of the best indications of that laxity is the number of relevant incidents exposed by civil suits rather than criminal prosecutions. Some births of bastards came to light only because the master of the female servant sued the reputed father of the child for damages; the men in such cases never faced criminal charges. Furthermore, southern judges did not punish misbehavior that would have resulted in conviction in New England courts. So when Mr. Joseph Wickes, the Kent Island magistrate, was accused in late 1656 of fathering the bastard child of a Virginia widow, a hasty wedding allowed him to avoid any consequences other than a temporary suspension from his official position, because—once he had formally acknowledged his financial responsibility for the child by marrying its mother—the county court declined to assess any penalties on him. Similarly, the Virginia General Court gave a very generous benefit of the doubt to an unmarried couple observed by several others engaged in a "great bussleling and juggling of the bed" one night. Even though one of the witnesses warned the couple that "it was not a place fitting that such doing should be before soe much Company," the judges decided that the evidence was insufficient to convict them of any crime.[51]

A further example of the regional difference is the existence in New England of a type of offense (encompassing more than one fourth of all the sex-crime prosecutions initiated there) rarely if ever punished in the Chesapeake colonies. Conduct described variously in the court records as "most lacivious, abseane, and vild expressions and actions," the "frequenting of one & anothers Company In an unseemly & suspitious manner," or being "unseasonably . . . in the company of two women" comprised a congeries of misdeeds that can most accurately be designated as lewd behavior, or (to employ seventeeth-century terminology) lascivious carriage.[52] Connecticut's assembly put it this way in a statute adopted in late 1642: in addition to crimes specifically described, the legislators had seen "sad evidence" of "severall other wayes of uncleanes and lasivious caridges practised among us." Since those "evells" were "very pernitious and distructive to the welfare of the Comon weale," the assembly directed that "severe and sharpe punishement should be inflicted uppon such delinquents" at the discretion of the courts, even though it was impossible to draft "particular and expresse lawes and orders" delineating each offense.[53]

Thus New Englanders often faced prosecution simply for suspicious sexual conduct. Ensuring that sexual activity was confined to the marriage bed was so important to Puritan authorities that attempts were made to bring offenders into court *before* criminal sexual behavior was known to have occurred—that is, when observers had developed what was frequently termed "vehement suspicion" but prior to the gathering of definitive proof. So, for instance, in early 1665 New Haven charged a young couple, John Clarke and Mary Fuller, with having been "together alone at an unseasonable time of night, & in an uncomely manner." They had been seen late at night in the house rented by Mary's mother, Goody Hannah Finch, he with "his armes over her shoulders" while "shee Leaned upon him." Because John had visited Mary contrary to his master's explicit instructions and had at first "presumptuously" denied misbehaving, he was ordered "severely Whipt," and Mary was directed "to stand by him while the sentence of the Court is inflicted on him, for her shame." The couple acknowledged "that they were sorry for what they had done & hoped it should be a warneing to them, & that they should doe soe noe more." The justices undoubtedly hoped that Clarke's and Fuller's punishment would also serve as a warning to other young people not to venture so close to the boundaries of acceptable behavior.[54]

John Clarke's "severe" lashing for what seems to have been a relatively innocent evening spent with his sweetheart might have been excessive punishment, but it was commonplace. Although there were significant variations depending on the sex of the defendant, the specific offense, and the geographic area in which the crime occurred (all of which will be discussed later in this section), defendants in sex-crime cases were more likely to be sentenced to at least a possibility of whipping than were defendants in nearly every other type of criminal prosecution.[55]

Whipping was a humiliating penalty—especially for women, who were stripped to the waist—a fact formally recognized in a clause of the Laws and Liberties. No one shall be whipped, the provision entitled "Torture" declared, "unles his crime be very shamefull, and his course of life vitious and *profligate*." New Haven's 1656 code employed different wording, but to the same end: whipping was appropriate, the statute read, "where the offence is accompanied with childish, or brutish folly, with rude filthiness, or with stubborn insolency, with be[a]stly cruelty, or with idle vagrancy." Criminal defendants fully understood the meaning of the sentence. So one Salem man begged the Essex County court to remit his sentence of a heavy fine (which he could not afford) or a whipping, asserting that "to be Whipp[ed] will Ever be the Ruine of your humble petitioner." Similarly, in 1662 a Dutch merchant asked the New Haven justices to alter a whipping imposed on his son as a penalty for premarital fornication, explaining that among the Dutch "to be corporally punished was such an infamy . . . that they looked upon such noe better then a dog & not fit for Commerce with them & soe his sonne would be undone thereby." Although insisting that their sentence had been appropriate, the judges agreed to change it to a fine.[56]

Colonial courts in general and New England courts in particular therefore prosecuted single women and single or married men for a wide spectrum of sexual misdeeds centering on fornication (premarital or nonmarital) and bastardy, but not limited exclusively to those transgressions. As was already indicated, a number of the offenses involved the promise or expectation of marriage. What must have been a common dynamic in many such cases was revealed in 1662 when a young woman, Mercy Payne, gave the New Haven Magistrates Court a uniquely detailed description of how John Frost, a farm worker occasionally hired by her father, had persistently pursued and eventually seduced her.[57]

Frost made a series of tentative advances over a period of months, giving Mercy a ribbon, attempting to feel her body, talking with her about his desire for a wife—initially in general terms, then asking her to marry him. Mercy rebuffed all his moves, telling no one but a female friend about any of them and informing John that she thought her parents would not agree to their marriage. Finally, one day while they were working together on the farm, he told her "let us set downe together & recreate ourselves a litle," and the following exchange took place:

John: come let us see if we be fit to marry together.
Mercy: noe, John, then I would be a whore.
J: you will not be except you be with child.
M: then I shalbe hanged.
J: I wonder you talk soe sillily you will neither be hanged nor whipt, what if we are whipt that is nothing.
M: it is a greivous sin.
J: noe, every one doth soe & must doe soe before they are married.

M: I will not beleeve it.

J: indeed they doe.

M: noe, its a greivous sin.

J: I will doe it.

M: what if any[one] sees us?

J: noe they will not.

M: one above will.

J: come let us. If any one sees us I will have them to the court & fined a great deale for I am of good esteem in the towne.

And so, Mercy concluded her account of the conversation, John Frost "would whether she would or not . . . & soe did lie with her & had the use of her body at that time."[58]

Mercy Payne then revealed that on several subsequent occasions she had engaged in sexual intercourse with John Frost at his instigation. She portrayed herself to the court as a reluctant participant in the relationship who had often refused his importunities or sought to avoid him. For his part, Frost admitted putting his hand under her clothes once but "denied those sinfull actings with her in that way of uncleanenes." The judges did not believe him, observing that it would have been surprising if she had concocted "such a longe relation" that brought to light "such a thing . . . to her owne shame." After a group of "skilful women" testified that "she was defiled," and Mercy assured the court that she had had no other sexual partner than John Frost, they were both sentenced to be whipped; he was also ordered to pay a fine for courting her without her parents' consent. Mercy's father, referring to "some weakenes upon her since the women had searched, which was not fit to be mentioned here," asked that his daughter's sentence be reduced to a fine, and the court agreed. Eventually, Mercy Payne married John Frost.[59]

The New Haven magistrates probably believed Mercy Payne's story not only because they thought she would have been hard pressed to make up a "longe relation" but also because she sounded so many themes familiar to them from other cases, some of which have already been discussed in different contexts: a persistent, sexually aggressive male, a woman frightened by his advances who complained to no one in authority but instead shared the information with a friend, a proposal of marriage, the man's minimizing the offense and ultimately denying responsibility. Furthermore, Mercy's account—with its emphasis on the need for her parents' approval, her fears that someone would see them, her belief that she would be thought a whore and receive harsh punishment, and her insistence that they would be committing "a greivous sin"—was wholly in character for a young woman raised in Puritan culture. Even her marriage to Frost was entirely in keeping with contemporary practice, since one of the legal remedies for fornication was, after all, "enjoyning to Marriage."

In contemporary terms, Mercy Payne was fortunate. Her father's successful plea allowed her to escape the whipping commonly inflicted on sexual delinquents, and although John Frost denied the truth of her story, he ultimately married her. She did not share the fate of other young colonial women who experienced in real life the classic tale of seduction and abandonment, being impregnated by seemingly sincere suitors who later refused to marry them and who perhaps absconded to avoid the financial responsibility for bastard children.[60] Some of those women, desperately attempting to conceal their plight, went so far as to kill the infants or to try to hide the births, thus opening themselves to prosecutions for the capital offense of infanticide.[61]

When the charge was lewd or promiscuous behavior rather than fornication or bastardy, most of those prosecuted were male. New England's men were convicted of such crimes as "attempting lewdnes with divers woomen," "unmeet dalliance with two or three girles," "Lascivious carriages towards young persons of the Female kinde," or "uncivell carrages towards severall weomen att severall times."[62] The behavior that lay behind these charges was occasionally detailed in court records: "he came into the roome, threwe her upon the bed, and discovered [revealed] her nakedness and his owne too"; he "pulled [her] upon his knee, put his hands under her coats, towards her naked belly, pulled out his member, and bid her take it in her hands"; he "intic[ed] her by words, as alsoe by taking out his instrument of nature that hee might prevaile to lye with her in her owne house."[63]

The crude aggression of these advances exposes the sexual frustrations of New England's unmarried men. Some, like John Frost, tried to seduce the virginal, others sought out sexually experienced wives or widows, still others—like Patrick Morran, the ironworks supervisor—approached any female who seemed potentially receptive to a proposition. Regardless of the specific circumstances, such prosecutions were as unique to New England as were trials for premarital fornication. It is difficult to believe that Chesapeake men behaved differently from their northern counterparts, but the south witnessed no similar prosecutions of men for lascivious carriage. The courts there showed no interest in penalizing men for lewd conduct that fell short of sexual intercourse causing illicit pregnancy—again, an indication that in a nascent Lockean society the morality of individual colonists was viewed as largely irrelevant to the health of the state.

The New England courts used such language as "disorderly carriage," "Suspitious company keeping," or "suspittion of Incontiency" to describe misconduct among married as well as unmarried sexual delinquents.[64] Indeed, that many of the prosecutions for lewd behavior involved single men and other men's wives raises the question of whether such charges were deliberately substituted for the far more serious one of adultery. As was indicated earlier in this chapter, conviction on a charge of adultery—defined as sex by any man (married or unmarried) with a married or engaged woman—carried the death penalty for both parties in Massachusetts and its imitators, Connecticut and New Haven. Yet the law was rarely enforced in any of the three jurisdictions. Its history and the controversies over its application suggest that even though Puritan leaders adamantly insisted on the importance of marital fidelity, they were extremely reluctant to condemn people to death for heterosexual misbehavior alone.[65]

The Bay Colony's Court of Assistants first made adultery a capital offense in 1631. Yet although the General Court formally reaffirmed that law seven years later, it simultaneously demonstrated its unwillingness to subject adulterers to the ultimate penalty by merely ordering severe whippings and banishment for the three malefactors (two men and their married female partner) whose offense it was then considering. In 1641, adultery charges filed against another couple clearly aroused Bostonians' fears that the death-penalty law might actually be applied, for eleven people, eight of them high-status men, helped the adulterous pair to escape from custody for a time. Wisely, given the sympathy the community obviously felt for the recaptured couple, the Court of Assistants ordered only a symbolic hanging, directing them to sit on the gallows for an hour with ropes around their necks, and thereafter banishing the woman but not the man.[66]

In March 1643/4, for the only time in its history, the Court of Assistants issued death sentences in an adultery case. Mary Latham of Marshfield, a young wife unhappily married to a much older man, and James Britton of Weymouth, described as "a great enemy" to "church government" in Massachusetts, were hanged for their acknowledged adultery. "When she came to die, she suffered very penitently, (as did the man,) exhorting young maids to be obedient to their parents, and take heed of evil company, which brought her to an untimely end," wrote the Reverend William Hubbard.[67]

Despite the appropriately repentant demeanor of the condemned couple, Massachusetts never again hanged anyone for adultery. Instead, the courts found reasons to declare defendants not guilty of the capital crime "according to lawe," but instead to convict them of "much shameful and unchast behavior" or simply of "lieing in bed" together. Occasionally, accused adulterers were acquitted, even when there was seemingly irrefutable evidence of their misconduct—that is, the birth of a child the woman's husband could not have fathered.[68] Such outcomes suggest that Thomas Gorges, the early Maine governor, and Roger Williams—both of whom expressed their skepticism about designating adultery as a capital offense—were not the only New Englanders to question the wisdom of the policy.[69]

Even repeat offenders escaped capital punishment. Take, for instance, Mary Clay, the wife of a Maine fisherman who was often absent from home. Between 1655 and 1660, Goody Clay was presented on six separate occasions for "frequenting the Company" of three different men. It was said that she consorted with John Davis "in such a suspitious manner as caused the neighbours to suspect them [of] incontinency"; that she entertained Robert Cooke "day & night" in spite of the "perswations" of his neighbors; and that she "too often & frequently suspitiously keept Company with James Harmon from whome shee hath beene forwarned." Her reputation must have been truly sordid, for in October 1660 her own mother, Elizabeth Batson, was fined and ordered to apologize publicly for "very scandelous & unnaturall accusations" that Mary was her stepfather's "Hoore & that they were naught togeather." Mary Clay was repeatedly fined or ordered to post bond to stay apart from one or the other of her reputed lovers, but only once was she sentenced to a whipping, and then her stepfather paid her fine to free her from that penalty.[70]

Further details from a Maryland case already examined at some length in chapter four disclose a primary reason why adultery charges were relatively rarely tried under that rubric in either north or south: all the participants in such episodes often thought it in their best interest to keep the story quiet. That desire was clearly evident in the events that followed Mary Taylor's reluctant admission to the midwives and her female relatives in December 1652 that the Virginia planter George Catchmey had fathered her newborn son.[71]

In her deposition, the midwife Ann Johnson reported that after Robert Taylor had learned of his wife's confession, "She came and fell upon her knees and Said Good husband forgive me, for Gods Sake Good husband forgive me, O! thou wicked base woman how can I forgive thee, I cannot forgive thee, the Law will take hold of thee." But instead of immediately informing the authorities of his wife's transgression, as his exclamation indicated he would, Taylor first confronted George Catchmey. Catchmey, after denying it, finally acknowledged paternity, and he and Robert then discussed "what they Should doe in the busieness." When Robert mentioned the possibility of prosecuting the adulterers, George described the consequences: "the Court would Record him Cuckold and Catchmey Should keep the Child."

Taylor, less than pleased with that possibility, suggested that if George would "disburse a little Tobacco he would keep the Child as his owne." Catchmey agreed with Taylor's reasoning: "rather then to have his name brought in question," he would pay "a Little Tobacco." The two next agreed on a price: two thousand pounds of tobacco. But no payment ever changed hands. After George later informed Robert that he had no tobacco, "Robert Taylor told him that he would give him tenn thousand pounds of Tobacco to deny what was past, and George Catchmey Said that he told Robert Taylor if hee were never questioned, he would never question it."

Thus each man decided that preserving his good name was his most important goal. Rather than be publicly identified as a cuckold, Robert Taylor agreed to raise George Catchmey's son as his own; rather than be publicly accused of adultery, George Catchmey offered to pay a substantial bribe. Mary Taylor also had good reason not to publicize the tale. So the fact that Catchmey fathered Mary Taylor's baby came to light only because Mary exchanged insults with Ann Johnson, who thereupon took the story to the authorities. Although he was eventually afforded two separate opportunities to prosecute his wife, Robert Taylor declined to do so both times. And Maryland's judges also did not want to pursue the case. They officially concluded that "the offence wherewith She Seems to Stand Charged (if any be) is Charged as done in Virginia under another Government, and of which the Court or Government here is conceived to have no Cognizance."[72]

The long-distance adulterous relationship of Mary Taylor and George Catchmey was unusual, for prosecutions involving relationships within the same household were more characteristic of Maryland. It is perhaps not surprising that the province's imbalanced sex ratio led to the existence of ménages à trois, in which two male partners in a plantation shared sexual access to one woman. These cases reveal a good deal about the sexual dynamics of life specific to the Chesapeake region.

The best-documented such household was composed of the planter

Robert Holt, his wife, Dorothy, and his partner, Edward Hudson.[73] Witnesses interviewed by Maryland officials revealed that during the summer of 1650 Dorothy Holt lived with Edward Hudson. The two had been seen several times going "to bed together as if they had been man and wife," and they explained to curious inquirers "that Robert Holt which was the Said Dorothy's husband was dead." Yet Robert had not died; rather, Dorothy had deserted him to move in with Edward. Robert evidently responded to Dorothy's action not by charging her with adultery but instead by inviting her to return and to bring Edward with her. By February 1650/1, the three were living together, the two men partners in a tobacco plantation.[74]

Less than a year later, the arrangement was already coming apart. When Rose Gilbert Smith, their matronly neighbor (and the local mid-wife), visited the Holts in September, Robert told her "that his wife would kill him." Rose protested that surely he was mistaken, but Dorothy broke in with the comment that "She were as good kill him as live as She did." When Rose replied that Dorothy "would be hanged then," Dorothy told her that "then there was an end of two." Another witness reported that "he heard Dorothy Holt to cry for many Curses to God against her husband, that he might rott limb from limbe, and that she would daily pray to God that Such Casualties might fall upon him."

In November 1651, Robert finally complained to an official of the Provincial Court that "Dorothy his wife hath threatned him divers times to take away his life." Moreover, Holt added, Edward Hudson "hath divers times been Compacted with her the Said Dorothy to abuse me . . . between them both I goe daily in fear of my life." Holt did not disclose to the authorities that their family had been a ménage à trois, but that fact emerged from the subsequent investigation, which was conducted with remarkable swiftness. Just four days after the complaint was first filed, Dorothy Holt and Edward Hudson were convicted of "divers lewd Incontinent and Scandalous actions and practices." Although the penalties were severe—Hudson was ordered whipped with thirty lashes and Dorothy Holt with fifty—at their "humble Submission and Suit for pardon acknowledging their great Offence and faithfull promiseing future amendment," the court suspended the sentences and required only that Hudson pay costs. The judges encouraged the Holts to live together "as man and wife ought to doe," but testimony in a subsequent prosecution of Robert for bigamy showed that Dorothy continued her liaison with Hudson and bore him at least two children. This sexual triangle, though evidently embarked upon willingly by all its participants, accordingly did not long endure. It is impossible to know how many others might have lasted longer.[75]

Prosecution for consensual heterosexual offenses was therefore sporadic in the Chesapeake and more systematic in New England. The penalties inflicted on convicted malefactors in the two regions differed as significantly as did the patterns of prosecution. Whereas in the Chesapeake couples convicted together of the same sexual offense received the same penalties less than one third of the time, in New England couples were punished the same way in more than half the cases.[76] Moreover, the divergent prosecutions pursued in the two regions had measurable consequences for the punishment of individual male and female defendants. As has been observed, in New England many men faced criminal charges for behavior that in the Chesapeake carried no legal consequences at all. In the Chesapeake, nearly as many women stood trial alone for bastardy as did so with their lovers, while in New England most bastardy prosecutions involved couples. The northern men accused of lascivious carriage and the southern women tried alone for bastardy had few counterparts in the other region.[77]

The regional disparity can be pointed up in other ways as well. In New England, more men than women were charged with sex crimes; in the Chesapeake, the reverse was true. As has already been indicated, Chesapeake defendants (male and female alike) were somewhat less likely to be convicted than were northern defendants, but the most important difference lay not in conviction rates but rather in punishments inflicted.[78] Although women everywhere were more often penalized by whipping in sex-crime cases than were men, a majority of New Englanders of both sexes found guilty of these offenses was sentenced to punishment that included at least the alternative of whipping. By contrast, whereas a majority of Chesapeake women incurred at least the possibility of whipping, only one fifth of Chesapeake men received a like punishment.[79]

The key point is that New England courts treated men and women more equally in sex-crime prosecutions than did courts in the Chesapeake. A clearly evident double standard of sexual behavior guided the authorities in Virginia and Maryland: women comprised a majority of those tried for sexual offenses, even though in all such crimes the women involved had had at least one male partner; and, once convicted, women were sentenced to different and harsher punishments than were men, even when couples were charged together with the same offense. In New England, by contrast, male defendants outnumbered women in

sexual prosecutions (largely because of the male-dominated crime of lascivious carriage, which did not exist in the Chesapeake) and were punished nearly as severely as women when convicted, especially when they
and their female partners were tried together for the same crime.[80]

In the Filmerian world that emphasized the maintenance of family
order, in short, men were held to be nearly as responsible as women for
violations of that order. In a nascently Lockean society, on the other
hand, men were more commonly freed from such responsibility: the
family was the domain of women, not of men, and violations of family
order could legitimately be charged primarily against women. At the
same time, the government of that Lockean world was less concerned
about familial disorder; consequently, fewer women (and in particular,
fewer men) were charged with such crimes in the first place. Greater
scrutiny led to more even-handed treatment of the sexes in the north,
whereas in the Chesapeake the courts' less-concentrated attention could
focus chiefly on the most obvious miscreant—the bastard-bearing
woman—and deal with other sexual offenders only when forced to
do so.[81]

Although fornication, bastardy, lewdness, and adultery together constituted the vast majority of prosecuted sexual offenses in both north and
south, rape and forms of deviant sexual behavior (especially same-sex
liaisons and bestiality) were also occasionally the subjects of court action. Few colonists were ever tried for such crimes (particularly in the
Chesapeake), but—because men were the primary objects of such
prosecutions—analyzing those cases can add another dimension to the
understanding of the intersection of sexuality and the system of gendered
power.

"FORSEMENT" AND "DEVILISH MILKING"

If the laws defining fornication and adultery were straightforward and
easily interpreted, those defining rape and sodomy were quite different,
at least in New England. Both crimes were capital offenses in Virginia
and Maryland, which adopted English law in that regard, and authorities
there saw no need to define what the terms meant or to adopt any
specific statutes on the subject.[82] In the Puritan colonies, on the other
hand, delineating both offenses—and deciding whether any form of rape
should be a capital offense—caused innumerable difficulties.

The problems were evident first in the Reverend John Cotton's
model code. Among Cotton's six capital sexual offenses was only one

form of rape: that of a married or espoused wife. "Forcing of a maid or
a rape, is not to be punished with death by Gods laws," Cotton observed, prescribing instead a fine (part to be paid to the young woman's
father), whipping, and marriage, if the woman consented. The Bay Colony then failed to include any form of rape among the capital crimes
listed in the Body of Liberties, but following the sexual abuse of John
Humfrey's daughters in 1642 (discussed in chapter two), the General
Court adopted a complicated capital rape statute. It ordered the death
penalty for any man who had "carnall copulation" with a girl under ten,
whether or not she had consented, and, as Cotton had proposed, also
made the rape of a married or espoused wife a capital offense. But when
a man was convicted of raping a single woman over ten, the death
penalty was optional. That law, however, remained in force only until
the adoption of the Laws and Liberties in 1648. It was thereupon deleted
from the new code, which retained only those provisions concerning
the rapes of single females over ten. Rapes of married or espoused
women, the codification assumed, would be prosecuted as capital offenses under the adultery statute. In the late 1660s, after the rape of an
eight-year-old girl, the law was revised once again to include the sexual
abuse of children. In the other Puritan colonies too, capital rape laws
were frequently revised and filled with qualifications.[83]

For two reasons New England's legislators had difficulties with rape
not evident among lawmakers in the Chesapeake. First, as has already
been seen, New England's emphasis on the establishment of orderly
marriages led to the legal privileging of a husband's sexual access to his
wife. Accordingly, adultery (a crime defined by the marital status of the
female participant) was punished more severely than any other consensual heterosexual offense. The only sort of rape Bay Colony lawmakers
unhesitatingly designated as deserving the death penalty was that of a
married or espoused wife, whether they dealt with the crime explicitly
in a rape statute or implicitly in an adultery law. Rape and adultery, the
legislators believed, were more heinous than any other heterosexual offenses because both injured husbands and threatened the integrity of
marital households. Even girls under ten did not receive the same protection the statutes afforded to wives.

Second was the matter of consent, which played a major role in the
permutations of the laws. Unlike later generations of lawmakers, who
would eventually come to assume that women felt little sexual passion
and so would not seek out illicit sexual relationships, Puritans saw females as at least equal participants in heterosexual involvements. Only
girls under the age of ten were believed incapable of properly consenting

to sexual intercourse; any older girl or woman, married or unmarried, could well have been complicit in a sexual act. Hence the reluctance to include the rape of single women in the list of capital offenses, at least not without qualifications. And hence the coverage of the rape of married women under the adultery statute after 1648; prosecutions under that law always carried the implication that the female participant might have consented.[84]

Sodomy was no easier for legislators and courts to deal with, though superficially it might have seemed so. The New England colonies, like Virginia and Maryland, followed English practice in declaring "sodomy" a capital offense, but the New Englanders' reliance on the Old Testament caused them definitional difficulties. As the Reverend Thomas Shepard remarked to John Winthrop in 1642, "in discussing these questions, we generally walke in untrodden paths." Since few nations had ever tried to integrate biblical sexual proscriptions into their legal codes, Shepard observed, there had been few attempts to "cleare up there proportions"; that is, to determine the exact definitions of edicts derived from the Old Testament.[85]

The statutes themselves, from Cotton's proposed laws through the first New Hampshire code of 1680, were uncompromising. Cotton wrote: "unnatural filthiness to be punished with death, whether sodomy, which is carnal fellowship of man with man, or of woman with woman; or buggery, which is carnal fellowship of man or woman with beasts or fowles." The Body of Liberties removed Cotton's application of the sodomy law to women's same-sex relationships and added that, in the case of bestiality, "the beast shall be slaine, and buried and not eaten." The Laws and Liberties largely copied the Body of Liberties but exempted from the death penalty a male participant in sodomy who was under fourteen or forced into the act, though providing that even in such cases "he shall be seveerly punished." As was true with the Laws and Liberties in general, the other New England colonies, with the exception of Rhode Island, followed the Bay Colony's lead.[86]

New Haven's 1656 code is particularly revealing because that most Filmerian of all colonies elaborated on the sodomy statutes as did no other jurisdiction. The basic bestiality and sodomy clauses it took from the Laws and Liberties. But New Haven did not stop there. Like the Reverend Cotton, that province applied the sodomy law to women who shall "change the naturall use, into that which is against nature." It also included in the capital crime "other kinds of unnaturall and shamefull filthines," which it defined as "carnall knowledge of another vessel then God in nature hath appointed to become one flesh" and identified as such anal intercourse with any partner and sexual knowledge of the "unripe vessel of a Girle." The statute went on to encompass male masturbation "in the sight of others . . . by example, or counsel, or both, corrupting and tempting others to doe the like," declaring that such behavior "shall be punished according to the nature of the offence," including the possible use of the death penalty if "aggravating circumstances" were involved. Like the Bay Colony, New Haven exempted from the death penalty an unwilling participant, who—"crying out, or in due season complaining"—would not be penalized, or a willing participant under fourteen, who would be "severely" punished but not executed.[87]

The many offenses comprised in the New Haven statute point up the interpretive problem facing those who wanted to include crimes other than male same-sex relationships within the term "sodomy." To the New Haven authorities, any sexual activity that did not involve a man's "naturall use" of a woman fell within the scriptural proscription against "going after strange flesh," thus requiring the death penalty. But not all New Englanders, not even all Puritan clergymen, agreed with such a sweeping definition. That fact emerged when in the spring of 1642 Governor Richard Bellingham addressed ministers throughout New England in the wake of the abuse of Dorcas and Sarah Humfrey, asking them, "What sodomitical acts are to be punished with death, and what very fact (*ipso facto*) is worthy of death; or, if the fact itself be not capital, what circumstances concurring may make it capital?" The question arose because, as has been seen, the Bay Colony at the time did not define rape or sexual abuse of a child as a capital offense, but did designate sodomy as such. Could Daniel Fairfield and the other abusers of the children be tried as violators of the sodomy statutes? That was what the Massachusetts magistrates wanted to know.[88]

The responses did not offer definitive or unified conclusions. The Reverend Thomas Shepard modestly declined "to define anything" but instead indicated that he intended "to enquire and to propound to your wisdom some things considerable, and to be considered of, at your leysure, that so if yow find them weake and inconsistent with truth yow may cast them by." Governor William Bradford of Plymouth told the Bay Colony officials that "we rather desire light from yourselves and others" on such points "than to presume to give our judgments in cases so difficult and of so high a nature." Although he expressed what seems to have been the consensus of Plymouth's civil leaders that "if there be not penetration" no capital offense had been committed, all three of the Plymouth clerics whose detailed replies have been preserved came to

the opposite conclusion. One, for example, commented that "the unclean acts punishable with death by the law of God are not only the
gross acts of uncleanness by way of carnal copulation, but all the evident
attempts thereof." But in the end, as will be recalled from chapter two,
since the abusers had not confessed to penetration and since there were
no witnesses other than the victims, no one was executed and Daniel
Fairfield, the chief offender, was ordered whipped, facially mutilated,
and subjected to a symbolic hanging.[89]

Linking the New Englanders' seemingly distinct obsessions with defining the capital crimes of rape and sodomy is the fact that both acts
involved sex that was simultaneously nonmarital and nonprocreative.
Since the Puritans believed that all sexual activity should be both marital
and procreative, these crimes in particular presented a frontal challenge
to the maintenance of the families that, in New Englanders' minds, constituted the bedrock of society. Therefore, each had to be severely punished, perhaps even with death. The convoluted New Haven sodomy
statute attempted to encompass a wide variety of sexual practices; what
anal intercourse, sex with young girls, male masturbation, and bestiality
had in common was that they could not lead to the conception of a
human fetus. So too rape was not only nonmarital but also believed to
be nonprocreative. As has already been observed earlier in another context, seventeenth-century people believed that a woman could not conceive unless she had an orgasm. If a woman had been forcibly raped,
she would not feel sexual pleasure (indeed, if a woman conceived a child
after claiming to have been raped, it was viewed as evidence that her
charge was false). Thus, in the eyes of colonial judges and lawmakers,
rape and sodomy shared two fundamental characteristics that rendered
them particularly odious.[90]

Yet the rape of a single woman or a child was a less serious crime
than was the rape of a wife. For the same reason, fornication was a less
serious offense than adultery. Neither fornication nor the rape of a single
woman contested a husband's right to exclusive sexual access to his wife,
and it was precisely the violation of the marital bond, the foundation of
society as it was the basis of individual households, that transformed rape
into an unqualified capital offense. Not the offense against the woman
but the offense against her husband was the key in determining the
severity of the penalty prescribed by law.

Consequently, it is ironic that—probably because of the ambiguity
surrounding the question of whether an adult woman had consented to
sexual intercourse or not—most rape prosecutions and convictions in
the colonies (both north and south) involved the abuse of teenaged girls

or young children. Indeed, the only two instances in which it is clear
that convicted rapists were hanged fell into that category: the 1627 prosecution of Thomas Hayle for raping "fower Mayden Children" in Virginia and the 1669 Massachusetts prosecution of Patrick Jennison for
raping the eight-year-old sister of one of his friends (who was whipped
for taking part in the abuse of his sibling). In two more Bay Colony
cases, involving victims aged thirteen and twelve, juries returned guilty
verdicts, but the sentences are not recorded.[91]

In other instances in which children had been raped and men convicted of those crimes, death penalties were not imposed on the perpetrators, even when the statutes specifically allowed such a sentence.
Thus in March 1642/3 the Bay's Court of Assistants tried two "boyes"
for "ravishing two yong girles." The girls were found by searchers "to
have bin defloured" and the boys confessed to "filthy dalliance," but
the jury found them "not guilty, with reference to the Capitall Law."
They were fined and ordered whipped on two separate occasions. So
too in 1654 the General Court, considering the case of a man accused
of raping a "girle," did "not finde him guilty of death, but justly
deserving a high and severe censure." He was also sentenced to two
lashings and was ordered to wear a rope visibly around his neck at the
court's pleasure. Seven months later, the magistrates allowed him to
remove it.[92]

On a number of occasions, young women who accused men of
attempted or completed rape were themselves punished for complicity
in the sexual act "for yeilding to him, and not makeing such resistance
against him as shee ought," "for not crying out when shee was assaulted," or "for concealeing it soe long."[93] Such penalties were fully in
accordance with the belief (as expressed by Roger Williams) that "a
woman that [is raped] can not but cry when she is forct and ravished:
she that cries not, she is a whore before God and Men." So when in
1655 Hannah Spencer accused William Ellit of raping her on shipboard
as they were sailing from Milford to Stamford, the New Haven magistrates' court questioned the truth of her story because a witness who
"lay closs by" did not "hear her cry out, onely one time he heard her
say with a mild voyce, William Ellit let me aloane." The judges decided
that it was an episode of "hainous filthyness" that "likely was begun in
a way of force" but which eventually involved her consent, and it ordered her to stand by the post as Ellit was whipped "that she may in
some measure beare the shame of her sin."[94]

That few adult women, married or single, seem to have complained
of rapes implies that older women believed that courts would greet their

claims of rape or attempted rape with considerable skepticism. If even young, virginal women were penalized for suspected complicity with the men they claimed had raped them, a sexually experienced woman might well have concluded that it would be nearly impossible to convince judges or jurors that she had not consented to sexual intercourse with an attacker. Recall that New Haven's Goodwife Fancy endured a long series of sexual assaults from Thomas Robinson before she told anyone other than her husband about them. Even married women with better reputations than Goody Fancy were caught in a serious bind: if they claimed they had been raped, they raised questions about their own sexual probity; yet if they failed to report a rape that later somehow came to light, they might find themselves being punished for adultery. It is thus hardly surprising that women found it difficult to know what to do and delayed reporting such crimes.[95]

The circumstances surrounding one of the rare prosecutions involving the rape of a wife are suggestive in this regard. Jane, the wife of Nicholas Bond, a Maine fisherman frequently absent from home for long periods, deposed in May 1650 that a few nights earlier Robert Collins had broken into her house and "forsed" her twice in the presence of her children, despite her cries for help and her "struggling." A simple tale, one might think: but Jane's testimony revealed that Collins's visit to her house that night was in fact his *fourth*. A year earlier, Collins had "strived with hir but hardly knew hur boddy fully," and six months after that she "could not save hir selfe" from him, even though she had told him, "meddell not with me, if not I will make you a shame to all New England." On the third occasion, the only one she reported to her husband, she did manage to prevent Collins from entering the house.[96]

Jane Bond thus told her husband only about Collins's least successful attack on her. Nor did she fully inform a sympathetic female friend about the second rape. The morning after her fourth encounter with "fat Robert," Jane met a neighbor, Mary Tappe. She sighed to Mary that "hir heart was heavey and she was troubled to be alone and she was afrayd to live soe & that some body was at hir house last night." When Mary pressed Jane for details, she replied "divers times," "I dare not reveale it." So the information about Collins's final sexual assault on Goody Bond reached the ears of court officials not because of anything Jane said, but through another means altogether.

The crucial revelation came from Henry Simpson, Jane's six-year-old son by her first marriage. When Collins raped her, Jane was up late "making a cake for [her children] against the next day to leave them." The following morning, a neighbor came to stay with the children while

Jane was away, and—he testified—"the eldest boye sayd there was a man heare to night: he asked who. The boye sayd Robert: he being asked what hee did hee sayd hee lay with my mother all night." The rape was therefore revealed and prosecuted only because Goody Bond's six-year-old (one of the youngest witnesses ever to testify in a colonial courtroom) blurted the sorry tale out to a male neighbor, who thereupon reported it to the authorities.

A jury found Robert Collins "guiltie of the ackt of Incontinencie, not guilty of the forsement," and he was sentenced to pay a substantial fine (half to Nicholas Bond) and to be whipped thirty-nine lashes. Goody Bond was not formally punished, but the ambiguous verdict surely raised just the sort of questions about her sexual behavior that she had hoped to avoid by failing to report Collins's attacks. Her husband and her neighbors probably regarded her with suspicion thereafter.

Patterns of prosecution and the evidence in specific cases therefore suggest that certain kinds of rape (of married women in particular) were but rarely reported. The same observation can be made about incidents of sodomy and bestiality, especially in the Chesapeake. Maryland recorded no such prosecutions in the years covered by this book, and Virginia just two—one for sodomy, one for bestiality. Yet the absence of prosecutions for such crimes occurred in a society with an exceptionally imbalanced sex ratio (three to four men for every woman) throughout much of the century, and in a context in which pairs of men commonly lived together as "mates," jointly running tobacco plantations. Since it is clear, as in the case of Robert and Dorothy Holt and Edward Hudson, that some Chesapeake households were heterosexual ménages à trois (arrangements clearly resulting from the limited number of women in the population), it would be truly remarkable if all the male-only partnerships lacked a sexual component.[97]

That most of the men prosecuted for sodomy or bestiality in New England fell into the same demographic groups as a large majority of the male population of the Chesapeake also implies that such sexual activities may have been commonplace in the south. Although four married New England men were charged with these offenses,[98] in most cases defendants were explicitly identified as young, unmarried servants. Among those executed for bestiality, for example, were teenaged manservants from Plymouth, Salem, and New Haven, and twice the New Haven magistrates considered incidents involving several young men who "had committed much wickedness in a filthy corrupting way one with another."[99]

In one of those cases, heard at a court convened solely for that purpose in August 1652, the judges took special care to expose the mis-behavior "because it was spread abroade amonge many youthes, and they would be in danger of being further corrupted if they were not publiquely witnessed against." Upon examination, the three young men (two of whom were servants) acknowledged that, at the instigation of one of their number, they had over the preceding two years engaged in a series of sexual acts in a shifting series of pairs—they "did put downe their breeches and whipt one another and handled one anothers mem-bers," they "laye one upon another, some time their bellyes together, some times belly to backe, some time the one upermost, some time the other." Yet the three resolutely denied "indeavor[ing] to enter on[e] anothers body." The judges, concerned by information that "sundrie youthes had heard of these miscarriages and that they had bine talkeing one to another aboute it," questioned several young gossipers as well, but learned nothing new. The three miscreants were consequently sen-tenced to be "severly corrected by whipping publiquly, according as their yeares and strength will beare, that themselves by the blessing of God may have the benifit of it, and otheres which have heard of it may bee thereby warned to take heed of such sinnfull courses."[100]

Whatever the impact on the onlookers or the other two young men, one of the participants failed to reform. He was none other than John Frost, who ten years later not only seduced Mercy Payne but also per-suaded her brother John to engage in the same sort of sexual horseplay for which he had previously been punished. John Payne testified in 1662 that when he and John Frost were watching the family's cows together a year earlier, Frost "pulled downe his breeches and said to him come John let us play with our things together." Although Payne refused, he did agree to a suggestion that they "whip one another with some ffernes," evidently on their bare buttocks. The story of Frost's trans-gressions with *both* the Payne children came to light only because John Payne became ill and, "troubled" by the "bad thing" he had done, confessed to his mother, perhaps to clear his conscience on what he feared was his deathbed.[101]

John Payne's account, coupled with testimony in other cases, iden-tifies the context of livestock herding as important for young men's sexual knowledge and acts. For example, Thomas Granger, the servant executed in Plymouth in 1642, revealed before his death that he learned about bestiality "by another that had heard of such things from some in England when he was there, and they kept cattle together," and one of John Frost's two youthful sexual partners explained to the court that "as hee and Esborne Wakeman was keepeing oxen in the feild in his fathers lott, Esborne Wakeman begane to playe with him in a filthy way." One of the sexual encounters between Wakeman and Frost likewise took place "as they were at the Stony Brooke together lookeing to their hoggs."[102]

It is thus not surprising that many incidents of bestiality came to light when a witness happened unexpectedly on a servant assigned to tend livestock. William Hackett, executed in the Bay Colony in 1641, was "espied in the very act" on a sabbath by a woman "detained from the public assembly by some infirmity that day and by occasion looking out at her window." Nathaniel Moore, a Virginia servant, was seen "Buggering [a] Calfe Fower or Five tymes" by a couple walking home in the early morning after spending a night at a neighbor's, and a witness saw John Ferris of Stamford "at or aboute sun-set" with a "cowes tayle in his hand, and his privy member in the other hand." The witness, Henry Accerly, who pronounced himself "in a maze" at the sight, asked Ferris what he was doing. "Milkeing," Ferris replied, to which Accerly riposted, "it is Devillish milking, which would bring him to the Gallows." But since Accerly was the only witness and Ferris confessed no more than "that he Attempted to Doe it, but did it not," he escaped hanging. Instead, he was fined, ordered severely whipped at both Stamford and New Haven, and directed to wear "allwayes" a halter around his neck "vissibly, without hiding or putting it off."[103]

Even in New England, with its statutory abhorrence of these crimes, Ferris's punishment—harsh, but falling short of execution—was the one most commonly inflicted on men convicted of sodomy or bestiality.[104] The fate of the three women found guilty of engaging in same-sex liaisons was similar, though less severe. In Plymouth Colony in March 1648/9, Mary Hammon and Goody Sarah Norman, presented "for leude behavior each with other upon a bed," were both admonished; Norman, who was also found guilty of "divers lasivious speeches," was in addition directed "to make a publick acknowlidgment" of her "unchast behavior." In the Essex County court seven years earlier, the maidservant Elizabeth Johnson was fined and ordered "severely whipped" for a series of offenses, including what the judges described as "unseemly & filthy practises betwixt hir & another maid, attempting To Doe that which man & woman Doe."[105]

As was true in adultery cases, some colonists expressed their dissatisfaction with the application of the death penalty to those found guilty of sodomy and bestiality. John Winthrop recorded in his diary that when William Hackett was tried in 1641 "much scruple there was with many" because there had been only one witness to his misconduct and because he had not fully confessed to the crime of bestiality. Indeed, after Hackett was convicted, Governor Richard Bellingham refused to pronounce sentence on him, so that task was performed by Deputy Governor John Endicott. The execution of Richard Cornish for sodomy in Virginia led to contempt charges against two men who declared that Cornish had been "wrongfully" convicted, and a Rhode Islander accused of bestiality in the mid-1650s was protected by his neighbors for a considerable period of time. Although many of them reportedly knew that he had twice been seen committing "Buggerie" with a heifer, they did not tell the authorities and later helped him to resist arrest when the story finally came out.[106]

DISSENTING VOICES were therefore raised about the conviction and punishment of sexual offenses of all descriptions in the Anglo-American colonies. Even within the ranks of the magistracy, men differed on the question of the proper penalties for such misconduct. But in New England there was, at least, a consensus that all sex crimes were serious, whereas in the Chesapeake opinions were more mixed. In the south, sexual misbehavior that did not involve some form of intercourse rarely resulted in prosecutions, and the only sexual offense consistently and severely punished was bastardy. The northern colonies energetically prosecuted a wide range of crimes, from lascivious carriage to sodomy and bestiality, because of the emphasis they placed on the need to confine sexual activity to the marriage bed. Though they seldom imposed the death penalty, even for the most serious offenses like adultery and sodomy, New England's leaders nevertheless regarded illicit sexual activity with alarm. If husbands, wives, or the unmarried were allowed freely to violate the rules of proper sexual conduct, then marriage, the only acceptable context for sexual activity and the basis of society and government in the Filmerian worldview, would be called into question. Left unpunished, sexual offenses could thereby shake the very foundations of the commonwealths New Englanders had worked so hard to establish.

Although the operations of the system of gendered power are thus especially noticeable in the prosecution of sex crimes, they are also visible in other sorts of criminal cases as well. The pattern of prosecution for crimes against authority exposes the nature of the demands placed on men by colonial governments and also provides a mechanism for determining the relative stability (or, more precisely, instability) of those governments. The fact that women were rarely charged with such offenses reveals their indirect relationship with the Filmerian and especially the Lockean state, as do the specific characteristics of the prosecutions that were or were not pursued against them.

Yet even if women were largely denied direct access to the polity in both authoritarian and contractual systems of thought, nevertheless they held markedly different positions in Filmerian and Lockean schemas. In the Lockean worldview, they were pushed to the margins of political life, their contacts with it wholly determined by their fathers and husbands, who alone were conceived as political actors. In the Filmerian world, by contrast, women could stand close to the center of political and social power by virtue of their position in the family, that key Filmerian institution. High-status widows and fictive widows— women like Mistress Ann Hibbens, Mistress Anne Eaton, and Mistress Margaret Brent—played crucial roles in the early history of the colonies and became focal points for conflict precisely because of their roles as symbolic mothers deserving of "honor" under the Fifth Commandment. The most important such woman in colonial America was unquestionably Mistress Anne Hutchinson, the subject of the final chapter in this book.

CHAPTER 8

✦

Husband, Preacher, Magistrate

You have stept out of your place, you have rather bine a
Husband than a Wife and a preacher than a Hearer; and
a Magistrate than a Subject.

—*Hugh Peter, 1638*[1]

THE REVEREND HUGH PETER'S WORDS, directed to Mistress
Anne Hutchinson during her church trial on March 22, 1637/8,
summed up the Massachusetts Bay authorities' view of the troublesome
woman whose religious beliefs they were soon to deem sufficiently unorthodox to warrant excommunication. Yet in this statement he spoke
not of her ideas or even of her specific offenses. Rather, Mr. Peter
focused on her general behavior and demeanor, her refusal to occupy a
woman's proper place: she was to be wife, hearer, subject—not husband,
preacher, magistrate.

Hugh Peter's list is remarkable not only for its succinctness but also
for its inclusion of the final pair: magistrate/subject. Anyone even generally familiar with the famous confrontation between Mistress Hutchinson and the civil and religious leaders of the Bay Colony between
1636 and 1638 is not startled by the clergyman's terming her "husband"
(she had taken the lead in her family's religious affairs) or "preacher"
(she had been speaking regularly about religion to large groups of people). But "magistrate"? Unlike her somewhat younger contemporary in
Maryland, Mistress Margaret Brent, Anne Hutchinson never, by word
or deed, sought any power in the secular realm. Her interests were
profoundly spiritual. Nevertheless, Governor John Winthrop and most
of the other magistrates perceived her activities and those of her followers
as a threat to the governance of Massachusetts Bay. In the Filmerian
world of unified authority they mentally inhabited, her challenges to the
church and the family translated into a challenge to the state. She could
not assert her autonomy, independence, and leadership abilities in the

first two without also attempting (in their minds) to seize power in the third as well.

The danger Mistress Hutchinson posed to the Bay Colony and its founding leaders went beyond the symbolic. At a time when the northern colonists were engaged in their first major conflict with the continent's native inhabitants—the Pequot War—at least some of her followers refused to muster with the militia because they deemed its officers ungodly. In a commonwealth becoming notable for its insistence on religious orthodoxy of a particular variety, members of her group began questioning and resisting the ministers at every turn. And she won to her side many of the most prominent women and men of Boston, along with similarly circumstanced people from surrounding communities like Charlestown and Roxbury. If they did not truly threaten the existence of the commonwealth, they at least jeopardized the power wielded by its current rulers.[2]

Yet still the word *magistrate* jars: how, exactly, had Anne Hutchinson claimed to be a magistrate rather than a subject? Hugh Peter's characterization in fact makes little sense outside the context of the system of gendered power that has been explicated at length in this book. And that context too helps to explain the general phenomenon historians usually term the "Antinomian Controversy," although "Antinomian" is not a word Anne Hutchinson would have applied to herself. Nor was it one commonly employed by her opponents, who most often called her and her followers "Opinionists" or "Familists."[3] Scholars who have studied the episode—seeing it variously as a theological dispute among the clergy, a revolt of the laity against the clergy, a political problem confronted ably by the elite, even a proto-feminist movement—have all overlooked the significance of Mistress Anne Hutchinson's position as a symbolic mother in the Filmerian world. The account that follows will accordingly focus on the controversy as a grave crisis in the system of gendered power.[4]

"MEETINGS OF THE WOMEN"

Mistress Anne Marbury Hutchinson and her large family—including husband, eleven children, and several collateral relatives—arrived in Boston, Massachusetts Bay Colony, in mid-September, 1634.[5] She had been born in 1591, the daughter of the Reverend Francis Marbury, an orthodox clergyman of the Church of England who had served parishes in Lincolnshire and London during her childhood and youth. Although nothing is known of her education, in America she proved herself to be intelligent, articulate, and able to match quotations and interpretations of biblical passages with clerics and well-educated laymen alike. At age twenty-one, Anne Marbury married Mr. William Hutchinson, a merchant, and the couple moved to his home in Alford, Lincolnshire.

Twenty miles away, in the village of Boston, preached the Reverend John Cotton, who arrived there about the same time as the newlywed Hutchinsons settled in Alford. Anne Hutchinson came to regard Cotton as her spiritual mentor, and when he was forced to flee England in 1633 after Archbishop William Laud began to persecute clergymen with Puritan leanings, she was, she later said, in "great trouble." As she often did in such circumstances, she turned to meditation and to her Bible, recounting that "the 30th of Isaiah was brought to my mind. Though the Lord give thee bread of adversity and water of affliction . . . thine eyes shall see thy teachers." Interpreting the passage as a call to emigrate, she recalled that she "could not be at rest" until she followed Cotton. Her husband, who thought her "a dear saint and servant of God," acceded to her wish. Thus at her instigation the family moved to Boston in New England, where they were given a prime building lot in the heart of town, her husband (as befitted his wealth and standing) was soon elected to the General Court, and she quickly assumed a prominent role among Boston's women, as befitted *her* position.[6]

Yet at the very outset of her residence in Boston questions were raised about her religious orthodoxy. The Reverend Zechariah Symmes, who had sailed to New England on the same ship as the Hutchinsons and had only met her "once or twice" previously, was sufficiently disturbed by "the corruptness and narrowness of her opinions" expressed to him on shipboard that he (and perhaps others) alerted then-Governor Thomas Dudley to the problem she potentially posed to the colony. Mr. Dudley accordingly warned the Reverend John Wilson, the Boston church's pastor, and John Cotton, its teacher, to question her with unusual care, presumably on the topic that most concerned Symmes, "the evidencing of a good estate" (that is, proof of salvation). But on the occasion of her membership examination she satisfied Dudley, Cotton, Symmes, and the others that "she held nothing different from us," and so she was admitted to the church in early November, a week after her husband.[7]

What happened over the next months must be reconstructed from fragmentary remarks in accounts written by her opponents and those to whom they later spoke. At the time of the Hutchinsons' arrival, Boston was in the midst of a revival, initiated by laity hungry for the religious

expression they had been denied in their homeland and furthered by
Mr. Cotton's "insinuating and melting way in his preaching," through
which (the Reverend William Hubbard later wrote) "he would usually
carry his very adversary captive after the triumphant chariot of his rhet-
orick." Town residents were thus notably receptive to religious messages, and Thomas Dudley recalled at Anne Hutchinson's civil trial that
"within half a year after" her admission to the church, or by May 1635,
"she had vented divers of her strange opinions and had made parties in
the country." Mistress Hutchinson initially spread her ideas in a context
from which the colony's male leaders were excluded, so they did not
know what was happening or its importance until many months had
passed.[8]

With the benefit of hindsight, John Cotton's grandson near the end
of the century described the conversations that for a crucial period took
place without the knowledge of the clerics or officeholders of the Bay
Colony. "At the meetings of the women, which used to be called *gos-
sippings,*" Cotton Mather wrote, "it was her manner to carry on very
pious discourses, and so put the neighbourhood upon examining their
spiritual estates." In particular, she pointed out to her hearers "how far
a person might go in 'trouble of mind' . . . without ever coming to a
'saving union with the Lord Jesus Christ.'" As a result, Mather noted,
"many of them were convinced of a very great defect in the settlement
of their everlasting peace, and acquainted more with the 'Spirit of the
gospel,' than ever they were before."[9]

Mistress Anne Hutchinson was not the Boston midwife—that role
was filled by Goodwife Jane Hawkins, who became one of her staunch
allies—but she was one of those high-status women whose expertise in
health care in general and childbirth in particular was greatly valued in
the early settlements. John Cotton put it this way in a pamphlet he
published twelve years after the events in question: "At her first com-
ming she was well respected and esteemed of me," not only because he
had known her in England or because she had emigrated "for conscience
sake," but "chiefly" because "she did much good in our Town, in
womans meeting at Childbirth-Travells, wherein shee was not only skil-
full and helpfull, but readily fell into good discourse with the women
about their spiritual estates."[10]

It is not difficult to imagine the scene, repeated again and again in
the small, dark houses of early Boston. A group of women summoned
to the bedside of a woman in travail. . . . The highest-ranking woman
among them, respected for her knowledge and skill in midwifery, a
person of "a nimble wit and active spirit, and a very voluble tongue,"

inquiring earnestly "about their spiritual estates." . . . A woman facing death in the midst of giving life, surrounded by female friends and neighbors recalling previous similar experiences, anticipating still others in the future. . . . All of them Puritans who had immigrated to North America because, like Anne Hutchinson, they were deeply concerned about the state of their souls, convinced of "the falseness of the constitution of the church of England" and searching for spiritual assurance. . . . Listening intently as Mistress Hutchinson explained that "the Soul might find some tastes and flashes of spirituall comfort" even if they had not truly been saved. . . . That observing "all knowen duties, as secret Prayer, Family Exercises, Conscience of Sabbaths, Reverence of Ministers, Frequenting of Sermons, Diligence in calling, honesty in dealing and the like" was inadequate to demonstrate salvation. . . . Thinking carefully about her assertions that many pious church members would "never see or feel the need of Christ, much lesse attain any saving Union, or Communion with him," but instead would be deluded into a false belief in their salvation by "Legall work"; that is, by outward signs of piety.[11]

Mistress Hutchinson's message to her female audience was unmistakable: too much reliance on what the Puritans termed the "Covenant of Works"—the notion, crudely put, that one could earn one's way into heaven through good deeds and pious behavior, or at least that such signs ("sanctification") could serve as evidence of salvation—was a snare for the unwary. All that mattered, she proclaimed, was the "Covenant of Grace": God's free gift of salvation, which the recipient could in no way influence, and knowledge of which could be attained only through intensely personal spiritual searching. The state of salvation, or "justification," was thus wholly separate and distinct from sanctification.[12]

When he first learned of Anne Hutchinson's labors with the women of Boston, the Reverend John Cotton later recalled, he applauded them. Her emphasis on the significance of God's free gift of grace "suited with the publike Ministery, which had gone along in the same way, so as these private conferences did well tend to water the seeds publikely sowen." He commented that "many whose spirituall estates were not so safely layed, yet were hereby helped and awakened to discover their sandy foundations, and to seek for better establishment in Christ." And the "many" of whom he spoke included men as well as women, for the women who absorbed her teachings conveyed those ideas to their husbands as well. In retrospect, the upholders of New England orthodoxy would liken Anne Hutchinson to Eve, or to a "Trojan horse . . . covered with womens aprons," but initially she seemed to be a welcome ally for the Bay Colony's clergy in general and for John Cotton in particular.[13]

Precisely when Mistress Hutchinson moved from speaking informally to women in the context of childbirths to holding meetings in
her own home is not known. At her civil trial she explained that when
she first came to Boston she did not attend any private religious gatherings, which were then commonplace among pious colonists seeking
to engage in collective Bible study or to gain a better understanding of
church teachings. Consequently, she noted, "it was presently reported
that I did not allow of such meetings but held them unlawful and therefore in that regard they said I was proud and did despise all ordinances."
In light of the position she was advancing in the childbed conversations,
it was not illogical for the Boston rumor mill to conclude that Anne
Hutchinson disdained such gatherings. If attendance at private meetings
constituted the sort of sanctification she rejected, she might indeed "despise all ordinances." But that was not the message she intended to
convey. So, when "a friend came unto me and told me of it . . . I to
prevent such aspersions took it up."[14]

Her language makes it appear that she took the need to squelch the
gossip as a signal not to attend gatherings at others' houses but rather to
initiate her own meetings. "We began it but with five or six," she later
recounted, "and though it grew to more in future time, yet being tolerated at first, I knew not why it might not continue." Mistress Hutchinson's statement was more than slightly disingenuous, for by the time
the Bay Colony authorities acted to put a stop to her meetings, they
had grown to a remarkable size. According to her neighbor John Winthrop, who would have seen the attendees with his own eyes, "shee
kept open house for all commers, and set up two Lecture dayes in the
week, when they usually met at her house threescore or fourescore
persons"—that is, sixty to eighty people at a time. There, reported one
witness, "the custome was for her Scholars to propound questions, and
she (gravely sitting in the chaire) did make answers thereunto." Another
New Englander, viewing such behavior, charged that "the weaker Sex
prevailed so farre, that they set up a Priest of their own Profession and
Sex." Indeed, since chairs were relatively scarce and usually reserved for
household heads, the conduct of the gatherings must have evoked just
such images of priesthood for Anne Hutchinson's listeners.[15]

When these meetings began, declared John Winthrop, "the pretence
was to repeat Sermons," especially those of her spiritual mentor and
guide, John Cotton. However, once she had finished that task, Winthrop
continued, "she would comment upon the Doctrines, and interpret all
passages at her pleasure, and expound dark places of Scripture." Moreover, Cotton added, she became the primary authority on the content

of his sermons: "what she repeated and confirmed, was accounted sound, what shee omitted, was accounted Apochrypha."[16]

At some point, according to her opponents, Mistress Hutchinson thus made a crucial transition: going beyond the "wholesome truths" she had originally advanced, she started "to set forth her own stuffe." Specifically, she "taught that no sanctification was any evidence of a good estate, except that justification were first cleared up to them by the immediate witnesse of the Spirit." This dangerous notion, asserted Mr. Winthrop, "tended to quench all indevour." In other words, once Bostonians were fully convinced that good works bore no relationship to salvation, once they came to believe that church attendance, Bible study, and so forth had nothing to do with the spiritual assurance they sought so desperately, even "many good soules, that had been of long approved godlinesse, were brought to renounce all the work of grace in them, and to wait for this immediate revelation." Such a doctrine especially appealed to "many prophane persons," Winthrop commented, because "it was a very easie, and acceptable way to heaven, to see nothing, to have nothing, but waite for Christ to do all."[17]

Mistress Hutchinson's doctrine presented the clergymen of the Bay Colony with a formidable challenge, one that became evident as her influence spread. Puritanism in general was built in part on a rejection of the Church of England as overly concerned with the covenant of works, and Calvinism's central message was that salvation was the free gift of God, not a goal that could be attained by earthly actions. So Anne Hutchinson based her theology on one of Puritanism's key tenets, carrying it to an extreme but nevertheless superficially advancing an idea wholly in accordance with orthodox beliefs. As the Reverend John Cotton noted, it was thus "no marvell" that initially "shee found loving and dear respect both from our Church-Elders and Brethren." Nor, given the arenas in which she promulgated her ideas, was it surprising that Boston men were for many months less than fully aware of their import. First in the context of gossipings at childbirths, then in all-female religious meetings in her own home, Anne Hutchinson developed and explicated a series of notions that together constituted a frontal challenge to the power of Massachusetts Bay's civil and religious elite—but the men did not realize that until it was nearly too late.[18]

The dangers the Bay Colony's leaders eventually perceived in the movement she led are revealed in the venom of their later descriptions of her: she was an "American Jesabel" who spread "poyson" through "the very veines and vitalls of the People in the Country," a "proud dame" with an "ambitious spirit" who acted with "impudent boldnesse"; she "insinuated her selfe into the hearts of much of the people" through "skill and cunning."[19] Behind the inflated rhetoric lay a recognition that they faced a worthy opponent, a woman whose standing in the community made her an adversary with the clear potential for success.

Several times the critics alluded to Mistress Hutchinson's status. In commenting upon Mary Oliver of Salem, a woman repeatedly charged with contempt of civil and religious authority and holding unorthodox views in the late 1630s and early 1640s, John Winthrop observed that "she was (for ability of speech, and appearance of zeal and devotion) far above Mrs. Hutchinson, and so the fitter instrument to have done hurt, but that she was poor and had little acquaintance." Anne Hutchinson, in other words, was successful at least in part because she was a well-known, high-ranking woman, not like Goody Oliver, who was "poor" with "little acquaintance." John Cotton's first formal admonition to Mistress Hutchinson, delivered at the midpoint of her church trial, carried a similar implication. Because of her place among "eminent Christians" with reputations for "Wisdome and Understandinge," he remarked, even if she merely asked a question about a doctrinal point, "others that hear of it will conclude them possitively and thay will thinke: suer thear is some thinge in it if Mrs. Hutchinson makes a Question of it."[20]

It was thus Mistress Hutchinson's high rank and her standing in the women's community that afforded her a hearing, but it was the content of her message that won her adherents. Her ideas were attractive not only because they offered what the Reverend Thomas Weld called "a faire and easie way to heaven," but also because they provided her followers with a means of challenging the increasingly repressive political and religious orthodoxy that prevailed in Massachusetts Bay. Moreover, her doctrines gave believers the assurance of salvation once they had experienced the "immediate revelations" of which she spoke. Although such assurance was also available to those who saw unmistakable evidence of sanctification in themselves, she seems to have imparted a special confidence to her followers. She herself so "clearly discerned her Justification" that John Cotton warned her against hubris even "in the times of her best acceptance." That confidence, indeed, may have caused her downfall, for her regular listeners, emboldened by the assurance of salvation she offered, began to proselytize among other Bostonians, both newcomers and longtime residents. Those efforts to spread her ideas beyond the usual attendees at the Hutchinson house appear to have at last alerted the authorities to the extent of the peril they faced.[21]

Certainly an attempt to enlist in their cause the Reverend John Wilson and his wife had that result. Wilson, according to Cotton, at first "thought well of" Hutchinson and her adherents, showing them "much forbearance." But "afterwards in some private conference, which one or more of them had with him, and (our beloved Sister) his Wife, he discerned some more rottennesse in them, and their way, then he suspected before," and he subsequently "grew more zealous against them."[22]

The mention of Mistress Elizabeth Wilson in this passage is sufficiently unusual to direct attention to her presence at the "private conference" and to speculate about its implications. As will be recalled from chapter four, Mistress Wilson a decade later took the lead in petitioning the General Court on behalf of the midwife Alice Tilly. That suggests that she, like Mistress Hutchinson, was deeply enmeshed in the community of women that developed from childbirth associations. It accordingly seems likely that she was one of the women influenced by Anne Hutchinson's ideas, and that the meeting the Hutchinsonians held with her and her husband was an attempt to use her to reach him. She might even have initiated the encounter herself, which would account for her presence. Since clerics' wives did not commonly observe their husbands' "private conferences" with parishioners, her participation would have been highly irregular had she not played a central role in the meeting.

All the reports of the recruitment activities come from Mistress Hutchinson's opponents, and so they must be interpreted critically. Nevertheless, they paint a consistent and compelling picture. In his introduction to John Winthrop's *Short Story*, the Reverend Thomas Weld described how Anne Hutchinson's followers "laboured much to acquaint themselves with as many, as possibly they could, that so they might have the better opportunity to communicate their new light unto them." Then they adopted what could be termed feminine tactics, using "loving salutes, humble carriage, kind invitements, friendly visits" to "insinuate themselves" into the affections of their new friends, especially targeting those newcomers who were "men of note, worth, and activity." They would "offer them roome in their owne houses, or of some of their owne Sect, and so having gotten them into their Web, they could easily poyson them by degrees; It was rare for any man thus hooked in, to escape their Leaven."[23]

Although Thomas Weld's account emphasized the Hutchinsonians' success at attracting high-ranking male followers—as well it might have, for one notable recruit was Sir Henry Vane, elected governor in May 1636—most of the evidence suggests that the core of Mistress Hutchinson's support lay with the women of Boston, who comprised her

earliest audiences. As shall be seen, her opponents were deeply concerned about her influence on female Bostonians, who were (in the
Reverend Weld's words), "the weaker to resist; the more flexible,
tender, and ready to yeeld," and able "as by an Eve, to catch their
husbands also." Both Thomas Weld and John Winthrop alluded to differences between husbands and wives stemming from Anne Hutchinson's teachings, and Weld asserted that she had advocates "almost in
every family." Since Mistress Hutchinson's position in the women's
community was unparalleled, it is likely that women were the Boston
residents responsible for the dissidence that, Winthrop observed, "spreads
into the families, and sets divisions between husband and wife, and other
relations there, till the weaker give place to the stronger, otherwise it
turnes to open contention."[24]

One man who resisted the message was Edward Johnson, an immigrant who moved his family to Boston in the spring of 1636 and later
vividly described his encounter with a follower of Anne Hutchinson:

> Come along with me, sayes one of them, i'le bringe you to a
> Woman that Preaches better Gospell then any of your black-coates
> that have been at the Ninneversity, a Woman of another kinde of
> spirit, who hath had many Revelations of things to come, and for
> my part, saith hee, I had rather hear such a one that speakes from
> the meere motion of the spirit, without any study at all, then any
> of your learned Scollers.[25]

The dialogue Johnson recorded, whether precisely accurate or not,
starkly revealed the nature of Mistress Hutchinson's challenge to the
clergymen of New England: if "spirit" and "revelation" were more important components of religiosity than "learning," college-educated clerics would have only a peripheral role in the spiritual lives of the members
of their churches. That, indeed, seemed to be the case for Anne Hutchinson herself, for although she had followed Cotton to Massachusetts,
he recorded rebuking her early on for the fact that "her Faith was not
begotten nor . . . strengthened, by publick Ministery, but by private
Meditations, or Revelations onely." Such doctrine, Johnson charged,
was devised "especially to please the Femall Sex," and surely women—
who were denied access to advanced education—would have found
Anne Hutchinson's elevation of personal spirituality and denigration of
formal learning very attractive. To Johnson, however, nothing but
"phantasticall madnesse" could cause "silly Women laden with diverse

lusts" to be held "in higher esteeme . . . then those honoured of Christ, indued with power and authority from him to Preach."[26]

In mid-1636, what the Reverend Thomas Weld called the Hutch-insonians' "boldnesse, pride, insolency," and "the disturbances, divisions, contentions they raised amongst us, both in Church and State, and in families, setting division betwixt husband and wife," finally prompted a counterattack from the Bay Colony's civil and religious leaders. They chose to move first not against Mistress Hutchinson herself but against her most prominent, and thus most vulnerable, male allies, notably John Cotton. Cotton later defended his long-standing failure to repudiate her publicly by claiming that he had had no adequate proof of her "corrupt opinions," for they were "maintained . . . in private, and not before such witnesses, as might reach to publick conviction." He had even dispatched "some Sisters of the Church on purpose to her Repetitions, that I might know the truth," he declared, "but when shee discerned any such present, no speech fell from her, that could be much excepted against."[27] Undoubtedly Cotton's critics among the clergy, who were many, recognized his statements for what they were, self-serving defensiveness; and Mistress Hutchinson's allies, learning of the spies, would have attributed her caution to revelatory prescience.

COUNTERATTACK

As a first step, the ministers Thomas Shepard and Peter Bulkeley addressed letters to John Cotton, asking him to clarify his theological views. His answers were not fully satisfactory, so in October 1636 the clergymen met with him and the Reverend John Wheelwright, Anne Hutchinson's brother-in-law, who had recently arrived in the colony and had aligned himself with the dissidents. The chief point at issue, according to John Winthrop, was whether "sanctification did help to evidence justification." Cotton and Wheelwright both satisfied the church leaders that their views were orthodox in that regard. Shortly thereafter the Hutchinsonian members of the Boston church tried to persuade the congregation to add John Wheelwright as a second teacher, but the effort failed after Mr. Winthrop vigorously opposed it. Relations between the two camps then deteriorated until, near the end of the year, "a very sad speech" by John Wilson blamed "these new opinions risen up amongst us" for "differences and alienations among brethren" that required an immediate remedy. This speech, Winthrop noted, "was taken very ill" by the Reverend Cotton and most of the members of the Boston

church, and Wilson barely escaped formal censure by his own congregation.[28]

Hoping to achieve a reconciliation, the General Court proclaimed
a fast day for January 19, 1636/7, asking Mr. Wheelwright to preach the
sermon. Instead of dampening the dispute, however, John Wheelwright
added fuel to the flames by attacking the very concept of a fast day. He
contended that "those that do not know the Lord Jesus, they are usually
given most unto fasting," and declared that "those under a covenant of
works, [the] more holy they are, the greater enimyes they are to Christ."
He concluded by specifically enlisting himself in the ranks of his sister-
in-law's supporters: "If Christ be present, there will be no cause of fasting
and mourning: therefore let me (in the name of God) incourage all those
that hold forth the wayes of grace, and do indeavour to make knowne
the Lord Jesus Christ."[29]

Thereafter, Mistress Hutchinson's advocates began to confront the
colony's established ministers directly. The Reverend Thomas Weld later
recalled that, after clergymen had completed their sermons, the "opinionists" would raise objections "in the open Assembly against our doctrine delivered," like "halfe a dozen Pistols discharged at the face of the
Preacher." They would even attend a minister's church "with a purpose
to oppose him to his face." Some wrote letters "of defiance and challenge" to clerics, and the Reverend John Wilson became a special target.
"When he began to pray or preach," Weld recorded, Wilson's critics
would "contemptuously" turn their backs on him and leave the congregation. John Cotton specifically identified Anne Hutchinson as one
of those who adopted this tactic, but noted that it was not easy to prove
that the exodus was motivated by contempt for the pastor, because
"most of them were women, and they pretended many excuses for their
going out."[30]

The conflict between the Hutchinson group and the majority of the
Bay Colony's clergymen focused on two closely related issues: first, the
question of whether sanctification was linked to justification; and second,
whether, if one answered yes to that, one was "under a covenant of
works." The topic was raised most sharply in a conference between
several ministers and Mistress Hutchinson herself in December 1636.
Having heard that she "did conceive our ministry to be different from
the ministry of the gospel, and that we taught a covenant of works, &c.,
and this was her table talk," reported the Reverend Hugh Peter, they
asked her to meet with them at Mr. Cotton's house, a request to which
she "willingly" acquiesced.[31]

At her civil trial, Mistress Hutchinson and her supporters disputed the clergymen's recollections of her statements at this conference, but it seems clear that she declared, as Mr. Peter testified, that "there was a wide and a broad difference between our brother Mr. Cotton and our selves." How precisely she characterized that "wide and broad" difference became a major point at issue between her supporters and her opponents. According to the Reverend Peter and the clerics she had criticized, she asserted that "he preaches the covenant of grace and you the covenant of works." By contrast, she—backed up by her allies John Cotton and Mr. Thomas Leverett, the ruling elder of the Boston church—maintained that she had rather averred that "one may preach a covenant of grace more clearly than another." She insisted further that a clergyman could unknowingly preach the covenant of works even if he were among the saved.[32]

The distinctions appear minute, but everyone understood that they were crucial, which is why testimony about this conversation occupied many pages of the record of Mistress Hutchinson's civil trial. The ministers, including Hugh Peter, charged that Anne Hutchinson had defamed them by maligning their ministry and terming them purveyors of the covenant of works. She and her adherents, by contrast, declared that she had simply (in effect) said that she preferred the Reverend Cotton's preaching to theirs—no harm in that—and that she had never meant to imply that the targets of her criticism were unregenerate. Anne Hutchinson tried to explain her position by comparing most of the Bay Colony clergy to the apostles prior to Christ's resurrection: in Elder Leverett's words, she affirmed that "as the apostles were for a time without the spirit so until they had received the witness of the spirit they could not preach a covenant of grace so clearly." Even though her supporters contended that such a comparison could not be deemed "offensive," it only added to the charges against her by again revealing her disdain for the doctrines advanced by all the ministers except Mr. Cotton and Mr. Wheelwright.[33]

Such confrontations, after which the participants could not even agree on what had been said or on the meaning of the words exchanged, did little to calm the storm. When the General Court next met, in early March 1636/7, John Winthrop believed that it could not ignore "the heat of contention and uncharitable censures which began to over-spread the Countrey." Attributing the overt hostility now being expressed to Wheelwright's incendiary sermon, the court examined the clergyman at considerable length over a period of several days, rejected a petition on his behalf signed by about forty members of the Boston church, and found him guilty of sedition. To those who argued that his sermon was a "matter of conscience" not subject to secular authority, the court responded that "in some cases of religious nature, as manifest heresie, notorious blasphemy, &c. the Civill power may proceed." The court told Mr. Wheelwright to return in November to learn his sentence, hoping that in the interim some sort of accommodation could be reached. In May, after a two-year absence from that post, John Winthrop was elected governor, replacing the Hutchinson ally Sir Henry Vane. At the same session, the General Court refused to receive yet another petition drafted by Wheelwright's supporters.[34]

Efforts to achieve accommodation then proceeded on two fronts. With respect to the laity, the authorities employed what were described by the Reverend Thomas Weld as "private meanes"—conferences with Hutchinsonians "sometimes in private before the Elders onely, sometimes in the publike Congregation for all comers" designed to refute their arguments and to show them the error of their ways. But even though (Weld claimed) the "opinionists" were "oftentimes brought to be either silent, or driven to deny common principles, or shuffle off plaine Scripture," they "would not yeeld to the truth." Instead of admitting their mistakes, they would meet to reinforce each other "in the old way," so that "when we dealt with them next time, we found them further off then before."[35]

To handle Mr. Cotton and Mr. Wheelwright, the clergymen summoned a synod to Newtown (Cambridge) in August 1637. Since Mistress Hutchinson's lay adherents had demonstrated such adamance, the synod was opened "to any of the Countrey to come in and heare," with even the dissidents being accorded "liberty of speech, (onely due order observed)." For two weeks the clergymen worked to restore harmony in their own ranks, if not to remove all disputes among the laity. And in that goal they largely succeeded: although John Wheelwright remained outside the fold, John Cotton at last surrendered to the importunities of his fellow clerics and nominally joined their consensus, papering over the previous points of disagreement. Like other dissident colonial men in other times and places, he yielded to the heavy conformist pressures placed on him by his male community, the clergymen of the Bay Colony, thus revealing his recognition that his standing within the community of men depended on his willingness to bow to a widely accepted position. The Reverend Cotton thereupon initiated a long process of distancing himself from his one-time follower. He continued that same endeavor during her trials and in his later writings, which downplayed the closeness and significance of their relationship and failed to acknowledge that his position in Boston had been substantially enhanced by her support.[36]

The ministers concluded by adopting four resolutions designed to quash the dissidents. One allowed a member to be censured by a church even in his or her absence; another attempted to prevent church members from moving easily among congregations. But the two most important tried to restrict church members' ability to question clergymen after their sermons and specifically condemned the ongoing meetings at Anne Hutchinson's house. "Though a private member might ask a question publicly, after sermon, for information; yet this ought to be very wisely and sparingly done, and that with leave of the elders," the synod declared, rebuking those who "with bitterness" currently "reproached" the leaders of their churches or "reproved" church doctrines. And it unhesitatingly denounced "such a set assembly, (as was then in practice at Boston,) where sixty or more did meet every week, and one woman (in a prophetical way, by resolving questions of doctrine, and expounding scripture) took upon her the whole exercise." Although the clerics concurred that "women might meet (some few together) to pray and edify one another," they insisted that what Mistress Hutchinson had done was "disorderly, and without rule."[37]

If the clergymen thought that achieving reconciliation with John Cotton and condemning the practices in which Mistress Hutchinson and her adherents regularly engaged would silence her, they were badly mistaken. John Winthrop recounted that following the synod John Wheelwright continued to preach "after his former manner"; that Anne Hutchinson likewise continued "her wonted meetings and exercises"; and that she and others persisted in leaving the Boston church whenever the Reverend Wilson rose to speak. Moreover, several Bostonians withdrew from the General Court, "with professed dislike of their proceedings, and many evidences brake forth of their discontented and turbulent spirits." The magistrates concluded that the situation had become "desperate" and that the state needed to take formal steps against the dissidents, since actions by the church had failed. They chose as their vehicle the petition presented on behalf of John Wheelwright in March, terming it a "seditious writing" because it had proclaimed his innocence and had accused the General Court of allying itself with "Satan, . . . who hath raised up such calumnies against the faithfull Prophets of God." These, declared Winthrop, were "scandalous and seditious speeches," worthy of censure.[38]

At the November 1637 meeting of the General Court, Governor

Winthrop and the other magistrates therefore acted decisively. First they refused to allow Mr. William Aspinwall (who had signed the petition) and Mr. John Coggeshall (who acknowledged his agreement with it) to take their seats as deputies from Boston. Then, having deprived the Hutchinson group of two prominent supporters, they called Mr. Wheelwright before them. When he continued to defend himself and refused to acknowledge any errors, they ordered him disfranchised and banished, asserting that the penalty of banishment was as appropriate as when Cain, Hagar, and Ishmael "were expelled as troublers of the families, (which were then as commonwealths)." Coggeshall and Aspinwall were likewise disfranchised, with the latter—who was particularly unrepentant in his appearance before the court—being banished as well. Over the next few weeks, the magistrates also disfranchised and disarmed other recalcitrant signers of the petition. Somewhat belatedly, the General Court adopted a seditious libel law, allowing for the fining, disfranchising, imprisonment, or banishing of anyone who "shall hearafter openly or willingly defame any court of justice," its sentences, proceedings, or members.[39]

But John Coggeshall, William Aspinwall, and even John Wheelwright were not, of course, the authorities' most important target. That was Anne Hutchinson, the woman whom Edward Johnson termed "the grand Mistris of all the rest" and Governor Winthrop called "the breeder and nourisher of all these distempers."[40] *She* was the person who had to be silenced if order was to be restored in the Bay Colony. Her movement had succeeded in part because of who she was—a high-status woman with an unassailable position within the women's childbirth community—and in part because of the attractiveness of her doctrine to laywomen and men alike. The first rendered her difficult to attack, the second rendered her vulnerable.

THE CIVIL TRIAL

On November 7, 1637, the Massachusetts Bay General Court summoned "Mrs Hutchinson, (the wife of Mr William Hutchinson,)" to appear before it on a charge of "traduceing the mi[niste]rs & their ministery in this country." The official record of her trial is brief and to the point: "shee declared volentarily her revelations for her ground, & that shee should bee delivered & the Court ruined, with their posterity, & thereupon was banished." She was remanded to the custody of Mr. Joseph Weld of Roxbury until her final expulsion from the colony the following spring, for not even the vengeful Bay Colony magistrates would force her to move her large household during the harsh New England winter.[41]

Fortunately for historians, this succinct summary is not the only surviving account of the civil trial of Mistress Anne Hutchinson. Governor John Winthrop included a description of it—more detailed in some places than in others, and at times carefully shaped to his own purposes—in his 1644 pamphlet, *A Short Story of the Rise, reign, and ruine of the Antinomians, Familists & Libertines*. In addition, Anne Hutchinson's great-grandson, the loyalist historian and governor Thomas Hutchinson, in 1767 printed what seems to be a transcript of the trial, perhaps based on notes taken by a supporter or family member, as an appendix to the second volume of his *History of the Colony and Province of Massachusetts Bay*. The account that follows is based primarily upon the latter (which will be called "the transcript") but relies cautiously on the former for one set of exchanges missing from the longer record.[42]

At the very outset of the civil trial Mistress Hutchinson signaled her unwillingness to yield to the authorities without resistance.[43] Informed by Governor Winthrop that she had been called before the General Court "as one of those that have troubled the peace of the commonwealth and the churches here," as someone who had spoken in "very prejudicial" terms about the clergymen and churches of the colony, and as one who had "maintained a meeting and an assembly in your house that hath been condemned by the general assembly as a thing not tolerable nor comely in the sight of God or fitting for your sex," she responded with a demand to be told the specific charges against her. Well prepared, she recognized that nothing Mr. Winthrop listed would necessarily open her to criminal prosecution.

The governor ventured a detail, asking her, as he had asked Mr. William Aspinwall and Mr. John Coggeshall, "whether you do not justify Mr. Wheelwright's sermon and the petition." Mistress Hutchinson did not answer directly, understanding that either a "yes" or a "no" would be fatal to her cause. A "no" would repudiate her brother-in-law and her most prominent supporters; a "yes" would inextricably tie her to the "seditious writing" that had already led to two banishment orders. Because she was a woman, she had not been involved in the formal protests against John Wheelwright's conviction. Accordingly, she was shielded from prosecution for sedition unless she explicitly aligned herself with the petitioners. That Mistress Hutchinson refused to do. When Governor Winthrop charged lamely that she "did harbour and countenance those that are parties in this faction," she replied that she did so as a "matter of conscience," thereby recasting the question in religious terms.

The two sparred at length over the nature of her relationship to Mr. Wheelwright and the petitioners and whether it constituted an offense against the state, properly subjecting her to legal action. Governor Winthrop insisted that the protesters had broken "the law of God and of the state" and that she had participated in the lawbreaking by "entertaining" them. When she again asked for specifics, the governor fell back on the Fifth Commandment: they, and by implication she, were guilty of "dishonouring of parents." Mistress Hutchinson then demonstrated the argumentative ability that had no doubt regularly awed the attendees at her meetings by posing an incisive hypothetical question to the governor.

What if I honor my parents, she asked, but my parents forbid me to entertain the godly? May I not rightly disobey such an improper order? Her inquiry exposed one of the key problems of the universalized family analogy—the ambiguous relationship between the powers of real and symbolic parents—and it must have given Mr. Winthrop pause. If the parents be "the fathers of the commonwealth" and those entertained be "of another religion," then you do "dishonour your parents and are justly punishable," he instructed his wily antagonist, explaining that "you by countenancing them above others put honor upon them." This gave Mistress Hutchinson the opening to return the debate to the ground she preferred: "I may put honor upon them as the children of God and as they do honor the Lord."

Governor Winthrop was either unwilling or unable to debate her uncontestable assertion that earthly authority must bow to God's greater power. He sputtered in response, "We do not mean to discourse with those of your sex," and then merely restated his position that by "adher[ing]" to the dissidents Anne Hutchinson dishonored the magistrates. After she retorted, "I do acknowledge no such thing," he abruptly abandoned the field and changed the subject. She had won their first exchange.[44]

The focus of the verbal combat then shifted to the meetings at Anne Hutchinson's house. "Why do you keep such a meeting at your house as you do every week upon a set day?" inquired the governor. Mistress Hutchinson initially defended herself by declaring that she did no more than follow Boston custom, since religious meetings were already common when she arrived in town. Although admitting that such gatherings were indeed customary, John Winthrop developed two distinct lines of attack on Mistress Hutchinson's position. He both challenged her scriptural authority for the meetings and tried to differentiate systematically between her meetings and all the others.[45]

Anne Hutchinson cited two passages of scripture to justify the regular gatherings in her home: Titus 2:3-5 and Acts 18:26.[46] In Titus, which described older women as "teachers of honest things," she found "a clear rule . . . that the elder women should instruct the younger." If she was to teach, "then I must have a time wherein I must do it." And the verse in Acts, she pointed out, explained how Priscilla and Aquila "expounded unto [Apollos] the way of God more perfectly." The passage from Titus offered a model of all-female instruction, while that from Acts suggested that a woman might "expound" religion to a man, even one described in a previous verse as "eloquent" and "mightie in the Scriptures." A marginal note in the Geneva Bible, which Anne Hutchinson used, explicitly adopted the interpretation of Acts she intended: "Apollos, a godly and learned man, refuseth not to profit in the schoole of a base and abject handicraftsman, and also of a woman: and so becometh an excellent minister of the Church."

John Winthrop countered by contesting her readings of the two passages. He observed accurately that Titus specified that "elder women must instruct the younger about their business, and to love their husbands and not to make them to clash," questioning whether such instructions in fact constituted the bulk of Mistress Hutchinson's teaching. And he treated her reference to Acts scornfully: "Priscilla with her husband, tooke Apollo[s] home to instruct him privately, therefore Mistris Hutchi[n]son without her husband may teach sixty or eighty."

Furthermore, he countered with two scriptures of his own: I Corinthians 14:34-35 (Paul's instructions to all women to keep silent in church and to wives to ask their husbands for spiritual guidance) and I Timothy 2:12 ("I permit not a woman to teach, neither to usurpe authoritie over the man, but to be in silence"). This time the Geneva Bible's marginal note (on the verse in Timothy) favored the governor's position: if women should teach "in the Congregation," it read, "they should be placed above men, for they should be their masters: which is against Gods ordinance."

The battle of the biblical passages ended in a standoff, with Governor Winthrop refusing to accept Titus and Acts as adequate justification for Mistress Hutchinson's instruction of others, and she refusing to admit that the verses in I Corinthians and I Timothy forbade such activities. The impasse is evident in the trial transcript, with Anne Hutchinson repeatedly insisting that John Winthrop "set me down a rule by which

I may put them away that come unto me," and Mr. Winthrop just as adamantly insisting instead that "you must shew your rule to receive them." The two, in other words, engaged in an inconclusive contest in which each denied the other's basic premise. He argued that the meetings were lawful only if they were supported by a definitive scriptural rule, whereas she contended that they could proceed in the absence of an equally definitive rule against them.

The frustrations felt by both combatants were revealed in sharp exchanges. At one point, the governor asserted that his position should prevail because "I have brought more arguments than you have." At another, his persistent refrain—"you shew us not a rule" for the meetings—elicited from her a sarcastic riposte, "Must I shew my name written therein [the scriptures]?"[47]

The circular discussion of Biblical interpretation was intimately connected to the magistrates' effort to distinguish Mistress Hutchinson's meetings from the other ongoing Boston gatherings. Yet the transcript and *Short Story* disagree on the precise nature of the argument. In the transcript, the point at issue is the presence or absence of men at Anne Hutchinson's meetings. In *Short Story*, by contrast, the dispute revolves around distinctions between *public* and *private*.

The difficulty of interpreting the divergent accounts is further heightened by the fact that this section of the transcript, the document that has heretofore served as the primary basis for analysis, appears faulty. Unless Governor Winthrop wholly fabricated certain exchanges (which seems unlikely, since he knew *Short Story* would be read by people who had attended the trial), the transcript as printed in Thomas Hutchinson's *History* omits some passages and garbles others. Perhaps a page or two of the transcript was lost in the 130 years before it was published, or possibly the family's scribe failed to take notes for a brief period. Portions of Mr. Winthrop's version of the dialogue nevertheless echo surviving parts of the transcript, suggesting that the governor shortened and carefully edited the exchanges on the subject of Anne Hutchinson's meetings.

The discrepancy in the two accounts begins after Anne Hutchinson explains why she instituted her gatherings (as was indicated earlier in this chapter, she said she did so to put a halt to the gossip that she thought such conferences "unlawful"). In both versions, that exchange is followed by Governor Winthrop's attempt to differentiate between the meetings at Mistress Hutchinson's house and other such private religious conferences. In the transcript, he tells her: "your meeting is of another sort for there are sometimes men among you." In *Short Story*, he states instead: "There were private meetings indeed, and still are in many places, of some few neighbours, but not so publick and frequent as yours, and are of use for increase of love, and mutuall edification."

A careful reading of the dialogue that follows in the transcript illuminates the relationship of the two records and suggests why, in his published account of the trial, Winthrop chose to refocus the exchange. To John Winthrop's charge that "there are sometimes men among you," Mistress Hutchinson responds in the transcript with a flat denial: "There was never any man with us." Later, however, in answering an inquiry from Deputy Governor Thomas Dudley, she acknowledges that "there is a meeting of men and women and there is a meeting only for women." Still, she insists that neither she nor any other woman ever taught in the meeting that included men. No magistrate disputed her statement, so it can be assumed to have been accurate—or at least that no one present had sufficient evidence to refute it. To Anne Hutchinson, the absence of men from the meetings in which she "taught" was a key aspect of her defense. Accordingly, she relied more heavily on the passages from Titus than on the verse in Acts as her scriptural authority for hosting the gatherings.

Governor Winthrop might thus appear to have been stymied in his attack on her meetings. Not being able to prove what initially seemed to be his key point, that Mistress Hutchinson had inappropriately instructed men, he thereafter shifted his ground. Although he himself introduced the issue of the sexual composition of her audience, he refuses in the transcript to accept her assessment of its importance: "men and women all is one for that," he asserts.[48] His version of the dialogue in *Short Story*, which does not include that statement, then adopts that conclusion as its silent starting point, ignoring gender and instead raising a set of other issues: the number of attendees, the frequency and presumably the regularity of the meetings, the content of the teachings, and a conceptual separation of public and private.

Because this part of the transcript is either faulty or lacking, it is impossible to assess the precise accuracy of John Winthrop's reporting. Yet it appears likely that he reshaped a dialogue that focused in the first instance on the presence or absence of men into one that took a minor theme of Anne Hutchinson's examination (a public/private distinction) and gave it a prominence not present in the original exchanges. He must have expected to gain clarity from those emendations, but instead demonstrated once again that Filmerian thinkers like John Winthrop and Anne Hutchinson found it impossible to develop mutually exclusive, widely acceptable definitions of *public* and *private*.

In *Short Story*'s account of their dialogue, the governor contends that although under the doctrine in Titus Anne Hutchinson can teach younger women "privately, and upon occasion," the verse does not permit "such set meetings for that purpose." Citing the text of I Timothy, John Winthrop argues that since all concur that Anne Hutchinson could counsel an individual man "in distresse of conscience" who came to her "in private" (the latter phase appears only in *Short Story*, although the same hypothetical situation is also discussed in the transcript), the passage in Timothy proscribed not teaching men per se, but rather "teaching in publick."

In response, Mistress Hutchinson defines *public* differently from Mr. Winthrop. "I teach not in a publick congregation," she insists in *Short Story*, denying that she was what the governor termed "a publick instructor." She spells out her practice in a series of statements omitted from the transcript: "We do no more but read the notes of our teachers Sermons, and then reason of them by searching the Scriptures." She did not summon her listeners, "but if they come to me, I may instruct them." When she instructs them, "they must not take it as it comes from me, but as it comes from the Lord Jesus Christ, and if I tooke upon me a publick Ministery, I should breake a rule, but not in exercising a gift of Prophecy." And, she observes, "if God give me a gift of Prophecy, I may use it."

In the relevant portion of the transcript, by contrast, the word *publick*—which appears repeatedly in *Short Story*'s exposition—is used only once, in Mistress Hutchinson's response to Governor Winthrop's explication of the passage in Titus and his reference to I Corinthians: "I do not conceive but that it is meant for some publick times." To what specifically did that ambiguous "it" allude? There are three possibilities in the scriptural texts: times when older women should instruct the younger to be subject to their husbands; when women should keep silence; and when women should ask their husbands for religious instruction. All three, in fact, make some sense in the context of the exchange, and none of them—Mistress Hutchinson seems to say—applies to her meetings, which, as has already been made clear, she resisted interpreting as public.

John Winthrop tried to prove the contrary—that the gatherings were public—because they then would fall under the proscriptions of I Corinthians and I Timothy and would also be more obviously subject to regulation by civil authorities. The elements that made him deem the gatherings *public* were: first, the number of people involved; second, their "set" meeting times; and third, Anne Hutchinson's pre-eminent role.[49]

She denied the importance of all three. The number of attendees did not matter; instead, the significant fact was that she did not summon them. The regular times were merely a convenience: to follow the rule in Titus to instruct younger women, "I must have a time wherein I must do it." Finally, she minimized her role, admitting that she would "breake a rule" if she assumed "a publick Ministery," but declaring that she had not done so.

How then did Anne Hutchinson define *public?* Two responses to that question are clear: *public* had to include men (any all-female group was by her definition *not* public), and *public* also meant adopting a formal role—teaching regularly, as a clergyman did, "in a publick congregation," or herself engaging in scriptural exegesis rather than simply "exercising a gift of Prophecy." She and the governor thus disagreed on two fundamental aspects of the definition of *public.* First, he applied the word to a large number of people, regardless of their sex, while she insisted that women alone could not compose a public group, no matter how numerous they were. Second, he asserted that her role as the leader of a group was automatically a public activity, whereas she distinguished among different sorts of leadership.

In sum, their disagreement boiled down to this: Mistress Hutchinson defined *public* as what has been called in this book *formal public;* since she did not teach "in a publick congregation" (in other words, one of the established churches that people were compelled by law to attend), she was not engaging in public activity. People came to her meetings voluntarily, and there she sought only to exercise her "gift of Prophecy." Governor Winthrop, by contrast, included what has been called herein the *informal public* in his definition of the broader term: a large group of women meeting at someone's house at regular intervals could endanger the state and therefore be proscribed.

If the usage of *private* in the recorded exchanges is examined instead, the disagreements between the two antagonists are just as evident. In neither the transcript nor *Short Story* does Mistress Hutchinson ever employ the word *private* in the context of the discussion of her meetings. The governor, on the other hand, does use *private.* He explicitly applies it (a word here identifying matters outside the boundaries of public authority) to a conference of a man and a woman about religious subjects and to small, occasional gatherings of women that "teach . . . that which the Apostle commands."

It was imperative that John Winthrop not allow Anne Hutchinson to claim that her meetings were beyond the reach of the state, and therefore even though he acknowledged the validity of the concept *pri-*

vate he sharply restricted the word's meaning. Although Mistress Hutch-inson's argument implied that a claim that her actions were *private* would have two components—it would apply solely to prophetic activity, and it would involve only women—she did not explicitly adopt such a de-fense. Consequently, by implication she rejected Mr. Winthrop's attempt to divide *public* (formal and informal together) from *private* and insisted instead that *public* applied only to civil or religious activity officially sanc-tioned by the state. She thus maintained the unified view of authority that simultaneously characterized Filmerian thinking and served as the basis for her own standing in the community. Yet that same Filmerian worldview rendered her vulnerable, for within its confines she could not develop a rationale that would protect her from prosecution.

The result of these conflicting definitions was confusion. If John Winthrop had hoped to clarify matters and to bolster his position by introducing a public/private distinction into the trial (either at the time or later in print), he failed miserably. Just as the first debate of the trial —whether Anne Hutchinson could be charged with sedition—ended without a satisfactory resolution from Winthrop's perspective, so too did the discussion of the meetings in her house. Governor Winthrop, aban-doning his efforts to persuade her to accede to his interpretations of scripture and to his use of *public* and *private*, raised an entirely new issue: "it will not well stand with the commonwealth that families should be neglected for so many neighbours and dames and so much time spent, we see no rule of God for this." Mistress Hutchinson refused to dignify this self-serving masculinist comment with a direct response, leading Mr. Winthrop again to a remark born of frustration: "We are your judges, and not you ours." After several ineffectual interventions by other mag-istrates, the topic then abruptly shifted once more.

This time Deputy Governor Thomas Dudley took the lead, accusing Mistress Hutchinson of having "disparaged all our ministers in the land that they have preached a covenant of works, and only Mr. Cotton a covenant of grace."[50] Again Anne Hutchinson challenged her judges to offer proof of the charges. As the examination wore on, it became ob-vious that Mr. Dudley was basing his accusation on statements she had reputedly made during her conversation with the Bay Colony ministers the previous December. And that raised yet another public/private issue, one more fully in accord with contemporary usage, but nevertheless posing a dilemma for Governor Winthrop and the other magistrates. Discussion of this subject proceeded in counterpoint with the main topic, which was the determination of the exact content of Mistress

Hutchinson's statements (a dispute already discussed in the previous section of this chapter).

Superficially, the issue was simple: was Mistress Hutchinson's conversation with the clergymen public or private? If the former, they could testify freely about what she had said; if the latter, they could instead be expected to keep her views confidential. As shall be seen, Anne Hutchinson repeatedly insisted that she had treated the meeting at John Cotton's house as a private conference, whereas the governor and deputy governor in particular saw it as public. Most of the clergy, including Mr. Cotton, were troubled by the ambiguity surrounding the conference and had difficulty deciding how to categorize it.

That the very clerics involved in this debate did indeed acknowledge the confidentiality of private conversations with parishioners is demonstrated in two other episodes connected to the Antinomian controversy. As was noted earlier, the Hutchinsonians made a failed attempt to use Mistress Elizabeth Wilson to recruit her husband, after which Mr. Wilson "grew more zealous against them." In his account of the incident, John Cotton added the following comment: "the occasion of the offence was private, and (for a good space) unknown both to mee and the Church." In short, even though the Reverend Wilson had "discerned . . . rottennesse" in his "private conference" with a Hutchinson supporter or two, and even though he thereafter opposed them vigorously, he did not reveal the specific circumstances behind his change of heart "for a good space," precisely because "the offence was private." Likewise, when Mary Dyer gave birth to her "monster" in October 1637 (an incident discussed at length in chapter four), Anne Hutchinson immediately sought the counsel of John Cotton about whether the stillbirth should be publicly recorded. He advised her to ignore the law and to bury the deformed fetus in secret, and he thereafter told no one what had happened. Thus the story came to light only by chance the following March.[51]

The debate at Mistress Hutchinson's civil trial accordingly revolved nearly as much around the question of whether the clergymen could properly testify against her as around the issue of precisely what she had said. And so in this matter too the determination of public and private was of critical importance. Despite the fact that this time the definition of the terms was not at issue—*private* meant "concealed, secret" and *public* meant "widely known"—their application was in dispute, and the outcome of the debate was crucial to Mistress Hutchinson's fate.

As soon as it became evident to Anne Hutchinson that one or more of the ministers with whom she had spoken eleven months earlier had revealed what she had said to Deputy Governor Dudley, she declared that "if one shall come to me in private" to ask for her opinion, "I must either speak false or true in my answer."[52] Governor Winthrop tried to downplay her objection by observing, "it is well discerned to the court that Mrs. Hutchinson can tell when to speak and when to hold her tongue." Anne Hutchinson's response focused sharply on the central issue: "It is one thing for me to come before a public magistracy and there to speak what they would have me to speak and another when a man comes to me in a way of friendship privately there is difference in that."

But just as Mr. Winthrop had earlier insisted that "men and women all is one" in countering her defense of her meetings, he now declared, "what if the matter be all one," thereby rejecting the notion that the context in which she spoke made any difference to the admissibility of the evidence. He did, though, add a dual justification that acknowledged the potential validity of her point in the process of denying it: "This speech was not spoken in a corner but in a public assembly, and though things were spoken in private yet now coming to us, we are to deal with them as public." Thus the governor offered two alternatives to those dissatisfied with his initial statement that the public/private distinction was irrelevant. Either her meeting with the clergy constituted a "public assembly," or, even if the words were originally private, their being brought to the court's attention had made it necessary to consider them to be public.

Of the Bay Colony clergymen who thereafter offered their recollections of the gathering, only the Reverend Hugh Peter appeared as certain as the governor that it was proper for the clerics to reveal the contents of their discussion with Mistress Hutchinson. Mr. Peter was eager to describe the conversation, although even he asked "that we may not be thought to come as informers against the gentlewoman." Others, including her staunch opponents Thomas Shepard and Thomas Weld, indicated that they were "loth to speak in this assembly concerning this gentlewoman" or that they spoke chiefly because it was "desired by the honoured court." They thereby disclosed their uneasiness at the situation in which they found themselves, one that was created by the Reverend Nathaniel Ward, who had been present at the December gathering but was not at the court session. Several months after the meeting, Mr. Ward had written an account of it for Thomas Dudley, who referred to that document while questioning Mistress Hutchinson.[53]

Several participants in the meeting, including Mr. Peter and Anne

Hutchinson, indicated that at first she was reluctant to speak freely with the ministers; she declared that she had opened her mind to them only when urged to do so by the Reverend Peter, who had informed her, "Mrs. Hutchinson we come for plain dealing and telling you our hearts." In response, she recalled, "I said I would deal as plainly as I could." Soon a dispute developed over the question of when in the conversation she had cited a particular line from Proverbs 29:25, "The fear of man is a snare why should I be afraid." Although Hugh Peter denied the importance of the debate, the timing of her remark was in fact crucial: if she cited it early (as the ministers claimed), her action indicated that she knew she was speaking words that might eventually become public; if she cited it later (as she claimed), it meant that at the outset of the meeting she did indeed regard it, as she insisted during the trial, as "a private conference and with a promise of secrecy."[54]

As did the earlier debates, this too proved inconclusive, at least initially. The first day of the trial ended before the difficulty was resolved, and on the morning of November 8 Mistress Hutchinson moved to the attack by asking the clergymen to swear to the truth of their statements. She furthermore challenged the accuracy of their memories by insisting that notes she had consulted over the intervening night (taken at the time of the meeting by the Reverend John Wilson) had shown their testimony to be incorrect in several particulars. John Winthrop, some of the other magistrates, and the clerics at first denied the necessity for an oath, but when the governor asked the General Court if its members were "satisfied" without one, the transcript reveals, "Many say.—We are not satisfied." The reasons for that displeasure were made evident by Mr. Increase Nowell of Charlestown: "I doe hear it affirmed, that things which were spoken in private are carried abroad to the publick and thereupon they do undervalue the ministers of congregations."[55]

The people of Massachusetts, in short, were deeply troubled by the implications of Mistress Hutchinson's contention that her conversation with the ministers had been private. If clergymen could report "abroad" what one person said to them in a private conference, could any residents of the colony expect to have confidential talks with their spiritual advisors in the future? This very point was presumably what bothered the ministers as well. Oaths would resolve the problem: not only would the testimony then be unquestionable, but it would also be clear that the clerics regarded the conversation as public, since part of the testimony given under oath would be their characterization of the circumstances surrounding the meeting.

Yet the ministers proved reluctant to take an oath. As has been

indicated previously in this book, oaths were regarded with great seriousness by all colonists, but that was especially true of the clergy. The
conversation had occurred eleven months earlier; not all of them recalled
the same aspects of it; only some had taken notes, and those that existed,
as John Wilson admitted of his, were "somewhat imperfect." In spite of
their detestation of Mistress Hutchinson, the clerics were understandably
reluctant to risk violating the Third Commandment against taking the
name of God in vain. Recognizing that the case against Mistress Hutchinson would fall apart if the ministers' testimony could be successfully
challenged, she and her supporters alike clamored for an oath. She also
asked that her own witnesses be called to testify. Mr. Thomas Leverett,
Mr. John Coggeshall, and Mr. John Cotton, all of whom had been
present at the December conference with the ministers, then gave accounts that tended to back up Mistress Hutchinson's version of events.
Moreover, the examination deteriorated as the ministers began to question each other's recollection of who had said what, and when.[56]

At this moment, Mistress Anne Hutchinson made what has long
been viewed by scholars as her fatal mistake: she told the General Court
about a series of revelations she had received from God. Most have found
those statements unaccountable, attributing them to fatigue, illness, care-
lessness, or a failure of the caution she had hitherto exhibited. Yet such
interpretations misread the evidence; and historians who have adopted
them have been misled by Governor John Winthrop's deliberate distor-
tion of the dynamic of the trial in his *Short Story*.[57]

The governor's account, not surprisingly, omitted all mention of the
embarrassing dispute about the admissibility of the clergymen's testimony. Instead, he summarized only the arguments over the contents of
the conversation and over her demand that the witnesses against her
swear to the truth of their statements. More significantly, he misrepresented the timing of a key event: the taking of the oath by the clergymen. In *Short Story*, that occurs precisely at this juncture.[58]

According to the transcript, however, the clerics took the oath only
after she had disclosed her revelations and *after* their nature had been
considered at length (a discussion John Winthrop also largely omitted,
in another alteration that conveys a false impression of the trial). In *Short
Story*, Anne Hutchinson's declaration of her revelations appears to be a
desperate move by a defendant whose defense has just collapsed because
of irrefutable sworn testimony. The transcript, however, demonstrates
that the opposite was true: she had emerged from this latest debate essentially unscathed, as she had from the first two in the trial, and she felt
victory within her grasp. Her cause seemed won. Confronted with her

insistence—which was seconded by "many" members of the General Court—that they swear to the truth of their allegations, the primary witnesses against her had fallen into utter disarray. At that moment of triumph, she began to teach the court, as she had long taught the eager listeners in her household. And if she made a fatal mistake, it was that: emboldened by her success, she came to believe that she could convince most of the members of the General Court of the truth of her teachings. In so doing, she in effect abandoned an essential aspect of her defense—that she never instructed men.[59]

"I shall give you the ground of what I know to be true," Anne Hutchinson told her judges. She described scriptures "brought unto" her to enable her to see "which was the clear ministry and which the wrong," informing them "if you do condemn me for speaking what in my conscience I know to be truth I must commit myself unto the Lord." God had spoken to her "by an immediate revelation," by "the voice of his spirit to my soul." She had even foreseen her own current "affliction," for God in a revelation had promised to deliver her, as he had delivered Daniel from the lion's den. "Therefore I desire you to look to it, for you see this scripture fulfilled this day," she declared, and continued:

> You have power over my body but the Lord Jesus hath power over my body and soul, and assure yourselves thus much, you do as much as in you lies to put the Lord Jesus Christ from you, and if you go on in this course you begin you will bring a curse upon you and your posterity, and the mouth of the Lord hath spoken it.[60]

The court then discussed aspects of her revelations in considerable detail. One deputy who had known her in England recalled her being even then "very inquisitive after revelations." At the request of a magistrate, the Reverend John Cotton discoursed learnedly on types of revelations and offered possible interpretations of what she had just said, in the process asking her for several clarifications. Moreover, the court members exchanged opinions on the revelations. John Winthrop, for one, pronounced them "the root of all the mischief" the colony had experienced. Although Mr. Cotton declared that a revelation directly linked to scripture, as hers seemed to be, was "not only lawful but such as christians may receive," few members of the General Court were prepared to entertain seriously the notion that a revelation predicting doom for themselves and their children was legitimate. Their negative reaction to her message was evident in the formal verdict they rendered—quoted at the beginning of this section—which emphasized above all the content of her revelation.[61]

Still, a few diehard supporters did not surrender. Mr. William Coddington, a deputy who would later go into exile in Rhode Island with the Hutchinsons, proposed a new line of defense: "What if she designed to edify her own family in her own meetings may none else be present?" After Governor Winthrop summarily rejected that ploy, Mr. Coddington raised the issue of the validity of the charges and the adequacy of the evidence: "I do not see any clear witness against her," he argued; "here is no law of God that she hath broken nor any law of the country that she hath broke." She had not truly maligned the clergymen, and her revelations were such as those God commonly offered to people who read the scriptures. Moreover, her only accusers were the ministers, "and she spake nothing to them but in private, and I do not know what rule they had to make the thing publick, secret things ought to be spoken in secret and publick things in publick, therefore I think they have broken the rules of God's word."[62]

Mr. Coddington's belated interjection therefore returned the discussion to the nature of Mistress Hutchinson's December 1636 conference with the clergy. His charge that the ministers were violating "the rules of God's word" by reporting what she had said to them "in private," coupled with calls by others for an oath, finally led three of the clergymen, Hugh Peter among them, to swear to the truth of their previous testimony. That sealed Anne Hutchinson's fate.

Once the oaths were on record, all that remained was for Governor Winthrop to ask for a vote (only three members of the court failed to favor conviction) and to pronounce the sentence of banishment, a task he must have performed with considerable pleasure. The court is "satisfied . . . concerning the troublesomeness of her spirit and the danger of her course amongst us," he declared. He told her that "you are banished from out of our jurisdiction as being a woman not fit for our society." Still defiant, Mistress Anne Hutchinson asked, "wherefore I am banished?" Governor John Winthrop dismissed her final query: "Say no more, the court knows wherefore and is satisfied."[63]

THE CHURCH TRIAL AND ITS AFTERMATH

When she faced the Boston church in mid-March 1637/8, Mistress Hutchinson was not the same energetic woman who had so vigorously combated the General Court the preceding November. Weakened by a winter of confinement and noticeably ill, she was incapable of defending herself with a verve comparable to that which she had shown in her civil trial. Repeatedly she wavered under the harsh questioning of church leaders and members, at times admitting her beliefs had been wrong, at others acknowledging "my Expression to be Ironious" but still insisting that "my Judgement was not Ironious."[64]

Early in the trial she again raised a public/private issue, though one that differed from both of those discussed in the General Court. Much of the evidence presented against her came from the clergymen Thomas Weld, Thomas Shepard, and John Eliot, all of whom had conversed with her during the winter since her civil trial. So she inquired,

> By what Rule of the Word whan these Elders shall come to me in private to desire Satisfaction in some poynts, and doe professe in the sight of God that thay did not come to Intrap nor insnare me, and now without speakinge to me and expressinge any Unsatisfaction would come to bringe it publickly unto the Church before thay had privately delt with me?

She declared that she thought their conduct constituted "a Breach of Church Rule, to bringe a Thinge in publicke before thay have delt with me in private."[65]

This time the ministers were not unsettled by her objection. The Reverend Thomas Shepard took the lead in contesting her account of their interactions. He explained that he spoke with her twice, was troubled by her ideas, and "left some Testimony behind me agaynst her Opinions." At first, he said nothing to others about their meeting. Yet he was bothered by "the Flewentness of her Tonge and her Willingness to open herselfe and to divulge her Opinions and to sowe her seed in us that are but highway side and Strayngers to her," worrying about her effect on "them that are mor nearly like to her." So he visited her a third time to try to persuade her to abandon her erroneous ideas. Consequently, he observed, "I do marvell that she will say that we bringe it into publicke before I delt with her in private." Anne Hutchinson had no adequate response to this recital of what all would have seen as acceptable behavior on the part of Mr. Shepard, and thereafter (though she did contest the ministers' interpretations of what she had said) she made no attempt to block the admission of their testimony against her.

Understandably, the examination at the church trial revolved around her theological errors. One in particular assumed a prominent place in the discussions—a failing known as the mortalist heresy. Briefly, the clerics charged that she believed that souls were mortal unless people were saved by Christ and that actual "fleshly bodies" would not be resurrected. Such an opinion not only called into question the prospect of eternal damnation for the unregenerate but also (in the minds of the Bay Colony's clergymen) raised issues involving marriage, the foundation of all social stability. The problem was this: Mistress Hutchinson seemed to be arguing that the promised resurrection of the body was in a measure symbolic, a representation of the union with Christ of the souls of the saved. The Puritan clergy found the implications of such a doctrine to be frightening. The reason lay in their interpretation of a passage that appears three times in the New Testament.[66]

When a group of Sadducees questioned Jesus about the resurrection of the body, he replied, according to Mark 12:25, "when they shall rise againe from the dead, neither men marrie, nor wives are married, but are as the Angels which are in heaven." Consequently, as one of the appalled clergymen pointed out, "after the Resurrection is past, marriage is past." If the resurrection were purely symbolic and occurred when people experienced saving faith, then thereafter the saved would not be married. And with no marriage, "if thear be any Union betwene man and woman it is not by Marriage but in a Way of Communitie." In heaven, the absence of marriage did not present a problem, but if a metaphorical resurrection occurred while people still lived on earth, sexual chaos would result.[67]

To the clergymen who interrogated Anne Hutchinson and attempted to refute her ideas, that "foule, groce, filthye and abominable opinion . . . of the Communitie of Woemen" linked her to the infamous Familists—the Family of Love, radical Protestant followers of the sixteenth-century Dutch mystic Hendrick Niclaes. (The Familists were perfectionists erroneously believed to engage in adulterous sex.) The members of the Boston church and her clerical questioners ignored Mistress Hutchinson's assurance that "if any such practice or Conclusion" could be drawn from her ideas, "I must leave it, for I abhor that Practise." Instead, they insistently accused her of the "dayngerous Error" of advocating the "Communitie of Weomen."[68] Her expressions of admiration for a female mystic from the Diocese of Ely—according to the Reverend Hugh Peter, she "did exceedingly magnifie her to be a Womane of 1000 hardly any like to her"—probably confirmed the clerics in their belief, for Ely was known to have been a hotbed of Familist activity.[69]

In the church trial as in the civil proceedings against her, Anne Hutchinson's influence on other women was of deep concern to the witnesses and judges. The Reverend Thomas Shepard, for example, made it clear that when he alluded to "those mor nearly like to her" than himself, he was referring to women. "She is of a most dayngerous Spirit and likely with her fluent Tounge and forwardnes in Expressions to seduce and draw away many, Espetially simple Weomen of her owne sex," he asserted.[70]

The same theme sounded in the Reverend John Cotton's formal admonition to his parishioner, delivered at the close of the first day of her church trial. Remarkably, even before he addressed Mistress Hutchinson directly, he spoke to the other women of the church, "many of whom I fear have bine too much seduced and led aside by her." He advised them "to looke to your selves and to take heed that you reaceve nothinge for Truth which hath not the stamp of the Word of God from it." Acknowledging that they had "receaved much good from the Conference of this our Sister and by your Converse with her," he nevertheless warned them that "she is but a Woman and many unsound and dayngerous principles are held by her." So, he told them, "doe not harden her in her Way by pittyinge of her or confirminge her in her opinions," but instead "deale faythfully with her soule in baring Witnesse agaynst any unsound Thinge that at any Time she hath held forth to you." His message to the sisters of Boston church was, in short, "Let not the good you have receved from her, make you to receve all for good that comes from her."[71]

Then, turning to Anne Hutchinson, who must have been deeply wounded by the criticism of the clergyman she revered above all others, he again admitted that "you have bine an Instrument of doing some good amongst us." Acknowledging her "sharpe apprehension . . . and abilitie to expres yourselfe in the Cause of God," he even so spoke of the "dayngerous Consequences" of her ideas. "The Evell of your Opinions doth outway all the good of your Doinges," the Reverend Cotton insisted, telling her she had misled many "poor soules" and had perhaps poisoned some of her followers forever. He explicitly aligned himself with those who had asserted that her beliefs about resurrection implied "that filthie Sinne of the Comunitie of Woemen and all promiscuous and filthie cominge togeather of men and Woemen without Distinction or Relation of Marriage." And in what must have been the worst blow of all, he told her "though I have not herd, nayther do I thinke, you have bine unfaythfull to your Husband in his Marriage Covenant, yet that will follow upon it . . . and soe more dayngerous Evells and filthie Unclenes and other sines will followe than you doe now Imagine or conceave."

John Cotton went on to inform his parishioner that "I have often feared the highth of your Spirit and being puft up with your owne parts, and therfore it is just with God thus to abase you." Her ideas, he declared, "set an open Doore to all Epicurisme and Libertinisme; if this be soe than come let us eate and drinke for to morrow we shall dye." He compared her doctrines to "a Gangrene" and "a Leprosie" that "infect farr and near, and will eate out the very Bowells of Religion." Concluding, he returned to his concern about her effects on other women: "take heed how you Leaven the hartes of younge Weomen with such unsound and dayngerous principles, but Labor rather to recover them out of the Snaers as opertunetie shall serve; which you have drawen them to."

The concern about sexual license that permeated the clergymen's examination of Anne Hutchinson was more than incidental. Since in the Filmerian system acquiesence in one role implied acquiescence in all, resistance to one likewise carried the implication of resistance to all others. Mistress Hutchinson had undeniably been, as the Reverend Hugh Peter said in the statement that provides this chapter with its title, "a preacher [rather] than a Hearer." That accordingly indicated that she was not appropriately subordinate in her marriage. Taking the lead in her family's religious affairs, being "a Husband," suggested that she could misbehave in other ways as well. And the most damaging possible misbehavior by a wife, as the criminal statutes demonstrated, was adulterous conduct. With "all things . . . turned upside down among us," as John Winthrop commented, nothing was certain, not even the sexual fidelity of wives to their husbands, the very foundation of state and church. John Cotton admonished female Bostonians, as well as the woman who had been their acknowledged leader, because he feared that Anne Hutchinson's ideas—implying, to his mind, "Communitie of Woemen"— could lead to a breakdown of marriage and thus to the collapse of the entire social structure.[72]

The very language of the charges exposed the nature of the clergyman's thinking about sexual relationships: Anne Hutchinson's doctrine led to the possible violation of "his" marriage covenant, not "hers"; her ideas implied "Communitie of Woemen," not "community of men." Men's need to control their wives' sexuality was crucial. The dangers lay primarily in women's promiscuity, in the prospect that a wife might engage in sexual intercourse with a man (or, worse yet, men) to whom she was not married. But the implications extended beyond adultery to sodomy and other deviant sexual activity. To John Cotton, Familism signified "promiscuous and filthie cominge togeather of men and Woemen without Distinction or Relation of Marriage." If men and women came together "without Distinction," that pointed to the likelihood of same-sex relationships, which were particularly "filthie." And Cotton, as was seen in chapter seven, advocated the death penalty for all practitioners of such crimes.[73]

After the powerfully evocative admonition, what happened next must have seemed anticlimactic to the members of Boston church. A week intervened between the first and second days of Mistress Hutchinson's trial. During that week, John Cotton later recalled, he and the Reverend John Davenport (who resided in Boston that winter, along with the other settlers bound for New Haven) engaged in "serious debate and conference with her." The result, on March 22, 1637/8, was that Mistress Hutchinson (in Mr. Cotton's words) "did openly recant every errour and heresie, and professed her repentance for every miscarriage against Magistrates and Elders, which farre exceeded the expectation of the whole Congregation, which then consisted of many Churches, and strangers." She apologized for her use of scriptures "in Censuringe the Cuntrie" at her civil trial and acknowledged having spoken "rashly and unadvisedly." Yet again she fell back on the explanation she had previously employed—her primary fault was simply misstating her position—and furthermore declared that she had developed the erroneous ideas for which she had been admonished the previous week only after her civil trial. The clergymen greeted both claims with considerable skepticism.[74]

Again Thomas Shepard expressed concern for "all those Weomen and others that have bine led by her and doted soe much upon her and her Opinions." The Reverend John Wilson was especially harsh in his condemnation of his parishioner, terming her "a dayngerous Instrument of the Divell." Accusing her of working not "to set up the Ministry of the Word ayther hear or elce whear, but to set up her selfe and to draw disciples after her," he declared that "the Misgovernment of this Woman's Tounge hath bine a greate Cause" of the disorder in the colony. "If the Botome hath bine unsound and corrupt, than must the Building be such," Mr. Wilson contended as he argued for her excommunication. John Cotton joined in the recommendation that she be separated from the church, and although a few of her supporters advocated another admonition, they were overruled. She was formally excommunicated by the Reverend Wilson, who declared her "from this time forth to be a Hethen and a Publican and soe to be held of all the Bretheren and Sisters of this Congregation."[75]

As Mistress Anne Hutchinson left the Boston church for the last time, a flash of her old defiance returned. Governor Winthrop reported in his *Short Story* that a person standing by the door said to her, "The Lord sanctifie this unto you." She replied, "The Lord judgeth not as man judgeth, better to be cast out of the Church then to deny Christ."[76]

The occasion of Anne Hutchinson's leaving the church, as was already pointed out in chapter four, was also the event that led to the discovery of the birth the preceding October of Mary Dyer's "monster." Subsequently, for the Bay Colony leaders who reflected on the Antinomian controversy, that birth, and another "monster" born to Mistress Hutchinson herself in her Rhode Island exile, came to symbolize the women's erroneous opinions. Governor Winthrop and the clergymen showed an inordinate interest in the physical character of the "monsters," interpreting them as concrete representations of deformed doctrines. Winthrop included detailed descriptions of both "monsters" in his journal and sent letters to correspondents in both England and New England informing them of the births.[77]

The gossip about the births circulated widely. Other colonists wrote and spoke of them, conveying reports that were often garbled but retained the key element of a connection among "monstrous" religious ideas, immoral behavior, and the physical manifestations thereof. One of the most remarkable tales was a version told in London to an undersecretary of state in 1667 by a traveler recently returned from America: "Sir Henry Vane in 1637 went over as Governor to N. England with 2 women, Mrs Dier & Mrs Hutchinson, . . . where he debauched both, & both were delivered of monsters."[78]

Better-informed contemporaries like John Winthrop, Thomas Weld, and Edward Johnson did not make such factual errors, but they were no less impressed with the symbolism of the births. Governor Winthrop commented in his *Short Story* that the Dyers were "of the highest forme of our refined Familists" and that William Dyer was "called before the Church for some of his monstrous opinions" at approximately the same time as his wife experienced her stillbirth. Johnson similarly declared that Mary Dyer's deformed fetus was a sign of the "loud speaking hand of God against them . . . setting forth the view of their monstrous Errors in this prodigious birth." And the Reverend Thomas Weld, the least restrained of all, declared in his introduction to *Short Story* that God had intervened in the Bay Colony "as clearly as if he had pointed with his finger, in causing the two fomenting women in the time of the height of the Opinions to produce out of their wombs, as before they had out of their braines, such monstrous births as no Chronicle (I thinke) hardly ever recorded the like." He concluded: "see how the wisdome of God fitted this judgement to her [Anne Hutchinson's] sinne every way, for looke as she had vented mishapen opinions, so she must bring forth deformed monsters; and as about 30. Opinions in number, so many monsters."[79]

The story of Mistress Hutchinson's "monster" was just one of the pejorative tales told in Massachusetts Bay about the subsequent life of the woman who had so disrupted the colony. John Winthrop inscribed them in his journal; Edward Johnson, the Reverend William Hubbard, and other authors repeated them in their summaries of later events. According to the governor, the Hutchinson exiles, who moved to Aquidneck in Rhode Island, fell into "new errors" and "strange delusions," engaged in "very tumultuous" political activities, and gathered a church "in a very disordered way." Indeed, asserted Mr. Winthrop, they "broached new heresie every year." Edward Johnson regarded the news from Aquidneck as an indication of how the Hutchinsonians "hamper'd themselves fouly with their owne line, and soone shewed the depthlesse ditches that blinde guides lead into." And Hubbard later described their "new errours" as "the issue of their depraved minds, more misshapen than those monsters, which were credibly reported to be born of the bodies of some of them."[80]

One of the tales that spread in Massachusetts even raised the specter of witchcraft. The midwife Jane Hawkins, known to John Winthrop as a "rank familist" and a close ally of Mistress Hutchinson, was suspected of witchcraft, in part because she gave young women "oil of mandrakes and other stuff to cause conception." Serious inquiry, reported the Reverend Cotton, could prove "no familiarity with the Devill" on her part, but she was nevertheless ordered to leave the Bay Colony by May 1638, and in spite of numerous petitions submitted on her behalf over the next two decades, was never allowed to return for more than a brief visit.[81] Anne Hutchinson's association with New England's first suspected witch led John Winthrop to speculate in 1640 that she herself might have been in league with the devil, especially because in Rhode Island she was able to convert to her beliefs Mr. William Collins, a young minister with a good reputation. Although Mr. Collins warned a friend to beware of Mistress Hutchinson's wiles, Mr. Winthrop recorded in his journal, he himself not only fell prey to her "heresies" but also joined the family by marrying her daughter. Such incidents, the governor wrote, "gave cause of suspicion of witchcraft."[82]

Given the Massachusetts magistrates' expressed detestation of the Hutchinson exiles, it is perhaps not surprising that they refused "to have any treaty with them." The Boston church did make one attempt, approximately a year after their departure, to inquire whether the apostates were interested in rejoining the church, but the civil authorities deliberately severed all contact with the exiles. Yet when individual male followers of Anne Hutchinson acknowledged their remorse, the magistrates proved willing to listen. Mr. William Aspinwall, Mr. John Underhill, and even Mr. John Wheelwright eventually made their peace with the Massachusetts government and were allowed to return.[83]

More strikingly still, the Bay Colony—and John Winthrop personally—dealt very differently with Roger Williams than with his fellow Rhode Island exile Anne Hutchinson. For years Williams, who was expelled from the Bay in 1635 for "dyvers newe & dangerous opinions, against the aucthoritie of magistrates," carried on a cordial correspondence with John Winthrop. Roger Williams even remarked to Mr. Winthrop in 1638 that "notwithstanding our differences concerning the worship of God . . . you have bene always pleased lovingly to answer my boldnes in civill things." Although Williams himself fell under a Hutchinsonian-inspired influence (through the vehicle of Mistress Hutchinson's Baptist sister, Katherine Scott), that did not interrupt the regular communications between the two men. Clearly, John Winthrop was comfortable dealing with a dissident clergyman; a dissident high-status woman was another matter entirely.[84]

The Bay Colony leaders offered their final commentary on Mistress Hutchinson in reporting her death. She had moved with her family to New Netherland and was killed there by Indians in September 1643, along with fifteen others, including Mr. William Collins. John Winthrop reported the news dispassionately; Edward Johnson noted the irony in the fact that although she claimed "strange Revelations" she could not see her own approaching peril; and Thomas Weld saw providence in her fate, as in so much else: "therefore Gods hand is the more apparently seene herein, to pick out this wofull woman, to make her and those belonging to her, an unheard of heavie example of their [the Indians'] cruelty above al others."[85]

Yet these were not the only verdicts on Mistress Hutchinson's death. Other Rhode Islanders also exiled from Massachusetts for their religious beliefs located the guilty not among the dead but the living. "Who was the cause of Mrs. Hutchinson, her departure from amongst you? was it voluntary?" asked Randall Holden rhetorically of the Bay Colony's General Court. He asserted that "no less are you the original of her removal" from Rhode Island, because she feared that the long arm of the vengeful Bay authorities would reach her even there. "We say their death is causeless," Holden declared, "for we have heard them affirm, that they would never heave up a hand, no, nor move a tongue against any that persecuted or troubled them." The "effusion of blood" lay on the hands of the Massachusetts magistrates. As had Mistress Hutchinson, he warned them that unless they repented they would meet a terrible fate.[86]

THE ANTINOMIAN CONTROVERSY was above all a crisis in the system of gendered power. Mistress Anne Hutchinson's initial success, the content of her ideas, and her ultimate fate were all intricately linked to her identity as a symbolic mother in a Filmerian society.

She promulgated her unorthodox teachings and gained her first following within the women's childbirth community, a context in which her position as a high-ranking woman with medical skills gave her regular access to a respectful and receptive female audience. Although she was unique in employing that forum for religious proselytizing, much evidence drawn from court cases throughout the colonies (especially those involving Mistress Ann Johnson Dorrington and Mistress Alice Tilly) suggests that high-status women with knowledge of midwifery occupied places of particular prominence within the female community. Mistress Hutchinson used a setting from which men were excluded and of which they were wholly ignorant to recruit a large number of faithful followers.

Although John Winthrop and her other opponents subsequently lamented their own failure to take firm steps to suppress her and her followers at an early stage, in fact they had little opportunity to move against her effectively. By the time the men realized what had been going on, first in the gossipings, then in the formal meetings at her house, it was already too late. And indeed that was precisely why the Hutchinsonians' challenge to the survival of Bay Colony orthodoxy proved to be more serious than that posed by any other dissident group in the seventeenth century. The other dissenters were men, whom the authorities knew how to control. Men could be convicted of sedition, disarmed, and disfranchised, as were Anne Hutchinson's male supporters. But silencing women, especially a high-ranking fictive widow with a firm base in the women's community, was far more difficult. As John Winthrop discovered to his dismay, her indirect relationship to the state made it difficult to use secular power against her. Mistress Anne Hutchinson stood outside the community of men and consequently could not be controlled by it as readily as could male dissenters.

Moreover, Mistress Hutchinson's ideas, because they made the requirements for salvation understandable and directly accessible to all, were particularly appealing to women, who were systematically denied education and formal training in theology. Under the doctrines of orthodox Massachusetts Puritanism, lay members of the churches, though encouraged to read their Bibles and to engage in serious religious reflection, were to look to their pastors and teachers for spiritual guidance. Anne Hutchinson's reliance on revelations, on an individual believer's direct relationship to God, did more than merely circumvent ministerial authority, it also fundamentally questioned the clergy's standing. That was evident in the insults Bay Colony clerics experienced during the months of the Antinomians' ascendancy, recorded by the Reverend Thomas Weld. These men, accustomed to being accorded the greatest respect, were treated with "contempt"; said to be "ignorant," "grossely Popish," or "under a Covenant of workes"; had "dung cast on their faces"; and were described as "no better then Legall Preachers, *Baals* Priests, Popish Factors, Scribes, Pharisees, and Opposers of Christ."[87] No wonder John Winthrop pronounced the situation "desperate."

Yet if Anne Hutchinson's success resulted largely from the combination of her high rank and her identity as a woman, so too did her eventual downfall. Unlike her mentor John Cotton and even (eventually) her brother-in-law John Wheelwright, she failed to recognize the necessity of conforming to a consensus reached in the community of men. As was the case with the other high-status New England women who would follow in her footsteps—Mistress Ann Hibbens, Mistress Anne Eaton, Mistress Lucy Brewster, and Mistress Moore—her status was both an asset and a liability. Had she, or they, been of ordinary rank, no one would have paid much attention to them; yet once they drew the authorities' ire, none had a previous experience of enforced conformity to an established male consensus to instruct them in how to avoid disaster.

The New Englanders, along with their Chesapeake counterpart, Mistress Margaret Brent, achieved their powerful position in their communities because of their standing as Filmerian mothers who were also widows or fictive widows, but the fates of all the women showed the limitations of the system of gendered power. It offered certain women the short-term potential for wielding authority while at the same time in the long run depriving them of its reality. Just as John Cotton and the male Bay Colony leaders applauded Mistress Hutchinson's teaching when it evidently worked to uphold their vision of orthodoxy but suppressed it when she challenged their own standing, so too Maryland's rulers relied on Mistress Margaret Brent to repair the colony's finances but deprived her of the "vote and voyce allso" that would have granted her full equality in their ranks. Ultimately, then, the gender identity that opened the door for women in the Filmerian system also closed it.

Conclusion

FROM A VANTAGE POINT late in the twentieth century, the Filmerian Anglo-America of the early and middle years of the seventeenth century seems alien indeed. The context that produced a female religious leader who nearly tore a colony apart, a female financier who saved a second colony from dissolution, a group of four women whose gossip session elicited a lengthy criminal prosecution, and a person officially designated as both male and female is inexplicable in modern terms. An emphasis on the capacity of better or older documentation to provide legitimacy for government perhaps appears not quite so distinctive at a time when arguments rage about the "original intent" of the framers of the Constitution. Yet the seventeenth-century insistence that proper authority in the long run rests not on the consent of the people but rather on a grant of power from a symbolic father, coupled with beliefs that state and family were analogous and that society was appropriately organized in a rigidly hierarchical fashion, points up the conceptual gulf that separates the world of the first English settlers in North America from our own.

Only by understanding the Filmerian worldview that infused those settlers' thinking can we fully comprehend a series of superficially familiar events. The demise of Plymouth's original communal plan, the political disputes that continually wracked Maryland and Virginia, Massachusetts Bay's successful takeovers of New Hampshire and Maine: all, like the events identified above, are best understood within the context of a unified theory of power. That a combination of demographic and religious differences caused such a manner of thinking to take less firm root in the Chesapeake than in New England explains the dramatically divergent patterns of criminal prosecution in the two regions. Northern authorities were both more likely to intrude into the functioning of individual families and less likely to overlook instances of sexual misconduct than were Chesapeake officials. The diverse records of law enforcement in the two regions arose not from settlers' differing behavior but rather from the distinctive concerns of their leaders—in New England, Filmerian thinking insisted that orderly families were prerequisites to a properly organized society; in the Chesapeake, demography made the prevalence of such normative families an impossibility and directed civil officials' attention instead to violations of political order.

Since in a Filmerian world the family governor occupied the lowest rung of the political ladder, events inside the seventeenth-century household took on societal significance. In New England, a male household head who wielded his authority inappropriately, an undeferential wife, a rebellious child or servant could all face prosecution for misbehavior. Even in the Chesapeake a particularly egregious violation of the rules governing intrafamilial conduct could draw the wrath of neighbors or judges. Under these circumstances, what was *public*—and thus properly subject to regulation by the community—was difficult to distinguish from what was *private*—and thus exempt from such supervision. Accordingly, definitional contests over these terms emerge repeatedly from seventeenth-century records. Were Mistress Anne Hutchinson's religious meetings, and her conversation with a group of clergymen, public or private? Should family governors be able to shield certain misconduct within their households from public scrutiny? Should Mistress Anne Eaton's misdeeds (and those of other offending church members) be discussed in public, before a large congregation, or in private, in front of church elders only?

The arguments reached a peak of frequency and acrimony when women were their primary objects. The public/private differential applied clearly only in ungendered settings (when the words meant "widely known"/"secret") or when the household activities of men holding political or religious office were at issue. Matters were far less readily resolved when the distinction pertained to women. To be sure, females were for the most part excluded from participation in the formal public—but not always, as the experience of Mistress Margaret Brent demonstrates. Within the informal public, they were expected to defer to men—but not always, as is shown by the actions of female Virginians in the case of T Hall and by the Boston women's petition campaign on behalf of Mistress Alice Tilly. Yet regardless of the ambiguities surrounding their participation in either aspect of the public, there was no ambiguity with respect to women's relationship with the private. Neither they nor men applied the word *private* to themselves. Mistress Hutchinson and the New Haven gossiping women, including Mistress Eaton at her church trial, failed to rely on its potential protections, and men like Governor John Winthrop and the Reverend John Davenport refused to acknowledge that women had any preemptive claim to a realm deemed *private*.

Not by coincidence did many of the most contentious incidents in the seventeenth-century colonies revolve around high-status widows or fictive widows. Under the theory of unified power, such women occupied an especially problematic position in the social hierarchy. Subject to no one man yet simultaneously commanding the deference of lower-ranking male and female colonists, such women as Mistress Anne Hutchinson and Mistress Margaret Brent exposed the logical contradictions in Filmerian thinking—a conceptualization of power that on the one hand glorified the power of fathers and on the other offered mothers, symbolic and real, unparalleled access to the wielding of legitimate authority. That high-ranking seventeenth-century women therefore confronted simultaneous opportunities and perils is not surprising. Under the proper conditions, such as those involving Mistress Brent, their status could be a major asset to themselves and their communities. Under other circumstances, such as those confronting Mistress Ann Hibbens in 1641 or Mistress Lucy Brewster in 1646, their rank could blind them to the special dangers they faced (Mistress Hibbens) or make them an obvious target for the authorities (Mistress Brewster).

It is also not coincidental that most such incidents occurred in New England and within two decades of the colonies' founding. Before the American polities were firmly established, symbolic mothers, like other recognized leaders of English society, helped to fill the perceived void at the top of colonial hierarchies. When lines of authority had not yet been unambiguously drawn, high-status women could contend for a share of social and (perhaps) political power. But once each colony had established its independent existence and its right to at least partial self-governance, and once provincial leaders had successfully advanced their own claims to the legitimate exercise of power, then even in the Filmerian societies high-ranking widows and fictive widows rarely presented significant challenges to existing structures. Still, the disrupted conditions in the first decades of English settlement in America revealed the fundamental paradox of the Filmerian conception of society: an intellectual scheme based on the Fifth Commandment and designed to enhance the power of "fathers" could not exclude high-status independent women from the ranks of potential wielders of gendered power.[1]

Embedded in the day-to-day functioning of the Filmerian system were the seeds of its own destruction. Egalitarian interactions within a myriad of Anglo-American communities belied the theoretical emphasis on hierarchy and offered an alternative model for society, one that rested on consensus among neighbors and a mutual acceptance of norms rather than on the imposition of values from above. In both same-sex and mixed-sex groups, colonists negotiated their differences and learned to acquiesce in communal judgments. Because of its unstable religious environment and imbalanced sex ratio, the Chesapeake in particular fostered the development of a nascent Lockean world that built upon the relationships of the informal public. That Maryland had no established church and Virginia only an enfeebled one, and that both colonies contained many households aberrant by English standards, together accounted for the Chesapeake's style of law enforcement. By creating a de facto zone of privacy within the household, the actions of the seventeenth-century Chesapeake judicial system presaged the eighteenth-century's more laissez-faire attitude toward familial disorder, including an increasing lack of attention to such crimes as premarital fornication and infanticide.[2]

Indeed, by the middle of the eighteenth century, the Filmerian world that has been examined in this volume had largely disappeared. Its rhetoric lingered, but with a sexual transformation that emphasized maternal care rather than paternal power: "The public is, as it were, one great family," wrote an American essayist in 1783; "we are all children of one common mother, our country; she gave us all our birth, nursed our tender years, and supports our manhood." Such language drew on the familial analogy common a century and a half earlier, but with significant changes signaling the end of authoritarian thinking. A parent who gave birth, nursed "tender" young, and "supported" adult sons in no way compared to the Filmerian father who coldheartedly arranged for the death or disinheritance of disobedient offspring.[3]

So too eighteenth-century writers found it easier to distinguish public and private than did their seventeenth-century forebears. Letters written during the American Revolution, especially by members of the extended Adams family, referred unselfconsciously to public/private distinctions and relationships in equal measure. "Private and publick Vices, though not always apparently, are in Reality . . . nearly connected," Samuel Adams told James Warren in 1775. Similarly, John Adams informed James Warren's wife, Mercy, the following year that "public Virtue cannot exist in a Nation without private, and public Virtue is the only Foundation of Republics." Such usage simultaneously linked and separated the public and the private, nominally connecting two qualities that were nevertheless definitively distinguished by the authors' choice of words.[4]

Just as public/private distinctions in general had become both clearer and more common by the revolutionary era, the private also had come to be more appropriately associated with women, primarily through the vehicle of the family. Thus in 1788 Dr. Benjamin Rush observed that "it is in private families only that society is innocent or improving. Here manners are usually kept within the bounds of decency by the company of females, who generally compose a part of all private families." Even more explicit were John Adams's remarks on the death of his mother-in-law in 1775. "Were not her Talents, and Virtues too much confined, to private, social and domestic Life"? he asked his wife, contrasting the deceased's self-imposed limits to the life he preferred, which required "a very extensive Connection with society at large, and the great Interest of the public."[5]

Rush and Adams, republicans in a Lockean mold, thus not only accepted Locke's distinction between family and state, they also in the process tied women explicitly to the family. Even more important, they designated the life of women in the family as, in some sense, *private*. By so doing, they revealed their distance from the Filmerian mindset that had long failed to make precisely that connection—indeed, had resisted creating such a bond, even when (as in Mistress Anne Hutchinson's defense of her meetings) the link had considerable persuasive potential.

How did the Anglo-American Filmerian world come to be replaced by one organized along Lockean lines? The answer to that key question is not clear and remains to be addressed.[6] But replaced it most definitely was. By the era of the American Revolution, the unified world of gendered power had been supplanted by a theory of dichotomous power, by pervasive public/private distinctions, and by a world in which all women were categorically excluded from the public. Not until nineteenth-century women began to challenge that exclusion vigorously would female Americans once again be conceptualized as a part of the public.

Author's Note

As I was completing the final manuscript for this book, I discovered to my astonishment that I am descended from John Wheelwright and his wife, Mary Hutchinson, through their daughter, Rebecca Wheelwright Maverick Bradbury, and my paternal grandmother, Jessie Kirk Norton. Mistress Anne Hutchinson is therefore my aunt by marriage, eleven generations removed. I hope I have done her justice; and I rededicate this book to the memory of Anne Hutchinson, a courageous foremother in more ways than I had hitherto realized.

Appendix: Data and Methodology

This study draws upon a database created for it by a small army of Cornell graduate and undergraduate students, who worked with me for a decade coding civil and criminal cases heard in the courts of seventeenth-century Anglo-America. The result is a main database with 4,878 cases from New England and 3,170 from the Chesapeake. With rare exceptions, only published materials were coded, because so many records are available in print that in most instances it seemed unnecessary to consult unpublished documents. Published records were coded for the main database from the following jurisdictions: Maryland (all records included in the *Archives of Maryland* series, along with the separately produced volume of Prince George's County records), Virginia (Accomack-Northampton County and the surviving early General Court records), New Haven Colony and town, Maine, Plymouth Colony, the Massachusetts Bay General Court (including the early Court of Assistants records), and Suffolk and Essex counties, Massachusetts (for Essex County, only criminal and defamation cases were coded after 1656). The bulk of the coded records fall into the three decades between 1640 and 1670.

In addition, two supplementary databases focus solely on defamation cases, both civil and criminal. The first, with 1,158 entries, mirrors the main database but encompasses all defamation suits and prosecutions located during the course of the research, including cases heard in jurisdictions that were not coded for the main database. Primarily places for which only scattered records have been published, such jurisdictions include New Hampshire, Rhode Island, Connecticut, Lower Norfolk County (Virginia), and the New Amsterdam city court. The second contains only those cases in which the nature of the slanderous statement was identified; these number 717. This database links the content of defamatory words to the sex and status of the parties involved and to the outcome of the case.

The main database was created by coding all cases in which women appeared in any capacity—as plaintiffs or civil defendants, witnesses, criminal defendants, or victims of a crime. Then, for most jurisdictions and types of legal actions, a randomly selected, approximately equal number of civil and criminal cases with male participants alone was coded for comparative purposes. (The exception is that all criminal prosecutions in the Chesapeake were coded in order to produce an adequately sized data set.) I chose this method rather than sampling all cases because women tend to appear infrequently in the court records, for reasons having to do with their status under the common law. I wanted to accomplish two goals that would have been impossible with universal random sampling: first, to have a sufficient body of data to justify generalizations about the relationships of gender and status in a wide variety of circumstances; and second, to follow the courtroom experiences of specific women over time. The drawback is that the New England data and the Chesapeake civil-case data can be analyzed only in distinct sets defined by sex of the participants, because the figures for men and women are not comparably derived (men being represented by a sample, whereas all cases with female participants are included).

Great care was taken in coding to identify a group of women I have termed "passive participants." These were women (usually wives, occasionally daughters, rarely widows) who did not file or respond to civil lawsuits independently, but whose male relatives appeared for them—not as their attorneys but rather as plaintiffs or defendants of record, because of custom or common-law procedures. An alternate mode of court appearance for wives was as a part of what I call a "legal couple"—that is, an instance in which a woman's husband joined her in a lawsuit to fulfill the requirement of the common law that a married woman not sue or be sued in her own name. A woman was coded as a "passive participant" or part of a "legal couple" only when it was evident from the case record that the matter at issue involved her alone, not her husband or the two of them as a couple. Examples of such cases include slander suits in which only the wife was a target or a defamer, but in which her husband rather than, or in addition to, herself was named as a litigant; or cases in which a wife was suing or being sued for something that happened before her current marriage. Most commonly, such lawsuits involved debts owed to or by a previous husband.

Coding categories focused on the gender and status of all participants in civil and criminal cases, including male and female witnesses as well as litigants, attorneys, and criminal defendants. The cases were analyzed using the Statistical Package for the Social Sciences. Throughout the project I made frequent use of Cornell computer consultants, both in the central offices of Cornell Information Technologies and, especially, the consultants for the History Department—first Steve Jackson, then Karel Sedlacek. They patiently answered a myriad of inquiries with good humor and wisdom, and I thank them all most sincerely.

In reproducing seventeenth-century language in quotations, I have retained the creative and often eccentric spelling of the original documents. I have nevertheless expanded common abbreviations—such as "dept" (deponent), "ct" (court), "wch" (which), "p" (pro-, per-, pre-), and "wth" (with)—have lowered superscript letters, and have changed "u" to "v" and "i" to "j," or vice versa. I have also silently transcribed the thorn, a letter no longer used in English, as its modern equivalent, "th" (rather than "y," as it is sometimes rendered). Where the meaning of specific words or phrases is obscure, I have added bracketed clarifications. To adhere as closely as possible to contemporary seventeenth-century materials, all biblical quotations contained herein are from the Geneva Bible, which was commonly used by seventeenth-century Protestants.

Likewise, all dates are "Old Style," based on the Julian calendar, which was employed in the English colonies until 1752, although that calendar had been abandoned in 1582 in Catholic countries in favor of the more accurate "New Style" Gregorian calendar. During the period covered in this book, the Julian calendar was ten days out of phase with the sun, and some modern authorities accordingly convert O.S. to N.S. by adding ten days to the dates recorded in seventeenth-century sources, a procedure not adopted herein. (By the time Britain and its colonies changed to N.S. in 1752, eleven days had to be added.) Because the first day of the year in Old Style reckoning was March 25, when a seventeenth-century court clerk wrote the date March 12, 1658, he meant the day a twentieth-century person would call March 12, 1659. Thus all dates between January 1 and March 24 are presented in this book in dual format: March 12, 1658/9.

Abbreviations Used in the Notes

AN Ct Recs — I: Susie M. Ames, ed., *County Court Records of Accomack-Northampton, Virginia, 1632–1640 (American Legal Records, VII)*. Washington, D.C.: American Historical Association, 1954.
II: Susie M. Ames, ed., *County Court Records of Accomack-Northampton, Virginia, 1640–1645*. Charlottesville: University Press of Virginia, 1973.

BOL — "The Body of Liberties (1641)," *MHS Colls*, 3d ser., VIII (1843), 216–37.

Conn Col Recs — J. Hammond Trumbull and Charles J. Hoadly, eds., *The Public Records of the Colony of Connecticut, 1636–1776*. Hartford, Conn.: Lockwood & Brainard, 1850–90.

CSM Pubs — *Publications of the Colonial Society of Massachusetts*.

Ct Assts Recs — John A. Noble, ed., *Records of the Court of Assistants of the Colony of the Massachusetts Bay 1630–1692*. Boston, Mass.: Suffolk County, 1901–28.

EC Ct Recs — George Francis Dow, ed., *Records and Files of the Quarterly Courts of Essex County Massachusetts*. Salem, Mass.: Essex Institute, 1911–21.

JWJ — James Kendall Hosmer, ed., *Winthrop's Journal "History of New England" 1630–1649*. New York: Charles Scribner's Sons, 1908.

L&L — Thomas G. Barnes, ed., *The Book of the General Lawes and Libertyes Concerning the Inhabitants of the Massachusets* (San Marino, Cal.: Huntington Library, 1975).

Mass Col Recs — Nathaniel B. Shurtleff, ed., *Records of the Governor and Company of the Massachusetts Bay in New England, 1628–1674*. Boston, Mass.: White, 1853–54.

Md Archs — William Hand Browne et al., eds., *Archives of Maryland*. Baltimore: Maryland Historical Society, 1883–1972.

Me Ct Recs — Charles Thornton Libby and Robert E. Moody, eds., *Province and Court Records of Maine*. Portland: Maine Historical Society, 1928–47.

MHS Colls — *Collections of the Massachusetts Historical Society*.

MHS Procs — *Proceedings of the Massachusetts Historical Society*.

New Ams Ct Recs — Berthold Fernow, ed., *The Records of New Amsterdam from 1653 to 1674 Anno Domini*. New York: Knickerbocker Press, 1897.

NH Ct Recs, XL — Otis Hammond, ed., *New Hampshire Court Records 1640–1692*. *New Hampshire State Papers Series*, 40 (1943).

NHCP Recs	I: Charles J. Hoadly, ed., *Records of the Colony and Plantation of New Haven, 1638–1649*. Hartford, Conn.: Case, Lockwood, 1857. II: Charles J. Hoadly, ed., *Records of the Colony or Jurisdiction of New Haven, 1653 to the Union*. Hartford, Conn.: Case, Lockwood, 1858.
NHT Recs	Franklin B. Dexter, ed., *Ancient Town Records: New Haven Town Records, 1649–1684*. New Haven, Conn.: New Haven Colony Historical Society, 1917, 1919.
NPCL	William Brigham, ed., *The Compact with the Charter and Laws of the Colony of New Plymouth*. Boston, Mass.: Button and Wentworth, 1836.
OED	*Oxford English Dictionary*. Oxford: Oxford University Press, 2d ed., 1991.
Plymouth Col Recs	Nathaniel B. Shurtleff and David Pulsifer, eds., *Records of the Colony of New Plymouth in New England*. Boston, Mass.: White, 1855–61.
Pynchon Ct Rec	Joseph H. Smith, ed., *Colonial Justice in Western Massachusetts (1639–1702): The Pynchon Court Record*. Cambridge, Mass.: Harvard University Press, 1961.
RI Col Recs	John Russell Bartlett, ed., *Records of the Colony of Rhode Island and Providence Plantations*. Providence, R.I.: A. Crawford Greene, 1856–65.
SAL	William W. Hening, ed., *The Statutes at Large: Being a Collection of all the Laws of Virginia, from the First Session of the Legislature, in the Year 1619*. New York: the author, 1823.
Suffolk Ct Recs	Samuel Eliot Morison, ed., *Records of the Suffolk County Court 1671–1680*. (*CSM Pubs*, 29, 30). Boston: Colonial Society of Massachusetts, 1933.
Va Ct Recs	H. R. MacIlwaine, ed., *Minutes of the Council and General Court of Colonial Virginia 1622–1632, 1670–1676*. Richmond: Virginia State Library, 1924.
WP	*Winthrop Papers, 1498–1649*. Boston: Massachusetts Historical Society, 1929–47.

Notes

INTRODUCTION

1. "A Relation or Journal of a Plantation Settled at Plymouth in New England, and Proceedings Thereof: First Printed in 1622," *MHS Colls*, 1st ser., VIII (1802), 205.

2. William Hubbard, *History of New England from the Discovery to 1680, MHS Colls*, 2d ser., V (1815), I, 62. That the government established by the Mayflower Compact ended up administering Plymouth Colony until it was absorbed into Massachusetts Bay in 1692 was not the fault of the settlers; they tried repeatedly but unsuccessfully to acquire the charter that would legitimize their rule in traditional terms. See Charles M. Andrews, *The Colonial Period of American History* (New Haven, Conn.: Yale University Press, 1934), I, 290–96.

3. See, among other works, Peter Gay, *The Enlightenment: An Interpretation*, 2 vols. (New York: Alfred A. Knopf, 1966, 1969); Michael P. Winship, "A Theater of God's Judgments: Providentialism and Intellectual Change in Early Massachusetts Orthodoxy" (unpub. Ph.D. diss., Cornell University, 1992); and Richard Godbeer, *The Devil's Dominion: Magic and Religion in Early New England* (New York: Cambridge University Press, 1992).

4. The fullest expositions of Filmer's theory are Gordon J. Schochet, *Patriarchalism in Political Thought: The Authoritarian Family and Political Speculation and Attitudes Especially in Seventeenth-Century England* (New York: Basic Books, 1975) and James Daly, *Sir Robert Filmer and English Political Thought* (Toronto: University of Toronto Press, 1979). See also Alan Craig Houston, *Algernon Sidney and the Republican Heritage in England and America* (Princeton, N.J.: Princeton University Press, 1991), chapter 2, for an assessment of Schochet and Daly. (I owe this reference to Rachel Weil.)

5. One of the few other scholars who has examined the implications of Filmerian thought for the development of American society, Melvin Yazawa, in *From Colonies to Commonwealth: Familial Ideology and the Beginnings of the American Republic* (Baltimore, Md.: The Johns Hopkins University Press, 1985), ignored both gender issues and the Chesapeake region, focusing exclusively on men in New England. Thus our approaches to the subject differ substantially. Because the words "patriarch" and "patriarchal" were not applied to non-biblical subjects before the nineteenth century, and because common twentieth-century feminist usage is confusing ("patriarchal" has been used to refer to both "the power of fathers over families" and "the power of men over women"), I will avoid employing "patriarch" and its variants in this book in the interest of achieving greater precision and adhering to terminology appropriate to the seventeenth century. (*OED*, q.v. "patriarch," "patriarchal.")

6. See J. P. Sommerville, *Politics and Ideology in England 1603–1640* (London: Longman, 1986) on John Locke's precursors, and Schochet, *Patriarchalism*, passim, for paternalistic thinkers who differed in specifics from Filmer. Although Filmer's best-known work, *Patriarcha*, was also published late in the century, several of his shorter essays appeared in the 1640s and 1650s.

7. The most thorough and influential examination of the concept of gender as it applies to historical works is Joan W. Scott, *Gender and the Politics of History* (New York: Columbia University Press, 1988). Feminist scholars have increasingly questioned the utility of a rigid distinction between "biological" sex and "cultural" gender, arguing that sex is also culturally constructed. Although agreeing with such caveats, I find the precision of the two terms too useful to discard completely. See Gisela Bock, "Women's History and Gender History:

Aspects of an International Debate," *Gender & History*, I (1989), 7–30, esp. 10–15, and Bock, "Challenging Dichotomies: Perspectives on Women's History," in Karen Offen et al., eds., *Writing Women's History: International Perspectives* (Bloomington: Indiana University Press, 1991), 1–23, esp. 7–9. Insightful works by anthropologists include Peggy Reeves Sanday, *Female Power and Male Dominance: On the Origins of Sexual Inequality* (New York: Cambridge University Press, 1981); Carol MacCormack and Marilyn Strathern, eds., *Nature, Culture, and Gender* (New York: Cambridge University Press, 1980); Sherry B. Ortner and Harriet Whitehead, eds., *Sexual Meanings: The Cultural Construction of Gender and Sexuality* (New York: Cambridge University Press, 1981); and Stephanie Coontz and Peta Henderson, eds., *Women's Work, Men's Property: The Origins of Gender and Class* (London: Verso, 1986). The philosopher Linda Nicholson addresses some of the same issues in *Gender and History: The Limits of Social Theory in the Age of the Family* (New York: Columbia University Press, 1986). See also Nicholson's recent essay, "Interpreting *Gender*," *Signs*, XX (1994–95), 79–105.

8. J. Franklin Jameson, ed., *Johnson's Wonder-Working Providence 1628–1651* (New York: Charles Scribner's Sons, 1910), 262; Thomas Lechford, "Plain-Dealing: or, Newes from New-England (London, 1642)," *MHS Colls*, 3d ser., III (1833), 103. A book exploring such contrasts is James Axtell, ed., *The Indian Peoples of Eastern America: A Documentary History of the Sexes* (New York: Oxford University Press, 1981).

9. Scott, *Gender and Politics of History*, 42. See also Joan Kelly's essay "The Social Relationship of the Sexes" in her *Women, History, and Theory* (Chicago: University of Chicago Press, 1984). Research for this book was already in progress when Scott's essay "Gender: A Useful Category of Historical Analysis" (reprinted in *Gender and Politics of History*) first appeared in the *American Historical Review* in 1986. A recent book exploring some of these issues in the contemporary United States is Sandra Lipsitz Bem, *The Lenses of Gender: Transforming the Debate on Sexual Inequality* (New Haven, Conn.: Yale University Press, 1993).

10. George Alsop, "A Character of the Province of Mary-land, 1666," in Clayton Colman Hall, ed., *Narratives of Early Maryland 1638–1684* (New York: Charles Scribner's Sons, 1910), 370–71, 377. For a similar comment by a New Englander, see Axtell, ed., *Indian Peoples*, 121. European settlers of course noted many additional contrasts between the two societies, but none of the other distinctions related so directly to the wielding of gendered power.

11. The passage analyzed in this and the following eight paragraphs is from William Bradford, *Of Plymouth Plantation*, ed. Samuel Eliot Morison (New York: Random House/ Modern Library, 1967), 120–21. The communal system had been controversial from its outset; see ibid., 361–64, for a response to early critics by one of its originators. Fred Martin usefully points out that, in the agreement in question, "equal" profits (due to the planters and investors at the end of seven years) meant "equal to the number of shares one possessed," not an entirely egalitarian distribution. Since some settlers had more shares than others, even the communal system was thus not without some distinctions by wealth. See John Frederick Martin, *Profits in the Wilderness: Entrepreneurship and the Founding of New England* (Chapel Hill: University of North Carolina Press, 1991), 135–36.

12. For example, George D. Langdon, Jr., in his *Pilgrim Colony: A History of New Plymouth 1620–1691* (New Haven, Conn.: Yale University Press, 1966), 29–30, quotes only the explanation of young men's wishes and analyzes the episode solely in terms of the benefits of private property ownership. Larzer Ziff, *Puritanism in America: New Culture in a New World* (New York: Viking Press, 1974), 38, summarizes the entire passage but interprets it wholly in familial, not gender, terms.

13. For a useful summary of current scholarship on the work roles of English women, which varied somewhat by region, see Kathleen M. Brown, "Gender and the Genesis of a Race and Class System in Virginia, 1630–1750" (unpub. Ph.D. diss., University of Wisconsin, Madison, 1990), I, 20–32. A particularly insightful article is Carole Shammas, "The World Women Knew: Women Workers in the North of England During the Late Seventeenth Century," in Richard S. Dunn and Mary Maples Dunn, eds., *The World of William Penn* (Philadephia: University of Pennsylvania Press, 1986), 99–118.

14. See Schochet, *Patriarchalism*, passim, and, for a feminist commentary, Carole Pateman, *The Sexual Contract* (Stanford, Calif.: Stanford University Press, 1988), chapter 2.

15. *WP*, II, 282–83.

16. Keith Wrightson, *English Society, 1580–1680* (London: Hutchinson, 1982), 17, 21.

17. The precise demographic composition of the Plymouth population in 1623 is unknown, and it is conceivable, though unlikely, that the colony contained no widows at that time. Appendix XIII of Bradford's *Of Plymouth Plantation*, 441–48, which recounts the biographies of the first settlers, makes it clear that high mortality rates sundered many families, creating both widows and widowers. Orphaned young women were present in some numbers in 1623, though Bradford's narrative ignores them.

18. Other scholars have also pointed out that women were perceived as potential sources of disorder in early modern European societies, but they have not singled out high-ranking women for special attention. See Carolyn Merchant, *The Death of Nature: Women, Ecology, and the Scientific Revolution* (San Francisco: Harper & Row, 1989), chapter 5; Natalie Z. Davis, "Women on Top," in her *Society and Culture in Early Modern France* (Stanford, Calif: Stanford University Press, 1975), 124–51; and Joy Wiltenburg, *Disorderly Women and Female Power in the Street Literature of Early Modern England and Germany* (Charlottesville: University Press of Virginia, 1992).

19. Although this formulation is my own, it is informed by the discussions in Arlene W. Saxonhouse, *Women in the History of Political Thought: Ancient Greece to Machiavelli* (New York: Praeger, 1985), chapters 1–5; Susan Moller Okin, *Women in Western Political Thought* (Princeton, N.J.: Princeton University Press, 1979), chapters 1–4; and Jean Bethke Elshtain, *Public Man, Private Woman: Women in Social and Political Thought* (Princeton, N.J.: Princeton University Press, 1981), chapters 1–2. See also Diana H. Coole, *Women in Political Theory: From Ancient Misogyny to Contemporary Feminism* (Boulder, Colo.: Lynne Rienner, 1988).

20. On the impact of Christianity, see Saxonhouse, *Women in the History of Political Thought*, chapter 6. For the egalitarian practices of English local government, see Wrightson, *English Society*, 35–36; David G. Hey, *An English Rural Community: Myddle under the Tudors and Stuarts* (Leicester: Leicester University Press, 1974), 218–31; Peter Clark, *English Provincial Society from the Reformation to the Revolution: Religion, Politics and Society in Kent 1500–1640* (Hassocks, Sussex: Harvester Press, 1977), chapter 4; C. S. Orwin and C. S. Orwin, *The Open Fields*, 2d ed. (Oxford: Oxford University Press, 1954), chapter 10; Carl Bridenbaugh, *Vexed and Troubled Englishmen 1590–1642* (New York: Oxford University Press, 1967), 243–45.

21. See Ortner and Whitehead, eds., *Sexual Meanings*, 1–27, esp. 8–9, 22–23.

22. Elizabeth Janeway, *Powers of the Weak* (New York: William Morrow, 1981), 111.

23. Readers familiar with David Hackett Fischer's *Albion's Seed: Four British Folkways in America* (New York: Oxford University Press, 1989) will recognize that I here part company with his contention that regional differences in North America stemmed from the varying customs and beliefs of English migrants coming from divergent regional traditions. Social historians have described in detail such regional variations in early modern England; see, for example, David Underdown, *Revel, Riot, and Rebellion: Popular Politics and Culture in England 1603–1660* (New York: Oxford University Press, 1985), and Margaret Spufford, *Contrasting Communities: English Villagers in the Sixteenth and Seventeenth Centuries* (New York: Cambridge University Press, 1974). But there is no evidence of disagreement among the migrants about the fundamental points that concern me (the requisite obedience of wives to husbands and children to parents, and the general validity of a unified theory of power). Moreover, because Fischer assumes continuity in colonial life, he uses sources from the eighteenth century to describe seventeenth-century Virginia "gender ways," a strategy I seriously question. Although Fischer and I agree that the Chesapeake and New England differed in their social, political, and familial organization in a number of crucial ways, in short, we disagree about both the nature of those differences and their origins. For Fischer's discussion of families and gender, see *Albion's Seed*, 68–111 (Massachusetts) and 274–326 (Virginia).

24. Cotton, *The Way of the Churches of Christ in New-England* (London, 1645), 4, as quoted in Darrett Rutman, *Winthrop's Boston: A Portrait of a Puritan Town, 1630–1649* (New York: W. W. Norton, 1965), 50. Virginia DeJohn Anderson, *New England's Generation: The*

Great Migration and the Formation of Society and Culture in the Seventeenth Century (New York: Cambridge University Press, 1991), 128, points to the importance of covenants in establishing authority "in a society made up of comparative equals."

25. For a summary of the literature on the demographic differences between the Chesapeake and New England and their impact on women, see Mary Beth Norton, "The Evolution of White Women's Experience in Early America," *American Historical Review*, LXXXIX (1984), 595–601 (hereafter cited as *AHR*). Jack P. Greene, in *Pursuits of Happiness: The Social Development of Early Modern British Colonies and the Formation of American Culture* (Chapel Hill: University of North Carolina Press, 1988), discusses the regional demographic differences but does not pursue their gendered consequences. He also notes that in the context of other colonial American societies, New England—not the Chesapeake—was unusual in familial terms. I agree with that assessment, but my reference point here is England, not the West Indies; and Greene's assertion that Chesapeake society resembled that of England seems to me mistaken in its lack of attention to the consequences of the skewed Chesapeake sex ratio (see *Pursuits*, chapter 2, esp. 35–36).

26. The database created for this study (described in the appendix) identifies just 26 prosecutions of Africans and 44 prosecutions of Indians. Both groups were even less likely to appear as civil litigants: the data set includes just 3 blacks and 4 Indians who filed or responded to civil suits. In the years after 1670, Indian families were more likely to be regulated by English courts; see Ann Marie Plane, "Colonizing the Family: Marriage, Household, and Racial Boundaries in Southeastern New England to 1730" (unpub. Ph.D. diss., Brandeis University, 1994).

27. In my 1984 *AHR* article, cited n. 25 above, I concluded that change began in the 1660s but now I think that date twenty years too early. The Restoration colonies (New York, New Jersey, Pennsylvania, and the Carolinas) have been omitted from this volume because they were founded at the very end of the period under consideration. On the late-seventeenth-century events that wrought so many changes, see Russell Bourne, *The Red King's Rebellion: Racial Politics in New England 1675–1678* (New York: Oxford University Press, 1990); Stephen Saunders Webb, *1676: The End of American Independence* (New York: Alfred A. Knopf, 1984); and David Lovejoy, *The Glorious Revolution in America* (Middletown, Conn.: Wesleyan University Press, 1987). Two recent dissertations concur that Bacon's Rebellion and the large-scale importation of African slaves had major consequences for gender relations in Virginia. See Brown, "Gender and Genesis of Race and Class System," and Terri L. Snyder, " 'Rich Widows are the Best Commodity This Country Affords': Gender Relations and the Rehabilitation of Patriarchy in Virginia, 1660–1700" (unpub. Ph.D. diss., University of Iowa, 1992). Legal historians have identified 1680–1720 as a key era of transition; see Cornelia Hughes Dayton, "Turning Points and the Relevance of Colonial Legal History," *William and Mary Quarterly*, 3d ser., L (1993), 9–11.

28. On the familial metaphors of the revolutionary era: Edwin G. Burrows and Michael Wallace, "The American Revolution: The Ideology and Psychology of National Liberation," *Perspectives in American History*, VI (1972), 169–254; and Jay Fliegelman, *Prodigals and Pilgrims: The American Revolt against Patriarchal Authority, 1750–1800* (New York: Cambridge University Press, 1982).

29. For information about the free families: T. H. Breen and Stephen Innes, *"Myne Owne Ground": Race and Freedom on Virginia's Eastern Shore, 1640–1676* (New York: Oxford University Press, 1980), and, for a later period, Douglas Deal, "A Constricted World: Free Blacks on Virginia's Eastern Shore, 1680–1750," in Lois Green Carr et al., eds., *Colonial Chesapeake Society* (Chapel Hill: University of North Carolina Press, 1988), 275–305. Brown, "Gender and Genesis of Race and Class System," II, chapter 6, supplies further information, but her discussion too focuses on the decades after 1680. The southern population estimate is from Allan Kulikoff, *Tobacco and Slaves: The Development of Southern Cultures in the Chesapeake, 1680–1800* (Chapel Hill: University of North Carolina Press, 1986), 40; the northern, from *Historical Statistics of the United States, Colonial Times to 1970* (Washington, D.C.: Government Printing Office, 1975), series Z, 1–19.

30. A similar point is made by Victoria Bynum, in *Unruly Women: The Politics of Social and Sexual Control in the Old South* (Chapel Hill: University of North Carolina Press, 1992),

40. Accordingly, not by chance do most studies of the development of slavery (e.g., Kulikoff, *Tobacco and Slaves*) begin about 1680. For my own previous work on the lives of enslaved people, which relies on the sorts of materials not available for this early period, see, e.g., Mary Beth Norton, Herbert Gutman, and Ira Berlin, "The Afro-American Family in the Age of Revolution," in Ira Berlin and Ronald Hoffman, eds., *Slavery and Freedom in the Age of the American Revolution* (Charlottesville: University Press of Virginia, 1983), 175–91.

31. See, on Virginia, Jon Kukla, "Order and Chaos in Early America: Political and Society Stability in Pre-Restoration Virginia," *AHR*, XC (1985), 275–98; on Maryland, Russell Menard, "Maryland's 'Time of Troubles': Sources of Political Disorder in Early St. Mary's," *Maryland Historical Magazine*, LXXVI (1981), 124–40; on New Haven, Isabel Calder, *The New Haven Colony* (New Haven, Conn.: Yale University Press, 1934). There is no adequate study of early Maine.

32. According to the *OED*, this definition first appeared in the mid-sixteenth century. Earlier (from 1400) *family* had applied solely to the servants of a household. David Herlihy, in "Family," *AHR*, XCVI (1991), 2, points out that the Latin *familia* similarly meant a group of slaves; thus the English usage derived from it implied "an authoritarian structure and hierarchical order, founded on but not limited to relations of marriage and parenthood."

33. Although co-residence alone is often used to define the colonial family, such a criterion provides an inadequate definition because, as is clear from colonial censuses, it was possible for more than one family to share the same living space. See Robert V. Wells, *The Population of the British Colonies in America to 1775* (Princeton, N.J.: Princeton University Press, 1975), 325–33.

34. *OED*, q.v. "rank," "status," "class."

35. Peter Laslett provides a useful chart giving the hierarchy of forms of address in Stuart England; see *The World We Have Lost*, 3d ed. (New York: Charles Scribner's Sons, 1984), 38–39; Fischer, *Albion's Seed*, 174–80, 382–89, 798–802, discusses the employment of a more limited set of terms in America.

36. Among those who do not recognize the distinctions noted here are George F. Dow, the editor of the Essex County court records, who in his extensive summaries of depositions often used "Mrs." and "Mr." in a twentieth-century rather than a seventeenth-century manner, and Lyle Koehler, who in *A Search for Power: The "Weaker Sex" in Seventeenth-Century New England* (Urbana: University of Illinois Press, 1980), sometimes calls women of ordinary rank "Mistress" (e.g., 138–39, 143).

37. *NHT Recs*, I, 476; *Va Ct Recs*, 194. According to the *OED*, "mister" is a corrupted pronunciation that evolved from "master" via the abbreviation "Mr." over the course of the seventeenth century. That one word stood for the two concepts "male governor of servants" and "high-ranking man" throughout most of the century (although the meanings eventually separated), whereas the two roles were from the beginning explicitly distinguished for women reveals the crucial significance of the designator *mistress* for high-status women. (The *OED* observes that *mistress* usually connotes "a woman who rules, or has control.") The substitution of *dame*, a word applying to ordinary women after the sixteenth century, for "female governor of servants" was especially common in New England. *OED*, q.v. "master," "Mr.," "mister," "mistress," "Mrs.," "dame."

38. For example, William Nelson in *Dispute and Conflict Resolution in Plymouth County, Massachusetts, 1725–1825* (Chapel Hill: University of North Carolina Press, 1980), 46, defines community simply as "those people who attended the same church." James E. Perry, in *The Formation of a Society on Virginia's Eastern Shore, 1615–1655* (Chapel Hill: University of North Carolina Press, 1990), relies instead on patterns of economic and social interaction as shown in legal documents. David Konig, in *Law and Society in Puritan Massachusetts: Essex County, 1629–1692* (Chapel Hill: University of North Carolina Press, 1979), xiv, adopts a definition requiring common goals and ways of acting. Martin, *Profits in Wilderness*, 235, is one of the few who divide New England towns into different communities; he distinguishes among residents, proprietors, voters, and church members in each New England town. By contrast, Helena M. Wall, *Fierce Communion: Family and Community in Early America* (Cambridge, Mass.: Harvard University Press, 1990), fails to define either "family" or "community." On the problems of definition, see Darrett Rutman, "The Social Web: A Prospectus for the

Study of the Early American Community," in William O'Neill, ed., *Insights and Parallels: Problems and Issues of American Social History* (Minneapolis: University of Minnesota Press, 1973), 57–89; and Richard Beeman, "The New Social History and the Search for 'Community' in Colonial America," *American Quarterly*, XXIX (1977), 422–43.

39. David Warren Sabean, *Power in the Blood: Popular Culture & Village Discourse in Early Modern Germany* (New York: Cambridge University Press, 1987), 95. The *OED* notes that the definition of *community* I am using here, "life in association with others; society, the social state," first appeared in 1652. This usage does not appear in the colonial records; rather, those colonists who employed the word adopted the earliest meaning identified by the *OED*, "common ownership" (e.g., "community of goods"), which dates to the mid-sixteenth century.

40. Although the *OED* states that *neighbor* as a term for one who dwells nearby is found in English as early as the ninth century, *neighborhood* defined as "a certain number of people who live close together" is first noted in 1625. The colonists tended to use the word most frequently in its oldest sense, "friendly relations among neighbors" (usually termed "good neighborhood"), which dates to the middle of the fifteenth century.

41. Wall, by contrast, conflates the two in *Fierce Communion*. Another synonym for the latter list, more commonly used in recent scholarship on the eighteenth and nineteenth centuries, would be *civil society*.

42. *Va Ct Recs*, 59; John Clark, "Ill Newes from New-England," *MHS Colls*, 4th ser., II (1854), 10; *Md Archs*, III, 400.

43. *NHCP Recs*, II, 235; *MHS Colls*, 4th ser., VII (1865), 499; *NHT Recs*, II, 292; *WP*, II, 293. Thus a man holding political office could refer to himself as "a publike person" (*WP*, III, 282). See, in this context, Morton J. Horowitz, "The History of the Public/Private Distinction," *University of Pennsylvania Law Review*, CX (1982), 1423–28.

44. The exception is Mistress Margaret Brent of Maryland, discussed in the prologue to the third section. Another possible exception is Lady Deborah Moody; for more on her, see chapter three, n. 53.

45. On this point, see my essay, "Gender, Crime, and Community in Seventeenth-Century Maryland," in James Henretta et al., eds., *The Transformation of Early American History* (New York: Alfred A. Knopf, 1991), 123–50, esp. 143–48. Because the best-known commentator on the concept of the *public*, Jürgen Habermas, failed to consider the role of women therein, his often-cited work has little relevance to my discussion.

46. *RI Col Recs*, I, 420; *Me Ct Recs*, III, 64; *Mass Col Recs*, IV, pt 1, 82; "The Autobiography of Thomas Shepard," *CSM Pubs*, XXVII (1927–30), 383.

47. *CSM Pubs*, XIV (1911–13), 193; Increase Mather, Diary, March 25, 1675, American Antiquarian Society, Worcester, Mass. (hereafter AAS); *WP*, I, 288.

48. *SAL*, I, 172.

49. Clark, "Ill Newes," *MHS Colls*, 4th ser., II (1854), 30; "Plymouth Church Records," *CSM Pubs*, XXII (1920), 163.

50. *Md Archs*, I, 389; *Mass Col Recs*, IV, pt 1, 3; Hubbard, *History of New England*, I, 65. Thus a "private howsekeeper" was one not licensed to keep an inn or sell liquor by the glass; see *Mass Col Recs*, IV, pt 1, 203; and *NH Ct Recs*, XL, 140.

51. Robert E. Moody, ed., *The Letters of Thomas Gorges, Deputy Governor of the Province of Maine 1640–1643* (Portland: Maine Historical Society, 1978), 11, 124; *The Calvert Papers* (Baltimore: Maryland Historical Society, 1889), I, 174–75. For "private occasions," see *Md Archs*, I, 319; *JWJ*, II, 3; *Mass Col Recs*, III, 19.

52. Robert G. Pope, ed., "The Notebook of the Reverend John Fiske," *CSM Pubs*, XLVII (1974), 5–6, 17–18, 20–21; Lechford, "Plain-Dealing," *MHS Colls*, 3d ser., III (1833), 72, 108–9.

53. Samuel Eliot Morison, ed., "The Reverend Seaborn Cotton's Commonplace Book," *CSM Pubs*, XXXII (1933–37), 330; *JWJ*, I, 107. That John Cotton's policy was continued by the Boston church after his death is evident in Mather diary, passim (e.g., April 14, July 7, 21, Sept. 29, 1665), AAS. The best discussion of the membership examination issue (which does not, however, systematically consider its gender dimensions) is Charles L. Co-

hen, *God's Caress: The Psychology of Puritan Religious Experience* (New York: Oxford University Press, 1986), 140–57.

54. Lechford, "Plain-Dealing," *MHS Colls*, 3d ser., III (1833), 68; Pope, ed., "Fiske Notebook," *CSM Pubs*, XLVII (1974), 4. John Cotton and the Wenham church were both interpreting 1 Corinthians 14:35, which reads, in part, "it is a shame for a woman to speake in the Church." Private examinations were also available to some "bashful" men, especially after the adoption of the Cambridge Platform of 1648; see Jameson, ed., *Johnson's Wonder-Working Providence*, 217; "Plymouth Church Records," *CSM Pubs*, XXII (1920), 163; and George Selement and Bruce Wooley, ed., "Thomas Shepard's Confessions," *CSM Pubs*, LVIII (1981), 20.

55. The phrase *private families* does appear occasionally in colonial discourse. But in context it is evident that the meaning of that phrase relates to one of the definitions of *private* already discussed, as when John Winthrop referred to those who lived in England only "for their owne private familys" rather than for "a more com[mon] good," or in an early policy proposal for Virginia stating that the governor should enforce order "aswell in the publique governement of the colonie as in the private families." In both cases, *private* meant "not public," though the senses of *public* and thus of *private* varied, with Winthrop's usage referring to economics and the Virginia statement being concerned instead with social regulation. See *WP*, II, 115; and Susan M. Kingsbury, ed., *Records of the Virginia Company of London* (Washington, D.C.: Government Printing Office, 1935), IV, 425.

56. Much of current feminist scholarship on women's history, including my own previous work, employs this dichotomy, or at least uses the terms *public* and *private* as though they were unproblematic. I have now come to question the applicability of these concepts to at least the pre-Enlightenment world, if not to much of the eighteenth century as well. For an insightful examination of a similar and related problem of terminology in the field, see Linda K. Kerber, "Separate Spheres, Female Worlds, Woman's Place: The Rhetoric of Women's History," *Journal of American History*, LXXV (1988–89), 9–39.

57. *L&L*, 22. And so in 1656 the town of New Haven gave a "verey helpfull" midwife a "convenient" house and home lot "rent free" (*NHT Recs*, I, 265). The only other persons so rewarded were the colony's officials, clergymen, and teachers, who—like the midwife— had acknowledged responsibilities to the people at large.

58. As shall be seen in the prologue to the first section, there were some contested applications of the word *private* within the family.

SECTION I PROLOGUE: THE GOVERNMENT OF FAMILYES

1. *Conn Col Recs*, I, 92.

2. *EC Ct Recs*, I, 134–35, 138; Essex County Quarterly Court File Papers, WPA Transcripts, I, f 90/1, Phillips Library, Peabody Essex Museum, Salem, Mass. (hereafter ECFP); *Mass Col Recs*, II, 243. That she was charged with two counts hints at a second adulterous relationship, but no other man's name is linked with hers in the records, and she faced trial alone. For a discussion of the Lynn ironworks and Nicholas Pinion's role therein, see Stephen Innes, *Creating the Commonwealth: The Economic Culture of Puritan New England* (New York: W. W. Norton, 1995), chapter 6, esp. 260–63.

3. *EC Ct Recs*, I, 173, 198, 254, 271, 305, II, 195–96, III, 83. The sexual horseplay involved the five people piling in a group on a bed, feeling each other's "nakedness," and much "laughinge" and "Shreekeinge," according to a disapproving witness (ECFP, I, f 114/2).

4. *NHT Recs*, II, 121, 161.

5. This and the next four paragraphs are based on *NHT Recs*, II, 117–22.

6. Ibid., 122–23, 204. In January 1666/7, Morran assaulted Nicholas Pinion, who won damages from him; see ibid., II, 201.

7. *NHT Recs*, II, 119–20.

8. Ibid., 123.

9. Ibid., 134.

10. The next three paragraphs are based on ibid., 148–51. The case record does not indicate whether Morran was still living in the Russell household.

11. *Plymouth Col Recs*, IV, 154. Thomas Pinion appears to have escaped prosecution in the theft case because of illness.

12. The next four paragraphs are based on *NHT Recs*, II, 159–62. Ruth was still "Moore" at the time of her brother Robert's August trial, so she had been married to Briggs for no more than four months. See ibid., 151.

13. This paragraph and the next two are based on ibid., 181–83.

14. See, e.g., *EC Ct Recs*, II, 234–36.

15. *NHT Recs*, II, 222–23.

16. This paragraph and the next three are based on Connecticut Archives, Crimes & Misdemeanors, Ser. 1, I, doc. 32, Connecticut State Library, Hartford (hereafter CSL), a record of the examination of Ruth Briggs and other witnesses, Feb. 21-March 4, 1667/8. I am grateful to Cornelia Dayton for supplying me with a transcript of this important document. The examination revealed that Ruth had been in Wethersfield in December 1667, but she was in New Haven the following month, for her father was called to court and asked "why he entertained Ruth Brigs soe Contrary to the mind of the towne & of authority here" (*NHT Recs*, II, 215). See also her account of her sexual conduct in New Haven after December 1665, below.

17. Her execution is recorded in "[Simon] Bradstreet's Journal, 1664–83," *New England Historical and Genealogical Register*, IX (1855), 44 (hereafter *NEHGR*).

18. *EC Ct Recs*, V, 21–22.

19. Appropriately enough, when Nicholas Pinion died, his debts amounted to twice his assets. See the inventory of his estate, March 16, 1675/6, Probate Court Records, New Haven District, I, f 171, CSL. I owe this reference to Cornelia Dayton. Eli Faber, in "Puritan Criminals: The Economic, Social, and Intellectual Background to Crime in Seventeenth-Century Massachusetts," *Perspectives in American History*, XI (1977–78), 83–144, esp. 127–35, argues (based on records from Middlesex County not consulted for this study) that some families were more prone to criminal conduct than others. The Pinions seem to confirm Faber's thesis.

20. *Mass Col Recs*, II, 55–56. For a similar argument, see Carole Shammas, "Anglo-American Household Government in Comparative Perspective," *William and Mary Quarterly*, 3d ser., LII (1995), 104–44. But cf. Daniel Scott Smith, "The Meanings of Family and Household: Change and Continuity in the Mirror of the American Census," *Population and Development Review*, XVIII (1992), 421–36.

21. John Reyner et al. to Boston church elders, Aug. 5, 1639, Cotton Papers, Prince Collection, Boston Public Library, as quoted in Darrett Rutman, *Winthrop's Boston: A Portrait of a Puritan Town, 1630–1649* (New York: W. W. Norton, 1965); 97; *WP*, IV, 19. A vast literature examines the early modern English family and the prescriptive writings that described the proper role of fathers therein. See Lawrence Stone, *The Family, Sex and Marriage in England, 1500–1800* (New York: Harper & Row, 1977); Susan Amussen, *An Ordered Society: Gender and Class in Early Modern England* (Oxford: Basil Blackwell, 1988); and Ralph Houlbrooke, *The English Family 1450–1700* (New York: Longman, 1984).

22. As early as November 1633 the leaders of Massachusetts Bay were already concerned about "excessive" wages and prices, which had created disorder by allowing workmen to "get as much in four days as would keep them a week" and to spend their money on "tobacco and strong waters" (*JWJ*, I, 112; and *Ct Assts Recs*, II, 39). On the frequent prosecutions for contempt of authority in the colonies, see chapter six.

23. See *Md Archs*, I, 20–21, for the March 1637/8 Maryland assembly session that adopted a series of laws to establish and regulate manors. For discussions of Lord Baltimore's original plan for the colony and the manorial system, see Russell R. Menard and Lois Green Carr, "The Lords Baltimore and the Colonization of Maryland," in David B. Quinn, ed., *Early Maryland in a Wider World* (Detroit, Mich.: Wayne State University Press, 1982), 167–215; and Lois Green Carr et al., *Robert Cole's World: Agriculture & Society in Early Maryland* (Chapel Hill: University of North Carolina Press, 1991), 119–37. One of the few

incidents of spouse abuse that attracted judicial attention in Maryland was heard in a manorial court (*Md Archs*, LIII, 628).

24. *NPCL*, 36; *Md Archs*, I, 84, 254; *Me Ct Recs*, I, 224; *NPCL*, 63, 68; *Conn Col Recs*, I, 61, 64; *Mass Col Recs*, I, 322. The Maryland laws mentioned here, the first of which was regularly renewed (*Md Archs*, I, 160–61, 251–52, 349–50), were the only two adopted in that colony that fit this category of legislation. Although the corn-planting statute placed the obligation on all persons planting tobacco, a Marylander in 1666 observed that the responsibility fell on the "Domestick Governor" to raise "so much Corn . . . as shall be sufficient for him and his Family" (George Alsop, "A Character of the Province of Mary-land," in Clayton Colman Hall, ed., *Narratives of Early Maryland 1638–1684* [New York: Charles Scribner's Sons, 1910], 350). In 1644 Massachusetts required heads of families to register all demographic events in their households; two years later, Plymouth and New Haven followed suit (*Mass Col Recs*, II, 59; *NPCL*, 86–87, 271–72; *NHCP Recs*, I, 192). One of the most eccentric of these laws (which was, not surprisingly, repealed just three months after its passage) was the 1642 Massachusetts statute requesting that householders collect "the urine of their families" to facilitate the making of gunpowder (*Mass Col Recs*, II, 17, 29).

25. *Mass Col Recs*, IV, pt 1, 59–60; *Conn Col Recs*, I, 289–90; *NPCL*, 147–48 (see also 153).

26. *SAL*, I, 286 (partners); I, 126, 152, 419, II, 123 (corn); I, 525 (guns); I, 542 (registration); II, 306–7 (hemp and flax); *Va Ct Recs*, 105 (prayer); *SAL*, I, 151 (ashes); I, 152, 164, 189, 205–6 (tobacco); I, 263 (guns); I, 361, 454–55, II, 19, 82–83, 187 (taxables); I, 483 (runaways); II, 108–9 (letters); II, 195 (servants). On the disorders of early Virginia, see Edmund S. Morgan, *American Slavery, American Freedom: The Ordeal of Colonial Virginia* (New York: W. W. Norton, 1974). Local justices of the peace (whose records have not survived) may have attempted to enforce the Virginia laws.

27. *NHCP Recs*, II, 608. The phrase "well governed families" comes from a Plymouth law of 1669 (*NPCL*, 156). See also ibid., 273; *L&L*, 51; *Conn Col Recs*, I, 8.

28. *NHCP Recs*, I, 47, 70; *Plymouth Col Recs*, I, 118; *Me Ct Recs*, II, 288.

29. *EC Ct Recs*, V, 104; *NHT Recs*, I, 370–71. See also ibid., I, 424, 426, and *Plymouth Col Recs*, III, 52, for concerns about unauthorized boarders.

30. For a more expansive interpretation of the meaning of family privacy in this period, see David H. Flaherty, *Privacy in Colonial New England* (Charlottesville: University Press of Virginia, 1972), part 1.

31. *Virginia Magazine of History and Biography*, XI (1903–04), 34; *SAL*, I, 365.

32. *JWJ*, I, 126. Evidently they could not find additional evidence, for *Mass Col Recs*, I, contains no record of such a trial.

33. *BOL*, 226; *L&L*, 47.

34. This case is discussed at length in chapter three. The statement from the servant, Job Hall, is in *NHCP Recs*, I, 252. For a mistress's complaint about a maidservant's "discovering [revealing] the secretts of the famyly," see *WP*, IV, 232.

35. *WP*, IV, 461–62.

36. This paragraph and the next are based on *NHCP Recs*, I, 118–19, 128–29.

37. Ibid., 335–36.

38. *NHT Recs*, I, 191–92; *Suffolk Ct Recs*, I, 255. See also *NHT Recs*, II, 23; *Suffolk Ct Recs*, II, 645.

39. *EC Ct Recs*, V, 306; *Suffolk Ct Recs*, I, 478–79. See also, e.g., *Ct Assts Recs*, II, 80, and *New Ams Ct Recs*, II, 299–301, III, 315, V, 2–3. Children could also be ordered punished by "the Governor of the Familie wher the[y] had offended" (*EC Ct Recs*, I, 11).

40. In the Chesapeake, I have identified only one case in which a parent was ordered to "Corect" a child (a seven-year-old girl), and two incidents in which punishment in the household was substituted for a public penalty (*Va Ct Recs*, 149; *Md Archs*, LIV, 443, LX, 233–35).

41. On Virginia's changing approach to family regulation in the early 1660s, see Kathleen M. Brown, "Gender and the Genesis of a Race and Class System in Virginia, 1630–1750" (unpub. Ph.D. diss., University of Wisconsin, Madison, 1990), II, 339–48. On New England's persistence in prosecuting such cases until the 1730s, see the summary in Mary Beth

Norton, "The Evolution of White Women's Experience in Early America," *American Historical Review*, LXXXIX (1984), 611–12.

42. The discussion in the following five paragraphs is based on *Va Ct Recs*, 176–77 (see also 166). Biographical details on the Beheathlands and the Wests are taken from entries in Virginia M. Meyer and John F. Dorman, eds., *Adventurers of Purse and Person Virginia 1607–1624/5*, 3d ed. (Richmond: Order of First Families of Virginia, 1987).

43. The quoted passages come from *Me Ct Recs*, II, 261; *Suffolk Ct Recs*, I, 231, II, 646, 599. See also, e.g., *Me Ct Recs*, I, 137, II, 263, 305, III, 143. Ministers too engaged in similar supervision of household heads; e.g. Increase Mather, Diary, April 27, 1665, American Antiquarian Society (Worcester, Mass.).

44. *NHT Recs*, I, 284–85. The couple, Henry and Blanche Morrell, remained in New Haven. It was at their house that Robert Pinion in 1665 threatened to seek revenge on the magistrates who had put him in the stocks; see n. 10, above.

45. *NEHGR*, XLVI (1892), 172; *EC Ct Recs*, IV, 290. Smith may have been held for as long as two years (*Suffolk Ct Recs*, II, 1101–2). Conversely, when in 1678 neighbors refused to testify against a man accused of "disorders in his family," he was acquitted (ibid, 940).

46. The next seven paragraphs are based on *NHCP Recs*, I, 233–39.

47. Ibid., 89.

48. If Medcalfe and Robinson were ever penalized, no record of their punishment survives. That the case aroused much comment in New Haven is indicated by the fact that it was discussed in the May 1646 gossip session which drew the magistrates' ire (n. 34, above). Four years later Meggs again offended in the same way, this time approaching Nathaniel Seely's wife, whose husband (unlike William Fancy) promptly complained to the magistrates. Meggs was ordered to stand in the pillory, was whipped once again, and was warned "to take heed least his unruly lust brought him to an untimely death"; i.e., execution for adultery (*NHT Recs*, I, 30–32).

49. For this case, heard May 28, 1655, see *NHCP Recs*, II, 137–39. Charles Hoadly, the editor of the New Haven records, expurgated much of the material from the printed version. The full story is in New Haven Colonial Records, I-B, ff 89–91, CSL. Quotations in the three paragraphs in the text are drawn from both the printed and manuscript records. See chapter seven, n. 101, for more on the sodomy prosecution of Knight.

CHAPTER 1: THE FIRST SOCIETY

1. John Locke, *Two Treatises of Government*, ed. Peter Laslett (Cambridge: Cambridge University Press, 1988), II, § 77 (p. 319).

2. See Keith Wrightson, *English Society 1580–1680* (London: Hutchinson, 1982), chapter 6, for a recent general discussion of early modern English people's concern with order, and Susan Dwyer Amussen, *An Ordered Society: Gender and Class in Early Modern England* (Oxford: Basil Blackwell, 1988), for a survey of the topic from a gender perspective. In *The Sexual Contract* (Stanford, Calif.: Stanford University Press, 1988), 3, Carole Pateman also stresses the significance of the fact that paternal power originated in conjugal right.

3. T.E., *The Lawes Resolutions of Womens Rights; or, The Lawes Provision for Woemen* (London: John Moore, 1632), 6.

4. Edmund S. Morgan, ed., *Puritan Political Ideas 1554–1794* (Indianapolis, Ind.: Bobbs Merrill, 1965), 56. On the centrality of marriage for Protestants, see Lyndal Roper, "Luther: Sex, Marriage and Motherhood," *History Today*, XXXIII (1983), 33–38.

5. John Cotton, *A Discourse about Civil Government in a New Plantation whose Design is Religion* (Cambridge, Mass., 1663), 10; *JWJ*, II, 239; David Leverenz, *The Language of Puritan Feeling* (New Brunswick, N.J.: Rutgers University Press, 1980), chapter 4. Cotton's *Discourse* has commonly been misassigned to John Davenport; for a persuasive attribution to Cotton, see Isabel Calder, "The Authorship of a Discourse about Civil Government in a New Plantation whose Design is Religion," *American Historical Review*, XXXVII (1931–32), 267–69 (hereafter *AHR*).

6. My colleague Rachel Weil has also analyzed political works for their familial content

in chapter 2 of her unpublished Ph.D. dissertation, "Sexual Ideology and Political Propaganda in England, 1680–1714" (Princeton University, 1991). For excellent discussions of contemporary prescriptive writings aimed more directly at familial behavior, see Amussen, *Ordered Society*, chapter 2, and Kathleen M. Brown, "Gender and the Genesis of a Race and Class System in Virginia, 1630–1750" (unpub. Ph.D. diss., University of Wisconsin, Madison, 1990), chapter 1.

7. For example, in more than 100 pages in *Ornaments for the Daughters of Zion* (Cambridge, Mass., 1692), Cotton Mather never felt the need to explain why wives should be subordinate to their husbands; rather, he simply described the components of that subordination.

8. Mary Astell, *Some Reflections upon Marriage* (2d ed., London: R. Wilkin, 1703), 97, 47–48. Six years later, in the preface to the third edition, Astell adopted a more secular approach, arguing that the need for a final authority in the family and women's physical weakness had combined to give men their superior position. (Bridget Hill, ed., *The First English Feminist: Reflections Upon Marriage and other Writings by Mary Astell* [New York, St. Martin's Press, 1986], 75.) An excellent biography of Astell is Ruth Perry, *The Celebrated Mary Astell* (Chicago: University of Chicago Press, 1986). See also the insightful discussion in Weil, "Sexual Ideology," chapter 3.

9. Peter Laslett, ed., *Patriarcha and Other Political Works of Sir Robert Filmer* (Oxford: Basil Blackwell, 1949), 245, 283, 57. Contemporaries who reasoned similarly are discussed in Gordon J. Schochet, *Patriarchalism in Political Thought: The Authoritarian Family and Political Speculation and Attitudes Especially in Seventeenth-Century England* (New York: Basic Books, 1975), 110–13.

10. Thomas Hobbes, *Leviathan. Parts One and Two*, intro. by Herbert W. Schneider (New York: Liberal Arts Press, 1958), chapter XX, 164–65.

11. For useful analyses of Locke's writings from a feminist perspective, see, in addition to Pateman, *Sexual Contract*, Lorenne M. G. Clark, "Women and Locke: Who Owns the Apples in the Garden of Eden?" in Lorenne M. G. Clark and Lynda Lange, eds., *The Sexism of Social and Political Theory: Women and Reproduction from Plato to Nietzsche* (Toronto: University of Toronto Press, 1979), 16–40; and Linda J. Nicholson, *Gender and History: The Limits of Social Theory in the Age of the Family* (New York: Columbia University Press, 1986), chapter 5.

12. Locke, *Two Treatises*, ed. Laslett, I, §§ 44, 46, 47 (pp. 172–73).

13. Ibid., I, § 47 (pp. 173–74).

14. Ibid., I, §§ 47, 48 (p. 174). In § 48 Locke also mentions the "Subjection . . . every Wife owes her Husband" and in § 49 (p. 176) "the Subjection that is due from a Wife to her Husband." In just three paragraphs, then, Locke employs similar wording in seven separate phrases. See also I, § 67 (p. 190).

15. Ibid., II, §§ 77, 78, 82 (pp. 319, 321). For more generous interpretations of Locke's position on marriage, see Melissa Butler, "Early Liberal Roots of Feminism: John Locke and the Attack on Patriarchy," *American Political Science Review*, LXXI (1978), 135–50; and Mary Lyndon Shanley, "Marriage Contract and Social Contract in Seventeenth Century English Political Thought," *Western Political Quarterly*, XXXII (1979), 79–91.

16. *Lawes Resolutions*, 51–52.

17. See ibid., passim, 52–64 (quotations 53, 57). A useful collection of English case studies is Lawrence Stone, ed., *Uncertain Unions: Marriage in England 1660–1753* (New York: Oxford University Press, 1992). See also Stone's *Road to Divorce: England, 1530–1987* (New York: Oxford University Press, 1990), part 1; and R. B. Outhwaite, *Clandestine Marriage in England, 1500–1850* (Rio Grande, Ohio: Hambledon Press, 1994).

18. The most comprehensive discussion is Martin Ingram, *Church Courts, Sex and Marriage in England, 1570–1640* (Cambridge: Cambridge University Press, 1988), chapters 4, 6. See also Ingram's useful essay "The Reform of Popular Culture? Sex and Marriage in Early Modern England," in Barry Reay, ed., *Popular Culture in Seventeenth-Century England* (New York: St. Martin's Press, 1985), 129–65.

19. Examples of early marriage laws are: *Mass Col Recs*, I, 275; *RI Col Recs*, I, 187; *Md Archs*, I, 97; *Conn Col Recs*, I, 47–48; and *Va Ct Recs*, 167.

20. E.g., *Md Archs*, X, 293–96; and *Suffolk Ct Recs*, II, 1153–57. Both couples were called "servants" by court clerks but could have been enslaved. In early 1635, Massachusetts considered adopting a law governing marriages "betwixt Englishe & Indeans," but evidently took no action (*Mass Col Recs*, I, 140). See also T. H. Breen and Stephen Innes, *"Myne Owne Ground": Race and Freedom on Virginia's Eastern Shore, 1640–1676* (New York: Oxford University Press, 1980), 83–84, and Brown, "Gender and Genesis of Race and Class System," chapter 5.

21. *L&L*, 37; *SAL*, II, 281. The novelty of the requirement was revealed when a young man charged with breaking the parental consent laws in New Haven in 1660 protested that "there was no such Law in the places where he hath beene, nor did he know that there was any such law here." The judges were not impressed, informing him "that he must (if he live heare) acquaint himself with the Lawes established, & submitt to them" (*NHT Recs*, I, 426–27).

22. *NPCL*, 79–80, 272 (see also 246, 61); *BOL*, 230; *L&L*, 11; *RI Col Recs*, I, 330.

23. For a summary of and citations to the key demographic works, see Mary Beth Norton, "The Evolution of White Women's Experience in Early America," *AHR*, LXXXIX (1984), 597–98. See *Md Archs*, I, 373–74, 441–42; *SAL*, I, 252–53, 332, 438–39, II, 114. Servants could negotiate with their masters for permission to marry: *AN Ct Recs*, I, 154, and *Virginia Magazine of History and Biography*, XII (1904–05), 292 (hereafter *VMHB*). An exception to the New England rule was the Rhode Island code of 1647, which penalized a young man who married a woman clandestinely by ordering him to pay a fine to her parents (*RI Col Recs*, I, 174, 187).

24. *NPCL*, 61; *RI Col Recs*, I, 174; *L&L*, 37; *NHCP Recs*, II, 600.

25. Ingram, *Church Courts*, 134–36, notes that the Church of England explicitly refused to make parental consent the prerequisite for a valid marriage, though the church did encourage "respectful attention to parental guidance."

26. The data set identifies only 8 women, along with 26 men (some of the latter clergymen or magistrates who performed illegal ceremonies) who were tried for violating marriage laws in New England (N=24 cases) or the Chesapeake (N=5 cases).

27. The few prosecutions include those recorded in *Suffolk Ct Recs*, I, 221, 559; *Conn Col Recs*, I, 115, 124; and *Va Ct Recs*, 469. On youthful marriage ages for women, see Lois Green Carr and Lorena Walsh, "The Planter's Wife: The Experience of White Women in Seventeenth-Century Maryland," *William & Mary Quarterly*, 3d ser., XXXIV (1977), 564 (hereafter *WMQ*), and Philip J. Greven, *Four Generations: Population, Land, and Family in Colonial Andover, Massachusetts* (Ithaca, N.Y.: Cornell University Press, 1970), 33–37.

28. For examples of fornication laws, see *L&L*, 23; *NHCP Recs*, II, 590; and *NPCL*, 43. Coding identified just 7 southern men and 6 women accused of premarital fornication; four of the Chesapeake trials occurred at one 1639 court session in Accomack County, Virginia (*AN Ct Recs*, I, 151). The database includes 153 prosecutions for premarital fornication in New England. See Ingram, *Church Courts*, chapter 7, on the handling of premarital fornication in English ecclesiastical courts; and the articles by P. E. H. Hair, "Bridal Pregnancy in Rural England in Earlier Centuries," *Population Studies*, XX (1966), 233–43, and "Bridal Pregnancy in Earlier Rural England Further Examined," ibid., XXIV (1970), 59–70.

29. For examples of cases in which the timing is given: *NH Ct Recs*, XL, 160, 304; *Pynchon Ct Rec*, 255. The shortest recorded interval is "within two Months" (*Me Ct Recs*, III, 269), the longest that resulted in conviction, "within thirty weeks" (*Plymouth Col Recs*, III, 6). But a woman who had a child "about thirty-two weeks after marriage" was acquitted (*EC Ct Recs*, II, 101). The Plymouth laws are in *NPCL*, 79–80, 246. The more lenient treatment in such cases is revealed in *Plymouth Col Recs*, II, 109–10, IV, 83, VI, 201.

30. *NHCP Recs*, I, 75, 77–78; *VMHB*, XL (1932), 141, XLI (1933), 119, 343. English couples likewise regarded contracts as legitimizing sexual relations, and the penalty inflicted on the Tuckers resembled punishments for premarital fornication ordered by English ecclesiastical courts; see Ingram, *Church Courts*, 228–29, 236.

31. *EC Ct Recs*, III, 151–52.

32. *EC Ct Recs*, I, 23; *JWJ*, II, 43–44. See *Plymouth Col Recs*, VII, 101, 108–9, 111, 115, for examples of such lawsuits; and *EC Ct Recs*, I, 44, and *Va Ct Recs*, 15, 17, for

prosecutions related to marriage contracts. On two other occasions Winthrop became directly involved in marriage-contract disputes (*WP*, IV, 169, 230–32).

33. *Md Archs*, X, 499; *Suffolk Ct Recs*, II, 840; Anna Keayne Lane, quoted in Edmund S. Morgan, "A Boston Heiress and Her Husbands: A True Story," *CSM Pubs*, XXXIV (1937–42), 503. For the lament of a man unable to find a wife because he was thought sexually "insufficient," see N. S. to [Thomas Cotton], Feb. 28, 1710/11, Curwen Papers, box 2, folder 1, American Antiquarian Society, Worcester, Mass. (hereafter AAS).

34. My New England data set includes 336 married couples charged with crimes of all descriptions, of which 45.5% (N=153) were for premarital fornication. The Bay Colony was the site of 71% (N=109) of those prosecutions. Married women were the objects of 804 New England prosecutions; of the 781 cases in which crimes are known, 163 were identified as fornication (10 married women were accused of fornication before marriage with men other than their eventual husbands). Most such women were never charged with any other crime; the handful (13) who appeared in court on other occasions had usually committed such minor offenses as not attending church services.

35. The percentage of married men is artificially inflated because in most cases it is impossible to tell from court records whether an accused male criminal was married or single. This percentage thus pertains only to the select group of men known to be married at the time of their trials (N=172 of 369); in addition to couples, it includes the men whose wives were not prosecuted for offenses the couple had committed together (19 premarital fornication cases fall into this category).

36. Virginia, it is true, did prosecute some couples for this offense, including, as noted above, Edy and Thomas Tucker. But the few such trials had largely ceased by the early 1660s. See Brown, "Gender and Genesis of Race and Class System," II, 339–48, and the tables in her appendices 4 and 5.

37. *Md Archs*, LIII, 599, XLI, 229. For other self-defined Maryland marriages see ibid., LIV, 10, 172–73, XLI, 456–57, and LVII, 433.

38. *Me Ct Recs*, I, 238, 240, 333–34, II, 119, 169 (quote), 252–53 (quote), 288, 461–62, 468. Sarah Mills and her children were Quakers, but whether Garland joined them in such beliefs is unknown. Perhaps Maine did not recognize the validity of Quaker marriages and Garland hoped to take advantage of that when he left Mills for Hitchcock.

39. *NHCP Recs*, II, 122; *Essex Institute Historical Collections*, XXXV (1899), 197–98. The trials in the last case are in *EC Ct Recs*, VI, 293, 373–74. For lies about marriage records, see ibid., V, 222; and *Plymouth Col Recs*, IV, 5.

40. Essex County Quarterly Court File Papers, WPA Transcripts, VII, ff 40/2, 40/1, 39/2, Phillips Library, Peabody Essex Museum, Salem, Mass. (hereafter ECFP); printed (in altered form) in *EC Ct Recs*, II, 340–41. The trial of the Woodrows is recorded in ibid., 217. In March 1656/7, Thomas was identified as a servant; he perjured himself in a case involving the Cantleburys in November 1656 (ibid., 38, 11). Similar cases are in ibid., I, 159, III, 189–90, and III, 338, V, 68.

41. *Lawes Resolutions*, 79–90, 116–229, describes the legal status of wives (quotations 119, 129–30, 204). The wills quoted are in *Md Archs*, XLI, 43; and *WP*, IV, 147.

42. *Md Archs*, I, 527, 533–34.

43. *Lawes Resolutions*, 128, 206. In 1647 Rhode Island thus provided that penalties for being accessory to a criminal offense did not apply to "a Wife towards her husband" (*RI Col Recs*, I, 172).

44. *BOL*, 229–30; *Mass Col Recs*, IV, pt 1, 26; *NPCL*, 273.

45. *RI Col Recs*, I, 161. The published records contain no explanation for the adoption of this unique statute. See G. B. Warden, "The Rhode Island Civil Code of 1647," in David D. Hall et al., eds., *Saints and Revolutionaries: Essays on Early American History* (New York: W. W. Norton, 1984), 138–51.

46. Adultery laws and prosecutions are discussed at length in chapter seven.

47. See *L&L*, 37, and Prologue, above, n. 43. For presentments of men for living apart from their spouses (a common offense, especially in fishing communities): e.g., *Me Ct Recs*, II, 12–13, 63, 83, 105.

48. *Lawes Resolutions*, 4; Hill, ed., *First English Feminist*, 75.

49. *Mass Col Recs*, IV, pt 2, 288; *New England Historical and Genealogical Register*, VI (1852), 39 (hereafter *NEHGR*). The same complementary advice appears repeatedly; see, e.g., John Saffin's poem, "To his dear friend W. T.," John Saffin Notebook, 29–33, AAS.

50. Jeannine Hensley, ed., *The Works of Anne Bradstreet* (Cambridge, Mass.: Harvard University Press, 1967), 225. See also John Saffin's many poems lauding his first wife: Saffin Notebook, 19, 20, 83–85, 187–89, 190–92, AAS.

51. "The Autobiography of Thomas Shepard," *CSM Pubs*, XXVII (1927–30), 373, 392; for the Winthrop letters, see *WP*, I and II, passim.

52. *NHCP Recs*, II, 123. On seventeenth-century scientific opinion about conception: Thomas Laqueur, *Making Sex: Body and Gender from the Greeks to Freud* (Cambridge, Mass.: Harvard University Press, 1990), 99–103 and passim.

53. Edward Everett Hale et al., eds., *Note-Book kept by Thomas Lechford, Esq, 1638 to 1641* (1884; repr., Camden, Me.: Picton Press, 1988), 177; *AN Ct Recs*, I, 85. John Demos's emphasis in *Entertaining Satan: Witchcraft and the Culture of Early New England* (New York: Oxford University Press, 1982), 72–73, on the negative implications of childlessness for women is thus partially misplaced, because husbands shared the blame for that condition. See Linda Pollock, "Embarking on a Rough Passage: The Experience of Pregnancy in Early-Modern Society," in Valerie Fildes, ed., *Women as Mothers in Pre-Industrial England* (London: Routledge, Chapman, and Hall, 1990), 40–41.

54. Quotations: *WP*, IV, 260; *NHT Recs*, I, 209; *NHCP Recs*, I, 368. The cases of the three men are printed in *NHT Recs*, I, 344–45; *NHCP Recs*, II, 261; ibid., II, 182–85, 255–57, 284–85, 309–11, 367–69; and ibid., II, 242–47. For defamation suits raising these sorts of issues: *Md Archs*, LIV, 222–23; *EC Ct Recs*, VII, 262; *NHT Recs*, I, 485.

55. *WP*, III, 279–80 (see also 368). The Winthrop papers are filled with reports of other husbands and wives disagreeing over emigration; e.g., ibid., 33, 36, 87.

56. Quotations variously from *JWJ*, I, 286–87; *WP*, IV, 31; *RI Col Recs*, I, 16. Jane Verin obviously set her own religious course; in 1639 she was presented in Salem for failure to attend church (*EC Ct Recs*, I, 10).

57. Outside Massachusetts or Maine, prosecutions for spouse abuse (by either party) were rare: the data set identifies formal charges of this nature brought against just two women and three men in New Haven, four men and one woman in Plymouth, two men in Virginia, and one man and one woman in Maryland. Overall, 33 women and 66 men were accused of abusing their spouses. Massachusetts and Maine together accounted for 75 (or 85%) of the 88 total prosecutions. That the Bay Colony was unusual in its attention to wife abuse is suggested not only by the relative absence of prosecutions in other jurisdictions but also by the matter-of-fact way in which the offense was occasionally referred to in court (e.g., *New Ams Ct Recs*, I, 326–27). On the handling of spouse abuse by English courts, see Susan Dwyer Amussen, " 'Being Stirred to Much Unquietness': Violence and Domestic Violence in Early Modern England," *Journal of Women's History*, VI, no. 2 (Summer 1994), 70–89.

58. *Va Ct Recs*, 70; *Me Ct Recs*, I, 264–65, 300; Dukes County Court Records, I, f 24, County Courthouse, Edgartown, Mass. Mistress Sarah Morgan was later prosecuted for abusing her husband (*Me Ct Recs*, II, 224).

59. ECFP, I, f 97/1; Essex County Quarterly Court Records, 2d ser., II, 229, Phillips Library, Peabody Essex Museum, Salem, Mass. (printed, in altered form, in *EC Ct Recs*, I, 136). He was fined, threatened with a whipping, and ordered to post a substantial good-behavior bond. Two years later, Mary was charged with throwing a trencher at him (*EC Ct Recs*, I, 184). In May 1663, living in Rhode Island, they asked the colony's highest court to divorce them (*RI Col Recs*, I, 503). For a man's assault on his wife on a public highway, see *EC Ct Recs*, V, 377. Yet despite the evidence of beatings, few men were charged with killing their wives; rare cases are *Md Archs*, LVII, 599–600; George Percy, "A Trewe Relacyon of the Proceedings and Ocurrents of Momente wch have hapned in Virginia . . . ," *Tyler's Quarterly Historical and Genealogical Magazine*, III (1922), 267.

60. *NH Ct Recs*, XL, 145; *EC Ct Recs*, VI, 116, VII, 381.

61. *AN Ct Recs*, II, 195, 202–8, 211–12, 225, 253; *Md Archs*, X, 464–65. See also ibid., XLI, 164, in which the information that a man had "kickd' his wife about the howse" three years earlier was offered casually in the course of testimony about another matter.

62. Astell, *Some Reflections*, 43; *WP*, I, 189. For wives who fought back: *Md Archs*, LIII, 628; *EC Ct Recs*, V, 377, VI, 193. Attempted murders of husbands: *Ct Assts Recs*, II, 108; *JWJ*, II, 218–19 (see also *Ct Assts Recs*, II, 47, 74, on this couple).

63. See, e.g., cases involving particularly contentious and long-standing marital disputes: *Plymouth Col Recs*, III, 75, IV, 4–5, and *Pynchon Ct Rec*, 235–36; *Me Ct Recs*, II, 43, 57, 92; *NH Ct Recs*, XL, 20, 83, 115, 161–62, 485–86.

64. Robert Keayne, a member of the Boston church, recorded the excommunication trial of Mistress Hibbens in his notebook. Overlapping but not identical portions of Anita Rutman's transcription of Keayne's notes have been published in two documentary collections. The quotations in these five paragraphs are taken from John Demos, ed., *Remarkable Providences* (New York: Braziller, 1972), 229, 238; and Nancy F. Cott, ed., *Root of Bitterness: Documents in the Social History of American Women* (New York: E. P. Dutton, 1972), 54–56. For a detailed discussion of the part of the trial dealing with the business matter (negotiations with carpenters over some work on their house), see chapter three.

65. Ann Hibbens's reference to Richard Bellingham's first wife, Elizabeth, who died in 1634, as "my Sister" stretched already loose contemporary usage of familial terms to a near breaking point. William Hibbens's first wife was Hester Bellingham, probably a cousin (not a sibling) of Richard Bellingham. Sisters-in-law referred to each other as "sister," but it was uncommon to adduce such a relationship through the previous marital partner of one's spouse. Some authors have erroneously concluded from this phrase that Ann Hibbens was the sister of Richard Bellingham. (Biographical information from Thwing Index, Massachusetts Historical Society, Boston.)

66. One male Bostonian, a follower of Anne Hutchinson, did cite Genesis 21:12 approvingly; see John Underhill, "Newes from America . . . ," *MHS Colls*, 3d ser., VI (1837), 6.

67. In New England, husbands more often appeared on their wives' behalf (59% to 41%), whereas in the Chesapeake, husbands and wives more commonly appeared together (54% to 46%). The difference seems to be more of form than of substance, because either method complied with common-law rules forbidding wives from acting independently of their spouses.

68. Thus those historians who have posited increased legal freedom for women in the early colonies have misconstrued the evidence, particularly as it pertains to wives. Cf. John Demos, *A Little Commonwealth: Family Life in Plymouth Colony* (New York: Oxford University Press, 1970), 82–91, and Joan Gunderson and Gwen Gampel, "Married Women's Legal Status in Eighteenth-Century New York and Virginia," *WMQ*, 3d ser., XXXIX (1977), 114–34. See the comprehensive discussion of land-sale procedures in Marylynn Salmon, *Women and the Law of Property in Early America* (Chapel Hill: University of North Carolina Press, 1986), chapter 2. Land-conveyance laws requiring wives' separate consent are printed in *NPCL*, 86; *Md Archs*, II, 307; *NHCP Recs*, II, 303–4; *SAL*, II, 317.

69. My data set includes 726 civil suits (500 in the Chesapeake, 226 from New England) in which married women appeared as plaintiffs or defendants; wives were unaccompanied by husbands in just 148 of those cases. Percentages for New England and the Chesapeake are nearly congruent: 22.5% of New England wives and 19% of Chesapeake wives came to court alone. The percentages did shift dramatically over time, due largely to the application of common-law rules to defamation cases in both regions after the mid-1660s. In both regions, 33% of wives came to court alone before 1665, whereas after that date the comparable figures were 10% (New England) and 7% (the Chesapeake). But fully 51% of the independent wives before 1665 (and 45% throughout the century) appeared in slander or divorce suits; if those cases are removed from consideration, the proportion of cases in which married women came to court alone before 1665 drops to 20%. For a description of how ecclesiastical courts handled slander cases, see Ingram, *Church Courts*, chapter 10.

70. For a postnuptial agreement, see William Sargent, ed., *York Deeds* (Portland, Me.: Brown, Thurston, & Co., 1888), IV, f 45. Examples of husbands' gifts to wives: *Md Archs*, LX, 278–79; Sargent, ed., *York Deeds*, II, f 70; *WP*, III, 178. For gifts to married women: *AN Ct Recs*, I, 134–35, II, 437–38; Sargent, ed., *York Deeds*, I, pt 1, f 131. Wives' wills are

recorded in, e.g., *EC Ct Recs*, IV, 313–14, and *Essex Antiquarian*, II (1898), 45–46. None of these examples contains any evidence of prenuptial agreements.

71. *MHS Procs*, 2d ser., VII (1891–92), 146; *Va Ct Recs*, 110; *AN Ct Recs*, II, 260, 262–63, 288–89; II, 11; I, 15. Two of the Virginia agreements were nullified in whole or in part, though not because the wives in question lacked the power to make them.

72. E.g., *NH Ct Recs*, XL, 380, and *NHT Recs*, II, 2, 9–10, 227 (selling); *AN Ct Recs*, II, 92–93, 95 (buying); *Md Archs*, X, 318, 336 (receiving payment); *Md Archs*, LIV, 467, 471, and *NHT Recs*, I, 344 (paying debts). Laurel Thatcher Ulrich has termed wives who acted thus "deputy husbands"; see her *Good Wives: Image and Reality in the Lives of Women in Northern New England 1650–1750* (New York: Oxford University Press, 1982), chapter 2.

73. *NHCP Recs*, II, 121; *AN Ct Recs*, I, 86. In neither of these cases is the court's decision recorded. For husbands' confirmations of wives' previous bargains, see *AN Ct Recs*, I, 42–43, II, 4. Two cases in which courts upheld agreements wives reached in the absence of their husbands (and without formal powers of attorney) are recorded in *NHT Recs*, I, 89–90, and *EC Ct Recs*, II, 62–63.

74. The suits, filed by Captain Richard Lockwood and Mr. Robert Pattishall (later pursued by Nathaniel Fryar) can be tracked in *Me Ct Recs*, II, 166–67, 402, 458, 494 (contempt citation, 403); the promissory notes from Joan that led to Lockwood's suit are printed in Sargent, ed., *York Deeds*, II, ff 91–92. For examples of other women deflecting suits in the same way: *Md Archs*, LIII, 15, and XLIX, 147. The voiding of a challenged postnuptial agreement is recorded in *Suffolk Ct Recs*, I, 5–9, 98–99, 131, 201, II, 569.

75. His petition, heard Oct. 11, 1661, is printed in *Md Archs*, XLI, 483. The two cases in question: ibid., 347, 494, 528–29. Hammond's power of attorney to his wife, April 16, 1655, is in ibid., X, 471–72. The matters in which she represented him (not all of which required court appearances) are recorded in ibid., X, 492ff, and XLI, 1–452 passim.

76. The data set identifies just 26 such lawsuits in the Chesapeake and 15 in New England. For examples of powers of attorney or wives acting as such in court: *Md Archs*, X, 16, 443, LIV, 236; and *Me Ct Recs*, III, 24, 29–30. The husband and wife in the last case, Rowland and Joanna Young, are my ancestors.

77. For example: *EC Ct Recs*, V, 49–51. Matters became even more tangled when the debts at issue were not a wife's but her previous husband's, a common problem in the Chesapeake because of women's multiple marriages (e.g., *Md Archs*, X, 453–54, 469–70, XLIX, 221–23, 242, 273–75, 300–1).

78. *Va Ct Recs*, 35; *Me Ct Recs*, II, 201–2. See also, e.g., *NHT Recs*, I, 459–61, 503; *Mass Col Recs*, IV, pt 1, 342, pt 2, 300, for husbands who claimed ignorance of illegal liquor sales by their wives but were ordered to pay fines nonetheless.

79. *Ct Assts Recs*, II, 89; *EC Ct Recs*, I, 158, 286. In 357 prosecutions of married women for offenses committed without the participation of their husbands, 190 (53%) resulted in the imposition of a fine or order to post bond. In 140 of those cases, that was the only punishment. In 37 additional instances, fines or posting bond were alternate penalties; that is, if a woman's husband so chose, he could save her from whipping or shaming by paying a monetary penalty. Thus the 357 prosecutions included 227 (63.5%) in which financial punishment was at least an option. The vast majority of all such trials of married women occurred in New England; just 14 with known outcomes were heard in the Chesapeake. In 151 cases, 16 of them in the Chesapeake, the outcomes are unknown.

80. See Nancy Folbre, "Patriarchy in Colonial New England," *Review of Radical Political Economics*, XII, no. 2 (summer 1980), 4–13, for a useful critique of scholars who have paid insufficient attention to husbands' economic power. Comments on the value of wives' labor are contained in, e.g., James P. Baxter, ed., *The Trelawny Papers. Documentary History of the State of Maine* (Collections of the Maine Historical Society, 2d ser., III [1884]), 86, 285; and Everett Emerson, ed., *Letters from New England: The Massachusetts Bay Colony, 1629–1638* (Amherst: University of Massachusetts Press, 1976), 82.

81. *Md Archs*, LIV, 394; *WP*, IV, 294–95; *Md Archs*, LIII, 39. Their wives' ability to wet-nurse orphaned babies became a lucrative source of financial support for some men (e.g., *AN Ct Recs*, II, 67–68, 160, 269–70, 426–27).

82. Figures tabulated from *Md Archs*, passim. On the terminology of court records, recall

from the prologue to this section that the key participant in the New Haven sex scandal of 1646 was called "Fancy his wife." For rare examples of prenuptial agreements and jointures not involving widows, see *Md Archs*, X, 12–13, LXV, 684–86; Sargent, ed., *York Deeds*, IV, f 86. Widows' prenuptial agreements are discussed in chapter three.

83. Robert G. Pope, ed., "The Notebook of the Reverend John Fiske," *CSM Pubs*, XLVII (1974), 6, 14–16, 19, 30. The same emphasis on male primacy can also be found in other sorts of documents. Increase Mather, for example, referred to his niece and her husband as "my Cousin Williams, & his wife" (Increase Mather, Diary, March 11, 1703/4, AAS).

84. *NHCP Recs*, II, 586 (also 479). See also *RI Col Recs*, I, 231, 311–12. On the English law of divorce: *Lawes Resolutions*, 64–68. For Cotton Mather's summary of justifiable grounds for divorce in New England: *Magnalia Christi Americana* . . . (Hartford, Conn.: Silas Andrus & Son, 1853), II, 253–54.

85. *Me Ct Recs*, I, 287 (see also 319–20). A useful introduction to colonial divorce is Nancy F. Cott, "Divorce and the Changing Status of Women in Massachusetts," *WMQ*, 3d ser., XXXIII (1976), 586–614. In New Amsterdam, judges granted separate maintenance but not permission to remarry; e.g., *New Ams Ct Recs*, III, 63–64, 72–74, II, 335, 338, 374, IV, 304, 328.

86. *Md Archs*, X, 471, LVII, 131, LIII, 33–34 (also, XLI, 20, 50–51, 79, 83, 85, LIII, 4). And see *Ct Assts Recs*, II, 60. Just 20 suits for divorce appear in the data set (13 brought by women, 7 by men) but many additional consensual separations are noted in the records. At least two couples signed separation documents courts deemed illegal (*Plymouth Col Recs*, IV, 66; *Md Archs*, XLI, 229).

87. See, e.g., *EC Ct Recs*, I, 135, 199, V, 65–67; *Suffolk Ct Recs*, I, 517. Cf. *Me Ct Recs*, II, 304, 308.

88. Examples of Connecticut divorces issued for desertion alone: *Conn Col Recs*, I, 275, 301, 376, 379. Divorce decrees in other colonies: *Ct Assts Recs*, III, 146; *Plymouth Col Recs*, VI, 44–45; *NHCP Recs*, II, 425–26. A detailed but unsuccessful divorce petition is printed in *MHS Procs*, XLVI (1912–13), 479–84 (see *Mass Col Recs*, IV, pt 2, 426–27).

89. *Suffolk Ct Recs*, II, 754–55, 837–41 passim (quotations 839, 841).

90. *Ct Assts Recs*, III, 131–32, and *EC Ct Recs*, III, 110–11; ibid., VI, 295–96, VII, 78. When a Plymouth man contested his wife's description of him as "misformed" and "always unable to perform the act of generation," judges agreed to separate maintenance but not to a divorce; see *Plymouth Col Recs*, VI, 190–93.

91. See *EC Ct Recs*, I, 221 (the Rowlandson divorce), and III, 419–20, 443–44 (hearings on two suits filed by William Beale after the brawl), but G. F. Dow's editorial omissions from the published text obscure the dynamic of the confrontation. Most of the details in the next three paragraphs accordingly come from ECFP, XII, ff 87–91, 136–42.

92. Again, Dow's deletions obscure some of the crucial details of these confrontations. Cf. *EC Ct Recs*, IV, 161–63, 269–71, 280–82, with ECFP, XIV, ff 126–31, XVI, 49–55, 66–67 (quotations in this and next two paragraphs from the unpublished material).

93. For example, a young New Haven wife, Hannah Uffitt, whose husband, John, had some difficulties with sexual functioning at the outset of their marriage, told him that "if he would confesse himselfe insufficient, she would live with him halfe a yeare longer." He agreed to this arrangement, he later admitted, because "in that time he hoped it might appeare otherwise." But he was unable to consummate the union, and his acknowledged impotence eventually led to a divorce. Hannah's scheming came to light when John later impregnated his father's maidservant (*NHCP Recs*, II, 201–2, 209–12 [quotation, 209]).

94. Exactly what Mr. Hollingworth said, or to whom, does not appear in the published or unpublished records.

95. *EC Ct Recs*, IV, 269–71 (Dow printed the petition verbatim). The Beales were involved in two more defamation suits (ibid., 286–87, V, 245), but the conviction of Mistress Hollingworth seems to have quieted most of their critics. Another divorced and remarried woman who aroused her neighbors' antagonism was Mary Lewis Parsons of Springfield, who was eventually convicted of witchcraft; see *WP*, V, 45–46, 50; Demos, *Entertaining Satan*, 74; and Carol Karlsen, *The Devil in the Shape of a Woman* (New York: W. W. Norton, 1987), 22–23.

CHAPTER 2: A LITTLE MONARCHY

1. Thomas Hobbes, *Leviathan. Parts One and Two*, intro. by Herbert W. Schneider (New York: Liberal Arts Press, 1958), chapter XX, 167.

2. On Hobbes's view of the family, cf. Richard Allan Chapman, "*Leviathan* Writ Small: Thomas Hobbes on the Family," *American Political Science Review*, LXIX (1975), 76–90, esp. 80; and Carole Pateman, *The Sexual Contract* (Stanford, Calif.: Stanford University Press, 1988), 43–50, esp. 47–48.

3. On the importance of the Fifth Commandment, see Edmund S. Morgan, *The Puritan Family* (rev. ed., New York: Harper & Row, 1965), 12, 19; Gordon J. Schochet, *Patriarchalism in Political Thought: The Authoritarian Family and Political Speculation and Attitudes Especially in Seventeenth-Century England* (New York: Basic Books, 1975), 14–16, 73–74; and Susan Dwyer Amussen, *An Ordered Society: Gender and Class in Early Modern England* (Oxford: Basil Blackwell, 1988), 36, 58–59.

4. John Locke, *Two Treatises of Government*, ed. Peter Laslett (Cambridge: Cambridge University Press, 1988), II, §§ 66, 68; I, §§ 61–64 (pp. 311, 313, 184–87); Peter Laslett, ed., *Patriarcha and Other Political Works of Sir Robert Filmer* (Oxford: Basil Blackwell, 1949), 62.

5. Laslett, ed., *Patriarcha*, 62, 188, 233, 283 (only once [245] did he quote it in full); Hobbes, *Leviathan*, ed. Schneider, chapter XX, 163; Locke, *Two Treatises*, ed. Laslett, II, §§ 52, 74, 170 (pp. 303, 316, 381).

6. Laslett, ed., *Patriarcha*, 74, 96, 188 (see also 77).

7. Locke, *Two Treatises*, ed. Laslett, I, §§ 56–59 (quotation: § 58, p. 181); II, §§ 58–59 (pp. 306–7).

8. Ibid., II, §§ 72, 73 (p. 315); cf. I, §§ 88–90, 93 (pp. 206–10); Laslett, ed., *Patriarcha*, 65.

9. Laslett, ed., *Patriarcha*, 58 (for other examples, 72–73, 287); Locke, *Two Treatises*, ed. Laslett, I, §123 (p. 230).

10. Sir Robert Filmer, "In Praise of the Vertuous Wife," in Margaret J. M. Ezell, *The Patriarch's Wife: Literary Evidence and the History of the Family* (Chapel Hill: University of North Carolina Press, 1987), 176. See Hanna Fenichel Pitkin, *Fortune Is a Woman: Gender and Politics in the Thought of Niccolò Machiavelli* (Berkeley: University of California Press, 1984), chapters 5 and 6, for a brilliant discussion of women/woman as a disruptive influence in another philosopher's political system.

11. On the American side of the Atlantic, historians have demonstrated that the theme of father-son conflict permeated early New England (and Virginia as well, if it is there defined in broad generational terms). On New England, see, most notably, Philip J. Greven, Jr., *Four Generations: Population, Land, and Family in Colonial Andover, Massachusetts* (Ithaca, N.Y.: Cornell University Press, 1970), passim. Edmund S. Morgan, in *American Slavery, American Freedom: The Ordeal of Colonial Virginia* (New York: Oxford University Press, 1975), has argued that much of the colony's early history was shaped by the struggle between the ex-servants he calls "terrible young men" (figurative "sons") and Virginia's leaders, who could be characterized as "fathers." Virginia DeJohn Anderson, in *New England's Generation: The Great Migration and the Formation of Society and Culture in the Seventeenth Century* (New York: Cambridge University Press, 1991), 160, contends that intergenerational conflict was muted because sons knew they would eventually inherit their fathers' lands and paternal powers. Intrafamilial lawsuits are discussed below.

12. Within the context of women's history, some attention has been paid to relationships of mothers and daughters in the colonies. See, e.g., Mary Beth Norton, *Liberty's Daughters: The Revolutionary Experience of American Women, 1750–1800* (Boston: Little, Brown, 1980), 102–5.

13. *SAL*, I, 156–57; *L&L*, 11; *NHCP Recs*, II, 376. See also ibid., 583–84; *NPCL*, 270–71. The earliest Bay Colony law on the subject of negligent parents and masters was adopted in 1642 (*Mass Col Recs*, II, 8–9). Note that "children" (presumably including daughters) were to be catechized and to learn to read, but that only sons had to be taught to write.

14. *RI Col Recs*, I, 332; *NHCP Recs*, II, 367; *Mass Col Recs*, IV, pt 1, 150–51.

15. *RI Col Recs*, I, 171; *SAL*, II, 266.

16. *NHCP Recs*, II, 611; *L&L*, 39, 6; *SAL*, II, 117–18.

17. For a comprehensive discussion of this process in Virginia, see Kathleen M. Brown, "Gender and the Genesis of a Race and Class System in Virginia, 1630–1750" (unpub. Ph.D. diss., University of Wisconsin, Madison, 1990), I, 177–211. The first relevant Maryland law appears in *Md Archs*, I, 342; it was later followed by many others.

18. *SAL*, II, 270 (quotations), 299–300, 480–81.

19. For example, *Md Archs*, I, 493–95, II, 325–30, and *SAL*, I, 260–61, 416–17, II, 92–94, 444–45. See Lois Green Carr, "The Development of the Maryland Orphans' Court, 1654–1715," in Aubrey C. Land et al., eds., *Law, Society, and Politics in Early Maryland* (Baltimore, Md.: The Johns Hopkins University Press, 1974), 41–62.

20. Recording contracts: *NPCL*, 58, and *SAL*, II, 388; terms of service: *Md Archs*, I, 409–10, II, 147–48, and *SAL*, I, 257, 442; apprenticing orphans: *L&L*, 11–12; forbidding sale: *NHCP Recs*, II, 177; pregnant maidservants: *SAL*, II, 114, 167. Massachusetts included a list of "Liberties of Servants" in *BOL*, carrying them over into *L&L*.

21. *SAL*, I, 538; *BOL*, 231; *RI Col Recs*, I, 162, 158 (quotations) (see also 182–83). For a sampling of the runaway laws adopted in the Chesapeake: *Md Archs*, I, 348–49, II, 146–47; *SAL*, I, 253–55, 401.

22. *L&L*, 6; *NHCP Recs*, II, 578; *NPCL*, 245. Although twelve of the fifteen capital offenses listed in the Laws and Liberties had originated in the Body of Liberties, these two laws were new in 1648. John Cotton first proposed the death penalty for rebellious children in his draft legal code for the Bay Colony (see Thomas Hutchinson, comp., *Hutchinson Papers. Publications of the Prince Society*, I [1865; reprint, New York: Burt Franklin, 1967], 197). Connecticut, declaring that "incorigiblenes" in children or servants was a "forerunner" of capital crimes, directed in 1642 that such rebels be committed to houses of correction for an indefinite period (*Conn Col Recs*, I, 78). See also *RI Col Recs*, I, 163.

23. William Bradford, *Of Plymouth Plantation*, ed. Samuel Eliot Morison (New York: Random House/Modern Library, 1967), 25.

24. *Mass Col Recs*, IV, pt 2, 395–96. For a 1655 call for "more severity" in enforcement, see *MHS Colls*, 3d ser., III (1825), 48–49, and for a futile 1674 attempt to do just that, *EC Ct Recs*, V, 378.

25. Increase Mather, Diary, American Antiquarian Society, Worcester, Mass. (hereafter AAS), passim. Quotations: Oct. 3, 1696; July 17, 1697. See, e.g., on children's illnesses, Apr. 23, 29, June 4, Aug. 25, 1665; wife's illness, Jan. 16, Feb. 10, Mar. 10, 1704/5; thanksgiving for Cotton and Samuel, Mar. 10, 1694/5; July 10, 1697; "disposing of" daughters, Sept. 16, 1691; Mar. 24, 1693/4. But when his daughters were successfully married off, that became grounds for thanksgiving (e.g., Aug. 22, 1696).

26. *WP*, I, 283, IV, 366, III, 263. On Henry, ibid., II, 67, 78–79, 94, 101.

27. *WP*, II, 285; John Saffin, Notebook, "Sundry Readings Epitomiz'd," 58 (typescript), AAS; *WP*, IV, 239–40. Some New Englanders even thought that "the ancient practice in England of children asking their parents' blessing upon their knees" should be revived, but not everyone agreed (*JWJ*, II, 324).

28. *Me Ct Recs*, II, 487; *NHT Recs*, 443–44. For other cases in which family governors were held responsible for offenses of servants and children, see, e.g., *Ct Assts Recs*, II, 60, 66; *Me Ct Recs*, II, 23, 286; *NH Ct Recs*, XL, 370. My data set includes 16 prosecutions for inadequate supervision of misbehaving children or servants, 15 of them in New England.

29. Essex County Quarterly Court File Papers, WPA Transcripts, XII, f 73/3, Phillips Library, Peabody Essex Museum, Salem, Mass. (hereafter cited as ECFP); printed in altered form in *EC Ct Recs*, III, 412.

30. Because James Hosmer omitted Winthrop's detailed account of this incident from his edition of *JWJ*, these two paragraphs rely on an earlier edition, James Savage, ed., *The History of New England from 1630 to 1649 by John Winthrop, Esq.* (2d ed., Boston: Little, Brown, 1853), II, 54–58 (quotations 54–55). The trial is described in *Mass Col Recs*, II, 12–13. Humfrey planned to assume the governorship of Providence Island, a Puritan colony in Central America, but the island fell to the Spanish prior to his arrival. See Karen O. Kup-

perman, *Providence Island, 1630–1641: The Other Puritan Colony* (New York: Cambridge University Press, 1993), passim, esp. 322–25.

31. Two years later, Fairfield was allowed to go as far as Roxbury (*Mass Col Recs*, II, 61), but he was not permitted to stop wearing the noose until 1652 (ibid., IV, pt 1, 91). The rewritten law is in ibid., II, 21–22. Hubbard's account, which relies heavily on Winthrop's journal, is in his *History of New England from the Discovery to 1680, MHS Colls*, 2d ser., VI (1817), 376–79. On Dorcas's later life, see *WP*, IV, 451–52.

32. For examples of these strategies: *EC Ct Recs*, VI, 156–58, 353; *Md Archs*, LIV, 523, 546; William Sargent, ed., *York Deeds* (Portland, Me.: Brown, Thurston, & Co., 1888), II, ff 123, 159; *NH Ct Recs*, XL, 337. Indentures for girls tended to require less of masters and mistresses than did those for boys.

33. *WP*, II, 175. Marylanders recorded many gifts of livestock to children; e.g., *Md Archs*, X, 84–85, 168, 299, 393–94, 406. Such strategies could be very successful: by 1666 two cow calves given to a girl around 1654 by friends of her deceased father, augmented with three other calves she inherited at the death of her stepfather in 1661, had become a substantial and valuable herd of six cows, six heifers, and a newborn calf, along with a manservant who had been purchased in exchange for six more of her cattle (ibid., LIV, 47, 219, 401).

34. *New England Historical and Genealogical Register*, XIII (1859), 203 (hereafter cited as *NEHGR*); *EC Ct Recs*, V, 380–82 (quotation 380). See also ibid., 57.

35. The following three paragraphs are based on *WP*, IV, 502 (Mr. Pester); IV, 303, 305, 312, 321 (James); V, 295–310 passim (Lucy Jr.). Emmanuel married Lucy Winthrop in 1622, after the death of his first wife, Ann, who had borne him three children: James, Susan, and Mary. Susan, the older girl, was probably the object of Mr. Pester's affections, since Mary married Mr. Anthony Stoddard before the end of 1639. Susan eventually married Robert Roberts.

36. For two examples of marriages without consent and their dire consequences, see Sargent, ed., *York Deeds*, III, 52–53, 66, 84; and *New Ams Ct Recs*, I, 155–73 passim, II, 33–87 passim (Maria Verleth and Johan Van Beeck).

37. *Md Archs*, LIV, 109–10.

38. Sargent, ed., *York Deeds*, II, f 79.

39. See *BOL*, 230; *NPCL*, 281–82, 299; *NHCP Recs*, II, 614; *Md Archs*, I, 156–57, 353–54; *SAL*, II, 303. On the problem of interpreting men's wills: Mary Beth Norton, "Reflections on Women in the Age of the American Revolution," in Ronald Hoffman and Peter J. Albert, eds., *Women in the Age of the American Revolution* (Charlottesville: University Press of Virginia, 1988), 482–88. On legal provisions for widows, see chapter three.

40. Detailed wills: Bernard Bailyn, ed., *The Apologia of Robert Keayne: The Self-Portrait of a Puritan Merchant* (New York: Harper & Row, 1965); *Md Archs*, X, 88–90; Sargent, ed., *York Deeds*, II, ff 27–31. Unborn children: *Md Archs*, LIV, 208–9; *AN Ct Recs*, II, 302. Approval of marriages: *NHCP Recs*, I, 411n–12n, 479n, II, 447n–48n.

41. *Md Archs*, LIV, 670; Job Chandler, will, August 24, 1659, Testamentary Proceedings, I (1659), f 31, Maryland Hall of Records, Annapolis (hereafter MHR).

42. For intergenerational disputes, see *Plymouth Col Recs*, V, 27, 44, 45, 50, and *Ct Assts Recs*, III, 90–93; for an intragenerational one (among sisters) that reached the Virginia House of Burgesses: *SAL*, I, 405.

43. The following five paragraphs are based on Mellen Chamberlain, ed., *A Documentary History of Chelsea* (Boston: Massachusetts Historical Society, 1908), I, 392–632 passim. Quotations, in the order used in the text, are from 395, 399, 405, 573, 405. A similar contentious case arose in 1665 when Governor John Endicott's will favored his younger son, Zerobabell, over his older son, John. See *CSM Pubs*, XX (1917–19), 259–63; "The Govr Endecott Estate," *Essex Institute Historical Collections*, XXV (1888), 137–57.

44. On daughters inheriting land, see, e.g., the essays in part 1 of Hoffman and Albert, eds., *Women in Age of American Revolution*, and Vivian Bruce Conger, " 'Being Weak of Body But Firm of Mind and Memory': Widowhood in Colonial America, 1630–1750" (unpub. Ph.D. diss., Cornell University, 1994), chapter 6. Carol Karlsen, in *The Devil in the Shape of a Woman: Witchcraft in Colonial New England* (New York: W. W. Norton, 1987),

passim, contends that such female landowners were particularly liable to be accused of witchcraft.

45. The data set identifies 43 such prosecutions in the Chesapeake, 11 with female defendants and 38 with male defendants (6 married couples were charged together). In New England, the comparable total in cases involving women was 17 (5 against women, 14 against men, 2 of these involving couples); an additional random sample of 10 represents a larger universe (approximately 30) of cases with male participants alone. Prosecutions enumerated herein are for child abuse (15) and the mistreatment (39) or murder (16) of one's servants or slaves. Infanticide, quintessentially a crime of unwed mothers and one with very different patterns of prosecution and conviction in both regions, is discussed in chapters four and seven.

46. Fourteen of the 21 mistreatment cases in the Chesapeake were brought to court by the victims, but the same was true in only 4 of 18 New England cases (22%). Just 2 of the 16 servant-murder prosecutions in the data set took place in New England, and I have identified only 2 additional northern cases in records not coded. Convictions were obtained in 57% (N=19 of 35) of Chesapeake cases with known outcomes and in 85% (N=22 of 26) of New England prosecutions. New England churches also occasionally excommunicated members who abused children or servants; see Richard D. Pierce, ed., *The Records of the First Church in Boston 1630–1868, CSM Pubs*, XXXIX (1961), 20, 44.

47. *NHT Recs*, I, 436; *EC Ct Recs*, III, 224.

48. The account in the next three paragraphs is based on *JWJ*, I, 310–14 passim; see also ibid., II, 20–21. The trial is recorded in *Mass Col Recs*, I, 275. Nathaniel Eaton was the brother of Governor Theophilus Eaton of New Haven; see *WP*, IV, 253–54.

49. "The Autobiography of Thomas Shepard," *CSM Pubs*, XXVII (1927–30), 389.

50. I can identify six such cases in the Bay Colony and one in Plymouth (e.g., *EC Ct Recs*, I, 174, 257).

51. *EC Ct Recs*, I, 257; *Plymouth Col Recs*, V, 16; *New Ams Ct Recs*, IV, 12; *Md Archs*, LX, 233–35. The spouse-abuse cases are *NHT Recs*, I, 246–47; *EC Ct Recs*, V, 312. For the opposite conclusion drawn from the same lack of prosecutions for child abuse, see John Demos, "Child Abuse in Context: An Historian's Perspective," in John P. Demos, ed., *Past, Present, and Personal: The Family and the Life Course in American History* (New York: Oxford University Press, 1986), 68–91. But Elizabeth Pleck concurs with me; see chapter 1 of her *Domestic Tyranny: The Making of American Social Policy against Family Violence from Colonial Times to the Present* (New York: Oxford University Press, 1987).

52. *Plymouth Col Recs*, III, 83; *EC Ct Recs*, V, 417–19, VII, 421–22. On the Beales and Stacys: chapter one, n. 91. For trustees' suits, *EC Ct Recs*, I, 258; *Md Archs*, LVI, 234; *Plymouth Col Recs*, III, 156, 160–61, 166.

53. *Va Ct Recs*, 201; *Md Archs*, LXV, 90. See also ibid., LIII, 410–11. For equally rare cases in which relatives interceded on behalf of Chesapeake children or servants, see *AN Ct Recs*, I, 1, and *Md Archs*, XLI, 334–35, 493–94.

54. Quotations: *AN Ct Recs*, I, 79; *Md Archs*, X, 474, XLIX, 318, X, 484. Two thirds of the Chesapeake complaints (11 of 16 with known outcomes) met with positive responses from the courts.

55. *EC Ct Recs*, II, 238, V, 351, I, 361–62. See also *Plymouth Col Recs*, III, 75; *NH Ct Recs*, XL, 113–14.

56. *EC Ct Recs*, I, 380, V, 351, II, 257. Most scholars, like the Essex court, have concluded that Elizabeth Dew was lying when she accused Zerobabell Endicott of fathering her child (another man admitted having sexual intercourse with her), but the evidence of sexual abuse is stronger than that for paternity.

57. *Md Archs*, XLI, 270–75. See also *Va Ct Recs*, 468–69.

58. John Josselyn, "An Account of Two Voyages to New-England," *MHS Colls*, 3d ser., III (1833), 231.

59. The Maryland records contain numerous reports of this nature (e.g., *Md Archs*, X, 52, 73–74, XLI, 385, XLIX, 215–16, LIV, 360–62).

60. *Md Archs*, XLIX, 166, LVII, 60–61. (The full records of the trials of Alvey and

Carpenter are in ibid., XLIX, 166–68, 230, 233–34, and LVII, 59–64.) One case in which a Marylander did intervene is in ibid., XLI, 478–80.

61. This and the next two paragraphs are based on *Va Ct Recs*, 22–24. Testimony about the earlier death of another Proctor servant is intermingled with that relating to Abbott. For a similar New England case, in which a young male servant futilely sought assistance from others prior to his death, but in which they repeatedly returned him to his abusive master, who then went unpunished, see Edward Everett Hale et al., eds., *The Note-Book of Thomas Lechford Esq 1638 to 1641* (1884; repr., Camden, Me.: Picton Press, 1988), 229–31; and *Mass Col Recs*, I, 319.

62. Examples: *Md Archs*, XLIX, 251, 307–12, LIV, 9, 125; *Me Ct Recs*, I, 261–62, 272, 286; *Plymouth Col Recs*, III, 71–73, 82, 143, VII, 75. One of the most gruesome accounts of continued brutality is in *Ct Assts Recs*, III, 24–34 (see also *Mass Col Recs*, IV, pt 1, 145). Several convicted men, most notably Pope Alvey and Francis Carpenter (n. 60 above), escaped capital punishment by pleading benefit of clergy. If a man (the option was not open to women until 1723) pleaded benefit of clergy after having been convicted of a capital crime, he was branded on the thumb and released, but only the first such conviction was "clergyable."

63. The two Marylanders were Joseph ffincher and John Dandy; see *Md Archs*, XLIX, 303–7, 310–14 (ffincher), and ibid., X, 522, 524–25, 534–45 (Dandy). The New Englander was a man named Franklin (*JWJ*, II, 187–89). Dandy could not plead benefit of clergy because of a previous murder conviction, though his death penalty for that was remitted (*Md Archs*, IV, 254–55, 260, III, 98, 146); ffincher was found guilty of acting with "malice aforethought" and so was not allowed clergy. Massachusetts did not permit miscreants to plead benefit of clergy (Edgar J. McManus, *Law and Liberty in Early New England* [Amherst: University of Massachusetts Press, 1993], 112–14).

64. This paragraph and the next three are based on *Md Archs*, XLI, 190–91, 204–6. For a prosecution in the abuse and death of a New England slave, see Dukes County Court Records, I, ff 29–30, Dukes County Courthouse, Edgartown, Mass.

65. George Alsop, "Character of the Province of Mary-land," in Clayton Colman Hall, ed., *Narratives of Early Maryland 1638–1684* (New York: Charles Scribner's Sons, 1910), 354.

66. *Ct Assts Recs*, II, 78–79.

67. The data set identifies 3 prosecutions of daughters and 14 of sons; 10 of the defendants (2 girls, 8 boys) were found guilty. No similar charges were ever filed in the Chesapeake colonies.

68. *Ct Assts Recs*, III, 144–45; *NHT Recs*, I, 88–89, 238–39. The Porter case can be traced in *EC Ct Recs*, passim, from II, 335ff (quotation 336) through V, 345–46; *Ct Assts Recs*, III, 138–39; and *Mass Col Recs*, IV, pt 2, 195–97, 216–17 (quotation 217). Rare incidents involving physical resistance are recorded in *Plymouth Col Recs*, IV, 10, VI, 20; *EC Ct Recs*, IV, 186–87. For a case in which a son acknowledged to be "dutiful" and "carful" nevertheless aroused antagonism from neighbors by suing his father (who had not fulfilled a promise to him), see *EC Ct Recs*, IV, 381–82, V, 176–78.

69. See *WP*, I, 323, for the description of a son/father lawsuit as "scandalous." A suit by a son against his father's estate, alleging an unpaid marriage gift, is in *Mass Col Recs*, IV, pt 1, 412–15. Another ongoing dispute among a father and his two sons may be traced in John Hull's letters to the squabbling trio, Thomas, George, and John Broughton, 1673–1676, Hull Letterbook, AAS.

70. For examples of dowry suits: *Plymouth Col Recs*, VII, 218; *EC Ct Recs*, III, 156–57, V, 148, 194–95. Carol Karlsen argues that one such lawsuit helped to lead to a witchcraft accusation (*Devil in the Shape of a Woman*, 89–95).

71. *NHCP Recs*, I, 81, 84; *JWJ*, II, 93. Martha's subsequent history is unknown, but the Malbon family returned to England in the early 1650s (*NHT Recs*, II, 63, 81).

72. This paragraph summarizes material in *NHCP Recs*, I, 469–71. On her sister: ibid., 480; for the Meekeses' subsequent history, see below, n. 88. Rebecca also flirted openly with a married Dutch merchant prior to her liaison with Meekes (ibid., 308).

73. This paragraph is based on *NHT Recs*, I, 497–99, 505–507, II, 8–9. Patrick Morran lived at the Russells' house, and Mary Hitchcock Russell convinced Elizabeth Pinion not

to report Patrick Morran to the magistrates the first time she threatened to do so. During a drinking bout at the Russell house, Thomas Pinion told William Collins he could have sex with his wife. Moreover, Mary Russell, along with Hannah Pinion, was accused of "unseasonable familiarity" with Patrick Morran in 1667. She also deposed in the infanticide/adultery prosecution of Ruth Pinion Briggs. See the prologue to this section, passim.

74. This paragraph is based on *NHT Recs*, II, 65–71.

75. Ibid., I, 506, II, 71, 68–69.

76. The data set contains 132 prosecutions for resistance by dependents, only 17 involving children. The most common crime was running away (99 cases, 58 of them in the Chesapeake). The following discussion will consider not only these 132 cases but also other categories of crimes committed by servants against their masters (for example, theft and arson) and lawsuits for freedom (48 in the Chesapeake, 4 in New England).

77. In the Chesapeake, just 18% (2 of 11) of female servants and 26% (10 of 39) of male servants were whipped, whereas 66% (33 of 50) of all servants suffered no penalties other than extended service. In New England, though, 65% (28 of 43) of servants were whipped and just 23% (10 of 43) escaped with only an additional term of service (the data set includes too few female servants to allow for a useful breakdown by sex for New England).

78. Quotations, in order: *Ct Assts Recs*, II, 104; *WP*, III, 221; *AN Ct Recs*, II, 5. Also, *NHT Recs*, I, 428–29 (lying), *EC Ct Recs*, III, 376–77 (threats), and *Md Archs*, LI, 211 (false accusations); ibid., LIV, 478 (slander). Servants could also resist by revealing criminal activity in which their masters and mistresses had engaged: e.g., *AN Ct Recs*, I, 89; *NH Ct Recs*, XL, 39–40, 42–43.

79. *Md Archs*, IV, 306, XLIX, 8–10, X, 521, IV, 166. But contract provisions exempting servants from having "to beat at the mortar" did not always protect them; see the complaints of a maid in 1640 in *Va Ct Recs*, 465.

80. The exact figure for the Chesapeake is 72% (33 of 46). The success rates of men and women did not differ appreciably. Servants in New England were much less likely to be successful: in the 4 cases in the data set, two plaintiffs lost and two gained a divided verdict.

81. E.g., *Md Archs*, XLI, 7–8, 67, 485, 499–500, XLIX, 81–84, 220–21, 237–38, 380–81, 387–88. For an unsuccessful Massachusetts freedom suit, see *EC Ct Recs*, II, 293–97.

82. Anglo servants going home: *Me Ct Recs*, II, 29; *Pynchon Ct Rec*, 275; *Plymouth Col Recs*, II, 58–59. Indian runaways: *WP*, III, 509, V, 164–66; *EC Ct Recs*, II, 240–42; *Suffolk Ct Recs*, II, 1086–92.

83. Comments on the Dutch and the Swedes: *AN Ct Recs*, I, 120; *Va Ct Recs*, 467; *Md Archs*, X, 511. The saga of the Virginia maidservants (originally three, one of whom seems to have died) may be traced in *AN Ct Recs*, II, 273–74, 276–78, and *Md Archs*, IV, 205ff passim, esp. 210–11, 215–16, 224, 294, 358, 524.

84. *NHT Recs*, II, 23; *Md Archs*, LIV, 692, 184, 297. The Virginia General Court complained in July 1643 that masters were being too lax in bringing runaways in to be punished by the judicial system; see Norfolk County Deeds and Orders, I, f 237, microfilm 1a, Virginia State Library, Richmond.

85. *NHT Recs*, I, 476–77.

86. Charges that children had run away from parents or stolen from members of their own families are extremely rare. See, e.g., *EC Ct Recs*, I, 404 (runaway son); *Plymouth Col Recs*, II, 149, Dukes Cnty Ct Recs, I, f 36, and the case of Martha Malbon, n. 71, above (intrafamily thefts).

87. *Md Archs*, LX, 251–54 (quotation 252); *NHT Recs*, II, 246–47 (quotation 246). For a sample of thefts by northern servants, see, e.g., *EC Ct Recs*, II, 307–10, V, 141–43; *NHT Recs*, I, 427–28, II, 91–94; *Suffolk Ct Recs*, II, 751–53. Laurel Thatcher Ulrich, "It 'went away shee knew not how': Food Theft and Domestic Conflict in Seventeenth-Century Essex County," in Peter Benes, ed., *Foodways in the Northeast* (Boston, Mass.: Boston University Press, 1984), 94–104, examines this phenomenon. On the paucity of household furnishings even in wealthy Chesapeake households, see Lois Green Carr et al., *Robert Cole's World: Agriculture & Society in Early Maryland* (Chapel Hill: University of North Carolina Press, 1991), chapter 4.

88. This paragraph and the next are based on *NHT Recs*, I, 3–17.

89. Laws against trading with servants may be found in, e.g., *SAL*, I, 274–75; *NHCP Recs*, II, 601; and *Md Archs*, I, 500–1.

90. For assaults, see *EC Ct Recs*, IV, 200; *NH Ct Recs*, XL, 209; and *Ct Assts Recs*, II, 62. A sexual assault on a mistress by a male servant is recorded in *EC Ct Recs*, I, 324–25. For murders, two by slaves, see *Va Ct Recs*, 479; *Md Archs*, XLIX, 486, 490–91; and *Virginia Magazine of History and Biography*, III (1895–96), 308–10 (hereafter *VMHB*).

91. *NHCP Recs*, II, 169–71, 384–86, 399–400, 504–10. For other arson prosecutions of servants, see *EC Ct Recs*, IV, 56–57; *Ct Assts Recs*, II, 100; *Me Ct Recs*, II, 335. A slave woman was convicted and executed for arson in Massachusetts in 1681 (*CSM Pubs*, VI [1899–1900], 323–35). Arson, like theft by servants, does not seem to have been as much of a problem in the Chesapeake, probably for the same reason: the lack of good targets. Only by burning a master's tobacco house at very limited times of the year could a servant arsonist have caused much damage.

92. *VMHB*, V (1897–98), 353.

CHAPTER 3: FREE IN LIBERTY

1. T.E., *The Lawes Resolutions of Womens Rights; or, the Lawes Provision for Woemen* (London: John Moore, 1632), 232.

2. Ibid., 6.

3. Sir Robert Filmer, "In Praise of the Vertuous Wife," in Margaret J. M. Ezell, *The Patriarch's Wife: Literary Evidence and the History of the Family* (Chapel Hill: University of North Carolina Press, 1987), 181. Yet in this same essay Filmer acknowledged the political logic of his schema; see the discussion in the prologue to section three, below. Mary Astell, in *Some Reflections upon Marriage* (2d ed., London: R Wilkin, 1703), mentioned motherhood only briefly (see 36, 93) and did not deal with widowhood at all. Even Cotton Mather, who in *Ornaments for the Daughters of Zion* (Cambridge, Mass., 1692) devoted as many pages to mothers and widows as he did to daughters and wives, failed to emphasize such women's authority over others, stressing instead the ways they could be of service to their families and communities (see 88–103 passim).

4. Thomas Hobbes, *Leviathan. Parts One and Two*, intro. by Herbert W. Schneider (New York: Liberal Arts Press, 1958), chapter XX, 164. That Hobbes and Locke were not alone in their concerns is suggested by the seven essays included in part 1 ("The Politics of Patriarchy: Theory and Practice") of Margaret W. Ferguson et al., eds., *Rewriting the Renaissance: The Discourses of Sexual Difference in Early Modern Europe* (Chicago: University of Chicago Press, 1986).

5. Hobbes, *Leviathan*, ed. Schneider, chapter XX, 164–65.

6. John Locke, *Two Treatises of Government*, ed. Peter Laslett (Cambridge: Cambridge University Press, 1988), II, § 77; I, § 59 (pp. 319, 183).

7. Ibid., I, § 55 (p. 180); and see above, chapter two, n. 4. See, in general, ibid., I, §§ 21–43 (pp. 156–71).

8. Ibid., II, § 170 (p. 381).

9. *RI Col Recs*, I, 161; *L&L*, 6.

10. For examples of colonial bastardy and fornication statutes, see, e.g., *Md Archs*, I, 373–74, 441–42; *SAL*, I, 252–53, 438–39, II, 114–15, 168; *NPCL*, 43. Bastardy prosecutions are discussed in chapter seven.

11. *BOL*, 229; *RI Col Recs*, I, 189–90; *NPCL*, 33. Another early law is *Conn Col Recs*, I, 38. For details of the English laws of widowhood, see *Lawes Resolutions*, 231–330.

12. *Md Archs*, I, 156–57, 190–91, 353–54. Details varied, but an intestate's widow commonly was given a life interest in a third of her husband's land and outright ownership of one third of his personal property. See, e.g., *NPCL*, 43, 133. New Haven's 1656 intestacy law allowed some discretion on the part of the judges as to the division of property between widow and children (*NHCP Recs*, II, 404–5, 614). If a Virginia woman had more than two children, she received only a child's share of her husband's personal estate but still succeeded to a life interest in one third of the real estate (*SAL*, II, 212, 303). Gloria Main, "Probate

Records as a Source for Early American History," *William and Mary Quarterly*, 3d ser., XXXII (1975), 91, estimates the proportion of men dying intestate as one fifth to one third.

13. *SAL*, II, 303; *NPCL*, 281. Even before 1671, Plymouth courts assisted widows whom they regarded as "a true labourer with him in the procuring of his estate" or "a frugall and laborious woman in the procuring of the said estate" (*Plymouth Col Recs*, III, 207, IV, 46).

14. *L&L*, 17; *NHCP Recs*, II, 586–87; *NPCL*, 299.

15. E.g., *EC Ct Recs*, II, 275–76, *NH Ct Recs*, XL, 427 (protecting children); *Plymouth Col Recs*, I, 54, III, 45 (wedding gifts); *Me Ct Recs*, II, 82, *Plymouth Col Recs*, I, 35 (rebellious servants); *Md Archs*, LXVI, 474 (servant abuse); *Mass Col Recs*, IV, pt 2, 453–54, *Plymouth Col Recs*, VII, 132–33 (suits by sons-in-law).

16. Frances Quilter, petition to Massachusetts General Court, May 29, 1679, Miscellaneous Manuscripts, Massachusetts Historical Society (hereafter MHS); *Me Ct Recs*, III, 224; *Md Archs*, LVII, 207, LIV, 212. I thank Vivian Bruce Conger for the Quilter reference. Despite the lack of evidence for this early period, the emotional state of these colonial widows probably resembled that of their later counterparts described in Mary Beth Norton, *Liberty's Daughters: The Revolutionary Experience of American Women, 1750–1800* (Boston: Little, Brown, 1980), 133–35.

17. For courts' dealings with poor widows, see, e.g., *Md Archs*, X, 75, XLI, 65–66, 320; *AN Ct Recs*, II, 202; *NHT Recs*, I, 417–18, 422. The Salem widow: *WP*, III, 22–23. Some widows were so poor they had to bind out their children: e.g., *Md Archs*, LIV, 28.

18. John Jarbo, deposition, Feb. 23, 1660/1, Testamentary Proceedings, I (1660), f 16, Maryland Hall of Records, Annapolis (hereafter cited as Test. Procs., MHR); *EC Ct Recs*, IV, 306–9 (quotations 308). For wills containing restrictions on widows, see *Me Ct Recs*, I, 329; *AN Ct Recs*, II, 46–49, 402; William Stone, will, December 3, 1659, Test. Procs., I (1659), ff 19–23, MHR. Studies of men's testamentary practices are summarized and cited in Mary Beth Norton, "The Evolution of White Women's Experience in Early America," *American Historical Review*, LXXXIX (1984), 603–4.

19. E.g., *NHT Recs*, II, 38, 80–81; *NHCP Recs*, II, 159–61; and *Mass Col Recs*, I, 292, II, 160, III, 124, 283. For rejected petitions: ibid., IV, pt 1, 98, 302.

20. Glenn W. LaFantasie, ed., *The Correspondence of Roger Williams* (Providence: Rhode Island Historical Society, 1988), II, 483–84; *Early Records of the Town of Providence* (Providence: Snow & Farnham City Printers, 1892), I, 30–34. A similar strategy was implied in the agreement signed by a Suffolk County widow and her grown children in early 1675 (*Suffolk Ct Recs*, I, 550–54).

21. For a few examples of such disputes: *Me Ct Recs*, II, 302–3, 501; *Suffolk Ct Recs*, II, 791, 848, 1040–41, 1139; *Md Archs*, LIV, 654, 658; *Mass Col Recs*, IV, pt 2, 525, 540. Not surprisingly, most such contentions occurred in New England. Chesapeake widows, who remarried quickly and tended to be younger, lacked the extended kinship networks that helped to produce lawsuits by expanding the number of potential heirs.

22. This paragraph and the next two are based on *Md Archs*, XLI, 164, 455, 518, 521, XLIX, 30. William Martin's will is in Test. Procs., I (1661), f 20, MHR.

23. Patience and her first husband, Henry Needham, arrived in Maryland in 1659, so she had been married to William Martin for less than two years. At some point between early 1663 and late 1665, Patience Martin married a man named Thomas Hawker (or Hooker), who thereby came into possession of Francis Martin's land (*Md Archs*, XLIX, 538, 563–64). The fate of the Needham daughters is unknown.

24. This paragraph and the next draw on *EC Ct Recs*, II, 443–46, III, 16, and Essex County Quarterly Court File Papers, WPA Transcripts, VIII, ff 66–70, 89–91, Phillips Library, Peabody Essex Museum, Salem, Mass. (hereafter cited as ECFP).

25. The account of this case in this and the next four paragraphs is drawn from *EC Ct Recs*, VII, 100, 255, 266–70, 383; ECFP, XXXI, ff 116–19, XXXII, ff 2–11; *Ct Assts Recs*, I, 156; and Frances Quilter, petitions to General Court, May 29, 1679, n.d., and related documents, Miscellaneous Manuscripts, MHS. I owe the latter references to Vivian Bruce Conger. Mark Quilter had beaten Frances at least once (*EC Ct Recs*, I, 140–41, 192). For another example of a brother-in-law pressuring a recent widow, see *EC Ct Recs*, V, 46–47, 111–12 (esp. 112).

26. For the Smiths and Rowlands, see *EC Ct Recs*, III, 414 through V, 181 passim; the Dorchester estate litigation is in *Suffolk Ct Recs*, I, 426–33, 472, 508–9, 543–46.

27. For Rachel Clinton, *EC Ct Recs*, III, 372 and ff passim; for the Nickerson suit, *Ct Assts Recs*, III, 121–28 (quotation 124). Rachel Clinton was later accused of witchcraft; her story is narrated in greater detail in both Carol Karlsen, *The Devil in the Shape of a Woman: Witchcraft in Colonial New England* (New York: W. W. Norton, 1987), 108–10; and John P. Demos, *Entertaining Satan: Witchcraft and the Culture of Early New England* (New York: Oxford University Press, 1982), 19–35.

28. The quoted phrase: *Md Archs*, LVII, 241. The much-married women of Maryland often distributed property to their children before reentering wedlock; e.g., ibid., X, 395–96, 419, LIII, 221–22, LVII, 215–18, LX, 133–34. For agreements allowing women to retain control of property in a new marriage, see ibid., LIV, 45–46, LVII, 468–69; *AN Ct Recs*, II, 127; *Plymouth Col Recs*, IV, 163–64; William Sargent, ed., *York Deeds* (Portland, Me.: Brown, Thurston, & Co., 1888), III, f 138. Marylynn Salmon, *Women and the Law of Property in Early America* (Chapel Hill: University of North Carolina Press, 1986), chapters 5–6, offers a comprehensive discussion of marriage settlements, though focusing on a later period.

29. *EC Ct Recs*, VI, 195, 297–98, VII, 150, 242. For the prenuptial agreement with Francis Plummer, see ibid., V, 159–60. See chapter one, n. 40.

30. Historians have disproportionately emphasized colonial widows' management of independent businesses, rather than focusing on their more common task of administering their husbands' estates. (This theme has been dominant in the literature since the publication of Elisabeth Anthony Dexter's influential *Colonial Women of Affairs* [Boston, Mass.: Houghton Mifflin, 1924; rev. ed., 1931].) Yet as Lyle Koehler has shown in his *A Search for Power: The "Weaker Sex" in Seventeenth-Century New England* (Urbana: University of Illinois Press, 1980), 118–22 and appendix 2, few widows in this early period engaged in enterprises other than innkeeping, and even female innkeepers were scarce before the final decade of the century. For a recent book on widows that properly stresses estate management, see Lisa W. Wilson, *Life after Death: Widows in Pennsylvania 1750–1850* (Philadelphia: Temple University Press, 1992).

31. The precise figures from my data set are as follows: in the Chesapeake, 57% (234 of 413) of named female plaintiffs were widows, and 80% (182 of 227) of their cases were suits for debt; 50% (223 of 447) of named female civil defendants were widows, 92% (200 of 218) of those lawsuits being for debt. In New England, 61% (91 of 150) of named female plaintiffs were widows, with 54% (44 of 82) of the suits being for debt; 51% (77 of 150) of female civil defendants were widows, while 56% (38 of 68) of the cases were debt suits. Fewer than 5% of female civil litigants in either region were single (never married).

32. *NHT Recs*, I, 107; *Md Archs*, LI, 47; *Mass Col Recs*, IV, pt 1, 296; *Md Archs*, LVII, 412; *NHCP Recs*, I, 397. On male assistance, see, e.g., *Md Archs*, X, 365, XLIX, 200.

33. Examples of cases widows lost on technicalities are: *Me Ct Recs*, II, 302; *NH Ct Recs*, XL, 147; and *Md Archs*, LIII, 371–72. Maryland creditors were particularly likely to file quickly against widows; see, e.g., *Md Archs*, X, 127–31 (12 suits against Rebecca Manners); LIV, 275–76, 283–84 (7 suits against Mistress Ann Blunt); LIV, 446–52 (12 suits against Frances Armstrong, then a month later 10 suits against her new husband, all claims on her previous husband's estate).

34. *WP*, III, 125; *SAL*, II, 36; *Md Archs*, LIII, 424–25; ibid., XLIX, 51 (on Mistress Hammond, see chapter one, n. 75). See also *Mass Col Recs*, IV, pt 1, 215–16, for a widow who took more than her third of her husband's estate and "carried this whole some already out of the country" even though her inheritance should have been "for terme of life only."

35. In the Chesapeake, 79% of widowed plaintiffs (N=168) were victorious in lawsuits, as were 74% (N=135) of married plaintiffs; 14% of widowed defendants (N=30) and 24.5% of married defendants (N=55) also won their cases. In New England, 59% (N=50) of widowed plaintiffs won, as did 58% (N=60) of married couples, while 34% (N=26) of widowed defendants and 29% (N=26) of married couples were victorious.

36. Both her first husband, Thomas Smith, "gent.," and her third, Mr. William Elton-head, ended up on the wrong side of Maryland's endemic political quarrels and were exe-

cuted, Smith in 1638, Eltonhead in 1655. Her second, Captain Philip Taylor, was a Virginian.

37. For the controversy surrounding William Eltonhead's will, see Test. Procs., I (1657), f 10, MHR; *Md Archs*, XLI, 178–80, XLIX, 206–7. Jane Eltonhead's will is in Test. Procs., I (1659), ff 27–28, MHR; the challenges to Thomas Taylor's claims to the land may be traced in *Md Archs*, I, 432–33, 466–67, LVII, 295–97, 439–44. See also *The Calvert Papers* (Baltimore: Maryland Historical Society, 1889), I, 231–32. In 1668 John and Gartrude Anderton tried unsuccessfully to win possession of land owned thirty years earlier by her father, Thomas Smith (*Md Archs*, LVII, 246–49, 381).

38. Jane Eltonhead's long-running suit against Edmund Scarborough and Simon Oversee's suit against her may be traced in *Md Archs*, X, XLI passim. Thomas Taylor's suit against John Anderton is in *Md Archs*, XLIX, 99–100, 196. See also Test. Procs., I (1657), f 9, MHR, evidently a piece of evidence in the case.

39. The database contains information on 1299 prosecutions of women with known marital status: single, 348; widowed, 68; married, 883. Since the 68 widows in the data set were charged with 25 different crimes, it is impossible to deduce much from the pattern of accusations. The most frequently committed offenses other than liquor-sale violations (N=8) and fornication (N=10) were not attending church services (N=7), neglect of duty (N=4), and lewd behavior (N=4). On widows as innkeepers, see n. 30, above.

40. This case may be followed in *Md Archs*, IV, 422–45 passim. On Roger Oliver's estate, see ibid., 209–10, 222–23. Baker and another perjured witness seem to have escaped punishment, though why is not clear.

41. *Md Archs*, XLIX, 44–45, 53, 76–77, 86–87. Elizabeth Potter had skated close to the edge of legality in March 1659/60, but escaped with only a monetary penalty; see ibid., XLI, 356–57. Men who married widows sometimes had to pay judgments against previous husbands' estates out of their own pockets; see, e.g., the decision against John Wright, who married the widow of Bartholomew Glevin, in ibid., LVII, 179.

42. The database identifies no other women in the Chesapeake accused of these crimes, and just 3 men; in New England, the comparable figures are 6 women and 20 men. The data set includes 20 prosecutions for perjury and 8 for forgery, with 5 of the cases involving more than one offender. In the 24 cases with known outcomes, 21 defendants (6 women and 15 men) were found guilty in 18 prosecutions. The only defendants sentenced to mutilation were Oliver, Greene, and one man; most commonly, men were punished by fines or shaming. The other four guilty women were fined, shamed, or whipped. It is impossible to know whether Oliver and Greene were treated more harshly because of their sex or because their offenses were regarded as particularly heinous, but the one male Marylander who received a sentence of mutilation was, like Oliver, tried in 1648 (*Md Archs*, IV, 391–93).

43. This paragraph and the next four are based on John P. Demos, ed., *Remarkable Providences* (New York: Braziller, 1972), 228–39 passim; and Nancy F. Cott, ed., *Root of Bitterness: Documents in the Social History of American Women* (New York: E. P. Dutton, 1972), 47–58 passim. The quotations are from: Demos, ed., *Remarkable*, 229, 228, 230–31, 237–38, and Cott, ed., *Root*, 50, 54. See chapter one, above, for more on Ann Hibbens's trial. The official record of the excommunication is in Richard D. Pierce, ed., *The Records of the First Church in Boston 1630–1868* (*CSM Pubs*, XXXIX [1961]), 31–33. At the time, Boston carpenters were being fined for overcharging their customers; a May 1640 petition on that theme is in Edward Everett Hale et al., eds., *The Note-Book of Thomas Lechford Esq 1638 to 1641* (1884; repr., Camden, Me.: Picton Press, 1988), 242. For a recent feminist interpretation of the Hibbens trial with a somewhat different focus, see Jane N. Kamensky, "Governing the Tongue: Speech and Society in Early New England" (unpub. Ph.D. diss., Yale University, 1993), chapter 3.

44. *Mass Col Recs*, I, 327. For a contemporary account noting the importance of the fact that Mistress Hibbens acted "without her husband," see Thomas Lechford, "Plain-Dealing: or, Newes from New-England (London, 1642)," *MHS Colls*, 3d ser., III (1833), 73.

45. Unfortunately, no detailed records of her witchcraft trial survive. For a convenient compilation of the remaining fragmentary accounts, see David D. Hall, ed., *Witch-Hunting*

in *Seventeenth-Century New England: A Documentary History, 1638–1692* (Boston: Northeastern University Press, 1991), 89–91.

46. *Essex Institute Historical Collections*, IX (1868), pt 1, 19–21; *Plymouth Col Recs*, III, 24; *RI Col Recs*, I, 31; *Mass Col Recs*, IV, pt 1, 275–76. At least two widowed landowners in Providence did not sign the 1640 document (cf. *RI Col Recs*, I, 24). See also a petition from Charlestown residents signed by six men and one widow in Hale, ed., *Lechford Note-Book*, 364–65.

47. Widows spoke for themselves (it appears) in New Haven: *NHT Recs*, II, 294, 306. The directive is in *NHCP Recs*, II, 5. On a similar ambiguity in the roles of women as shareholders in land corporations, see John Frederick Martin, *Profits in the Wilderness: Entrepreneurship and the Founding of New England* (Chapel Hill: University of North Carolina Press, 1991), 172, 220–21.

48. Twice Locke remarked that if Filmer could read the Fifth Commandment as meaning "all Power were Originally in the Father," it was just as logical to read it to mean, "all Power were Originally in the Mother." Locke clearly believed that his readers would find that idea ridiculous and thus accept his contention that the analogy between family and state should be rejected (Locke, *Two Treatises*, ed. Laslett, I, §§ 11, 66 [pp. 149, 188–89]).

49. Lillian Handlin, "Dissent in a Small Community," *New England Quarterly*, LVIII (1985), 193–220, examines these same incidents, but our interpretations differ significantly, most notably because Handlin insists that gender was not a factor in the confrontations. See also, on Anne Eaton, Mary Maples Dunn, "Saints and Sisters: Congregational and Quaker Women in the Early Colonial Period," *American Quarterly*, XXX (1978), 587.

50. The biographical data on Anne Eaton are taken from S. E. Baldwin's article on Theophilus Eaton, *New Haven Colony Historical Society Papers*, VII (1908), 1–33 (hereafter cited as *NHCHS Papers*). The descriptive phrase is Cotton Mather's, in *Magnalia Christi Americana . . .* (Hartford, Conn.: Silas Andrus and Son, 1858), I, 151.

51. *NHCP Recs*, I, 93, 258 (the quotation), 334. Her first husband was lost at sea, along with several other leaders of the colony, in early 1646. At the time of the events considered here, their deaths were suspected but not yet confirmed. On her later life, see Robert Bolton, *A History of Westchester County*, 2d ed. (New York: A. S. Gould, 1848), II, 43–44.

52. For fragmentary information about Edmund Leach, see *NHCP Recs*, I, 199; *WP*, V, 358; and *A Volume Relating to the Early History of Boston Containing the Aspinwall Notarial Records from 1644 to 1651* (*Boston Record Commissioners' Reports*, XXXII [1903]), 239–41, 386–87.

53. The account of Mistress Eaton's conversion to Baptist reasoning in this and the next three paragraphs is drawn from Newman Smyth, ed., "Mrs. Eaton's Trial (in 1644); as it Appears upon the Records of the First Church of New Haven," *NHCHS Papers*, V, 134–36 (hereafter cited as "Mrs. Eaton's Trial"). On Lady Moody: *JWJ*, II, 126; *EC Ct Recs*, I, 48; Koehler, *Search for Power*, 240–42; and Linda Biemer, *Women and Property in Colonial New York: The Transition from Dutch to English Law, 1643–1727* (Ann Arbor, Mich.: UMI Research Press, 1983), 11–31. The book was A. R. [Andrew Ritor], *A Treatise on the Vanity of Childish-Baptisme* (London, 1642). On the implications for Puritanism of the denial of infant baptism, see William McLoughlin, *New England Dissent 1630–1833* (Cambridge, Mass.: Harvard University Press, 1971), I, 26–48.

54. On religious practices in the Eaton household: Mather, *Magnalia*, I, 153. First Corinthians 14:35: "And if they will learne any thing, let them aske their husbands at home: for it is a shame for a woman to speake in the Church." Davenport also cited Malachi 2:7 (advising men to talk to their priests) as pertinent to her failure to consult him.

55. Her comments during the sermon are noted in "Mrs. Eaton's Trial," 143. Although the timing of Anne Eaton's initial conversion is nowhere specified, it probably occurred during the early months of 1644. In April of that year, one of John Winthrop's correspondents told him that "by meanes of a booke shee [Lady Moody] sent to Mrs. Eaton, shee questions her owne baptisme and it is verie doubtefull whither shee will be reclaymed, shee is so farre ingaged" (*WP*, IV, 456).

56. The account in this and the following paragraph comes from "Mrs. Eaton's Trial," 136–37. On the friendship of Theophilus Eaton and John Davenport: Leonard Bacon, *Thir-*

teen Historical Discourses on . . . the First Church in New Haven (New Haven, Conn.: Durrie & Peck, 1839), 88–89. Appropriately, perhaps, the author of an elegy on the death of Theophilus Eaton, comparing him successively to such Old Testament figures as Abraham and David, chose Job as the archetype for the verse dealing with Mistress Eaton (*MHS Colls*, 4th ser., VII [1865], 479).

57. Perkins: Edmund S. Morgan, ed., *Puritan Political Ideas* (Indianapolis, Ind.: Bobbs Merrill, 1965), 58. I thank Natalie Z. Davis for alerting me to the importance of Davenport's motivation. So crucial was household order to Theophilus Eaton's reputation that Cotton Mather, writing about him years later, ironically lauded his household management. "As in his government of the commonwealth, so in the government of his family, he was prudent, serious, happy to a wonder," asserted Mather, going on to quote unnamed "observers" who had supposedly exclaimed, "They never saw a house ordered with more wisdom!" (Mather, *Magnalia*, I, 153).

58. This paragraph and the next draw on "Mrs. Eaton's Trial," 137–38.

59. Matthew 18:17: "And if he refuse to heare them [visitors encouraging reformation], tell it unto the Church: and if he refuse to heare the Church also, let him bee unto thee as an heathen man, and a Publicane."

60. The charges, summarized in this and the following two paragraphs, are listed in "Mrs. Eaton's Trial," 138–44. Of the sixteen complaints about Anne Eaton's conduct in her household, six pertained to her relationships with her mother-in-law or stepdaughter, two to her treatment of her husband, and eight to her behavior toward her servants. In the mind of her prosecutors, breaking the Fifth Commandment involved her mistreatment of both superiors and inferiors; the Sixth ("Thou shalt not kill"), a figurative, not literal, "killing" of others; and the Ninth ("Thou shalt not bear false witness"), telling lies, primarily about her servants.

61. Cotton Mather, in *Magnalia*, I, 153, states that at times up to thirty people lived in the Eaton household.

62. The account in this and the next two paragraphs is drawn from "Mrs. Eaton's Trial," 144–48. For an example of how an admonition could successfully end in the reconciliation of its target to the New Haven church, see Bacon, *Thirteen Historical Discourses*, 307–9.

63. See Lechford, "Plain Dealing," *MHS Colls*, 3d ser., III (1833), 73, on New Haven's policy of excluding excommunicates from sabbath services.

64. "The Trial of Ezekiel Cheever, 1649," *Connecticut Historical Society Collections*, I (1860), 44–45 (see also 29, 35) (hereafter cited as *CHS Colls*). Cheever also insisted that one charge against Mistress Eaton was technically incorrect, for she admitted striking Elizabeth Eaton on the breast, not in the face.

65. *NHCP Recs*, I, 268–70. The circumstances under which this deposition was to be presented in court are obscure, but seem to be related to the 1646 trial of the gossiping women discussed in the following pages. See, in particular, a comment on 269 that this evidence "would nothing advantadg Mrs. Brewster," and a similar brief reference to a dispute between Mr. Perry and Mistress Brewster in "Trial of Cheever," *CHS Colls*, I (1860), 34.

66. *Mass Col Recs*, II, 85.

67. *NHCP Recs*, I, 242–57 (quotation 242). Anne Eaton herself was neither charged in the case nor called as a witness. The only charge not related to the women's conversations was an accusation that Mistress Brewster had been retailing liquor without a license. She demonstrated the hypocrisy of that charge by pointing out that the magistrates' own families had been among her best customers.

68. *NHCP Recs*, I, 242, 247, 252. After the trial of the women, Smith and her lover Philip Galpin (whom she soon married) were convicted of fornication, but she ultimately escaped whipping, just as Lucy Brewster had predicted (ibid., 259, 327).

69. Ibid., 252, 243.

70. Ibid., 246–47. The confrontation among Mistress Brewster, Smith, and Hall occurred on May 9, so the original conversation among the women took place some time in early May, though the date is nowhere given. The New Haven magistrates frequently employed such private examinations; see Gail Susman Marcus, " 'Due Execution of the Generall Rules of Righteousness': Criminal Procedure in New Haven Town and Colony, 1638–

1658," in David D. Hall et al., eds., *Saints & Revolutionaries: Essays on Early American History* (New York: W. W. Norton, 1984), 99–137.

71. *NHCP Recs*, I, 244–45. Mistress Brewster denied having said precisely the words reported, though she admitted uttering some of the statements in a general way. See above, prologue, n. 46 (Fancys); and *NHCP Recs*, I, 221–25 (Fugill).

72. Ibid., 253, 243 (quotations). See 244–45, 256–57, for Mistress Leach's remarks; 242–44 for Mistress Brewster's; and 253–56 for Mistress Moore's.

73. Ibid., 245, 247–50. Parker's trial also took place on June 2 (ibid., 257–59). The two had married by July 7 (ibid., 262).

74. Ibid., 249, 244, 243, 246.

75. Ibid., 251, 255, 257.

76. Although the records of the penalties have been lost, that the defendants were heavily fined can be inferred from Thomas Pell's repeated refusal to pay a substantial fine imposed on Lucy Brewster prior to their marriage. See ibid., 334, 362–63, 402, 456.

SECTION II PROLOGUE: SEARCHERS AGAINE ASSEMBLED

1. *Va Ct Recs*, 194.

2. Anthropologists have been in the forefront of the investigation of the various relationships of sex and gender. A good introduction to such work is Sherry Ortner and Harriet Whitehead, eds., *Sexual Meanings: The Cultural Construction of Gender and Sexuality* (New York: Cambridge University Press, 1981). The handling of cross-sexed individuals in Native American societies is analyzed in Walter L. Williams, *The Spirit and the Flesh: Sexual Diversity in American Indian Culture* (Boston, Mass.: Beacon Press, 1986). For an account of how contemporary American society handles sexually ambiguous babies at birth, see Suzanne J. Kessler, "The Medical Construction of Gender: Case Management of Intersexed Infants," *Signs*, XVI (1990), 3–26.

3. Three other scholars have written about the case. Alden Vaughan, in "The Sad Case of Thomas(ine) Hall," *Virginia Magazine of History and Biography*, LXXXVI (1978), 146–48, reviews the facts, compares Hall to Hester Prynne, and remarks on Hall's probable "mental anguish." Jonathan Ned Katz interprets Hall as a possible male cross-dresser in *Gay/Lesbian Almanac: A New Documentary* (New York: Harper & Row, 1983), 71–72. Kathleen M. Brown, in "Gender and the Genesis of a Race and Class System in Virginia, 1630–1750" (unpub. Ph.D. diss., University of Wisconsin, Madison, 1990), I, 88–90, uses Hall to introduce her discussion of women's roles in the colony. Brown has also written an unpublished paper focusing on Hall; our interpretations coincide on some points and differ on others. I wish to acknowledge the work of Tom Foster, Cornell '91, whose term paper on the Hall case in a seminar in autumn 1989 first alerted me to its importance. My discussion of the case has also benefited from the comments of members of the Cornell Study Group on Women and Gender, especially Biddy Martin, and of the Chesapeake Area Early Americanists, especially Toby Ditz.

4. Unless otherwise indicated, all quotations and details in the account that follows are taken from the record in the case, *Va Ct Recs*, 194–95.

5. Clive Holmes and Nicholas Canny alerted me to the fact that "Cales Accon," in which T's brother participated, was the attack on Cadiz (anglicized at the time as "Cales") in October 1625. The expedition in which Thomas later took part was an ill-fated English attack on the Isle de Ré during the summer of 1627. The troops who futilely tried to relieve the French Protestants besieged in the city of La Rochelle embarked on July 10, 1627; most of them returned to Plymouth in early November. It is, however, possible that Hall returned sooner than that.

6. *Va Ct Recs*, 159, 162–64 (quotation 163). Yet it is possible that the Thomas Hall in this case was the other man, the one who came to Virginia in 1620. (For him, see Virginia M. Meyer and John F. Dorman, eds., *Adventurers of Purse and Person Virginia 1607–1624/5*, 3d ed. [Richmond: Order of First Families of Virginia, 1987]. The Virginia muster of 1624/5 [ibid., 42] lists Thomas Hall and John Tyos as residents of George Sandys's plantation in James City and as 1620 immigrants on the *Bona Nova*. Also, in March 1625/6 Tyos men-

tioned Thomas "Haule" in a deposition [*Va Ct Recs*, 96].) In the theft prosecution Thomas Hall is not explicitly identified as a servant, though he was living with T's eventual master and mistress. Thus he could have been the free man who was Tyos's earlier acquaintance, perhaps a partner. Moreover, the birthplaces differ: T, as already indicated, described a birthplace "at or neere" Newcastle; this Thomas Hall identified his birthplace as a village in Cambridgeshire—not especially "neere" Newcastle, yet still in the same general area northeast of London. But the conclusion that the later T and this Thomas are the same seems justified not only by the thieving Thomas's sewing abilities but also by the difficulty of believing that within the same year two *different* persons both named Thomas Hall—who were approximately the same age (25 or 26) and who both knew how to sew—lived at the house of John and Jane Tyos, which would be a remarkable coincidence. Katz, Vaughan, and Brown do not link the Thomas Hall of the theft case with T.

7. Since the conversation overheard by England took place at Atkins' Arbor, the home of T's second master, it possibly occurred *after* T had been officially ordered to don women's clothing (see below). But then the element of voluntarism in both the question and the answer would seem misplaced, unless T's wearing women's apparel on that occasion was recognized as one of a number of similar episodes rather than a break with a past pattern that had occurred only because of orders from a superior.

8. Little can be discovered about the three women. At the time of the muster in 1624/5, Alice Longe was listed as living with her husband, Richard, on Nathaniel Basse's plantation. Roger Rodes, probably Dorothy's eventual husband, was then a servant of Thomas Allnut. The name Barbara Hall does not appear. A "boy" named Nicholas Eyres was resident on the Sandys plantation with John Tyos and the other Thomas Hall. See Meyer and Dorman, eds., *Adventurers*, 32, 41, 48. In *Va Ct Recs*, the name of Tyos's partner is rendered as "Eyros," not "Eyres," but since handwriting styles at the time make it difficult to distinguish "o" and "e," and the presence in Virginia of men surnamed "Eyres" is well documented, I have altered that spelling. I have discussed the role of female searchers of women's bodies in "Gender, Crime, and Community in Seventeenth-Century Maryland," in James Henretta et al., eds., *The Transformation of Early American History* (New York: Alfred A. Knopf, 1991), 144–48.

9. The two newcomers were the wife of Allen Kinaston and the wife of Ambrose Griffen. Allen Keniston is listed as a single man and a resident of Pasbehays in James City on the muster of 1624/5 (Meyer and Dorman, eds., *Adventurers*, 25). There is no mention of Griffen or his wife.

10. Vaughan and Brown (n. 3, above) argue that the fornication rumor was the key to the case, which they both interpret as preliminary to the possible prosecution of T for that crime (that is, T would first have to be defined as male before a fornication charge could be filed). I disagree with them over the centrality of the fornication rumor, but agree that the gossip must have been part of the reason why T was brought to court.

11. On February 9, 1632/3, the administration of Thomas Hall's estate was awarded to a man named Francis Poythres, but there is no way of knowing which Thomas Hall had died (*Va Ct Recs*, 202). A Thomas Hall also appears occasionally in the Lower Norfolk County records in the early 1640s; see Norfolk County Deeds, vol. 1, microfilm 1a passim, Virginia State Library, Richmond.

12. The best discussion of the one-sex model of humanity and its implications is Thomas Laqueur, *Making Sex: Body and Gender from the Greeks to Freud* (Cambridge, Mass.: Harvard University Press, 1990). See 126–30 for an analysis of Marie-Germain. See also, on persons with ambiguous sexual organs, John Money and Anke Ehrhardt, *Man & Woman, Boy & Girl* (Baltimore, Md.: The Johns Hopkins University Press, 1972), chapters 6, 8; Julia Epstein, "Either/Or—Neither/Both: Sexual Ambiguity and the Ideology of Gender," *Genders*, no. 7 (Spring 1990), 99–142; and Anne Fausto-Sterling, "The Five Sexes: Why Male and Female Are Not Enough," *The Sciences*, XXXIII, no. 2 (March/Apr. 1993), 20–24. Fausto-Sterling believes that T was either a true hermaphrodite or what she calls a "ferm"—a female pseudohermaphrodite, or a person with XX chromosomes and female sex organs but also with masculinized genitalia (Fausto-Sterling, personal communication, 1993).

13. See Lois Green Carr et al., *Robert Cole's World: Agriculture & Society in Early Maryland*

(Chapel Hill: University of North Carolina Press, 1991), 90–114, on "the standard of life" in the early Chesapeake.

14. See *Mass Col Recs*, IV, pt 1, 60–61, IV, pt 2, 41–42. Carolyn Merchant, *The Death of Nature: Women, Ecology, and the Scientific Revolution* (San Francisco: Harper & Row, 1989), 174–77, points out the importance of clothing in establishing status in Francis Bacon's utopia, described in his 1624 *The New Atlantis*.

15. Laqueur observes, in *Making Sex*, 124–25, that "in the absence of a purportedly stable system of two sexes, strict sumptuary laws of the body attempted to stabilize gender —woman as woman and man as man—and punishments for transgression were quite severe." A relevant recent study is Marjorie Garber, *Vested Interests: Cross-Dressing and Cultural Anxiety* (New York: Routledge, 1991).

16. For another case in which a master ordered a maidservant's body searched (it is not clear by whom), see *Suffolk Ct Recs*, II, 690.

17. A good general discussion of the colonists' attitudes toward sexuality is John D'Emilio and Estelle B. Freedman, *Intimate Matters: A History of Sexuality in America* (New York: Harper & Row, 1988), 1–52, especially (on the regulation of deviance) 27–38.

18. Brown interprets the statement literally in her "Gender and the Genesis of Race and Class System," I, 88. The suggestion that the phrase might have meant "earning a living" is mine, developed after consulting the *OED* (q.v. "bit"). Katz speculates that T's phrase had the erotic meaning suggested here, though he recognizes that such an interpretation is problematic (*Gay/Lesbian Almanac*, 72).

19. I owe the identification of the probable French origin of this phrase to Marina Warner and, through her, to Julian Barnes, whom she consulted (personal communication, 1993). My colleague Steven Kaplan, a specialist in the history of early modern France (and scholars he consulted in Paris), confirmed that "bite" and "chat" were used thus in the late sixteenth century and that the interpretation appears plausible. My thanks also go to the many historians who futilely tried to assist me in interpreting the phrase when I thought it was English in origin.

20. See the discussion in chapter one, ns. 53, 88–90. On the importance of marital sexuality in the colonies: D'Emilio and Freedman, *Intimate Matters*, 16–27.

21. See, on this point, Rudolf M. Dekker and Lotte C. van de Pol, *The Tradition of Female Transvestism in Early Modern Europe* (London: Macmillan, 1989).

22. *AN Ct Recs*, I, 85.

23. *Plymouth Col Recs*, III, 83; *WP*, III, 472; *BOL*, 218. See also *L&L*, 1. For a use of "inhabitants" excluding women, see *Mass Col Recs*, IV, pt 2, 173. See also *WP*, III, 181–85, for an essay by Winthrop that implies a society composed exclusively of males.

24. *WP*, IV, 478–79. See also William Bradford, *Of Plymouth Plantation*, ed. Samuel Eliot Morison (New York: Random House/Modern Library, 1967), 127, for a statement indicating that "useful persons" and "wives" were different sets of people.

25. *WP*, II, 282–83.

26. Edmund S. Morgan, ed., *Puritan Political Ideas 1554–1794* (Indianapolis, Ind.: Bobbs Merrill, 1965), 39, 51, 57. Such beliefs were not confined to Puritans; recall the Marylander George Alsop's equally hierarchical vision of society quoted in chapter two (n. 65). See also John Bargrave, "A Form of Policy for Virginia," c. December 1623, in Susan M. Kingsbury, ed., *Records of the Virginia Company of London* (Washington, D.C.: Government Printing Office, 1935), IV, 408–34.

27. Bradford, *Of Plymouth Plantation*, 370; *MHS Procs*, 2d ser., VIII (1893–94), 209; Everett Emerson, ed., *Letters from New England: The Massachusetts Bay Colony, 1629–1638* (Amherst: University of Massachusetts Press, 1976), 105; *WP*, III, 18. See also *JWJ*, I, 271; *WP*, II, 125, III, 432–33; and, on the importance of manorial lords in plans for Maryland, Section III, prologue, below.

28. Bradford, *Of Plymouth Plantation*, 369–70; *WP*, II, 294. See also *JWJ*, II, 83–84, for Winthrop's impassioned criticisms (from the standpoint of communal obligation) of those who moved to other colonies or returned home.

29. *NPCL*, 48. For prosecutions of people for disturbing their neighborhoods, see, e.g.,

Plymouth Col Recs, IV, 11, V, 27; *Me Ct Recs*, II, 57, 197; *NH Ct Recs*, XL, 11–12; *Suffolk Ct Recs*, I, 225, II, 785.

30. *SAL*, I, 164, 189, 244, II, 101–2, 280; *Me Ct Recs*, I, 268. See also *Ct Assts Recs*, II, 38.

31. *Md Archs*, III, 509.

CHAPTER 4: COMMUNITIES OF MEN, COMMUNITIES OF WOMEN

1. Statement printed in Roger Heamans, "An additional brief narrative of a late bloody design against the Protestants in Ann Arundel County Severn in Maryland in the Country of Virginia," *Maryland Historical Magazine*, IV (1909), 152 (hereafter *MHM*).

2. Boston women to magistrates, n.d. [c. 1649], Massachusetts Archives, IX, f 11, Massachusetts State Archives, Columbia Point, Boston (hereafter MA). Similar undated petitions are ff 8–9 (c. March 1648/9, signed by 68 Boston women), 10 (c. March 1648/9, 21 Dorchester women), 12–13 (c. May 1650, 43 Dorchester women), 14 (c. May 1650, 130 Boston women). Photostats of these petitions are also available at the Massachusetts Historical Society, Boston; some passages are easier to read in the MHS copies than in either the originals or the photostats at the state archives.

3. For competing accounts of the conflict, see the Heamans narrative, n. 1, above, 140–52 passim; John Hammond, "Hammond versus Heamans or an Answer to an audacious Pamphlet, published by an impudent and ridiculous Fellow," *MHM*, IV (1909), 237–51; Leonard Strong, "Babylon's Fall in Maryland," and John Langford, "A Juste and Cleere Refutation of . . . Babylon's Fall in Maryland," in Clayton Colman Hall, ed., *Narratives of Early Maryland 1638–1684* (New York: Charles Scribner's Sons, 1910), 235–46, 254–75.

4. MA, IX, ff 11, 8. Mistress Tilly had also committed a previous offense; in November 1647, she petitioned the General Court about a fine of £4 that had been levied on her. See *Mass Col Recs*, II, 207, III, 154. For her age, see n. 7, below.

5. MA, IX, ff 14, 11, 10, 12. See n. 2, above, for details of the individual petitions. The Court of Assistants records for this period have been lost, but Mistress Tilly's trial seems to have occurred in the spring of 1649, for the sole surviving deposition from it is dated March 8, 1648/9 (MA, IX, f 7). At its session of May 1649, probably as a consequence of the charges filed against Mistress Tilly, the General Court adopted a law forbidding midwives or other medical personnel from exercising "violence" or "cruelty" to the bodies of their patients, even "in the most difficult & desperate cases" (*Mass Col Recs*, II, 278–79).

6. MA, IX, ff 14, 10, 8, 11. That she was convicted is evident from the magistrates' comment in June 1650 (*Mass Col Recs*, III, 209).

7. Quotations: MA, IX, f 11 (the deputies' comment is written on the bottom of the petition), 12. The General Court formally responded to petitions from both women and men at its session of May–June 1650, but no petition signed by men survives in the records (*Mass Col Recs*, III, 197, 208–9, IV, pt 1, 24–25). It is not clear when or if the court wholly freed Mistress Tilly. The Tillys did not leave Boston; in 1665 they had some marital difficulties (*Mass Col Recs*, IV, pt 2, 288), and in 1668, when she was 66, she gave a deposition in an estate dispute (Suffolk Files #931, MA; my thanks to Elizabeth Bouvier of the archives staff for this latter reference).

8. *Mass Col Recs*, III, 197; MA, IX, f 14.

9. MA, IX, ff 8, 14.

10. Since the largely illiterate Chesapeake settlers did business chiefly on the basis of oral agreements instead of written documents, the court records of Virginia and Maryland serve as particularly rich sources for studying men's values. For books focusing on men's civil litigation that take a different approach from mine, see, e.g., David Thomas Konig, *Law and Society in Puritan Massachusetts: Essex County, 1629–1692* (Chapel Hill: University of North Carolina Press, 1979); William E. Nelson, *Dispute and Conflict Resolution in Plymouth County, Massachusetts, 1725–1825* (Chapel Hill: University of North Carolina Press, 1980); and Bruce Mann, *Neighbors and Strangers: Law and Community in Early Connecticut* (Chapel Hill: University of North Carolina Press, 1987). After reading numerous volumes of court records, I

have concluded that formulaic "lawsuits" often provided a way for illiterate people to record their obligations to each other. Many defendants failed to contest plaintiffs' claims, instead acknowledging the validity of demands in a perfunctory manner.

11. *Md Archs*, X, 458, IV, 465, 205, XLI, 6, 526–27. For similar deals involving residents of other colonies, see, e.g., *AN Ct Recs*, II, 170–71; *Plymouth Col Recs*, II, 50; *NHCP Recs*, I, 176–78.

12. *Md Archs*, IV, 15; *AN Ct Recs*, I, 86–87; *Md Archs*, LIII, 34–37. Undoubtedly it was such dealings as these that led George Alsop to observe that Maryland planters engaged in "crafty and sure bargaining" that could "over-reach the raw and unexperienced merchant." (Alsop, "Character of the Province of Mary-land," in Hall, ed., *Maryland Narratives*, 379.)

13. *Md Archs*, LIV, 74; *AN Ct Recs*, II, 67; *Md Archs*, XLIX, 158–59. See also, e.g., *AN Ct Recs*, I, 141; and Dukes County Court Records, I, f 88, Dukes County Courthouse, Edgartown, Mass. For rare instances of mistrust, see *Md Archs*, LIV, 190, XLIX, 162.

14. See *WP*, IV, 208–9, for the unsent letter. Winthrop's letters for 1640, passim, ibid., and *JWJ*, II, 3–4, give more details on the financial fiasco. See also John Hull Letterbook, I, passim, American Antiquarian Society, Worcester, Mass. (hereafter AAS), for a merchant's emphasis on the importance of fulfilling debt obligations—both those he owed and those owed to him.

15. *Md Archs*, XLIX, 238. Recall, in this context, the unenviable fates of the convicted perjurers Elizabeth Greene and Blanch Howell, discussed in chapter three. In New Haven, though, Governor Eaton thought oaths unnecessary, since men should always speak the truth (see *NHCP Recs*, I, 224).

16. *Md Archs*, LIV, 83, 159, LIII, 15. Many such cases may be found in ibid., IV, passim (e.g., 114, 227, 262, 333, 364). In 1648 the Provincial Court explicitly outlined "the Custome of the province" regarding oaths in civil suits (ibid., 414–15, 419).

17. Commins's difficulties may be traced in *Md Archs*, IV, 393 (quotation), 440–41, 448 (quotation), 451. For other men with the same problem: *Md Archs*, IV, 549; *Va Ct Recs*, 58; *Suffolk Ct Recs*, II, 763, 786; *Me Ct Recs*, III, 179.

18. *Virginia Magazine of History and Biography*, VIII (1900–01), 31 (hereafter *VMHB*); *Md Archs*, LIII, 447. For a man still contesting a negative decision about his veracity five years later: *Plymouth Col Recs*, III, 75, 156–57.

19. Quotations: *A Volume Relating to the Early History of Boston Containing the Aspinwall Notarial Records from 1664 to 1651 (Boston Record Commissioners' Reports*, XXXII [1903]), vii; *NHT Recs*, I, 496; *EC Ct Recs*, VI, 274. For examples of "credit" used as a synonym for "good name," see *Md Archs*, XLIX, 21; Hull Letterbook, I, 185, AAS; and *WP*, III, 37.

20. As shall be seen in the next chapter, men also attacked defamers physically and sometimes counterattacked with verbal charges of their own. Lawsuits could have significant financial consequences for the losing party. Defamers were often fined (sometimes heavily), and the losing party was also commonly required to pay the winner's fees as well as his own. Although attorneys were rarely involved in such litigation, clerk's fees and the required compensation for witnesses on both sides (expenses plus allowances for lost work) could amount to substantial sums.

21. See Mary Beth Norton, "Gender and Defamation in Seventeenth-Century Maryland," *William and Mary Quarterly*, 3d ser., XLIV (1987), 35, for more on this point (hereafter cited as *WMQ*). Most studies of colonial slander suits have focused on defamers and the insults they employed rather than on targets and their reasons for filing suit. Yet since the target, not the defamer, chose to bring the case to court, and since targets always had other options, that focus seems to me misplaced. See, e.g., Peter N. Moogk, " 'Thieving Buggers' and 'Stupid Sluts': Insults and Popular Culture in New France," *WMQ*, 3d ser., XXXVI (1979), 524–47; Robert B. St George, " 'Heated' Speech and Literacy in Seventeenth-Century New England," in David Grayson Allen and David D. Hall, eds., *Seventeenth-Century New England (CSM Pubs*, LXIII [1984]), 275–322; and Roger Thompson, " 'Holy Watchfulness' and Communal Conformism: The Politics of Defamation in Early New England Communities," *New England Quarterly*, LVI (1983), 504–22. But cf. Cornelia Dayton,

"Women Before the Bar: Gender, Law, and Society in Connecticut, 1710–1790" (unpub. Ph.D. diss., Princeton University, 1986), chapter 4, for a more balanced treatment.

22. These observations are based on 493 civil defamation suits with male plaintiffs and defendants of known status. Sixty-three percent of those cases (N=310) involved two litigants of ordinary rank; 9% (N=46), two high-status litigants; 20% (N=99), high-ranking plaintiffs and low-ranking defendants; and 8% (N=38) low-ranking plaintiffs and high-status defendants. The relative paucity of lawsuits among high-status male litigants suggests the efficacy of the informal dispute-resolution processes employed in the upper ranks of colonial society, while the failure of low-status men to file many suits against high-ranking defamers reveals those men's respective positions in the social hierarchy. Men of ordinary status usually did not seek legal redress from higher-ranking slanderers, to whose opinions they were expected to defer.

23. Analysis based on 136 prosecutions for criminal defamation with male defamers and male victims of known status. In 27% (N=38) of the cases, both were of ordinary or servant rank; 8% (N=11), both of high rank; 60% (N=82), high-ranking victims and low-status defamers; and 4% (N=5), low-ranking victims, high-ranking defamers. For the purposes of this tabulation, ordinary men serving as constables (or the like) have been counted as "high-ranking," since they held official positions that entitled them to government protection for their "credit."

24. The content of the slander is known in 386 of the civil (N=305) and criminal (N=81) cases with exclusively male participants. In 47% (N=71) of the 151 cases with epithets only, some form of the terms "rogue" or "knave" was used; in another 36% (N=55) of the cases, theft, lying or perjury, or cheating was charged in nonspecific terms. Accordingly, just 17% of the cases (N=25) exclusively involved epithets of other sorts ("cuckold," "dog," "drunk," and so forth). *OED*, q.v. "rogue," "knave." It is important to point out that the *OED* notes no sexual implication in either "rogue" or "knave"; "roger," as a synonym for sexual intercourse, did not appear until the early eighteenth century.

25. Based on 284 cases in which specific charges were employed (sometimes in conjunction with general epithets); 53% (N=151) of the accusations involved dishonest dealings. (Theft, accounting for 27% (N=77) of the slanders, was the single largest category.) Charges of political malfeasance or challenges to an official's authority constituted 12% (N=35) of the defamatory statements. (These figures do not include prosecutions for contempt of authority, instead enumerating personal insults.) The only other substantial grouping of slanders alleged sexual misconduct (12%, N=35).

26. *NH Ct Recs*, XL, 207; *AN Ct Recs*, II, 28; Dukes Cnty Ct Recs, I, f 56; *Md Archs*, LIV, 531.

27. *Md Archs*, LIV, 78, 383. According to the *OED*, *cozen* meant "to cheat or defraud by deceit" as early as the sixteenth century, and *shark* referred to "financial swindling" by the early seventeenth century.

28. *Plymouth Col Recs*, VII, 304; *AN Ct Recs*, I, 117; *VMHB*, XLI (1933), 339; *Suffolk Ct Recs*, I, 134. Of the 386 civil cases, 235 (61%) involved only a specific charge, and 51 (13%) represented some combination of a general epithet and a specific charge.

29. *Plymouth Col Recs*, II, 80; *Suffolk Ct Recs*, I, 228–29 (on the controversy over Richard Bellingham's will, see chapter two, n. 43).

30. *NHCP Recs*, II, 250; *Md Archs*, LXX, 11.

31. *Ct Assts Recs*, II, 49; Joseph Smith and Philip A. Crowl, eds., *Court Records of Prince George's County, Maryland, 1696–1699* (Washington, D.C.: American Historical Association, 1964), 256. For examples of such prosecutions, 97% of which ended in convictions, see *EC Ct Recs*, III, 447; *NHCP Recs*, I, 257–58, 315–17. "Just ass" seems to have been a favorite defaming pun for a judge; see, e.g., *Ct Assts Recs*, II, 35.

32. *Md Archs*, LXVIII, 91; *Plymouth Col Recs*, VII, 173, 153. Of 247 incidents in which both the context and the content of the men's defamations of other men are known, nearly one fifth (N=48) of the lawsuits involved deliberate public slanders spoken to sizable groups, and slightly more than one fifth (N=57) arose from face-to-face confrontations in the presence of several witnesses.

33. Based on 82 cases with known outcomes in which general epithets alone were

employed. Success rates were 83% when *rogue* (N=33 of 40) and its equivalents or a term like *perjurer* or *cheater* (N=19 of 23) was used, but only 68% when other epithets were at issue (N=13 of 19).

34. *Md Archs*, XLI, 433; *NHT Recs*, I, 214–15 (see also 211–12). Plaintiffs who sued after having been accused of cheating, theft, or the like won 63% of their cases (81 of 129), while those who alleged other slanders were slightly more successful, winning 68% of their suits (85 of 125). One indication that "truth" could serve as a successful defense when specific charges were at issue is that 23.5% of the defamers (N=60) who employed them actually won the lawsuits or gained a divided verdict. By contrast, defamers who used only epithets won a full or divided verdict just 9% of the time (N=8). (Other possible outcomes included withdrawal of the charges or referral to another body.)

35. This paragraph and the next two are based on *EC Ct Recs*, I, 339–45, and Norfolk County Court Records, Box I, items 4–15, Phillips Library, Peabody Essex Museum, Salem, Mass. Robert and Frances Swan (Quilter) were later involved in one of the will disputes discussed at length in chapter three (see n. 25).

36. The next four paragraphs are drawn from *NH Ct Recs*, XL, 172, 474–76, 487–97, 503 (quotations: 474, 476, 492, 493).

37. For *Turner v. Bouling*, see *Md Archs*, LIII, 369–71, 375–76; for *Stanley v. Paggett*, see ibid., XLIX, 208–9, 243, 255, 265–70.

38. *JWJ*, I, 75–114 passim (quotations 77, 85, 91).

39. Ibid., 171. See also *WP*, IV, 403–4, 410, and Everett Emerson, ed., *Letters from New England: The Massachusetts Bay Colony, 1629–1638* (Amherst: University of Massachusetts Press, 1976), 146–53, for other disputes among Bay Colony leaders and their resolutions. The church policies mentioned here are described in the introduction to this volume.

40. *JWJ*, I, 85, 270.

41. Mistress Hutchinson is discussed at length in chapter eight. On New England church governance and the role played by pastors therein, see David D. Hall, *The Faithful Shepherd: A History of the New England Ministry in the Seventeenth Century* (Chapel Hill: University of North Carolina Press, 1972).

42. "Plymouth Church Records," *CSM Pubs*, XXII (1920), 174; John Saffin, Notebook (typescript), 180, AAS. On church voting practices: *JWJ*, II, 281; Thomas Lechford, "Plain-Dealing: or, Newes from New-England (London, 1642)," *MHS Colls*, 3d ser., III (1833), 58, 74. A similar desire to avoid overt dissent was displayed by the New Haven town meeting in early 1675 (*NHT Recs*, II, 329).

43. "The Trial of Ezekiel Cheever, 1649," *Collections of the Connecticut Historical Society*, I (1860), 38. In the same vein, when Increase Mather objected to the calling of a synod in 1664, his brother-in-law told him that he had "acted disorderly . . . & that being disorderly was as bad as drunkenesse or Scandall." (Increase Mather, Diary, June 21, 1664, AAS.)

44. *Md Archs*, III, 33–41 passim (quotations 38, 33, 36). See also "Extract of a Letter from Captain Thomas Yong . . . ," in Hall, ed., *Maryland Narratives*, 58–61. Claiborne was a thorn in Maryland's side for many years. See *Md Archs*, III, 16–44, V, 157–239; and *The Calvert Papers* (Baltimore: Maryland Historical Society, 1889), I, 182–89, on his challenges to Maryland's authority.

45. For a brief and balanced summary of these events: Aubrey C. Land, *Colonial Maryland: A History* (Millwood, N.Y.: KTO Press, 1981), chapter 3. For Giles Brent: *Md Archs*, IV, 126–64 passim (quotation, 129). Given the context, it was perhaps remarkable that two men who both claimed the governorship in June 1647 did *not* engage in a violent confrontation (*Md Archs*, III, 188–91).

46. Politics in Maine are discussed at length in chapter six.

47. An insightful overview is Adrian Wilson, "The Ceremony of Childbirth and Its Interpretation," in Valerie Fildes, ed., *Women as Mothers in Pre-Industrial England* (London: Routledge, Chapman, & Hall, 1990), 68–107. Isabel Hull has pointed out to me that early modern Europe contained other female-dominated spaces, such as markets, so that the colonies may have been unique in having only one such all-female locus.

48. The most comprehensive examination remains Daniel Scott Smith, "Population, Family and Society in Hingham, Massachusetts, 1635–1880" (unpub. Ph.D. diss., University

of California, Berkeley, 1972). I have discussed these same issues for a later period in *Liberty's Daughters: The Revolutionary Experience of American Women, 1750–1800* (Boston, Mass.: Little, Brown, 1980), 72–84.

49. Recall the slanderous encounter of three women at the Accomack cowpen (chapter one) or the abused Virginia servant Elizabeth Abbott's search for a female ally at the local well (chapter two). Laurel Thatcher Ulrich, *A Midwife's Tale: The Life of Martha Ballard Based on Her Diary, 1785–1812* (New York: Alfred A. Knopf, 1990), is the best introduction to the practice of midwifery and the centrality of the midwife's role in early America. Male physicians did not enter the birth process until after 1750; see Judith Walzer Leavitt, *Brought to Bed: Childbearing in America* (New York: Oxford University Press, 1986), and Jane Donegan, *Women and Men Midwives: Medicine, Mortality, and Misogyny in Early America* (Westport, Conn.: Greenwood Press, 1978). The only men who seem to have been nearby at seventeenth-century births were the fathers-to-be; e.g., *Md Archs*, LIII, 61; William Sargent, ed., *York Deeds* (Portland, Me.: Brown, Thurston, & Co., 1888), II, f 1; *New Ams Ct Recs*, II, 221. But cf. *WP*, V, 290.

50. For example, officially recorded births in the small Massachusetts town of Andover (probably excluding stillbirths and perhaps even some early infant deaths) averaged 10 annually before 1674 and 28 a year through the rest of the century. Thus Andover women would have gathered at childbeds about once a month in the early years of the settlement and at least biweekly thereafter. See Philip J. Greven, Jr., *Four Generations: Population, Land, and Family in Colonial Andover, Massachusetts* (Ithaca, N.Y.: Cornell University Press, 1970), table 14 (p. 180) and graph 4 (p. 182). In another New England town, births annually averaged 36 per 1000 people; see Kenneth A. Lockridge, "The Population of Dedham, Massachusetts, 1636–1736," *Economic History Review*, XIX (1966), 329.

51. *OED*, q.v. "gossip," "gossiping." For a use of *gossip* in the older sense of "godparent," see *Md Archs*, XLI, 328.

52. For instance, at a child's death bed—again, when only women were present—a terrified young wife blurted out to two older women a story of how a man had raped her, then afterwards threatened her with violence or an adultery prosecution if she revealed what had happened (*NHT Recs*, II, 256–57).

53. Johan Winsser, "Mary Dyer and the 'Monster' Story," *Quaker History*, LXXIX (1990), 31 (quotation from a letter written by John Eliot, May 19, 1660).

54. Winthrop's comments in the next two paragraphs are taken from his two detailed accounts of the monstrous birth and its discovery: *JWJ*, I, 266–68; and David D. Hall, ed., *The Antinomian Controversy, 1636–1638* (2d ed., Durham, N.C.: Duke University Press, 1990), 281–82. See also Valerie Pearl and Morris Pearl, eds., "Governor John Winthrop on the Birth of the Antinomians' 'Monster': The Earliest Reports to Reach England and the Making of a Myth," *MHS Procs*, CII (1990), 21–37.

55. Liddea Williams, Deposition, March 8, 1648/9, MA, IX, f 7.

56. MA, IX, ff 10, 14, 11, with Dudley's comment referred to on f 11.

57. *Va Ct Recs*, 111; *Md Archs*, XLI, 207–13, 221–23, 255, 258 (Clocker prosecution); Mary White, oral will, Testamentary Proceedings, I (1659), ff 3–4, Maryland Hall of Records, Annapolis. Both the Oversee and White babies survived. Clocker and her primary accomplice in the theft—each blaming the other—were convicted and sentenced to death but were pardoned by the governor. Mistress Oversee was the woman involved in the abuse of the slave Antonio (chapter two, n. 64).

58. Examples of female juries: *Md Archs*, LIV, 233, 250; *Suffolk Ct Recs*, I, 91; "Ordeal of Touch in Colonial Virginia," *VMHB*, IV (1896–97), 187.

59. On patterns of witnessing by women in Maryland courts, see Mary Beth Norton, "Gender, Crime, and Community in Seventeenth-Century Maryland," in James Henretta et al., eds., *The Transformation of Early American History* (New York: Alfred A. Knopf, 1991), 143–44, 292–93 n. 54. Statutes assuming that women had to tell the truth at the moment of birth are in *Md Archs*, I, 441–42, and *Mass Col Recs*, IV, pt 2, 393–94. The midwife Mistress Dorothy Cromwell, for example, made four appearances as a witness in Essex County between 1662 and early 1669 (*EC Ct Recs*, II, 444, III, 118, 460, IV, 91).

60. Quotations: *NH Ct Recs*, XL, 320; *Suffolk Ct Recs*, II, 719. See also, e.g., *EC Ct*

Recs, V, 298, VI, 171, VII, 137–38. A rare case in which the court did not believe the woman's childbed accusation is in Norfolk County Deeds and Orders, I, f 218, film 1a, Virginia State Library, Richmond.

61. *NH Ct Recs*, XL, 293–94. See also a defamation suit arising from the charge that a woman had failed to call a midwife: *EC Ct Recs*, II, 10.

62. *Md Archs*, LIV, 206, 211–12. Her age is given in ibid., 127. Although the gossip seems to have been incorrect in this case, Read was formally accused of impregnating a maidservant about a year later (ibid., 233).

63. E.g., *Va Ct Recs*, 194; *EC Ct Recs*, V, 291–92; *Md Archs*, XLI, 329–31, LIV, 394–95. In an unusual 1683 case, two Indian women were named to search the body of a young tribeswoman accused of infanticide (*Plymouth Col Recs*, VI, 113).

64. Connecticut Archives, Crimes & Misdemeanors, Ser. 1, I, doc. 32, Connecticut State Library, Hartford (my thanks to Cornelia Dayton for a transcript of this document); *Md Archs*, XLIX, 212, 217–18, 231–36 (quotations: 232, 218, 233). Conversely, if women refused to cooperate, conviction was impossible. An infanticide case involving Hannah Lee Price and her maidservant Mary Marler (ibid., 476ff passim, LIII, 617, LVII, 16–124 passim, LX, 12) occupied the courts for a full year and ended without a conviction because no witnesses would appear.

65. She was granted administration of Johnson's estate in March 1655/6 (*Md Archs*, X, 439) and had married Dorrington by the following September (ibid., 460). For the family's immigration, see Gust Skordas, ed., *The Early Settlers of Maryland* (Baltimore, Md.: Genealogical Publishing Company, 1968), 259, 161.

66. *Md Archs*, X, 516, and XLI, 14–18 (Jane Palldin); LVII, 598–99 (Joane Colledge). Palldin was ordered whipped, Norton was assessed for child support, and the Dorringtons were told to keep the two apart.

67. The account in the following eight paragraphs is based on *Md Archs*, X, 280–90, primarily on the depositions of Ann Johnson (280–82), Margaret Broome (282–84), and Sarah Goulson (284–85).

68. If the dates on the depositions presented to the court are accurately recorded, Ann Johnson was not the first to depose about some of the events surrounding the birth of Mary Taylor's son. On April 6, Cornelius Abraham reported a conversation he had had in January with George Catchmey, in which Catchmey described being threatened by the Taylors (an aspect of the case discussed in chapter seven) about "the child [Robert's] wife Laid to him." But court officials sought no further information until after Ann Johnson testified; the Abraham deposition primarily pertained to the threat to Catchmey, not to Mary's adultery (ibid., 288).

69. Ibid., 289. Two men deposed about the argument between Ann Johnson and Mary Taylor, which occurred, according to Sarah Goulson, "as we were Comeing home [from Pope's]" (ibid., 284). One of them, whose account is quoted here, was recounting Ann Johnson's later description of the incident. The other might possibly have been present.

70. Conversation reported by Ann Johnson, ibid., 282.

71. These conclusions are based on 79 defamation cases involving only women as defamers and targets. In 75% (N=59) of the cases, defamer and target were of similar rank. In 39 suits, general epithets were employed; of those, 54% (N=21) consisted of "whore" or a similar term. The only other significant category was "witch," constituting 15% (N=6). In 51 instances in which specific charges were at issue, 47% (N=24) were sexual in nature. Other than theft (N=13) or witchcraft (8%, N=4), no charge accounted for more than 4% of the total. Female targets won over 80% of all the defamation cases in which they were involved, regardless of the nature of the slander—with one significant exception. When charged with specific acts of theft or cheating, they were successful in winning redress just 67% of the time.

72. See, e.g., *Md Archs*, X, 473, 477–78; *Suffolk Ct Recs*, II, 688; *EC Ct Recs*, VII, 257–58; *NH Ct Recs*, XL, 448. A theft accusation spread along a gossip chain of at least four, and possibly six, women can be traced in *New Ams Ct Recs*, V, 194, 197, 246–47, 272–73.

73. *Me Ct Recs*, III, 198; *AN Ct Recs*, I, 20, II, 292, 103.

74. *Md Archs*, IV, 258, LIV, 575; *VMHB*, XLI (1933), 117; *Suffolk Ct Recs*, II, 818. For another slander case in which the husband of a woman accused of adultery was termed a "wittal," or willing cuckold, see *EC Ct Recs*, I, 62, 78. That husband in turn called their female neighbors "in a libelling way . . . some captains, some lieutenants"—implying an organized campaign against his wife (ibid., 81).

75. *NHCP Recs*, I, 180–81. The cucking, or ducking, stool, was a standard English punishment inflicted on women deemed scolds; they were tied to a stool or chair and ducked several times in a pond or other body of water.

76. This paragraph and the next are based on ibid., 473–76.

77. *NHT Recs*, I, 120, 126, II, 135–36. Hannah Finch was ordered to apologize and to pay court costs. For the prosecution of Mary Fuller, see chapter seven, n. 54, below.

78. *WP*, IV, 297–98 (see also 309–10, and *Ct Assts Recs*, II, 102–3); *Suffolk Ct Recs*, II, 839, 838. By contrast, Lydia Drury's five brothers and two sisters-in-law attested that she never said anything comparable to them; clearly, she concealed her husband's sexual incapacity from her own family (ibid., 838). See also chapter one, n. 89.

79. Quotations: Essex County Quarterly Court File Papers, WPA Transcripts, X, ff 35/1, 35/3, 37/5, Phillips Library, Peabody Essex Museum, Salem, Mass.; see *EC Ct Recs*, III, 192–94, for an expurgated version that omits the reason why Perkins and Ewens spoke to Mary Howe. Interventions to avert mistreatment are noted in, e.g., *EC Ct Recs*, V, 221, 363; *Suffolk Ct Recs*, I, 7.

80. This paragraph and the next are based on *NHCP Recs*, II, 77–89, 122 (quotations 81–83, 89).

81. *Va Ct Recs*, 62.

82. Captain Martin, though a resident of Virginia at the time of the whipping of Laydon and Wright, held no official position in Dale's government and probably had nothing to do with his harsh policies, which were carried out under martial law. Ann Laydon arrived in Virginia as a maidservant in 1608; "Jane" Wright is undoubtedly the left-handed midwife Joane Wright, who is listed in the muster of 1624/5 with a husband and two Virginia-born children. When Wright was accused of witchcraft in 1626, Mistress Perry testified on her behalf (*Va Ct Recs*, 112). For biographical details: Virginia M. Meyer and John Frederick Dorman, eds., *Adventurers of Purse and Person Virginia 1607–1624/5*, 3d ed. (Richmond, Va.: Order of First Families of Virginia, 1987), passim. On Captain Martin, see David Thomas Konig, "Colonization and the Common Law in Ireland and Virginia, 1569–1634," in Henretta et al., eds., *Transformation*, 84ff.

83. The infanticide trial: *Md Archs*, X, 456–58. The next five paragraphs are based on ibid., 464–65, 488.

84. Claxton also testified in a third case at that session (ibid., 460). Because timing is not given, the object of the abuse could have been either Francis Brooke's first wife, Ann, who died by May 1654, or his second wife, Mary, by whom he had two children at the time of his death in late 1658 or early 1659. Elizabeth Claxton was present in the colony at least by February 1653/4 (ibid., 383), so she could have witnessed abuse of Ann, possibly even abuse that contributed to her death. That Mr. Brooke was formally (though briefly) charged with "murder" implies that Ann was the battered wife, for feticide was not a crime commonly prosecuted in the colonies.

85. Rose Smith's deposition in the Holt case (discussed at greater length in chapter seven) is printed in ibid., X, 109–10. For biographical information: Skordas, ed., *Early Settlers*, 181–82, 428, and *Md Archs*, IV, 5–6, 51. She also testified twice in 1658; see ibid., XLI, 161, 181.

CHAPTER 5: AMONGST THE NEIGHBORS

1. *NHCP Recs*, II, 352.

2. The cases on which this and the next two paragraphs are based are printed in ibid., 349–54. A similar case involving women is in *NHT Recs*, I, 413–16, 514.

3. I have borrowed the phrase "small politics" from the anthropologist F. G. Bailey

("Gifts and Poison," in Bailey, ed., *Gifts and Poison: The Politics of Reputation* [Oxford: Oxford University Press, 1971], 2).

4. *NHT Recs*, II, 163–64, 25. For studies of neighborhood interactions in the colonies, see David Thomas Konig, *Law and Society in Puritan Massachusetts: Essex County, 1629–1692* (Chapel Hill: University of North Carolina Press, 1979), chapter 5; and Lorena Walsh, "Community Networks in the Early Chesapeake" in Lois Green Carr et al., eds., *Colonial Chesapeake Society* (Chapel Hill: University of North Carolina Press, 1988), 200–41. An examination of some of the same themes in England is J. A. Sharpe, " 'Such Disagreement betwyx Neighbours': Litigation and Human Relations in Early Modern England," in John Bossy, ed., *Disputes and Settlements: Law and Human Relations in the West* (Cambridge: Cambridge University Press, 1983), 167–87.

5. In my data set, prosecutions for drunkenness constitute 12% of accusations against New England men and 5% of charges against Chesapeake men. In both regions such offenses represent 2% of charges brought against women.

6. *Me Ct Recs*, I, 333, 263; *EC Ct Recs*, V, 315. See *NHT Recs*, I, 245–46, for details of how one woman created "discord among neighbours."

7. *Plymouth Col Recs*, III, 6–7, 102.

8. *Md Archs*, X, 459–60, LIV, 623, 625–28.

9. Quotation: *NHCP Recs*, II, 205. The Maryland case is in *Md Archs*, XLI, 217–20, 277–79. Prolonged disputes were common; e.g., ibid., XLIX, 108, 118, 158, 172, 196–200. The difficult New Haven cases are in *NHCP Recs*, II, 294–97, 349, 390–92, 463–65.

10. *AN Ct Recs*, II, 51–52.

11. Hannah Jones's campaign can be followed in *NH Ct Recs*, XL, 127, 137, 148–49, 413–14, 455–64 passim (quotation 464). Thomas Walford's wedding gifts of marsh to his other daughters and his bequests to grandchildren created disputes as late as 1686 (ibid., 226–27, 359–60, 378–79, 397). Another similar case involving New Hampshire women is in ibid., 280, 309–10, 315, 317, 322.

12. *EC Ct Recs*, II, 199–202, 279–80; also, Essex County Quarterly Court File Papers, WPA Transcripts, V, ff 79–83, VI, f 84, Phillips Library, Peabody Essex Museum, Salem, Mass. (quotations V, f 81/3, VI, f 84/2). Examples of scuffles caused by roaming stock: *EC Ct Recs*, II, 100–1, III, 273–74.

13. This paragraph and the next three are based on *Md Archs*, LIV, 116–22. A "rundlett" (runlet) was a liquor cask of varying capacity (*OED*).

14. *Md Archs*, LIV, 399, 404; *Va Ct Recs*, 110, 114. For an analysis of some of the same dynamics in England, see Cynthia Herrup, "New Shoes and Mutton Pies: Investigative Responses to Theft in Seventeenth-Century East Sussex," *Historical Journal*, XXVII (1984), 811–30.

15. *Md Archs*, LIV, 508, XLI, 21, IV, 396, XLI, 211. Two thieves (one who had stolen a shirt, the other a handkerchief) had the misfortune to encounter their victims while they were wearing the loot (ibid., XLIX, 504–5; *EC Ct Recs*, II, 420–21).

16. *Suffolk Ct Recs*, I, 222; *Plymouth Col Recs*, VI, 176; *New Ams Ct Recs*, V, 93–94; William Hubbard, *History of New England from the Discovery to 1680*, *MHS Colls*, 3d ser., VI (1817), 347–48. But a statement from 16 neighbors, attesting that they had seen only "sober comly & modest behaviour" on the part of a young Lynn woman, did not prevent her from being admonished for "light and lascivious carriage" (*EC Ct Recs*, III, 111–13).

17. *NHT Recs*, II, 163–64. The classic work on witchcraft that first explored the way in which contentions in small communities produced such accusations was Keith Thomas, *Religion and the Decline of Magic* (New York: Charles Scribner's Sons, 1974); on this point, see esp. 526–30. The best comparable discussion in the American context is John P. Demos, *Entertaining Satan: Witchcraft and the Culture of Early New England* (New York: Oxford University Press, 1982), part 3.

18. According to Carol Karlsen, who has compiled the most comprehensive list of accused witches in New England before 1725, 342 persons of known sex, 22% of them male, faced such charges in one way or another. See *The Devil in the Shape of a Woman: Witchcraft in Colonial New England* (New York: W. W. Norton, 1987), 47, 280–81, ns. 1–2. John Demos includes a chapter on John Godfrey, one of the few men accused of witchcraft, in

Entertaining Satan (chapter 2). On contentions, see Karlsen, *Devil in the Shape of a Woman,* passim, and Demos, *Entertaining Satan,* passim, esp. chapter 3.

19. Such an argument is more characteristic of scholarship on European than American witchcraft, as is evident in Joseph Klaits, *Servants of Satan: The Age of the Witch Hunts* (Bloomington: Indiana University Press, 1985), a convenient synthesis of scholarship. But cf. Karlsen, *Devil in the Shape of a Woman,* chapter 4.

20. See, e.g., the discussion in Ian Maclean, *The Renaissance Notion of Woman* (Cambridge: Cambridge University Press, 1980).

21. Karlsen, *Devil in the Shape of a Woman,* table 9, 72, shows that 73% of women charged with witchcraft at times other than the Salem Village outbreak were married, as were 52% of the women accused in 1692–93. The reduction in the latter proportion was anomalous, caused largely by the fact that 30% of the accused Salem witches were young women, most of them related to older suspects. John Demos speculated in *Entertaining Satan* that the accused witch John Godfrey's career might "reflect an intensification of certain themes which, in the lives of women, created a strong presumption of guilt [36]," but does not identify as one of those themes the fact that Godfrey, like most wives, owned no landed property. He was, instead, a herdsman notable for his mobility.

22. See the discussion in Karlsen, *Devil in the Shape of a Woman,* 60–61, and n. 11, above.

23. This paragraph is based on *Ct Assts Recs,* III, 179–80; Suffolk Court Files, case #762, Massachusetts Archives, Boston; and *EC Ct Recs,* III, 420–21. The Crawfords sued the owner of the house for defamation but eventually withdrew the complaint.

24. This paragraph and the next five are based on *NHCP Recs,* II, 29–36, 151–52; and *NHT Recs,* I, 249–52, 256–57. When Mr. Goodyear died in 1659, he owed her over £150; at her death in 1660, the property in her hands amounted to more than £46 (*NHCP Recs,* II, 306; *NHT Recs,* I, 462). Although both Carol Karlsen and John Demos describe Elizabeth Godman as a widow, there is no evidence that she had ever been married. Indeed, one of the charges against her was that she had hoped to marry Mr. James Bishop and was subsequently jealous of his wife and babies, which suggests that she was of childbearing age. She might have therefore been one of the high-status Englishwomen who came to the colonies to find husbands; for references to other such women, see *The Calvert Papers* (Baltimore: Maryland Historical Society, 1889), I, 244, 269.

25. On her deathbed, she gave legacies to several members of that family, thus demonstrating her affection for them (*NHT Recs,* I, 462–67, 478–79, 481). The court dismissed her 1653 defamation suit, finding that she had behaved like a witch, and in the 1655 witchcraft prosecution it declared that "though the evidenc is not sufficient as yet to take away her life, yet the suspitions are cleere and many" (*NHCP Recs,* II, 30–31, 152).

26. Quoted phrases: *SAL,* II, 166, 109; *Md Archs,* I, 343.

27. So women, who participated as litigants or witnesses in just 18% of other civil cases in the Chesapeake and 13% in New England, appeared in 58% of civil defamation suits in the south and 42% in the north. Moreover, whereas in other types of civil actions the vast majority (90%, Chesapeake; 80%, New England) of cases with women had just one female participant, in civil slander suits a substantial proportion (45%, Chesapeake; 35%, New England) had two or more female participants. Women also appeared as victims, witnesses, or defamers in just over half the criminal defamation prosecutions in the two regions (Chesapeake, 51.5%; New England, 53%). For a more detailed discussion that cites the relevant anthropological scholarship, see Mary Beth Norton, "Gender and Defamation in Seventeenth-Century Maryland," *William and Mary Quarterly,* 3d ser., XLIV (1987), 5–7. See also James Scott, *Weapons of the Weak: Everyday Forms of Peasant Resistance* (New Haven, Conn.: Yale University Press, 1985), which argues that gossip is a valuable "weapon of the weak"; Sally Engle Merry, "Rethinking Gossip and Scandal," in *Toward a General Theory of Social Control,* ed. Donald Black (New York: Academic Press, 1984), I, 271–302; and Jorg R. Bergmann, *Discreet Indiscretions: The Social Organization of Gossip* (New York: Aldine de Gruyter, 1993).

28. *NH Ct Recs,* XL, 167, 480, 484–85. Laurel Ulrich speculates that this confrontation occurred at a childbed, or at least at a time when no men were present (*Good Wives: Image*

and Reality in the Lives of Women in Northern New England 1650–1750 [New York: Oxford University Press, 1982], 191). On the Chesley-Hall case, see chapter four.

29. James P. Baxter, ed., *The Trelawny Papers. Documentary History of the State of Maine* (*Collections of the Maine Historical Society*, 2d ser., III [1884]), 127; *WP*, IV, 376. Letters in the Curwen Papers, box 2, folder 1, American Antiquarian Society, Worcester, Mass. (hereafter AAS), attest to New England clergymen's obsession with their vulnerability to gossip; see also Increase Mather, Diary, Oct. 10, 1664, and Sept. 8, 1676, AAS.

30. *Md Archs*, XLI, 153; *Suffolk Ct Recs*, II, 880; *Me Ct Recs*, I, 85–86.

31. Quotation: *Me Ct Recs*, III, 204. See ibid., II, 23, 184, 199, III, 225, for examples of such presentments. Often, Maine presentments named as the relevant witness the "[grand] jury," the equivalent of citing "common fame" as a reason for a charge (e.g., ibid., II, 261–69 passim).

32. *Md Archs*, LVII, 597, 601; *MHS Procs*, XLIX (1915–16), 105; *NH Ct Recs*, XL, 114–15. Although the Marylander was cleared, more than a decade later he was still combating the same gossip (*Md Archs*, LXIX, 118–21).

33. *SAL*, I, 310, II, 51–52; *Conn Col Recs*, I, 394; *NHCP Recs*, I, 244. And note the reference to "comon fame" in Maryland's 1666 hog-stealing statute (*Md Archs*, II, 140).

34. *NHCP Recs*, II, 227–29. Occasionally, though, investigation proved that gossip networks were wrong; e.g., *EC Ct Recs*, I, 388; *NHT Recs*, II, 272–73.

35. *Md Archs*, LIII, 106–8, 113; *New Ams Ct Recs*, I, 184–282 passim (quotations: 250, 201, 265).

36. The next five paragraphs are based on *Md Archs*, LIV, 42–43, 49–51, 60. A similar case, beginning when (male) visitors were served pork that aroused their suspicions, is in *NHT Recs*, I, 169–74.

37. *Pynchon Ct Rec*, 300; *Md Archs*, LIV, 85; *New England Historical and Genealogical Register*, LI (1897), 68–69 (hereafter *NEHGR*).

38. *AN Ct Recs*, II, 287, 298–300; *Va Ct Recs*, 183; *NH Ct Recs*, XL, 518–19. Incidents involving both physical conflict and an exchange of insults seem to have occurred frequently in New Amsterdam (e.g., *New Ams Ct Recs*, II, 148, 332, V, 247–48).

39. *Va Ct Recs*, 46; *AN Ct Recs*, II, 211–12, 383–84.

40. E.g., *Suffolk Ct Recs*, I, 139; *EC Ct Recs*, V, 347.

41. *Md Archs*, LIV, 207; *EC Ct Recs*, VII, 327. See also, e.g., *NHT Recs*, II, 199, and *AN Ct Recs*, I, 145.

42. The English legal background is discussed by J. A. Sharpe, *Defamation and Sexual Slander in Early Modern England: The Church Courts at York* (Borthwick Institute of Historical Research, University of York, Paper No. 58 [1980]), 1–9; and Martin Ingram, *Church Courts, Sex and Marriage in England, 1570–1640* (Cambridge: Cambridge University Press, 1988), chapter 10. Some manorial and borough courts also heard slander cases in England. For a detailed account of the English law of defamation see Sir William Holdsworth, *A History of English Law* (2d ed., London: Methuen, 1937), VIII, 333–78 (355–56 on the rules of interpreting slanderous words). My thanks to Clive Holmes for assistance on English defamation law.

43. *SAL*, I, 156; *L&L*, 35–36; *Md Archs*, I, 343; *RI Col Recs*, I, 184.

44. Quotation: *SAL*, II, 72. The changes in Maryland law may be traced in *Md Archs*, II, 201, 273–74. See also Norman Rosenberg, *Protecting the Best Men: An Interpretive History of the Law of Libel* (Chapel Hill: University of North Carolina Press, 1986), chapter 1, for a concise survey of colonial defamation law that describes the transition from general slander statutes to an emphasis on protecting officials from libelous statements.

45. See chapter four, ns. 22–25, 71.

46. Observations based on 393 defamation suits involving both sexes, in 239 of which the content of the slander is known. In 111 of the cases with known content men sued or prosecuted women; in 128, women sued or prosecuted men. (All couples [N=27] are included in the "female" totals.) Seventy percent of cases with male targets and female defamers (N=78) involved people of equivalent rank, as did 69% (N=89) of cases in which the roles of men and women were reversed. Eleven percent (N=14) of cases with female targets and

20% (N=21) of cases with male targets involved low-status defamers and higher-ranking targets.

47. Based on 50 cases involving epithets alone, 64 specific charges, and 14 combinations thereof. Of 64 epithets, 66% (N=42) were "whore" or the equivalent; of 78 charges, 56% (N=44) were sexual in nature. The only other sizeable categories were the epithet "witch" (14%, N=7) and specific witchcraft accusations (6%, N=5).

48. Based on 31 cases employing general epithets only, 74 specific charges, and 6 combinations. "Rogue" or equivalents composed 60% (N=22) of the epithets; theft, 12% (N=13) of the specific charges. Sexual slanders amounted to 42.5% (N=34) of the individual accusations. By contrast, only 5% (N=4) of male targets complained of charges of cheating.

49. E.g, *Md Archs*, IV, 183; *WP*, IV, 182; *EC Ct Recs*, V, 155, 231, 267.

50. The record of the Taylor/Catchmey case, discussed in chapter four, is in *Md Archs*, X, 272, 276, 279–90, 339, 366. For a detailed examination of just such an episode of sexual gossip, see Eldon R. Turner, "Gender, Abortion, and Testimony: A Textual Look at the Martin Cases of Middlesex County Massachusetts, 1681–1683," in William Pencak and Wythe W. Holt, Jr., eds., *The Law in America 1607–1681* (New York: New-York Historical Society, 1989), 73–113.

51. *Md Archs*, X, 114; *EC Ct Recs*, I, 210; *Plymouth Col Recs*, IV, 7, VII, 157.

52. *AN Ct Recs*, II, 313; *NHT Recs*, II, 7.

53. *Md Archs*, LIV, 42, 55–56; the outcome of Carline's suit is not recorded. For an overheard remark: *NHCP Recs*, I, 478; for a shouted joke: *New Ams Ct Recs*, I, 51–76 passim.

54. *Plymouth Col Recs*, VII, 148; *NHT Recs*, I, 455–56, 461.

55. *Me Ct Recs*, III, 223; *AN Ct Recs*, II, 238; *NHCP Recs*, I, 327. See also *EC Ct Recs*, II, 52–54, V, 239–40. Only one woman—who said that "James Watts followed after her like a dog"—ended up as a defendant in such a defamation suit (ibid., II, 208).

56. *WP*, IV, 300; *EC Ct Recs*, V, 43, 52–55.

57. Mary Lewis Gibson: *WP*, IV, 96, and *Me Ct Recs*, I, 68–69; Hannah Phelps: *EC Ct Recs*, I, 267–68, II, 237–39, 261, 310. The deposition about Hannah's conduct on shipboard is undated though included with materials from 1652. It is unclear when the voyage took place.

58. *Plymouth Col Recs*, I, 132; *Me Ct Recs*, I, 176–77. See also an account of a nine-year-old rape accusation that surfaced to damage a Massachusetts woman's credibility in 1640: Edward Everett Hale et al., eds., *The Note-Book of Thomas Lechford Esq 1638 to 1641* (1884; repr., Camden, Me.: Picton Press, 1988), 259–61.

59. E.g., *NHT Recs*, II, 256–57; *Md Archs*, LIV, 576–77; *Suffolk Ct Recs*, I, 43; *EC Ct Recs*, III, 438–39, VII, 299–300.

60. *Me Ct Recs*, I, 70–71, 73–75, 77, 80. On Burdett's reputation, *JWJ*, II, 8–9. A Maryland planter was able to stop gossip *after* he had been convicted of fornication by arguing that he had already been punished for his offense and should not be subjected to further talk about it (*Md Archs*, LIV, 366, 371, 387).

61. A brief biography of Lumbrozo is included in Lois Green Carr et al., *Robert Cole's World: Agriculture & Society in Early Maryland* (Chapel Hill: University of North Carolina Press, 1991), 258. The quoted phrase: *Md Archs*, LIII, 390. Lumbrozo's activities undoubtedly attracted his neighbors' close scrutiny because of his identity.

62. This paragraph and the next are based on *Md Archs*, XLI, 588–91.

63. This paragraph and the next are based on ibid., LIII, 352, 355–57. The story of Lumbrozo's proposition may have been circulating as much as four months earlier, for in January 1662/3 the Goulds sued Giles and Elizabeth Glover for calling Margery a whore. (It was at the Glovers' "loged hows" that Lumbrozo first outlined his proposal to the Goulds.) Lumbrozo served as John and Margery's attorney in that suit, which they did not pursue beyond filing a complaint and a single deposition (ibid., 316, 319–20).

64. Probably the "scriptur" to which Lumbrozo referred was Genesis 16:1–5, in which Abraham sleeps with Hagar, his wife's servant.

65. This paragraph and the next three are based on *Md Archs*, LIII, 387–91.

66. Subsequent litigation involving the Lumbrozo estate, Elizabeth, her second husband,

John Browne, and her third husband, John Robinson, may be found in *Md Archs*, LX, passim.

67. The talk probably destroyed Mistress Hammond's reputation also. After John died, she married the brutal Pope Alvey, hardly a desirable husband for a respectable high-status woman (see chapter two on Alvey's beating a maidservant to death). After committing a second major felony, Alvey barely escaped the gallows (*Md Archs*, XLIX, 538–46).

68. For the 1662 cases, see *Md Archs*, LIII, 198, 204–6; the two-cow dispute, ibid., 26–28 (with a countersuit by Robisson). Robisson was so outraged by the outcome of that case that he slandered George Thompson, the court clerk who recorded the judgment. Robisson had to apologize to Thompson and pay court costs in May 1659 (ibid., 47). Gust Skordas, ed., *The Early Settlers of Maryland* (Baltimore, Md.: Genealogical Publishing Company, 1968), 20, lists several Thomas Bakers among the first immigrants to Maryland. It is impossible to tell which one is this man, who first recognizably appears in the court records in April 1653 (*Md Archs*, X, 265). He could, however, have been the ex-servant of Mr. Francis Pope of the same name for whom Blanch Oliver committed perjury in 1648 (chapter three, n. 40). Baker was named to the Charles County court when the incumbent commissioners were replaced following the Fendall Rebellion (ibid., LIII, 104–5); he was thereafter termed "Mr." in the records.

69. The material in this paragraph and the next two is drawn from *Md Archs*, LIII, 231–34. The court record does not make clear precisely when the childbed incident occurred, but it must have taken place several years previously, because when Empson died in March 1660/1 he was married to a woman named Elenor (ibid., XLI, 454, LIII, 147–48). Joan Porter Nevill was John's second wife; he had immigrated in 1646 with his first wife, who died soon thereafter. He transported Joan in 1651 and married her early in 1652. (Skordas, *Early Settlers*, 333, 367.)

70. This paragraph and the next draw on *Md Archs*, LIII, 220, 235–37. The 1658 defamation suit against Baker is in ibid., 13. There is much more in the testimony, including a similarly bawdy sexual insult aimed at a man and Robisson's claim that in 1655 Baker and Mary Empson had tried to persuade him to steal a wealthy man's silver plate. Mr. John Hatch and Mr. Francis Pope, the husbands of the women Baker defamed, were both magistrates and, as indicated above, Baker may once have been Mr. Pope's servant.

71. This and the following paragraph are based on *Md Archs*, LIII, 237–39. On page xvii the editor of the records notes that Baker disappeared from the court after this case.

72. Baker's career can be traced chiefly in the Charles County records, ibid., passim, esp. 44, 50–51, 74–75, 140–41, 173.

73. The cases, which are inevitably intertwined, are in ibid., 367, 376–83, as follows: assault, 382–83; defamation of Richard Dod, 380–82; defamation of Mary Dod, 376–80. Richard Dod was a freeholder; he and his wife were married, with a small child, by the fall of 1658 (ibid., XLI, 293).

74. *Md Archs*, LIII, 376–78. Another female witness, who was not present at this altercation, testified that Joan Nevill had slandered Mary Dod in the same way several months before. At one point Joan Nevill also referred to "that pockei whore" Mary Empson. Captain William Batten, who had moved to Maryland in 1651 with his wife (Skordas, *Early Settlers*, 29), died in October or early November 1662 (*Md Archs*, LIII, 269).

75. *Md Archs*, LIII, 378–79. The *OED* entry for "bald" reveals a seventeenth-century English custom of shaving the head of an adulteress. "Gammer" Belayne was an older woman in the neighborhood.

SECTION III PROLOGUE: HIS LORDSHIP'S ATTORNEY

1. *Md Archs*, I, 215.

2. Ibid.

3. See Lois Green Carr's biographical sketch of Margaret Brent in Edward T. James et al., eds., *Notable American Women* (Cambridge, Mass.: Harvard University Press, 1971), I, 236–37, and Julia Cherry Spruill, "Mistress Margaret Brent, Spinster," *Maryland Historical Magazine*, XXIX (1934), 259–68 (hereafter cited as *MHM*). Lois Carr suggested to me that Brent may have been a lay sister; see Marie B. Rowlands, "Recusant Women, 1560–1640,"

in Mary Prior, ed., *Women in English Society 1500–1800* (London: Methuen, 1985), 149–80, esp. 166–74. A ceremony of "fealty to the Lady" on one of Mistress Mary Brent's manors is described in *Md Archs*, XLI, 94.

4. Her first recorded appearance was as a claimant for 66 pounds of tobacco from the estate of three Irishmen who had fled the colony in 1641 (*Md Archs*, IV, 68). She was to make more than 100 such court appearances during her time in the colony. On Calvert's deathbed designations: ibid., 312–14 (Brent); ibid., III, 190–91 (Greene).

5. Russell Menard, "Maryland's 'Time of Troubles': Sources of Political Disorder in Early St. Mary's," *MHM*, LXXVI (1981), 124–40, offers a succinct description of the early years of the colony; see also "Richard Ingle in Maryland," ibid., I (1906), 129–39. Contemporary references to this period as "the plundering time" are in *Md Archs*, IV, 362, 375. Ingle revealed his aims to Parliament in February 1645/6 (ibid., III, 165–66).

6. *Md Archs*, I, 226–27, 217. On the soldiers' demands: ibid., IV, 312–13, 338, 353.

7. Quotation: ibid., IV, 358. Her activities as Baltimore's attorney and executrix of his brother's estate can be followed in ibid., 353–490 passim.

8. Quotations: ibid., 358, 434–37. For Howell, see chapter three, n. 40; for Bradnox, chapter five, n. 15, and *Md Archs*, IV, 444, 447–48.

9. *Md Archs*, IV, 439–40, 321–22, 324. The contempt for Greene continued after he had left the governorship (e.g., ibid., X, 26). On his contest with Hill: ibid., III, 171–72, 188–91. Hill's claim to be governor rested on Calvert's having named him to that post when he left the province in July 1646; Hill's selection was then confirmed by the colony's Council prior to Leonard Calvert's return.

10. Ibid., IV, 355–56.

11. Peter Laslett, ed., *Patriarcha and other Political Works of Sir Robert Filmer* (Oxford: Basil Blackwell, 1949), 78; Filmer, "In Praise of the Vertuous Wife," in Margaret J. M. Ezell, *The Patriarch's Wife: Literary Evidence and the History of the Family* (Chapel Hill: University of North Carolina Press, 1987), 183, 186–87.

12. *Md Archs*, I, 268, 239. Lord Baltimore's comments are taken not from his first letter to the Maryland authorities, which is now lost, but rather from a later one, dated August 26, 1649.

13. As was seen previously, public/private distinctions were successfully being made with respect to the official and familial responsibilities of public officeholders. Baltimore's dilemma lay in the fact that for him that distinction was not so readily drawn; in the Filmerian worldview, his duties as "lord [ruler]" and those as "proprietor [chief landholder]" inextricably shaded into each other, as was indicated in his title itself.

14. *Md Archs.*, I, 268–69. In 1650, Lord Baltimore surrendered to the inevitable and accepted the Marylanders' financial arrangements (ibid., 316–17).

15. The best book-length examinations of Maryland's seventeenth-century society are Gloria Main, *Tobacco Colony: Life in Early Maryland, 1650–1720* (Princeton, N.J.: Princeton University Press, 1982) and Lois Green Carr et al., *Robert Cole's World: Agriculture & Society in Early Maryland* (Chapel Hill: University of North Carolina Press, 1991). On the eighteenth-century hierarchy, see Allen Kulikoff, *Tobacco and Slaves: The Development of Southern Cultures in the Chesapeake, 1680–1800* (Chapel Hill: University of North Carolina Press, 1986).

16. The first three questions are discussed in chapter three; see ns. 46, 47. On the fourth, see *Md Archs*, I, 40–41: in early 1639, the Maryland assembly debated, but did not adopt, a law requiring every person in the colony aged 18 or over to swear an oath of allegiance to King Charles I, under pain of banishment. That widows were included was indicated by an exemption from the penalty for "women covert" but no one else.

17. Both Gordon Schochet, in *Patriarchalism in Political Thought: The Authoritarian Family and Political Speculation and Attitudes Especially in Seventeenth-Century England* (New York: Basic Books, 1975), and Peter Laslett, editor of *Patriarcha*, observe that Filmer was replying to such early contract theorists as Hugo Grotius and John Milton. This important point has too often been ignored by other scholars, including Carole Pateman, who in her otherwise provocative and insightful book *The Sexual Contract* (Stanford, Calif.: Stanford University Press, 1988) presents the theories sequentially rather than as a dialogue.

18. The quotation: John Locke, *Two Treatises of Government*, ed. Peter Laslett (Cambridge: Cambridge University Press, 1988), II, § 123 (p. 350). Locke alluded briefly to marriage contracts that might allow wives to retain some control over property, but largely assumed that, as he put it, husbands would "determine all things of their common Concernment." See ibid., I, §48 (p. 174), and, on marriage contracts, II, §§ 82, 83 (pp. 321–22). A feminist analysis that emphasizes the significance of men's control of property in Locke's schema is Lorenne M. G. Clark, "Women and Locke: Who Owns the Apples in the Garden of Eden?" in Lorenne M. C. Clark and Lynda Lange, eds., *The Sexism of Social and Political Theory: Women and Reproduction from Plato to Nietzsche* (Toronto: University of Toronto Press, 1979), 16–40.

19. Laslett, ed., *Two Treatises*, II, § 138 (p. 360). The only time Locke indicated that a wife might hold property was in the context of conquest: a conqueror, he remarked, could not rightfully seize the possessions of a defeated enemy's wife and children (II, § 183 [p. 390]). See also ibid., II, §§ 4, 57 (pp. 268, 306).

20. Ibid., II, §§ 118, 122 (pp. 347, 349). See also II, § 85, in which Locke argued that because slaves "are not capable of any Property," they could not be said to be members of civil society.

21. T.E., *The Lawes Resolutions of Womans Rights; or, The Lawes Provision for Woemen* (London: John Moore, 1632), 2.

22. For a useful general survey of the process through which women were incorporated into the Lockean public, see Glenna Matthews, *The Rise of Public Woman: Woman's Power and Woman's Place in the United States, 1630–1970* (New York: Oxford University Press, 1992).

CHAPTER 6: FATHERS AND MAGISTRATES, AUTHORITY AND CONSENT

1. Peter Laslett, ed., *Patriarcha and Other Political Works of Sir Robert Filmer* (Oxford: Basil Blackwell, 1949), 63; John Locke, *Two Treatises of Government*, ed. Peter Laslett (Cambridge: Cambridge University Press, 1988), II, § 2 (p. 268).

2. In addition to the works cited in the introduction, n. 4, see (on Filmer), R. W. K. Hinton, "Husbands, Fathers, and Conquerors, I," *Political Studies*, XV (1967), 291–300; and, on the English tradition of local government, R. B. Goheen, "Peasant Politics? Village Community and the Crown in Fifteenth-Century England," *American Historical Review*, XCVI (1991), 42–62.

3. Few scholars have systematically examined the colonial dialogue in these terms. For example, Michael Kammen, *Deputyes & Libertyes: The Origins of Representative Government in Colonial America* (New York: Alfred A. Knopf, 1969), and Edmund S. Morgan, *Inventing the People: The Rise of Popular Sovereignty in England and America* (New York: W. W. Norton, 1988), trace the development of the Lockean construct but devote little attention to Filmerian thought. Cf., though, Aviam Soifer, "Assaying Communities: Notes from the Tempest," *Connecticut Law Review*, XXI (1989), 871–95, which considers the "pervasive dispute [in Virginia and New England] about what gave anyone authority to claim to be in charge [884]." I thank David Konig for calling this article to my attention.

4. Quotation: Laslett, ed., *Patriarcha*, 53.

5. Ibid., 63. Elizabeth Janeway, in *Powers of the Weak* (New York: William Morrow, 1981), 93, usefully points out that this paternal model of political power "includes not only control over, but also affectionate regard for, their subjects among 'wise rulers.'"

6. Laslett, ed., *Patriarcha*, 283, 289, 57.

7. Ibid., 232, 60–61, 96, 84.

8. Ibid., 287, 231 (see also 211, 225, 255). Hobbes dealt with Filmer's objection by contending that even infants implicitly consented to the power of their parents and thus to the state (see Carole Pateman's discussion of this point in *The Sexual Contract* [Stanford, Calif.: Stanford University Press, 1988], 45–46).

9. On such less venturesome contract theorists as Algernon Sidney and James Tyrrell, see Rachel Weil, "Sexual Ideology and Political Propaganda in England, 1680–1714" (un-

pub. Ph.D. diss, Princeton University, 1991), chapter 2. Pateman, *Sexual Contract*, 91, correctly observes that "the full theoretical and practical significance of Locke's separation of what he calls paternal power from political power is rarely appreciated." (See, in general, 77–116 for her discussion of that significance, which differs in emphasis from mine, but concurs in its broad outlines.)

10. Locke, *Two Treatises*, ed. Laslett, I, §§ 48, 65, 66 (pp. 174, 188, 189).

11. Ibid., II, §§ 2, 71, 86 (pp. 268, 314, 323). Locke twice remarked that a husband did not have the power of life and death over his wife, and thus that his authority over her could not be likened to that of a king over his subjects (I, §48; II, § 82 [pp. 174, 321]).

12. Ibid., II, §§ 65 (pp. 310–11).

13. Ibid., II, § 61 (p. 308).

14. Ibid., II, §§ 74, 76 (pp. 316–18). See Gordon J. Schochet, "The Family and the Origins of the State in Locke's Political Philosophy," in John W. Yolton, ed., *John Locke: Problems and Perspectives* (Cambridge: Cambridge University Press, 1969), 81–98.

15. Locke, *Two Treatises*, ed. Laslett, II, § 105 (p 336); Laslett, ed., *Patriarcha*, 61–62. For an extended discussion of this aspect of Filmer's theory, see James Daly, *Sir Robert Filmer and English Political Thought* (Toronto: University of Toronto Press, 1979), chapter 4.

16. Isabel M. Calder, *The New Haven Colony* (New Haven, Conn.: Yale University Press, 1934), chapters 1–2; Sydney V. James, *Colonial Rhode Island: A History* (New York: Charles Scribner's Sons, 1975), chapter 4. A similar process undoubtedly occurred in Connecticut, but events prior to the drafting of the Fundamental Orders of Connecticut in January 1638/9 are undocumented. See Mary J. A. Jones, *Congregational Commonwealth: Connecticut, 1636–1662* (Middletown, Conn.: Wesleyan University Press, 1968), chapter 3.

17. This and the next two paragraphs are based on *WP*, III, 296–97. For the dating of this important letter, see Glenn LaFantasie, ed., *The Correspondence of Roger Williams* (Providence: Rhode Island Historical Society, 1988), I, 53, 55n.

18. *RI Col Recs*, I, 52, 112 (see also 14).

19. LaFantasie, ed., *Williams Correspondence*, I, 331; *MHS Colls*, 3d ser., no. 3 (1825), 3–4. Roger Williams seemed to agree with the complainants near the end of his life; he wrote in early 1682 that without a "Setled Govrment," no man could be "sure of his Howse, Goods Lands Catle Wife Children or Life" (LaFantasie, ed., *Williams Correspondence*, II, 775).

20. LaFantasie, ed., *Williams Correspondence*, II, 612. For a contemporary observation that Rhode Island lacked government, see *Plymouth Col Recs*, II, 37. When the freemen of Rhode Island reconstituted the government in 1647, they insisted that it was "DEMOCRATI-CALL" in form, resting on "the free and voluntarie consent of all, or the greater parte of the free Inhabitants" (*RI Col Recs*, I, 156), yet what gave that consent its legitimacy was the imprimatur of Parliament, the appropriate higher authority.

21. The next two paragraphs summarize material from *NHCP Recs*, I, 11–15. The dissenter described in the second paragraph is believed to have been the Reverend Samuel Eaton, Theophilus Eaton's brother.

22. The dissenter was prescient, for the restriction of the vote to male church members became a major source of trouble in the colony. See, e.g., ibid., II, 52–66, 94–95.

23. Ibid., 473–74 (see 465–75 passim). New Haven's 1663 negotiating position and Connecticut's reply are printed in ibid., 491–95. See also *Conn Col Recs*, I, 415.

24. *NHCP Recs*, II, 528–29; *MHS Colls*, 4th ser., VII (1865), 524 (see 521–29, 546–48, 552–55 passim).

25. *NHCP Recs*, II, 530–37 (quotations 535–36).

26. Ibid., 544–57 passim (quotations 551, 554).

27. *RI Col Recs*, I, 158. For examples of references to colonial leaders as "fathers," see, e.g., *WP*, IV, 302; *Md Archs*, XLI, 540. For the English monarch as a parent, see John Hull, Letterbook (typescript), II, 410–11, American Antiquarian Society, Worcester, Mass.

28. *Collections of the Connecticut Historical Society*, I (1860), 20; *SAL*, I, 502.

29. *Md Archs*, IV, 458–59. According to this deposition by Thomas Bradnox, essentially the same thing happened when Claiborne tried again two years later. He at first convinced a group of Kent Islanders that "hee had lawfull Authority" to lead them in an attack on St. Mary's City. But skeptics "desryed to bee made acquainted by him, with the Authority that

should justify them in the said Act. which he denying to shew[,] the said Inhabitants drew of[f] from the designe."

30. Clayton Torrence, *Old Somerset on the Eastern Shore of Maryland* (1935; repr., Baltimore, Md.: Regional Publishing Company, 1966), 388.

31. Augustine Herrman, "Journal of the Dutch Embassy to Maryland," in Clayton Colman Hall, ed., *Narratives of Early Maryland 1638–1684* (New York: Charles Scribner's Sons, 1910), 321–32 passim (quotation 321).

32. Torrence, *Old Somerset*, 388–89. Horsey was undoubtedly referring to the 1638 execution of Mr. Thomas Smith, an ally of William Claiborne's (see chapter three, n. 36).

33. Roger Heamans, "An additional brief narrative of a late bloody design against the Protestants in Ann Arundel County Severn in Maryland in the Country of Virginia," *Maryland Historical Magazine*, IV (1909), 152, 145 (hereafter cited as *MHM*); John Langford, "A Juste and Cleere Refutation of . . . Babylon's Fall in Maryland," in Hall, ed., *Maryland Narratives*, 259.

34. Leonard Strong, "Babylon's Fall in Maryland," in Hall, ed., *Maryland Narratives*, 240–41; John Hammond, "Hammond versus Heamans or an Answer to an audacious Pamphlet, published by an impudent and ridiculous Fellow," *MHM*, IV (1909), 238.

35. Sorting out the conflicting claims is difficult. Two useful discussions are John Frederick Martin, *Profits in the Wilderness: Entrepreneurship and the Founding of New England* (Chapel Hill: University of North Carolina Press, 1991), 101–5; and Robert E. Moody, ed., *The Letters of Thomas Gorges, Deputy Governor of the Province of Maine 1640–1643* (Portland: Maine Historical Society, 1978), 59n–60n. See also "Stephen Bachiler and the Plough Company of 1630," *Collections of the Maine Historical Society*, 3d ser., II (1906), 342–69 (hereafter cited as *MeHS Colls*), and Charles M. Andrews, *The Colonial Period of American History: The Settlements* (New Haven, Conn.: Yale University Press, 1934), I, chapters 16, 19.

36. *WP*, IV, 101; Nathaniel Bouton, ed., *Documents and Records Relating to the Province of New-Hampshire* (Concord, N.H.: George Jenks, 1867), I, 46. Winthrop's comments on the validity of Indian titles were addressed to the settlers at Exeter; see their "certen combination," drafted in June 1639 so that they "should not live without wholsome lawes & government amongst us," ibid., 131–34, and *JWJ*, I, 294.

37. This paragraph and the next are based on *WP*, IV, 185–88 (quotations 186); Bouton, ed., *New-Hampshire Docs*, I, 126–27, 158–59; *JWJ*, II, 42–43.

38. Letters addressed to the leaders of Massachusetts by both sides are printed in *WP*, V, 14–16, 33, 39–40, 60–62 (a response is on 66–67). On Thomas Gorges's administration: Moody, ed., *Gorges Letters*, passim, and Robert E. Moody, "Thomas Gorges, Proprietary Governor of Maine, 1640–1643," *MHS Procs*, LXXV (1963), 10–26. See also James P. Baxter, *George Cleeve of Casco Bay, 1630–1667* (Portland, Me.: Gorges Society, 1885).

39. *WP*, V, 75–76; *JWJ*, II, 266–67.

40. *Me Ct Recs*, I, 133. For Maine residents' complaints between 1646 and 1649, see *WP*, V, 152, 173, 259–60.

41. The documents detailing this fascinating dialogue are printed in William Sargent, ed., *York Deeds* (Portland, Me.: Brown, Thurston, & Co., 1888), pt 1, ff 20–28, 65 (quotations f 23); and *Mass Col Recs*, IV, pt 1, 70–362 passim.

42. *Me Ct Recs*, II, 138–43 passim. In all, 17 men were prosecuted for contempt during this one court session.

43. Ibid., I, 209; *New England Historical and Genealogical Register*, V (1851), 264; *Mass Col Recs*, IV, pt 2, 236–53, 265–73 passim (quotation 249).

44. The quotations are from "Nathaniel Phillips' Relation," *MeHS Colls*, 2d ser., V (1894), 189–94; for the Massachusetts version of the same events, see *Mass Col Recs*, IV, pt 2, 400–4. The May 1668 decrees that proclaimed Bay Colony control over Maine are printed in ibid., 370–73.

45. An excellent brief biography of Winthrop that discusses these disputes in greater detail than is possible here is Edmund S. Morgan, *The Puritan Dilemma: The Story of John Winthrop* (Boston, Mass.: Little, Brown, 1958). See also Darrett B. Rutman, *Winthrop's Boston: A Portrait of a Puritan Town, 1630–1649* (New York: W.W. Norton, 1965); and Robert

Emmet Wall, Jr., *Massachusetts Bay: The Crucial Decade, 1640–1650* (New Haven, Conn.: Yale University Press, 1972).

46. Winthrop's account of these early disputes is in *JWJ*, I, 74–151 passim. The demand for codification eventually led to the drafting of the Body of Liberties (1641) and the Laws and Liberties (1648). On the latter: Ronald G. Walters, "New England Society and the *Laws and Liberties* of Massachusetts, 1648," *Essex Institute Historical Collections*, CVI (1970), 145–68.

47. On these developments, see David D. Hall, ed., *The Antinomian Controversy, 1636– 1638: A Documentary History* (2d ed., Durham, N.C.: Duke University Press, 1990), 7–9 (hereafter cited as *AC*).

48. This paragraph and the next are based on *WP*, III, 422–24. Winthrop's similar argument (also offered during this period) about the need to expel troublemakers from families and states is in *AC*, 254, 261. After Winthrop's June 1637 essay was attacked by Sir Henry Vane, who had served as governor from May 1636 to May 1637, Winthrop produced in August a "Further Defense" of the court order (*WP*, III, 463–76). Vane's tract is printed in Thomas Hutchinson, comp., *Hutchinson Papers. Publications of the Prince Society*, I (1865; repr, New York: Burt Franklin, 1967), 84–96.

49. *JWJ*, I, 303. The Reverend John Cotton likewise cited the Fifth Commandment in a 1641 sermon supporting the magistrates (*JWJ*, II, 49).

50. Quotation: *WP*, IV, 383. Wall, *Massachusetts Bay*, 51–64, narrates the case with particular attention to its political consequences. For a longer treatment and transcripts of some of the relevant documents, see Arthur P. Rugg, "A Famous Colonial Litigation: The Case between Richard Sherman and Capt. Robert Keayne, 1642," *Proceedings of the American Antiquarian Society*, new ser., XXX (1920), 217–50. Goody Sherman's first name is nowhere indicated in the official records, but that it was Elizabeth is revealed in the Thwing biographical index, Massachusetts Historical Society, Boston.

51. John Winthrop wrote two accounts of the case, which differ slightly in wording but largely agree in content (*WP*, IV, 349–52, and *JWJ*, II, 64–66, 116–21). His summaries form the basis for the narrative in the next seven paragraphs even when not specifically cited. (Quotation: *WP*, IV, 349).

52. See Richard D. Pierce, ed., *Records of the First Church in Boston, 1638–1860, CSM Pubs*, XXXIX (1961), 25; and *JWJ*, I, 315–18, and *Mass Col Recs*, I, 281, 290. Keayne's anguish was made fully evident in his will (Bernard Bailyn, ed., *The Apologia of Robert Keayne: The Self-Portrait of a Puritan Merchant* [New York: Harper & Row, 1965]). The most thorough recent examination of Keayne's case, which revises earlier interpretations, is Stephen Innes, *Creating the Commonwealth: The Economic Culture of Puritan New England* (New York: W. W. Norton, 1995), chapter 4.

53. The official record of the proceedings is *Mass Col Recs*, II, 12, 31, 51. Pettford's deposition, June 30, 1641, is in the Essex Quarterly Court File Papers, WPA Transcripts, I, f 8/2, Phillips Library, Peabody Essex Museum, Salem, Mass. (summarized in *EC Ct Recs*, I, 27). The vote was 17 for her, 15 for Keayne, 7 abstentions. Some scholars have speculated that the deputies favored her in part because some of them lodged at her house during sessions of the General Court (e.g., *Mass Col Recs*, II, 116).

54. *WP*, IV, 351; *JWJ*, II, 65, 118–19; *WP*, V, 36. See *WP*, IV, 359–60, for Winthrop's October 1642 comments on the case and its aftermath.

55. Edward Everett Hale et al., eds., *The Note-Book of Thomas Lechford, Esq. 1638 to 1641* (1884; repr., Camden, Me.: Picton Press, 1988), 430–31. See *JWJ*, II, 119, on Keayne's offer. The account in Winthrop's journal asserts that Mr. George Story was the chief instigator of the lawsuit, but no other evidence supports that contention.

56. *JWJ*, II, 66. See also ibid., 119–21, and *Mass Col Recs*, II, 40, 58–59. The separation, of course, confirmed rather than ended the magistrates' veto in legislative matters. Subsequently, it was decided that when the houses sat together as the colony's final court of appeal, a majority of the whole would decide the case. Thus the more numerous deputies could outvote the magistrates; that was what sealed Mistress Ann Hibbens's fate at her 1656 witchcraft trial (see above, chapter three, n. 45).

57. Winthrop described the circumstances that produced these documents in his journal

(*JWJ*, II, 217, 229–37). The dispute over the leadership of the Hingham militia may be followed in *Mass Col Recs*, II, 97, 113–14, III, 17–26.

58. *WP*, IV, 468, 482. Much of the text (468–88) was devoted to the specific point at issue; that is, whether the law should prescribe penalties for each criminal offense or instead leave specific punishments to the discretion of the judges.

59. *JWJ*, II, 229–37 passim (quotations 233, 236).

60. The next two paragraphs summarize this "discourse on civil liberty," as printed in ibid., 238–39. For Winthrop's reflections on the episode, see ibid., 240–44, 264–66.

61. John Cotton, *A Discourse about Civil Government in a New Plantation whose Design is Religion* (Cambridge, Mass., 1663), 9–10. On the authorship of this pamphlet, see chapter one, n. 5. For other examples of Cotton's use of the marital metaphor, see Edmund S. Morgan, ed., *Puritan Political Ideas 1554–1794* (Indianapolis, Ind.: Bobbs Merrill, 1965), 170, 176, 215.

62. On contemporary uses of the marital metaphor in England, see Mary Lyndon Shanley, "Marriage Contract and Social Contract in Seventeenth-Century English Political Thought," *Western Political Quarterly*, XXXII (1979), 79–91; and Richard Braverman, *Plots and Counterplots: Sexual Politics and the Body Politic in English Literature, 1660–1730* (Cambridge: Cambridge University Press, 1993), 29–30 (I owe this latter reference to Michael Winship).

63. *Mass Col Recs*, IV, pt 1, 384–90 passim (quotations 388–89). Even when Massachusetts clerics formally denied the family analogy, they still used it. See, e.g, John Davenport's election sermon of 1669 (preached after he left New Haven for Boston), reproduced in *CSM Pubs*, X (1904–06), 6–7, in which he on the one hand asserted that "we must distinguish between Family-Rulers, and Commonwealth-Rulers" and on the other hand analogized between a woman's choice of a husband and the colonists' election of their "publick Rulers."

64. *Mass Col Recs*, IV, pt 2, 157–275 passim, narrates the crisis from the Bay Colony's perspective (quotations: 162, 197). On the abandonment of the voting policy: ibid., 117–18.

CHAPTER 7: MARVELOUS WICKEDNESS

1. William Bradford, *Of Plymouth Plantation*, ed. Samuel Eliot Morison (New York: Random House/Modern Library, 1967), 316.

2. Ibid., 317.

3. For example, Maryland's courts heard approximately eight times as many civil as criminal cases, whereas in New Haven criminal prosecutions outnumbered civil suits by about 2.5 to 1. The only other scholar to compare systematically patterns of prosecution in New England and the Chesapeake is David Hackett Fischer, *Albion's Seed: Four British Folkways in America* (New York: Oxford University Press, 1989); see esp. 189–96, 398–405. I concur with Fischer's observation that prosecution rates per capita in Maryland county courts were less than half those in Massachusetts Bay. But on the whole Fischer's and my conclusions (and sometimes our data) differ considerably. Fischer's figures, for example, rely on the work of a student who appears neither to have included in his tally of Maryland crimes the cases initially pursued as civil suits nor to have utilized the Provincial Court records (see 404, n. 21). Consequently, Fischer's data are less complete and differently distributed than the data analyzed below.

4. On the crucial role played by victims in identifying crimes and criminals in the Chesapeake: Mary Beth Norton, "Gender, Crime, and Community in Seventeenth-Century Maryland," in James Henretta et al., eds., *The Transformation of Early American History* (New York: Alfred A. Knopf, 1991), 126–34. See also J. A. Sharpe, "Enforcing the Law in the Seventeenth-Century English Village," in V. A. C. Gatrell et al., eds., *Crime and the Law: The Social History of Crime in Western Europe since 1500* (London: Europe Publications, 1980), 97–119, for a discussion of some of these same issues in the English context.

5. Recall, for instance, that the first laws defining widows' rights to shares of their husbands' estates were vague and required revision (chapter three, n. 13). The Virginia codes: *SAL*, I, 239–82, 432–94, II, 41–138. The sole exception to early fragmentation was Gov-

ernor Dale's short-lived draconian legal code for Virginia; see *Lawes Divine, Morall and Martiall* (1612) in Peter Force, ed., *Tracts and other Papers* . . . (1844; repr., Gloucester, Mass.: Peter Smith, 1963), III, no. 2.

6. For Maryland's 1642 criminal laws, which relied jointly on English precedent and judicial discretion, see *Md Archs*, I, 147–48, 158, 184, 192. On Virginia: Hugh Rankin, *Criminal Trial Proceedings in the General Court of Virginia* (Williamsburg, Va.: Colonial Williamsburg, 1965). A useful general discussion of the carryover of English law is Zechariah Chafee, Jr., "Colonial Courts and the Common Law," *MHS Procs*, LXVIII (1944–47), 132–59. On New England, see Edgar J. McManus, *Law and Liberty in Early New England: Criminal Justice and Due Process, 1620–1692* (Amherst: University of Massachusetts Press, 1993); chapter 2 contains a useful discussion of the relationship of New England capital crimes and Old Testament scriptures.

7. Quotation: *Mass Col Recs*, I, 174. Cotton's code is printed in Thomas Hutchinson, comp., *Hutchinson Papers. Publications of the Prince Society*, I (1865; repr., New York: Burt Franklin, 1967), 181–205 (hereafter *Hutchinson Papers*). The imitations of *L&L* may be consulted in *Conn Col Recs*, I, 509–63; *NHCP Recs*, II, 146–47, 571–615; *NPCL*, 242–93; and Nathaniel Bouton, ed., *Documents and Records Relating to the Province of New-Hampshire* (Concord, N.H.: George Jenks, 1867), I, 382–408.

8. The lists of capital offenses were not mutually exclusive in north and south; that is, the Bay Colony code threatened habitual thieves with execution, and Maryland too designated sodomy, rape, and "Sacriledge" as capital crimes. But the overall thrusts of the codes—and their enforcement, as shall be seen below—were very different. See *Md Archs*, I, 158, 192; *BOL*, 232–33; *L&L*, 5–6; *Conn Col Recs*, I, 77–78; *NHCP Recs*, II, 576–78, 593; *NPCL*, 244–45; Bouton, ed., *New-Hampshire Docs*, I, 384–85. Both Plymouth (1658) and New Hampshire (1680) dropped adultery from the list of capital crimes. Rhode Island was the only northern colony to follow English practice (*RI Col Recs*, I, 163–66). On the death penalty in England, see Cynthia Herrup, "Law and Morality in Seventeenth-Century England," *Past & Present*, no. 106 (1985), 102–23.

9. Based on 35 people (7 women, 28 men) sentenced to death—22 in the Chesapeake, 13 in New England. All but one of the women (86%) were hanged (4 had been convicted of infanticide), whereas 8 of the men (7 of them in the Chesapeake), or 29% of the males originally sentenced to death, escaped execution. Women could not plead clergy because the origins of the practice lay literally in the claim that a convicted felon was a clergyman exempt from civil law and subject only to his ecclesiastical superiors. For more on benefit of clergy in the colonies, see chapter two, ns. 62–63.

10. More precisely, 19% of female delinquents in the Chesapeake (N=37) and 8% of those in New England (N=100) were accused of crimes against property, while 16% (N=30) in the south and 12% (N=150) in the north were charged with crimes against persons. Comparable figures for men must be derived by considering only the cases with male defendants and no female participants, since the coding of all sexual offenses in New England otherwise distorts the ratios for the sample of men from that region. (Although all Chesapeake criminal cases were coded, the following proportions are for male-only cases in that region to allow appropriate comparisons to the New England data.) The figures for men are: property crimes, 28% of offenders in the Chesapeake (N=137) and 14% (N=242) of those in New England; crimes against persons: 16% in the Chesapeake (N=80) and 11.5% (N=198) in New England.

11. In the Chesapeake, 35% (N=172) of prosecutions of men were offenses against authority, whereas in New England 26.5% (N=458) of accusations against men fell into that category (see n. 10, above, on the derivation of these figures). Relatively few women in either region were charged with such misbehavior; see the extended discussion below.

12. Precise figures from the data set are: in the Chesapeake, only 9 women and 97 men were tried for these offenses; in New England, 460 female defendants (36%) and 778 male defendants (45%) faced such charges. See n. 10, above, for the origins of the figures for men.

13. The ratio of prosecutions for victimless crimes to crimes with victims was 1.7:1 in Maryland and 1.6:1 in Virginia. In New England, the ratios ranged from a low of 2.3:1 in

Plymouth to a high of 3.2:1 in Maine. Sexual offenses—some of which fell into each category—are discussed at length in the final two sections of this chapter.

14. For examples of the statutes: *L&L*, 29–31; *Conn Col Recs*, I, 153–54; *Md Archs*, I, 159, 342–43, 375; *SAL*, I, 433, II, 268–69.

15. In New England, crimes associated with drinking composed 22% of prosecutions of men (N=376) and 10% of prosecutions of women (N=123); in the Chesapeake, the comparable figures are 7% of men (N=46) and 3% of women (N=5). (See n. 10, above, for the derivation of the figures for men.)

16. *Md Archs*, LIII, 193–95, 207–10 (quotations 194, 209), XLIX, 29, X, 219, 202; *Va Ct Recs*, 20.

17. *NHCP Recs*, I, 133, 170–71, II, 124–27. Of the first fourteen offenses considered by the New Haven court, ten were related to drunkenness (*NHCP Recs*, I, 26, 28–29). New Amsterdam might not have penalized people for drunkenness alone, but its court records are filled with prosecutions for drunken brawls and violations of liquor-sale laws (e.g., *New Ams Ct Recs*, II, 296–300, 325–26, 332, 352–53).

18. Quotation: *Me Ct Recs*, I, 236 (see 235–40 passim); 1666 session: ibid., 263–64. For more on alcohol consumption on the islands, see, e.g., ibid., 222, 288–89, II, 101–2. I am descended from Mr. Walter Matthews, a grand jury man at the Shoals, who is mentioned in the November 1665 record.

19. *NHCP Recs*, I, 306; *NHT Recs*, I, 494; *NHCP Recs*, II, 430.

20. The lowest conviction rate in New England was 86% (N=239 of 279), for women charged alone with an order violation; the highest, 100% (N=13 of 13), for couples charged with crimes against property.

21. The lowest conviction rate in the Chesapeake was 56.5% (N=13 of 23), for men charged alone with a sexual offense; 93% (N=50 of 54) of couples tried together were convicted of sexual offenses. The next highest Chesapeake conviction rate was 85% (N=146 of 172), for men charged with crimes against authority.

22. Take, for example, the fate of those convicted of crimes against property: 64% of New England women, 73% of New England men, 62% of Chesapeake women, and 66% of Chesapeake men were fined or required to post a good-behavior bond. In three of these four groups—all but New England women, where the proportion was 40%—more than 50% of the guilty parties suffered *only* financial penalties. Yet at the same time New Englanders were more likely to incur multiple penalties than were Chesapeake residents. Again, considering the punishment of crimes against property: 78% of Chesapeake men and 90% of Chesapeake women received only one penalty for committing such an offense, whereas 44% of New England men and 41% of New England women were sentenced to combined or alternate penalties: most commonly, whipping and/or a fine, but also such combinations as a fine and shaming or whipping and shaming.

23. For committing crimes against property, 34% of New England women and 35% of New England men were sentenced to at least the possibility of whipping, whereas the comparable figure for Chesapeake men was 23% and for Chesapeake women 26%. Total numbers of cases in the data set for each group described in this and the preceding note are: Chesapeake men, 100; Chesapeake women, 19; New England men, 273; New England women, 83.

24. The data set includes 318 New England prosecutions of men (more than one fourth of them in groups of two or more), or 11% of all cases with male offenders, charged with neglect of a duty, and 155 prosecutions of men (or 4.5% of cases with male offenders) accused of contempt of authority. In the Chesapeake as well, 11% of prosecutions of male offenders, nearly one third involving groups of two or more (N=77), charged men with neglecting a duty, but 14% of such cases (N=101) accused men of contempt or treason. The only other categories of cases identified as authority crimes (desertion from military service, harboring fugitives, perjury, and malfeasance in office) had many fewer miscreants in both regions. Although the same proportions of men in both regions were charged with neglecting duties, the duties in question were different. In the Chesapeake, the vast majority fined for this delinquency did not appear in court as a witness or did not turn up for jury duty; in New

England, most of the delinquents failed to muster with the militia, refused to labor at public works or to maintain their fences properly, or did not take their turn at guard duty.

25. For examples of such laws, see the prologue to the first section of this book, n. 26.

26. See, e.g., *AN Ct Recs*, II, 105, and *NHCP Recs*, I, 392 (carrying arms); ibid., I, 143, 261–62 (public works projects). For a case in which an inexperienced juror wreaked havoc in a civil suit: *Md Archs*, IV, 414–23 passim, X, 26.

27. The rules were most fully set forth in April 1644 (*NHCP Recs*, I, 131–32), but even before then men were being fined for failure to comply with the requirements (ibid., 122–23). The rules for the watch in particular needed constant tinkering (ibid., 374–75, 381–83, 464–65; *NHT Recs*, I, 34–36). For other colonies' militia regulations: *Plymouth Col Recs*, II, 61–62; *Md Archs*, I, 412–13, III, 345.

28. *NHT Recs*, I, 326–27, 37–38. Some men malingered or slept on duty (ibid., 189, 191, 194; *NHCP Recs*, I, 488–89). Occasionally, one would challenge the watchmaster and refuse to serve (ibid., 386–87).

29. *NHCP Recs*, I, 317; *NHT Recs*, I, 76, 405, 46; *NHCP Recs*, I, 410–11.

30. *NHT Recs*, I, 141; *NHCP Recs*, I, 420–21.

31. *Mass Col Recs*, II, 208, 197; *L&L*, 23; *NHT Recs*, I, 475, 484. See also ibid., 523–24; *NHCP Recs*, I, 457, 461, 466.

32. Quotations on grand jurors' duties: *L&L*, 32; *Mass Col Recs*, I, 275. Resistance to them: *Me Ct Recs*, II, 41; *Suffolk Ct Recs*, II, 995; *Me Ct Recs*, I, 288, III, 133. Resistance to other minor officials: *Pynchon Ct Rec*, 291; *Me Ct Recs*, I, 304, 307. For similar problems in England, see Keith Wrightson, "Two Concepts of Order: Justices, Constables, and Jurymen in Seventeenth-Century England," in John Brewer and John Styles, eds., *An Ungovernable People* (New Brunswick, N.J.: Rutgers University Press, 1980), 21–46.

33. *NPCL*, 127–28, 264; *Mass Col Recs*, IV, pt 1, 324–27 (quotation 327). See also ibid., I, 302; *L&L*, 13.

34. Rebuffs: *Me Ct Recs*, I, 284, II, 151. Verbal abuse: ibid., II, 106, III, 212, 257.

35. *NH Ct Recs*, XL, 508; *Plymouth Col Recs*, VI, 180; *Me Ct Recs*, I, 104. A popular form of resistance was taking the constable's staff, the symbol of his office (e.g., *NH Ct Recs*, XL, 367; *Suffolk Ct Recs*, I, 256–57; on the staff, see *NPCL*, 123, 265). A few such incidents also occurred in the Chesapeake (e.g., *AN Ct Recs*, I, 71–72; *Md Archs*, IV, 171, 395), but they were nowhere near as common as in New England.

36. Thus unstable Maine was the only New England jurisdiction represented in the data base in which prosecutions for contempt (61%, N=49) outnumbered prosecutions for neglecting duty (39%, N=31); in the other colonies, those proportions were reversed, at the very least, and in New Haven contempt prosecutions represented just 10% of the whole. In Maryland, 42.5% (N=34 of 80) of all contempt prosecutions occurred during the particularly disrupted five-year period from 1655 through 1659. Another 17% (N=14) of prosecutions took place in the 1640s.

37. *AN Ct Recs*, II, 3; *Me Ct Recs*, I, 2; *Md Archs*, LIV, 566. Those who waited several weeks or months to complain to acquaintances fared no better: e.g., *Md Archs*, LIV, 433–35, 449–50, 458–59.

38. *Md Archs*, II, 55–56; *Va Ct Recs*, 476; *NHCP Recs*, II, 93; *Me Ct Recs*, II, 41.

39. *Md Archs*, X, 94, 229, 434. For other cases from the same period: ibid., III, 354–58, IV, 308, 544–46, LIV, 2. In more stable colonies, such prosecutions clustered in the early years (e.g., *Ct Assts Recs*, II, 16; *Va Ct Recs*, 12, 14) or followed the Stuart Restoration of 1660 (e.g., *Plymouth Col Recs*, V, 54, 61).

40. In New England, 86% (N=250 of 291 cases with known outcomes) of men charged with neglecting duty were convicted, and 94.5% (N=239) of those convicted were fined. Nearly one quarter (N=71) of the northern defendants were of high status; another 6% were groups of men with mixed status. In the Chesapeake, too, about one quarter of the defendants (N=20 of 74) were high-status men; 90% (N=67) of those charged with this offense were found guilty, and all were fined.

41. Conviction rates for contempt were 83% in the Chesapeake (N=74 of 91) and 95% (N=123 of 129) in New England. Unsurprisingly, twice as high a proportion of high-status men were prosecuted for contempt in the tumultuous Chesapeake (35% of offenders were

so designated) than in more stable New England (17%). Nearly two thirds (63.5%) of those found guilty in the Chesapeake were fined, with another 23% being whipped or shamed. In New England, a majority of men (53%) were also fined, with 45% of those defendants receiving such additional penalties as shaming or posting a good-behavior bond. (Only 25% of Chesapeake men were given multiple penalties.) Another 19% of New England men were sentenced to alternate penalties that included fines as an option (e.g., whipping or fine). New England also occasionally disfranchised men convicted of contempt, sentenced them to short jail terms, or—in especially serious cases—banished them from the colony. In only a few cases in either region were penalties wholly or partially remitted (12.5%, New England; 17%, Chesapeake).

42. Women faced charges of neglect in just 2 Chesapeake cases and 14 New England prosecutions. For a widow's problem with fences, see *NHT Recs*, I, 27–53 passim. For recalcitrant female witnesses: *Md Archs*, XLIX, 536, LVII, 16, 36. Women, unlike men, were rarely assigned civic duties and so were equally rarely charged with failing to carry them out. But for female estate appraisers, see *NHT Recs*, I, 287–88. In New Amsterdam, women arbitrated disputes among other women: *New Ams Ct Recs*, IV, 136, 140, 147, 151, 308.

43. Quotations: *Me Ct Recs*, I, 165, 267. Resisting constables: ibid., II, 355, 391–92; *Plymouth Col Recs*, III, 75.

44. The data set includes just 5 cases in which Chesapeake women were prosecuted for authority crimes, and I found only 2 more in records that were not coded. In New England, women were involved in 63 prosecutions for authority crimes. The larger number means little in and of itself, because more northern crimes in general are included in the data set, yet those prosecutions amount to 10% of the offenses charged against New England women, whereas the comparable figure for the Chesapeake is 3%. And additional New England cases also turned up in records not coded.

45. The three cases described in the text are *AN Ct Recs*, II, 118–19; *Md Archs*, LVII, 453 (the haircut), LXVI, 328. An unusual case in which a wife actually was prosecuted for such conduct is ibid., LVII, 198–99, but her sentence of whipping was wholly remitted because of pregnancy. In a comparable Maine case (*Me Ct Recs*, II, 391–92), the wife's sentence was merely postponed until after she had delivered the baby. Women rarely even appeared as *witnesses* in Chesapeake contempt prosecutions (N=5 of 101); a rare instance of such testimony is in *Va Ct Recs*, 62. (By comparison, male witnesses testified in 28 of those same 101 cases.)

46. These conclusions are based on 34 cases with known penalties involving New England women: 52% were fined (31% of those defendants received additional penalties); 10% were given alternate penalties including fines; 35% were sentenced to whipping or shaming. In just 3 cases were penalties wholly or partially remitted. Proportional distribution of penalties across categories resembled that for New England men, with no noticeable sexual differentials in sentencing. Conviction rates for women were exactly the same as men's (95%).

47. The exact figures are: Chesapeake, 68% (N=91 of 134); New England, 59% (N=421 of 721). On confusions caused by uncertain marriage definitions, see chapter one; for one of many fornicating couples ordered to marry, see *NHCP Recs*, I, 88–89, 105. See *L&L*, 23, for the quoted law; and *NHCP Recs*, II, 590; *NPCL*, 43; and *RI Col Recs*, I, 355, for similar statutes.

48. In the Chesapeake, bastardy prosecutions constituted precisely 50% (N=67 of 134) and fornication 18% (N=24) of sex crimes. In New England, fornication prosecutions constituted 49% (N=351 of 741) and bastardy 10% (N=70) of sex crimes. As will be recalled from the data in chapter one, 153 married couples (43.5% of fornication defendants) were accused of that crime in New England. Whenever a bastard birth was mentioned in a prosecution for "fornication," the case was coded as "bastardy" to permit an analytical distinction between the two crimes.

49. One Maryland servant couple, after having been whipped for bastardy, won their master's permission to marry when they promised to "make Sattisfaction by way of Servetude unto there said Master for Every Child the[y] Shall have In his Sarvis" (*Md Archs*, LIV, 513). On the demography of the Chesapeake: Russell Menard, "Immigrants and Their Increase: The Process of Population Growth in Early Colonial Maryland," in Aubrey Land et al., eds.,

Law, Society, and Politics in Early Maryland (Baltimore, Md.: The Johns Hopkins University Press, 1977), 88–110, and Lois Green Carr and Lorena Walsh, "The Planter's Wife: The Experience of White Women in Seventeenth-Century Maryland," *William and Mary Quarterly*, 3d ser., XXXIV (1977), 542–71 (hereafter cited as *WMQ*).

50. Chesapeake bastardy laws emphasized the economic consequences of the offense: *Md Archs*, I, 373, 441–42; *SAL*, II, 114–15, 168. For a further discussion of prosecutions for bastardy in Maryland: Norton, "Gender, Crime, and Community," in Henretta et al., eds., *Transformation*, 136–38. Massachusetts did not overlook the financial consequences of bastardy; see *Mass Col Recs*, IV, pt 2, 393–94.

51. Wickes: *Md Archs*, LIV, 78–121 passim; the Virginia case: *Va Ct Recs*, 139–42, 148 (quotations 140). Suits for the support of bastards: *Md Archs*, X, 336–37, 365–66, 525–26, LIV, 610–59 passim (Susanna Brayfield). Moreover, Chesapeake judges assessed lower penalties when bastard children died (e.g., *Md Archs*, LIV, 324–25, 329; XL, 519). By contrast, the deaths of bastards did not alter the penalties for the offense in New England (e.g., *NH Ct Recs*, XL, 354).

52. *Plymouth Col Recs*, V, 42; *Me Ct Recs*, I, 239; *Suffolk Ct Recs*, II, 912–13. In New England, fully 27% (N=194) of prosecuted sexual offenses fell under this rubric, whereas in the Chesapeake only 2% (N=3) did so. Cases so coded were those in which it was impossible to identify a specific offense from a court's language (precisely what, for example, was "sinfull dalliance" or "light" behavior?); those in which judges assigned penalties even though they had no convincing proof of illicit sexual activity; and those in which the behavior in question clearly stopped short of sexual intercourse. When phrasing or terminology obviously encompassed fornication ("committing folly with," "being naught with") the offenses were coded in that category even if the word "fornication" was not utilized.

53. *Conn Col Recs*, I, 78.

54. *NHT Recs*, II, 132–33. See also ibid., I, 450–52, for a similar prosecution. For "vehement suspition," see, e.g., *Me Ct Recs*, II, 502; *Suffolk Ct Recs*, I, 94.

55. The sole exception was Chesapeake men convicted of crimes against property; 23% were ordered whipped, as was already indicated in n. 23, above, whereas just 20% of Chesapeake men convicted of sexual offenses were so sentenced (N=10 of 49). In all other categories of offense (divided by region, type of crime, and sex of defendant), a lower percentage of miscreants was ordered whipped than was true in sex-crime cases.

56. *L&L*, 50; *NHCP Recs*, II, 611; *New England Historical and Genealogical Register*, XXXIV (1880), 268 (hereafter *NEHGR*); *NHT Recs*, II, 12.

57. The next two paragraphs are based on New Haven Colonial Records, I-B, ff 328–30, Connecticut State Library, Hartford (hereafter CSL). This material was omitted from the printed version of the case in *NHCP Recs*, II, 466–67.

58. Mercy Payne recounted this conversation in the third person. I have changed the pronouns and some verb tenses but otherwise the dialogue is precisely as she reported it.

59. They were married some time before February 1664/5 (*NHT Recs*, II, 131).

60. Many such stories are found in the records. For just a few: *Ct Assts Recs*, II, 91; *Suffolk Ct Recs*, I, 409, 435, 487; *Plymouth Col Recs*, V, 83–84, 87–88, 94, VII, 173–74; *Me Ct Recs*, III, 202, 212. Couples who subsequently married usually had bastardy penalties reduced (e.g., *Me Ct Recs*, I, 292–93, 296, 305, II, 169, 406).

61. Infanticide was essentially a crime committed by unwed mothers, other perpetrators being unusual. For two prosecutions not cited earlier (chapter four, ns. 63–64), see *Md Archs*, XLI, 430–32; *JWJ*, II, 317–18. A related offense, abortion (not officially termed a crime by any colony), was most often attempted by the fathers of bastards. See *Md Archs*, X, 80–81, 175–78; and the account of John Lumbrozo in chapter five (n. 65).

62. *Ct Assts Recs*, II, 81, 126; *Suffolk Ct Recs*, II, 697; *Plymouth Col Recs*, III, 159. Men (alone or in couples) constituted 63% of the defendants (N=144 of 227) in prosecutions for lewd behavior in New England. This is the only category of sexual offense in either region in which men outnumbered women, except for rape or homosexual behavior, offenses almost exclusively charged against men. But cf., for women accused of promiscuity, *NHT Recs*, II, 228–29; *Suffolk Ct Recs*, II, 915; *Pynchon Ct Rec*, 230–31.

63. *NHT Recs*, I, 182; New Haven Col Recs, I-B, f 92, CSL (omitted from published

text, *NHCP Recs*, II, 139); *Plymouth Col Recs*, III, 97. See also, e.g., *Pynchon Ct Rec*, 290; *EC Ct Recs*, II, 11–12.

64. Quotations: *Suffolk Ct Recs*, I, 443, 518; *Me Ct Recs*, I, 334. Although the following discussion will focus on consensual relationships between wives and men to whom they were not married, many cases prosecuted under this rubric involved attempted seductions of and sexual assaults on unwilling married women (e.g., *Me Ct Recs*, II, 42, 426; *Plymouth Col Recs*, III, 36, IV, 88, V, 8, VI, 178).

65. Adultery statutes: *BOL*, 233; *L&L*, 6; *Conn Col Recs*, I, 77; *NHCP Recs*, II, 577. In England, the Puritan-dominated Parliament also applied the death penalty to the crime, with similar results; see Keith Thomas, "The Puritans and Adultery: The Act of 1650 Reconsidered," in Donald Pennington and Keith Thomas, eds., *Puritans and Revolutionaries* (Oxford: Oxford University Press, 1978), 257–82. By contrast, the Puritans had fewer qualms about employing the death penalty in cases of bestiality or same-sex relationships involving men (see the next section of this chapter).

66. *Ct Assts Recs*, II, 19, 66, 67, 70, 108–9; *Mass Col Recs*, I, 225. Also, *JWJ*, I, 262–63.

67. *Ct Assts Recs*, II, 139; *WP*, IV, 445–46; William Hubbard, *History of New England from the Discovery to 1680*, MHS Colls, 2d ser., VI (1817), 426–27 (all quotations).

68. The quotations are from cases heard in 1654 (*Mass Col Recs*, IV, pt 1, 193–94) and 1667 (*Ct Assts Recs*, III, 191–93). For similar cases: *JWJ*, II, 257–59; *Mass Col Recs*, IV, pt 1, 212–13, and pt 2, 309; *Ct Assts Recs*, III, 150–51. If convicted of some offense, defendants were usually subjected to whipping or symbolic hanging or both. A detailed examination of the life of a prominent adultery defendant (Anna Keayne Lane Paige) is Edmund S. Morgan, "A Boston Heiress and Her Husbands: A True Story," *CSM Pubs*, XXXIV (1937–42), 499–513. In 1650, Connecticut hanged a woman, Elizabeth Johnson, for adultery, but her partner, Thomas Newton, escaped from custody, taking refuge in Rhode Island and eventually New Netherland (*Conn Col Recs*, I, 209, 222, 226, 232; *RI Col Recs*, I, 235). (William K. Holdsworth, "Adultery or Witchcraft? A New Note on an Old Case in Connecticut," *New England Quarterly*, XLVIII [1975], 394–409, concludes erroneously that Johnson was not executed.) John Winthrop's own daughter-in-law (the wife of his dead son Henry), Elizabeth Fones Winthrop Feke Hallett, escaped prosecution for adultery in Connecticut in 1649 only by a timely flight to New Netherland. Her saga may be followed in *WP*, V, passim; or, in fictionalized form, in Anya Seton's 1958 novel, *The Winthrop Woman*.

69. Roger Williams commented at length on the death penalty for adultery in the context of the Johnson-Newton case (n. 68, above); see Glenn W. LaFantasie, ed., *The Correspondence of Roger Williams* (Providence: Rhode Island Historical Society, 1988), I, 308–9, 316, 320–21. For Gorges: Robert E. Moody, ed., *The Letters of Thomas Gorges, Deputy Governor of the Province of Maine 1640–1643* (Portland: Maine Historical Society, 1978), 36–37, 55.

70. *Me Ct Recs*, II, 34–92 passim, 367–69 (quotations 43, 42, 367); see also *NH Ct Recs*, XL, 90. Another repeat adulterer in Maine (who was whipped and fined, but not hanged) was Mistress Mary Bachiler, the estranged third wife of the Reverend Stephen Bachiler, who himself confessed to attempted adultery. After she had been presented four times for adultery or "vehement suspicion of incontinency" (three times with one man, once with a second), Mistress Bachiler petitioned the Massachusetts General Court for a divorce in 1656. The response to her request is unknown. On the Bachilers, see *JWJ*, II, 45–46; *WP*, V, 153; *EC Ct Recs*, I, 191; and, on Mary's adulterous career, *Me Ct Recs*, I, 146–77 passim, II, 31. The divorce petition is in *Mass Col Recs*, IV, pt 1, 282.

71. The next two paragraphs are based on *Md Archs*, X, 282–83, 285–86. See chapter four, n. 67. Recall, in this context, the drunken orgy at the Bradnox household on Kent Island in 1658 (chapter five, n. 13), where adultery accusations were freely voiced but never formally pursued for the same reason.

72. Ibid., 339, 366.

73. This paragraph and the next two are based on ibid., 109–12. For what seem to have been other such households: ibid., LIV, 63–91 passim (Robert and Elizabeth Martin and

Henry Ashley); X, 188–498 ff passim, esp. 296–97 (Walter Pakes, his wife, and his partner Paul Simpson); and LIV, 534–38 (Bridgett and David Johnson and John Clymer; here the husband appears to have been ignorant of his wife's adulterous liaison with their servant).

74. See ibid., X, 64, 222.

75. For the adultery law under which Dorothy and Edward were tried, see *Md Archs*, I, 286. For Robert Holt's attempted second marriage and its disastrous consequences: ibid., XLI, 149–593 passim, III, 463; and Testamentary Proceedings, I (1662), ff 23–25, 29, Maryland Hall of Records, Annapolis. Ironically, Dorothy Holt and Edward Hudson seem to have escaped later prosecution because they did not try to legalize their union.

76. In 279 prosecutions of couples in New England for fornication, adultery, bastardy, or lewdness, 156 (56%) of the men and women received the same penalties as their partners; in the Chesapeake, the comparable proportion was 32% (N=12 of 38).

77. Of New England prosecutions for lewd behavior, 52% (N=90 of 173) targeted men alone, and just 36% of the men in cases with known outcomes (N=30 of 84) escaped with nothing but a financial penalty or an order to stay away from the woman or women in question. The others faced combinations or alternatives of financial penalties and whipping or shaming. In 40% of Chesapeake bastardy cases (N=19 of 47) women stood trial alone. Fully 44% (N=7 of 16) were ordered whipped with no opportunity to avoid that penalty by paying a fine. In New England, by contrast, just 28% of bastardy cases involved women tried alone (N=18 of 64), and only 28% of those defendants (N=5 of 18) were ordered whipped without the alternative of paying a fine.

78. Based on 134 Chesapeake prosecutions and 721 in New England. In the Chesapeake, men were defendants in 59% (N=79) of the sex-crime cases and women in 81% (N=109); in New England, men were defendants in 79.5% (N=573) and women in 67% (N=480) of sex-crime cases. Conviction rates were: in the Chesapeake, women 85% (N=93), men 82% (N=65); in New England, women 97% (N=466), men 96% (N=548). In addition to the crimes already analyzed and rape, sodomy, and bestiality (to be discussed in the next part of this chapter), categories of offenses included as sex crimes in this tabulation are incest, abortion, bigamy, prostitution, and "other" (including cohabitation by a divorced couple and lascivious speech without allied conduct). These total fewer than 5% of offenses in either region.

79. Precise percentages for sexual miscreants sentenced to at least an alternative penalty of whipping are: New England women, 56% (N=267 of 422 cases with known penalties); New England men, 51% (N=248 of 490); Chesapeake women, 69.5% (N=45 of 59); Chesapeake men, 20% (N=10 of 49). For more on the Chesapeake pattern of differential punishment of men and women in sex crimes: Norton, "Gender, Crime, and Community," in Henretta et al., eds., *Transformation*, 136–43.

80. This is not to claim that northern men and women were treated absolutely evenhandedly, especially when they were tried separately for similar offenses. New England women who stood trial alone for fornication or bastardy, for instance, were more liable to be sentenced to a possibility of a whipping than were any other defendants, with the exception of the small number of Chesapeake women (N=6) convicted of adultery, all of whom were ordered whipped. Just 10% (N=9 of 90) of such New England women escaped a whipping penalty, whereas 56% (N=29 of 52) of male defendants did so. Presumably, such women were more likely to be whipped because they refused to name their partners or had been sufficiently promiscuous that they could not identify a bastard's father.

81. Historians hitherto have tended to stress the unequal, if not oppressive, treatment of women in New England. Yet in contrast to the Chesapeake the handling of female defendants in Puritan courts was relatively evenhanded. Cf. Lyle Koehler, *A Search for Power: The "Weaker Sex" in Seventeenth-Century New England* (Urbana: University of Illinois Press, 1981), and Carol Karlsen, *The Devil in the Shape of a Woman: Witchcraft in Colonial New England* (New York: W. W. Norton, 1987).

82. According to the *OED*, "rape" first came to mean "the ravishing of a woman" in the late fifteenth century, after having initially been employed to mean "the act of taking anything by force." Likewise, from the late thirteenth century, "sodomy" meant "an unnatural form of sexual intercourse, esp. that of one male with another." For the seventeenth-

century English law of rape, see T.E., *The Lawes Resolutions of Womens Rights; or, The Lawes Provision for Woemen* (London: John Moore, 1632), 375–402.

83. The history of New England's rape laws is succinctly summarized in McManus, *Law and Liberty*, 31–33; only Rhode Island—which, like Virginia and Maryland, copied English law—did not engage in some variation of this sort of waffling. Significantly, the rape laws in the northern colonies differed from one another in specifics, exposing the problem by their very divergence. The quotation: *Hutchinson Papers*, 200. See also *Mass Col Recs*, II, 21–22, IV, pt 2, 437–38.

84. See Laurel Thatcher Ulrich, *Good Wives: Image and Reality in the Lives of Women in Northern New England, 1650–1750* (New York: Oxford University Press, 1982), chapter 5, and Edmund S. Morgan's classic article "The Puritans and Sex," *New England Quarterly*, XV (1942), 591–607. Cf. Nancy F. Cott, "Passionlessness: An Interpretation of Victorian Sexual Ideology, 1790–1850," *Signs*, IV (1978–79), 219–36.

85. *WP*, IV, 345. For a flawed but pioneering study focusing primarily on Plymouth Colony, see Robert Oaks, " 'Things Fearful to Name': Sodomy and Buggery in Seventeenth-Century New England," *Journal of Social History*, XII (1977–78), 268–81; the most recent detailed examination is Richard Godbeer, " 'The Cry of Sodom': Discourse, Intercourse, and Desire in Colonial New England," *WMQ*, 3d ser., LII (1995), 259–86.

86. *Hutchinson Papers*, 199; *BOL*, 233; *L&L*, 5–6. See also *NPCL*, 244; Bouton, *New-Hampshire Docs*, I, 384; *Conn Col Recs*, I, 77; *RI Col Recs*, I, 172–73.

87. *NHCP Recs*, II, 576–77.

88. Ibid., 577; question quoted from Bradford, *Of Plymouth Plantation*, 404. John Winthrop's comments in another case make it appear that he thought the answer was yes: *JWJ*, II, 38.

89. *WP*, IV, 345; Bradford, *Of Plymouth Plantation*, 318–19, 410 (appendix X, 404–13, reprints the ministers' replies in full). See chapter two, n. 31.

90. See chapter one, n. 52, and Thomas Laqueur, *Making Sex: Body and Gender from the Greeks to Freud* (Cambridge, Mass.: Harvard University Press, 1990), 161–62.

91. *Va Ct Recs*, 149; *Ct Assts Recs*, III, 199–200; and *NH Ct Recs*, XL, 247–48, 261. The other two cases are those of John Simple (*Ct Assts Recs*, III, 191; Suffolk County Court Files, #814, Massachusetts Archives, Boston [hereafter MA]); and Peter Croy (*Ct Assts Recs*, III, 258; Suffolk Court Files #1254, MA).

92. *Ct Assts Recs*, II, 121; *Mass Col Recs*, IV, pt 1, 212. See also *Ct Assts Recs*, III, 216–17, for an Indian man convicted of raping a nine-year-old Indian girl and sentenced to sale in the West Indies. In 1654, the Bay Colony had no rape law explicitly applying to children, but the absence of one did not prevent the colony from adopting that penalty in the case of Patrick Jennison; it was *after* his 1669 trial that the law was rewritten once again.

93. *Plymouth Col Recs*, IV, 22, III, 97; *Conn Col Recs*, I, 28. See also, e.g., *Plymouth Col Recs*, II, 35, and *Ct Assts Recs*, II, 79.

94. LaFantasie, ed., *Williams Correspondence*, II, 588; *NHCP Recs*, II, 134–37. Even two of the "four mayden children" (aged 8 and 10) raped by Thomas Hayle were ordered whipped by the Virginia General Court, but it is not clear why (*Va Ct Recs*, 149–50). The ages of Avis Partin and Ann Usher are given in the muster of 1624/5, printed in Virginia M. Meyer and John Frederick Dorman, eds., *Adventurers of Purse and Person Virginia 1607–1624/5*, 3d ed. (Richmond, Va.: Order of First Families of Virginia, 1987), 13.

95. See Section I, Prologue, n. 46, and chapter four, n. 52. Once women did complain in New England, though, the accused men were convicted—though usually not of a capital offense. Of 21 northern rape prosecutions in which the outcomes are known, all ended in conviction. By contrast, in 6 Chesapeake cases, only one man (Thomas Hayle) was found guilty. See, e.g., *Md Archs*, LVII, 353–58, 597, 604. It is perhaps significant that several of the New England prosecutions involved Indian men and English women or girls (e.g., *EC Ct Recs*, IV, 230–32; *Plymouth Col Recs*, VI, 98); women might have concluded that they were more likely to be believed if the attack had been interracial. One case involved a black assailant: *Suffolk Ct Recs*, II, 1067.

96. This paragraph and the next three are based on *Me Ct Recs*, I, 140–43 (among the witnesses in the case are two of my ancestors, Robert Knight and his wife). Another example

of delayed reporting by a wife may be traced in *Mass Col Recs*, IV, pt 1, 271, and *Pynchon Ct Rec*, 389–91. See also n. 64, above, for trials of men accused of less serious sexual assaults on wives.

97. The Virginia prosecutions are *AN Ct Recs*, II, 371–73; and *Va Ct Recs*, 34, 42, 47. (I have not surveyed the unpublished Virginia records, and they may contain a few other such cases.) Without making a systematic search, I identified 33 Chesapeake households headed by two unmarried men, many of whom termed themselves "mates." See, e.g., *Md Archs*, IV, 24, 162, X, 171–72, 290–91; *AN Ct Recs*, I, 31, 47. That such arrangements were substitutes for marriage was demonstrated when partnership agreements referred explicitly to what would happen when one of the men married (*Md Archs*, LIV, 218, LX, 103).

98. The four married men, the first two of whom were executed, were William Potter of New Haven (*NHCP Recs*, II, 440–43); William Plain of Guilford (James Savage, ed., *The History of New England from 1630 to 1649 by John Winthrop, Esq.* [2d ed., Boston: Little, Brown, 1853], II, 324); John Rogers of New London (*MHS Colls*, 4th ser., VII [1865], 584–86; *NEHGR*, VIII [1854], 329); and Nicholas Sension of Windsor (see Godbeer, " 'Cry of Sodom,' " *WMQ*, 3d ser., LII (1995), 259–60, 273–77.

99. Plymouth: Thomas Granger, aged c. 16 or 17 (Bradford, *Of Plymouth Plantation*, 320–21; *Plymouth Col Recs*, II, 44). Salem: William Hackett, c. 18 (Savage, ed., *Winthrop's History*, II, 58–60; *Mass Col Recs*, I, 339, 344). New Haven: Walter Robinson, 15 (*NHCP Recs*, II, 132–33; New Haven Col Recs, I-B, ff 85–86, CSL). The quotation is from the March 1652/3 trial of six young men, all of whom were ordered "whipt publiquly." A seventh, who denied complicity, was remanded to his master "to give him that correction in the family which he should see meete" (*NHT Recs*, I, 178–79).

100. New Haven Town Records, ff 142–44 (typescript), CSL. All information but the fact that an "extraordinary" court session was held on this day was omitted from *NHT Recs*.

101. New Haven Col Recs, I-B, f 328, CSL. Another New Haven sexual-offense recidivist was John Knight, hanged in 1655 as "a leud, prophane, filthy, corrupting, incorridgable person," after he committed "filthyness in a sodomitticall way" with Peter Vincon and sexually assaulted Mary Clarke, both of whom were his fellow servants in the household of William Judson. Knight had previously been severely whipped and ordered to wear a hangman's noose for his "loathsome filthyness" with the children of Francis Hall (*NHCP Recs*, II, 137–39 [quotations 138]; New Haven Col Recs, I-B, ff 89–91, CSL). For more on Knight, see Section I, Prologue, n. 49.

102. Bradford, *Of Plymouth Plantation*, 321; New Haven Town Recs, 142–43 (typescript), CSL.

103. Savage, ed., *Winthrop's History*, II, 58; *AN Ct Recs*, II, 372; *NHCP Recs*, II, 223–24; New Haven Col Recs, I-B, ff 145–46, CSL. So the case of George Spencer, executed for bestiality in New Haven in early 1642 after initial suspicions were aroused because it was thought that a recently born deformed piglet resembled him, was anomalous in its origins (*NHCP Recs*, I, 62–73). (See also ibid., 295–96, and *NHT Recs*, I, 158–59.)

104. Of 20 prosecutions of men for various forms of bestiality or same-sex sexual activity (13 with known outcomes) included in the data base, 5 ended in executions. All the men who were not hanged were punished by whipping, about half the time (as in Ferris's case) in conjunction with fines and shaming penalties.

105. *Plymouth Col Recs*, II, 137, 163; *EC Ct Recs*, I, 44, and Essex Quarterly Courts, Record Books, 2d ser., I, f 123, Phillips Library, Peabody Essex Museum, Salem, Mass. George F. Dow, the editor of the Essex court records, expurgated all but the charge of "unseemly practices" between Elizabeth Johnson and another maidservant from his published text. For the fragmentary record of what could be either a rape or a third such presentment, see *Me Ct Recs*, I, 291.

106. Savage, ed., *Winthrop's History*, II, 58; *Va Ct Recs*, 78, 81, 83, 85, 93; LaFantasie, ed., *Williams Correspondence*, II, 464–81. See also *Plymouth Col Recs*, I, 64, for the 1637 sodomy prosecution of John Allexander, said to have been "formerly notoriously guilty that way, and seeking to allure others thereunto," which implies similar concealment on the part of those Allexander had tried to "allure." Richard Godbeer likewise concludes that Nicholas

Sension's sexual activities were well known to his neighbors long before he was brought to trial (see above, n. 98).

CHAPTER 8: HUSBAND, PREACHER, MAGISTRATE

1. "A Report of the Trial of Mrs. Anne Hutchinson before the Church in Boston," in David D. Hall, ed., *The Antinomian Controversy, 1636–1638* (2d ed.; Durham, N.C.: Duke University Press, 1990), 382–83 (book hereafter cited as *AC*; document as *AC* [Church]). This chapter has benefited from a close reading by my former student Michael P. Winship.

2. The most comprehensive discussion of these points appears in Emery Battis, *Saints and Sectaries: Anne Hutchinson and the Antinomian Controversy in the Massachusetts Bay Colony* (Chapel Hill: University of North Carolina Press, 1962). For briefer summaries: Darrett Rutman, *Winthrop's Boston: Portrait of a Puritan Town, 1630–1649* (New York: W. W. Norton, 1965), 114–24; and Philip Gura, *A Glimpse of Sion's Glory: Puritan Radicalism in New England, 1620–1660* (Middletown, Conn.: Wesleyan University Press, 1984), chapter 9.

3. See *AC*, 3. The pejorative term "Antinomian" was evidently first used in the title of John Winthrop's pamphlet *A Short Story of the Rise, reign, and ruine of the Antinomians, Familists, & Libertines*, published in London in 1644 and reprinted in *AC*, 199–310 (hereafter cited as *AC* [Story]).

4. For a useful compilation of some of the most important early articles, see Francis Bremer, ed., *Anne Hutchinson: Troubler of the Puritan Zion* (Huntington, N.Y.: Krieger Publishing Co., 1981). More recent scholarship includes Amy Schrager Lang, *Prophetic Woman: Anne Hutchinson and the Problem of Dissent in the Literature of New England* (Berkeley: University of California Press, 1987), chapters 2, 3; Marilyn J. Westerkamp, "Anne Hutchinson, Sectarian Mysticism, and the Puritan Order," *Church History*, LIX (1990), 482–96, and "Puritan Patriarchy and the Problem of Revelation," *Journal of Interdisciplinary History*, XXIII (1992–93), 571–95; Amanda Porterfield, *Female Piety in Puritan New England: The Emergence of Religious Humanism* (New York: Oxford University Press, 1991), chapter 3; Darren M. Staloff, "The Making of an American Thinking Class: Intellectuals and Intelligentsia in Puritan Massachusetts" (unpub. Ph.D. diss., Columbia University, 1991), chapters 4, 5; and Jane N. Kamensky, "Governing the Tongue: Speech and Society in Early New England" (unpub. Ph.D. diss., Yale University, 1993), chapter 3.

5. Biographical details in this paragraph and the next are drawn from *AC*, 5–6, and Battis, *Saints and Sectaries*, chapters 1–5.

6. Quotations from "The Examination of Mrs. Anne Hutchinson at the Court at Newtown," in *AC*, 337 (hereafter cited as *AC* [Court]); *AC*, 392.

7. *AC* [Court], 322, 317; Richard D. Pierce, ed., *The Records of the First Church in Boston, 1630–1868, CSM Pubs*, XXXIX (1961), 19.

8. Quotations: William Hubbard, *The History of New England from the Discovery to 1680, MHS Colls*, 2d ser., V (1815), 175; *AC* [Court], 317. On the revival: *AC*, 13–16.

9. Cotton Mather, *Magnalia Christi Americana . . .* (Hartford, Conn.: Silas Andrus & Son, 1853), II, 516–17.

10. John Cotton, "The Way of Congregational Churches Cleared," in *AC*, 411–12 (hereafter cited as *AC* [Way]). For a discussion of other such women, see chapter four.

11. *AC* [Story], 263; *AC* [Court], 336; *AC* [Way], 412.

12. This paragraph overly simplifies a complex theological position. For more detail, see William Stoever, *"A Faire and Easie Way to Heaven": Covenant Theology and Antinomianism in Early Massachusetts* (Middletown, Conn.: Wesleyan University Press, 1978).

13. *AC* [Way], 412; *MHS Colls*, 4th ser., I (1852), 206. See also *AC* [Story], 263, and, on the Eve analogy, *AC* [Story], 206; Hubbard, *History*, I, 283–84; and Mather, *Magnalia*, II, 509.

14. *AC* [Court], 314.

15. *AC* [Story], 267, 264, 207–8; J. Franklin Jameson, ed., *Johnson's Wonder-Working Providence 1628–1651* (New York: Charles Scribner's Sons, 1910), 131. On the use of Winthrop's *Short Story* as a source for information about Hutchinson's civil trial, see n. 42, below.

Battis, *Saints and Sectaries*, 69, gives the relative location of the Hutchinson and Winthrop houses.

16. *AC* [Story], 264; *AC* [Way], 413.

17. *AC* [Story], 263–64.

18. Quotation: *AC* [Way], 413.

19. Quotations variously from *AC* [Story], 308–9, 206, 275; Mather, *Magnalia*, II, 516. Recall that John Cotton too was called "insinuating"; n. 8, above.

20. *JWJ*, I, 285–86 (see, on Mary Oliver, *Ct Assts Recs*, II, 80; *EC Ct Recs*, I, 12, 34, 61, 99, 138–86 passim; and *Mass Col Recs*, II, 258, III, 182); *AC* [Church], 372–73. See also *AC* [Story], 207, for Thomas Weld's comment on how the "great respect" accorded her caused the magistrates and elders to "wink at" her meetings for too long.

21. Quotations: *AC* [Story], 203, 264; *AC* [Way], 413.

22. *AC* [Way], 420.

23. *AC* [Story], 204.

24. *AC* [Story], 206, 209, 253.

25. Jameson, ed., *Johnson's Wonder-Working Providence*, 127.

26. *AC* [Way], 413; Jameson, ed., *Johnson's Wonder-Working Providence*, 127, 28. See also *MHS Colls*, 4th ser., I (1852), 213, for a 1648 comment that, in 1636, "divers, who love the preheminence of both sexes, . . . began to inveigh against learning, Scholars, and Colledges," thus explicitly linking women's standing in the Hutchinson movement with its antagonism to higher education.

27. *AC* [Story], 209; *AC* [Way], 422, 413. Cotton also claimed that Anne Hutchinson and her followers dissembled when he asked them about the ideas they were advancing (ibid., 398–99).

28. *JWJ*, I, 195–99, 201–7 passim (quotations 196, 204). For the clerics' correspondence with Cotton, which continued for months as others joined the fray, see *AC*, 24–151.

29. *AC*, 152–72 (quotations 157, 164, 171). Wheelwright's wife Mary was William Hutchinson's sister.

30. *AC* [Story], 209–10; *AC* [Way], 423.

31. Quotation: *AC* [Court], 320. I have followed Battis, *Saints and Sectaries*, 128–33, and Hall, *AC*, 6–7, in placing this crucial conversation in December 1636, but it is nowhere dated precisely in the surviving records.

32. Ibid., 320, 318, 325; see 333 for Leverett and Cotton.

33. Ibid., 333, 345.

34. See Winthrop's extended discussion and defense of Wheelwright's trial in *AC* [Story], 282–300 (quotations 283), and his account of these events in *JWJ*, I, 208–18. The brief official record is in *Mass Col Recs*, I, 189.

35. *AC* [Story], 212.

36. Ibid., 212–13. Cotton's description of his theological position is in *AC*, 173–98. In his later comments on Hutchinson, he described himself merely as "one amongst the rest" who respected her and claimed that she "seldome resorted to mee" for "private speech" or rarely "tarried long" when she did come (*AC* [Way], 413, 434).

37. *JWJ*, I, 234–35 (see, in general, 230–35).

38. *AC* [Story], 248–50 (see also 213); *JWJ*, I, 239. On the "desperate" situation, see *JWJ*, I, 230, for the story of a woman so troubled by her "spiritual estate" in August that she threw her baby into a well, saying, "now she was sure she should be damned," and John Clark, "Ill Newes from New-England," *MHS Colls*, 4th ser., II (1854), 23–24.

39. These events are recounted in *AC* [Story], 252–62 (quotation 254); *Mass Col Recs*, I, 205–13 passim (quotation 213); and *JWJ*, I, 239–41. For the expulsion of Cain, see Genesis 4:12–16; of Hagar and Ishmael, Genesis 21:9–14.

40. Jameson, ed., *Johnson's Wonder-Working Providence*, 127; *AC* [Story], 262.

41. *Mass Col Recs*, I, 207.

42. Both records can most conveniently be consulted in *AC*. For the transcript, herein cited as *AC* [Court], see 312–48; for the relevant part of *Short Story*, 262–76. The two versions will be compared in some of the following notes. Winthrop's account makes him look better by omitting certain exchanges in which he was bested, making his questions

seem more coherent, and misrepresenting the trial's dynamic in one crucial way. Yet where there is overlap Winthrop's version and the transcript roughly accord with each other and clearly represent different reports of the same oral exchanges. Winthrop may well have kept his own notes during the encounter.

43. The next five paragraphs are based on *AC* [Court], 312–14. Winthrop's phrase "general assembly" referred to the August synod rather than to a prior civil action against her.

44. Winthrop's version of the foregoing discussion (*AC* [Story], 266–67) shortened it, restructured his questions, and omitted his frustrated statement about not "discoursing" with women.

45. The next nineteen paragraphs are based on *AC* [Court], 314–17, and *AC* [Story], 267–69. The themes discussed separately here are intextricably interspersed in the exchanges, which accordingly cannot be divided neatly into individual footnotes.

46. Titus 2: "[3] The elder women likewise, that they be in such behaviour as becommeth holinesse, not false accusers, not subject to much wine, but teachers of honest things, [4] That they may instruct the yong women to bee sober minded, that they love their husbands, that they love their children, [5] That they be temperate, chaste, keeping at home, good & subject unto their husbands, that the word of God be not evill spoken of." Acts 18:26: "And he [Apollos] began to speake boldly in the Synagogue. Whom when Aquila and Priscilla had heard, they tooke him unto them, and expounded unto him the way of God more perfectly."

47. References to Titus appear in both the transcript and *Short Story*, to Corinthians only in the transcript, and to Acts and Timothy only in *Short Story*. The passage in Acts offered potentially powerful support to Mistress Hutchinson, but she relied more heavily on Titus, for reasons that shall shortly become evident. See the speculations below on the possible reasons for differences between the two accounts of the debate over the meetings at her house.

48. In the transcript, the questions and answers preceding this comment by the governor seem garbled, yet it is clearly responsive to her insistence that the sex of her listeners was an important factor in assessing the legitimacy of her meetings.

49. These conclusions are based on his allusions (in *Short Story*) to acceptable meetings being composed of "some few neighbours," to his concerns about the frequency and regularity of her gatherings, and to his repeated insistence that "your Ministery is publicke."

50. *AC* [Court], 318.

51. *AC* [Way], 420; *JWJ*, I, 267–68. It could be argued that Cotton had reason to conceal the stillbirth, since it might be seen as reflecting on his "monstrous" ideas as the source of the dissension, but by October 1637 he had been formally reconciled to his fellow clergy, and Wilson had no similar motive for his act of concealment. Thus both clearly understood the importance of confidentiality in certain dealings between clerics and the lay members of their churches.

52. This paragraph and the next are based on *AC* [Court], 319.

53. Ibid., 319, 323, 321, 325.

54. Ibid., 320–30 passim (quotations 325, 330).

55. Ibid., 326–28. Mistress Hutchinson probably obtained her transcription of John Wilson's notes from her supporter Sir Henry Vane, for the Reverend Wilson indicated in this dialogue that the then-governor had copied his notes.

56. Ibid., 326–35 passim (quotation 327). The absence of detailed, definitive notes of the meeting supports Anne Hutchinson's characterization of it. Had the clergymen regarded the conference as *public* at the time it occurred, they would surely have designated one or more of their number to record the proceedings accurately.

57. See the works cited above, n. 4. Only one other work has not been misled by the implications of Winthrop's clever deception; see Anne F. Withington and Jack Schwartz, "The Political Trial of Anne Hutchinson," *New England Quarterly*, LI (1978), 226–40 (hereafter cited as *NEQ*).

58. *AC* [Story], 269–71. Winthrop's account (271) reads as follows: "The Court . . .

required three of the Ministers to take an oath, and thereupon they confirmed their former testimony. Upon this she began to speake her mind. . . ."

59. An insightful recent study of the tradition with which Anne Hutchinson hereby aligned herself is Phyllis Mack, *Visionary Women: Ecstatic Prophecy in Seventeenth-Century England* (Berkeley: University of California Press, 1992), esp. part 1. See also Rosemary Radford Ruether, "Prophets and Humanists: Types of Religious Feminism in Stuart England," *Journal of Religion*, LXX (1990) 1–18.

60. *AC* [Court], 336–38 passim. By her statement that the verses from Daniel were "fulfilled this day," Mistress Hutchinson might have meant not just her trial, but also the triumph that she at the time anticipated. In *Short Story*, Winthrop misrepresented her revelatory speech, just as he misrepresented the sequence of events leading up to it: he placed the statement about her "immediate revelation" at its end, rather than in the middle; wrote that she claimed she would be delivered by a miracle (she did not); and said that the "immediate revelation" concerned her deliverance (which it did not, but rather her ability to distinguish among ministers). See *AC* [Story], 271–75.

61. *AC* [Court], 338–44 passim (quotations 342, 340). Many scholars have erroneously concluded that the key issue was the fact of the revelations rather than their content.

62. This paragraph and the next are based on ibid., 344–47 passim.

63. Ibid., 347–48.

64. Quotation: *AC* [Church], 361. As David Hall explains, 349–50, the sole surviving record of Anne Hutchinson's church trial is an incomplete 18th-century copy (made by the Reverend Ezra Stiles) of a lost 17th-century transcript. See also John Winthrop's description of the church trial in *AC* [Story], 300–8, and *JWJ*, I, 259–64.

65. This paragraph and the next are based on *AC* [Church], 352–54. She was relying on the injunction in Matthew 18:15: "Moreover, if thy brother trespasse against thee, goe and tell him his fault betweene thee and him alone: if hee heare thee, thou hast wonne thy brother." Verses 16 and 17 then explain that if this tactic does not work, first witnesses should be obtained, then the entire church informed of the offense.

66. Quotation: *AC* [Church], 364. See, in general, 354–64. The scriptural passages, which are very similar, are Mark 12:25, Matthew 22:30, and Luke 20:35. A useful article is J. F. Maclear, "Anne Hutchinson and the Mortalist Heresy," *NEQ*, LIV (1981), 74–103.

67. *AC* [Church], 362.

68. Ibid., 362–63. See Christopher Marsh, *The Family of Love in English Society, 1550–1630* (Cambridge: Cambridge University Press, 1994). When two of Anne Hutchinson's most prominent supporters, Captain John Underhill and the Reverend Hansard Knollys, later acknowledged having committed adulterous acts, her opponents acquired specific evidence that her ideas fostered marital infidelity. See *AC* [Story], 276–77; *JWJ*, I, 276–77, 280–81, 329, II, 12–14, 27–28; Pierce, ed., *Boston Church Recs*, 28–29.

69. *AC* [Church], 380. See Felicity Heal, "The Family of Love and the Diocese of Ely," in Derek Baker, ed., *Schism, Heresy and Religious Protest* (Cambridge: Cambridge University Press, 1972), 213–22. No one has yet definitively identified the woman to whom she referred, but see Gura, *Glimpse of Sion's Glory*, 365 n. 12, for a concrete suggestion. See also Robert G. Pope, ed., "The Notebook of the Reverend John Fiske," *CSM Pubs*, XLVII (1974), 83, for a 1648 reference to a woman in Wenham who "declared herself of the opinions of the women of Eli."

70. *AC* [Church], 365.

71. This paragraph and the next three are based on ibid., 370–73. That Cotton had reason to be concerned is indicated by the subsequent excommunication of Mistress Harding "for having said in open Court that Mrs. Hutchinson neyther deserved the Censure which was putt upon her in the Church, nor in the Common Weale" (Pierce, ed., *Boston Church Recs*, 25; see *Mass Col Recs*, I, 259).

72. Quotation: *AC* [Story], 253. Cotton, it should be recalled, held a very restricted view of women's proper role; most notably, he argued that women should not undergo public examinations for church admission (see Introduction, n. 51). See also *AC*, 393, for a Cotton statement disclosing his assumption that *men* were the prime instigators of the move

to Rhode Island, even though he acknowledged that *women* were especially attracted to Mistress Hutchinson's ideas.

73. See chapter seven, n. 86. According to the *OED*, the word *distinction* did not carry the meaning of "rank" until the 18th century; at this period it denoted only categorization in general. Thus the *distinction* to which Cotton referred must have been sex, not social standing or marital status, the subject of his final phrase.

74. *AC* [Way], 431; *AC* [Church], 374–86 passim (quotation 377). It is highly likely that Mistress Anne Eaton witnessed Anne Hutchinson's church trial, since the migrants bound for New Haven spent that winter in Boston and so many "strangers" were noted as being present in the church; and it is probable that Mistress Ann Hibbens (whose husband was a leader of the Boston congregation) also attended. Accordingly, the tactics they later adopted during their own church trials—in the case of Mistress Hibbens, refusing to speak at all in the later stages; in that of Mistress Eaton, asking to speak to the church at large rather than to the elders—may well have been influenced by what happened to Mistress Hutchinson, who spoke freely to both elders and church throughout the process (see chapter three).

75. *AC* [Church], 384–88 (quotations 384, 388). For the record of the excommunication: Pierce, ed., *Boston Church Recs*, 21.

76. *AC* [Story], 307.

77. See *JWJ*, I, 267 (the Dyer fetus); James Savage, ed., *The History of New England from 1630 to 1649 by John Winthrop, Esq.* (2d ed., Boston: Little, Brown, 1853), I, 326–28 (the Hutchinson "birth," probably a hydatitiform mole, described in a passage expurgated by Hosmer); *WP*, IV, 23, 25; and Valerie Pearl and Morris Pearl, eds., "Governor John Winthrop on the Birth of the Antinomians' 'Monster': The Earliest Reports to Reach England and the Making of a Myth," *MHS Procs*, CII (1990), 21–37. A more detailed examination of this topic is Anne J. Schutte, " 'Such Monstrous Births': A Neglected Aspect of the Antinomian Controversy," *Renaissance Quarterly*, XXXVIII (1985), 85–106.

78. *MHS Procs*, 1st ser., XIII (1873–74), 132. See also John Josselyn, "An Account of Two Voyages to New-England," in *MHS Colls*, 3d ser., III (1833), 231; *MHS Procs*, 2d ser., XIII (1899–1900), 126; and Everett Emerson, ed., *Letters from New England: The Massachusetts Bay Colony, 1629–1638* (Amherst: University of Massachusetts Press, 1976), 229–30.

79. *AC* [Story], 281–82; Jameson, ed., *Johnson's Wonder-Working Providence*, 187; *AC* [Story], 214.

80. *JWJ*, I, 284, 297, 299, II, 39; Jameson, ed., *Johnson's Wonder-Working Providence*, 185; Hubbard, *History of New England*, II, 341–42.

81. *JWJ*, I, 266, 268; *AC* [Way], 437; *Mass Col Recs*, I, 224, 329. For the petitions, dating between 1646 and 1656, see ibid., III, 63, 190, 228, 394, 413.

82. *JWJ*, II, 7–8, 39–40.

83. Quotation: ibid., 19. See also ibid., 56, and *Mass Col Recs*, II, 3 (Aspinwall); ibid., I, 301 (Underhill) (see also n. 68, above); and ibid., II, 32, 37, 67, IV, pt 1, 187; *JWJ*, II, 122, 165–67; *WP*, IV, 414–15, 449–50 (Wheelwright). By 1645, Wheelwright was consciously distancing himself from Anne Hutchinson's "strange fancies"; see Charles H. Bell, *John Wheelwright* (1876; repr., Freeport, N.Y.: Books for Libraries Press, 1970), 197. The report of the Boston church's emissaries (one of whom was Mr. William Hibbens): *AC*, 389–95.

84. Quotations: *Mass Col Recs*, I, 160–61; *WP*, IV, 2. See *WP*, III and IV, passim, for letters from Williams, all of which presumably elicited cordial responses from Winthrop; *JWJ*, I, 184–273, passim, for accounts of contacts between the two; and ibid., I, 309, for Winthrop's comments on Williams's conversion to Baptism. Hubbard, *History*, II, 338–40, gives a more complete description of Mistress Scott's role. In 1658, she wrote to John Winthrop, Jr., informing him that she had heard that his father was "trobled . . . upon his death bed" about the banishing of her sister (*MHS Colls*, 5th ser., I [1871], 96). Whether there was any truth to the rumor is unknown.

85. *JWJ*, II, 137–38; Jameson, ed., *Johnson's Wonder-Working Providence*, 186–87; *AC* [Story], 218. See also Hubbard, *History*, II, 345.

86. *MHS Colls*, 3d ser., III (1825), 13–14.
87. *AC* [Story], 209.

CONCLUSION

1. A similar woman who emerged amid the disruptions of the pre–Civil War era in England was Lady Eleanor Davies, a self-styled prophet. See Phyllis Mack, *Visionary Women: Ecstatic Prophecy in Seventeenth-Century England* (Berkeley: University of California Press, 1992), passim; and Esther Cope, *Dame Eleanor Davies: Never Soe Mad a Ladie* (Ann Arbor: Univesity of Michigan Press, 1993).

2. See, e.g., Peter Hoffer and N. E. H. Hull, *Murdering Mothers: Infanticide in England and New England, 1558–1803* (New York: New York University Press, 1981), passim; and Cornelia Hughes Dayton, "Women Before the Bar: Gender, Law, and Society in Connecticut, 1710–1790" (unpub. Ph.D. diss., Princeton University, 1986), esp. chapter 3.

3. "An Essay on Patriotism," *Boston Magazine*, I (November 1783), 13; reprinted in *American Museum*, VI (December 1789), 445. For an extended examination of this theme (but with a more "masculine" emphasis), see Gordon S. Wood, *The Radicalism of the American Revolution* (New York: Alfred A. Knopf, 1992), chapter 9, "Enlightened Paternalism."

4. *Warren-Adams Letters . . . 1743–1814*, MHS Colls, LXXII (1917), 172, 222.

5. Lyman H. Butterfield, ed., *The Letters of Benjamin Rush* (Princeton, N.J.: Princeton University Pres, 1951), I, 464; Lyman H. Butterfield et al., eds., *Adams Family Correspondence* (Cambridge, Mass.: Harvard University Press, 1962), I, 316. And see a letter from Abigail Adams to Thomas Jefferson in 1786, wherein she applied to herself the common public/private distinction employed only for men a hundred years earlier: "In a private station I have not a wish for expensive living . . . [and] I will most joyfully exchange Europe for America, and my public for a private life" (Julian Boyd et al., eds., *The Papers of Thomas Jefferson* [Princeton, N.J.: Princeton University Press, 1950–   ], IX, 277).

6. As was indicated in the introduction, I intend this question to be the focus of my future research.

Index

Abbott, Elizabeth, 124–25, 136
Abbott, Sarah, 253
Abbott, Walter, 332
abortion, 36, 267, 467n. 61
Accerly, Henry, 356
Accomack County (Va.), 76, 197, 245, 334
Adam and Eve: Filmer on, 59, 98; Locke on, 60–61, 296
Adams, Abigail, 405
Adams, John, 404–5
Adams, Samuel, 404
adultery: 238; in New England, 28, 37, 74–75, 87, 264–65, 341–46, 468nn. 68, 70; and divorce, 90, 93–95; and midwives, 228–31, 343–44; in Maryland, 246–47, 265–67, 348–49; importance of, 392
Africans, 247; and colonial courts, 15–16; and marriage, in colonies, 63–64. See also slaves
Alford (Eng.), 361
Allen, Rev. James, 212
Alsop, George, 6, 127
Alvey, Pope, 123, 456n. 67
Ames, Robert, 213–14
Anabaptism, 166–67, 173, 178, 396
anatomy: and gender identity, 188–90, 194
Anderton, John, 158
Andrews, Joan, 85
Andrews, John, 85
Anne Arundel (Md.), 307
Anthony (slave), 46, 170
Antinomian controversy. See Hutchinson, Mrs. Anne
Antonio (slave), 125–26
Aquidneck (R.I.), 395
Arbella (ship), 9

arson, 135–36, 250
Aspinwall, Mr. William, 374–75, 396
assault, 28, 92, 135, 253, 257–58, 332, 334; sexual, 35, 52–53, 353, 468n. 64. See also children; servants; spouse abuse
Astell, Mary, 59, 62, 75, 81
Atkins, John, 186–94, 196
Atwater, Mrs., 251–52
Atwell, Philip, 85
authority: reliance on, for legitimate government, 11–12, 401; challenges to, by high-status women, 165–80, 359–99; of men, over women, 206; and women, 285; and consent, 293–94, 298, 308–12; demand for, in Rhode Island, 301–2; of Connecticut charter, and New Haven, 303–4; arguments for, 305–8, 320–21; Winthrop on, 317–19; regional differences in crimes against, 329–34. See also contempt of authority; state
Axey, Frances, 148
Axey, James, 148

Baker, Thomas, 160, 269–76
Ball, Allen, 251
Baltimore, Lord (Cecilius Calvert), 200, 204, 220–21, 306–7; and Margaret Brent, 281–87
Baptists. See Anabaptism
Baskel, Hannah, 264
Basse, Capt. Nathaniel, 186–97
Bassett, William, 330–31
bastardy, 69, 130, 144, 336–37; and midwives, 225–26. See also infanticide

theft: in New Haven, 33, 36, 51, 53; and servants, 45–47, 134–35, 185; and midwives, 225, 248; and neighbors, 247–48, 255–56; and capital punishment, 325–26

Thomas, Goodwife, 53

Thompson, Ellen, 234

Thompson, Mr. George, 270–72

Thorpe, Goodwife, 251–52

Tilly, Mrs. Alice, 203–6, 224–25, 236, 239, 277, 367, 397, 402

Tilly, Mr. William, 205

Tinsin (Indian), 264

Tomkinson, Giles, 70

Tucker, Thomas, 67

Turner, Mr. Arthur, 209, 216–17, 242

Turner, Rebecca. *See* Meekes, Rebecca

Tuttle, Mr. William, 330

Two Treatises of Government (Locke), 5, 143, 289. *See also First Treatise of Government* (Locke); *Second Treatise of Government* (Locke)

Tyler, Francis, 37

Tyos, Jane, 185

Tyos, John, 185–87, 189–90, 192, 194, 196

Underhill, Capt. John, 308–9, 396

Usher, Robert, 53

Vane, Sir Henry, 367, 372, 394

venereal disease, 122–23

Verin, Jane, 77–78

Verin, Joshua, 77–78

Vincent, William, 247

Vincon, Peter, 54–55

Vines, Mr. Richard, 309

Virginia, 20–21, 43, 200, 247, 282, 305, 324–25, 333, 337, 404; and family governors, 40–41; and familial offenses, 48–49; and prosecution of Thomas Flint,

49–51; family laws in, 63–65, 101–3, 145, 329; husbands and wives in, 67–68, 79–80, 84–86; child abuse in, 120; abuse of Elizabeth Abbott in, 124–25; unruly servants in, 133–34, 136; widows in, 157; Thomas(ine) Hall in, 183–97, 206; men's business dealings in, 207–8, 210; political disputes in, 220–21, 401; J(o)ane Wright in, 225, 236–37; and adultery, 229–30, 343–44; defamation in, 76, 197, 232, 257–59, 262; gossip in, 254, 263; soldiers from, in Maryland, 283–84, 286, 333; disputes of, with Maryland, 306–7; rape and sodomy in, 347, 352, 354, 357; bestiality in, 354, 356. *See also* Accomack County (Va.)

Wakeman, Esborne, 355–56

Waltham, Grace, 76

Waltham, John, 76, 197

Walton, George, 245, 250

Ward, Rev. Nathaniel, 384

Ward, Thomas, 150

Warren, James, 404

Warren, Mercy Otis, 404

Weld, Mr. Joseph, 374

Weld, Rev. Thomas, 366–70, 372, 384, 389, 394–96, 398

Wenham (Mass.), 23, 88

West, Govr. Francis, 49–51

West, Mrs. Temperance, 49

Weymouth (Mass.), 234, 342

Wharton, Mr. Richard, 212

Wheelwright, Rev. John, 313, 369–76, 396, 398, 407

Wheelwright, Mrs. Mary Hutchinson, 407

whipping, 338–39

White, Mary, 225

Whittaker, Abraham, 213–14, 217

Wickes, Mr. Joseph, 111, 209, 246–47; and maidservant, 121–22; and bastardy, 337

A NOTE ON THE TYPE

The text of this book was set in Bembo, a facsimile of a typeface cut by Francesco Griffo for Aldus Manutius, the celebrated Venetian printer, in 1495. The face was named for Pietro Cardinal Bembo, the author of the small treatise entitled *De Aetna* in which it first appeared. Through the research of Stanley Morison, it is now generally acknowledged that all oldstyle type designs up to the time of William Caslon can be traced to the Bembo cut. The present-day version of Bembo was introduced by the Monotype Corporation of London in 1929. Sturdy, well balanced, and finely proportioned, Bembo is a face of rare beauty and great legibility in all of its sizes.

Composed by PennSet, Inc., Bloomsburg, Pennsylvania
Printed and bound by Quebecor Printing, Fairfield, Pennsylvania
Designed by Robert C. Olsson